ALSO BY WALTER RUSSELL MEAD

God and Gold
Power, Terror, Peace, and War
Special Providence
Mortal Splendor

The Arc

of a

Covenant

The United States, Israel,
and the Fate of the Jewish People

WALTER RUSSELL MEAD

ALFRED A. KNOPF   New York

2022

THIS IS A BORZOI BOOK
PUBLISHED BY ALFRED A. KNOPF

Copyright © 2022 by Walter Russell Mead

All rights reserved. Published in the United States by Alfred A. Knopf,
a division of Penguin Random House LLC, New York, and distributed
in Canada by Penguin Random House Canada Limited, Toronto.

www.aaknopf.com

Knopf, Borzoi Books, and the colophon are registered
trademarks of Penguin Random House LLC.

Library of Congress Cataloging-in-Publication Data
Names: Mead, Walter Russell, author.
Title: The arc of a covenant : the United States, Israel,
and the fate of the Jewish people / Walter Russell Mead.
Description: First edition. | New York : Alfred A. Knopf, 2022. |
"This is a Borzoi Book published by Alfred A. Knopf." |
Includes bibliographical references and index.
Identifiers: LCCN 2021037997 (print) | LCCN 2021037998 (ebook) |
ISBN 9780375414046 (hardcover) | ISBN 9781101946985 (ebook)
Subjects: LCSH: Arab-Israeli conflict. | Zionism—United States. |
Religion and politics—United States. | United States—
Foreign relations—Israel. | Israel—Foreign relations—United States. |
Israel—Strategic aspects. | United States—Politics and government.
Classification: LCC E183.8.I7 M423 2022 (print) |
LCC E183.8.I7 (ebook) | DDC 327.7305694—dc23
LC record available at https://lccn.loc.gov/2021037997
LC ebook record available at https://lccn.loc.gov/2021037998

Jacket photographs by Oleksii Liskonih /iStock/Getty Images
Jacket design by Mark Melnick

Manufactured in the United States of America
First Edition

To Ravenel B. Curry III

May the father of all mercies scatter light and not darkness in our paths, and make us all in our several vocations useful here, and in his own due time and way everlastingly happy.

—GEORGE WASHINGTON,
Letter to the Hebrew Congregation in Newport, Rhode Island, 18 August 1790

Contents

The Arc

of a

Covenant

1

The Mystery of Zion

A T A TIME WHEN so many books are being written, and so many of them are so long, the reader of any book is entitled to ask why it had to be written at all and, if the book absolutely had to exist, why it couldn't have been shorter.

That is particularly true when it comes to books about the U.S.-Israel relationship. There are few subjects in American foreign policy that get as much attention as the relationship between the world's only Jewish state and the global superpower. Professors and students offer teach-ins and hold demonstrations on university campuses; pastors, rabbis, and imams speak about it from the pulpits; politicians make speeches; candidates get questioned on Middle East policy during election debates; think tanks issue voluminous reports; foundations sponsor a never-ending deluge of roundtables and panel discussions; journalists report and talking heads debate. Enough books on this subject have been published to fill a respectable library; do we really need another one?

I believe we do. One hates to belabor the obvious, but American diplomacy in the Middle East in recent decades has neither been wreathed in glory nor crowned with success. War in Iraq, war in Afghanistan, an ill-considered "humanitarian" Libyan intervention that led to years of chaos, a generation of failure for the Israeli-Palestinian peace process, helplessness in the face of Iran's drive for regional hegemony, failure to prevent a malignant Russia from reentering the Middle East: Americans and the peoples of the Middle East alike deserve better.

When we look at the intense national debate over Middle East policy and, especially, over our policy toward Israel, the discussion is often angry, accusatory, and simplistic. One thinks of the lines from *The Dun-*

porting "self-determination" for ethnic groups across Europe. Zionism itself can't be understood without some background in the history of the rise of national movements in the Austro-Hungarian, Russian, and Ottoman empires that once dominated Central and Eastern Europe and the Middle East. I was either going to have to give up the Israel book project, or steel myself for a deeper dive and a longer book than I originally expected.

Meanwhile, during the years in which I was slowly coming to appreciate the difficulty of this task I had so rashly taken on, American society and American foreign policy were hurtling into crisis. As Russia and China stepped up their challenge to the American-led "liberal world order" abroad, Americans were losing faith in their national institutions at home and, weary of endless wars in far-off lands, American public opinion questioned the country's ambitiously globalist post–Cold War strategy. Increasingly it looked as though some of America's central assumptions about international politics in the twenty-first century were fundamentally flawed. The focus of American foreign policy was in any case moving from the Middle East to the Indo-Pacific. Did it still make sense, I found myself asking, to focus on a parochial subject like the U.S.-Israel relationship in such dangerous times?

What kept me plugging away was my growing realization that the very problems that made the book so hard to write brought me to the heart of the challenges facing a divided America in the Age of Trump. The wide-ranging survey of the relationship between American domestic politics and our foreign policy that the Israel story required would help Americans gain perspective on the foreign and domestic policy challenges that have tested us so severely in recent years.

Rather than fighting the complexity of my subject, I decided to embrace it. I would follow the thread to the heart of the labyrinth. If the story took me to Theodor Herzl's meetings with Kaiser Wilhelm II in Constantinople and Jerusalem, I would follow it there. If the story led into the politics of nineteenth-century human rights movements, if it led to a study of the religious and secular roots of the unique American approach to the integration of Jewish immigrants, if it challenged the pious legends that the American Jewish community produced about its role in the emergence of Israel, I would pursue it.

To write about the American relationship with the Jewish state and the Jewish people is to sketch a portrait of the American spirit at work in the world. That, at any rate, is what I came to believe and what I have tried to do in these pages.

======

Writing this book has forced me to think much more systematically and deeply about international affairs. My own engagement with American foreign policy began in childhood. I was ten years old at the time of the Cuban Missile Crisis of 1962, when newspaper headlines spoke of imminent war and our schools conducted air raid drills to protect us from nuclear bombs. In the fifth grade, my friends and I used to argue about whether our hometown of Chapel Hill, North Carolina, was on the Soviet target list for destruction. The playground consensus was that yes, we would be hit early, because the NASA astronauts used the University of North Carolina Planetarium for training. There was, we agreed, no way that the Soviet leaders would leave such an important asset untouched. We did not, by the way, think this was a gloomy forecast. We knew that the lucky ones in a nuclear war would be the ones who died first.

Six decades later, I am as transfixed by the spectacle of American foreign policy as I was during that historic October. For one thing, it matters: American foreign policy remains of supreme importance for the well-being and even the survival of the American people and of humanity itself. Beyond that, it is interesting; few areas of study can match the sheer intellectual challenge of a subject that requires its students to engage with an almost infinite variety of disciplines and perspectives. American culture, economics and the history of economic institutions and policies, religion and religious movements, technological change and its impact on human societies, political ideologies and political history, social movements and intergroup relations, immigration, the histories of foreign countries—these are only some of the subjects to which the study of American foreign policy leads. Any serious student in this genre should travel widely in the United States and abroad, immerse herself in diplomatic history, grapple with issues of strategy and war, and gain some knowledge of practical affairs.

This study is so complex and so far-reaching that nobody ever comes to the end of it. Great foreign policy figures like Henry Kissinger, George Shultz, Zbigniew Brzezinski, and George Kennan were still learning and still making discoveries and new connections well into their eighties and nineties. The subject is a mountain whose summit can never be reached, but the higher one ascends, the more comprehensive and far-reaching the views.

The student of American foreign policy must also engage with some of the most basic questions about the meaning and direction of life. American foreign policy must be shaped to some extent by our beliefs and intuitions about human nature, our ideas about the meaning if any of the historical process, and the ultimate values that for some take the form of religious belief and for others form the ideological foundations of their sense of identity and purpose.

It is more difficult than it looks to bring one's deepest convictions into effective foreign policy. Most of those who have sought to turn international relations into a form of religious or ethical mission have been disappointed in the results. This is often because they fail to think the thing through. To act with real moral effect in the world of foreign policy, it is not enough to understand one's own convictions and the ethical guidance they provide. One must also seek to understand how other people from different religious and philosophical backgrounds understand the world, how those beliefs shape the way others see the world and provide a filter through which they analyze events, and how they seek to translate their beliefs into policy. One will then need to study how these conflicting moral visions interact with unyielding realities and less elevated motives in surprising and sometimes explosive ways, and how the international system in which all these forces collide is more mysterious, more dangerous, and more unpredictable still.

"A statesman cannot create anything himself," said Otto von Bismarck. "He must wait and listen until he hears the steps of God sounding through events; then leap up and grasp the hem of His garment."[2] Discerning the steps of God in the rush of world events is not easy; history teaches that many world leaders have listened in vain.

Yet difficult as it is to bring our religious and ethical convictions to bear in American foreign policy, some understanding of and sympathy for the worlds of religion and spiritual hunger remains indispensable for serious policymaking. It is not just that a subject like the Jewish state with its inevitable religious associations brings these questions to the fore. In a world of nuclear weapons, people everywhere come to foreign policy questions and questions of peace and war conscious that, at the extreme, such questions potentially involve the survival of the human race. Periodically other issues erupt into foreign policy debates in which, potentially, the future of the human race is at stake: extreme climate change, the consequences for disaster inherent in the development of technologies like cyberwar software, genetic modification, and artificial intelligence. Foreign policy in our time cannot exclude the consideration of existential threats to human civilization and survival, and debates over foreign policy often lead into or proceed from debates over what human beings should do to preserve our species and even our planet.

The extreme stakes in the world of international politics make it more necessary to think clearly about foreign policy, but they also make that clear thought more difficult. Our emotional responses to the potential for world-ending conflicts and apocalyptic disasters built into international relations today—responses that range from panic to denial—can affect the ability of both elites and mass opinion in the United States and abroad to assess distressing realities in a cool and balanced way.

There have been few moments in the last sixty years as tension-filled as the Cuban Missile Crisis, but in recent years it has become apparent that, after a long period in which global tensions appeared to be easing, the world is drifting steadily into more danger. Since the attacks of 9/11 the international scene has continued to darken; today we worry not only about the threat of terror attacks, but about possible conflicts among the great powers. Problems like climate change add to the challenges and difficulties with which the feeble tools of diplomacy must cope. Just as the twentieth century saw the challenge of foreign policy become more difficult and more consequential for the United States than it had been in the nineteenth, so the tasks of foreign policy in the twenty-first century look to be more difficult and more consequential still. In this often frightening world, Americans are going to have to study foreign policy again, and external events are likely to play an increasing role in our domestic political contests and debates.

Israel policy will inevitably play a role in the debates that lie ahead. Israel occupies a unique place in American foreign policy because it occupies a unique, and uniquely charged, place in the American mind. The U.S.-Israel relationship is not and never has been the most important relationship in American foreign policy. Israel is neither America's most important ally nor its most valuable trading partner. But the idea that the Jews would return to the lands of the Bible and build a state there touches on some of the most powerful themes and cherished hopes of American religion and culture. America's long immersion in biblical Christianity and in a theory of progress that both secular and religious Americans have built on those foundations has given the Jewish people and the Jewish state a distinctive place in American historical consciousness and political thought. The state of Israel is a speck on the map of the world; it occupies a continent in the American mind.

That continent is terrain that any serious student of American politics and culture needs to explore for reasons that include, but go well beyond, the study of American foreign policy in the Middle East. The ideas that have shaped Americans' approach to first the idea and then the reality of the Jewish state are ideas that play an immense and often underappreciated role in virtually every aspect of our domestic life. Debates about Israel policy in the United States often have more to do with debates over American identity, the direction of world politics, and the place that the United States should aspire to occupy in world history than about anything that real-world Israelis and Palestinians may happen to be doing at any particular time.

At a time when Americans are fundamentally divided over the meaning of their heritage and the future of their country's role in the world, understanding the "Israel factor" in American life has become more important than ever. This is not just a foreign policy story, a story about Jews, or a story about American history; it is a story about American values, America's role in the world, American identity, and about the fight between conflicting visions of America now dominating our politics. Dispensing with bad theories—like the idea that a cabal of American Jews controls America's Israel policy—is important, but this book is less about dispelling some rancid urban legends about American Jews than about examining some of America's deepest and most contested values at a time of great social change.

This will not be a book of policy proposals or of policy advocacy. I did not write it to advance my personal views about Middle East peace or to establish myself as a moral arbiter subjecting Israelis and Palestinians alike to the cool and balanced judgment of my keen, all-seeing eye. I am not going to use these pages to evangelize for my pet ideas about peacemaking, or to draw lines in the sand to divide the Holy Land between its inhabitants. That said, I have views, and I am not seeking credibility by pretending to an indifference that I do not feel. I am glad that the State of Israel exists, though I regret the tragedy that befell the Palestinian people as a result, and I hope someday to visit a free Palestinian state. Overall, I believe that the alliance between the United States and Israel serves American interests well, although Americans need to remember that Israel is a separate state whose interests are not always the same as ours, and as circumstances change the interests of both countries could develop in ways that make the alliance less useful. When it comes to the Israeli-Palestinian dispute, I have long believed that a two-state solution in which both peoples can shape their own futures through the exercise of self-determination is the approach that best reconciles the interests of the two parties with American interests and principles. There is nothing new about this idea; in one form or another it has been on the table for generations, and it was the basis for the United Nations decision in 1947 to partition British Palestine into Arab and Jewish states. Stating this goal is easy; implementing it has eluded generations of diplomats. This book does not attempt to find the magic, conflict-ending formula that so many past leaders have sought in vain.

I share the concerns of those who fear that the two-state solution is becoming less feasible, but the "one-state solution" of Israelis and Palestinians living peacefully together in a single country seems even less realistic. A one-state solution would require what today is an unimaginable degree of reconciliation between the two peoples.

Having visited Palestinian refugee camps from Gaza to Damascus and beyond and spoken with Palestinian leaders and ordinary people, I am clear that the Palestinians are a people whose tragic history deserves a compassionate and constructive response. It is unjust that Palestinians living on the West Bank do not control their own future. While the United States cannot give the Palestinians a state, I hope we can help them build one. Ending the occupation with the establishment of an independent Palestine would, under the right conditions, be good for both peoples. Even if full peace isn't possible, it is in the interest of the United States to seek ways in which both Israelis and Palestinians can live in peace and security, to reduce the injustice occupation inevitably entails, and to find methods to make this ongoing dispute less of a blistering sore in international relations.

GETTING IT WRONG

There are many reasons why so much of the American debate over the U.S.-Israel relationship produces more heat than light, but the most common and widespread problem is easy to identify: American foreign policy debates often contain a strong moralistic component, and debates over Israel policy are no exception.

Proponents and critics of the U.S.-Israel alliance often agree that the question of American policy toward Israel is primarily a moral one, though they disagree on who is more moral. One side criticizes the morality of Israel's policies toward the Palestinians and argues that American policy should uphold the human rights of a people struggling under occupation, denied a state of their own, and suffering from the loss of their homes and possessions. The other side points to the suffering of the Jewish people, their right to self-determination, and the long record of terrorism and intransigence among Arab opponents of Israel to claim that the moral balance tilts toward the Jewish state rather than away from it. Both sides make some important points, but as a student of foreign policy I find the tendency to reduce a complicated practical question to a question of moral accounting unhelpful. Morality has a vital and irreducible place in foreign policy, but the relationship of the morality of American foreign policy overall to the rights and wrongs of any specific dispute is much more complicated than many advocates of either the Palestinian or the Israeli causes acknowledge.

The prime directive of American foreign policy since the start of the Cold War, which is to say since Israel became an independent state, has been to preserve the American way of life while preventing World War III. During the Cold War and beyond, the pursuit of this goal involved a wide range of economic, political, and military initiatives aimed at creating a world in which the United States and like-minded allies could flourish while managing relations with nuclear-armed great power rivals that avoided triggering the ultimate conflagration. In order to achieve these overarching goals, American presidents have made a number of decisions that were, to put it mildly, morally questionable. They have taken actions that many would call criminal, turned a blind eye to some terrible evils, and they have tolerated human rights abuses and wholesale looting by rulers who were prepared to support Washington's agenda.

Sometimes from a pragmatic American perspective these morally compromised actions worked out for the best. Sometimes they did not. Foreign policy is hard, and the game of thrones doesn't work like an academic examination where giving the right answers yields a perfect score. International life is more like a competitive sport in which even the greatest athletes commit fouls, make errors, and lose games. War excepted, the conduct of foreign policy is the most complex and dangerous activity that human beings undertake. In this field, even true genius cannot safeguard a policymaker from error. But while many argue differently, Americans have generally felt that even taking the sometimes appalling cost of our errors fully into account, the national effort to prevent global great power war while preserving the American way of life was both practically beneficial and morally right.

The rights and wrongs of the Israeli-Palestinian dispute need to be viewed in perspective. Even if everything advocates for the Palestinians say about Israeli bad behavior and American complicity in it is true, there might be compelling reasons for the United States to look beyond these issues in the interest of its global peace policy. On the other hand, if everything that the most intense and impassioned Israeli nationalists say about the crimes and shortcomings of the Palestinians is true, it might still be necessary for the United States to overlook those crimes and shortcomings to achieve some other goal of more importance to the security of the United States or the peace of the world.

The rights and wrongs of the Israeli-Palestinian dispute are not irrelevant to American foreign policy, but they are not and cannot be determinative, either. Tibet has not driven America's China policy; the Kurds have not driven our Turkey policy; rampant and vicious discrimination against Christian and other religious and sexual minorities across much of the Islamic world has not driven our Middle Eastern, North African, or South Asian policy; the continued unfair treatment of the Romani people by some European states doesn't drive our policy toward the European Union (EU). This is a hard truth, but an inescapable one: in the Middle East as elsewhere it is the prime directive, not the rankings of the world's various peoples on a hypothetical Global Victimization Index, that must guide American policy. Our policy toward the rival parties should take note of the moral elements of the dispute, but it cannot be driven or defined by them.

There is another problem with using, or attempting to use, moral judgment as the decisive criterion for foreign policy choices: it is much easier and more common for human beings to feel strongly about moral issues than to judge wisely about them. In the 1940s and 1950s, for example, support for Israel in both the United States and Western Europe was a cause favored by the political left. For the progressives and social democrats of that era, the Jewish people were the most prominent victims of the fascist and obscurantist right. Antisemitism was the mark of Cain branding religious and political conservatives as, at heart, fascist sympathizers, and deep sympathy for the Jewish people was a mark of leftist virtue. Not only had the Jewish people suffered under the Nazis, the Jews had also accepted the 1947 U.N. vote to partition Palestine into Jewish and Palestinian states. The Arabs, on the other hand, had rejected the U.N. vote. Worse still, the leader of the Palestinians, the Grand Mufti, had been closely allied to Adolf Hitler and supported his campaign to exterminate the Jewish people.[3] Other Arab leaders were either royal puppets of the British (like the kings of Iraq, Egypt, and Jordan), whose opposition to Israel reflected British imperial interests as much as any Arab nationalist aspiration, or they were, as the left at the time saw things, bigoted Islamist clerics opposed to all forms of enlightenment and modernity. For twenty years liberals and progressives in the United States, and their allies in Europe, attacked the more pro-Arab American Republicans for cynically preferring Arab oil wealth to the cause of human rights and Israel.

In recent decades, the left has shifted to a different narrative, one in which Zionism is a form of European and American racism and neo-colonialism. The Jews of Israel were no longer seen as desperate refugees from a Europe that sought to exterminate them, but as a vanguard of western domination. The dispossession of the Palestinians was the consequence of Israeli brutality in the war of independence, not of the Palestinian rejection of the U.N. partition plan. As Israeli politics have shifted away from the social democratic left toward a more nationalistic and pro-capitalist right since 1980, and as Israeli settlements in the West Bank have proliferated, the leftist critique of Israel has sharpened. By imposing an unjust occupation on the Palestinian territories, and by building Israeli settlements on Palestinian land beyond the 1949 dividing line, Israel was said to be doubling down on bad behavior. To sympathize with Israel was increasingly seen as a sign of racism, sympathy for imperialism, and support for antihuman systems of domination and oppression. Much of the American right, meanwhile, has embraced a version of the old leftist narrative that justifies Israel and makes support for it a moral imperative.

Both narratives achieve their moral power in part by obscuring important facts. The old pro-Israel narrative of the left did not do justice to the suffering and displacement of the Palestinians, to the role of the Israelis in stimulating the mass flight of Palestinians in 1948–49, or to the origins of the mandate system (which gave the United Nations the legal authority to rule over the future of British Palestine) in European colonialism. The Palestinians never consented to become a British mandate under either the League of Nations or the United Nations; Britain seized Palestine from the Ottoman Empire in a classic act of great power politics with no regard whatever for the views of its inhabitants. From the perspective of the Palestinian Arabs, the Balfour Declaration in which Great Britain committed itself to the establishment of a "national home for the Jewish people" in Palestine was the illegitimate act of an imperial power. The moral balance between Israelis and Palestinians was never as one-sided as the old leftist narrative had it.

Yet the new anti-Israel narrative also overlooks crucial events. To take just one example, only a minority of Israeli Jews are European by origin or descent. The plurality have no European roots; they came to Israel from other countries in the Muslim Middle East.[4] Many of these Mizrahi Jews fled or were driven out of their homes by Arab governments and mobs in retaliation, it was claimed by their persecutors, for Israeli behavior against the Palestinians. Others fled brutal mistreatment and unconscionable discrimination. No one speaks of compensation for these refugees; no one commiserates with them; no one seeks to hold anyone to account for the crimes committed against them.

The "European colonizer" narrative about Zionism ignores this reality as studiously and as unjustifiably as the earlier "unspotted Zionist" narrative passed over the suffering of the Palestinians. But the story of the Mizrahi Jews is no small factor in the tangled situation that exists today. Absent Arab persecution of Middle Eastern Jews, Israel today might not even exist; it would certainly be a smaller, weaker, and more left-wing country than is currently the case. The turn to the right in Israeli politics after 1980 and the increasing popularity of hardline nationalist policies in Israel was driven in large part by these refugees from Arab and Muslim persecution. Much of the cynicism in Israel about the moral bona fides of European human rights activists and the U.N. comes from the bitterness of a community whose suffering and losses are a matter of near-universal indifference around the world. Much of the distrust of Arabs and Muslims that plays such a significant role in Israeli politics is grounded in the bitter experiences of this community and its descendants.

The point is not that the old leftist narrative should be preferred to the new one, or vice versa; nor is the point that the suffering of Jews does or should cancel out or obscure the suffering of Palestinians. If we want to think clearly about world politics we can never forget that both on our own part and on the part of those we encounter, it is much easier and more common to feel strongly and speak loudly about the moral imperatives of foreign policy than to reach an accurate, just, and comprehensive understanding of the complex and subtle moral balance that so often exists in our complicated and disorderly world.

Identity Politics

If moralism distorts the American discussion of Israel policy, identity politics inflames it. Israel policy is never just a foreign policy issue in the United States, and many of the ethnic, religious, and racial groups who compose the American people feel a special connection either to the Israelis or to the Palestinians.

Identity politics does not always work in an obvious way. It is precisely because of their strong sense of Jewish identity that many American Jews became strong critics of Israeli policies under Prime Minister Benjamin Netanyahu. To persuade the American government to oppose Israeli policies like settlement construction seen as unjust to Palestinians is, for many of the majority of American Jews who fall on the left side of the political spectrum, much more than a foreign policy challenge. It is a test of moral integrity. American Jews in groups like J Street are not just making arguments about foreign policy; their political activism is a way of rising above tribal loyalties and fulfilling what they see as their responsibility to stand up for Jewish values before the world.

Liberal American Jews are not the only Americans whose deepest beliefs and sense of personal identity influence both the intensity and the nature of their convictions about U.S.-Israel relations. There are other American Jews who believe that to call for the U.S. to oppose

Israeli policies amounts to a betrayal not only of Jewish values but of the Jewish people. The controversies among American Jews about American policy toward Israel, and the role if any that the Jewish community should take in that debate, are also controversies about the meaning of Jewish experience, Jewish faith, and Jewish identity. They are disputes about which elements of the American Jewish community should be dominant, whether the Democratic or Republican parties should rule in Washington, and about the meaning of Jewish identity in the modern world. Should Jews bear witness to the universal ethical principles embedded in Jewish tradition, or should they think first about the security and power of the Jewish fatherland?

It is not only American Jews for whom arguments about Israel policy are about more than the American national interest in the Middle East. For many American Christians and Muslims, Israel policy involves questions of identity and group standing. Millions of American Christians believe that loyally supporting Israel is part of America's special world mission. Other American Christians, also numbering in the millions, believe that the pro-Israel bias in American evangelical religion is a gross religious and cultural error that needs to be purged. Many American Muslims believe that correcting what they see as an American pro-Israel bias based on racist, orientalist, and Islamophobic ideas will help improve their standing and acceptance in American society. Are ideas about the Israeli-Palestinian conflict that are mainstream in much of the global Islamic community to be ruled out of bounds in American politics? Does this mean that the American political system has no room for Muslims who are loyal to their own core beliefs?

The passions stirred by Israel policy go deeper. Many Americans historically sympathized with the Zionists because the Zionists, like the early American settlers, were pioneers, bringing civilization and progress, as they saw it, to new lands. Both Israeli Zionists and American pioneers drew inspiration from passages in the Hebrew scriptures about the advance of the "Chosen People" into the land of Canaan, where they displaced the original inhabitants in obedience, as they believed, to a divine mandate. But "settler state colonialism" is controversial, and rightly so.

In the United States today, many people identify with the victims of settler colonialism. For some Native Americans, Hispanics, and African Americans, it can make more sense to identify with the Palestinian victims of Zionist expansion than to hail the heroism of the Zionist pioneers. For other Americans, rejecting the heritage of settler colonialism is seen as an important step on the road to building a more just society. From this perspective, one's attitude toward Israel is a test case: those who support Israel have aligned themselves with the history of western rapacity and colonialism responsible for so much injustice and misery around the world, while those who oppose Israel have joined the resistance.

Far from seeing support for Israel as a form of dual loyalty, many Americans view sympathy with Israel's enemies as something close to treason against the United States. Israel's enemies are America's enemies, they believe. Islamic triumphalism, postcolonial hostility to western capitalism and Israel, hatred of western civilization and perhaps of Christianity itself are seen as hostility to American values and the American way of life. However we come down on the issues, what is important to observe is that while the object of these policy debates is U.S.-Israel relations, the energy driving this activism comes from Americans' deepest beliefs about themselves and their identity.

The issues brought forward by these different perceptions are real, and the questions they pose are deep. The passions raised by these issues may be grounded in skewed and one-sided perceptions about the facts on the ground, but they are still, from a political standpoint, facts; in no state can policymakers avoid taking strong public sentiments into account. Inescapably in American politics, Israel policy is a domestic political issue, not just another foreign policy debate.

We can acknowledge this reality, but we must also acknowledge its consequences: the passions of identity politics make us angry and they keep us engaged, but they do not always make us wise.

The Strategic Vacuum

America's Israel policy, like its China policy, its NATO policy, or its Russia policy, cannot be assessed or debated in a vacuum, yet that is what many people on both sides of the Israel debate would like to do. Perhaps the establishment of the Jewish state on Palestinian land was a ghastly blunder and a horrible crime. Perhaps it was the legitimate exercise of self-determination by the Jewish people. Perhaps it was the fulfillment of biblical prophecy. Perhaps it was a mix of one, two, or all three of these.

Nevertheless, the state—a nuclear state and a regional superpower in a region many think vital for American interests—exists. What should we seek to achieve through our relationship with it?

That question can only be answered on the basis of a considered national strategy, and it is at this level that the problems with our national debate on Israel policy mix with the problems of our larger national conversation on foreign policy. What is America's global strategy? What role should our Middle East policy play in that strategy? And what role can or should Israel play in both our regional and our global strategies? The election of President Trump, a man determined to break with conventional Washington establishment foreign policy, led to the most intense debate over American global strategy in many years and, at the time of writing, that debate is still in its early phases.

In the twentieth century, there were four distinct moments when the United States had to develop a new approach to foreign policy. One was in the aftermath of World War I, when the United States reexamined old assumptions and methods to develop an approach to the international situation that dominated our politics through the start of World War II. The second came after World War II, when the Soviet challenge forced the Truman administration to develop what would become America's basic strategy during the Cold War. The third came in the early 1970s when the Vietnam defeat, the collapse of the Bretton Woods monetary system, the rise of OPEC, and the Soviet achievement of nuclear parity forced a difficult strategic reappraisal on the Richard Nixon administration. The last shift came at the end of the Cold War, when the American foreign policy establishment decided that the promotion of a "new world order" based on liberal market economics and democracy promotion should drive American strategy in the wake of the Soviet collapse.

At each of these decision points, the American position toward the Zionist movement and, later, the State of Israel was one of the questions Americans wrestled with. In every case, the policy we adopted toward Zionism and Israel was of a piece with the larger national strategy, even as the national strategy was influenced by perceptions of a special relationship between American and Jewish destiny.

With the decay of the post–Cold War consensus, American society is now conducting a foreign policy debate as consequential as any of the earlier ones. These debates are likely to continue as the twenty-first century brings new challenges. Will the United States press forward with the global-order-building agenda that characterized our policy during the Clinton, Bush, and Obama administrations? Will we pursue similar goals in different ways, adjusting our responses and priorities to changing conditions? Will we slash our international commitments and responsibility, trusting more to allies and to the balance of power to keep the peace? Will we walk away from the whole global order project? Whatever we decide, the consequences for the United States and for the rest of the world will be immense and, as in the past, the course of our national debate over Israel policy will likely both reflect and help shape the broader debate. In any case, the question of Israel policy must be placed in the strategic context of American foreign policy as a whole.

The Perils of Theory

There is another reason why American discussions about foreign policy in general and, especially, Middle East policy so frequently fall short. Half-digested generalizations resting on weak readings of history or careless assumptions about large groups of people often lead us astray when the national conversation turns to the Middle East.

Dogmatism is one of the great enemies of clarity when it comes to the study of American foreign policy. Political theory is an important subject and from Plato to our own time brilliant intellectuals have illuminated the choices societies face. Without generalizations we could not think at all; the world is too complex, and our minds too limited, to make sense of events without resorting to simplifications and generalizations. It is when theory degenerates into dogma and laws that the trouble begins.

At its best, theory can challenge our assumptions, point us toward interesting questions, and alert us to important facts that we might otherwise miss. But theory can and often does hide as well as uncover; without deep wells of historical knowledge and personal experience, a too confident reliance on abstractions and generalizations frequently creates an illusion of knowledge, concealing our ignorance and blinding us to forces and facts that cannot safely be ignored.

International relations constitute one of the most intricate forms of human interaction, and, thanks to the global range of American engagements and the complicated nature of the American political process, American foreign policy is the most complex phenomenon in the field of international relations. After a lifetime of study, I for one am still learning new and surprising things about it all the time. Yet not many people can immerse themselves in this study, and in any case, we cannot wait until a lifetime of reflection and experience makes us wise in order to deal with the crises of the passing day. For this reason, the production of theory, of generalizations about and simplifications of foreign policy, is necessary for public and democratic debate, and presidents and other policymakers must make decisions about subjects whose depths they will never have the time to plumb.

Academic theories about international relations, however recondite they sometimes become, are one of the ways that scholars try to make the complex realities of foreign policy more comprehensible to more people; myths or narratives are another way in which people try to make sense of large forces that affect their daily lives. The importance of American foreign policy is so great, the amount of knowledge required to really make sense of it is so daunting, and the hunger of people to understand forces that have so much impact on their lives is so unappeasable, that sweeping generalizations can always find a receptive audience. I have made some of these generalizations myself. Some are deeply considered, good-faith efforts by serious observers to find useful patterns; some are simply popular prejudice in crystallized form; some are conspiracy theories formulated by immature minds who've spent too much time in the steamier zones of the internet. The good theories can be useful aids to comprehension as long as we don't rely on them blindly; the bad ones lead the unwary into endless mazes of illusion and error, where far too many people wander in the pathless dark.

Elaborate and highly developed theories about international relations are also necessary for bureaucratic policymaking. Before World War II, American foreign policy was, at least in comparison to what it has become, a semi-artisanal activity carried out by small groups of people all mostly sharing a common background and a common set of cultural and social beliefs. Since then, the massive growth of the national security state, and the proliferation of immense and lumbering bureaucratic behemoths from the Pentagon to the State Department to the intelligence community and beyond, have vastly increased the role of academic theory in policy planning. The bureaucratic structures that produce contemporary foreign policy do not favor sensitive, intuitive observers whose delicate senses can detect subtle shifts in the wind of international affairs; they favor administrators and managers who are less interested in the significance of small differences between countries and situations than in broad theoretical principles and generalizations that enable bureaucrats to create, for example, "development policies" intended to operate in countries as different as Guatemala and Guinea-Bissau.

Unfortunately, when it comes to American Middle East policy discussions, glib theories about how the world works, how the peoples of the Middle East think, how liberal societies work, and about the roles that American Jews play in American politics work together to confuse and frustrate both policymakers and the general public. Whether it is orientalist caricatures of Middle Eastern peoples or antisemitic caricatures about Jews, bad theories about how groups of people think and behave—stereotypes—usually lead to bad analysis. When, as has happened more than once in American discussions about the Middle East, stereotypes about ethnic, racial, or religious groups combine with poorly grasped abstract theories about international relations, major confusion results, and the policies that flow out of this muddle rarely lead to success.

This is not a right-wing problem or a left-wing problem; it is a human problem and an American problem. Liberals and conservatives, isolationists and interventionists, realists and idealists all struggle to balance, and sometimes they all fail to balance, the inescapable need for theories and simplifications against the ineradicable truth that reality is more complicated than our sometimes crude mental approximations of it. There is no real way to solve the problem of theory; like so many other difficult and uncomfortable realities in the world of foreign policy, it is something that we have to live with, and it is yet another reason why we must so often resign ourselves to the disappointing and compromised results that flow from the policies we make.

The Problem of Progress

Americans are usually optimists; our history has made us so. The belief that history is ascending toward a future of more freedom, more justice, more abundance, and higher spiritual values is one of the foundations of American thought. It has been a powerful and often benign force in American politics and policy; it helped propel both the antislavery and women's suffrage movements to success, and its optimism about the

American future was a powerful influence on George Kennan's ideas about containment at the onset of the Cold War.

In many ways this optimism is a positive national trait, but the fit between American expectations and Middle East realities has never been smooth. Optimistic American missionaries in the nineteenth century believed that their work among the Armenians and other Christian minorities in the Ottoman Empire would promote harmony between Christians and Muslims and, eventually, lead Muslims to convert to Christianity.[5] In reality, the missionary work contributed to the national and sectarian conflicts that led to genocidal massacres of Middle Eastern Christians and brought some of the world's oldest Christian communities to the brink of extinction. Optimistic Americans believed that the establishment of a Zionist state would accelerate the economic and social development of the Middle East, and that the Arabs would learn from their Zionist neighbors and build prosperous democratic societies of their own.[6] Optimistic Americans believed that the newly independent Arab states were ripe for democracy after World War II. They believed that the Shah of Iran's so-called White Revolution would modernize and ultimately democratize Iran.[7] They believed that the Oslo Accords would lead to a permanent, stable peace between Israelis and Palestinians. After 9/11, optimistic neoconservatives believed that a new wave of democracy and prosperity would destroy the political appeal of jihadi ideology. They believed that an American intervention would lead to stable democracy in Iraq. Optimistic Americans believed that the Egyptian "revolution" of 2011 was creating a new Egypt, liberal, democratic, and westward looking.[8] They believed that overthrowing Muammar Qaddafi would bring better governance and safer living conditions for civilians in Libya.[9] They believed that Turkish Islamist Recep Tayyip Erdoğan was a democrat who would modernize Turkey and overcome the gap between Islam and western-style democracy.[10] They believed that Crown Prince Mohammed bin Salman was a forward-looking, modernizing reformer who was interested in moving Saudi Arabia toward a democratic future. Many now appear to believe that an American withdrawal from the region would leave it more tranquil without any serious negative impact on American interests worldwide.[11]

The disappearance of American optimism would be a bad thing. Much of the dynamism of American life springs from the habits of risk taking, innovation, and entrepreneurialism that an optimistic mindset creates. A more pessimistic America might be a wiser country that made fewer foreign policy blunders, but it would be weaker, poorer, and less influential than the America we know. Nevertheless, a sober analysis of America's Middle East track record leads to an inescapable conclusion: when it comes to analyzing events in the Middle East and crafting policies, a naive and deterministic optimism has led Americans to one grave error after another.

With respect to the Israeli-Palestinian dispute, American optimism leads to three very damaging mistakes. First, we continually overestimate the chances that negotiations for a lasting peace will actually succeed. These negotiations may someday succeed, and, speaking personally, I very much hope that they do. But every American president who has tried to reach this goal has fallen short, and these repeated failures have made the region less stable, further inflamed the dispute, and reduced American prestige while diverting American resources from other, more achievable goals.

Second, when negotiations fail, Americans, still overestimating the prospects for success, blame the intransigence of the two parties rather than acknowledging the difficulties of the task. Americans demonized Palestinian leader Yasser Arafat after he failed to respond to President Clinton's last-minute peace appeals in the closing weeks of his power; a more sober reading of Palestinian politics would have revealed that a final accord was exactly what Arafat could not endorse. Similarly, Israeli leaders are sometimes blamed when ambitious but impractical American initiatives fall to the ground. Much more than Americans see or are willing to admit, the obstacles to peace lie less in the intransigence of individual leaders than in the politics of both sides and the situation in the region at large.

Third, American optimism leads both elite and popular observers to mistake the nature of American power. The United States is a very powerful country, but Washington's ability to force smaller and weaker countries to take steps against the wishes of their leaders is much less extensive than most Americans appreciate. One American president after another has tried and failed to persuade Saudi leaders to provide equal rights for women, to introduce more democratic reform into the kingdom, and to soften the harsh nature of the dominant form of Islam preached in its mosques. While Saudi officials know that the United

States has been the kingdom's protector of last resort for seventy years and its most reliable source of weaponry, American pressure is only one of the forces the Saudis must negotiate, and they will continue to resist American pressure that, in their view, threatens their hold on power at home.

There are similar limits on Washington's ability to wring concessions on human rights from Egypt, on settlements from Israel, on financial support for terrorists' families from Palestinians, on final status negotiations from both Israelis and Palestinians, and on much else besides.

This overestimation of American power creates political difficulties for American presidents whatever their party or whatever their approach to the Middle East. If Washington is as powerful as many Americans think it is, then any problem in the Middle East must ultimately be the responsibility of bad political decisions taken in Washington. If Israel is not being forthcoming enough in peace negotiations, if the Palestinians aren't doing enough to suppress terrorist incitement in their schools, or if democracy isn't on the march across the Arab world, this is because the American president is doing something wrong.

America-centrism is another form of this tendency to overestimate American power. Alice Longworth once said that her father, Theodore Roosevelt, wanted to be the "bride at every wedding, the corpse at every funeral, the child at every christening." That is not a bad description of what many Americans, even relatively well-educated and experienced Americans, think the American role in world history has been. As we shall see, America's role in Middle East politics has often been much less significant than both pro-Zionist and anti-Israel observers assume. Harry Truman was, for example, less significant than Joseph Stalin in the diplomacy surrounding the emergence of an independent Israel, and France, not the United States, was Israel's most important ally right up through the 1967 war. Americans not only overestimate what their country can do to shape the future in the Middle East; we often overestimate what we have accomplished in the past.

ORIENTALISM

In 1978, Columbia University professor Edward W. Said published the groundbreaking book *Orientalism,* and the discussion of Middle East policy will never be the same. Said noted, quite rightly, that the peoples of the Middle East were perceived through a thick fog of preexisting prejudices, cultural incomprehension, and a political context shaped by colonialism and western domination. Said's book was not without problems, and his assessment of earlier scholarship was sometimes both inaccurate and unfair, but overall, it cannot be denied that the portrayal of Arabs, including Palestinians, and Islam in the western world was and to some degree still is distorted. Islam was reduced to an intellectual and spiritual caricature; Middle Easterners were seen as simple people who needed redemption through westernization and modernization.

There is no doubt that prejudice and orientalism played a significant role in the development of American attitudes toward the Zionist movement and its enemies. American travelers in nineteenth-century Palestine portrayed the country as a thinly populated desert whose inhabitants were, at best, indolent and backward.[12] They were, perhaps, picturesque, but few Americans considered the townspeople, farmers, and herders of Palestine as their equals.

Orientalism is still a factor in American perceptions of the Middle East, and the tendency to substitute caricatures and stereotypes for real knowledge and understanding continues to darken our counsel. These orientalist stereotypes become a civil rights issue when immigrants, refugees, visiting students, and others face hostility, discrimination, and in some cases violence because of fears and hatreds rooted in a distorted vision of the world. The effect of these ideas on American debates about Israel and about Middle East policy is still felt; popular prejudices about the peoples of the Middle East make sensible policy discussions about Israel and its neighbors more difficult to have.

Orientalism is often seen as a problem of the right and as a carrier of anti-Arab and even Islamophobic images and ideas, but western liberals struggle with an orientalism of their own. Sympathetic caricature is still caricature, and it remains an obstacle to full understanding of a rich and complicated political culture. In terms of the Arab-Israeli conflict the most common form of what could be called the orientalism of the left involves a romanticization and simplification of Arab reactions to the Jewish state. In recent years, the wide variety in Arab approaches to Israel has become more visible as the Gulf states turn to Israel as a valuable if not beloved ally against both Iranian and Turkish ambitions. If anything, Egypt under President Abdel Fattah el-Sisi and the Palestinian Authority on the West Bank have usually pursued a harder line against the radical Islamist Hamas government in Gaza than Israel has done. But the Arab relationship with the Zionist movement and Israel has never been as monolithic as many believe. Most of the land that Zionists settled before 1947 was freely sold to them by Arabs. In the 1948–49 war, no Arab state really wanted to see an independent Arab Palestine emerge from the conflict. The Jordanians, at the time the most militarily formidable of the Arab states, negotiated with both the British and the Israelis to conquer the part of Palestine designated as an Arab state by the 1947 U.N. partition resolution. The Egyptians, once it was clear that they could not conquer it for themselves, preferred an Israeli presence in the Negev Desert to Jordanian control. Jordan at the time was an ally of the U.K., and the British hoped to use the Negev as a base to defend the Suez Canal against a possible Egyptian takeover. Iraq and Jordan, both ruled at the time by Hashemite kings, hoped to unite the fertile crescent into the state that, they believed, the British had promised them during World War I. The Syrians were more interested in keeping the Iraqis and the Jordanians at bay than in helping the Palestinians establish a state. After the Israeli War of Independence, Jordan controlled the West Bank, including the Old City of Jerusalem, and Egypt controlled Gaza. Either country could have set up an independent Palestinian state in the territory they held; neither country encouraged Palestinian independence in those territories until the Israelis conquered them in the 1967 war.

The mix of public hostility and quiet cooperation between Arab states and Israel that we see today is nothing new. Security cooperation between Jordan and Israel was a reality long before the two countries signed a peace treaty. As early as the 1960s, Israel helped Saudi Arabia thwart Egyptian president Gamal Abdel Nasser's ambitions in Yemen.[13] Neither Arabs as a whole nor Palestinians are nor ever have been a monolithic people unanimously opposed to Israel. The picture of an Arab world united in an unrelenting hatred of the "Zionist entity" contributes to a sense of Arabs as in some way less human, less enlightened than westerners. It is as orientalist to claim that all Arabs are fanatical members of the anti-Zionist resistance as it is to say that all Arabs or Muslims are religious fanatics.

This form of orientalism doesn't just lead to mistaken ideas about Arabs. It also distorts the American discussion over Israel policy. One reason some observers have exaggerated the power of the "Israel lobby" is their belief that policy battles over issues like military aid for Israel involve a bitter zero-sum contest between pro-Israel forces and a united and determined "Arab lobby." Arab alienation from the United States over the Israel issue, many have believed over the years, puts U.S. access to Arab oil at risk and imperils the fortunes of American oil companies.

If that is all true, the Israel lobby must be awesome indeed. But it hasn't been true. It has always been the case that their own security—the security of their countries, the security of their dynasties, their own personal security—has been the major priority of the oil sheikhs. Some have been more anti-Zionist than others in their private feelings, but in their foreign policy these states are too weak and too surrounded by envious rivals and enemies to privilege visionary projects like throwing the "Zionist entity" back into the sea over the quiet pursuit of more important, more attainable, and more immediate goals.

THE JEWISH QUESTION AND THE JEWISH STATE

Left and right orientalism muddles American thinking about the Arab world; the widespread belief, especially abroad, but frequently found in the United States, that a sinister "Israel lobby" somehow controls America's Middle East policy is also a source of distortion and error.

Antisemitism is a tricky subject to discuss. Many of modern Israel's most bitter critics in the United States are proud and passionately committed Jews whose critique of Israel is grounded in their understanding of Jewish ethics; clearly, one can be a critic, even a bitter and persistent critic, of Israel without harboring feelings of hatred toward the Jewish people as a whole.

There is nothing inherently antisemitic about criticizing a given Israel policy on moral or pragmatic grounds, and still less is there anything inherently antisemitic about arguing that the interests of the United States might lie in opposing Israel on a particular issue rather than supporting it.

There is nothing inherently antisemitic about believing that the Balfour Declaration was unjust to Palestinians or that American interests would be better served by withdrawing from the Middle East rather than remaining engaged with it. Arguments about ideas and about policies generally deserve and indeed demand to be addressed on the merits, rather than with a flurry of ad hominem attacks about the imputed motives of those making them.

Yet it would be obtuse to deny that reactions to Israeli actions are often fueled by passions and perceptions grounded in antisemitic memes and ideas, and that antisemitism is deeply entrenched in the culture and thought processes, not only of that misguided and unfortunate portion of humanity that consciously espouses antisemitic ideas, but of many others who do not always perceive the antisemitic origins or implications of false but plausible-seeming ideas that have long been a part of the mental furniture of our civilization.

Antisemitism itself is related to a broader phenomenon, something my brilliant former colleague Adam Garfinkle has written a book about. Many people—Jews, antisemites, and others—share a tendency to think that Jews play a larger role in human society than they actually do. Garfinkle's term for this phenomenon is "Jewcentricity."[14] Both the pro-Zionist and anti-Zionist narratives about the birth of the Jewish state exaggerate the Jewish role in the events that created Israel and overlook the critical importance of gentile support in making the Zionist movement powerful among Jews. As I studied the degree to which the Zionist movement's unique ability to get critical gentile support gave Zionism a prominence and power among Jews that it otherwise could never have had, I was frequently tempted to subtitle this book "Don't Blame Israel on the Jews."

I resisted that temptation, but the mistaken impression that Zionism is an agenda that powerful Jews imposed either on the United States or on the gentile world at large remains a major reason why so much of our national conversation about Middle East policy consumes so much energy but produces so little good policy. Antisemitism is not just an invidious prejudice, and therefore a moral error; it is an intellectual error, and an example of a bad political theory. Antisemitism commits its adherents to a set of damaging errors about how power works in the modern world. Those who think that "the Jews" control finance don't understand how economic power works. Those who think that "the Jews" control American politics understand neither the United States nor its political system. Those who think that "the Jews" control the American media and abuse that power to create an American consensus behind support for Israel don't know much about American Jews, the

American media, or the many millions of non-Jewish Americans who have their own reasons for supporting an American alliance with the Jewish state.

If we are to have a serious and effective national conversation about Israel policy, we will have to clear away the mistaken ideas and perceptions that any conversation about the Jewish people naturally and inevitably attracts. We need a less Jewcentric narrative of both Zionist history and of America's engagement with the Zionist project.

2

The Quest for Planet Vulcan

A NYONE INTERESTED IN both the benefits and the drawbacks of theory can learn from the career of Urbain Le Verrier, a distinguished French astronomer of the nineteenth century. Compared to American foreign policy, the mechanics of the solar system are relatively simple and easy to make good theories about; as early as the late seventeenth century Sir Isaac Newton had mastered many if not all of the concepts needed to explain the motion of the various planets, meteors, and comets that sweep around the sun. But every now and then some loose ends cropped up. In the 1840s, scientists observing the orbit of Uranus noted that its motion didn't conform to the known laws of gravity. Instead of traveling around the sun in a smooth and undisturbed ellipse, Uranus's orbit was subtly irregular. Either the laws of gravity were wrong, or something was pulling the distant planet out of place. Le Verrier, an acknowledged expert on celestial mechanics, did the math and predicted the location of an undiscovered planet perturbing the Uranian orbit. In a letter to Johann Gottfried Galle, a young German astronomer, Le Verrier included his calculations about the unknown planet, asking Galle to see whether its existence could be confirmed. Galle pointed his telescope to the predicted location and there, almost exactly at the spot Le Verrier predicted, the planet Neptune swam into view.[1]

The news caused a sensation and made celebrities out of both Galle and Le Verrier. Both men have craters on the moon and rings of Neptune named after them; Le Verrier was one of seventy-two distinguished persons to have his name engraved on the Eiffel Tower. But Le Verrier didn't stop with Neptune. Flush with success, he took a look at another loose end in the tidy world of Newtonian cosmology: Mercury's motion was also irregular. Unless the laws of Newtonian physics were wrong, something must be operating on Mercury to explain its mysterious shifts. Le Verrier hypothesized that a hidden planet must be responsible, and, based on its effects, he calculated the size and predicted the orbit of a mysterious planet even closer to the Sun than Mercury. Astronomers all over the world began to comb the skies, hoping for the glory and fame that would follow the new planet's discovery.

The search did not take long. Edmond Modeste Lescarbault, a French amateur astronomer, had observed what at first appeared to be a sunspot, but on closer examination looked more like a small planet transiting the sun. Le Verrier took the train to the village of Orgères-en-Beauce, reviewed Lescarbault's observations, and on January 2, 1860, at a meeting of the French Academy of Sciences he proclaimed the discovery of a new planet to the world. There was another sensation, and the government of Napoleon III awarded the Légion d'honneur to the newly famous Lescarbault.[2]

The new planet was named Vulcan, in honor of the Greco-Roman blacksmith god whose work kept him close to the blazing hot forge. While some thought it surprising that a planet so close to the earth had escaped the observation of astronomers for so long, Le Verrier's allies pointed out that the very brightness of the sun made an object as small as a planet easy to miss. It was only when Vulcan crossed or transited the sun, or during an eclipse, that the small planet could be observed from the earth. Over the next few years a series of astronomers in Britain, France, and Turkey spotted transits of Vulcan. The most impressive confirmations came from the United States. Lewis Swift, an amateur astronomer from Rochester, New York, saw Vulcan from an observation post near Denver; Professor James Craig Watson of the University of Michigan, accompanied by the famous inventor Thomas Edison, traveled to the remote hamlet of Separation, Wyoming, to observe a solar eclipse. As the sun's light dimmed, Planet Vulcan duly appeared.[3]

With so many professors and eminent observers in so many places spotting it, the existence of Vulcan seemed to be settled science. Yet there were problems. The observations of Vulcan didn't follow predictable patterns. Different astronomers made different calculations of its size, its speed, and its path around the sun, but none of the models quite worked. Astronomers both professional and amateur continued to spot Vulcan, but the observations never quite tallied with the predicted orbits. At one point, the confusion was so great that it was suggested that one planet wasn't enough; there had to be two planets inside the orbit of Mercury.[4]

It took Albert Einstein to sort things out. Einstein's theory of relativity offered another, and more convincing, explanation for Mercury's motion. Mercury's irregularities had nothing to do with another planet, but were caused by effects of the sun's gravity on the space-time fabric that Newtonian physics knew nothing about. The astronomers who spent decades hunting for Planet Vulcan had fallen victim to bad theory; their conviction that Planet Vulcan must exist led them to misinterpret what they saw even as it blinded them to the richer and more comprehensive worldview that lay beyond the physics they understood.

It is rare for solar astronomers to go off on wild-goose chases like the hunt for Planet Vulcan, but students of foreign policy lead less predictable lives. In the world of foreign policy, even experts go badly wrong, and history is full of examples in which very serious and thoughtful people have fundamentally mistaken the nature of the forces with which they were trying to deal. As noted earlier, a common source of often very damaging mistakes comes when foreign policy practitioners mix stripped-down and simplified assumptions about how groups of people behave—stereotypical ideas about ethnic groups, religious communities, and ideological movements, for example—with simplistic theories about the international system. The result is almost always confusion, and the consequences are often grim. As shrewd and as ruthless as Joseph Stalin was, crude Marxist ideas about how "bourgeois" and "imperialist" governments behaved often led him astray. Adolf Hitler's foreign policy was distorted by his belief that "the Jews" were behind both the capitalist and communist governments that he faced. During the Cold War, Americans frequently missed the subtleties and complexities of important international developments because they viewed events through a simplistic "us vs. them" paradigm. Had Americans understood how estranged the Soviet Union and China had become by the early 1960s, the most tragic American misadventure of the Cold War era might have been avoided.

We've seen that stereotypes and illusions based on oversimplified political theories have played a significant role in American policy in the Middle East. Crude ideas about the nature of Iraqi society and its prospects for democracy led the George W. Bush administration to misread the realities of Middle Eastern politics in Iraq; just a few years later the Obama administration would make eerily similar mistakes about the Arab Spring in countries as important as Egypt. We've seen that orientalist stereotypes about Arabs and Muslims have frequently led Americans to miss opportunities and make false steps in the Middle East. Similarly, stereotypes about Jews, in the United States and abroad, have often confused analysts about the sources and aims of American policy.

Indeed, the way many observers have thought about America's relationship with Israel bears an uncanny resemblance to Le Verrier's approach to Planet Vulcan. The United States and the other states in the international system are seen to circle the sun of the national interest on steady and predictable orbits—except for a certain wobble in the American orbit when the subject of Israel comes up. The search for Planet Vulcan, the mass of dark matter whose gravitational pull is responsible for America's deviation from the true path of the national interest, has engaged many minds.

Down through the years there has been no shortage of books and articles claiming that an "Israel lobby" that prioritizes Israel's interests over those of the United States, composed largely of American Jews and empowered by their wealth ("It's all about the Benjamins," as a first-term congressional representative inelegantly but forcefully put it)[5] largely controls both the public discussion of U.S.-Israel relations and the actual policy. We can call this the Vulcan Theory of American Israel policy: it is the belief that Jewish power exerted in the interest of a foreign state is subordinating American policy to the will of another state.

There is more than one version of this modern Vulcan Theory, just as there was more than one theory about Planet Vulcan. Some observers see two planets at work: fundamentalist Christian support is also involved in the force that pulls the United States away from its true national interest. With or without the evangelical embellishment, the belief that American Jews control America's Israel policy is an article of faith in much of the world.

Vulcan Theory is somewhat less popular in the United States than it is abroad, but over the years many Americans have accepted it. In 1974, General George S. Brown, then chairman of the Joint Chiefs of Staff, bemoaned Israel's influence in Congress and said that Jews "own, you know, the banks in this country, the newspapers."[6] Columnist and onetime candidate for the Republican presidential nomination Pat Buchanan called Capitol Hill "Israeli occupied territory" on national television in 1990.[7] Minister Louis Farrakhan, one of America's leading Vulcanists, told an audience that "the Israeli lobby controls the government of the United States of America."[8] Senator J. William Fulbright, longtime chairman of the Senate Foreign Relations Committee, charged in 1973 that "the Senate is subservient to Israel," and that the United States could not use its economic leverage to affect Israeli policy because "Israel controls the Senate."[9]

To have an intelligent discussion about Vulcan Theory is hard. Those who accept it do not think of themselves as victims of prejudice; as they see it, they are drawing obvious conclusions from overwhelming evidence. When, after stating what they see as obvious facts about American foreign policy, they find themselves widely attacked for antisemitism, they see those attacks as confirming the truth of their original conclusions. Anybody who dares to tell the truth about Jewish power in the United States, they claim, is subjected to nonstop vituperation and driven to the margins of public life. What more proof could one want that "the Jews" dominate the media and the policy debate?

Even so, for reasons that Vulcan Theory proponents sometimes do not understand, many Americans, and not only Jewish Americans, find some of the ideas that inform Vulcan Theory—and some of the language in which its ideas are often expressed—problematic in the extreme. Any allegation that American Jews are powerful string-pullers who secretly control our political system immediately strikes many people as a form of vicious and ignorant bigotry. Similarly, the allegation that American Jews are less loyal than other Americans, that as a group they have what is known as a "dual loyalty," preferring the interests of Israel over those of the United States, is seen by many people as an ugly smear, an expression of the kind of hate and prejudice that no honest and intelligent person should embrace.

Discussions of Israel policy often break down at this point. When charged with antisemitism after voicing what they see as perfectly reasonable ideas, Vulcan proponents become more deeply convinced that a powerful and well-organized Jewish lobby group is trying to curtail all discussion of an important topic. And the more Vulcan Theorists refer to these ideas, the more vociferous the cries of antisemitism become.

the history of U.S.-Israel relations, wrong about the way foreign policy works, wrong about the American political process, wrong about American Christians, and, last but by no means least, it is wrong not only about American Jews but about the political context of Zionism. This never was, and given the power relationships between gentiles and Jews, never could be an agenda that "the Jews" imposed on the gentile world. The triumph of Zionism in the Jewish community was driven less by the spontaneous appeal of Zionism to Jews than by the recognition, late and reluctant in many cases for many Jews, that unshakable gentile preferences and priorities, which all the Jewish power in the world was helpless to alter, made the odd and unlikely ideology of Zionism the only program that offered many of the world's Jews a hope however modest for both personal and cultural survival. Israel is not a project that Jews imposed on gentiles; for better or for worse it is something that gentiles, antisemites included, and Jews made together.

THE NATIONAL INTEREST

The heart of Vulcan Theory is the idea that America's Israel policy does not serve America's national interest, but serves Israeli interests instead. When Israeli interests are at stake, the United States deviates from its "true orbit" around the sun of the national interest, and the quest for Planet Vulcan is the quest to identify the lump of dark matter responsible for this otherwise inexplicable behavior.

This picture is, to use Secretary of State Dean Acheson's phrase, a great deal "clearer than truth."[11] In the real world, as opposed to the simplified cosmos of an IR—international relations—theory textbook, the national interest is rarely clear and almost always in dispute; politicians and national leaders are often much more interested in preserving their own power than in anything so abstract and patriotic as the national interest, even if they could be sure what it was.

As soon as we begin to think seriously about the national interest, we face some very tough questions. It is difficult to define the national interest, and it is difficult to identify with any certainty the policies by which it can best be served. People come to politics with very different ideas about what the national interest is and how we can advance it. Some Americans, for example, believe that America's national interest requires us to build a global order based on democracy, free markets, and the rule of law. Only this, they believe, can prevent the eruption of new wars between the great powers that could exterminate our species, while offering the scope for American enterprise to operate on a global scale in ways that assure American prosperity in a stable and affluent world. To achieve this goal, they believe that the United States should engage in an active, global foreign policy aimed at strengthening organizations like the United Nations and the International Criminal Court. American forces should be used, preferably in association with others but if necessary on our own, to protect human rights.

This approach has its critics. Some Americans believe that a global foreign policy of this kind leads to endless wars overseas. Others believe that the economic policies like free trade that this approach involves actually work to the detriment of American workers. Some believe that the project is unrealistic, and that the nations of the world will never create the kind of order that these Americans are hoping to build.

My book *Special Providence* centers on a discussion of four very different traditions of American thought about the national interest—Jeffersonians, Hamiltonians, Wilsonians, and Jacksonians all care about the American national interest—who often disagree profoundly about what that interest is or how it can best be achieved. Wilsonians believe that the United States should promote the establishment of a world order based on human rights, international law, and powerful multinational institutions. Hamiltonians believe that we must build a strong federal government that can act to support American business abroad and economic development at home. Jeffersonians believe that too much activity overseas will increase the risk of war, promote inequality in the United States, and reduce individual freedom at home. Jacksonians share Jeffersonian skepticism about Wilsonian interventions to promote human rights and Hamiltonian support of a strong central government and pro-corporate economic policies; but unlike Jeffersonians, they believe that the United States will not be safe unless other countries respect our willingness to use force to defend our honor, our interests, and our allies. These schools argue for very different foreign policies. The quarrel is more than two hundred years old; it is no closer to being settled now than it was when George Washington was president.

The political history of American foreign policy is not a struggle between patriots wanting to advance the national interest and traitors who seek to undermine it; it is a history of conflicting ideas about what the national interest means and how to pursue it under particular circumstances. When Secretary of State William H. Seward supported the annexation of Alaska and opponents denounced it as "Seward's Folly" and "Andrew Johnson's Polar Bear Garden," the opponents were not a Russia lobby or a British lobby seeking to prevent American territorial expansion in order to help foreign governments. They were patriotic Americans who believed, wrongly as it turned out, that the addition of a large but largely empty expanse of territory on the far northern fringes of the American continent would not be worth the purchase price of $7.2 million.[12] Intelligent people can and frequently do disagree in good faith about what the national interest is—which means that the national interest is anything but self-evident much of the time.

Even if we could agree on what the national interest is, it is unlikely that we would often find a consensus about what policies are most likely to achieve it. The history of American foreign policy is in part a history of disappointment—when policies do not work out as planned— and partly a history of surprise, when unexpected developments catch American policymakers off guard. American officials were unable to predict the Iranian Revolution of 1979; neither did they predict the fall of the Soviet Union ten years later. The administration of George W. Bush failed to anticipate the 2008 Russian invasion of Georgia; Barack Obama's administration failed to anticipate Russia's intervention in Syria or the boost to Russian influence that the intervention—which the Obama administration, wrongly, predicted would fail—ultimately provided. Over thousands of years of human history we can see how great leaders and great states have been repeatedly surprised by both positive and negative events that they could not predict and did not expect.

In the Middle East, the predictions of those who supported and those who opposed closer U.S.-Israel relations have repeatedly been proven wrong. Pro-Israel observers argued in 1948 that Arab hostility to the new state would rapidly diminish. Anti-Israel observers argued that U.S. relations with Israel would frustrate our efforts to build a Cold War alliance with the Arabs against the extension of Soviet power. Both predictions were wrong. Arab bitterness over the establishment of Israel remains a powerful force in the Middle East even today; on the other hand, during the Cold War and beyond no other power has been able to develop and maintain the range of deep, cooperative, and strategic relationships the United States has built with many countries in the Arab world.

The political struggle over foreign policy is never and can never be an intellectual contest in a seminar room, where calmly rational arguments lead to a stable consensus. Many participants in the political debate have only very hazy ideas about the national interest; they are much more interested in the interests of a particular domestic constituency— sugarcane farmers and orange juice growers opposed to a free trade agreement with Brazil, Armenian Americans opposed to a deeper U.S.-Turkey relationship, gay activists opposed to close relations with African governments that criminalize homosexuality, arms manufacturers fighting to lift controls on the export of powerful weapons to unstable but well-heeled rulers abroad, politicians who only want reelection, and many others. If we add to these self-interested voices in the debate the voices of those who do care about the national interest but disagree fundamentally about how the national interest can be defined and how it should be pursued, we begin to understand how chaotic, how unpredictable, and how contingent the formation of American foreign policy actually is.

No umpire is capable of issuing an objective and infallible ruling about which of the possible courses is actually correct; historians, we can be sure, will debate the merits of important American foreign policy choices for years to come without necessarily reaching a consensus. If historians often do not agree about whether our policies in the past were effective and wise, what kind of agreement can we expect from policymakers and politicians today about whether a given policy will work?

America's Israel policy, like our NATO policy, our trade policy, our Venezuela policy, and our human rights policy, poses a set of complicated questions, and Americans do not always or even usually agree about what we should be trying to achieve, much less the best strategy for achieving it. Lacking certain knowledge about future developments, we seek to steer our policies based on different ideas about how the world works, what America needs, and what our priorities should be. No side in these debates is always right, and no side is always wrong. This is politics, not algebra. It is art, not science.

Vulcanism assumes a clarity that does not exist: that the "correct" foreign policy in the Middle East is obvious, that this correct policy rarely if ever involves a close U.S.-Israel relationship, and that the only people who dispute this obvious truth are Jews driven by dual loyalty, evangelical Christians blinded by superstitious ideas about the end of the world, and opportunistic scoundrels who follow the Benjamins wherever they lead.

THE HISTORICAL RECORD

One of the problems for Vulcan Theory is that American policy toward Israel has not been historically consistent. If an extremely powerful Israel lobby guided by Israeli rather than American interests was responsible for America's policy toward the Zionist movement and the Jewish state, we would expect that America's Israel policy would not show much change over time, and we would also expect to find that American support would be strongest when Israel needed help most.

That is not what happened. American policy toward the Zionist movement before 1948 and to the State of Israel after that date has varied widely. In 1937 Britain issued the Peel Report and sharply limited Jewish migration to Palestine even as Nazi persecution of the Jews was intensifying. The United States put no pressure on Britain to change its policy. During the 1930s and 1940s, despite vigorous efforts, American Jews were unable to mobilize America against Hitler, unable to persuade the American public to admit Jewish refugees from Nazi persecution, and unable even to persuade Franklin Roosevelt to bomb the rail tracks leading to Auschwitz. When the Jews needed the United States most, the United States was nowhere to be seen; if there was ever a time for American Jews to demonstrate their mastery of the American political process, from the standpoint of the interests of Jews around the world, that would have been the time to do it.

From ignoring Jewish powerlessness during most of the 1930s and 1940s, Vulcan Theory then highlights Jewish influence over the Truman administration. President Harry Truman's Palestine policy between 1945 and 1948 is seen to demonstrate the irresistible power of the apparently invincible Israel lobby.

Vulcan theorists do not even attempt to describe what must have been an extraordinary process of Jewish political development that transformed the hapless Jewish leaders vainly begging Roosevelt to spare a few bombs for the rail lines to Auschwitz in 1944 into the ruthless dictators of 1948 forcing a cowed Harry Truman to follow their bidding. A revolution so complete, so astonishing in American politics as a Jewish seizure of power in the mid-1940s ought to be the object of great interest by historians. The libraries should be full of books on this fascinating subject, and the memoirs of those who brought it about would be documents of great value. Yet somehow these books do not seem to exist.

The Vulcan hypothesis leads from one monstrous historical incongruity to another. The powerless Jews begging Roosevelt for bombs may have become the supreme rulers of American foreign policy under Truman, but by 1953 they must have all died of the plague. While there is an unthinking perception among many that the United States and Israel have "always" been allied, history tells a very different story. Under presidents Dwight Eisenhower and John F. Kennedy, the focus of American policy in the Middle East was Egypt, not Israel. In the hope of developing a relationship with Nasser, the United States worked to make Egypt its preferred partner in the Middle East at Israel's expense.

So how did those ruthless Jewish dictators who held Truman in thrall lose their grip? Why was Eisenhower able to defy the erstwhile hidden masters of American politics? How did the Jews lose their cunning? If American policy toward Israel has varied significantly, and it has, and we are supposed to believe that the power of a shadowy Israel lobby is the most important determinant of American policy in the Middle East, then a history of American foreign policy would need to include a history of the rising and falling fortunes of this lobby, explaining why it is more influential at some moments, less influential in others.

We will look at the historical record in more detail later; it is enough for the present purpose to note that American support for Israel has been both less consistent and less tied to Israel's needs than Vulcan Theory would have it. In the 1950s and early 1960s, when Israel was a weak regional power, the American attitude toward Israel was distant and cold. Israeli prime ministers did not visit the White House; the United States not only did not send Israel military aid but Israel was prevented from buying American weapons. It was only as Israel became a more influential and powerful country in the region that American attitudes shifted. Israel the victim never drew much American support; Israel the victor found America eager to cooperate.

Vulcan Theory does not seriously engage with the complicated actual history of American relations with the Jewish state and the Zionist movement; to do so would test the theory to destruction. There are many criticisms one can make about American Middle East policy in the last one hundred years, but the idea that the influence of American Jews—even with the help of evangelical Christians—shaped that policy to serve the interests of Zionism does not explain the historical record. If we want to understand the American Middle East policy we must dig deeper than Vulcan Theory.

Dark Planet

Vulcan Theorists are not wrong to ask why American policy is often so pro-Israel; nor are they wrong to look to politics and even to lobby politics for an answer. Foreign policy is always a political question; even in undemocratic societies foreign policy decisions reflect political calculations by rulers who worry about their hold on power at home as much as and sometimes more than they worry about defending their power abroad. The problem with the Vulcan approach to the politics of Israel policy is not that it is too focused on the political support for Israel in American society; it is that the Vulcanist analysis of American politics is too crude. Their fault isn't that they think too much about the Israel lobby; it is that they haven't thought about it enough.

The topic of lobbies in politics makes Americans uncomfortable today in much the same way and for much the same reasons that the topic of political parties made Americans uncomfortable in the Federalist Era. Politics is supposed to be about the general good; parties then— and lobbies now—are seen as chiefly interested in special as opposed to general interests. The sugar beet lobby cares a lot more about the financial well-being of sugar beet farmers than it does about the health of American democracy as a whole. The Founding Fathers were ashamed of being seen to act on the part of a special interest—of a "faction" in the language of the day—in much the same way an aspiring politician today would not want to be seen as the tool of a lobby.

Yet lobbies are as indispensable to the functioning of representative government now as factions were to the Federalists. Lobbies are organized groups that seek to influence the political process in a particular direction. With its large population, robust civil society, active federal government, diverse economic base, and far-reaching foreign policy, the United States leads the world in lobbies, whether one looks at commercial lobbies like the Chamber of Commerce, environmental lobbies like Greenpeace, or ideological lobbies like NARAL and Human Rights Watch. Religious organizations maintain lobbying offices in Washington; foreign governments funnel torrents of cash to public relations firms; and civil servants, elected officials, and congressional staffers toil at low-paid public-sector jobs in the sure and certain hope of a lucrative afterlife in the influence industry.

There is no other way in a complex society like ours that the various groups whose interests are directly affected by federal legislation or policy can make their views known to the officials whose actions will determine their fate, and while abuses and corruption sometimes occur, the existence and activity of lobbies are normal and necessary parts of the political process. To the extent that Vulcan Theorists believe that it is unusual or illegitimate for supporters of close U.S.-Israel relations to organize politically to advance their point of view, but they don't object to the presence of lobbies throughout American life, they are applying a different standard to pro-Israel groups than to other political movements.

One group of Vulcan Theorists argue that the Israel lobby is different from all other lobbies. This was the argument I heard during a seminar in Amman, Jordan, as Jordanian experts analyzed the politics of American foreign policy. It was, most of them felt, "the Jews" rather than "the oil companies" who ran the United States. The Jordanians reached this conclusion because the oil companies and other corporations—who presumably value good relations with the Arab countries where many of the world's most abundant oil resources are found—have been unable to prevent American presidents from choosing pro-Israel policies that Arabs dislike. Given the immense wealth and presumed power of the oil companies in American politics, a power that can defeat them must be awesome indeed. Planet Vulcan must be very large.

American as opposed to Jordanian academics who agree that the Israel lobby is qualitatively different from other lobbies reach this conclusion by a variety of routes. There are, for example, academics who teach that domestic politics is largely irrelevant to the foreign policy of a given state. The competitive and anarchic nature of the international system leaves governments no real choice in foreign policy. In the eat-or-be-eaten world of international politics, states—seen as rational actors whose goal is survival—do what they must. They circle the sun of the national interest on predictable orbits. Yet at the time of George W.

Bush's 2003 invasion of Iraq, in the minds of some analysts, America wobbled. American foreign policy appeared to diverge so far from the rational pursuit of state survival that it was necessary to seek the cause.

Only one factor appeared to be powerful enough to have pulled American policy into such a strange deviation from its expected orbit: the "Israel lobby" was playing the role of Planet Vulcan. The Iraq War might not have been in the American national interest, these analysts argued, but it was in Israel's interest.[13] A cabal of Jewish neoconservatives and big-money donors who privileged Israel's national interests over those of the United States must, they reasoned, somehow be controlling the Bush administration.

The claim that the pro-Israel lobby is uniquely powerful in American politics looks, on its face, antisemitic to many people. That's not quite fair to the proponents of this line of thought, and we will look more closely at this approach when our story reaches the Bush administration.

The claim that the Israel lobby is unique is Vulcan Theory in its purest form, but there is another approach to the question. Both on the left and on the right in American politics one can find people who object to the excessive power of all economically powerful lobbies, the Israel lobby included. For such people, the problem is not that America has a powerful Israel lobby, but that American policy in general is under the control of well-organized and well-funded lobby groups. Given the power of these special interests, America's pretensions to be a democratic government are fraudulent, and the special interests control virtually everything we do. Many people believe that this is the case: that the oil companies control our oil policy, other corporations control our policy toward Latin American producers of raw materials, and pro-Israel Jews control our Israel policy. This is a very common critique of American society and American foreign policy that informs the cynicism of Gore Vidal, the wrath of Noam Chomsky, and the disdain of Ron Paul. From this perspective, elite groups organized into powerful lobbies dominate American life. American democracy as currently practiced is essentially a sham, a theatrical performance behind which our real masters go about their business of controlling state policy. All the politicians spouting platitudes about "the issues" and "values" are simply there to make it harder for ordinary people to understand the hidden forces that in fact shape both foreign and domestic policy in our corporate and plutocratic state.

This is a classic antiliberal argument that long predates the existence of Israel and that has been used by Marxist and populist movements to attack liberal democracy since the nineteenth century. It treats foreign and domestic policy as largely interchangeable; the Israel lobby controls Middle East policy in much the same way that the employers' lobby controls labor policy. It is not totally without merit; clearly wealth plays a role in American politics and rich lobbies often have more success than poor ones.

Whether one takes the Chomsky position that the Israel lobby is one lobby among many that successfully reduce the democratic process to a charade or the competing position that the Israel lobby is different from all the others, both positions, if true, amount to fundamental critiques of the concept of democracy as practiced in the United States. Either way, the Israel lobby argument is not just an argument about Middle East policy; it is an argument about what kind of society we live in. It is an argument about the health of American democracy.

If Chomsky is right, we need something very like a revolution in the United States to replace our current ugly regime of state-sponsored terrorism with something at least marginally less awful. If the problem is just the Israel lobby, then we need to do something about the power of evangelical Christians and Jews.

While there are flashes of truth in both lines of analysis, both take one feature of American foreign policy and blow it out of proportion. Chomsky and company are surely right that corporate lobbies and similar groups exercise significant influence in American foreign and domestic policy, and that this influence isn't always or even often exercised in the service of a philanthropic vision of the common good. And no one in their right mind would deny that there are groups who lobby the American government on behalf of what they believe to be "pro-Israel" policies and that this lobbying is often successful.

But even so, these writers and thinkers are wrong about American politics. There are lobbies and they do have influence on matters of both domestic and, despite what some realists claim, foreign policy, but the American political system is more than the creature of powerful interest groups operating behind the scenes. Lobbies can win victories here and there, and a smart, well-financed lobby will do better than a foolishly led or poorly funded one, but American democracy is not just a slogan. To control the policy of the United States government over the long run on an issue that the public cares about, something else is needed: public support.

Take the tobacco lobby. In the middle of the last century, Big Tobacco was widely believed to be the most powerful lobby in Washington. It was political suicide to go up against it, and for years the tobacco lobby was able to get almost everything it wanted. But then the wind changed. Public opinion about smoking began to shift. The tobacco lobby had just as much money as before, and its lobbyists were just as skilled, but gradually the tobacco interests began to lose ground. Before long, it was political suicide for politicians to take money from tobacco companies. Public opinion changed and then policy changed. The tobacco lobby had to lower its sights. It could no longer fight smoking restrictions, suppress medical studies linking tobacco to cancer, or fight taxes on its products. The tobacco lobby has not disappeared, and tobacco companies continue to fund it, but it is a much less ambitious force in Washington and state capitols today.

Some of the most powerful lobbies in the United States today are powerful because they represent public opinion, rather than opposing it. The American Association of Retired Persons (AARP) with its membership of nearly 37 million[14] dues-paying people over fifty years of age has time and again brushed back well-funded attempts by Wall Street firms and their allies to privatize Social Security. Politicians fear such lobbies because they move votes. Politicians fear the National Rifle Association (NRA) less because of its money than because in much of the country being labeled "anti-gun" will end their hopes for reelection. They fear the AARP because being labeled "anti–Social Security" means political death.

Lobbies whose causes are unpopular, or to which the public is largely indifferent, are only as powerful as the money and the political skills they bring to the table. Their causes prosper best when their issues stay under the radar of public attention. The tobacco lobby was once popular and courted publicity for its defense of "smokers' rights"; today it prefers to do its business as far from the spotlight as possible.

Israel lobbies benefit from their ability to mobilize public support. In much of the country, being labeled "anti-Israel" is political poison—often among non-Jews as much or more than among Jews. Given that, politicians generally try to avoid falling afoul of groups that the public recognizes as reliably pro-Israel. Like it or not, most of the Israel lobby's influence comes from the popularity of its cause among the American people.

But, Vulcan hunters riposte, who makes public opinion? American policy may be pro-Israel because American public opinion is pro-Israel, but that public opinion itself, they believe, has been shaped by what they see as an American media industry dominated by Jews.

This is a very popular theory in some quarters, but it hardly fits the facts. The most pro-Israel coverage in American news today doesn't come from mainstream news organizations like *The New York Times*, CNN, or the three networks. To find coverage that was broadly sympathetic to the Israeli government under the right-leaning Likud leadership, one had to turn to Fox News. This news organization has been consistently the most conservative and the most pro-Israel major news source in the twenty-first century. It is owned by the Australian Christian Rupert Murdoch, it was built by the non-Jewish Roger Ailes, and its most prominent news hosts and commentators have had names like Bill O'Reilly, Sean Hannity, Tucker Carlson, and Mike Huckabee.

There is another problem with the idea that American public opinion is pro-Israel because of the powerful Jewish presence in the media. The idea that powerful Jewish cabals manipulate the public like puppets on a string thanks to their control of the American media is not just a theory about clever and ruthless Jews. It is also a theory about stupid and clueless non-Jewish Americans. If non-Jewish Americans are so easily manipulated on this subject, they are easily manipulated about almost anything, and American democratic governance is less about translating the preferences of the majority into public policy than it is about providing a veneer of legitimacy for the policies our Jewish media masters have devised for us.

No sane person will deny that Americans sometimes make foolish choices in their personal and political lives, but to believe that Jewish virtuosos play the country like a violin seems a little extreme. Are non-Jewish Americans really just sheeple, pawns of the Jews, manipulated by the clever, clannish Chosen People in ways that we simple sons and daughters of the soil can never fully comprehend? The American people have built the largest and most stable democracy in world history. We have built the world's richest and most advanced economy. Our predecessors helped defeat or contain some of the worst monsters in human form, mass-murdering psychotics like Hitler and Stalin. Thrust into world power in the middle of the tumultuous twentieth century, the Americans were remarkably successful at building a global political and economic system that has prevented great power war for seventy years, promoted the emergence of the developing world from colonialism, and allowed billions of people worldwide to enter into undreamed of prosperity. The United States built a global coalition against the Soviet Union that held the line against communist expansion until this backward and cruel system collapsed of its own weight. Patient American leadership helped Europe overcome a legacy of generations of warfare to move toward the kind of deep peace humanity could once scarcely imagine. Domestically, the American people attacked a host of evils, wrestling with the demon of racism and restructuring family life to provide increasing freedom and opportunity to women. The Americans sent astronauts to the moon, invented the internet, and they continue to produce more scientific and technical breakthroughs than any other country on earth.[15]

Are the people who accomplished all this, 98 percent of whom aren't Jewish,[16] really a bunch of ignorant peasants, "useful idiots" manipulated by clever and determined Jews? Is 98 percent of the American population a collection of ignorant and sniveling couch potatoes, passively accepting whatever ideas the Jewish puppet masters stuff into their feeble brains? This is a slur, not an argument, but many people lazily accept it without thinking through its implications for democracy.

Pro-Israel political groups play a significant role in American political life, but their role is both more normal and more nuanced than Vulcan Theory would have it. They operate less as a means to impose the will of a minority on the majority than as instruments through which a pro-Israel majority enacts its preferences into policy and law. They also operate in a cut-and-thrust world of lobby politics in which unexpected alliances and coalitions often form. If we want to understand the sources of the power of pro-Israel forces in American politics, it is the nature and the history of the American political process and of pro-Israel sentiment that we must examine, not the plots and machinations of "the Jews." American policy on Israel may be right or it may be wrong, but it emerges from the same kind of political process and struggle that produces the rest of our policies.

THE PLANET OF THE JEWS

Since Vulcan Theory is wrong about the history of U.S.-Israel relations, wrong about the politics of the national interest, and wrong about the role of pro-Israel lobby groups in the American political process, we should not be surprised that it is also wrong about American Jews. It is wrong not only about the amount of power "the Jews" wield in American society; it is wrong about what American Jews think and have thought about Israel policy, and wrong about the relationship of Israel policy and Jewish political commitments.

There are, of course, American Jews who support a pro-Israel foreign policy, and organizations like AIPAC (American Israel Public Affairs Committee) have a significant presence in Washington. AIPAC spends just over $100 million per year[17] and has over four hundred employees.[18] Presumably they are doing something, though AIPAC's opposition did not succeed in derailing President Obama's Iran policies. But the belief that AIPAC and its allies play the role in American foreign policy that Le Verrier thought Vulcan played in Mercury's orbit blinds the Vulcanologists to the existence of forces that can tell us much more about American politics and foreign policy.

The idea that "the Jews" control American policy on matters affecting Israel is absurd on its face. Throughout the twenty-first century, American Jews have consistently voted in greater numbers for candidates seen as more "dovish" on U.S. support for Israel than for the pro-Netanyahu, pro-Likud "hawks."[19] Barack Obama received more Jewish votes and more Jewish money than either of his Republican opponents; of the $160 million donated to the presidential nominees of the two major parties in 2012, President Obama's reelection campaign received 71 percent. The remaining 29 percent went to Mitt Romney.[20] American Jews consistently preferred George W. Bush's Democratic opponents to the author of an Iraq war allegedly undertaken in Israel's interest, voting heavily against Bush in both 2000 and 2004. Large majorities of American Jews voted against Donald Trump in 2016 and 2020, and the vaunted neoconservatives whose backing for Bush and the war in Iraq led some observers to conclude that the "Israel lobby" had taken over American foreign policy became leading voices in the Never Trump community. In 2016, while a small number of wealthy Jewish donors supported the Trump campaign, Hillary Clinton's presidential campaign raised substantially more money from Jewish donors than did the Trump effort, and she also received an overwhelming electoral mandate from Jewish voters.[21] Before President Trump could implement a series of policy changes ranging from repudiating President Obama's nuclear agreement with Iran to moving the American embassy to Jerusalem he had to defeat the presidential candidate that most American Jews strongly supported. It seems more than perverse to attribute these policies to the power of "the Jews," just as it had earlier been wrong to attribute George W. Bush's policies to a community that largely rejected him.

If the American Jewish community actually controlled American policy on Israel, the policy would be something well to the left of anything establishment Republicans like Mitt Romney and John McCain proposed; many leading Jewish donors, activists, and Obama White House staffers wanted President Obama to put more pressure on Israel over Palestinian issues. If American Jews controlled America's Israel policy, the U.S. embassy would still be in Tel Aviv, the annexation of the Golan Heights would not be recognized, and the United States would be pressing Israel on settlement policy. To blame the Jewish community for policies it dislikes made by presidents it rejects seems, if not virulently antisemitic, at least uninformed.

Those who see the American Jewish community as monolithically united behind a hardline Israel policy do not know much about American Jewish history. In the nineteenth century, most American Jews rejected the idea that Jews were exiles longing for a restoration to the Promised Land. The idea of a Messianic redemption was seen by the modernizing, enlightened Jews of that era as one of the elements of superstition that an enlightened Jewish culture should abandon. An important early prayer book issued for the use of American Jews, the *Minhag America* published in 1857, scandalized many Jews because it omitted the traditional prayers for a return to the Holy Land.[22] For many years Herzlian Zionism, the idea that Jews needed a Jewish state in order to fully express their identity, was unpopular among American Jews.[23] Once immigration restrictions in 1924 ended mass Jewish immigration to the United States, more American Jews came to support (both financially and politically) Jewish immigration to British-ruled Palestine, but Jewish leaders remained deeply skeptical about the idea of a Jewish state until Hitler's Final Solution was already under way.

American Jews were more supportive of Israel in the 1950s and 1960s.

Israel was weaker than it would later become, and the slender economic resources of the state were largely taken up with the need to resettle refugees from Europe and the Middle East. For American Jews, the idea of Israel as a refuge for persecuted Jews unable to settle in the United States was a unifying force, and their uneasiness about the state of Palestinian refugees was to some degree offset by the spectacle of hundreds of thousands of Jewish refugees coming into Israel from the rest of the Middle East. This united and fervent Jewish support did not have much effect on Eisenhower administration policy; U.S.-Israel relations touched their lowest point following Israel's invasion of the Sinai in 1956.

Israel's stunning victory in the 1967 Six-Day War led in the short term to an intensive surge in support for Israel among both Jewish and non-Jewish Americans,[24] but over the longer term many American Jews began to question Israeli policies in the territories seized from Egypt, Jordan, and Syria in the course of the conflict. As the balance in Israeli politics shifted toward right-wing, nationalist parties, older political divisions among American Jews began to reappear. The doubts that many American Jews voiced about Israeli policies in recent decades echoed concerns about Zionism that preceding generations had shared. Leaders like Judah Magnes, the founder of the Hebrew University in Jerusalem and, next to Golda Meir, the most prominent American Jew to take up a new life in Israel, had called for a binational state in the 1940s and spoken of the need for a "cultural home" for Jews in Palestine rather than a sovereign state. By the Obama administration, a new generation of American Jewish writers was expressing, often in the face of stiff criticism from other members of the American Jewish community, similar doubts and qualms about the direction of the Jewish state.

Later we will return to the deep debates among American Jews over Zionism and over Israel policy, but here we must note that as Jewish support for Israel became more nuanced and in some quarters less strong, support for Israel among non-Jewish Americans continued to grow. At the same time, as Israel itself became a stronger country and therefore, at least from some perspectives, a more valuable ally, the United States increased military aid to Israel and deepened its commercial and diplomatic relations.

The most important turning point in the U.S.-Israel relationship came in 1973. The president who laid the foundations for the Israeli-American alliance was Richard Nixon, hated by most American Jews and given to the crudest antisemitic rhetoric in private conversation, as his secret White House tapes reveal.[25] Nixon's diplomatic and material support for Israel in the 1973 Yom Kippur War helped save the Jewish state in an hour of crisis, but it brought him no surge of Jewish support and he did not expect that it would; the American Jewish community was viscerally and almost unanimously opposed to the best friend in the White House that Israel had ever had. Not until Donald Trump would a president appear who shifted American policy as decisively as Richard Nixon in a pro-Israel direction; not until Trump would a president appear who was as unpopular with American Jews as Nixon became.

The American Jewish community is not a dark planet that irresistibly pulls American policy in a pro-Israel direction. Insofar as the American Jewish community has an impact on American foreign policy, it is more to moderate and limit American support for Israel, and especially for Israeli governments of the right, than to press inexorably for ever greater support to Jerusalem from the United States. A political candidate whose sole goal it is to collect campaign contributions and votes from American Jews would do better running against pro-Likud policies than for them.

The relationship between Jewish support for Israel and gentile support for Israel is clearly more complicated than the caricature of Jewish manipulation that Vulcan Theorists too often put forward. This is nothing new; Zionism was never an agenda that a disciplined Jewish community imposed on the rest of the world. From the beginning of the Zionist movement, Zionism owed much of its power among Jews to its ability to attract gentile support. To see how this worked, it is worth turning away from American politics for a moment to look at how the founder of modern Zionism was able to persuade Kaiser Wilhelm II to endorse the idea of a Jewish state in Palestine. This "German Balfour Declaration" was not as long-lasting or as historically significant as the British one, but the process through which Theodor Herzl was able to get a great European power to support the Zionist project illustrates dynamics that are still at work in American politics today.

3

A Knock at the Door

A S THEODOR HERZL GREW UP in the Austro-Hungarian monarchy, the only thing that would have seemed less probable to
him and his family than a Jewish return to Palestine would be
that young Theodor would help start it. At the time of his birth in 1860,
his father, Jacob, was a successful timber merchant and businessman.[1]
In 1878, Jacob moved the family from Budapest to the larger and more
imposing city of Vienna. In Vienna, Theodor studied the law, as his
father wished.[2] Like many Jewish fathers across the German-speaking
world, Jacob was determined to see his son enter the professions.

The Herzl family was more successful than many, but the path they
followed was well trodden. Liberated from the ghettos, a steady stream
of young and eager Jews poured out into the wider world in search of
more adventure and success than they could ever hope to acquire within
the narrow confines of the Jewish community. In the 1860s and 1870s,
their future seemed bright. Across Europe, new generations of Jews were
making their mark in culture, business, and the arts. Even in politics,
Benjamin Disraeli (whose father had him baptized as an Anglican)[3]
led Britain, the most powerful nation in the world, and dominated the
European leaders at the Congress of Berlin.[4]

Like so many of the other changes that transformed European life
in the nineteenth century, the emancipation of the Jews had its roots in
the French Revolution. In the optimistic era of the closing decades of
the eighteenth century, the oppression of the Jews, their confinement to
ghettos in some countries, restrictions on their participation in business
and civic life, and the popular prejudice against them that for centuries
had broken out in murderous riots all looked like remnants of the medieval superstitions that the sun of reason was clearing away. The ideas

of brotherhood and equality at the heart of the French Revolution—universal freedom—surely meant freedom for the children of Israel.[5]

In 1791 the National Assembly gave French Jews their full legal rights.[6] They responded for the most part enthusiastically, and the emancipation of the Jews followed French power across Europe. While these changes never took hold in the vast Russian Empire, and while some of the most conservative European governments reestablished the restrictions on Jews following Napoleon's defeat, in much of Western Europe Jewish freedom was too important a change to be reversed, and for the first time in 1,500 years, significant numbers of European Jews lived under governments that recognized their equality under the law.[7]

Meanwhile, the Enlightenment that was challenging the old order of church and state among Europe's Christians was also felt among the Jews. While some Jews continued to observe the old laws and traditions, many others took a new look at the old ways. Viewed through the critical lenses of the Enlightenment, rituals and ancient dietary restrictions looked more like superstitions than acts of rational piety. As historians and scholars questioned the historicity of the Bible, and as theologians challenged traditional rabbinical interpretations, many western Jews discarded the practices that had once marked their ancestors as a people apart. The essence of Judaism, they now believed, lay more in the universal ethical principles that it taught than in rituals and dress codes. More and more Jews dressed like their neighbors, discarded kosher laws, embraced new political ideas, fell in love with European culture, interpreted the ancient religion in the light of the philosophy of the Enlightenment, and took pride in the history and culture of the nations among whom they lived.

This was the world the young Theodor Herzl enthusiastically joined. As a university student he fell in love with the arts and wanted to become a playwright, leaving his legal studies behind. While some of his plays were eventually performed, they never received either the critical acclaim or the popular success that he wanted for them.[8] His real talent turned out to be for a form of writing he did not much like—his feature pieces and feuilleton essays for newspapers, which were much admired and widely read. In the end, the editors of the *Neue Freie Presse*, the most influential liberal newspaper in Vienna, were so impressed with his journalistic abilities that they offered him one of the most prestigious posts in the field: he became their Paris correspondent.[9] Austria-Hungary was one of the European great powers; France was another. The *Neue Freie Presse* was closely read by Austrian statesmen and diplomats; it also circulated widely among informed readers throughout German-speaking Europe and beyond.

Herzl now moved freely in the highest political circles in Vienna. With a solid salary, support from his new wife's wealthy family,[10] and a handsome expense allowance from his newspaper, Herzl had the kind of social and professional stature that no Jew could have hoped to achieve in his grandfather's day. He attended sessions of the French National Assembly, consorted with cabinet ministers, dined with dukes, and regularly attended the plays and operas that made the City of Light the most glittering capital in Europe. As Herzl looked at his own life, it must have seemed as if the Jews of Europe were moving toward full integration, and that, even though his deepest literary ambitions remained unfulfilled, Theodor Herzl was living the dream.[11]

Herzl's Jewish roots seemed of less importance every year. When his son was born in 1891, Theodor gave him the very German name of Hans and refused to have the boy circumcised.[12] The Herzl family never darkened the synagogue doors but they decorated a Christmas tree every year. In the modern age opening up, Herzl was sure the quaint Jewish folkways of the past were fated to disappear.

Yet even as Herzl went from success to success, a wave of antisemitic reaction swept across Europe. In Russia, the assassination of the liberal Alexander II had ended a period of relative toleration and openness. His son, the bigoted Alexander III, embarked on a series of antisemitic measures, excluding Jews from universities, closing professions to Jewish applicants, imposing economic discrimination against Jewish businesses, forcing Jews to move from restricted areas, and, ultimately, failing to protect Russian Jews as the Orthodox clergy and nationalist agitators fomented violent, anti-Jewish mob action.[13] Asked how Russia intended to solve its "Jewish problem," Konstantin Petrovich Pobedonostsev, an advisor to Alexander III and a friend of Fyodor Dostoyevsky, is said to have replied that "a third of Jews will be converted, a third will emigrate, and the rest will die of hunger."[14]

While most enlightened Europeans regarded this fanaticism and occasional violence as typical products of Russian backwardness and brutality, hostility toward the growing Jewish presence in the professions and the business world was not confined to the Empire of the Tsars.

Indeed, as first tens of thousands and then hundreds of thousands and ultimately millions of Jews fled the Russian Empire, the Jewish population surged in Austria, Germany, and elsewhere in Europe, fueling a rise of antisemitism in these countries as well.[15] In Germany, a new generation of Pan-German nationalists took their inspiration from the vitriolic antisemitism of composer Richard Wagner. As these ideas spread through universities and into the officer corps, Jewish students and cadets found themselves increasingly isolated. Herzl resigned angrily from his old student fraternity when it signed an antisemitic declaration.

The new antisemitism was not simply a resurgence of the religious antagonism of past generations. Jews had been subjected to persecution in the Middle Ages because they refused to conform to the standards of the Christian world around them. In the late nineteenth century, Jews were accused of embracing the opportunities and customs of the Christian world too eagerly. The antisemites of the 1890s were less angry at the bearded Orthodox believers clinging to the old ways than at the elegantly mannered and impeccably dressed professional Jews who were making their way in gentile society.[16]

Little by little, Herzl found himself thinking about the problems of the Jewish people in a Europe that seemed to be rejecting them. In 1894 he wrote his first play on a specifically Jewish topic: *The New Ghetto,* an analysis of the difficulties facing assimilationist Jews.

In October of that year, Alfred Dreyfus, a French army officer of Jewish background, was arrested and charged with treason for passing military secrets to the Germans.[17] Early on Herzl, like most observers, assumed Dreyfus's guilt; it was hard to believe that France's highest military authorities were engaged in a systematic program of perjury and deceit with the aim of convicting a blameless man. But circumstances surrounding the case were suspicious enough that by the time Herzl witnessed the ceremony in which the convicted Dreyfus was degraded and stripped of his rank and honors, the journalist was convinced of Dreyfus's innocence. With crowds shouting *"Mort aux Juifs!"* ("Death to the Jews!") in the street, and both the Catholic Church and the French army joining in the anti-Dreyfus campaign, it was clear that something more than a miscarriage of justice was at work. A series of financial scandals in which some prominent Jews had conspicuously figured made banking and Jewish financiers objects of popular distrust and hate; antisemitic newspapers fanned the flames, and it began to look as if the country that had launched the emancipation of the Jews had come to regret its decision.

If events in France were disturbing, developments in Vienna brought the threat home to Herzl. Not only in aristocratic and court circles, but among the ordinary workers and citizens as well, a spirit of fanatical hatred was beginning to grow. In the 1895 municipal elections, two thirds of the seats went to the "United Christians" party grouping, making the vociferous antisemite Karl Lueger mayor. Lueger, whom Hitler would hail as an inspiration in *Mein Kampf,* went on to dominate Viennese politics until his death in 1910.[18] As Lueger denounced Jewish influence and Jewish dishonesty, drawing cheers when he denounced the Hungarian capital as "Judapest" due to its supposed domination by Jews, Herzl was overwhelmed by premonitions of a dark and terrible fate awaiting Europe's Jews.

The golden dream of assimilation and acceptance had been, Herzl concluded, an illusion. His always active and theatrical imagination perceived a wave of hate slowly building in Europe, and the distinguished and dapper journalist was seized by the conviction that unless the Jews could somehow escape, they faced mass murder and persecution on an unprecedented scale. Finding a way to avoid this fate became the dominant passion of the remaining nine years of his short life; Herzl would transform himself into the leader of the national movement of the Jewish people.

After much hesitation and agony of spirit, Herzl experienced what felt like a revelation, and wrote down his vision in a pamphlet, *Der Judenstaat (The Jewish State)*. Written in a frenzy of inspiration, it appeared on the streets of Vienna in February of 1896.[19] Lucid and penetrating in its analysis of the problems facing European Jews and of the options they faced, it skipped lightly over the problems that establishing a new state on territory currently inhabited by Arabs would cause. Several years later, when in 1902 Herzl fleshed out his vision of the Jewish commonwealth he hoped to build in the short novel *Altneuland,* he still assumed that the old inhabitants of Palestine would welcome their new, Jewish neighbors. When a European visitor asks an Arab citizen of the new Jewish state why the Muslims don't resent the Jewish intruders, he replies, "Christian, you speak very strangely. Would you consider him a robber who takes nothing from you, but gives you something? The Jews have made us rich. Why should we scorn them? They live with us as brothers. Why should we not love them?"[20]

Even at the time, Herzl should have seen how unlikely it was that the Arabs of Palestine would react to mass Jewish immigration in this calmly philosophical way. After all, the Jews of Europe were enriching rather than impoverishing their neighbors. Jewish doctors were curing the sick; Jewish bankers were making investments that promoted the well-being of all; Jewish scientists were making discoveries that led to new technologies; Jewish artists were enriching European culture: how much love had these contributions earned Europe's Jews from their gentile neighbors? If Jewish wealth creation and Jewish benevolence had failed to win acceptance for long-established Jewish communities in Austria and France, why would those same qualities make them beloved as immigrants in the Middle East?

If Herzl failed to understand the impact that his project would have on the Arab world, his analysis of the Jewish Question in Europe and his vision for how to proceed made him one of the most consequential figures of his time. Within a few months of the publication of *The Jewish State* Herzl's idea was being seriously discussed by crowned heads; before his death, Herzl would hold face-to-face meetings with the Kaiser of Germany, the sultan of the Ottoman Empire, Pope Pius X, Prince Ferdinand of Bulgaria, King Victor Emmanuel of Italy, the colonial secretary of the British Empire, and many of the other leading statesmen of the day. Twenty-one years after the pamphlet appeared, Great Britain would issue the Balfour Declaration committing itself to establish a "national home for the Jewish people" in the Palestinian territories wrested from the Ottoman Empire. France and the United States also endorsed the project, and a solemn commitment to the establishment of a Jewish national home in Palestine was enacted by the newly established League of Nations. Thirty-one years after the Balfour Declaration, the Jewish state declared its independence in May of 1948. The United States recognized the new State of Israel almost before the ink on the declaration was dry, and the Soviet Union, the other great power of the day, quickly followed suit. In just fifty-two years, the apparently impossible vision of a Jewish state had become a reality.

For many observers, the rapid rise of the Zionist movement and its success among non-Jewish elites was all the proof they needed to demonstrate that clever and powerful Jews in finance and the media pulled the strings of world politics. How else could such a development be possible? They saw every step in this process, from Herzl's meetings with emperors and kings to Harry Truman's recognition of Israeli independence as evidence that "the Jews" rule the world from invisible thrones.

But the antisemites were wrong. It was not the backing of Jewish financiers that opened the doors of the chancelleries of Europe; Herzl never had their support, funding his work out of his own pocket and from the contributions of the relatively poor and powerless Jews who came to make up the bulk of the membership of the Zionist Organization Herzl founded. Nor was it the power of Jewish press lords that induced these leaders to listen to him; the great Jewish newspapers of the day were almost uniformly anti-Zionist. Herzl's own newspaper refused to use the word "Zionism" during Herzl's lifetime.[21]

It was the powerful idea of Zionism, not the power of the Jews, that brought Herzl to the attention of Europe's crowned heads. In country after country, case after case, Zionism intrigued, interested, and ultimately drew the support of powerful gentile leaders, even as Jewish leaders often wanted nothing to do with it.

The core insight of *The Jewish State* was not that the world's Jews were so powerful that they could achieve anything they wanted if they would only unite. On the contrary, Herzl believed that the world's Jews, even with the help of western liberals, were too weak to make assimilation work. Herzl was a loyal, loving son of the Enlightenment who believed that the Enlightenment would fail. Even as he watched western gentiles fight the injustice of the Dreyfus affair, Herzl believed that these efforts would ultimately fall short. Émile Zola and Georges Clemenceau might rescue Captain Dreyfus from his unjust imprisonment on Devil's Island, but the tolerance and secularism that they represented would not save the French Jews as a whole.

So powerful was the wave of antisemitism, Herzl believed, that to save both themselves and the European Enlightenment the great mass of the Jewish population needed to leave Europe en masse. Outside Europe, the Jews could build an enlightened republic in their ancestral homeland. With the irritant of the Jews removed, Europe's descent into the abyss of barbarism and hate might end, and the peoples of Europe, including the small minority of Jews who did not join the Zionist emigration, could resume their progress along the path of enlightened modernity.

Migration had long been an option for persecuted Jews. Banned from England, France, and Spain during the Middle Ages, Jews had mostly gone east toward Poland and Russia. Faced with the antisemitic revivals of the 1880s and 1890s, European Jews were once again on the move. Hundreds of thousands came to the Americas, mostly to the United States but also to Canada, Argentina, and elsewhere. Jewish settlements were also springing up in Palestine, where one of the French Rothschilds subsidized Jewish settlement.

But conventional migration, Herzl warned, could not solve the problems of the Jews of his time. The sheer number of desperate migrant Jews was leading some countries, like Britain, to consider restricting migration; even the United States, long hungry for workers and the most important destination for Europeans looking for a fresh start, was beginning to discuss limits and quotas. Ultimately, Herzl predicted, the doors to immigration (open practically everywhere when Herzl wrote in 1896) would shut, leaving millions of Jews trapped in a Europe that would turn increasingly murderous in its Jew-hatred.

Sadly, he turned out to be right.

Herzl's pamphlet was an attack on the core political project and even on the identity of the assimilated, successful western Jews among whom he lived and whose culture and aspirations he basically shared. The assimilated upper-middle-class and upper-class Jews of London, Paris, Vienna, and Berlin believed that they were the vanguard of the Jewish masses, that the path of adaptation, assimilation, and conformity that led them to success was open to the Jewish masses of the East.

Not true, said Herzl. Not only was the road of assimilation closed to the Jewish masses, ultimately it would close to all. Successful assimilated Jews were already beginning to experience the blowback as gentiles reacted to Jewish success with greater hatred; not even the most assimilated and powerful Jews would be safe when the gentile reaction reached its peak. Zionism, Herzl believed, could change that because it offered a program for a Jewish future that gentiles who hated Jews or were indifferent to their fate could and would support. Antisemites would rejoice at the opportunity to get rid of their Jews; those who cared nothing for the Jews one way or the other might see business and political opportunities in the establishment of a prosperous Jewish state in what was then the backward and impoverished Ottoman Empire.

Herzl expected an unfavorable response to his pamphlet, and the Jews of Vienna did not disappoint him. A few weeks after publication, Herzl noted in his diary that "the Jews of the upper-class, educated circles . . . are horrified by me."[22] It was not just that the idea of a Jewish "return" to a homeland where no Jewish state had existed for almost two thousand years struck most sensible Jews as a fantasy rather than as a serious political proposal; it was that most western Jews had long ago renounced the idea that Jews were a nation. One could think of Jews as a race of people sharing a common descent, or as a religious community. But the world's Jews, who lived in many different countries, spoke many different languages, followed a wide variety of religious customs, ate different foods, and, at least in Western Europe and the Atlantic world, were finally beginning to enjoy the blessings of full citizenship in their respective home countries, were not a nation and were certainly not pining for a blighted, disease-ridden homeland that few had ever seen.

From the beginning, Herzl understood that winning Jewish support would be Zionism's hardest test. While he expected that some Jews would spontaneously support the idea of returning to their ancient homeland out of a mix of religious and Jewish nationalist sentiments, Herzl knew very well that the Zionist program would strike most western Jews as eccentric and impractical at best, dangerous at worst. A Jewish national movement raised uncomfortable questions about loyalty and patriotism that assimilated European Jews wanted to avoid. Could a British, German, or French government trust Jewish citizens who were helping to organize the rise of a foreign power? Assimilationist Jews spent enormous amounts of time convincing their gentile associates that they were as French, as German, or as British as everyone else. Now here came Herr Herzl with his nonsensical talk of a Jewish state, and for the sake of this impossible dream he would put at risk all the acceptance, all the trust that Jews across Europe had labored so long and so hard to win.

———

Herzl published his pamphlet, the Jewish world for the most part laughed at or ignored it, and here, it appeared, the matter would rest.

Then on March 10 came a knock at Herzl's door. The man calling was Rev. Mr. William Hechler, an Anglo-German cleric of the Church of England who served as chaplain to the British embassy in Vienna. Hechler had read a copy of Herzl's pamphlet and he wanted to meet the author.[23] The clergyman, unbeknownst to Herzl, came from a long tradition of pro-Jewish and proto-Zionist thinkers and writers in German and British Protestantism, and his father had served as a missionary in an 1840s Anglo-German attempt to establish a missionary diocese intended among other things to advance the cause of a Jewish return to the lands of the Bible.[24]

On the British side, the primary moving force behind this attempt had been Lord Ashley, later the 7th Earl of Shaftesbury, nephew to one British prime minister and stepson-in-law to another. The earl worked for decades to make support for a Jewish state in Palestine British policy. Although he died with his dream unrealized, his work laid the foundation for the Balfour Declaration of 1917.[25]

On the German side, King Frederick William IV of Prussia gave his backing to the proposal for an Anglo-German diocese in Jerusalem. This was partly for religious and partly for diplomatic reasons. From a religious standpoint, missions to the Jews combined with friendship toward the Jewish people (however incongruous such an agenda might sound to most Jews then and now) was a key tenet of Pietism, a movement of personal and social religious renewal that played an immense role in eighteenth- and nineteenth-century Protestant Germany—and, through its influence on the Wesley brothers and other American religious leaders, would become one of the most important influences on American evangelical religion. For political as well as religious reasons the Hohenzollern dynasty had long supported Pietism.[26] The Hohenzollerns, a Calvinist dynasty ruling a predominantly Lutheran Prussia at a time when theological differences could be politically explosive, welcomed the Pietist movement, which downplayed the importance of doctrinal differences among Protestants and taught its followers the duty of obedience to ruling princes.[27] Philipp Spener, the founder of the movement, had been named pastor of one of Berlin's most important churches; the network of Pietist institutions in Halle, including an early German school for the teaching of "oriental" languages such as Hebrew and Arabic, benefited from Hohenzollern generosity and patronage.[28]

Diplomatically, Frederick William believed that extending Prussian protection to the Jews and the Protestants of the Ottoman Empire would bring important political and economic benefits to his kingdom, including a closer relationship with Great Britain. By the 1840s, the decline of Ottoman power was creating both dangers and opportunities in what we now call the Balkans and the Middle East. Both Russia and France had established themselves as the protectors of Ottoman religious minorities, with Russia claiming a right to protect Orthodox Christians in the Muslim empire, and France claiming similar rights over Roman Catholics. The two countries used this position to good effect, establishing networks of economic and political influence through the sprawling Ottoman territories. At the same time, both the French and the Russian governments reaped political rewards at home among religious people for nobly protecting the rights of believers abroad. Prussia and Britain, the two great Protestant powers of the day, sought their own set of clients in the increasingly ramshackle empire; there were not enough Protestants to make a respectable group, but there was no shortage of Jews, and they were in enough need of protection at a time when anti-Jewish feeling was rising in the Ottoman world, that both London and Berlin saw advantages in taking up their cause.[29]

The Anglo-German missionary diocese was established, but did not succeed in converting many Jews or in persuading many to return to the Holy Land to take up agriculture as in biblical times, but the ideas and the networks survived. Hechler, who had once hoped to be appointed bishop in Jerusalem, still had access to exalted circles in both Germany and Britain.[30] In the 1890s Restorationism (the idea of "restoring" the Jewish people to their ancestral home in Palestine) was slowly declining as a force in British Christianity, but from Arthur Balfour to David Lloyd George many members of the political establishment still felt its force. Hechler struck more advanced contemporaries in the 1890s as old-fashioned and even embarrassing with his enthusiasm for biblical prophecy and a Jewish state, but he persevered, studying the prophetic literature and writing on the ways that, in his view, the Hebrew scriptures pointed to the return of the Jewish people to their ancient homeland sometime around the end of the nineteenth century.

Herzl knew very little about this earlier history, and he knew and cared less about the religious sentiment that brought Hechler to his doors. What electrified him was what Hechler told him about his connections. As Herzl's diary puts it, "He [Hechler] wants to have my work sent to a few German princes. He was tutor in the Grand Duke of Baden's house, knows the German Kaiser, and believes he can get me an audience."[31]

On the Sunday following their first meeting, March 16, Herzl returned Hechler's call, visiting the chaplain in his fourth-floor walk-up apartment overlooking Vienna's Schillerplatz. As Herzl describes the meeting in his diary, it was one of the strangest—and also most consequential—meetings in the long history of the Jewish people.

"Even while I was going up the stairs," wrote Herzl, "I heard the sound of an organ. The room which I entered was lined with books on every side, floor to ceiling.

"Nothing but Bibles. . . .

"Mr. Hechler showed me his Biblical treasures. Then he spread out before me his chart of comparative history, and finally a map of Palestine. It is a large military staff map in four sheets which, when laid out, covered the entire floor. . . .

"At this point we were interrupted by the visit of two English ladies to whom he also showed his Bibles, souvenirs, maps, etc. After the boring interruption he sang and played for me on the organ a Zionist song of his composition."

One can only imagine the feelings of Herzl, a convinced religious skeptic and a sophisticated connoisseur of Wagner and Debussy, as he watched this enthusiast sing what he imagined a song of Jewish religious rejoicing would be while pounding the keys of his house organ.

Herzl got to the point, telling Hechler that powerful gentile support was the key to making Jewish Zionism effective: "I told him: I have got to establish a direct contact, a contact that is discernible on the outside . . . with a minister of state or a prince. Then the Jews will believe in me, then they will follow me."[32]

When Hechler said that he thought he could arrange audiences with the grand duke and possibly the Kaiser, Herzl wondered whether this eccentric priest was simply trying to scrounge travel funds from him, but agreed to provide Hechler the money for travel, first to Berlin to meet with members of Kaiser Wilhelm II's entourage, and then to Karlsruhe, where the Kaiser was visiting Prince Frederick, the Grand Duke of Baden.

By April 14 Hechler reported that he had met with several members of the Kaiser's entourage and that they had been fascinated by the idea of a Jewish homeland. On April 23, two months after *Der Judenstaat* was published, Herzl, accompanied by Hechler, was en route to Karlsruhe to meet the Grand Duke.

Prince Frederick, married to a daughter of Kaiser Wilhelm I and therefore the uncle of Wilhelm's grandson Wilhelm II, occupied a strategic position in the political structure of the German Empire. At the time of the Franco-Prussian War, the duke was a close and trusted Prussian ally, and was the first of the ruling German princes to endorse the proclamation of a united German Empire in 1871. His association with the old Kaiser, the liberal reputation of the grand ducal family, and his personal reputation for integrity and dignity made him a trusted figure in German politics, and his support for his great-nephew Wilhelm II at critical points of the reign was much appreciated in Berlin. Having supported Wilhelm II at the time when his dismissal of Bismarck led many to doubt the wisdom of their new ruler, Frederick was seen as one of the few elder statesmen the young Kaiser respected, and the cliques around Wilhelm were careful to maintain good relationships with the grand ducal court in Karlsruhe.

Herzl was so overawed in the august surroundings of the grand ducal palace in Karlsruhe that he tried to calm himself by focusing on the details of the decor. At first he found it difficult to speak clearly and naturally with the grand duke. But, sensing a sympathetic audience, he quickly warmed to his work.

After listening with intense interest, Frederick expressed a worry: wouldn't endorsing Herzl's idea expose him to charges of antisemitism? This seems an odd worry today—that a gentile would worry that support for Zionism might mark him out for criticism as an antisemite, but in the context of late-nineteenth-century Germany the question was a shrewd one. Jews and their allies were arguing at that time that German Jews should be regarded as fully integrated, and as having just as much right as all other Germans to a place in the empire. Zionism, from this perspective, could be seen as a step away from civil equality and full participation. Wouldn't a German prince who endorsed a program founded on the separation of the Jews from Germany be playing into antisemitic hands? Would Frederick's support for Herzl's plan be seen as an invitation to the Jews of Baden to depart?

Frederick suggested to Herzl that it would be easier for him to endorse the proposal after it had received significant Jewish support. That posed a problem. Herzl knew very well that no body of respectable Jewish opinion in either Germany or Austria was anywhere close to endorsing what most of them regarded as a ridiculous proposal that ran directly counter to their goal of full acceptance and citizenship in the land of their birth. Herzl's idea had, at this point, no significant support from any organized body of Jews, and was very far from receiving it.

Herzl responded to the Grand Duke by hitting the ball back into the court of the gentiles: as he summarized his presentation in his diary, "Some princes should manifest their favorable disposition: this would enable the Society of Jews [Herzl's name for his proposed central committee of leadership for his still hypothetical Zionist movement] to act with more authority from the outset. And authority was necessary if such a big movement was to be carried out in an orderly way. For even during the migration the Jews would stand in need of education and discipline." After a discussion of the foreign policy implications of the idea—whether the project could revive the Anglo-German cooperation then beginning to fade, what the impact would be on the geopolitics of the Ottoman Empire and the Suez Canal—the grand duke endorsed the Zionist idea: "I should like to see it happen. I believe it would be a blessing for many people."

Herzl had achieved his first goal: endorsement of his Zionist program by a significant European prince. Better still, Frederick promised to discuss the idea with his great-nephew the Kaiser. At this point Herzl's pamphlet had only been published for two months, but was about to land in the in-basket of one of the most powerful rulers on earth.[33]

Meanwhile, Herzl's reception among the Jews he most wanted to reach continued to be disappointing. Jewish reviewers across the German-speaking world competed to pan the work—where it wasn't ignored. Friends in Vienna reported that Herzl was becoming a laughingstock thanks to his bizarre proposal. Leading Jews continued to reject the Zionist idea. When Herzl's supporter Max Nordau (an internationally famous author and the only Jewish convert to Zionism other than Herzl himself with a serious reputation at the time) met with the French banker Edmond de Rothschild on May 18, 1896, three months after publication of *Der Judenstaat* and three weeks after Herzl's meeting with the grand duke, Rothschild brusquely and comprehensively rejected Nordau and the Zionist idea. They met, Nordau reported to Herzl, for sixty-three minutes. Rothschild spoke for fifty-three of them; Nordau, "with difficulty and rudeness," spoke for ten. Rothschild told Nordau that the proposal was "dangerous" because it would create suspicions of dual loyalty against Jewish citizens of European countries, and that it would be harmful to the colonies Rothschild was supporting in Palestine.[34]

Gentile elites, on the other hand, continued to show interest in the idea. On July 26, Herzl was in Karlovy Vary. As he sat down to his hotel breakfast, Prince Ferdinand of Bulgaria and his entourage took a table nearby. Herzl watched as the group pointed Herzl out to the prince. Invited to join the royal party, Herzl quickly sketched out the outline of his proposal. "A magnificent idea," said Ferdinand. "Nobody has ever spoken to me about the Jewish question in this fashion before."[35] At times, Herzl must have felt somewhat like another Jewish writer dazzled by a vision, Paul, who found gentiles more receptive to the message. But Herzl, like Paul, hoped that ultimately his reception among the gentiles would provoke a new interest among Jews. In Herzl's case, over time the strategy worked. The Grand Duke of Baden was as good as his word, and wrote to Wilhelm about the impressive Jewish journalist with the crazy but interesting idea. Wilhelm was intrigued, but he wanted another opinion before agreeing to look more deeply into the matter. His ambassador to Vienna, a close friend and confidential advisor, was the natural choice, and Wilhelm forwarded Frederick's letters and notes to Prince Philipp zu Eulenburg, one of the most antisemitic men in Germany at the time.[36]

Eulenburg was an ally of Richard Wagner; when the Bavarian government balked at paying the costs of the Bayreuth Festival, Eulenburg persuaded Wilhelm to propose paying for them himself—a move that ensured the Bavarians would fund Bayreuth after all.[37] Eulenburg was also a close friend, and perhaps lover, of Arthur de Gobineau, the man whose massive treatise *On the Inequality of the Human Races* first put forward the idea of the Aryan "master race" and was a landmark in the construction of the new, modern antisemitism of nineteenth-century Europe.[38] As Wilhelm II's ambassador in Vienna, Eulenburg also befriended Houston Stewart Chamberlain, the British antisemite whose work on race powerfully influenced both Wagner and Hitler. Eulenburg's own antisemitism was visceral as well as ideological; after his duties as ambassador required him to attend a charity ball near Vienna organized by the local Jewish community, he described the attendees as having, among other equally charming characteristics, "noses like tapirs," "eye teeth like a walrus's," and "gaping jaws with hollow teeth."[39] This was the man to whom Kaiser Wilhelm ultimately referred the letters and documents that Prince Frederick of Baden sent him concerning Herzl's proposal. Eulenburg who considered himself a master geopolitician as well as a great artist, responded with enthusiasm, and agreed to meet Herzl at his castle north of Berlin.

Herzl's meeting with Eulenburg came two years after publication of *The Jewish State*. The Kaiser was looking to increase German influence in the Middle East, and had come to believe that the promotion of a Jewish national home in Palestine under German protection would strengthen Germany's hand. As part of his diplomatic offensive, the Kaiser was about to undertake what was advertised as a pilgrimage to Jerusalem. The (feeble) hope was that by describing the visit as a personal religious pilgrimage there would be fewer alarms about Germany's Middle Eastern ambitions set off in other European capitals.

The meeting went well. Herzl in his best suit and kid gloves and Eulenburg in hunting costume strolled around the grounds of the old manor that Eulenburg hoped to build into a residence suitable for his new princely rank. Eulenburg told Herzl that he also supported the Zionist idea, was keeping it before the Kaiser, and had persuaded the influential foreign minister Bernhard von Bülow to support it as well.[40] As Herzl thanked him, Eulenburg stared hard at Herzl. "Perhaps there will come a time when I shall ask favors of you," he said.

For Herzl, this was the beginning of the most dramatic episode in his career. In the next few weeks, he would meet face-to-face with Kaiser Wilhelm in Constantinople, travel for the first and only time in his life to Palestine, and have two further encounters with the Kaiser: on the road from Jaffa to Jerusalem and then again in Jerusalem when Herzl, at the head of a small Zionist delegation, formally presented the proposal to create a Jewish state under German protection to the Kaiser.

Herzl would not just see the Kaiser, he would persuade him. For the first time, the head of state of a major European power would not only approve of the establishment of a Jewish home in Palestine in principle, but would take concrete steps to bring it about. The initiative, like many of Wilhelm's diplomatic enthusiasms, was poorly thought through and it quickly failed. Nevertheless, Herzl had succeeded in raising the idea of a Jewish state to the highest levels of international diplomacy.

Following his meeting with Eulenburg, Herzl met the chancellor and foreign minister in Berlin. They seemed anything but enthusiastic;[41]

in fact these experienced officials considered the idea utterly impractical and wanted nothing to do with it. They knew, however, that overt opposition would only intensify the Kaiser's determination, and like the seasoned and effective bureaucratic infighters they were, they quietly worked to undermine the proposal while seeming to support it.

The idea, as Wilhelm summed it up in a letter to the Grand Duke explaining his reasons for supporting the proposal, was as follows:

> I am convinced that the settlement of the Holy Land by the financially strong and diligent people of Israel will soon bring undreamt-of prosperity and blessing to the land, something that may with further expansion grow into a significant resuscitation and development of Asia Minor. But that in turn means millions into Turkish moneybags—including those of the great lords, the effendis—and consequently a gradual curing of the so-called "Sick Man," which would quite imperceptibly avert the troublesome "Eastern Question" at least from the Mediterranean and gradually solve it.

The Kaiser's point was that the long decline and apparently impending collapse of the Ottoman Empire had destabilized Eastern Europe and the Middle East. In particular, the decline of Ottoman power in the Balkans had increased the tension between Germany's current ally, the Habsburg monarchy, and its former ally, Russia. From a German point of view, anything that supported Ottoman power would curb Russian ambitions in the Balkans and reduce the chance of war between Russia and Austria. If the Jews were willing to pay millions to the Turks for Palestine, the Ottoman Empire would stabilize, improving Germany's security situation.

But there was more. In this case, the Kaiser continued, "Then the Turks won't be sick anymore; they will build their roads and railroads themselves, without foreign companies, and it won't be so easy to partition Turkey then." Here the Kaiser alluded to the problems caused when the floundering Ottoman government borrowed money from foreign (mostly British and French) banks, and when the Turks defaulted on their loans western governments were able to use these loans to pressure Constantinople for various concessions, including the cession of lands inhabited by rebellious Christians. If the Turks could pay off their existing loans to British and French banks, Turkey would be free to support ambitious projects like the Berlin-to-Baghdad railroad that the Kaiser hoped would extend German power throughout the Middle East.

And there was another advantage to the Zionist idea that appealed to Wilhelm II: "the energy, creative power and productivity of the tribe of Shem [a reference to the biblical account that traces the Jewish people to the descendants of Noah's son by that name] would be directed to worthier goals than to exploitation of Christians, and many a Semite who incites the opposition and adheres to the Social Democrats will move off to the East where there is more rewarding work and the end is not, as in the above case, the penitentiary." (At the time, the German socialist party, the Social Democrats, was illegal, and many members served prison terms.)

Finally, the Kaiser saw one more reason to support the idea. "We must not disregard the fact that, considering the tremendous power represented by international Jewish financial capital in all its dangerousness, it would surely be a tremendous achievement for Germany if the Hebrew world looked up to our country with gratitude."[42]

To geopolitical amateurs like Herzl, and the Kaiser, this all looked very straightforward. Persuading the sultan to accept the diminishment of his empire seemed to be the least difficult part of the problem.

Since the glorious days of the seventeenth century when the Ottoman Empire was the mightiest state in Europe, a long period of decline had set in. Bit by bit, pieces of the empire had been torn away. The Russians had conquered Crimea and pushed down through the Caucasus. With the help of Christian European powers, Greeks, Bulgars, Croats, Slovenes, Romanians, and Serbs all managed to throw off the Ottoman yoke. Egypt and the North African states, though still acknowledging the formal primacy of the sultan, had, for all practical purposes, become largely independent. Abdulhamid II, the canny and ruthless sultan who spent his long reign ceding territory to foreigners as slowly as possible while crushing all attempts at domestic reform, was clearly in the habit of making territorial concessions. Surely, a small additional concession in exchange for vast sums of Jewish gold was a reasonable thing to expect?

As for the sultan's pride, Herzl was willing to make the face-saving compromise that had been followed in other breakaway Ottoman provinces. Egypt, for example, for all practical purposes was ruled by its khedives after 1805, but nominally the sultan remained sovereign. Surely, with enough money, some arrangement could be found for Palestine.

This concept, at the core of Herzl's diplomatic strategy, was completely impractical. Sultans had, under duress, ceded territory in the past, but only after military defeats. And the territory that they had ceded was largely in Europe. To sell territory rather than losing it in battle, especially territory in the heartland of the Muslim world that contained one of the three holiest Islamic sites, would strike at the legitimacy of the Ottoman Empire among its Muslim subjects, a group who, after the progressive losses of mostly Christian territories in Europe, were increasingly powerful in what remained of the empire.

There was, of course, another problem with Herzl's proposal. Suppose the sultan agreed that for such and such a sum he would lease Palestine to the Jews under German protection. Where would Herzl get the money? By 1898, Herzl had succeeded in building a small and fractious Zionist movement, but its membership was largely composed of poor Russian Jews who could barely feed themselves. The Kaiser could dream of rich Jewish moneylenders and their overflowing vaults, but Herzl had no money, and no way to raise it.

Fortunately for Herzl, negotiations never reached this point. What the Kaiser did not realize, but what his chancellor and foreign minister did, was that Herzl's Palestine proposal was completely incompatible with Germany's overall diplomatic strategy.

During much of the nineteenth century, Great Britain had been the European power most concerned with propping up the declining Ottoman Empire, not out of any love of an empire most British people believed was both backward and cruel, but out of a desire to keep Russia, as generations of tsars dreamed, from taking Constantinople and making itself a great Mediterranean and Middle Eastern power. Nobody yet had any idea about the vast oil reserves of the Middle East that would have so much impact on the politics of the twentieth century, but Britain did not want Russia pressing on the Suez Canal, the vital lifeline between Britain and its vast imperial possessions in India and beyond. In the 1850s, Britain and France had fought the Crimean War to block Russia's ambitions to control the waterway linking the Black Sea and the Mediterranean; as recently as the Congress of Berlin in 1878, Britain had forced the Russians to disgorge most of their gains in the 1877 war that saw Russian forces reach the walls of Constantinople itself.

Since then, the Germans were gradually replacing Britain as the Ottoman Empire's patron and protector. British public opinion turned sharply against the pro-Turkey policy as communal massacres, especially of Christians, spread across an empire increasingly threatened by nationalism and religious discord. Tens of thousands of Armenians, Bulgarians, and others perished in violence that the sultan seemed to allow and perhaps to approve. From a geopolitical point of view, Britain was also losing some of its sensitivity to Russian expansionism in the Middle East. By 1898, Britain had consolidated its hold on the Suez Canal. Egypt had essentially been reduced to a British possession, and once the British gained control of Cyprus in 1878, their concerns about Russian power in the Mediterranean grew less acute. Meanwhile, the rapidly increasing power of imperial Germany meant that Germany was displacing Russia as Britain's greatest geopolitical concern. The Russian Empire, for all its giant size and population, seemed backward at a time when industrial development was increasingly the standard of international power; Germany, on the other hand, was beginning to challenge Britain across a wide range of technologies.

As the British worried less about Russia in the Mediterranean—and the Balkans—Germany worried more. Germany's one reliable ally, the dual monarchy of Austria-Hungary, was in direct competition with Russia in the Balkans, and every retreat of Turkish power opened the prospect of more conflict between Austria and Russia. In any confrontation between the two, Germany would have to stand by Austria or see its ally collapse, but a confrontation with Russia would likely land Germany in a European conflict in which France, bitterly determined to seek revenge for the loss of Alsace-Lorraine following its defeat in 1871, would look to side against Germany.

Additionally, German strategic thinkers saw a great opportunity in the Ottoman Empire. In a world in which Britain and France had already divided the great bulk of the world's colonial territories between them, Germany was looking for ways to develop clients and allies beyond Europe's boundaries. Even in its reduced state, the Ottoman Empire stretched from the Balkans to the Persian Gulf. The imperial authorities in Constantinople wanted to extend the European rail network across Ottoman territory, and competition among European banks and engineering firms to build the new railways was stiff. German firms had the inside track, and Berlin applauded the Ottoman intention to build its railway lines far enough from the coast so that British naval power could not threaten them. The prospect of a "Berlin-to-Baghdad" railway that would help revive the Ottoman Empire by stimulating its commerce and growth, and that would tie the empire more closely to Berlin, was already gaining favor.

It was as part of this eastward-looking German policy that the Kaiser embarked on the journey to Constantinople and Jerusalem that included his encounters with Herzl. The visit was intended to highlight the deepening ties between Constantinople and Berlin, and to pave the way for further German commercial and strategic links in the region. The Kaiser, elated by the geopolitical implications of Herzl's proposal, saw the Zionist idea as a marvelous scheme that would enlist Jewish money in the furtherance of German imperial projects. The money of the mythical Zionist Jewish bankers would allow the Ottomans to pay off their existing loans and to undertake large new development projects with, presumably, German partners. But from the Turkish point of view, the only reason to side with Germany was to protect the territorial integrity of the weak Ottoman state. The Kaiser foolishly believed that the sultan would consider an offer of Jewish gold for worthless desert land as a way to escape his financial difficulties for good. From the sultan's point of view, there was no shortage of foreign powers looking to rip another province of his empire away; Germany interested him as a partner that might help him keep his empire, not as another bidder eager to profit from its decay.

Wilhelm however saw only the benefits, and when he met the sultan he urged him to accept the proposal. The sultan waved it away with vague phrases. Wilhelm returned to it; this was the solution to all of their difficulties, he said. Abdulhamid refused to budge. The dream of a Jewish revival under Ottoman sovereignty and German protection faded away.

Wilhelm clearly understood that the project had failed, and immediately backed away from it. Herzl, whom Wilhelm had greeted warmly and spoken with animatedly just the day before, was now an embarrassment. The ministers and counselors who had expected this all along knew what to do; Herzl was gently but firmly pushed to the margins of the Kaiser's program. The planned public meeting in Jerusalem would still occur, but von Bülow insisted on receiving an advance text of Herzl's proposed address—and crossed out everything but the blandest of remarks. Herzl was also forbidden to publicize his private meetings with the Kaiser and his senior advisors.[43]

Herzl traveled from Constantinople to Jaffa in Palestine and visited the small agricultural Jewish colonies that his nemesis Edmond de Rothschild sponsored. Torn between their fear of alienating their wealthy protector and their admiration for the prominent Zionist, the colonists did their best to prevent Herzl's visit from attracting any negative publicity. Hearing that Wilhelm was due to ride on horseback up to Jerusalem, Herzl thrust himself into a group of Jewish colonists waiting to greet the Kaiser along the side of the Jerusalem road. Recognizing Herzl, the Kaiser reined his horse to an abrupt stop and the two men chatted for a few minutes about the potential to develop the dry farmland through extensive irrigation. Then the Kaiser rode off to Jerusalem as Herzl, faint with the heat and weak from a malarial attack, watched the dust of the imperial procession disperse in the wind.[44]

William Hechler, the clergyman whose enthusiasm launched Herzl's career into the world of high politics, was in the Kaiser's entourage. He and the Grand Duke of Baden would remain among the most steadfast supporters of the Zionist movement. Wilhelm II was on to other things.

———

Herzl's first venture into diplomacy ended anticlimactically. He made his address to the Kaiser in Jerusalem, and made a public request for German help. "This is the land of our fathers . . . it cries out for people to build it up. We happen to have among our brethren a distressing proletariat. These people cry out for a land to cultivate. We wish to derive a new welfare from these two conditions of distress—of the land and of the people—by a carefully planned combination of both . . . we are requesting your Imperial Majesty's exalted aid for the project."[45]

The Kaiser's reply was noncommittal, though he went as far as to remark that "your movement, with which I am well acquainted, contains a sound idea."[46]

As Herzl, the Kaiser, and von Bülow conversed, the conversation turned again to the need for water to revivify the land. "We can bring the country water," Herzl said. "It will cost billions but will yield billions."

"Well, money is what you have plenty of!" the Kaiser replied. "More money than any of us!"[47]

Those were among the last words Herzl ever heard from Kaiser Wilhelm II, who died hoping that Adolf Hitler would restore the House of

Hohenzollern to the German throne, and whose son August William joined the Nazi Party.

═══

At the time, this was very deflating and many of Herzl's fellow Zionists questioned his judgment over a very expensive and apparently fruitless trip. But while the approach to Wilhelm failed to deliver the Jewish state, it served as a proof of concept for Herzl's Zionist strategy. The Zionist program could win an extraordinary, even shocking amount of cooperation from powerful gentiles who might otherwise never lift a finger to help the world's Jews. Even a vicious and committed antisemite like Eulenburg was open to cooperating with Zionism on grounds that had nothing to do with sympathy for suffering Jews. One might object that the gentiles who aided the Zionists did so from a mix of motives, but Herzl would retort that that was the point. If the Jews only relied on gentiles who sympathized with their difficulties out of a common respect for the values of the Enlightenment, the Jews had no hope. It was only a program that could rally new allies to their side that could offer the Jews a way forward. After his first meeting with the Grand Duke, Herzl knew that Zionism could attract the non-Jewish support he required. The meetings with Wilhelm confirmed it.

William Hechler always thought of the idea in religious and biblical terms. As the heir of a long tradition of Protestant exegesis that believed that the biblical prophecies foretold the return of the Jews to the Holy Land as the Second Coming of Christ began to come closer, Hechler inevitably saw news of a spontaneous Jewish movement to return to Palestine as the fulfillment of his religious hopes and dreams. It was not only fundamentalists and literalists who responded to Zionism in this way. In an age when scholarship, and German scholarship especially, was beginning to question the historical and factual veracity of some biblical narratives, anything that suggested that the biblical prophecies were being fulfilled brought great comfort to believers. If 2,500-year-old prophecies foretold events that were actually coming to pass in the late nineteenth century, then Christian faith had little to fear from the textual critics and the modernist theologians. For Hechler, and for many other Christians in the twentieth century from many theological backgrounds, the skeptical and worldly Herzl was a miraculous figure; the more irreligious and secular Herzl was, the more convincingly his interest in Zionism demonstrated the power of the Bible.

The Grand Duke of Baden shared some of Hechler's religious beliefs but understood that Zionism needed to make sense at the level of international politics if it was to become a practical force. The condition of the Ottoman Empire combined with its need for great power protection put the idea of the sale or lease of an Ottoman province into the realm of possibility. Knowing his great-nephew's ambitions, he could see a match between the needs of the Jewish people—for which he seems to have felt some real sympathy—as expressed by Herzl and the ambitions of German foreign policy.

Neither Hechler nor Frederick seems to have been motivated either by the hope of Jewish gold or the fear of Jewish power. The third member of the group who ensured the meeting between Herzl and Wilhelm was a more complex case. Of Eulenburg's antisemitism there is no doubt; he had no philanthropic motive in mind as he considered Herzl's idea. For him, advocating Zionism made political sense. Eulenburg was one of the coterie around Wilhelm who increased their influence with the Kaiser by feeding his hunger for adoration and respect. Wilhelm needed uncritical admiration and he rewarded those who both fed his ego and enabled his quest to seize control of German policy from the bureaucrats and the professionals. Eulenburg, a diplomatic amateur whom Wilhelm had installed first as his ambassador to Bavaria and then, against the advice of the professionals in the foreign ministry, moved to the much more important post in Vienna, shared Wilhelm's romantic approach to foreign policy and liked the idea of the spectacular, theatrical diplomatic coup that the establishment of a German protectorate in Palestine would have been. His instincts for power were strong enough (and his knowledge of Frederick's influence was extensive enough) that he saw promoting Herzl's idea as serving his own interest.[48] At the same time, as his heavy hint to Herzl made clear, Eulenburg saw the potential for vast riches in facilitating the Zionist program. As an antisemite, Eulenburg believed the stories of untold Jewish wealth; he also believed that "the Jews" acted collectively. The man who made the dreams of the Jews come true would be showered with gold; Eulenburg wanted to be that man.

This was a fantasy that Herzl was willing to indulge—especially at a moment when he had no Jewish gold to offer. But Herzl had no scruples about using both Zionist funds and his own private means to pay agents and officials for access to important heads of state. He was in many ways a political naïf as late as 1898, but he understood that to achieve a great aim it was necessary to work with whatever tools came to hand. Herzl was always an impresario; the sultan was not the last European dignitary before whom Herzl dangled the specter of Jewish gold that he did not possess. The later history of Zionism would show that the uncritical belief of many western gentiles in the wealth and hidden power of "the Jews" remained a potent weapon in the hands of Zionist activists. Philipp zu Eulenburg was not the last politician to be led by his own fantastic notions of Jewish power to support the Zionist cause in the hope of a phantom reward.

═══

In 1898 Zionism was still a marginal, almost negligible movement among Jews. But the gentile public found the idea romantic and striking. The annual meetings of the Zionist Organization attracted press attention far in excess of the political importance of the delegates who attended. A movement that financially lived hand to mouth and struggled to carry out the most basic tasks basked in the attention of the civilized world.

Herzl's ability to engage the attention, sometimes sympathetic, sometimes not, of the most exalted personages and powerful politicians in Europe helped win public attention for Zionism, and cemented his place at the head of the movement. Which other Zionist, which other Jew could get the German Kaiser to ask the Ottoman sultan to turn the Holy Land over to the Jews? The marginalized, desperate Russian Jews at the heart of the Zionist movement saw Herzl meeting with emperors and popes; this told them that Zionism was a serious movement and that Herzl was its natural leader.

Before his death in 1904 (at the age of forty-four!), Herzl would negotiate as an equal with the British, who offered him a colonial charter in modern Kenya and seriously contemplated establishing a Jewish home in Sinai. He never spoke for a majority of Jews; he never won the great Jewish financiers and industrial titans to his side; he never controlled the press or bought and sold politicians. The Zionism that Herzl built into an important historical force was not a movement of Jewish power, but a movement that linked the preferences and passions of the gentile world to the needs of the Jewish people, and it was the unique power of Zionism to enlist powerful gentile supporters that made Zionism a power among Jews.

Many things would change over the twentieth century, and the Zionist movement saw many ups and downs after Herzl's death. Through it all, the secret weapon of the Zionists, the weapon that allowed them to dominate Jewish politics, was their ability to gather up the critical gentile support that other political currents in the Jewish world could never obtain.

4

George Washington and the Jews

I F THE SUPPORT OF powerful gentiles like the Grand Duke of Baden and Kaiser Wilhelm II helped Theodor Herzl launch the Zionist movement in Europe, Christian Zionist initiatives sprang up in the English-speaking world without any help from the Jews. Early Puritan leaders like John Cotton, who emigrated to the Massachusetts Bay Col ony in 1633, hoped to see "willing people among the gentiles" bring the Jews back to their ancestral home.[1] Five years before Herzl met William Hechler, some of the most powerful people in the United States sent a petition to President Benjamin Harrison asking him to use his diplomatic influence to further the project of a Jewish state.[2] Five years before Herzl published his pamphlet, at a time when leading Jewish families like the Rothschilds and the Warburgs had no interest in such an absurd idea, powerful Christian leaders like J. P. Morgan and John D. Rockefeller, among others, were on the record in support of a Jewish home in Palestine.[3]

Historically, the Anglo-American world had not always been so sympathetic to Jewish causes. Medieval England had if anything been more hostile to the Jews than medieval Spain; in 1290, King Edward I capped a century of intensifying persecution by expelling the three thousand or so Jews who lived in England at that time. The Edict of Expulsion would stand until the Protectorate of Oliver Cromwell, and Jews were forbidden to set foot in England or Wales without special permission.[4]

A century later, Geoffrey Chaucer's masterpiece, *The Canterbury Tales,* opens a window into the murderous prejudice against Jews that was widespread at the time. In one of the stories, a fatherless seven-year-old boy memorized a hymn to the Virgin Mary in his choir school. The boy was so struck with the beauty of the music and so eager to honor the

Mother of God that he would sing the hymn in his clear and carrying voice on the way to and from school. Unfortunately, his route passed through what the poet calls the town's "filthie Jewerye," or Jewish Quarter. As paraphrased into modern English, this is what happened next:

> Our waspish first foe, Satan, builds his nest
> Inside the heart that beats in Jewish breast.
> He asked the Jews: "O Hebrew folk, alas
> Is this the kind of thing you call OK,
> That such a boy will walk his merry way
> And fill your ears with some vile Christian song
> That teaches what your laws consider wrong?"
> From this time forth the Jews began to plan
> From out the world this guiltless boy to chase.
> They hired a desperate, homicidal man
> That in an alley had a hidden place
> And as the child passed by with heedless pace
> The cursed Jew grabbed him tight and held him fast,
> The throat he cut, the corpse in pit he cast.

The boy's distraught mother searched for her son throughout the town. At last she came to the Jewish Quarter, where they denied all knowledge of what had happened. But, the tale continues, after she had asked for help in vain, she sat down and began to cry for her son—and from the pit in which he had been cast, his clear voice was heard singing a hymn to the Virgin. Thanks to this miracle, the murder was discovered (the phrase "Murder will out" comes to us from this poem), and the nasty, murdering Jews got what they deserved: they were dragged by wild horses and then hung.[5]

This is how medieval England saw the Jews. Duplicitous, scheming, filled with hate—the Jews in the poem live by usury and guile. English hatred and fear of Jews didn't end with Chaucer. Shakespeare's *The Merchant of Venice* reveals a picture of Jews that is not very far from Chaucer's. Shylock seethes with resentment against the Christians who have oppressed and wronged him. Bitterness has eaten away the better part of his humanity, and he finds his joy in the suffering of the Christians he hates.

One hundred eighty-five years after King James I saw a 1605 performance of *The Merchant of Venice,* George Washington sent a letter to the small Jewish congregation in the Touro Synagogue in Newport, Rhode Island. In it, he declared that the Jews of the United States were full and equal citizens by right: "All possess alike liberty of conscience and immunities of citizenship. It is now no more that toleration is spoken of, as if it was by the indulgence of one class of people, that another enjoyed the exercise of their inherent natural rights. For happily the Government of the United States, which gives to bigotry no sanction, to persecution no assistance requires only that they who live under its protection should demean themselves as good citizens, in giving it on all occasions their effectual support."[6]

This was revolutionary. Jews did not need to swear a special oath, renounce Jewish personal law in their dealings with one another, or do anything else to be accepted as active members of the American commonwealth. Washington's sentiments in this letter are even more remarkable because they were uncontroversial in the America of that day; he was reflecting the common sentiment of his compatriots at that time about how their federal government should be organized. (Americans were more conservative when it came to state governments. Some states maintained religious establishments until the 1830s; North Carolina only dropped its religious test for officeholders in 1868.)[7]

Clearly, something fundamental had changed in the English-speaking world since the days of Geoffrey Chaucer and William Shakespeare. How and why did that happen? How did Jews go from being the enemy within to being fellow citizens worthy of trust and respect?

Four related sets of changes combined to create a new, more favorable view of the Jews in the English-speaking world. First, the British Reformation led to a reappraisal of the religious position of the Jews. Second, the English-speaking world embraced a historical and cultural vision that linked the fate of the Jews with the fate of the English speakers. Third, the English-speaking world moved away from the medieval "total society" toward a vision of a pluralistic society in which different faiths could coexist side by side. Finally, fears of capitalism and the disruptive forces of free markets gradually faded as the English-speaking world came to harness these forces as the engines of its own rapid development. As a result of these independent but related sets of changes, the English and the Scots came to see Jews in a more favorable light both at home and in their colonies overseas, and because American society was more profoundly affected by these forces, the different view of the Jewish people went further, struck deeper roots, and has lasted longer in the United States than elsewhere.

THE BRITISH REFORMATION AND THE JEWS

Like so many of the revolutions in sentiment that have changed human relations through the ages, the Anglo-American "new look" at the Jews had its origin in religion and went on to affect secular ideas and institutions. Specifically, the changes unleashed by the Reformation led to a revolutionary upheaval in the theological appraisal of Jewish-Christian relations, and those changes would reverberate in secular politics and social thought. The original Protestant Reformers gave little thought and (especially in Martin Luther's case) little sympathy to the Jews, but the changes the Reformers set in motion had many religious and secular consequences they didn't anticipate, and some of those had to do with the position of Jews in predominantly Christian societies.

In England and Scotland the change began with something very simple, but very profound: the translation of the Bible into English and the distribution of cheap editions to ordinary people all over the land who could, and did, read the book for themselves. In the Middle Ages, the Bible was not available in the language of ordinary people, and before the invention of printing, books of any kind were expensive and rare. All over Europe the appearance of Bible editions in local languages sparked generations of controversy and war. But in the British Isles, as readers spent more time with their Bibles, English and Scottish Christians came to take a second look at the Jewish people.

During the Middle Ages Christianity fanned the flames of antisemitism across Europe. Medieval Christians generally believed that the exile of the Jews was their just punishment for rejecting and crucifying the Savior sent by God. The Jews were cursed, and the consequences of the curse were both exile and blindness. People this wicked could be capable of anything; Jews were often objects of both fear and hate to their neighbors.

Additionally, before the Reformation, when the celebration of the Mass was the liturgical centerpiece of worship, the service each week revolved around the re-creation of the death of Christ in the sacrifice of the Eucharist. Each week the prayers repeated the story of Jesus's passion, crucifixion, and death; each week the congregation was asked to remember the cruel mistreatment of an innocent man by a vicious and depraved Jewish mob. Holy Week, the most intense and theatrical observances of the Christian year, often revolved around re-readings and reenactments of those terrible events. "Let him be crucified! Let him be crucified!" a crowd of actors representing the Jews of Jesus's day,* sometimes dressed up as contemporary Jews, would shout. "His blood be on us and on our children!"[8]

Rituals like the Stations of the Cross commemorated Jesus's suffering and death. Priests would lead groups of the devout to each station, at which point they would preach passionately about the evils Christ suffered, the mockery and scorn his pain attracted from the crowds lining his route, and the innocence and meekness with which the Lamb of God accepted his torment.

Nothing in the rest of the Bible received the kind of attention the Passion Narratives (as the accounts of Jesus's death in the four gospels are called) did, and those narratives, deprived of any context or explanation, helped strengthen popular dislike and suspicion of the Jews.

For those who wanted to hear more about the Bible stories, most of what they would hear came from the other sections of the four gospels, as the priests gave sermons about different episodes in Jesus's life. Many of these involved theological and social disputes with different Jewish religious factions of the time: the Pharisees and the Sadducees were well-known to Christians as the chief opponents and enemies of their Lord.

This situation changed dramatically at the time of the Reformation. With the translated Bibles, biblical study was no longer something that demanded advanced theological training, abundant leisure, and access to rare and expensive hand-copied texts. As the idea spread that God speaks directly through this book, and that he speaks to anybody who chose to read it with a humble heart, the Bible became the intellectual and emotional center of millions of lives. Reading the Bible in this way opened an avenue of escape and discovery for common people. In your day job you were at the mercy of your husband, your master, your landlord. When you were reading the Bible and reflecting on its meaning, you were speaking directly with the ruler of the universe. And in those

---

* Christian theologians today generally agree that any imputation of collective guilt either to the Jews of the first century or their descendants today cannot be justified on any reasonable reading of the biblical record.

moments of spiritual communion with the Almighty, you were the equal of any king, any priest, any bishop in the world.

As millions still do, those readers read the whole Bible, from Genesis to Revelation, over and over again during the course of their lives. (By age fourteen the future President Harry Truman had read the family Bible cover to cover three times.)[9] These readers were in closer touch with the Jewish scriptures than any group of Christians since the beginning of the Church. The Jewish scriptures are, for one thing, much longer than the Christian ones.* In my own copy of the King James Version, the four-hundred-year-old translation that most American Christians used until the middle of the last century, the thirty-nine books of the Old Testament take up 813 pages from Genesis to Malachi. The twenty-seven books of the New Testament from Matthew to Revelation are only one third as long: the Old Testament is 75 percent of the Christian Bible.

Christians who make a habit of reading the Bible regularly often therefore spend more time with the old Jewish scriptures than with the new Christian ones. The Passion Narratives, the angry disputes with the Sadducees and Pharisees, and the persecution of the early Christians by Jewish authorities were still in the Bible, but there were also stories of Jewish heroes of faith, of prophets and patriarchs, kings and warriors.

The Old Testament as read by the Protestants wasn't just longer than the New Testament; it was often more useful. The Old Testament had more to say about politics, government, and war than the New. Jesus was what Machiavelli called an "unarmed prophet," and as he told Pontius Pilate, his Kingdom was "not of this earth." He taught people how to approach God, how to love their neighbors, how to reorder their priorities, but he did not tell them how to organize their civic lives. Unlike Moses and Muhammad, who left detailed instructions for their followers about various political, civil, and even sanitary laws, Jesus had very little to say about the tax rate, the best organization of government, the civil law, and the rights and duties of magistrates. He does not say what makes for a just war, or how his followers should behave in a conflict. The gospels say not one word either in direct defense of slavery or

---

* Another important factor: scholars were rediscovering Hebrew. By 1644, England's Puritan Parliament was taking time out of the English Civil War to mandate that candidates for the ministry pass examinations in biblical Hebrew as well as Greek; at Harvard, the bastion of Puritan scholarship in the New World, Hebrew lessons were mandatory up until 1787. Barbara Tuchman, *Bible and Sword: England and Palestine from the Bronze Age to Balfour* (New York University Press, 1956), 116; Peter Grose, *Israel in the Mind of America* (Alfred A. Knopf, 1983), 5.

against it. There is nothing there about inheritance law, nothing about the proper age of consent for marriage, nothing about how a country should choose its rulers.

Jesus may not have spoken on these subjects, but the Bible did—often in the Old Testament. There, God judged kings and nations, gave victory in battle, established principles of civil law, and generally supplied the guidance that nations need. The New Testament was produced by and for a small sectarian movement; the Old Testament is the library of a people. Christians like the Protestant Reformers who believe that the Bible is the source of all the wisdom humanity needs must spend much of their time searching the Jewish scriptures for examples and advice.

If most Jews in the New Testament, with the exception of Jesus and his followers, are not very sympathetic as literary characters, the Jews of the Old Testament are presented as heroes (and heroines) of faith. Abraham, Gideon, Moses, David, Nathan, Solomon, Hannah, Deborah, Samuel, Joshua, Samson, Elijah: the children of the Reformation grew up among these familiar presences. Protestants gave Old Testament names to their children and to this day ancient Hebrew names like Joshua, Sarah, Samuel, Josiah, Hannah, Jesse, and Ruth are as American as apple pie. For centuries, comic writers trying to evoke the spirit of backwoods America gave Old Testament names to their characters—Ichabod Crane of Sleepy Hollow, Li'l Abner of Dogpatch, Gomer Pyle of Mayberry.

To read the literature of England, Scotland, and America from the seventeenth century into our own day is to find the Old Testament at every turn. Many of the most familiar hymns were metrical adaptations of the Hebrew psalms. Poets from John Milton to W. H. Auden were fascinated by the rhythms and themes of the Jewish scriptures. For many people, the history and the place names and the landscape of the Holy Land were almost as familiar as the villages in which they lived. From Bethesda, Maryland, to Berea, Kentucky, their hometowns often bore Old Testament names. The Anglo-American imagination was saturated in the Bible. Joseph and his coat of many colors, Jacob's ladder, the plagues of Egypt, Jonah and the whale, Daniel and the lion's den, David and Goliath: there was scarcely a farmhouse or cabin in the United States where these stories weren't among the most familiar of all—told by parents and grandparents, sounded out by children learning to read from the family Bible, turned into folk songs, echoing and reechoing in the mind from infancy to old age, generation on generation.

THE DOCTRINE OF THE JEWS

Familiarity with the Jewish scriptures and admiration for Jewish heroes was only the beginning. As Protestant theologians worked out the meaning of their new religious vision, many were drawn to a fundamental reconceptualization of the place of contemporary Jews in the divine plan.

Most of the early Church Fathers and the medieval theologians believed that when the Jews rejected Jesus's claim to be the Messiah, the Jewish people lost their special place in God's plan. The Church was the "new Israel," and Christians as the new Jews were the inheritors of all the promises made to Abraham and the patriarchs and kings. God had no more business with Jews as Jews; they could become part of the new Israel by converting and being baptized, but otherwise they had no further part to play in the sacred story of God's redemptive intervention in this world.

Technically, this idea is known as "supersessionism": the Church and the Christians have superseded or replaced Israel and the Jews in the divine plan. Many Calvinists and Puritans, however, came to reject it, believing that the Jews of the present day, without Christ though they were, still had a part to play in God's story. The Jews, they believed, may have turned their backs on God, but God is faithful when men are not and, in the end, the old Israel would once more be reconciled to its God. That reconciliation, they believed, would not just be spiritual; the Jews would return someday to the land that was promised to Abraham. In many circles, it became a mark of Calvinist doctrine to believe that Israel would be restored.

Against a thousand years of Catholic (and Eastern Orthodox) theology, the English Puritans insisted that the Old Testament had to be interpreted literally as well as figuratively, allegorically, and typologically. When God said to Abraham in verse 8 of chapter 17 of the book of Genesis, "And I will give unto thee, and to thy seed after thee, the land wherein thou art a stranger, all the land of Canaan, for an everlasting possession, and I will be their God," Christians were obliged to interpret that as a literal promise of the actual Holy Land to real-world, physical Jews. It was no good talking about the symbolism, or saying that this was an allegory representing God's promise of an eternal home in heaven to Christians; those interpretations might be and indeed were also true, but the plain, commonsense literal meaning of the text was not to be denied. Likewise, God's promise of an eternal relationship with the Jewish people also had to be understood by Christians as still true today. The "New Covenant" that Jesus established with Christians went beyond but did not negate the "Old Covenant" that God had established with Abraham. God was faithful and His Word once given would never fail.

If the Jews were still in a covenantal relationship with God, it followed that the Jews of the contemporary world were still a people, a nation. They had a history and a future, and they remained a special object of divine care.

Many Protestants' insistence on the literal meaning of the Old Testament combined with their close study of every page in the Word of God led them to another conclusion. What God says in chapter 12, verse 3 of Genesis to Abraham is also still true today: "And I will bless them that bless thee, and curse him that curseth thee. and in thee shall all the families of the earth be blessed."

When millions of Americans go into the voting booth today they bring with them a belief in this verse of the Bible. It doesn't mean that they will always prioritize Israel over other concerns or that they will assume that God wants the United States to do whatever a given Israeli prime minister is proposing. Nor does it automatically free people from prejudice and keep antisemitic stereotypes at bay. Still, many Protestants feel and felt obliged to take those words seriously.

Not every verse in the Bible gets an equal amount of attention from evangelical Protestants. (Paul's exhortations to remain single have never been popular, for example, among American evangelicals.) But the Abrahamic promises in Genesis became and remained prominent in the mind of American Protestantism because they are linked to what became a key concept in Protestant theology: the idea of a "covenant."

Covenants are legal agreements between two parties. In Protestant theology (especially, though not only, in Calvinism) a series of covenants between God and humanity mark the basic stages in God's work of redemption. God made covenants with Adam, Noah, Abraham, Moses and the Israelites at Sinai; with David, and through Jesus, he made the "New Covenant" that, Protestants taught, was the one toward which the others all pointed. These covenants come with commandments and are the basis of moral obligation. God's promise to Abraham came with the commandment to circumcise his male children on the eighth day. The Sinai covenant involved the acceptance by the Israelites of the Ten Commandments and the other laws in the Torah. The New Covenant of the New Testament offered a better path to a relationship with God and offered it to the whole world rather than only to the Jews. The Protestants took all the covenants seriously, and generations of preachers highlighted the texts that described them and made sure that the people in the pews understood what covenants were and why they mattered.

Once the promises made to the Jews were accepted as still valid today, something else became clear: at some point in the future God would bring the Jews back to the Holy Land. There are many biblical prophecies to this effect; one example is found in the book of the prophet Isaiah, chapter 11, verses 11 and 12:

> And it shall come to pass in that day, that the Lord shall set his hand again the second time to recover the remnant of his people, which shall be left, from Assyria, and from Egypt, and from Pathros, and from Cush, and from Elam, and from Shinar, and from Hamath, and from the islands of the sea. And he shall set up an ensign for the nations and shall assemble the outcasts of Israel, and gather together the dispersed of Judah from the four corners of the earth.

The first exile of the Jewish people is the so-called Babylonian Captivity, said to date from 586 to 538 BCE. Protestant exegetes read this passage from Isaiah as explicitly predicting a second return from a second exile.[10] The second exile was the one that began when the Romans crushed the Jewish Revolt forty years after the crucifixion of Jesus; was Isaiah predicting that this exile, too, would have an end?

Nothing could have seemed more unlikely in the seventeenth century than that such an event would take place, but Protestant theologians felt that their understanding of the holy books required this interpretation, and there is a long tradition of Protestant predictions of an ultimate return of the Jews. In 1666, Increase Mather took to the pulpit of the First Church of Boston, the largest and oldest congregation in Massachusetts Bay Colony, and told his congregation that "the time will surely come, when the body of the twelve Tribes of Israel shall be brought out of their present condition of bondage and misery, into a glorious and wonderful state of salvation, not only spiritual but temporal." They would "recover the Possession of their Promised Land." Mather would go on to publish this theory in London in 1669 in *The Mystery of Israel's Salvation Explained and Applyed.*[11]

The colonies did not have a publishing industry, and had to look to the mother country to publish and buy books. But the Puritan tradition of which Mather was a part flourished in seventeenth-century England as much as in New England. At the dawn of the century, theologian Thomas Brightman was writing of the Jews, "Shal they returne agayn to Jerusalem? There is nothing more sure: the Prophets plainly confirme it, and beat often upon it." Lawyer, MP, and leading Puritan Henry Finch wrote in a 1621 volume called *The Worlds Great Restauration, or, the Calling of the Iewes* that the Jews would defeat Gog and Magog (which he interpreted as a prophecy referring to Islam) at the end of days and "sit as a Lady in . . . true Tsion." He further emphasized to his readers, "Where Israel, Iudah, Tsion, Ierusalem, &c. are named in this argument [i.e., in the Bible], the Holy Ghost meaneth not the spirituall Israel, or Church of God collected of the Gentiles, no nor of the Iewes and Gentiles both (for each of these have their promises severally and apart) but Israel properly descended out of Iacobs loynes." These views were very much in the Puritan mainstream.[12]

This kind of thinking endured intact in the American colonies long after ardor for Puritanism had died down almost completely in England. Similar predictions would flow from generations of American theologians and religious leaders. The most famous of them all, Jonathan Edwards, maintained that the Jews would even increase the amount of land under their rule beyond the Israel of biblical times: "And it is the more evident, that the Jews will return to their own land again, because they never have yet possessed one quarter of that land, which was so often promised them, from the Red Sea to the river Euphrates. (Ex. 23:31; Gen. 15:18; Deut. 11:24; Josh. 1:4)."[13]

For American divines it remained a point of dispute whether the Jews would convert to Christianity before or after their return to the Holy Land. Nevertheless, a sea change had taken place. In the new, Puritan understanding, the Jews were back in God's plan, their covenant intact, with a role to play in the future under divine guidance. As the centuries wore on and the Ottoman Empire weakened in a way visible even from half a world away, divines in America from this intellectual lineage would continue to proclaim God's plan in this regard with mounting excitement as this once unimaginably improbable event began to look possible.

These early American thinkers drew not only on the Old Testament for their beliefs but also on the Epistles of St. Paul. These letters by the most active of the early Christian evangelists are both the earliest Christian documents that survive (scholars believe that most of the epistles were written before any of the gospels assumed their final form) and the closest thing the Bible contains to a systematic exposition of Christian theology and ecclesiastical guidance. From the time of Martin Luther, whose meditations on Paul's Epistle (letter) to the Romans led him to the key ideas on which he was to build his theology, Protestant laypeople and clergy combed these letters with the greatest possible attention for guidance on matters of faith and conduct.

Paul was a zealous Jew who led early efforts to persecute Christians until he had a vision of the risen Christ and embraced Christianity. Like Jesus, he would spend much time engaged in theological controversy with Jewish leaders (a story told at some length in the biblical book known as the Book of Acts). In the letters he wrote to various church communities of the day, he not only reflected on these controversies but also set out principles that in his view should guide the relations between Christians and Jews, principles that had apparently been neglected during the medieval period. As Protestants encountered Paul's thoughts on the subject, many came to believe that the treatment of Jews was yet another area in which the Roman Catholic Church had gone wrong.[14]

Paul's Epistle to the Romans is the longest and most theologically significant account of his thinking. In the eleventh chapter of the epistle, Paul examines the question of why the majority of the Jews, God's Chosen People, had not accepted the Christian message, what God's purpose was in this development, and what would happen in the future. First, Paul notes that it should not surprise Christians that only a minority of Jews had embraced the new teaching. Citing many Old Testament passages, he points out that over and over in Israel's history the majority rejected God's message and only a "saving remnant" remained faithful. But God was faithful even when humans failed. God stood by Israel even when Israel didn't stand by God.

For Paul, as many Protestants understood him, this was a vital theological point. His doctrine of human salvation held that Jesus came to die for human beings because humans simply can't do the right thing on their own. The failure of the Jews to remain faithful to God under their covenant wasn't evidence of some uniquely pathological Jewish blindness or the result of a curse; it was simply one aspect of humanity's larger problem. We all recognize that the moral law (however we might understand it) is correct and ought to be obeyed, yet none of us can live up to our own moral standards. If we are honest with ourselves, we have to admit that we all fall short. But, and this is for many Christians the essence of Paul's concept of religion, God loves us too much to leave us in this fix. From this perspective, the failure (as Christians understood it) of Israel to live up to the covenant of Moses begins to look less like an endpoint and more like a beginning. Israel's inability to live up to the Old Covenant or to accept the New is only what must be expected, but human failure does not mean the failure of God's plan. His plan for the Jews continues.

At some future date, as many Protestants interpreted him, Paul predicts, the Jews will be gathered to Christ and that moment, when it comes, will mark the culmination of world history. Noting that the failure of the Jews to embrace the gospel of Christ opened the door to the salvation of the gentiles, Paul speculates that the acceptance of the gospel by the Jews would mean even more. "For if the casting away of them [the unbelieving Jew] be the reconciling of the world, what shall the receiving of them be, but life from the dead?" (Romans 11:15).

Paul, as many Puritan theologians came to understand him, believed that the conversion of Jews was delayed to allow the gospel to be preached to the non-Jewish world, giving non-Jews the chance to embrace Christianity and find God. Rather than cursing and reviling the Jews for their failure to convert, non-Jewish Christians should thank God for his mercy in delaying the end times to allow people from all over the world to enter God's kingdom. God sent a "partial hardening" to the non-Christian Jews (i.e., they accepted some of his plan but not all of it), Paul wrote, so that there might be space before the end of the world for the full complement of gentiles to be converted and saved (Romans 11:25).

To medieval Christians the survival of the Jews was simply a sign of God's continuing wrath. The theologians who followed the Puritan reading of Paul came to a different conclusion. The unbelief of the Jews may have been a defiance of God's will, but it was also part of God's plan: "through their [the Jews'] fall salvation is come unto the Gentiles" (11:11). Additionally, the Jews were still a special people with a special role in world history. Their dramatic conversion would be part of the events at the end of the world that prepared for the return of Christ, the Last Judgment, and the establishment of God's true kingdom.

This new view of the Jewish future entered the wider cultural consciousness of the English-speaking world. In the seventeenth century, in Andrew Marvell's "To His Coy Mistress," the suitor says that if we had enough time, "And you should, if you please, refuse/Till the conversion of the Jews." Isaac Newton mentioned the restoration of the Jews, in a volume he wrote on the book of Revelation.[15] In *Paradise Regained*, John Milton wrote:

> *Yet He at length, time to himself best known,*
> *Remembering Abraham, by some wondrous call*
> *May bring them back, repentant and sincere,*
> *And at their passing cleave the Assyrian flood,*
> *While to their native land with joy they haste,*
> *As the Red Sea and Jordan once he cleft,*
> *When to the Promised Land their fathers passed.*
> *To his due time and providence I leave them.*[16]

Another doctrinal shift further influenced Protestants toward a less hostile attitude toward the Jewish people and their faith. From Martin Luther on, Protestant theologians stressed the role of election, of God's choice in the process of salvation. You didn't earn salvation by doing good deeds (or lose it by doing bad ones); indeed, it was blasphemous to think so. You were saved because God chose to save you in spite of your sins. As Protestants thought through the implications of this idea, many reached the conclusion that the question of salvation was entirely about God's predestination. The Jews weren't rejecting Christianity because they were particularly evil or rebellious; rather, it was part of God's plan to preserve the nation of Israel in unbelief until, in his own good time, he willed their conversion.

Seen in this light, persecuting the Jews was irrational, even blasphemous. You were protesting against the plan of the Divine Architect of the Universe. You were protesting against something that (per Paul) staved off your own destruction. Ultimately, you were protesting against omnipotent will.

These changes led to another very important shift in the attitude of many Anglo-American Christians toward the persistence among them of a Jewish minority. In the Middle Ages, Jews were seen as threats to Christianity. Their refusal to accept the truth of the Christian gospel or to worship Jesus as the Messiah was felt as an argument against the truth of Christianity: if Jesus's own people, who knew their scriptures best, thought he was a fraud, did this mean that Christianity was false? This fear meant less to the new generations of Protestant believers. The continuing existence of the Jewish people from the standpoint of Protestant theology went from being evidence that Christianity might be mistaken to evidence that the Bible was true. The world had once been full of many nations larger and more powerful than the Jewish people; that the Jews, small and persecuted, should have survived was a sign that God is real and that he keeps his word. God promised Abraham that the Jews would survive, and the Jews, unlike the Hittites, the Babylonians, and the Assyrians, are still with us today. And when and if the Jews should return to the Holy Land, Americans were predisposed to see that return as yet another sign that the God of the Bible is real and that the Christian religion is therefore true. The existence of the Jews was evidence for the existence of God; any sign that the Jews were returning to Palestine would be seen as proof that God was acting in history.

As a result of their theological reflections, American scholars and preachers came to several conclusions about the Jews:

- Although they do not, in unbelief, have the salvation that comes alone through Christ, Jews remain under God's special covenant and care.
- The Jews are a nation, not a religious minority or a racial group.
- To hate or persecute Jews is a crime against God, and it is a crime that almighty justice will avenge.
- The gift of the Holy Land to Abraham remains valid and the Bible prophesies that the Jews will someday return to it.
- It is a sign of God's blessing on America if the American people understand these truths and build a special relationship with the Jewish people.

It was never the case that all Americans were Protestants or that all Protestant Americans accepted these ideas about the Jews. Nevertheless, these ideas influenced millions of Americans from the colonial era through the present day. The power of religion in American life rises and falls across the generations, but the salience of these ideas in American religion and in the broader culture remains. These views helped shape the American mind for centuries, and they are shaping it still, among secular people as well as among religious ones.

HISTORICAL AND THEOLOGICAL IDENTIFICATION

If Protestants' theology led many of them to take a different and more positive view of the continuing role of the Jews in God's plans, a combination of theology and historical experience led them to a sense of connection and identification with Jews. In England and Scotland in particular a popular nationalism and identity arose which saw these countries as Chosen People standing in the same kind of relationship to God that the ancient Hebrews did: chosen by God and standing in a covenanted relationship with him. The failure of the Reformation to sweep Europe and the success of the Catholic Counter-Reformation meant that a solid majority of Europe remained faithful to the old religion. That left Protestants feeling exposed. Before the rise of Prussia in the mid-eighteenth century, England was the only Protestant great power, and from the time of the Spanish Armada (1588) through the Battle of Waterloo (1815) the English associated threats to their national security with great powers on the continent often in league with the pope.

The more radical Protestants in Britain and their American cousins felt themselves further embattled at home. Combating the backsliding, Catholicizing Stuart kings, the seventeenth-century dissidents saw themselves as a tiny minority of believers in a hostile world, utterly dependent on the power of God for their survival.

For Bible-reading people, the parallels with the situation of the ancient Hebrews were numerous and convincing. Like the Hebrews, they were the one faithful nation in a world of darkness. Like the Hebrews, they were surrounded by powerful enemies. And like the Hebrews, they could only survive by staying close to God.

One of the most powerful moments in the Hebrew scriptures comes in Exodus when the Hebrew people, newly rescued from slavery in Egypt, assemble before the presence of God on Mount Sinai, receive the Ten Commandments, and accept the Covenant that God has offered them. They will keep God's laws and worship him only, and God will protect the people. This is the moment that makes the Hebrew people a nation; it was a moment that echoed in the thoughts of the early Protestants who also saw themselves under a covenant with God.

The most dramatic expression of this current of thought politically was found among the Scottish Covenanters. As the storm clouds that would lead to civil war gathered over England and Scotland, radical Calvinists in Scotland interpreted current events through a biblical lens and came to believe that God had called the Scots as a people to a special relationship, just as God extended protection to Israel in the Bible when the Jews obeyed the biblical laws. As religious and political tension mounted, Calvinists summoned the Scottish people to make a national covenant with God, and in 1638 swore the Scottish National Covenant, in which they pledged to God and one another their determination to preserve and live by the Reformed (Presbyterian) Church in Scotland. Their decision to abide by this covenant and protect it by force directly precipitated the so-called Bishops' Wars and indirectly led to the English Civil Wars. The Scottish determination to stick by this covenant guided Scottish policy throughout the violent period that followed. It led various factions to split first with the king, then with the English Parliamentarians, then with each other. It encouraged popular uprisings and lonely martyrdoms alike. One of the last factions to adhere to it, the Cameronians, were almost an archetype of what would later become American religiosity: outlawed by their own government, they would meet and preach in fields, "worshipping defiantly with a Bible in one hand and a weapon in the other, and slaughtering the forces that were sent to suppress them."[17]

The New England settlements also believed themselves to be under a covenant with God. Through their experience, so like that of the biblical Hebrews, of moving into a land inhabited by others and making it their own, they came to see themselves as a Chosen People, like the ancient Hebrews, called to covenant with God and given a new land to possess on condition that they fulfilled the covenant.[18] This provided them with both psychological reassurance that God would protect them in the strange, dangerous, and remote corner of the world to which he had called them, and perhaps also justification to salve their consciences about taking land from the natives.

During all the wars of the colonial era and the Revolution itself, many Americans saw themselves as a Chosen People in the wilderness, protected by and accountable to the God of the Bible. When they won victories, they gave thanks to God; when they suffered defeat they looked for the faults in their conduct that had led God to punish them. Whether fighting off Native American tribes, French forces, or, during the Revolution, the armies of King George, many Americans compared their situation to that of the ancient Hebrews; they prayed to Jehovah and looked to his mighty arm for protection.

While only a relatively small number of Americans went as far as to think of the United States as God's "New Israel," the idea that God would deal with America with something analogous to the care—and discipline—that he showed the Hebrew people in the Bible was widely accepted. The American colonists formed their view of history by studying the books of the Bible that recount the adventures of the Hebrew people under the judges and kings, seeking parallels in the careers of those ancient leaders to the events of their own time. From the first English settlement in the New World to the Revolution and beyond, the Americans were immersed in the images, the language, and the historical ideas of the Hebrew Bible. Of the over three thousand citations catalogued in the works of the Founding Fathers by Professor Donald Lutz, 34 percent are to the Bible, marking it by far the most cited single influence on their thought, and many of those citations reference the Jewish scriptures.[19] In 1776, both Benjamin Franklin and Thomas Jefferson proposed designs for the Great Seal of the new nation that would appeal to the public: Franklin's showed Moses dividing the Red Sea as Pharaoh (often presented at the time as synonymous with King George III) is drowned, while Jefferson's showed the Israelites following the cloud and the pillar of fire through the desert.[20] (This was an appeal to popular sentiment on Jefferson's part; privately he wrote that the God of the Old Testament was "cruel, vindictive, capricious, and unjust.")[21]

The connection with Israel became a building block of American identity, and not just for free whites. Enslaved Blacks, as they turned to Christianity in large numbers during the waves of evangelical revivals in the generation after the American Revolution, saw themselves as God's Israel in Egyptian bondage. They awaited a Moses who would lead them forth, and spoke longingly of the year of jubilee, the biblical promise of freedom for the slaves.

Such ideas about the ancient Hebrews did not automatically make Americans lovers of modern Jews, but they steadily undercut the negative ideas and stereotypes that they inherited from the medieval past. Their direct experience with Jews was small.[22] The first written record of a Jewish presence in Maryland, for example, comes in 1658 when a Jew by the name of Jacob Lumbrozo was tried for blasphemy; convicted, he was released as the result of an amnesty issued on the occasion of Richard Cromwell succeeding his father in power that same year.[23] Only about one thousand Jews lived in the thirteen colonies at the time of the Revolution.[24]

THE DESACRALIZATION OF THE SOCIAL ORDER

A third set of changes brought about by the peculiar course of the Reformation in Britain and America ended by changing the core values of many people in both societies in ways that made it easier for Jewish individuals and organizations to find a comfortable place in the English-speaking world.

The medieval Christian world, as noted, was a holistic society that sought to bring all of society into harmony and unity under a set of basic values and rules grounded in the theology and the practice of the Roman Catholic Church. It was in many ways a beautiful vision, but it had no room for religious or social dissidents.

The Reformation did not at first challenge the medieval ideal of a united Christendom. Martin Luther and John Calvin wanted to correct the abuses they saw in the Catholic Church, but their goal was to set up a purified and reformed Christendom that would be just as holistic and united as the old one. Both Protestants and Catholics long struggled to unite Europe under one of the two competing faiths before reluctantly accepting the fact of division.

Even so, the ideal of the holistic society was dominant in most of the individual political units of the post-Reformation world. Europe as a whole might be divided, but Prussia was Lutheran, Spain was Catholic, Geneva was Calvinist, and Russia was Orthodox. The famous *cuius regio* principle from the Peace of Augsburg upheld the idea that the ruler of each state could choose the religion around which that particular country would be organized.

This meant that Europe was more religiously diverse than formerly, but each European kingdom, principality, and city-state held up an ideal of religious uniformity within its frontiers. The Jews still stuck out, however, and their presence was still seen by many, Protestant as well as Catholic, as containing moral, political, and economic threats to the social order.

But in England and Scotland, the lengthy and drawn-out process of the Reformation took a different turn. Protestant opinion continued to divide; the English, for example, read their King James Bibles in the hundreds of thousands, and they found that they could not agree on what the Bible meant. Should churches be governed by bishops? Should babies be baptized in infancy, or should baptism be for adults only? Was it necessary that Holy Communion be administered by an ordained priest, and what exactly happened to the bread and the wine during a Communion service? Were kings and lords appointed by God, or did the Bible teach that all people were equal? Was war against the law of God? Were stained glass windows and statues of saints useful reminders of divine truths, or did they tempt ignorant people to practice idolatry, worshipping an image rather than worshipping God alone?

All these questions and more divided British Protestants, and before long the differences were so deep and the passions aroused by the disputes so intense that more and more English and Scottish Christians began to leave the established churches in their respective kingdoms. The English Civil Wars of the 1640s and the upheavals of the next generation when England and Scotland executed one king, lived under a Lord Protector, overthrew a second monarch, invited three princes from overseas to come and reign over them, and ended by merging the two kingdoms of England and Scotland into the United Kingdom, saw the religious unity of the realms broken once and for all.

Communities of dissidents like the Presbyterians, the Baptists, the Quakers, the Congregationalists, and dozens of others broke off from the churches of England and Scotland for various reasons, until both countries were full of "nonconformists" who belonged to different religious sects or, as we now call them, denominations. Most Christians at the time thought this breakdown was terrible, and hoped that it was a temporary way station on the road back toward a unified, holistic Christian society. But as time went by, in Britain and much more in America, it became clear that this hope was an illusion. The religious differences between the denominations were too great for the restoration of a national church that everyone would belong to.

For some Christians, however, "denominationalism" wasn't just a

necessary evil. It was a positive good. For some of the more radical Protestants, the medieval ideal of a single church supported by and supporting the government was evil in and of itself. The union of church and
state corrupted both. People would belong to a church not because they
agreed with its doctrines and sought to work out their salvation in its
fellowship, but because church membership was the road to political and
economic power. Meanwhile, the government, with the powerful backing of the clergy, would soon become so powerful that civil liberty would
be lost.

For these Protestants, the traditional, all-encompassing vision of a
unified Christendom was losing its appeal. They believed that the civil
authorities should run the secular government and leave each religious
congregation free to manage its own affairs. The separation of church
and state became an ideal, especially for groups like the Baptists who
had known little except persecution and discrimination from governments aligned with religious establishments.

Along with the separation of church and state, another concept took
root: the sinfulness of religious persecution. During the religious wars
of the seventeenth century in Britain, every religious group underwent
periods of persecution. The Anglicans persecuted the radical Protestants until the civil war broke out. Once the king was defeated and
Cromwell was in power, the Anglicans could be stripped of their power
and wealth unless they were careful. When Charles II was restored to
the throne in 1660, the triumphant Anglicans forced savage persecution
laws through Parliament, and many nonconforming clergy and believers were deprived of their positions, fined, imprisoned, and worse.

As Reformed Protestants and their Baptist cousins endured persecution, they developed a new and radical religious idea: that persecution
was not, as generations of popes, archbishops, and kings had taught, a
religious duty. It was a terrible sin, and not just when Christians were
the victims. Out of the fires of religious persecution came a belief among
increasing numbers of Protestants that religious toleration, as well as the
separation of church and state, was God's will.

In 1644, Roger Williams, who had been expelled from Massachusetts
by the Puritans on religious grounds and had just secured the charter
for what would become the state of Rhode Island (then the colony of
Providence Plantation), published *The Bloudy Tenent, of Persecution, for
Cause of Conscience*. In it, he declared:

It is the will and command of God that since the coming of his Son the Lord Jesus, a permission of the most Paganish, Jewish, Turkish or anti-Christian consciences or worships be granted to all men in all nations and countries. . . . God requireth not a uniformity of religion to be enacted and enforced in any civil state. . . . True civility and Christianity may flourish in a state or kingdom notwithstanding the permission of divers and contrary consciences either Jew or gentile.[25]

It will not surprise the reader to learn that all denominations were tolerated in Williams's new colony, one of a growing number—mostly founded by groups that suffered persecution in England, such as the Quakers (Pennsylvania) or Catholics (Maryland)—that enshrined freedom of worship and of conscience into law.

By the eighteenth century, the United States was well on the way to a new kind of ideal for a Christian society. Each denomination would have its vision about how the church and family life ought to be structured. Society depended on the strength of these faith communities and associations and on their ability to form virtuous citizens who could provide the civil government with honest and public-spirited administration. But it was not the place of any one of these religious communities to remake the body politic in its own image. America would be a Christian republic in the dual senses that most of its citizens would be Christians and that the republic they built proceeded from their understanding of the kind of commonwealth Christians ought to build. However, the authorities of that republic had nothing to do with regulating the beliefs of the citizens. No special class of prelates would share in its tax revenues, no religious test would be required for any civil office whatever, and the republic would not favor one denomination or oppress another.

This idea of a nonreligious republic in a country of many independent religious societies could not have been more congenial to Jews. The synagogue became another denomination, and Jews who went to synagogue were one minority among many. In this kind of society, Jews no longer endangered the social compact simply by existing. As George Washington told the elders of Touro Synagogue, Jews who obeyed the general laws of the land stood on exactly the same footing with the government as any of their neighbors. The Jewish "denomination," like the denominations of the Methodists, Presbyterians, and Unitarians, was free to regulate itself in its own way, and it was the duty of the government to treat this denomination as it treated all others.

Without really thinking about Jews, and certainly without trying to change Christian society in a way that would benefit Jews, American Christians had, for their own mix of theological and historical reasons, developed a social structure in which Jews could comfortably fit. And the Jews among them no longer looked so much like the agents of chaos and the destroyers of communal life; they were a religious minority in a nation of religious minorities, and the counsels of religion, humanity, and civil order favored letting them live in peace.

CAPITALISM AND THE JEWS

The other great change that occurred in the English-speaking world between the time of Shakespeare and the time of George Washington was the transformation of society from a traditional agricultural economomy with elements of capitalism embedded in it to a capitalist economy with some traditional features. By the end of the eighteenth century, capitalism was increasingly accepted in the English-speaking world as the ethical as well as the practical foundation of modern life. The shift had large consequences for attitudes toward Jews.

In the Middle Ages, Jews were seen as both a resource to be exploited (by hard-pressed rulers who could tax them at will and confiscate their wealth without a murmur from the wider community) and a force to be feared. Whether as merchants or as moneylenders they dealt in forces that the rest of society did not like, did not understand, and dimly suspected were undermining the foundations of social order.

The rise of capitalism in the English-speaking world led to new attitudes toward economic exchange and even, to some degree, banking. Elites in particular came to view old prejudices against free markets and finance as relics of the past. The Bank of England, a fiercely capitalist institution, became the epitome of establishment respectability, and the upper and middle classes entrusted their savings to interest-bearing government bonds. As finance and financial markets became integral to the life of the English-speaking political classes, and as non-Jews engaged in the financial markets became increasingly powerful and respectable, one more element of the medieval fear of the Jews began to be undermined.

A spirit of commercial rivalry might lead to personal hostility between Jewish and Anglo-Saxon bankers, but it grew increasingly difficult to believe that the Rothschilds were doing anything different from the Barings and the Morgans. Dislike of the Jews and prejudice against them began slowly to soften as the logic of the religious and social changes in non-Jewish society gradually made themselves felt.

These changes, rooted in the shifting ideas and conditions of life in the Anglo-American world, helped prepare the ground both for rising social tolerance of the Jews and for the idea of a new Jewish state in Palestine. One more factor remained. As the English-speaking world reflected on its rising power and affluence in the eighteenth and nineteenth centuries, an optimistic philosophy of history took shape. That philosophy remains powerful in American life today; it regards the American story as part of a process of global enlightenment and transformation that will ultimately bring about the kind of global peace and brotherhood traditionally associated with the afterlife and the Kingdom of God. This sense of destiny would become a building block of American identity and this new liberal and enlightened form of civil religion was, as we shall see, if anything even more philo-Semitic and pro-Zionist than the old Protestant faith. Secular and liberal America, at least for a time, would be as ardently pro-Zionist as the older America had ever been.

5

The "End of History" and the American Mind

THE POLITICAL CULTURE OF the United States was shaped by an unusual period in world history. The Napoleonic Wars ended in 1815 and it would be a hundred years before another major war would engulf Europe. During much of that century, economic and social progress appeared to be transforming the world. The Industrial Revolution, the railroad, and the telegraph meant that the generation between 1815 and 1848 saw more change, and more dramatic change, than any previous generation in history.

For many Europeans and North Americans, this was one of the most optimistic eras our suffering species has known. The human condition was improving on every side. Major great power war began to look like a thing of the past. Slavery came under greater and greater pressure, and with Russia abolishing serfdom and the United States abolishing slavery in the 1860s it appeared that one of humanity's oldest scourges was fading away. Many felt that the intoxicating vision of the Enlightenment, that human reason could unlock the secrets of nature and that this knowledge could lead humanity to a golden age of affluence and peace, was being realized on every side. It was against this backdrop that Americans would develop a set of ideas about their national destiny and the role of the Jews in the modern world that, in darker times to come, would continue to influence American attitudes toward both the challenges of the twentieth century as a whole and the emergence of a Jewish state.

The early nineteenth century augured well for the Jews.[1] The Enlightenment created a new kind of public opinion and political consensus within which Jewish citizens could reasonably hope to be integrated into West European societies as free and equal citizens. The walls of the ghettos came down, and like the Herzl family in Budapest and Vienna,[2] Jews in many countries were able to participate in the economic and political life of their societies in a new way. European culture was profoundly changed as the creative talents of this once excluded people entered the mainstream.

In the nineteenth century, individual Jews played a much smaller role in the development of American thought, business, and the arts than was the case across most of Europe. Until the 1840s, there were very few Jews in the United States.[3] The failure of the 1848 revolutions in Germany combined with the economic stresses of the Industrial Revolution led to large numbers of German-speaking Jews coming to the United States before the Civil War.[4] A second and much larger wave of Jewish immigration began after 1881 as pogroms and antisemitic legislation spread across the vast Russian Empire following the assassination of the liberal Alexander II and the succession of his reactionary son Alexander III.[5] A sprinkling of American Jews entered public life before the Civil War, but it would be another generation before significant numbers of them joined the country's business, political, cultural, and intellectual leadership.[6] The United States was a country where the Jewish presence was smaller and less influential than in most of Europe, but it was in the American republic that an ideology would develop that, in due course, would prepare the American people to welcome and support the emergence of a Jewish state in the Holy Land.

AMERICAN IDEAS

Americans don't like to think of themselves as an ideological people, but in spite of the intellectual and cultural diversity found in the United States, many Americans share a set of convictions and ideas that mark them off from much of the rest of the world. It is perhaps less of a national creed than a set of national memes; for most of us this is less a set of abstract ideas than an array of mental habits, cultural predispositions, and unspoken assumptions that inform our approach to world events.

The foundations of this approach were laid down in the colonial era, then during the first century of American independence the political culture coalesced around the beliefs and assumptions that still influence us today. During those years, Americans worked out a series of ideas about the direction of world history and America's role in the historical process that reflected both the religious ideas of an increasingly individualistic American Protestantism and the individualistic and liberal ethos of British and American political life. Combined with the radical egalitarianism of the American frontier, this cultural inheritance, contested and challenged though it is, remains the most profound influence on the way contemporary Americans think about their society and its place in the world.

Just as American culture in the colonial era developed in ways that tended to weaken the grip of antisemitism on the American mind, the ideological constructions of the nineteenth century would bend the arc of American development in ways that predisposed public opinion toward a unique approach to the place of the Jewish people in the modern world. One consequence of that approach would be to privilege pro-Zionist political activism as a way in which American Jews could simultaneously act on behalf of a specifically Jewish cause and further their integration into the heart of American life. Indeed, many twentieth-century Jewish leaders in the United States would regret the degree to which American ideology often made Zionism virtually the only question on which Jewish activists could look to American public opinion for support.

The emerging American ideology was not constructed by Jews or built with Jews particularly in mind. The Americans of the first one hundred years after the Declaration of Independence, with only a tiny Jewish minority scattered across the country, were interested above all in the experiment in democratic governance they were conducting, and in interpreting its meaning and purpose in the history of the world. For our purposes it is useful to note that four basic propositions have widely influenced the way Americans think about their country and its world role:

- Free institutions and free markets, correctly understood and securely established, will over time deliver enough happiness and prosperity to enough people to change the arc of history, not only in the United States but throughout the world.

- This coming transformation of the world is the culmination and capstone of all that has gone before; it is the fulfillment of humanity's deepest hopes and fondest desires.
- The rise of such a country at such a time of world history indicates that providence has chosen Americans to play a leading role in the annals of the human race.
- Americans have a duty not only to themselves but to the whole human race to preserve and perfect their system at home, and to assist the global spread of these principles of civil and economic freedom.

Not everyone in the United States subscribed to these ideas in the nineteenth century any more than they do today. Even among the substantial majority who do accept these ideas, there are differences over what these ideas mean or how they should be applied. Franklin Roosevelt and Calvin Coolidge had very different ideas about how much regulation free markets required, but they both believed that American capitalism offered a path to prosperity for the whole human race.

However much contentiousness exists within this ideology, and however many people in the United States present and past have dissented from it altogether, these national ideas are deeply ingrained in our popular and political culture. A political candidate unwilling or unable to believe, or at least to assert with apparently heartfelt sincerity, that freedom is a gift that God has given to America and that the sacred gift of freedom needs to be shared with the rest of the world is unlikely to prosper at the polls.

This standard optimistic American ideology rests uneasily with the nation's Christian roots. In both its Catholic and Protestant forms, Christianity has usually taken a skeptical view about the possibility that human effort would create any kind of heaven on earth. "My kingdom is not of this world," Jesus told Pontius Pilate, but it was in this world that the hopeful heirs of the Enlightenment looked to build a new paradise. Christianity in its various forms became the dominant religious faith of the American people; Americanism in its various forms became the dominant civic faith of the country. Both faiths contained elements that would make the United States a largely pro-Zionist country in the twentieth century.

DESTINY MANIFEST

Americans came to their ideas about America's role in the historical drama through a process of observation and reflection. The world of the late eighteenth century and of the nineteenth appeared to be moving in ways that made faith in an age of progress through the global spread of American values look like the most natural and obvious truth in the world.

Part of the inheritance the first Americans brought with them from Britain was a belief that God was acting through British and American history to reshape the world. From the standpoint of the Founding Fathers, three centuries of rapid change had taken the English-speaking world from an abyss of poverty, ignorance, and superstition to a greater height of philosophical insight, civil virtue, and material prosperity than the ancient world had ever known.[7] The cobwebs of the Middle Ages had been swept away. Humanity had woken from its sleep and for the first time in 1,500 years stood erect and unblinking in the clear light of day.

There had been three stages in the work of regeneration. The Renaissance saw the scholars and humanists of Europe recover the knowledge of the ancients and begin to sift out the pure philosophy and political thought of Greece and Republican Rome from the medieval detritus, as they thought, of monkish superstition and papist deception. This was more than a mix of artistic innovation and literary criticism; it was a recovery of the free spirit of antiquity. Arguments from authority were no longer enough. One had to proceed by means of open, rational debate and, as the new sciences took hold, on the basis of solid evidence.

This initial step led to the second great movement that the American Founders and their contemporaries believed had remade the world: the Reformation. For most of them, the Reformation was the religious dimension of the Renaissance: just as the Renaissance swept aside the cobwebs of medieval tradition and monasticism to regain the free spirit of rational enquiry that characterized the golden ages of Greece and Rome, the Reformation in religion swept aside the corruption and contrivance of the Middle Ages to place Christian believers once more in the clear light of faith. The Protestant Reformers believed that they were uncovering the pure and uncorrupted Christian doctrine and practice as they existed in the golden age of Jesus and the first apostles.

The third stage as the Anglo-Americans saw it was the discovery of the principles of the open society. The "ordered liberty" on which both Britain and America prided themselves involved limited government, private initiative, and the principles of political economy as expounded by Adam Smith. The common law, representative institutions, the jury system, the rights of property, and the rights of man: these were, the English-speaking world of the day believed, the keys to both liberty and wealth.[8] With the Glorious Revolution of 1688 in Great Britain and, Americans insisted, the American Revolution of 1776, the true principles of civil government had at last been found.

By the eighteenth century, the Anglo-Americans believed that it was their privilege and destiny to go further and higher than the ancients.[9] After more than a thousand years in which European scholars lived in the shadow of the glorious classical past, the scientists and mathematicians of the eighteenth century were conscious of surpassing the ancients. Aristotle knew nothing of calculus; Newton's theories were as far beyond the ken of the philosophers and mathematicians of antiquity as the microscopes and telescopes of the new age were beyond anything the ancients possessed. The discovery of the circulation of the blood, the advances in chemistry, the knowledge of the civilizations of the East, and the settlement of the New World: by 1800 it could no longer be doubted that a new era in history was at hand.[10]

The intellectual and political excitement of this moment in history spread throughout the centers of European and Atlantic enterprise and thought, but the English-speaking world had its own special perspective on the age of Enlightenment. For the Anglophones on both sides of the Atlantic, the modern age was also a story of the rise of British power in world politics as well as of rising liberty and prosperity at home. The history of the modern world began for the English-speaking world with the dizzying sixteenth-century victory of Sir Francis Drake and his cohorts over the Spanish Armada. That story went on to feature the defeat of Louis XIV by the Duke of Marlborough in the late seventeenth and early eighteenth centuries and concluded magnificently with the defeat of Napoleon by the Duke of Wellington in 1815. Three times the might of great European empires strove to extinguish, as the British saw it, the light of liberty and true religion, and three times the assaults were rejected.

For Americans, their own triumph over the mother country in the

Revolution, and the rapid growth that followed, were signs of America's unique blessing and destiny. They saw an open continent before them, felt the growing power of their nation, tallied the rapid growth of population in the census, and believed that the wind of history was in their sails. They were the spear tip of humanity's rise, the pioneers of liberty, the leaders of humanity's advance into a new world of justice, freedom, and hope.

Thoughtful people increasingly believed that a radically new day had dawned. The events of the French Revolution and the Napoleonic Wars electrified the citizens of the English-speaking world. Napoleon was the greatest conqueror since Alexander the Great, and under the hammer of his armies, ancient institutions fell apart. The pope was temporarily cast down from power and the Holy Roman Empire fell even as the arrogant monarchs of Europe's reigning dynasties fled the Revolution. The Napoleonic Code ended feudalism in half of Europe; Napoleon's armies occupied the Pyramids and stormed across the Holy Land.

The American belief that history was moving to a glorious climax was the manifestation in American culture of one of the most important defining phenomena of the modern and postmodern eras. Humanity had always speculated on the meaning of life and the end of the world, but until modern times, the end of history had been a mythological rather than a political concept. Before the Enlightenment popularized the hope that the progress of science and education could transform the human condition and usher in a new and utopian stage of world history—without poverty, oppression, bigotry, despotism, or war—human beings generally thought that only some form of divine intervention could fundamentally alter the conditions of human existence. Jews hoped for the Messiah, Christians awaited the Second Coming. Other religions had visions of the end of days, of a final judgment, of the burning away of the imperfections of the world, or some other grand climax to the pageant of human history. But these were supernatural visions of a supernatural intervention. The idea that the day-to-day activities of human beings could dramatically change the human condition was something new.

This "historicization of the eschaton," the transfer of speculation about the end of history and/or the end of the world from the realm of theology and myth to the realm of practical politics, is one of the greatest differences between human culture and self-awareness in our times and in the premodern era. In the twenty-first century it is a common-place observation that human action or inaction can and indeed prob-ably will bring about the kind of total change in the human condition that Silicon Valley savants like Ray Kurzweil refer to as the "Singular-ity." Some of the possible transformations fill us with anxiety: a nuclear holocaust, a climate change catastrophe, the invention of an artificial intelligence that turns on its creators to create a post-human world. Oth-ers fill us with hope: the elimination of poverty, the indefinite extension of the human lifespan, the conquest of war, the prospect of a just and fair world system. But whether one looks at benign or more frightening scenarios, human beings all over the world today understand that the historical and political processes we see unfolding around us can bring the human story to a triumphant conclusion or to an ignominious end. We can build a utopian world order, or we can wipe ourselves out. At a time when the president of the United States and other world leaders can launch nuclear strikes that would end human life, it is painfully clear that human beings have seized powers that our ancestors believed could only be wielded by gods.

America's history as an independent country more or less coincides with the period in which the end of the world seemed to move from the realm of myth to the realm of politics, and the history of American political thought has been profoundly affected by the emergence of the change. The consciousness of growing American power and of the like-lihood that the United States would play a major role in world history was already a heady draught; that Americans imbibed this intoxicating beverage at exactly the moment when world history began to enter what appeared to be a decisive and climactic stage was headier still. Ameri-cans believed, as many still believe, that their country had a messianic vocation to transform the world.

Americans who thought that their country was playing a critical role in the unfolding of the divine plan for the culmination of world history would naturally follow Jewish affairs with unusual interest. Traditional Protestant theology had assigned a central role to the Jewish people in the events of the last days. Now that American opinion believed that the United States also had been called to the center stage for this last act, the destinies of the two people seemed linked. Any sign of a Jewish return to their ancestral home would, in this electric atmosphere, appeal to the American imagination. The perceived connection between America's future, the fate of the world, and the future of the Jewish people already influenced American thought in the first half of the nineteenth century; over time, the influence of these ideas would grow in line with the growth of American power, the developing crisis of the Jewish people, and the crisis of a world civilization that, increasingly, seemed to have acquired more power than it knew how to control.

The defeat of Napoleonic France opened the gates of an unprecedented era of progress. As Europe enjoyed its most peaceful century in almost two thousand years, the Industrial Revolution took the scientific and economic achievements of the post-Renaissance world into overdrive. Industrial manufacturing, the railroad, and the telegraph brought on the most rapid-fire and consequential changes in the known history of the world. For the English-speaking world, and especially for Americans, who felt they were on the cutting edge politically as well as economically, it was an era of almost inconceivable and intoxicating triumph and produced an overwhelming sense of vindication. The principles of political and economic liberty at the foundation of the American way of life were transforming the world in a way nothing else ever had.

Americans looked around the world and it appeared that the countries that adopted American principles (Protestant Christianity and the "ordered liberty" of democratic constitutional government) flourished, while those without them fell further behind with every passing year. The Protestant powers of Northern Europe were growing compared to the Catholic ones. The more liberal countries (including France after 1830 and, by comparison with Austria, Prussia after 1848) were gaining power while the dictatorships and feudal monarchies were visibly growing weaker. Christian Europe as a whole was gaining in wealth and influence compared to the rest of the world, and the Ottoman Empire, the great Islamic power that had once terrified all of Europe, was sinking in a mire of backwardness and ruin.

Meanwhile, even as they celebrated the triumph of their principles worldwide (not enough Americans had read Hegel to call this the end of history yet), Americans saw that the great revolution still had some distance to go even in the United States. The nineteenth century saw the emergence of the first modern nongovernmental organizations (NGOs) with an agenda for social change. Movements against slavery, for women's rights, for free public schools, for the education of the deaf and the blind, for vegetarianism, for the end of debtors' prisons, for prohibition, for prison reform, for the end of child labor, for the improvement of conditions in mental asylums, and many other causes both wacky and wise sprang up in the western world. Sometimes these movements focused on changes that were needed at home. Increasingly, though, the nineteenth century was also an era of international campaigns for human rights in foreign lands.

One of the first of those campaigns was the movement in support of Greek independence. Nineteenth-century education was heavily classical and biblical in its inspiration; most educated people were familiar with Greek literature and philosophy. To classically educated Europeans and Americans, the state of the Greek nation in the early nineteenth century was both shocking and sad. Under the increasingly decadent rule of a backward Ottoman Empire, most Greeks were poor, uneducated, and entangled in an ugly feudal system. The classical cities of Athens and Sparta had declined into mere villages; the countryside was desperately poor and centuries of overexploitation and overgrazing had destroyed the fertility and even the beauty of the countryside so gloriously painted and praised by the classical poets.

It seemed to many progressive-minded people in the West and especially in the English-speaking world that the time had come for the redemption and restoration of the Greeks. The Ottoman Empire was visibly losing its grip and seemed to stand for everything that the English-speaking world believed was on the way out: un-Christian, oppressive, economically backward. The Greeks, on the other hand, were a great people fallen on hard times. Let them get free of the Ottoman yoke and reestablish their country under democratic laws and sound business principles and the glories of the classical age would return.

Not for the last time, the modern Greeks and the liberal West would disappoint one another. The deeply Orthodox Greeks of the nineteenth century were often less interested in democracy and the glories of pagan Athens than they were in restoring the lost glories of the Byzantine Empire. Nevertheless, the Greek War for Independence became a great cause célèbre throughout the Atlantic world, complete with fundraisers, petitions for military intervention, human rights groups organizing to protest against Turkish atrocities, and celebrity spokesmen like the great British poet Lord Byron, who died in Greece while volunteering to help the revolution. American liberals, including Samuel Gridley Howe, the future abolitionist and husband to Julia Ward Howe, also volunteered.[11]

If the Greek state that resulted from these wars never fulfilled the hopes of its western midwives, its ultimately successful war of independence appeared to point the way toward a new kind of political action in the West: public support for progressive struggles could pressure governments to act in ways that advanced the cause of liberty and progress.

Just as the causes of the Uighurs and the Palestinians engage the sympathy and attention of many people interested in human rights today, in the nineteenth century the struggles of underdog national movements were a source of constant concern for the emerging world of progress-minded NGOs and individuals. The struggles of the Poles, whose country had been partitioned among the Austrian, Prussian, and Russian empires in what was seen as the archetypal example of cynical realpolitik by despotic rulers, were followed with great sympathy and attention. The Hungarian revolt against Austrian rule after the revolutions of 1848 led to some of the biggest demonstrations in American history,[12] with prominent politicians and civic leaders promoting U.S. intervention in the resulting war.

The struggle that had the deepest sympathy in the Atlantic world was the struggle for Italian unification. The Italians, like the Greeks, were one of the famous peoples of the ancient world. Roman history and literature were even more familiar to educated Anglo-Americans than the Greek classics. The Founding Fathers relied heavily on Roman history and Roman ideas as they thought through the problem of how to build a stable republic after they got rid of George III. The post-1815 map of Italy was a cynical carve-up of the peninsula by dynasts and intriguers, and the wretched state of the Italian people—poor, superstitious, oppressed—created intense sympathy and interest in the Anglo-American world for the Italian cause. A dashing and mediagenic group of gallant protesters opposed the ugly despotisms of the restored Bourbons and Habsburgs, and were imprisoned in ghastly fortresses and jails. Artists like Verdi challenged the limits of strict censorship. The pope still ruled the Papal States, badly for the most part, and the papacy followed its geopolitical interests in siding with the antiliberal autocracies of the day.

Anger at human rights abuses across Italy, fury at the misrule and oppression of bigoted popes, sympathy for a people seen as struggling to regain the nobility and honor of their classical forebears all combined to put the Italian struggle front and center in the liberal and progressive agitation of the day. The villains were ugly and stupid, the heroes dashing, and the struggle for freedom in Italy, which only ended when the French troops defending the pope in Rome were withdrawn during the crisis of the Franco-Prussian War, kept Europe enthralled for two generations.

American sympathy for Italian liberty, combined with the hatred of many Americans for what they saw as papist tyranny in both religion and politics, was so intense and so political that the U.S. Navy came to the aid of refugees from the collapsing Roman republic when the revolution of 1848 failed.[13] British concern was equally keen; William Gladstone's 1851 published letters recounting the atrocities of the hated Ferdinand II, King of the Two Sicilies—his rule, wrote Gladstone, was "the negation of God erected into a system of government"—helped make Gladstone's career.[14]

The Classical Nations Motif and American Proto-Zionism

There was, of course, a third ancient people that survived from antiquity into modern times—even more degraded and oppressed, most westerners thought, than the Italians and Greeks. Like the Greeks and the Romans, the Jews had a glorious past. Liberal opinion in the nineteenth century saw the Jews, like the Greeks and Italians, as an example of a once great people fallen on hard times. For many liberals, the extension of that sympathy to the Jews was a logical step.

In both Britain and the United States, a combination of Christian and liberal ideas gave the concept of a restored Jewish commonwealth in the lands of the Bible great appeal. Many of the reform movements of the day, like the abolitionist movement, were made up of devoutly religious evangelicals and less devout, even secular, liberals. The Jewish cause could bring them together; biblical prophecy and liberal sentiment pointed in the same direction.

For Americans, there was another angle. In the ancient world, as Americans saw it, the Greeks, Romans, and Hebrews had been much like Americans of the nineteenth century. They were mostly agrarian people, nations of family-owned farms. They had free institutions and their societies were grounded in virtue. But corruption, urbanization, and monarchy had wreaked their ugly work; in time, all three of the ancient peoples fell from their virtue and freedom into slavery, superstition, and oppression.

But now the sun was coming out from behind the clouds. Light from the West was illuminating the blighted landscapes of the East. As the classical peoples returned to their own core principles, the same principles on which American life was based, those nations would recover their freedom and dignity. As they rose from poverty and oppression, the whole world would realize that it was American principles that brought these changes about, and the renewal of the world would gain ground as others followed these examples.

The eastern landscapes, by the way, were literally blighted. In ancient times the Greek, Roman, and Hebrew homelands had been hailed by their inhabitants as rich, prosperous, and beautiful. The records of that beauty in the Bible and in the works of the classical poets remained part of the literary heritage of the educated world, but as the railway and the steamship made travel more practical for larger numbers of people, and as the development of photography allowed stay-at-homes to learn more about the outside world, there was a shock. Much of the ancient world had become a wasteland. Rome was a disease-ridden swamp; each summer malaria rose from the marshes to thin the poor and ignorant population. Greece was mostly barren and poor. The Holy Land, once flowing with milk and honey, impressed travelers as a dreary, stony waste.[15] A redemption of the ancient peoples would lead to the redemption of the land, many believed.

As the nineteenth century progressed, and the Greek and Italian independence movements advanced, the possibility of a restored Jewish commonwealth also began to gleam on the horizon. It wasn't just Bible-thumping preachers deciphering the Delphic prophecies of the holy books who saw the possibility of a new Jewish state emerging in the lands of the Bible. Liberals with no interest in literal interpretations of scripture also saw the obstacles in the path of a Jewish restoration beginning to melt.

The visible decline of the Ottoman Empire and more generally of the Islamic world before the rising power of the West was the key. After centuries of expansion, the Ottoman wave had crested at Vienna in 1683.[16] Since then the tide had receded. Napoleon had conquered Egypt easily and it took British intervention to defeat the French there.[17] It was evident that the balance of power between the Christian and Muslim worlds had dramatically changed.

As the technological and industrial revolutions of the nineteenth century swept ahead, the gap between the Ottomans and the other European powers perceptibly widened. More and more observers came to believe that the whole tottering Ottoman structure was doomed to fall. Out of that crash, it was clear that many new states would emerge. Most of the European states would be Christian as the Balkan nations and the Armenians shook free of Ottoman rule. But in the ensuing chaos, surely there would be opportunities for Jews to return to their homeland.

For many years Great Britain rather than the United States was the political center of Restorationism in the English-speaking world. By 1838, the Restorationists were influential enough to persuade the British government to appoint a vice-consul to the then obscure and impoverished settlement of Jerusalem with a special mission to protect the Jewish inhabitants of the Holy Land against the depredations and oppressions of Ottoman rule.[18] The 7th Earl of Shaftesbury played an important role in the Christian Zionist tradition that produced Herzl's friend William Hechler; through much of the nineteenth century he lobbied to see the establishment of a Jewish colony in Palestine under the protection of the British Crown.[19]

Shaftesbury, an evangelical who was active in a host of Victorian movements for social reform, saw the establishment of a Jewish commonwealth in Palestine primarily as a religious rather than as an imperial project.[20] But he knew it would be most productive to present the project to Lord Palmerston and other British leaders in terms of power politics.[21] With the British increasingly focused on the importance of the eastern Mediterranean, Shaftesbury argued that a colony of pro-British Jews in the Holy Land would help stabilize the region and protect British interests. Others argued that a Jewish presence in Palestine would protect the approaches of the future route of the Suez Canal.[22]

The British government had been interested in strategic questions in the Middle East since the late eighteenth century, when Turkish weakness and Russian power began to cause dangerous shifts in the balance of the great powers.[23] As the Ottoman "Sick Man of Europe" weakened throughout the century, Britain would get drawn further in. The decline of the Ottoman Empire was slow, and it took longer for Palestine to fall into British hands than Shaftesbury or his contemporaries imagined it would. But the ideas Shaftesbury espoused and the strategic idea he had inspired in Palmerston would leave a legacy to future generations of British politicians, while the popular enthusiasm such an idea commanded among low church Britons would play a role during the last great upsurge of imperialism in the early twentieth century.

In the United States, Restorationism was influential from the early years of the republic. "I could find it in my heart to wish that you had been at the head of a hundred thousand Israelites," wrote John Adams to a Jewish friend, "making a conquest of that country and restoring your nation to the dominion of it."[24]

For a handful of Americans, it was not enough to bemoan the ruined state of Palestine and dream of the restoration of the Jews. A sermon preached by Rev. John McDonald in Albany in 1814 was republished in pamphlet form and caused a considerable stir in religious circles. Citing the prophecies in Isaiah 18, Reverend McDonald argued that the United States was divinely appointed to bring the restoration about. Among those sympathetic to McDonald's message of American activism in the service of the Jewish restoration, some felt called to convert the Jews to Christianity as the first step in reestablishing a Jewish state.[25] Hoping to convert local Jews, the first American missionaries arrived in Jerusalem in the early 1820s. Discouraged by their reception, the missionaries shifted base to the predominantly Christian city of Smyrna. Subsequent missionaries began the educational and medical work that would have enormous consequences for the future of the region.[26]

Other Americans felt called by God to begin the restoration immediately. During the nineteenth century there were three separate attempts of Americans to establish settlements in the Holy Land.[27] The hope was that either by attracting Jews directly into agriculture or by setting an example of successful farming, the Americans could induce the Jews to establish flourishing agricultural settlements that would form the base of a new Jewish community. All the American efforts failed miserably, leaving the picturesque and refreshing American Colony Hotel as their most lasting legacy in Jerusalem today.

What was missing from these efforts was a Jewish national movement. Many Americans, without much experience of actual Jews, believed (wrongly) that the Jews of the day were consumed with longing for an end to exile. Reading Jewish experience primarily through the lens of the scriptures, Americans assumed that the Jews of Russia, Turkey, Iraq, and other countries were as homesick for Palestine as their ancestors had been during the first exile in Babylon. Americans looked at the rising national consciousness of the other peoples of the region and believed that the awakening of a Jewish national movement was only a question of time.

Just as William Hechler saw Herzl's pamphlet as the fulfillment of his own prediction of a divinely inspired Jewish movement to return to Palestine, many non-Jewish Americans felt that the Zionist awakening vindicated their beliefs about the direction of world history. They confidently looked forward to further developments in this unlikeliest of national movements: they expected that Jews would begin to return to Zion, that they would engage in farming there and establish a democratic society. When that happened, they predicted, Jews would stand proud, free, and strong in a land of their own, just as liberation from the Ottomans would launch the Greeks on a new and glorious career, and the overthrow of the pope and the Austrians would set Italy free.

Enlightened opinion in the Anglo-American world held that the perceived inadequacies and deformations in the Jewish national character (stereotypically seen at that time to be physically timorous, untrustworthy, underhanded, and acquisitive) were neither the consequence of Jewish religion nor of Jewish blood. Rather, they were the fault of bad institutions and bad living conditions. Forced to live in cities rather than in the healthy countryside, relegated to a handful of trades and professions and excluded from responsible positions in governance, Jews were seen to have developed many of the characteristics which antisemites disliked about them. Give them their own homeland, said the Restorationists, and these negative characteristics would disappear.[28]

This was a convenient position to hold. One could simultaneously dislike individual Jews and exclude them from one's social life while distancing oneself from conventional antisemitism and supporting greater political and economic emancipation for Jews at home—and for restoration as the grand solution to the problem of the Jews. It was also a convenient position for Jews trying to make their way in the Anglo-Saxon world. If the Jews could build a state of their own, said Benjamin Disraeli, the Jewish-born British statesman who rose to become one of the country's most important prime ministers, they would be more like the English: attached to conservative values and deeply rooted in the land.

In Israel, Jews would be manly and self-confident, the sort of people English Christians would like and admire. In identifying himself, however fancifully, with a Zionist movement that did not yet exist, Disraeli was able to reduce the perceived distance between himself and the land-owning Tory squires on whom his political prospects would depend. He was the first, but by no means the last, political figure in the English-speaking world whose political standing among gentiles would benefit significantly from embracing the Zionist cause.

THE PALESTINE FIXATION

Nineteenth-century Americans were fascinated by the lands of the Bible. Improvements in travel and political concessions extorted from the Ottoman authorities made it possible for a handful of intrepid travelers to visit that hallowed soil in the 1840s and 1850s. After the Civil War, the development of steamships and the end of a period of political instability in Palestine opened the gates to much more extensive American travel.[29] On the last day of his life, Abraham Lincoln discussed with Mary Todd Lincoln his hopes to visit the Holy Land after his second term. Ulysses Grant visited Palestine on his world tour following his presidency.[30] The young Theodore Roosevelt visited Palestine as a teenager.[31] Following his visit to Palestine, Herman Melville wrote *Clarel,* an almost unreadable epic poem about the love between a literary American and the daughter of a Jerusalem rabbi. Mark Twain's literary account of his visit helped make him a household name.[32] Lew Wallace, a Civil War general who served briefly as the U.S. minister (ambassador) to the Ottoman Empire, wrote the best-selling novel *Ben-Hur.*[33] After Harriet Beecher Stowe's *Uncle Tom's Cabin,* the best-selling book in the post–Civil War United States appears to have been an illustrated book of Holy Land travels by William M. Thomson (*The Land and the Book,* 1859). Chautauqua, the upstate New York institute whose conferences and lecture series became famous throughout the country, featured a scale model of the Holy Land on its grounds.[34]

Beyond the conventional travel destinations of Western Europe and the British Isles no spot on earth held a fascination for Americans greater than Palestine. Students and theologians pored painfully over the maps in their Bibles, tracing the movements of the ancient prophets and patri-archs across the sacred landscape. Lecturers could—and did—make an excellent living taking colored transparencies of Palestinian scenes from town to town across the United States.

Yet to American eyes, the land that the Bible famously described as "flowing with milk and honey" appeared bone dry and deserted in the nineteenth century, and its handful of inhabitants, Arabs and Jews, seemed deeply wretched and prey to disease and poverty. Mark Twain, in one of his popular travel columns, wrote: "From Abraham's time till now, Palestine has been peopled only with ignorant, degraded, lazy, unwashed loafers and savages."[35] For Twain (and for many Americans), the Holy Land was wasted on its current inhabitants, whose poor stewardship had turned the land of King Solomon and King David into, as Twain quipped, "the most hopeless, dreary, heartbroken piece of territory out[side] of Arizona."[36]

With their vision of the land shaped by the biblical stories, Americans found evidence of a biblical curse on both the people and the land. Travel accounts almost invariably looked forward to a future time when the Jews would return and the land would bloom once again—as prophesied in the holy books.[37] Twain mentioned this "long-prophecied assembling of the Jews in Palestine"[38] but was skeptical about the willingness of the Jews to move to such a barren place.

In any case, many people in the Anglo-American world had a vision of the future of the Holy Land by the 1880s.[39] As the Ottoman Empire continued to weaken, it would lose the power to block Jewish settlement in Palestine. Jews around the world, Restorationists imagined, would be stirred with a longing to return to the home from which their ancestors had been ejected two thousand years previously. From dozens of countries, they would spontaneously return, embrace farming and democracy, and make the deserts bloom. A desolate land would grow fertile; a weak people would become strong; a nation despised and rejected would become proud and free.

Additionally, Americans expected that the newly restored Israel would have a special relationship with the United States.[40] The restoration of the Jews would involve their adoption of the principles of American life as they built a democratic and capitalist state. The new, Americanized Jewish commonwealth would be proof positive that the American way was the way to happiness and success, bringing wealth and power to even the weakest and most despised of the world's peoples.

Once a Zionist movement formed among Jews and its leaders began to seek support among American gentiles, they were pushing on an open door. Many non-Jewish Americans did not see the Zionist movement as an attempt to impose a special Jewish agenda on the United States; rather, they saw it as an encouraging sign that at long last the Jews were climbing on an American bandwagon. The result, they were confident, would be the restoration of the Jews and the Americanization of the world.

PROGRESS AND THE JEWS

There was another element to the association between American values and the Jewish people. The march of liberal democracy was at the center of European politics in the optimistic atmosphere of the time. The great powers were divided between the liberal West and the reactionary East. Britain was the chief of the liberal powers and Russia the champion of reaction. There were free countries like the U.S., the U.K., and France (intermittently and sort of), and there were absolute monarchies like the Austrian, Russian, and Ottoman empires. The multinational empires, and the equally absolute petty principalities in Italy and Germany, opposed the cause of human freedom and opposed religious freedom. Protestants, for example, suffered discrimination and in some cases persecution in countries including Portugal, Spain, and the Papal States. The despotic rulers of these states were horrified by the French Revolution and by the Napoleonic Wars. Led by the Russian tsar and the Austrian emperor, the conservative European states instituted tough censorship laws, imposed dramatic restrictions on academic freedom (sometimes allowing only religious orders to staff universities), and did their best to hold the line against any form of representative government.[41]

The reactionary powers were predictable. Their rulers were usually committed to the theory of absolute rule. The legitimate emperor, king, prince, or archduke had a divine right to rule, and the people should be content with whatever constitution and limited rights he conceded them. The reactionary powers closely censored the press, used secret police agents and networks of domestic spies, and viewed religions other than that of the ruler with great suspicion. Where many different ethnic and religious groups lived under one imperial lord, as in the Austrian, Russian, and Ottoman empires, the rulers and their agents fought against the poison of nationalism, sensing that it was a deadly threat to the unity of their dominions.[42]

The progressives were also recognizable from country to country. Among them were heroic nationalists, daring journalists, victims of religious persecution, and idealistic young noblemen who followed the hallowed example of the Marquis de Lafayette to enlist in the cause of freedom. British and American newspapers and books recounted their exploits and the public followed their fortunes with sympathy and interest. At a time when most people did not yet realize what deadly forces nationalisms with their conflicting historical and geographical claims would awaken in due course, all nationalists seemed to be engaged in a common struggle against the despots. To be a nationalist was to be a democrat.[43] Nationalists everywhere wanted elected assemblies, confident that with a free press and free votes, their causes would triumph.

The evil reactionary powers organized themselves into a series of alliances with an overt antidemocratic agenda. Austria and Russia, two religious autocracies, worked together to crush democratic, nationalist movements within their territory and as far afield as Spain. The Austrians also supported despotic rulers throughout Italy and worked to protect papal rule in the Papal States around Rome. Americans felt at this time a great sense that the forces of darkness and evil were strong and determined, and that while the arc of history bent toward freedom and justice in the long run, it could sometimes use a helping hand.

One of the clear distinctions between the advanced, liberal, and progressive societies of the day and the authoritarian, backward-looking, and repressive societies was that almost universally the Jews were better off under liberal governments than under reactionary ones.[44] Liberal governments gave Jews civil and political rights. They could teach in universities, study for the professions, vote, and otherwise do everything that other citizens could do. Reactionary governments almost always kept their Jews under tight control. (Austrian chancellor Prince Metternich was an honorable exception.) The more backward the government, the more repressed were the Jews. Americans began to do something then that many still do today, using the way foreign cultures and regimes treated Jews to measure their degree of enlightenment and civilization.

Many of the Americans who looked askance at foreign mobs chasing Jews through the streets had no desire to see Jews in their own neighborhoods and social clubs. Even so, they saw zealous, conspiracy-spouting, and systemic antisemitism whether as mob violence or as government action as both a moral shortcoming and as a sign of civilizational backwardness. This was particularly the case when it came to Russia. Russian pogroms and restrictions against Jews helped create a climate of contempt in the United States for Russian backwardness and autocracy that still affects U.S.-Russian relations.[45]

The association of Jewish repression with absolute monarchy was a natural and logical one. The despotisms of the Old World were in most cases run by conservative, inquisitorial regimes that, desperately casting about for ideological legitimacy for absolute monarchical rule in a world where such policies seemed increasingly outdated, relied more and more on the authority of the Catholic or, in the Russian case, Orthodox Church. The Roman Catholic Church, which had been persecuted and proscribed under the French Revolution and which had lost vast landholdings in the era of upheaval, was happy to respond, and after the fall of Napoleon the Church for the most part blessed the return of the *ancien régime*. As they circled the wagons against the forces of democracy and modernity, princes and prelates tried to re-create the ideal of the Christendom of the Middle Ages. The state was a family, the prince was the father of the people, dissent was the work of the devil, and clerics sprinkled holy water over the edifice of tyranny restored. Such a political enterprise had no more place for the Jews than medieval Christianity. A prince relying on the Church to unify and pacify his dominions wouldn't want Jewish university professors, journal editors, or even poets to disturb the purity and tranquility of the realm.

There was another similarity between the medieval order and the reactionary post-1815 European movement: the neo-medievalists had as much trouble with economics as their predecessors.[46] The Industrial Revolution turned Europe upside down in the generation after Napoleon fell. No matter how conservative governments were in religion and politics, their dominions were being revolutionized by the new industries of the day. New social classes were emerging, financial markets were gaining importance, and society was changing in ways that made it progressively harder for monarchs to go on ruling in the traditional way. Just as their medieval predecessors hated and feared the Jews, who, they thought, were in league with dark economic forces that undermined the structure of their society, so the princes and autocrats of the day saw the Jews as a source of economic as well as social and cultural danger.

For Jews (and for many other people who were frozen out by the traditional social and economic structures) the changing economic opportunities of the nineteenth century were heaven-sent. Merchants and traders could invest in new technologies and industries and build new fortunes in the new economy. New businesses and new professions sprang up that were open to talent, even as the aristocracy continued to dominate military and diplomatic life.

The increased internationalization of the investment economy seemed to favor the Jews. In London, Amsterdam, Paris, and other cities Jews were part of a rising new world of international banking. Like other capitalists in this dynamic and competitive era they looked to extend their operations through the rest of Europe. Economically and technologically backward countries to the east and south of the heartlands of the Industrial Revolution needed to borrow money, import technology, and accept increasing inroads by foreign firms. That such investment, humiliating and destabilizing under any circumstances and often representing a challenge to the economic dominance of the traditional aristocracy, sometimes appeared under Jewish auspices only exacerbated the perceived need of these governments to fight Jewish influence. It was as if the international financial system exported Jewish emancipation from the West to the East, and many who opposed the inroads of capitalist modernity into their societies would develop elaborate conspiracy theories about Jews, Freemasons, and perceived other enemies of traditional society.

But if the medieval governments and their nineteenth-century emulators tried to hold Jews down, they often also didn't have much room for Protestants and liberals. The ideas of non-Jewish thinkers like Tom Paine were as destabilizing and dangerous as anything Jews might do. Indeed, one of the reasons the reactionaries feared Jews at home is they saw them as likely conduits for subversive liberal ideas from abroad.

Those who hated liberalism and who persecuted Jews and freethinkers, who censored the press and banned pro-democracy publications generally, also hated the United States and saw its democratic experiment as a danger to their own way of life. Aristocratic contempt of the transatlantic republic ran strong after 1815. It was no secret that most of Europe's crowned heads and their servants hoped that the United States would fail.[47] A reactionary clergy and intellectual class in these countries lambasted the follies and sins of what they claimed was an anti-Christian and dangerous social experiment. When Pius IX, whose brief flirtation with liberal ideas ended abruptly after the Roman people rose against papal rule, set out to combat the evil ideology of liberal democracy, his notorious antiliberal encyclical *The Syllabus of Errors* read like a direct attack on everything Americans believed.

At a time when America as much as Great Britain was seen as a Protestant nation (as well as a mercantile, trading nation), French reactionary journalist Alphonse Toussenel would write that "behind the Protestants there is always Jewish power." As a growing group of scholars including Ian Buruma, Michele Battini, Avishai Margalit, Andrei Markovits, and Philippe Roger have pointed out, from the reactionary period in the beginning of the nineteenth century onward, a nexus of prejudice against capitalism, Anglo-American culture, and the Jews was emerging in continental Europe. It would have its full flowering in the 1920s–1940s, not only in Germany but in France as well, and its influence can still be felt today.[48]

The association of liberal ideas and belief in human freedom with sympathy for the Jews was seen inside the United States and Britain as well as on the continent of Europe. In Britain, it was the liberal nonconformists and free trade advocates who wanted to tear down the last remaining barriers to full Jewish participation in British political and intellectual life. The socially conservative Anglicans and Tories were largely against it. One George William Finch-Hatton, 10th Earl of Winchilsea and 5th Earl of Nottingham, "violently opposed almost every liberal measure which was brought forward" during his tenure in the House of Lords, opposed the parliamentary reform of 1832 and both Jewish and Catholic emancipation. He went so far in his opposition to the Catholic Emancipation Act that he fought a duel with the Duke of Wellington while the latter was prime minister.[49]

The pattern was crystal clear. The people in Britain who supported democracy and wanted Britain to become more like America wanted British Jews to have full civil rights in Britain as they did in the United States. Those who wanted to preserve the remaining barriers (Jews could not take seats in Parliament or receive Oxford or Cambridge university degrees until after the American Civil War)[50] were often the same people who loathed American democracy, who mocked American ideas and values, and who fought the extension of American-style reforms as they tried to defend the privileges of the British aristocracy at home.

America was seen as the archetypal country of the democratic and modernizing revolution. In much of Europe, the Jews were seen as a prime beneficiary of and mover in that revolution. Those who hated and feared that revolution, hated and feared both the United States and the Jews. As the nineteenth century wore on, the vision of America and Britain as Jew-ridden plutocratic powers bent on imposing a heartless social system of naked greed on the rest of the world, destroying all civilized and social values in the lust for lucre that bound the calculating Yankee to the homeless Jew, gained ground. The anti-Dreyfusards in France were largely anti-American and antiliberal as well as antisemitic.[51]

For both liberals and reactionaries, attitudes toward the Jews were a "tell." Someone who favored full and open Jewish participation in the political and cultural life of the day was likely to be a liberal who favored capitalism, wanted to dismantle the remaining power of aristocracies and monarchies, wanted governments based on popular vote, and favored religious liberty and the free press. People who held these views were almost inevitably pro-American, and saw the country, in spite of its flaws and shortcomings, as a repository of the hopes of mankind.

People who opposed the emergence of the Jews into the wider society tended to be opponents of liberalism, capitalism, and democracy, and also saw the growth of power and influence of the United States as a dangerous thing. The identification of Protestant Anglo-American capitalism with Jewish power is significantly older than the Zionist movement, and the perception that America is a pro-Jewish power antedates significant Jewish immigration to the United States.[52]

The association of liberal values, market capitalism, American democracy, and freedom for the Jews made historical sense. A liberal world order opens doors to Jewish participation that a reactionary world keeps tightly closed. Even before it became a superpower on the global stage, America was clearly a liberal power whose success would entail the reconstruction of the world on liberal lines. American intellectuals saw those around the world who agreed with it as allies in the war against ignorance and tyranny. They saw their opponents as narrow-minded reactionaries who hated the entire liberal program in politics and economics. They weren't always wrong.

6

Maelstrom

THE RESTORATION OF the Jews and the Americanization of the world did in fact take place in the twentieth century, but the fulfillment of these hopes was not as satisfying as Americans had once dreamed. The twentieth century didn't just see the restoration of a Jewish state in Palestine; it also saw the most murderous outbreak of mass antisemitism in the thousands of years of Jewish existence.

It would have been simpler if either the hopes of the optimists or the fears of the pessimists had come true. Instead, the world of the twentieth century was one in which human progress exceeded the wildest hopes of past centuries—even as the century brought forth horrors that outstripped the worst nightmares of the past. Stalin's Soviet Union, Mao's China, Hitler's Germany took cruelty and the ruthless exercise of power to depths no previous era had seen. The wars of the twentieth century saw a marriage of technical skill and moral depravity beyond anything the world had known. Yet at the same time, the spread of democratic ideals, the miracles of modern medicine, and the wonders of industrial production allowed an unprecedented number of people around the world to live in a freedom and affluence that no human beings had ever known. In the United States during the Cold War, fewer parents than ever in history had to worry that their children would die from hunger or disease, but every parent had to worry about thermonuclear war.

If the first century of American independence was the century in which the prospect of the end of the world moved from the realm of myth into the realm of politics, America's second century saw the possibility of both apocalypse and utopia move from the realm of imagination to the realm of fact. What America's third century will bring we are only beginning to discover, but we already live in a world whose dangers and opportunities both surpass anything the human species has ever seen.

This change in the human condition is so familiar a part of our lives that we must struggle to remind ourselves both how unusual our circumstances have become, and how disruptive our ancestors found the transition from the relatively orderly and optimistic world of, say, the mid-nineteenth century through all the turbulence that has happened since. But we cannot understand American history, or any world history at all, without some grasp of the uniquely complex and startling concatenation of change that brought us to our current precarious perch.

For Americans, the transition from the simple and confident worldview of the pre–Civil War era to our current state first took the form of a rapidly deepening but largely unwelcome relationship with the people and the politics of the three great empires that between them controlled Eastern Europe, much of Central Europe, and most of what we now think of as the Middle East. The Ottoman Empire, the Russian Empire, and the Austrian Empire (the Austro-Hungarian Dual Monarchy after 1867) had not figured largely in American life before 1880, but as the imperial zone moved closer to the catastrophic wars and revolutions of the twentieth century, developments there played a steadily greater role in American life. A stream of migrants changed the ethnic and cultural composition of the United States in ways that many of the Founders would have found incomprehensible, while the conflicts that broke out as the empires declined ultimately gave birth to the two world wars of the twentieth century and transformed America's relationship with the world.

If the crisis in the imperial zone was a harrowing ordeal for the United States, it was transformational and catastrophic for the Jews. More than 90 percent of the world's Jews lived in the three empires when the upheavals began, and the destruction of the old order plunged the Jewish people into its greatest crisis since the emperor Hadrian devastated Judea in 135. The Holocaust was the crowning disaster of an age of disasters. The Zionist movement emerged from and was shaped by a social implosion on an unprecedented scale.

Neither the American people, the Jews of the imperial zone, nor anybody else had any idea what lay ahead of them in 1880. Just as the young Herzl believed that the economic and technological progress of the nineteenth century heralded a brighter future for Europe's Jews, many

Americans looked at the progress of liberal democracy, the Industrial Revolution, and capitalist economic development across Europe and predicted a future of democracy and peace: the end of history seemed to be at hand.

The international situation seemed to be improving in the 1870s and 1880s. Germany's liberal future seemed assured; Wilhelm I's son and heir, the future Kaiser Frederick III, was married to a daughter of Queen Victoria and espoused liberal principles. At a time of antisemitic rioting in Prussia, the crown prince attended a synagogue service in full dress uniform and ensured that his attendance at a university lecture on the evils of antisemitism was publicized.[1] Beyond Germany, the forces of freedom faced tougher challenges. But even in the East, light was beginning to dawn. Russia's reforming Tsar Alexander II had emancipated the serfs, relaxed censorship, and by 1880 was mulling plans to call a Russian parliament.[2] The Ottoman Empire was in the midst of badly needed reforms. Beginning in 1830, the so-called Tanzimat Era saw the introduction of legal, administrative, educational, and economic reforms intended to modernize and revitalize the empire. Christians and Jews were given legal standing equal to that of Muslims, and in 1876 an Ottoman constitution was adopted that converted the sultan into a constitutional monarch who shared power with an elected assembly.

Sadly, history still had some tricks up its sleeve. In Germany the liberal Kaiser Frederick III died of cancer after a reign of only ninety-nine days. His successor was the illiberal Wilhelm II, under whose erratic leadership German history lurched onto the path that would bring it and the world to catastrophe. In the Ottoman Empire, Sultan Abdulhamid II quickly overthrew the elected assembly, abrogated the constitution, and resumed his role as absolute monarch.[3] In what became known as the Austro-Hungarian Dual Monarchy after 1867, conservative elements in both the Austrian and Hungarian parts of the empire did their best to limit the nationalist movements that threatened to tear the monarchy apart. And in Russia, Alexander III, who came to power after his liberal, reforming father was assassinated, was even more antiliberal than Wilhelm II. Within days, riots against Jews spread across Russia; the police stood by as dozens of Jews were murdered and some twenty thousand were made homeless. Under Alexander III, antisemitism became official government policy. The May Laws limited Jewish participation in the professions and imposed restrictions on where they could live.[4] "But we must never forget that the Jews crucified our Lord and shed His precious blood," wrote the tsar to officials who proposed a relaxation in anti-Jewish policies.[5] Jews were seen as a "bacillus," a germ poisoning the pure Russian nation.

The hate that Alexander III unleashed in Russia permanently changed America's relationship to the Jewish people. More than two million Jews from the Russian Empire and Eastern Europe would emigrate to the United States between 1881 and the end of mass immigration in 1924.[6] The large majority of American Jews today are descended from this wave of emigration. Before 1881 the United States was essentially a spectator nation where Jewish issues were concerned; by the time the Russian immigration was over, the United States was home to one of the world's largest Jewish communities.

The resurgence of despotic rule and its alliance with antisemitism were only a small part of the deepening crisis that embraced the vast expanse of land that stretched from Warsaw to Vladivostok, and south through the Balkans to include most of what today we think of as the Middle East. As recently as 1870 there were only four states (the Russian, Austrian, and Ottoman empires plus Greece) in what we can think of as the imperial zone. The Russian Empire stretched well into modern Poland, and in addition to Russia itself its European territories included Finland, Lithuania, Latvia, Estonia, Belarus, Ukraine, Azerbaijan, Georgia, and much of Moldova. The Austro-Hungarian monarchy, successor state to the Holy Roman Empire of old, included not only modern Austria and Hungary, but also the Czech Republic, Slovakia, much of southern and western Poland, Croatia, Slovenia, and Romania. In Europe, the Ottoman Empire still controlled much of the Balkan Peninsula. Its African territory—where its grip was steadily weakening— nominally included Libya, Tunisia, Egypt, and Sudan. In Asia, the Ottomans controlled modern Syria, Lebanon, Israel and the Palestinian territories, Jordan, Iraq, and much of the Arabian Peninsula including the sacred cities of Mecca and Medina now controlled by Saudi Arabia.

It was in this part of the world that the shape of the twentieth century would be decided, and the tragedies that convulsed the region, killing close to 100 million people in military and political violence, and driving tens of millions from their homes, still haunt our lives today.

From the standpoint of educated middle-class American opinion, nothing could have been more surprising than the eruption of violence across so much of the world. Then as now, Americans liked to believe that all good things work together: that economic development promotes political democracy, that political democracy promotes tolerance and inclusion, and that all this progress leads to a more peaceful world. That liberal American faith may yet prove to be justified in the long run— I for one hope very much that it does—but the history of the decades following the assassination of Alexander II seemed to tell another story. Historians will long debate the causes of the great catastrophe that overtook the imperial zone, but a few big trends seem to stand out.

One of the most important differences between Western Europe and the imperial zone was the contrast between the relative linguistic and cultural uniformity of the nations of Western Europe and the complex, interwoven ethnic tapestry of the empires. Countries like France, Sweden, Britain, and Germany had their linguistic and ethnic diversity and sometimes, as in the bitter relationship between Ireland and the rest of the United Kingdom, national identity was a major political factor. But over more than a thousand years the lands of the imperial zone had developed an ethnic, religious, and cultural mix that was far more intricate and intimate than anything found in the West.

The Austro-Hungarian province of Transylvania, for example, was a mix of Romanians, Hungarians, Germans, Jews, and the Roma tribes often called gypsies.[7] The city of Constantinople included Turks, Kurds, Armenians, Greeks, Jews, Albanians, and Arabs. Vienna, another sprawling capital of a multiethnic empire, was almost as diverse.

The rich mix of ethnicities and religions across the imperial zone had deep roots. For generations the imperial powers in the eastern Mediterranean had facilitated and even promoted ethnic mixing and migration. Greek, German, Italian, Arab, Turkish, Crusader, and Russian leaders had planted colonies of their fellow-believers in newly acquired territories. Arab, German, Jewish, Genoese, and Venetian merchants had built long-established mercantile settlements on key trading routes.

When Americans think about ethnic diversity, they often have the image of the melting pot in mind. As generations go by, there is more intermarriage among groups and cultural differences diminish as members of all groups integrate more fully into a new and common identity. This is not what the imperial zone was about. The empires were more of a bouillabaisse than a melting pot; the different ingredients in the pot might swap flavors, but each preserved a distinct identity. Hungarians and Croats, to take just one of dozens of examples, could live together for hundreds of years without merging into a new and larger national group.

Today, this part of the world is mostly divided into nation-states. The Slovaks live in Slovakia and the Czechs in the Czech Republic and so on. In 1881 things were not so clear-cut; a transition was under way from the standards of an earlier time when ethnic groups did not yet always think of themselves as distinct nations who wanted or needed a distinct national home. For many people in this part of the world, ethnic groups and religious communities had been and to some extent still were more like castes in India than nations in the modern sense. That is, people from many different religious and cultural backgrounds lived together—sort of. The communities were quite distinct and intermarriage was rare.

Economically and politically, different communities had different roles. The peasants who labored on the farms might speak one language and have their own religion. The nobility frequently had a different language from the peasants—like the French-speaking Normans in medieval England. Often they had a different religion as well; Muslim, Turkish-speaking nobles lorded it over Orthodox peasants who spoke various Slavic languages in the southern Balkans, and Roman Catholic German- and Magyar-speaking nobles ruled Romanian Orthodox peasants farther north. Different ethnic and religious groups specialized in different trades and occupations in the cities and towns, and the ethnic mix found in cities and towns was often quite different from the makeup of the population in the surrounding countryside.

Under a system of government dating back to Greco-Roman times and before, the mixed ethnic and religious communities of this part of the world were often at least semiautonomous when it came to the regulation of their own cultural affairs. Orthodox, Protestant, Catholic, Muslim, and Jewish religious leaders oversaw questions like marriage and inheritance law among their coreligionists. Particularly in the Ottoman lands, but also elsewhere, each religious community maintained its own system of institutions and courts. The powers of these communal institutions were very real. Being cast out of an ethno-religious community was a kind of civic death; the system promoted cohesion within the religious groups of the region—and perpetuated their separation from each other. As a result, it was not uncommon to have people living in the same street who spoke different languages at home, followed different professions, practiced different religions, ate different foods, dressed in different clothes, paid different levels of tax to different authorities, and lived under different legal systems.

Jewish life in Europe and the Middle East was shaped by the political and social organization under which the vast majority of the world's Jews had lived since Roman and pre-Islamic times. Conditions varied immensely through space and time. Often an unpopular and besieged minority, Jews were periodically exposed to mob violence or organized persecution. Commercial and political restrictions, special taxation, campaigns for forced conversion, extortion by political authorities: Jews faced them all from time to time in every part of the imperial zone. If Jews in one city, duchy, or country faced harsh conditions, life went on normally in other places, and the sloth and venality of local officials often meant that harsh orders from the top were never quite fulfilled.

Jewish communities and families were scattered across the imperial zone. In two cities—Salonika, known today as Thessaloniki in modern Greece, and Jerusalem[8]—Jews made up a majority for at least part of the nineteenth century. More usually, however, they were one among many minorities in bustling urban centers. In parts of modern Poland and the Baltic republics, as well as in Baghdad, they were a substantial minority; one fourth of the residents of Baghdad in 1900 were Jewish.[9] In other places they were a smaller but still significant minority—about 4 percent of the population in Alexandria, about the same share as in Constantinople.[10]

These Jews differed tremendously among themselves, both on matters of Jewish legal doctrine and in matters of culture and practice. Some spoke Arabic and, in cities including Alexandria and Baghdad, lived in Jewish communities that were proudly conscious of thousands of years of history. Some still spoke Ladino, a language that developed in Spain under the centuries of Islamic rule and that persisted among the descendants of Spanish Jews for centuries after their expulsion. Many spoke Yiddish, a language grown out of the encounter between Hebrew and German with Russian and Polish words thrown in; in Germany, increasing numbers of Jews scorned this language of the ghetto as they embraced German culture. Others spoke the languages of the peoples around them: Polish, Russian, Turkish, Arabic, Bulgarian, Magyar, and many more.

As the Industrial Revolution spread south and east from its heartland in Britain, the Low Countries, and northern France, it put the imposing but brittle states of the imperial zone under stress. By the 1880s, the Industrial Revolution was reshaping the world, upending political arrangements within countries and transforming the global balance of power. Countries that were good at implementing the Industrial Revolution and managing its consequences rapidly grew in wealth, power, and prestige; countries that were slow to adopt the new ways or had difficulty with the social and political changes the new system required fell behind, and often fell victim to colonial powers who were quicker to master the new instruments of power.

The approach of modernity challenged the political order of the empires in complicated ways. Before modern times, governments in the imperial zone had been absolute in theory, but weak on the ground. Local officials hundreds or thousands of miles away enjoyed a great deal of practical autonomy. Signing a decree in Vienna or Moscow did not always result in anything happening in the provinces. Officials frequently were bribed by powerful local interests to ignore inconvenient policies. This was all part of an unwritten system of checks and balances that over the generations had limited the power of absolute rulers and allowed the very disparate communities and regions of these great empires to accommodate to the imperial system in different ways.

By the late nineteenth century, this no longer worked. The economic and technological revolutions both enabled and required the development of new and much more powerful and rational states. The telegraph and the railroad gave central authorities new possibilities to monitor and control the behavior of their far-flung subordinates. New forms of bureaucratic organization, while still very far from perfect, vastly enhanced the powers of the state.

To make capitalism work and to survive in an industrial era, governments had to be able to implement and administer uniform codes of law across their territories. Complex but necessary enterprises like railroads demanded legal and administrative uniformity and predictability in ways that changed the way government worked. Foreign investors insisted on consistent administration of centrally drafted laws. In the new era of mass technological warfare unleashed by Napoleon, the military forces required to defend the empires needed to be larger than ever before, requiring higher levels of tax and disrupting traditional forms of military and social organization.

The newly powerful and ambitious governments had a much greater impact on society, so people who previously had paid little attention to politics were suddenly and passionately interested in the policies of the state. Now that the government had an army of bureaucrats and officials to enforce its decrees, people cared much more about what those decrees commanded. But they also cared about who staffed the bureaucracies and what language they used. Why, asked the sons of both peasants and merchants, should they be conscripted into an army to defend an emperor who spoke a different language, practiced a different religion, and was clearly concerned to maintain a special, hegemonic power for his ethnic and religious brethren in the empire they were being forced to defend?

Ethnicity and religion started to matter more, and the old cautious peace among the region's plethora of ethnic and religious groups started to fray. The titanic forces of the Industrial Revolution were pulling society apart: the rich and the poor, industrialists and farmers, workers and bosses all had very different ideas about the ongoing transformation of the social fabric. Yet the challenges of modern life required a strong state and a united public. What force could bind peasants and intellectuals, workers and bosses, into enough of a unit to maintain political cohesion?

The lessons of West European history seemed clear. France and Britain, to say nothing of Bismarck's new Germany, were more or less nation-states. These were the success stories of the day. The embrace of the multiethnic empires became stifling. Many of the zone's inhabitants—Czechs, Serbs, Armenians, Ukrainians, Poles—felt they could do better for themselves if they were not held back by the ramshackle, ineffective imperial powers. The development of printing and distribution technology made it increasingly possible to publish newspapers and books in the once neglected "peasant" languages. New publics took shape, bound together by ties of language, history, and, often, grievance, and a bloody era of identity politics dawned on the imperial zone.

The problem with nationalism turned out to be that national movements did not agree on the brave new world they were trying to build. Everybody could find a golden age buried somewhere in the glorious past, and everybody wanted to rebuild it. Enthusiastic historians chronicled the past greatness of their peoples, producing maps that showed the vast historic extent of their homelands. Hungarians spoke of the "lands of the Crown of St. Stephen." Arabs were beginning to reflect on the glories of the Arab caliphates before the Ottoman Turks subjugated the last independent Arab states four hundred years earlier. Czechs hearkened back to the days when Bohemia was an independent kingdom and a force to be reckoned with. Poles dreamed with increased intensity of their lost independence and thought fondly of the days when Poland stretched almost to the Black Sea. Greeks dreamed of a rebuilt Byzantine Empire with its capital at Constantinople. Everybody in the imperial zone, it sometimes seemed, had a map, maps that didn't match. Greater Serbia included parts of Greater Albania; Greater Hungary included much of Greater Romania; Greater Armenia and Greater Greece both claimed large sections of what is now Turkey.

Ethnic groups often staked claims based on history. Kosovo might not have many Serbs in it now, but it was the heartland of "historic Serbia" and many Serb nationalists could not imagine a future without the province's "return" to the motherland. Kiev might be populated with Ukrainians today, but it was the birthplace of Russian culture. In many cases, a sense of historical grievance was closely connected to these historical claims. Just as Irish nationalists regarded the seventeenth-century settlements of Protestants in the north as illegitimate because they were imposed by an occupying power, so many Balkan nationalists saw the Turks and other Muslims among them as the unwanted consequences of an Ottoman conquest that was illegitimate and immoral in the first place. Nationalism quickly became identified with the idea of reversing historical wrongs, and that was often seen as justifying or even mandating the removal of long-established populations who inhabited the "wrong" place.

The rise of ethnic nationalism was about more than maps. It was about the creation of new bonds of solidarity between educated and privileged city dwellers and the peasant masses. Before the age of nationalism, a rich Prague merchant with, say, Czech blood in his veins might feel more closely connected to German, Hungarian, and even Jewish merchants than to the Czech-speaking peasants in the fields. Such a merchant was likely to speak German at home, send his children to German-language schools, and look to the Habsburg authorities in Vienna for political leadership. Frederick the Great had spoken French better than German.

Tolstoy's Russian aristocrats sometimes bragged about their bad Russian in flawless French. "I speak Spanish to God, Italian to women, French to men, and German to my horse," Holy Roman emperor Charles V is supposed to have said. It was a mark of wealth and breeding to have a cosmopolitan outlook and to scorn the rude jargon of the lowborn peasants.

The nationalists brought a new and compelling moral vision into these fractured societies: they taught the moral duty of caring for one's own. The Czech merchant ought to care about the Czech peasant, and ought to teach literacy in the Czech language to the peasant's children. People who shared the same language and the same blood, it was said, shared a common destiny and a common set of interests; they ought to care for one another. Nationalist movements and nationalist feeling went hand in hand with the establishment of early social safety nets. Politicians like Karl Lueger, the antisemitic populist mayor of Vienna whose rise to power helped to make Herzl a Zionist, combined a hatred of out-groups and immigrants with a call for solidarity and support for the poorer members of their favored national group.

This was, in many cases, a program that combined the virtues of democracy and social justice. Where Czechs were the majority, Czechs should rule, and Czechs should be able to choose the form of government that suited them best. At the same time, the privileged and learned Czechs ought to dedicate themselves to legislative programs and social activity that would elevate the poor Czech farmers and urban workers. To most people in Europe and America who thought of themselves as progressive, this seemed preeminently rational and just. The rise of nationalism was seen as part and parcel of the spread of the Enlightenment. Europe's brotherhood of peoples would weave a wonderful tapestry of diversity and mutual respect.

Linguistic revivals were an important part of the nationalist surge. Local languages and dialects lacked modern, scientific, and technical vocabularies. When nationalist intellectuals sought to revive these languages and turn them into instruments of communication fit for modern society, they often turned to ancient liturgical languages for a more elaborate grammar and vocabulary even as they "purified" their grammar and purged the spoken dialect of foreign loan words.

In the Ottoman Empire and the newly independent Balkan countries, western missionaries, many of them American, promoted the development of the new languages and encouraged the education of a new generation of nationalist intellectuals trained to use them. Partly in order to promote the study of the Bible, missionaries worked to establish printing presses and distribution services for publications in Armenian, Arabic, Turkish, Bulgarian, and other languages. Missionaries supported the translation of scientific and other works into these languages, and mission schools instructed children in languages that began to compete with the imperial languages of the Ottoman, Russian, and Habsburg administrations. Missionary-run American colleges in Constantinople, Beirut, and Cairo became centers of nationalist thought and activism, sometimes leading to clashes between the professors and the imperial governments.[11]

Nationalism and its ally democracy attacked the foundations of the power system in the imperial zone. Tsars, emperors, and sultans could have no place in a world of independent nation-states. Increasingly, the statesmen and rulers of the eastern empires saw mortal threats in the new ideas sweeping through their realms.

They were not wrong. Nationalism often tended to become more virulent and extreme as time went by. What began as a relatively innocent and peaceful desire for group solidarity and self-determination could turn fanatical and dark. From asserting the value of one's own religious and cultural traditions to seeing the Other as an evil and dangerous rival is a short step—especially as political and economic competition between ethnic groups sharpened in the increasingly unstable political conditions of the foundering imperial zone. Religious fanaticism and murderous ethnic chauvinism steadily gained ground among different groups in the years after 1881. After World War I the fascist movements and above all the Nazi Party would show the whole world just how poisonous and deadly these ideas could become. But ethnic cleansing and genocidal episodes had already become part of life in much of the imperial zone by 1920. Some of these episodes, like the Armenian genocide of 1915–16, are well-known; others, like the Circassian genocide in the 1860s and the mass killings of Bulgarians in the 1870s, are known mostly to historical specialists and to the descendants of the peoples involved. But by the early 1920s, massacres and ethnic cleansings associated with rival nationalisms had become almost commonplace in the disintegrating imperial zone.

Worse Was to Come

The old systems of the East confronted another powerful ideological challenge besides nationalism. All of the eastern empires depended on religion to assure their legitimacy. In even the most "modern" of them, Bismarck's Germany, the Hohenzollern monarchy saw itself as the protector of European Protestantism and Bismarck led a bitter battle against the influence of the Catholic Church (the so-called *Kulturkampf*). The Austrian Habsburgs posed as the upholders of Roman Catholic orthodoxy. The Romanovs in Moscow considered themselves the heirs of the Greek Orthodox rulers of Byzantium. The Ottoman sultan considered himself the Caliph of Islam, the divinely blessed ruler of the Islamic world and the political heir to the Prophet Muhammad.

The legacy of the French Revolution—anticlerical, republican, anti-traditionalist—was poison to all the empires. That all men were equal, that all should vote, that no religion should enjoy a special relationship to the state—these ideas were as revolutionary in some parts of the imperial zone in 1875 as they had been in Paris in 1789. Yet it seemed evident to more and more intellectuals and students—the people without whom no state could function in an age of expanding bureaucracy—that these "revolutionary" ideas were simple common sense. The brightest members of the rising generation were becoming increasingly skeptical of the very foundations of the empires they were expected to serve. The rise of a new and even more radical form of Enlightenment ideology—socialism—only heightened the threat to the existing order.

There was more. In the late nineteenth century, the western powers, grown arrogant and ambitious with their new wealth, shifted the focus of their geopolitical competition to a region that had been something of a strategic backwater in recent centuries. For millennia, trade between the Far East and the western world had passed through the territory that in the nineteenth century was controlled by the Ottomans and (in Central Asia) by the Russians. The age of European exploration and expansion had been driven by the desire to find alternative sea routes for the eastern trade. That quest succeeded, as voyagers like Vasco da Gama found ways to sail directly from Western Europe to the Far East. The West's focus on the Indian Ocean dealt the Islamic world an economic blow from which in many ways it has yet to recover. At the same time, however, the West's focus on the Indian Ocean and the Cape of Good Hope as the key avenues of eastern trade meant that outside powers were less interested in controlling the eastern Mediterranean and the lands around it.

That began to change as first the prospect and then the reality of the Suez Canal shifted the location of the major trade routes between Europe and Asia. The eastern Mediterranean was now the fastest and most important route not only between Great Britain and its vast domain in India, but between the West generally and Asia. Just as the completion of the Panama Canal fixed American attention on the Caribbean and Central America, leading to decades of meddling and intervention, the completion of the Suez Canal turned everything from the Black Sea to the Red Sea into a major theater of international great power rivalry. Britain, Russia, France, Germany, and Austria all sought to build influence in the neighborhood of the Suez Canal, and from southern Russia through the Balkans, into modern Turkey, Cyprus, Egypt, and Crete, the imperial rivalries began to feed into and embitter the ethnic and religious conflicts brewing across the region. Reeling from the impact of nationalism, struggling to manage the forces of the Industrial Revolution, the empires of the East were increasingly confronted with the power of the West. The emerging nationalist movements began to turn to these outside powers for protection and support; the eastern governments were increasingly forced to seek the friendship and support of the West on their own.

As the imperial zone and the eastern Mediterranean moved to the center of world politics, this competition led the Turkish and Islamic populations of the Ottoman Empire increasingly to resent Christian meddling in imperial affairs. Torn between resentment of Christian arrogance and the need for the financial and diplomatic support of the western powers, the Ottoman government gradually lost power and legitimacy as observers on all sides grew disgusted with what they saw as its vacillation and deceit. In 1878 the British took the island of Cyprus from the enfeebled Ottoman sultan and although they would wait until World War I to declare a formal protectorate, by 1882 the British were in full control of Egypt.

At the same time, geopolitical rivalries were taking a dangerous turn further west. The establishment of the German Empire in 1871 challenged the European balance of power. The creation of a powerful German state in the heart of Europe set a process of counterbalancing in motion that ultimately led to the division of Europe into the two alliance blocs that fought World War I. As the competition intensified, events in far-off Balkan or Middle Eastern locations suddenly had the potential to set off dangerous great power crises. In the end, the assassination of an Austrian archduke by a Serb ultranationalist set off World War I, but long before Franz Ferdinand's death diplomats everywhere understood that the tiny, bitter nationalist rivalries in the East had the power to plunge all of Europe into war. Given that the nationalist movements of the region understood that genocide and ethnic cleansing faced their peoples in the event of military defeat, the intensity of the nationalist struggles continually grew. Hungarians, Romanians, Bulgarians, Macedonians, Albanians, Circassians, Armenians, Chechens, Georgians, Germans, Croats, Slovenes, Turks, Serbs, and Greeks: these peoples and their neighbors knew that they all lived on the slopes of an active volcano.

The volcano has not yet gone dormant; the wars of ethnic survival continue to break out. The Yugoslav Wars of the 1990s, and the Syrian, Kurdish, and Ukrainian conflicts of the following decades demonstrate that the old dynamics are still there.

In 1880 Americans were generally optimistic about the future of nationalism and of the imperial zone. Over the next generation they learned how wrong they had been. But there was another difference. In 1880, Americans thought of the imperial zone as a remote, exotic part of the world that had little ability to affect American lives. Again, they learned to think differently. Not only did what started as a Balkan quarrel between Serbia and Austria-Hungary metastasize into a world war that drew the United States into the cauldron, but the unrest and economic dislocations in the region launched a massive wave of migration toward the United States, a wave of migration whose effects are still being felt today, and whose political and cultural consequences became the hottest issue in American politics in the opening decades of the twentieth century.

The Great Wave and the American Crisis

This wave of migration between 1880 and 1924 altered the face of America forever. In 1880 the population of the United States had just passed

50 million; between 1880 and 1920, 23.5 million new immigrants would arrive.[12] In 1890, the percentage of foreign-born Americans reached 14.8 percent, the highest level since colonial times.[13] In individual cities and neighborhoods, this could be felt much more acutely: in Chicago in 1900, 34.6 percent of the population was foreign-born, and 77.4 percent was either foreign-born or had parents who were.[14] Other cities saw similar changes. As political scientist Michael C. LeMay writes, "By 1920 . . . the new immigrant groups comprised 44 percent of New York's total population, 41 percent of Cleveland's, 39 percent of Newark's, and 24 percent of Boston's, Buffalo's, Detroit's, Philadelphia's, and Pittsburgh's."[15] Within individual parts of cities, such as the Lower East Side of New York, the transformation was even more overwhelming.

But it wasn't just scale that made the Great Wave so momentous. Before the 1880s, new American immigrants tended to come from the same places as eighteenth- and even seventeenth-century immigrants had done. The British Isles and German-speaking Europe had provided the bulk of America's free immigrants during Benjamin Franklin's time; this was still the case as late as the Civil War. This changed dramatically with the Great Wave. Russia, Austria-Hungary, and Italy overtook Germany and Britain as sources of immigration, even as immigrants from the Ottoman, Chinese, and Japanese empires clamored for entrance. The percentage of immigrants to the U.S. who came from Southern or Eastern Europe jumped from 7.1 percent in the 1870s, to 18.3 percent in the 1880s, 52.8 percent in the 1890s, and finally peaked at 71.9 percent in the 1901–10 decade. Conversely, while as late as 1870 the percentage of newcomers from Northern and Western Europe (including the traditional feeder nations of Ireland, Germany, and Scandinavia) made up over 80 percent of immigrants, by 1901–10 only about 20 percent of immigrants came from the "traditional" sources.[16]

This translated into a massive increase in Italian, Polish, and southeast European immigrants: as historian Howard M. Sachar wrote, the number of Polish, Ruthenian, Slovak, Croatian, and Serbian immigrants "rose from 17,000 in 1880, to 114,000 in 1900, to 338,000 in 1907. The emigration of southern Italians swelled from 12,000 in 1880 to 52,000 in 1890 to 100,000 in 1900—to 200,000 in 1910!"[17]

Jews did not dominate the immigrant wave: of the 23.5 million arrivals, approximately 2.25 million or just under 9 percent were Jewish.[18]

But Jewish immigration was conspicuous. In its peak years, Jews constituted the largest single group of migrants, and the impact of the new immigrants on the small pre-existing American Jewish population was immense. As one scholar of Jewish immigration to the United States describes the situation, "The influx of several millions of additional Jews totally altered the demographic and cultural profile of American Jewry. Of the 4,200,000 Jews who lived in the United States in 1928, 3,000,000 were of East European origin. American Jewry had been re-European-ized. Also, for the first time in their history they became a rather conspicuous minority. While the general population increased 112 percent between 1881 and 1920, the Jewish population increased by 1,200 percent."[19]

The speed, size, and cultural diversity of the Great Wave were not the only challenges the migration surge posed to American society. The millions of immigrants who entered the United States after 1880 entered a country whose economic and intellectual foundations were being shaken to the core. For hundreds of years the prospect of open, inviting farmland to the west had provided a safety valve for social pressures in American cities and towns: dissatisfied urbanites could always go west and farm. At the same time, since workers always had that option, employers were forced to keep wages high enough to keep their workers reasonably happy. The Homestead Act of 1862 enshrined the right to land ownership by offering 160 acres of land to anyone who settled on it,[20] but as the frontier pushed westward, the farmland became less productive and more marginal. Recognizing this, Congress passed the Enlarged Homestead Act of 1909 that doubled the acreage allotment to 320; the Stock-Raising Homestead Act of 1916 doubled that again to a full square mile (640 acres).[21] Yet in the windswept Dakota plains, the arid deserts of the Southwest, and the barren high country of the Rocky Mountains, even farms of this size often struggled to survive. Droughts and blizzards made farming in the Dakotas and the High Plains a much more challenging proposition than in Iowa and Missouri. Even the United States, it appeared, did not have an infinite supply of good farmland.

Beyond the problems of struggling pioneers on hardscrabble marginal farms, small farmers everywhere faced mounting difficulties. In its initial phases the Industrial Revolution had been a huge boon to family farms. Railroads allowed crops to get to global markets; new tools like sod-busting plows and mechanical reapers came on line; the rise of an industrial, urban working class meant millions of customers both in the U.S. and abroad who needed to buy the surplus production of the nation's farmers. But the same improvements in transportation and agricultural technique that opened up the Middle West and the Plains states to commercial farming also operated abroad: new lands in Argentina, Canada, Ukraine, Australia, and New Zealand also opened up. Improvements in agricultural machinery and fertilizer raised yields per acre but increased the amount of investment that profitable farming required. Small farmers found it harder and harder to earn a good living from the land.

With the frontier closing, farmers going out of business, and a high birth rate, American agriculture could no longer offer opportunities for most of the rising generation. The same decades that saw the Great Wave of foreign migration to American cities also saw a large internal migration; for the first time, Americans were moving from the wide-open spaces to the cities. As late as the time of the 1880 census, 71 percent of Americans lived in rural areas. By 1920, 51 percent of the population lived in cities.[22]

These developments raised basic questions about the American future. Battening on cheap labor and the magnificent opportunities for industrialists and financiers in an era of rapid technological progress, a new class of super-rich Americans rose to prominence. For the first time in American history, many people grew concerned about the well-being of the coming generation. Populist and socialist political movements began to appear, and many people started to worry about whether America's democratic system and egalitarian culture could survive the transition from a mostly rural and agricultural society built around independent small farmers to a mostly urban and industrial society where the mass of the people were wage-earning workers.

Rural and agricultural America might be endangered and declining, but its voting power—magnified by the large representation of farm states in the Senate—could not be ignored. Many of the early progressive reforms, like legislation to regulate railroad freight rates, were intended to protect the interests of small farmers against the financial interests behind railroads and other large corporations. The farmers sensed, rightly, that the rise of the cities would lead to a shift in political power and that rural interests, already endangered by the changing economic fortunes of an industrializing society, would be further weakened and marginalized as urban power grew.

That many of the inhabitants of the great cities were immigrants from faraway countries with religious and cultural traditions that many Americans found alien and threatening only added to the tension around migration. In this environment, outbreaks of nativism and xenophobia were only too likely to emerge, and emerge they did. Though they suffered nowhere near to the same degree as Black Americans, immigrants were sporadically targets of the lynching era; the largest mass lynching in American history occurred in 1891 in New Orleans, when a mob of thousands murdered eleven Italians for their alleged role in the recent assassination of the chief of police.[23]

By 1903, the United States was facing the same rate of inflow (800,000–1.2 million per year) into a country of roughly the same population that Germany would experience from the Middle East and Africa in 2015. The reaction against immigration grew into a serious political force and in some cases became violent.

In the spring of 1913, the night watchman of National Pencil Company in Atlanta, Georgia, discovered the beaten and strangled body of thirteen-year-old Mary Phagan, and despite evidence to the contrary, the crime was quickly pinned on the manager, Leo Frank, a Jew. For two years, Frank's trial, appeal, retrial, and commutation roiled Georgia and brought forth some of the worst antisemitism and anti-immigrant sentiment (even though Frank was native-born) yet seen in the South. This culminated in August 1915 with Frank's high-profile lynching, signaling that for some Georgians at least the Jews had been added to the list of "Others" who were outside the full protection of the law in the Jim Crow South.

Two months after the Frank lynching, William J. Simmons refounded the Ku Klux Klan. The old Klan had been largely crushed by federal counterterrorism actions during Reconstruction. The new Klan reinvented itself as an anti-Catholic and antisemitic organization as well as an anti-Black one and surged to new heights of popularity as it battled what it saw as alien influences corrupting and undermining traditional American life.

Over the next decade, the Klan exploded out of its old southern heartland to become a significant force in the Middle West and beyond. The peak of its political power came in 1924, when the Klan came in force to the Democratic National Convention in New York City to block the nomination of the Catholic governor of New York, Al Smith, for the presidency.[24]

World War I and the Bolshevik Revolution brought a heightened concern about dangerous radicals entering the country as immigrants. The Palmer Raids of 1919 and 1920, authorized by the Woodrow Wilson administration, targeted suspected anarchist and Bolshevik radicals, mostly immigrant Italians and Jews. Despite determined resistance from the U.S. Department of Labor (which then had jurisdiction over deportation cases and where lawyers and bureaucrats saw Palmer as overreacting), more than five hundred immigrants were deported.

To many Americans, the country seemed to be living through a terrible nightmare. Instead of the prosperity, stability, and freedom of the United States flowing out into the world to transform it, the poverty, terror, and tyranny of the imperial zone seemed to be invading the United States. The Great Wave and the Great War had transformed the United States and its place in the world. It remained to be seen how Americans would handle the new challenges that were coming their way.

Medieval England was one of the most antisemitic countries in Europe. Edward I expelled the Jews from England in 1290, more than two hundred years before the Jews were expelled from Spain.

Eminent Boston clergyman Increase Mather taught that the Bible predicted the return of the Jews to Palestine. His book *The Mystery of Israel's Salvation Explained and Applyed* was published in London in 1669.

Roger Williams founded Providence Plantation, which became Rhode Island. He wrote, "It is the will and command of God that since the coming of his Son the Lord Jesus, a permission of the most Paganish, Jewish, Turkish or anti-Christian consciences or worships be granted to all men in all nations and countries."

The Greek and Italian national movements electrified Americans fascinated by the historical glory of the great peoples of antiquity—Greeks, Romans, and Hebrews. Italian revolutionaries like Giuseppe Garibaldi were idolized by Americans who also hoped to see a national movement among Jews.

Pliny Fisk was among the first of the thousands of American missionaries to the Middle East. Although they had little success at winning converts, the universities and hospitals they built remain important across the region today.

John D. Rockefeller, oil baron and devout Baptist, was one of the many prominent Americans who signed the 1891 Blackstone Memorial advocating for a Jewish homeland in Palestine. His wildcat rivals in the oil industry funded the conservative theological and political institutions that defined evangelical Christianity and Sun Belt Republicanism.

Lord Anthony Ashley-Cooper, 7th Earl of Shaftesbury, an evangelical, lobbied the British Crown for decades to establish a Jewish colony in Palestine.

Philipp, Prince of Eulenburg and Hertefeld, was an amateur diplomat, Richard Wagner devotee, and notorious antisemite. He supported Herzl's vision of a Jewish state in Palestine to curry favor with the Kaiser and to gain fantastic riches from the (imaginary) wealthy Jews behind Herzl.

Convinced by Herzl's advocacy, in 1898 Kaiser Wilhelm II asked Ottoman sultan Abdulhamid II to create a Jewish state in Palestine under German protection. The Kaiser hoped to rid Germany of Jewish socialists while freeing the Ottoman Empire of its debts to British and French creditors.

Americans hoped that nationalism and democracy would bring peace to the Old World, but massacres, ethnic cleansing, and genocide resulted instead as the Austro-Hungarian, Russian, and Ottoman empires fragmented. Here, Russian soldiers look at the remains of the Armenian population of Sheykhalan in 1915.

Dr. Karl Lueger,
Bürgermeister von Wien.

Unlike his father, Czar Alexander III was a brutal autocrat. During his reign, millions of Jews and Muslims fled the Russian Empire. Over two million Russian Jews came to America from 1881 to 1924.

Karl Lueger, widely admired as a founding father of European Christian Democracy, was an antisemitic populist Hitler praised in *Mein Kampf*. His election as mayor of Theodor Herzl's home city of Vienna helped convince Herzl that Europe's Jews would soon face an unsurvivable wave of antisemitic persecution.

More than 23 million people immigrated to the United States between 1880 and 1924. As the percentage of foreign-born Americans climbed precipitously, the federal government set up immigration facilities like this one at Ellis Island to process the new arrivals.

Senator Henry Cabot Lodge defined U.S. foreign policy after World War I. He opposed Woodrow Wilson's League of Nations but favored American economic engagement in Europe, supported immigration restrictions, and authored the 1922 Lodge-Fish Resolution endorsing a Jewish homeland in Palestine.

Arthur James Balfour, 1st Earl of Balfour, championed restrictions on immigration to the United Kingdom while he was prime minister. As Britain's foreign minister during World War I, he supported the Balfour Declaration in favor of "the establishment in Palestine of a national home for the Jewish people."

Benjamin Disraeli, a baptized Anglican of Jewish birth, used proto-Zionism to gain acceptance from British Tories as he rose to the summit of British and European politics.

Henry Morgenthau Sr., a former U.S. ambassador to the Ottoman Empire, was one of the 299 prominent Jews who petitioned Woodrow Wilson in 1919 to reject the Balfour Declaration. The American Jewish establishment of the day rejected Zionism on both religious and political grounds.

Pastor John Hagee, the founder and chairman of Christians United for Israel (CUFI), the largest pro-Israel organization in the United States by membership.

Alfred Dreyfus, seen here in prison on Devil's Island, was a French army officer and assimilated Jew who was falsely accused of spying for Germany. The French left rallied to Dreyfus's support and he was eventually returned to active duty.

Many European liberals hailed Dreyfus's release as proof that liberal democratic values could protect Europe's Jews. Theodor Herzl concluded the opposite: that Europeans' attachment to liberal and democratic values was too weak to hold the forces of antisemitism in check.

Adolph Ochs, the publisher of *The New York Times* from 1896 to 1935, married Effie M. Wise, the daughter of prominent Reform Judaism in America leader Rabbi Isaac M. Wise. Wise described Judaism as "eminently humane, universal, liberal, and progressive." Under its previous, non-Jewish owner, the *Times* had supported the Blackstone Memorial. Under Ochs, the *Times* vigorously opposed the Balfour Declaration.

American Jewish leaders tried and failed to win public support for a boycott of the 1936 Olympics in Nazi Germany.

Henry Morgenthau Jr., left, and Rabbi Stephen S. Wise, right, leaving a White House meeting regarding German and Austrian refugees in April 1938. Like his father, Henry Morgenthau Jr. was an opponent of Jewish statehood in Palestine. As Nazi persecution of German Jews intensified, Zionist and anti-Zionist American Jews united to find places of refuge for European Jews, but they could not overcome the Lodge consensus on immigration restrictions.

Embittered by British support for the Palestinian Jewish community, Arab Palestinians turned to Italy and Nazi Germany for support. During World War II, Grand Mufti of Jerusalem Mohammed Amin al-Husseini visited Hitler in Berlin and supported Nazi campaigns against European Jews.

7

Great Decisions

A T THE END OF World War I, Americans faced two domestic issues and several foreign policy questions related to the situation of the Jews. In domestic politics, the issues were first, whether the United States would continue to offer its Jewish residents the equality that George Washington had promised now that the American Jewish population numbered in the millions rather than in the thousands. The second, related question, was how would the United States treat Jewish immigration in an era when all immigration was becoming controversial.

In the realm of foreign policy, one question had little to do directly with the Jewish people, but would have major implications for the future both of Zionism and of Jewish diaspora communities in Europe: What strategy would the United States pursue to avoid a new world war? Would it join institutions like Woodrow Wilson's League of Nations and use its power to promote democracy, human rights, and peace abroad? In that case American diplomatic muscle might become a defense for Jewish minorities in European countries where they suffered discrimination and persecution. Would the United States withdraw entirely from international affairs, trusting in the Atlantic and Pacific oceans to protect it from the troubles of the Old World? Finally, what attitude would the American government take toward the Balfour Declaration, the promise that the British cabinet made in 1917 to allow the construction of a "national home for the Jewish people" in Palestine, a province seized from the defeated Ottoman Empire and awarded to Britain under the League of Nations mandate system?

Some of the answers America gave to these questions were necessary and wise; others have been severely criticized by later generations. But in every case, the decisions were immensely consequential for the future of the Jewish people in the United States and abroad, and we still live with their consequences.

The debate over immigration restriction was one of the longest and most bitter debates in American history. Nativism, or as people might put it today, "white nationalism," was not enough to shift the long-established national consensus in favor of open immigration. The agricultural economy of small farms might be in crisis, but American factories were booming and the onset of the automobile age only increased the demand for factory labor. For factory owners, immigrant labor was close to ideal. Penniless foreign immigrants who spoke little or no English, had only the most basic education if that, and were used to low wages and hard work at home made for malleable and willing workers. Better still, a multilingual and multicultural working class was difficult to organize into labor unions. Belonging to different ethnic communities, worshipping in different churches or synagogues, divided by language and history, the large pool of industrial labor was less capable of supporting a strong labor movement or socialist party than the working class of most European countries at the time. Urban politicians also benefited from the presence of a large population of workers who could be converted into loyal voters for political machines. Given the economic and political forces in support of unlimited migration, the nativist reaction of rural America was unable to stop the tide.

But the nativists found unexpected allies among the nation's Progressives, a movement of upper-middle-class moral and political reformers then at the peak of their influence. Progressive intellectuals worried that masses of ignorant and, in some cases at least, anarchistic and socialist immigrants would cement the power of big-city political machines, block needed urban reforms, and doom the United States as a whole to the rule of the most backward and benighted political forces. In their fights with machines like Tammany Hall, Progressives learned that the newest immigrants were often the best recruits for the machine politicians: penniless "greenhorns," as fresh-off-the-boat immigrants were called, were much less concerned about municipal governance and civil service reform than about finding powerful political patrons who could help them get jobs. Progressive intellectuals well understood that the kind of patron-client relationships that were fostering corruption in the New World had deep roots in Old World politics and social structures.

They did not just fear that organizations like the Mafia would bring Italian criminal organizations to the United States. They feared that the mass of immigrants who had grown up under quasi-feudal relations of dependency with powerful patrons and godfathers would reproduce the political structures of the Old Country in American cities.

There were some Progressives who had other, deeper fears where the new migrants were concerned. The period between 1880 and the 1920s was the apogee of the deeply perverse set of misguided ideas that, at the time, went by the name of "scientific racism." Based in part on a misunderstanding of Charles Darwin's theory of evolution, many Progressive intellectuals tried to explain the differences between human cultural groups on the basis of Darwin's theory of natural selection. Like past generations, and like many Americans to this day, they believed that Great Britain and the United States were the most advanced societies of their time. Why was this so? It must, they argued, be that the "Anglo-Saxon" race had better genes than other human races and cultures. The Progressives were for the most part not so stupid as to fail to understand that both Britain and the United States are countries with long histories of ethnic mixing. They were, however, deeply worried about the mass migration into the United States of Asians, Greeks, Jews, Italians, Arabs, and others that their racial theories labeled as inferior and in some cases as "degenerate."[1]

The immigrants from the imperial zone, worried these eminent scientists, professors, civil society activists, foundation executives, public intellectuals, and politicians, would dilute the American "race." Beyond their presumed racial unsuitability was the question of culture. A number of leading Protestant clergy and intellectuals were also concerned that too great an infusion of Catholic, Orthodox, and Jewish immigrants would undermine the Protestant culture of ordered liberty and civic virtue that, they felt, lay at the foundation of American prosperity.[2]

The Progressives were realistic enough to understand that the new immigrants were here to stay. Their responses were sometimes constructive, sometimes reprehensibly misguided, and sometimes a curious mix of both. Among these initiatives, Progressives sought to "Americanize" the new immigrants by increasing support for public education and the establishment of "settlement houses" to inculcate healthy American values in poor urban neighborhoods. Simultaneously, they looked to police the unruly behavior of the immigrants by promoting prohibition, mandating sterilization for the unfit, legalizing and encouraging birth control to keep their burgeoning numbers in check, and above all by limiting the numbers of new immigrants and testing new entrants more aggressively for infectious diseases like tuberculosis and mental defects likely, in the view of Progressive eugenicists, to create a breed of subnormal hereditary paupers.

Labor unions, including unions many of whose members were themselves foreign-born, also came to support immigration restriction. As they reflected on the reasons why the owners of factories supported immigration, union members and leaders, despite their own immigrant roots, came to feel that restricted migration would offer those already in the United States a greater opportunity to advance. Blue-collar opposition to immigration was a powerful political force for many decades in the United States.

The coalition that ultimately put an end to the long era of open immigration to the United States was a strange one. Pro-labor Democrats, frank racists who believed that America should stay "white," populist farmers, and the Progressives were divided on many issues, but gradually their different concerns about the effects of mass immigration brought them together into what was ultimately an irresistible movement.

The political progress of the restrictionist movement was gradual and slow. The first victories came in the early 1880s. Of these, by far the most sweeping was the Chinese Exclusion Act of 1882, which ended a period of Chinese immigration, primarily to the West Coast. But those who were seeking similar measures against Eastern and Southern European immigration largely were stymied. A few bans on criminals, wards of the state, the insane, and the contagiously ill were passed, and Ellis Island was opened in 1892 to create a central depot to ensure that federal officials could screen the flow of new entrants. The idea was that the facility on Ellis Island (which only examined arrivals who traveled in "steerage"; better heeled travelers could land with less trouble) would sort out the sick and the unsuitable. In practice this did not significantly reduce immigration. While 20 percent of arriving passengers were quarantined or held for further examination, in the end only 2 percent of those who landed on Ellis Island were forced to return. Measures to impose substantial financial qualifications or literacy tests that would severely restrict the Great Wave immigration were defeated again and again, and similar measures at the state level were deemed unconstitutional by the courts.[3]

The pressure to limit immigration continued to grow. In 1907, Congress established the Dillingham Commission, which met from 1907 to 1910 and delivered an influential, strongly pro-restrictionist report based largely on the supposed science of eugenics.[4] Evidence of a changing approach to Irish immigrants can be found in a commission report on conditions in the coal mining industry. Workers of Irish ancestry were classified with other "old stock" Americans.[5] This marked a sharp break from decades of Anglo prejudice against the sons and daughters of St. Patrick, but the proponents of immigration restriction knew how to count. Only by separating the old immigrants from the new could a restrictionist consensus be forged. Had the Irish Americans thrown in their lot with the Great Wave immigrants and pro-immigration capitalists, the cause of restriction might never have prevailed.

After the Dillingham Report, the restrictionist cause gained momentum. Only presidential vetoes (1913 and 1915) prevented Congress from imposing a literacy test on would-be immigrants that would have excluded many immigrants from the imperial zone. Then World War I broke out and transatlantic passenger travel came largely to a stop. But there were widespread concerns that with the return of normal trade and travel patterns after the war, the torrent would resume. In 1917, Congress passed a law requiring a literacy test over President Wilson's veto: opposition to immigration had reached super-majority status.

But the literacy test proved not to be enough of an impediment because the demographic pressure from a war-wracked Europe was huge. When it came to Jewish migration, the literacy test had little impact. Given the emphasis on literacy even in impoverished Jewish communities, only 3 percent of Jewish arrivals were rejected for illiteracy when immigration resumed under the new law in 1921.[6]

Once it was clear that millions of Europeans were desperate to escape the poverty and dislocation of post–World War I Europe by migrating to the United States, it was only a question of time before immigration would be effectively curtailed. Two acts of Congress shut the Golden Door. First, in 1921, an Emergency Quota Act limited immigration from each nation to a fixed proportion based on the percentage of the U.S. population from each nation recorded in the 1910 census. Then in 1924, came the decisive step: the Johnson-Reed Act dropped the cap to 2 percent of the number of immigrants from each nation that had been living in America in, crucially, the 1890 census—before the Great Wave had radically changed the demographics. This system, building on the findings of the Dillingham Commission, effectively split the descendants of the old waves of migrants from the latest arrivals. Countries like Ireland and Germany received much larger quotas than countries like Italy and Poland.[7]

Additionally, the act set an overall cap on immigration from the Eastern Hemisphere at 150,000 per year. This slammed the door shut with a vengeance: immigration fell more than 90 percent in the following few years, from 700,000-plus newcomers in 1924 to 29,500 in 1934.[8] Because of the nationality quota provisions, the decline in immigration from Eastern and Southern Europe was even sharper. The Great Wave was over and the American Jewish community was quick to note that many of the countries from which immigration was most drastically limited under the quota system were countries from which, before 1924, most of America's Jewish immigrants came.

The American decision to slash migration from countries with large Jewish populations was partly, though not exclusively, motivated by antisemitism. Americans passed laws to ban whole groups of people: bans on Japanese and Chinese immigrants were the most conspicuous example. No such outright ban was adopted in the case of the Jews, and some of the restrictionist legislation, like the imposition of a literacy test, left Jewish migration largely untouched. However, there is no doubt that the presence of significant numbers of Jews among the waves of European migrants helped strengthen anti-immigrant sentiment in the United States.

Fundamentally, the decision to restrict immigration after 1924 reflected a decision by Americans of the time that migration to the United States, even by desperate refugees fleeing massacres and oppression in their homelands, could not be the solution to the humanitarian problems of the world. There were too many wars and there was too much oppression. To be open to the radically unsettled world of the time, they believed, was to risk losing America's cohesion and unity at home.

The 1924 Johnson-Reed Act was the most important single act of legislation in American history from the standpoint of the State of Israel and the Zionist movement. If the United States had not voted to restrict immigration so drastically, it is probable that the country of Israel would not exist today.

Whatever the number of Jewish immigrants, the question remained as to whether they, along with long-established residents, would be considered fully "American" in a country riven by nativist discord and an activist Ku Klux Klan.

The Place of the Jews

By 1920, there were almost four million Jews in America[9] and among both Jews and non-Jews there was a real concern that the earlier American tradition of relative acceptance of Jews would fade away in the face of rising antisemitism. It was quite possible, after all, that the early American tolerance for Jews was due in part to the very small number of Jews living in the United States. As we have seen, in the 1770s, only an estimated one thousand Jews lived in the thirteen colonies; by 1800 there were still fewer than two thousand. As late as 1830, the Jewish population of the United States was still less than five thousand.[10] At such levels, many Americans had no personal contact with Jews. There were only a handful of Jewish synagogues, no large Jewish neighborhoods or any other conspicuous signs of a significant Jewish presence.

This began to change around 1840 as a wave of mostly Ashkenazi Jews from German-speaking Europe came to the United States. By the outbreak of the Civil War, the American Jewish population reached 150,000, and as the Jewish presence in the United States became more conspicuous, the signs of growing antisemitism were increasingly evident.[11]

Even in colonial times there was evidence that, despite a general lessening of anti-Jewish feeling in the United States compared to conditions in Europe, old stereotypes had crossed the ocean. Increase Mather wrote that Jews "have been wont once a year to steal Christian children and to put them to death by crucifying out of scorn and hatred against Christians."[12] A century later, John Quincy Adams's reaction on visiting a synagogue in Amsterdam was that "I never saw in my life such a set of miserable looking people, and they would steal your eyes out of your head if they possibly could."[13]

Even as Jews gained voting rights and were elected to public office in the early American republic, antisemitic beliefs, caricatures, and abusive language continued to appear. Some of the most progressive figures of the day indulged in some of the ugliest rhetoric. William Lloyd Garrison loathed a prominent Jewish activist and writer, calling Mordecai Manuel Noah "the lineal descendant of the monsters who nailed Jesus to the cross. . . . Shylock will have his 'pound of flesh' at whatever cost."[14] A widely known Mother Goose rhyme of the era contained verses that would not have startled Chaucer:

> *Jack sold his egg*
> *To a rogue of a Jew*
> *Who cheated him out*
> *Of half of his due.*

The Rothschilds and the Jewish banking power they were believed to represent cast a long shadow in some American minds. *Niles Weekly Register* was the leading periodical of its time; published in Baltimore, it enjoyed a national distribution among business and political leaders. In 1829 it carried the "news" that the Rothschilds had purchased Jerusalem from the sultan and went on in 1835 to assert that the Jewish banking dynasty "govern[s] a Christian world. Not a cabinet meets without their advice. They stretch their hand with equal ease from Petersburgh [*sic*] to Vienna, from Vienna to Paris, from Paris to London, from London to Washington. Baron Rothschild, the head of the house, is the true king of Judah, the prince of the captivity, the messiah so long looked for by this extraordinary people. He holds the keys of peace of war, of blessing or cursing." Even as it repeated conventional antisemitic fantasies about secret Jewish power and influence, the *Register* could not conceal its admiration for the financier. The baron "possesses more real force than David—more wisdom than Solomon. What do they care for the barren seacoast of Palestine? . . . We understand that an accomplished and beautiful daughter of this house, is married to an American, and intends soon to make New York her permanent residence. The beauty of Judah is not departed, nor is the strength of the house of Israel weakened."[15]

Lydia Maria Child, like Garrison an abolitionist, and also one of the first women to carve out a solid place in American literary life, shared the *Register*'s awe at Rothschild power. "The sovereigns of Europe and Asia, and the republics of America, are their debtors to an immense amount. The Rothschilds are Jews; and they have wealth enough to purchase all Palestine if they choose; a large part of Jerusalem is in fact mortgaged to them."[16] In Julia Ward Howe's 1857 play *The World's Own,* a wicked queen hires a nasty, usurious Jew to kidnap the innocent child of the play's hero.[17] Describing New York's notorious Five Points neighborhood, a popular guidebook of the era described the Jewish receivers of stolen goods operating there as possessing "the elasticity of flesh, the glittering eye sparkle . . . the hook of the nose which betrays the Israelite as the human kite, formed to be feared, hated and despised, yet to prey upon mankind."[18] The attitude of James Gordon Bennett, publisher of the sensational and widely read *New York Herald,* also deserves comment; the *Herald* treated the Damascus blood libel of 1840 as straight news, accusing Syrian Jews of using the blood of Christians in their hellish feast, and blamed "Rothschild" for supposed efforts to cover up the affair.[19]

As the wave of Jewish immigration from German-speaking Europe made the Jewish presence in the United States more conspicuous, there was an increase in anti-Jewish activity. During the Civil War, a time when both North and South were swept by religious revivals, non-Jews in each section feared (mistakenly, on the whole) that the Jews in their region sympathized with the other side. That August Belmont, a Prussian-born Jewish immigrant who represented Rothschild interests in the United States from the 1830s onward, and who had supported the presidential candidacy of James Buchanan, was the national chairman of the Democratic Party during the Civil War attracted considerable comment and criticism. In 1864, *The Chicago Tribune* accused Belmont of buying Confederate bonds on behalf of the Rothschilds; the charges were false but widely disseminated.[20]

The presence of Judah P. Benjamin in Jefferson Davis's cabinet led many northerners to conclude that Jews backed the South, while many southerners saw him as an evil genius deliberately leading the Confederacy to its destruction. General Grant's infamous General Order Number 11, which specifically banned Jewish peddlers from Union lines was, as Grant himself came to realize, both wounding and unfair. Many of the German-speaking Jews who came to the United States began as itinerant peddlers and were not always highly thought of or warmly welcomed. However, Jewish peddlers were no worse, if also perhaps no better, than the many other itinerant sellers who followed the armies, and in an age of primitive commissaries and poor supplies, soldiers relied on private merchants for many essential goods.[21] John Wilkes Booth's brother

Edwin, perhaps the best-known Shakespearean actor of the time, compared Shylock to contemporary Jewish financiers like August Belmont,
Judah P. Benjamin, and, of course, the Rothschilds.[22]

In any case, after the war, there was murmuring on both sides that
few Jews had actually served in the front lines, while some Jewish businesses (like, it must be added, many more non-Jewish businesses) had
grown conspicuously prosperous during the conflict. When Union vet-
eran J. M. Rogers published an article in the prestigious *North American Review* in 1891 saying that he had served for eighteen months in the
front lines and never saw a Jewish soldier in the battle zone, Simon Wolf
published a book of names of Jews who served in the conflict, and the
Hebrew Union Veterans Association was founded in 1896.[23]

The number of American Jews and the signs of American antisemitism both continued to grow in the years following the Civil War. In
1866 a group of leading insurance companies agreed not to insure Jewish businesses against fire out of a belief that Jewish business owners
were setting fire to their own premises to collect insurance claims.[24] In
1877 Joseph Seligman, a prominent Jewish banker, was barred by the
exclusive Grand Union Hotel in Saratoga Springs, New York.[25] This was
the beginning of a long-term effort to exclude Jews from fashionable or
desirable hotels and residential developments.

All this and more had occurred when the Jewish population of the
United States was still around 200,000. As harassed and impoverished
Russian Jews fled persecution and violence in backward Russia, the
American Jewish population began to soar, and the eastern Jews looked
much less American or even assimilable than their German predecessors. Between 1880 and 1940 antisemitism in the United States would
become a much more formidable force than at any time in our history,
and while it never reached the depths struck in many European countries, in politics, business, and education antisemitism steadily and ominously grew.

A mix of sources contributed to the new antisemitism. Non-Jewish
immigrants brought the prejudices of the Old Country with them. The
embedded antisemitism in pre–Vatican II Catholic tradition became a
stronger force in American life as Catholicism increased its presence
and built up its institutional networks. Immigrant Jews lived in the same
working-class neighborhoods as immigrant non-Jewish Poles, Russians,
and other populations from countries where antisemitic sentiment was

widespread. Jewish pupils often faced ostracism or bullying in public schools; Jewish workers might face similar problems in factories. Occasionally these tensions resulted in larger-scale violence; in 1911 in Malden, Massachusetts, a group of young Irish men attacked and beat up older Jewish men. As Jewish immigration began to change the character of New York's Lower East Side, hundreds of Jews were beaten in what observers called a "police riot" led by members of the predominantly German American and Irish American police.[26]

At the other end of the social scale, the longtime genteel distaste with which many upper-class Americans had always viewed European Jews intensified after the Civil War and through the years of the Great Wave of immigration. It intensified partly because the new Jewish immigrants looked and acted more stereotypically "Jewish" than the assimilated, acculturated, and long-established Sephardic Jews who had been integrated into urban society in cities such as New York, Philadelphia, and Charleston from the colonial period. At the same time, as the children of Jewish immigrants began to compete for places in universities and professions, and as Jewish Wall Street firms began to play a larger role in the world of finance, an element of economic competition came into play. The WASP ascendancy of well-established families exercising power through informal networks was coming under increasing pressure as American society grew more diverse. Measures to limit the number of Jewish students and faculty in colleges gradually spread throughout the educational system. College after college adopted formal or informal (but very real) limits on the number of Jews admitted. It was extremely difficult for any Jew, however accomplished, to get a faculty job at an American university. Hospitals, often run by nonprofit corporations under the control of long-established WASP families, limited the number of Jewish doctors they would hire. Prestigious WASP law firms and banks refused to hire Jews. The State Department was for much of this time a bastion of antisemitic sentiment.[27]

Finally, nativist anxiety about demographic and cultural change mixed with agrarian fears and resentment connected to the decline of the family farm to create a toxic form of antisemitism whose dim echoes can still be heard among some on the antisemitic far right. William Jennings Bryan's cross of gold speech at the 1896 Democratic convention ("You shall not press down upon the brow of labor this crown of thorns, you shall not crucify mankind upon a cross of gold") would have been heard by many listeners as what today would be called an antisemitic dog whistle: the Jews crucified Christ and their successors, the bankers, seek to crucify the innocent again today. The hatred of financial and moneyed interests that swept through hard-pressed farming states and communities in the 1890s frequently singled out Jews as the villains of the drama. A journalist reporting on the Populist convention held in St. Louis in the year of Bryan's speech wrote that "one of the striking things about the Populist convention . . . is the extraordinary hatred of the Jewish race. It is not possible to go into any hotel in the city without hearing the most bitter denunciation of the Jewish race as a class and of particular Jews who happen to have prospered in the world."[28]

Muckraking journalism, which later generations have somewhat uncritically assumed to have been entirely on the side of virtue and truth, often stoked the fires of antisemitism. George Kibbe Turner was a prominent writer much of whose work focused on the sensational subject of the white slave trade, which today would be called human trafficking. Turner claimed that Jews dominated the human trafficking business, relying on links to corrupt urban politicians in Tammany Hall to protect them. His allegations about Jews turned out to have little foundation; when questioned under oath he was forced to acknowledge that in fact he lacked any "personal knowledge" about their involvement.[29] Beyond the world of human trafficking, Jews were accused of committing a disproportionate number of crimes; in 1908 the commissioner of police in New York falsely stated that half of all the criminals in the city were Jews.[30]

To many at the time, including many Jews, it seemed as if the United States had lost any immunity to antisemitism that it may once have possessed, yet the remarkable thing about this period of rising antisemitism in the United States is that the civil and legal equality of Jewish Americans was never endangered. Jews continued to hold political office, to advance—slowly and against resistance—in the professions, to build and to operate businesses, to organize advocacy organizations, open schools and colleges, own property (except where prohibited by restrictive covenants), and otherwise participate in American life. Antisemitism was a social force in America without any significant legal power.

Even at the height of the nativist backlash leading up to immigration restriction, Jews were not the object of special legislation. Immigration from China was banned by law, and immigration from Japan was restricted by virtue of a "gentleman's agreement" with that country, but no special legal test was ever imposed to exclude Jewish immigrants while letting others pass. The most important legislative act aimed at limiting migration before the quotas were introduced in the 1920s was the literacy test adopted over Woodrow Wilson's veto; this literacy test, as we have seen, had less impact on Jewish immigration than on other groups. Similarly, the quota system acted even more drastically against some other ethnic groups than against Jews. Jews from Germany, for example, benefited from the relatively large quota that German emigrants enjoyed under the Johnson-Reed Act; non-Jewish Italians and Poles had a harder time getting permission to immigrate to the United States than Jewish citizens of Weimar Germany.

Even on the far right, Jew-hatred never quite became a defining issue. Emanuel Steiner was a Jewish merchant who operated a store in Fairfield, Illinois. In 1924 he was startled and perhaps apprehensive to see a delegation from the local branch of the Ku Klux Klan. According to one account of the proceedings, the delegation's spokesman read the following declaration:

> Mr. Steiner, we are [here] today as your friends. You have lived here 50 years. You have been an honest, upright man. The Knights of the Ku Klux Klan respect and revere you. It is the constitutional right of every man to worship God according to the dictates of his conscience. The Ku Klux Klan never has and never will try to violate that right. You have built up by your honesty, uprightness and integrity a successful business. As a citizen there is no better. You have always been behind every proposition for the community and its welfare. As American citizens the Knights of the Ku Klux Klan congratulate you for the many things that you have done for the flag and for the country.

The Klan delegation then presented the Jewish storekeeper with a bouquet of American Beauty roses.[31]

Not every Klan branch shared this attitude, of course, but it remains the case that even for the Ku Klux Klan, America's Jews were, at worst, one of a number of problems that the country faced, and among those problems, they were neither the largest nor the most dangerous. Jews might be an unpopular minority, and they might, like many other

American minorities at the time, find themselves the victims of discrimination, but their status as citizens, voters, and economic actors was never seriously threatened in the United States.

In the end, the American answer to the Jewish Question, that Jewish Americans were part of America and would be treated more or less like other Americans, stood the test of the twentieth century. They might be liked, they might be disliked, but American Jews were basically one more minority in a nation that was full of minorities. America was a tribe of tribes, and the Jewish tribe had a place under the big tent.

There are several reasons why antisemitism in the United States, despite its growth between 1860 and 1940, never became the kind of political force it sometimes became in Europe. Not all of these reflect credit on American society. One factor was clearly that the centrality of what W. E. B. Du Bois famously called "the color line" in American life and politics significantly reduced the difference between Jewish Americans and other Americans in the minds even of bigots. The Ku Klux Klansmen of Fairfield, Illinois, might have been less fond of Emanuel Steiner if they were not more concerned about Black Americans in the area.

Despite the occasional hostility between the groups, American Jews also benefited from the presence of American Catholics. Both demographically and religiously, Catholicism was a larger problem for Protestant nativism than Judaism was or could ever be. In the eighteenth century Jews enjoyed more freedom of worship and more political rights in most American colonies than Roman Catholics did. During the nineteenth century, right up through the end of mass immigration in 1924, Catholic immigration caused considerably more unease than Jews among both upper- and lower-class Protestants. With the Catholic Church officially at least committed to a set of political beliefs directly opposed to many key tenets of American democracy, right up through the 1960 election of John Fitzgerald Kennedy many Protestant intellectuals and social leaders worried that a rising tide of Catholicism might swamp the American republic.

But there was an additional factor, rooted both in the differences between the European and American approaches to Jewish emancipation, one which to some degree still today informs attitudes on both sides of the Atlantic. Max Nordau spoke at the First Congress of the

World Zionist Organization about the degree to which Jewish emancipation cut across much popular feeling in Europe:

> As the French Revolution gave to the world the metric system and the decimal system, so it also created a kind of normal spiritual system which other countries, either willingly or unwillingly, accepted as the normal measure for their state of culture. A country which claimed to be at the height of culture had to possess several institutions created or developed by the Great Revolution; as, for instance, representation of the people, freedom of the press, a jury system, separation of powers, etc. Jewish Emancipation was also one of these indispensable articles of a highly cultured state; just as a piano must not be absent from the drawing room of a respectable family even if not a single member of the family can play it. In this manner Jews were emancipated in Europe not from an inner necessity, but in imitation of a political fashion; not because the people had decided from their hearts to stretch out a brotherly hand to the Jews, but because leading spirits had accepted a certain cultured idea which required that Jewish Emancipation should figure also in the statute book.[32]

As Shlomo Avineri explains in *The Making of Modern Zionism*,[33] Nordau's point was that the gap between "the formal, external norms of Emancipation and the real, concrete feeling toward the Jews in society" was a fertile environment in which new forms of antisemitism would and did grow. The French revolutionaries, said Nordau, formulated a syllogism: "Every man is born with certain rights; the Jews are human beings; consequently the Jews are born to own the rights of man." The result, he argued, was that emancipation was decided, "not through a fraternal feeling for the Jews, but because logic demanded it. Popular sentiment rebelled, but the philosophy of the Revolution decreed that principles must be higher than sentiments. The men of 1792 emancipated us only for the sake of principle."[34]

In the United States, both the Enlightenment itself and the emancipation of the Jews rested on different foundations. The ideas of the Enlightenment came to the United States, as to Great Britain, as a result of internal historical developments. The Anglo-American Enlightenment emerged in many places among many people at many different levels of society whose reflections on their own conditions of life led them to embrace as commonsense ideas that elsewhere burst out of a revolutionary thunder cloud or were carried on the bayonets of an invading revolutionary army. The Enlightenment in America was not the triumph of principle over popular sentiments; it was the expression in abstract form of widely felt popular sentiment.

Similarly, the place of Jews in American society rested less on abstract syllogisms about universal human rights than on a historical process that created the idea of ethnic and religious denominations existing peacefully in a common society. During and after the Great Wave, as both "old stock" and "new stock" Americans struggled to make sense of the new social reality in which they found themselves, the denominational model felt—and indeed still feels—to many Americans like the obvious, even self-evident approach. There are Irish-Americans; there are Mexican-Americans; there are Jewish-Americans; there are Polish-Americans. In every case, what comes before the hyphen is important to individuals and communities, but what comes after the hyphen is the foundation of the common life of the American people, still a tribe of tribes.

In the migration debates and in the domestic debates over the place of Jews in American life, Americans came to two conclusions. Abroad, Jews would be treated like other people; mass migration to the United States was not to be a solution for the Poles, the Greeks, the Armenians, or the Russians—or the Jews. The new quota system would not inflict any special penalties on Jewish immigrants, but neither would it offer them any special benefits. At home, Jewish Americans would be treated like other Americans. At the time, private discrimination was still legal and, for that matter, was widely accepted as natural and normal. Jews were no more exempted from its operation than were Italians, the Irish, or other ethnic groups. American Jews might not always be welcome at the High Table with the WASP ascendancy, but they were not going to be driven out from under the big tent of the American nation.

The Lodge Consensus

As American society worked its way to an understanding of the place of Jewish American citizens, it also confronted questions about American policy toward Jews overseas. The answers to these questions natu-

rally and inevitably depended on national debates about the role of the
United States in the twentieth century. In the aftermath of World War I,
now that the United States had clearly emerged as the greatest power in
the world, and now that it was clear that political disturbances in the
Old World could drag the United States into major conflicts, Americans
needed to develop a vision about a new foreign policy for the postwar
world. And of course, they also needed to decide how to respond to the
British promise to allow the creation of a national home for the Jews in
Palestine. To Americans at the time, the questions were related; most
Americans saw their policy in Palestine as the natural application to the
special condition of the Jewish people of the policies that guided American diplomacy worldwide.

In recounting this history and explaining why Americans thought
as they did, it is not my intention to defend all of these decisions. With
the clarity of hindsight it is evident that many features of American
global policy after World War I were ultimately unsatisfactory. And it is
also clear that American support of Zionist aspirations did not give the
weight to the wishes of the Palestinian Arab community that by today's
standards we would seek to apply. That racism influenced the thinking
of Americans in the 1920s is clear; in many ways, the United States at
that time was a deeply racist society, with "scientific racism" enshrined
as a serious academic subject in the minds of many prominent intellectuals, businesspeople, and politicians. Nevertheless, we will not understand American or world history unless we can learn to see the world at
least to some degree as our predecessors saw it. What we will find is that
even when they were wrong, our predecessors were for the most part
serious and even earnest people who, within the limits of the ideas and
values that shaped their mental horizons, did their best to puzzle out
a course through world politics that would keep the United States safe
while, as far as possible, promoting the emergence of a world that in the
future would be more peaceful, more prosperous, and more just than the
war-torn and staggering globe that they knew.

Henry Cabot Lodge, the Massachusetts Republican who was a close
friend and associate of Theodore Roosevelt and an inveterate enemy of
Woodrow Wilson, was one of the most influential American foreign
policy actors of his times, and the framework within which the Warren Harding and Calvin Coolidge administrations developed America's
post–World War I foreign policy owes enough to him that it is reason-

able to call this framework by his name. Best known today for his opposition to Wilson's version of the League of Nations, Lodge was also a leader in the movement to restrict immigration, a leading pro-Zionist, and both a lifelong proponent of a greater American role in world politics and a bitter enemy of what he saw as Wilson's idealistic overstretch. Lodge embodied the virtues and the vices of a new era in American foreign policy. Had he not died in 1924, it's likely that Lodge, an unabashed believer in the need for the United States to attend to the balance of power in Europe, would have fought the isolationist tide in the 1930s. As it happened, however, the policy mix he supported in the early 1920s was so solidly grounded in American opinion that it outlasted the circumstances that made it so appealing. In the end, the policies Lodge and his allies advocated contributed both to the Holocaust and to the success of the Zionist movement, a profoundly ambivalent legacy that reflects the uneasy relationship between American policy and Jewish history that marks the twentieth century as a whole.

Though often tagged as "isolationist" by later historians, the Lodge consensus was more of a transitional stage between what noted historian Walter McDougall has called the Old and New Testaments in American foreign policy. "Old Testament," nineteenth-century American foreign policy presupposed a strong British Empire capable of maintaining both the European balance of power and the emerging global system of commerce and investment. After World War II, the United States embraced a much more ambitious global policy when it seemed clear that the maintenance of world order was a vital American interest and that Great Britain could no longer do its old job. In the era of the Lodge consensus, when British power was waning but Americans were not yet convinced that it was Washington's job to replace the British colossus, Americans sought to minimize the costs and risks associated with their growing power and global interests while supporting efforts by Britain and its allies to maintain the global framework that offered both security and prosperity to the United States.

The Lodge consensus, the result of a maturing American view of the world that took shape between 1880 and the 1920s, sought to advance American interests in an unstable world while minimizing America's exposure to the endless entanglements and unending wars that the seething hellscapes of the imperial zone seemed fated to produce. The horrors of World War I, the war's disorderly aftermath in Europe, and the rise of communism tempered the optimism of earlier years, but Americans did not give up so easily on their hope for a better tomorrow. History might be more complicated than they had anticipated, and the road to a peaceful, democratic world might have more speed bumps and detours than they expected, but the American establishment and the progressive, educated middle classes of the post–World War I era were still convinced that history was on the side of American ideas, and that those ideas would carry the United States and the world to a triumphant post-historical utopia. Sustained by this belief, the Americans of that time wanted to see a world transitioning to a system of independent nation-states based on the principle of self-determination and self-rule. They wanted to see these nations, once established, operating under treaties, institutions, and disarmament agreements that would progressively reduce the risk of war. And they wanted all that to happen without a lot of heavy lifting on America's part. American diplomats and bankers would go abroad, and American diplomacy would play a more conscious leadership role on issues like disarmament, but, with the exception of America's immediate neighborhood in the Caribbean, American soldiers would mostly stay home—and America wouldn't join clubs like the League of Nations whose rules might interfere with the democratic sovereign will of the people of the United States or compel the United States to intervene in foreign lands against its better judgment.

In the 1920s Americans no longer believed that the world would heal itself while the United States cheered from the sidelines. But they still hoped that with relatively limited intervention on America's part the forces of progress could transform the world in line with our values and hopes. Writing with the grim hindsight that World War II provided, later generations of American historians would scoff at the naive optimism of the 1920s, but the diplomatic record of the 1920s was not all bad. Naval armaments were significantly reduced, the postwar chaos in Europe subsided, Germany began a process of rapprochement with the West, economic recovery was well under way, and Japan appeared to have embraced liberal domestic and foreign policy ideas. In 1929 the Lodge consensus seemed to have brought about a new and peaceful world order. Few anywhere guessed that a new mass slaughter even greater than the Great War of 1914–18 was about to be unleashed on the world.

Disarmament held a special place in the Lodge consensus. In an era before missiles and long-range jets, foreign powers could only threaten the United States and the Western Hemisphere with strong navies. Reducing the naval threat to American shores by global naval arms limitation treaties was a major goal of American policy during this era, and the Washington naval accords of the early 1920s succeeded brilliantly in doing just that—while they lasted. German submarine warfare had pulled the United States into World War I; policymakers in the postwar era devoted great attention to eliminating the danger that the naval forces of a rival nation could again compel the United States to go to war.

Accepting the idea that disarmament, and especially naval disarmament, could keep the United States out of harm's way, the postwar consensus rejected the idea of permanent alliances or substantial American ground deployments beyond the hemisphere. Foreigners would have to solve their own problems in their own way. At the time, this looked like a good bet. Germany had been defeated and diminished by the war, Russia was consumed in the flames of the Bolshevik Revolution, and Japan had accepted the constraints of naval disarmament. Britain and France seemed ready and willing to defend the power balance in Europe, and Japan did not seem eager to disrupt it in Asia. A peaceful world based on a natural balance of power seemed well within reach.

Economic cooperation also played a major role in the American policy of the era. As is characteristic of Americans, the postwar policymakers believed that a restoration of stable prosperity was the key to creating a durable peace, and the 1920s saw unprecedented levels of American engagement with Europe. American statesmen developed the Dawes and Young plans that were widely credited with ending the succession of postwar economic crises that were crippling European recovery and poisoning political relations.

The promotion of the rule of law in international affairs was another lodestone of American policy at this time. Americans did not particularly want to join international organizations or be bound by international laws themselves, especially when it came to anything that might restrict or circumscribe America's freedom of action in the Western Hemisphere, but (then as now) they very much wanted other people to join such groups and observe such laws. Winston Churchill once told an admirer who had praised him for being a "pillar of the Church" that he was more of a flying buttress, supporting it from outside. This was the policy the United States adopted toward the League of Nations, the World Court, and other international institutions of the time.

After the turmoil of a generation of mass immigration, world crisis, and the most brutal war up to that point in history, Americans wanted a quiet life. The postwar consensus was, first and foremost, about stability and risk management. Immigration restriction declared that the United States was no longer willing to serve as the global asylum of last resort; national and religious quarrels in foreign lands could no longer be resolved by unlimited immigration to the United States. The refusal to join the League of Nations was seen as a way to avoid any binding obligation to use American force outside the Western Hemisphere. The other elements of the consensus, many of which would continue to play a role in American foreign policy into the twenty-first century, were aimed at preventing foreign wars by preventing the causes of war: poverty, tyranny, arms races, and aggression.

The Lodge consensus was not, most Americans would later feel, a particularly effective or inspiring approach to twentieth-century problems, but it successfully incorporated what a generation of Americans saw as the lessons of their past. Its power and longevity came from the way that even as it prioritized American economic interests abroad it accommodated deep American beliefs in democracy and progress to the difficult circumstances of the times, enabling Americans to feel that they could advance their hopes for international peace and order without entangling themselves in risky commitments overseas.

THE NATIONAL QUESTION

One of the questions that continued to pose problems for American policy after the Great War was the "national question," the quest to build ethnic nation-states on the ruins of multinational empires. The Lodge-era American vision for the world's future united three quite distinct ideas already well entrenched in American thought which had direct application to the case of the Jews: that every "people" deserved a state of its own choosing and design; that the causes of democracy and of ethnically based self-determination were ultimately aligned; and that the transition from a world order based on dynasties and multinational empires to a world of ethnically based nation-states would lead to a less-conflicted era in international politics. Intellectually, a strong case can be made against any and all of these ideas, and many in the U.S. and elsewhere have frequently attacked them. Politically, despite all the theoretical and practical problems these ideas entailed, they remained America's default ideas about foreign policy for many years. They would be modified by America's rise to superpower status, the Cold War, and the complex politics of decolonization and state building, but they remain to this day very powerful in the American public mind, and policymakers can never safely ignore the need to take these ideas into account when seeking public support for policy ideas.

World War I challenged the deeply rooted optimism that informed the way most Americans looked at historical trends, but there seemed to be a silver lining to the storm cloud. In particular, the collapse of the Russian, German, Austro-Hungarian, and Ottoman empires and the rise of newly independent ethnic nation-states gave Americans reason to be hopeful about the future. Terrible as the war had been, its root cause could be seen as a crisis of the old imperial order, and its outcome reflected the triumph of exactly those forces that Americans hoped were remaking the world.

The fallen empires had all been nondemocratic, multinational polities. All suffered from erratic, incompetent, and warlike policymaking in the years leading up to the cataclysm. In every case, the nondemocratic structure of the imperial states was responsible, Americans believed, for the vainglorious and self-defeating policy choices that led to 1914, and in every case the nondemocratic power structure was connected to the denial of self-determination of the subject peoples of the imperial crowns. Offered free votes, Poles, Czechs, Serbs, Armenians, and others would have voted themselves out of the decaying imperial entities, and there would have been, could have been, no Great War.

Democracy based on ethnic nationalism was, it appeared, an antidote to the poison of great power wars. While the problem of drawing suitable frontiers between ethnic nation-states was a messy one, and while the new order might demonstrate teething pains in the form of bitter little wars and ethnic cleansing, quarrels between small countries were unlikely to metastasize into global conflagrations without jealous imperial powers using them as proxies.

The transformation of the imperial zone of jealous and undemocratic great powers into a zone of smaller, democratic nation-states looked like a very good thing from the standpoint of American interests. Small nation-states in Europe could never threaten the United States the way a large empire like Germany could. Better still, since this American goal coincided with what the peoples of the region desired, the reordering of the region wouldn't require military efforts by the United States.

And there was an additional factor. While the American consensus to restrict immigration was deep and strong, many Americans still felt a humanitarian responsibility about developments in the rest of the world. Supporting national self-determination struck many Americans as an excellent way to balance realism about American interests with a humanitarian and even a Christian solicitude for the well-being of people abroad. Why, Americans asked, had Poles, Irish, Jews, and others flocked into the United States in such overwhelming numbers? The answer was oppression at home. An independent Ireland would have handled the potato famine better than the distracted British; without Russian, German, and Austrian occupation the Poles could have solved their problems at home without streaming into the United States. Let every people govern themselves, Americans reasoned, and the need for mass migration would largely disappear. And if foreign self-governing nations made poor political and economic choices and got into trouble, Americans could keep their doors closed with a clear conscience. We had done everything we could to give those peoples the chance to run their own affairs in their own way. Now they must live with the consequences of the choices they made.

Two generations of increasing turmoil in the old imperial zone convinced educated Americans that ethnic and religious disputes were intractable, and in many cases insoluble. They were also unavoidable. Nationalist passions were so strong, and the influence of nationalist politics on the international situation so significant, that it was idle to hope that the national question would fade away on its own. Vociferous advocates for national groups, each convinced that his or her own little nationality was the moral center of the universe, each claiming to be acting on the highest principles, and each accusing rival nations of the most unspeakable crimes were to be found at every international gathering. Their stubborn preoccupation with the grievances, real or perceived, of their suffering people was a fact that could not be changed. Their ability to whip up the passions of millions and create violent new facts on the ground could not be ignored. They were irrational, they were bloody-minded, they were obstinately unwilling to consider things from the other side's point of view, they were monstrously selfish and epically egotistical—and they could neither be ignored nor wished away.

There was also a sense of weary despair about the ability of well-intentioned outsiders to mandate decent treatment for minorities through diplomatic means. European diplomatic archives contained masses of solemn agreements to protect this or that endangered minority in the Ottoman Empire. The first dated back to the eighteenth century in a treaty between Russia and the Ottomans. The sultans had signed agreement after agreement during the nineteenth century. None of these agreements had done much good. Americans could look back at decades of diplomatic pressure on Russia for its antisemitism with nothing to show for it. They could look at the inability of the European great powers to force Romania to live up to its promises concerning better treatment of Romanian Jews. Or they could look at the stacks of diplomatic correspondence with the Ottoman government about the fate of the Armenians.

The U.S. would support the rights of minority groups through diplomatic pressure falling well short of threats of force or official boycotts, but without much confidence that such pressure would actually work. Decades of experience by the 1920s had taught American diplomats and policymakers that little short of war, and perhaps not even that, would provide effective protection for ethnic or religious minorities caught up in the miserable conflicts of the day. Given that the American people lacked the will to go to war in places like Armenia or Transylvania to protect minority rights, diplomats were left to craft elegant but empty notes, communications that both the American diplomats who crafted them and the foreign diplomats who received them knew meant little and would accomplish less.

One red line was clear: after World War I, Americans were not going to intervene in national quarrels overseas. At various points during the Paris peace negotiations in 1919, Wilson expressed an interest in American mandates over what is now Turkey and Armenia, and proposals for an American rather than a British mandate over Palestine were also discussed. But even Wilson quickly realized the impracticality of a Turkish mandate, and the possibility of a major American presence in the Middle East died along with the League treaty.[35] American officials were not going to take on the thankless tasks of administering overseas territories where mixed national groups contended for power, and American troops would not defend them. Americans believed that every national group should have a state, but also believed that every people was responsible for its own defense and well-being.

As nationalist and anticolonial movements spread around the world, Americans responded by supporting an extension of these ideas to a global rather than a European scale. Americans sympathized with Gandhi in the 1930s in the same way they sympathized with Polish nationalists in the 1830s. In both cases most Americans didn't want to do much to help them concretely, but wished them well and believed that historical forces favored their ultimate triumph. Americans would not cross the street to win their independence for them, but to the degree that the United States had some influence over their future it would be used, when not too inconvenient, to support their aspirations.

Where ethnic groups weren't "ready" for self-rule, the League of Nations promoted the establishment of mandates as a kind of halfway house for independence. Nations entrusted with mandates for foreign territories were at least theoretically expected to see themselves as trustees and guardians rather than as colonial overlords. Their rule was justified insofar as they promoted economic and social development that would lead to a smooth transition to full independence.

From the perspective of many progressive-minded Americans, the emerging postwar order of the 1920s looked significantly better than the prewar system. The dynastic despots of the imperial zone had been driven from their thrones, more of the peoples of Europe were free, disarmament treaties were limiting the dangers of war, and the mandate system promised a gradual and peaceful end to imperial rule. The age of mass immigration into the United States had been brought to an end, but Americans could feel they had kept faith with oppressed people overseas by supporting the establishment of independent ethnic nation-states in which the peoples of the world would be free to build a better future on their own.

The American approach to the problems of foreign peoples had evolved during a generation in which as the world's problems became more urgent, as America's power in the international system grew, and as Americans increasingly saw connections between conditions overseas and the security and prosperity of the United States. When Alexander II was murdered in 1881, Americans still saw themselves as disinterested spectators watching the unfolding catastrophe of the imperial zone from a safe distance. By the end of World War I, Americans had learned just how costly to their own peace and security that catastrophe could become. They were not yet ready to assume the vast responsibilities that came to them in the 1940s, but they hoped that the ideas embedded in the Lodge consensus would keep the world peaceful and America safe. In the meantime, the Jewish Question was exactly the kind of question that the Lodge consensus sought to address, and the application of the principles of the Lodge consensus to the problems of the Jewish people would guide American policymakers through the most terrible and tumultuous era in the modern history of the Jews.

8

Blackstone and Lodge

O N MARCH 5, 1891, Secretary of State James G. Blaine presented William Blackstone of Chicago to President Benjamin Harrison. It was a miserable March, and the day was wet and dismal, with temperatures hovering around freezing.[1] But as Blackstone entered the White House, he was bathed in light. The White House of the day was not the austere Federalist mansion that we know today: in 1882 Chester A. Arthur sold the old decorations at auction and asked Louis Tiffany to redecorate the interior in a more modern style. Tiffany's pièce de résistance was a fifty-foot-long screen inlaid with stained glass that stood across the entrance hall.

In 1891, the rooms were already beginning to look dated. President Harrison had electricity installed that year, though both he and his wife, Caroline, refused to touch the light switches for fear they would be electrocuted. The garish light of early modern bulbs (far brighter than those of today) did no favors for the elaborate iridescent designs with which Tiffany, anticipating illumination by soft gaslight, had painted the rooms. In eleven years, Theodore Roosevelt would strip it all out and take the mansion back to its Federalist roots.

Blackstone's business with President Harrison that day was to present a document that history remembers as the Blackstone Memorial, a petition asking President Harrison to use his influence to persuade European leaders to prevail upon the Ottoman sultan to open the province of Palestine for Jewish settlement and the creation of a Jewish national home.[2]

Blaine, Harrison, and Blackstone were an odd trio. Harrison was a model of personal rectitude presiding over a corrupt administration that made, like many late-nineteenth-century presidencies, prodigious and unbecoming use of the spoils system. A devout Presbyterian, he had served as a brigadier general of volunteers in the Civil War before entering politics. Afflicted by dermatitis on his hands, when he greeted Blackstone he was probably wearing his trademark gloves. (The president's political opponents dubbed him "Kid Gloves Harrison" in an effort to portray him as a fop and an Anglophile.) Harrison almost certainly would have been smoking; he'd tried to quit and failed, and now relied on a supply of cigars provided by a tobacconist from his hometown of Indianapolis. Harrison was portly and, at five foot six, the second shortest president ever. As of 2022, he was the last bearded occupant of the White House.[3]

James Blaine, in contrast to Harrison, was so famously corrupt that his 1884 nomination for the presidency had caused the Mugwump revolt among Republicans who, like the Never Trumpers of a later time, would rather break with their party than support an unacceptable candidate. Blaine lost a close election to Grover Cleveland, but remained, as he had been for decades, a force to be reckoned with in national politics. As secretary of state, he focused on expanding America's role in Latin America. A Congregationalist, Blaine was also anti-Catholic: today he's mostly remembered as the man who promoted the "Blaine amendments" in many state constitutions that limit the parochial school system's access to public funding.

William Blackstone, the memorial's originator, was a self-ordained evangelical minister, a well-known Christian apologist, a best-selling writer, and a close associate of Dwight Moody, the most famous evangelist of the day. Blackstone, like Moody, was a biblical literalist; in the face of the skeptical theologies emerging in response to the critical insights of German biblical scholarship, Blackstone believed that the Bible was the literal Word of God and that it was an infallible guide to past, present, and future events. Like Moody, Blackstone was a premillennialist, believing that the transition from the realm of human history to a post-historical utopia under God would only happen after terrible wars and vast upheavals had overturned the existing order and demonstrated the futility of human reforms apart from God.[4] Blackstone's popularity, and Moody's, reflected the growing power of dystopian fears about the future in the world of American religion.

In the history of American religion, Dwight L. Moody's career marks the beginning of modern evangelicalism. Moody's movement rejected both the increasingly liberal theology of the American Protestant establishment and the reforming optimism of what would soon become the Social Gospel movement. Although a supporter of charitable organizations and movements for individual reform like the temperance movement, Moody held out little hope for political action aimed at producing deep social change. He famously summed up this view by saying, "I look upon this world as a wrecked vessel. God has given me a lifeboat and said, 'Moody, save all you can.'"[5] Moody's tireless preaching and impressive demeanor sparked major religious revivals in both Britain and the United States, with special appeal among those who felt deracinated and dispossessed thanks to the economic and social upheavals of the time, and the views he popularized remain influential in many evangelical and Pentecostal circles to this day.

But wrecked vessel though the world might be, there was one political cause that, to the eyes of Moody and associates like William Blackstone, had promise. While more liberal and optimistic Christians hoped that Jews returning to Palestine would succeed by adopting American democratic and economic principles and therefore demonstrate to the world that the way to usher in a triumphant utopia was to follow the American example, Moody and Blackstone looked for very different but equally significant consequences to flow from the still hypothetical return of the Jews to Palestine. The contemporary fulfillment of Bible prophecy would, they believed, dramatically confirm the power of the Bible. If texts that were more than two thousand years old could predict contemporary events better than conventional experts and practical politicians, this would clearly demonstrate the divine inspiration of the holy books. At the same time, the return of the Jews would confirm the theological views that Moody and Blackstone advanced. The Jews would return to Palestine in a darkening world, against a background of crisis and conflict. Their return was not a sign that God was blessing the work of earnest Protestant social reform by ushering in a new era of peace; it was a sign that God's long-suspended judgment was about to fall on a sinful world. The maelstrom in the imperial zone, the rising and falling of great nations, the wars and the tumult of wars, like the social conflict and decay at home, were the signs of a great purpose moving toward fulfillment. It was both a terrifying and a reassuring picture; the ship was sinking, but the lifeboat was sound.

There's no evidence that President Harrison had much interest in

Blackstone's theology, but he certainly intended to give the minister a friendly reception. Blackstone's associations with Moody were well-known, and like the later evangelist Billy Graham, Moody was a power in the land. In 1865, Moody had entered Richmond with Grant's victorious army. In 1876, Grant along with members of his cabinet attended one of Moody's services. Before his death in 1899 at the age of sixty-two, Moody is said to have preached to 100 million people in the United States and abroad; before the mass communications technologies of the twentieth century, no single person in human history had reached an audience of this scale.[6]

But it was not only the power of Blackstone's spiritual associations that won him an audience with President Harrison. Among the four hundred signatures on Blackstone's petition were the names of J. P. Morgan, John D. Rockefeller, Cyrus McCormick, the editors of most of the leading American newspapers, leading clergymen from the East Coast and the Middle West, the chief justice of the Supreme Court, and the speaker of the House of Representatives. It had also been signed by prominent media corporations, including *The New York Times*.[7] Not many such petitions cross a president's desk on any given day, and the bearer of such a document will inevitably receive a courteous hearing even when, as in this case, the petition asks for something outlandish.

We do not know very much about the motives of most of the people who signed the memorial, but it seems unlikely that Episcopalian men of the world like J. P. Morgan or hard-nosed Baptist businessmen like John D. Rockefeller believed that they were hastening the Second Coming and the end of the world by endorsing Blackstone's idea. For many of the signers, the petition merely expressed the long-held belief among both religious and secular people of the nineteenth century that the Jews, like the Greeks and the Italians, could regain some of their ancient glory and greatness if freed from foreign rule and oppression. Others were moved by the appalling spectacle of deliberate, state-sponsored cruelty in Russia and elsewhere against innocent and helpless people. Some may have been moved to some degree by the spiritual forces that drove Blackstone. Some may have wished to support Blackstone out of regard for Moody and his movement—not because they shared Moody's theology but because many upper-class Americans thought that the spread of revivalist ideas through the urban working class (and Moody's ministry was chiefly aimed at this group) would help keep socialism at bay. Some no doubt were chiefly drawn to the potential of the Blackstone proposal to divert Jewish immigration from the United States to a faraway land. And it is possible that, even at this early date, there were a few political calculators who understood that to advocate both for the creation of a Jewish homeland and for immigration restriction hit a sweet spot in American politics.

Most American Jews of the day had a different view. Blackstone presented his petition as though it were the brainchild of a joint Jewish-Christian meeting, but he was only able to persuade a handful of Jews to sign it (and only after he had granted them permission to print a reservation about some of the language).[8] In fact, there was significant Jewish pushback against the memorial, which can be summed up in the phrasing of a leading Reform rabbi, Emil G. Hirsch, whom Blackstone had approached early in his project: "We, the modern Jews, say that we do not wish to be restored to Palestine. . . . The country wherein we live is our Palestine."[9]

Rabbi Hirsch's observation was more than a casual aside. Reform Judaism was originally built around a modernization of Jewish faith that explicitly rejected the goal of a return from exile. For Reform Jews, steeped in the atmosphere of the European Enlightenment and its approach to Jewish emancipation, any talk of a Jewish state was an attack on the ideas that allowed Jews to participate in the life of the countries in which they lived. They not only dismissed the idea of a return to Palestine as a naive fantasy with no hope of realization; they deplored it as an assault on the values that, as they saw things, offered the only possible security for a Jewish minority in a non-Jewish state.

Despite the religious foundations of his interest in Palestine, Blackstone drafted his memorial in largely secular terms. Given the misery of the Jews in Russia, and the mass migration from Russia that was already ten years old, something needed to be done. "But where," the memorial asks, "shall 2,000,000 of such poor people go? Europe is crowded and has no room for more peasant population. Shall they come to America? This will be a tremendous expense, and require years."[10]

The answer seemed obvious. The European powers were already in the habit of carving slices off the Ottoman Empire to create homelands for its various minorities. Why not reserve a slice for the Jews? Or, in the language of the memorial, "Why shall not the powers which under the treaty of Berlin, in 1878, gave Bulgaria to the Bulgarians and Servia to the Servians now give Palestine back to the Jews? These provinces, as well as Roumania, Montenegro and Greece, were wrested from the Turks and given to their natural owners. Does not Palestine as rightfully belong to the Jews?"[11]

The Blackstone Memorial had no immediate impact on history. The president made some friendly remarks of appreciation and referred the document to the State Department, where horrified officials sat on it until all memory of the document, and even the original document itself, had vanished.[12]

Yet the ideas behind the memorial, both religious and political, lived on. For the next sixty years, whenever the Jewish Question emerged into world politics, non-Jewish Americans responded with the logic and program of the memorial. The United States should support the creation of a Jewish home in the Middle East; it should use diplomatic rather than military or even economic means to achieve this goal; and it should not do this work on its own but in concert with other powers.

The Blackstone Memorial was the first draft of America's proposed answer to the international Jewish Question. Blackstone would live to present a new version of his petition to Woodrow Wilson in 1916, see his principles enshrined in American law in 1922, and, by the time he died in the 1930s, see the establishment of a flourishing Jewish community in Palestine.[13] Had he lived longer, he would have seen President Harry Truman stubbornly stick to the Blackstone principles in the face of bitter criticism until he was able to recognize the existence of a Jewish state that, with American diplomatic (but not economic or military) assistance, had been voted into being by the United Nations.

The Balfour Declaration and the Lodge Consensus

It took a war to put the Blackstone Memorial back on the agenda. In 1914, the Ottoman Empire threw in its lot with the Central Powers against the alliance of Russia, Great Britain, and France, and plans for its partition and destruction took root in the allied capitals. The Russians, whose emperors considered themselves the heirs of the Byzantine Empire, wanted Constantinople and control of the straits that would give them unrestricted access from the Black Sea to the Mediterranean. France had long ties to the Levant; Paris wanted control over modern Syria and Lebanon. The British, already focused on the potential oil riches of the

Middle East, wanted to create friendly Arab states under puppet rulers and to bolster the security of the Suez Canal.

At the beginning of the war, Palestine was of little concern to anybody except those who lived there and to the struggling Jewish Zionist movement that, so far, had only managed to settle a few tens of thousands of Jewish settlers in a land they did not seem very close to conquering. But the British, newly attuned on the Middle East after Winston Churchill determined that oil should be the future fuel of the British navy, envisioned a Jewish settlement in Palestine that would cover one flank of the Suez Canal, and serve as a source of supply for British forces in the region.

Canal security and oilfields, however, were not the only motives behind the Balfour Declaration. A major aim of British policy up through 1917 in World War I was to draw the United States into the conflict. With American help, victory over Germany seemed likely; without it, the war might never be won. But drawing America into the war meant overcoming strong anti-British, anti-Allied sentiment inside the United States. Many Americans were descended from German-speaking immigrants who still sympathized with the worldview of their ancestral home. Many others had Irish backgrounds and were fervently anti-British at a time when the movement for Irish independence was moving to a climax. British diplomats searched frantically for groups they could persuade to support an American declaration of war.

American Jews were also largely unsympathetic to the Allied cause when war broke out. Leading Jews were mostly of German origin, and like other immigrants from Germany, often retained an ancestral sympathy for the fatherland. But if some Jews were pro-Germany, almost all American Jews were fervently anti-Russia. Hatred of the tsar, the most brutal and vindictive enemy of the Jewish people in the world at the time, was nearly universal among American Jews. If the Russian tsar was numbered among the Allies, American Jews did not want to help him survive.

The British government was an early believer in the Planet Vulcan thesis: like so many through history they believed that Jews were more powerful than was the case, more united than was the case, and more pro-Zionist than was the case. Drastically overestimating the power of the American Jewish community, and completely misreading its attitude toward Zionism, the British government hoped that the promise of

Palestine as a national home would swing the allegedly vast and united power of the American Jewish community behind the Allied cause.

These geopolitical and political concerns combined with a streak of pro-Zionist feeling that was relatively widespread in a Britain still impacted by the evangelical religious tone of the Victorian era. Britain's own immigration restriction law had been passed in 1905, limiting ships with more than twenty steerage emigrants from putting in at British harbors;[14] the act effectively put an end to large-scale Jewish immigration into Britain and was supported by, among others, a rising politician named Arthur Balfour.[15]

Around the same time as he pushed the immigration restrictions, Balfour made the acquaintance of Chaim Weizmann, one of the most important Zionist leaders of the twentieth century. Over the years, Weizmann would impress upon Balfour that for at least some British Jews, support for the creation of a Jewish homeland in the Middle East could bring Jewish gratitude even for British politicians who opposed open immigration. In 1917, Balfour himself visited America to float his idea with an explicit eye to this dynamic.[16] Shortly thereafter, with the approval of the British War Cabinet, Balfour as Britain's foreign secretary sent his famous letter to Lord Rothschild: "His Majesty's Government view with favor the establishment in Palestine of a national home for the Jewish people, and will use their best endeavours to facilitate the achievement of this object."[17]

While the British were debating the merits of what would become the Balfour Declaration, the young and fragile American Zionist movement sought to persuade Woodrow Wilson to endorse the plan. After learning that the State Department no longer had a copy of the memorial, Louis Brandeis, then a Progressive activist with ties to Wilson and the most conspicuous leader of the small American Zionist movement among Jews, tracked down William Blackstone.[18] Aged seventy-four, Blackstone busied himself with collecting new signatures to add to the impressive list already on the memorial, including a wide group of important Protestant leaders around the country. The Presbyterian church in which Wilson had been raised and of which he was a loyal member added its endorsement.

The United States had declared war on Germany in April of 1917; by October the first significant American forces were entering the trenches.[19] The Balfour Declaration was issued on November 2.[20] On

December 11, British forces under General Edmund Allenby entered Jerusalem unopposed as the Turks retreated, and for the first time since the Crusades a Christian power found itself in control of the city that witnessed the climactic scenes of Jesus's life.[21]

Coming so quickly after the Balfour Declaration, the conquest of Jerusalem ignited a media firestorm across the United States. Allenby, in a piece of inspired theater, entered the city on foot. This was a deliberate dig at Kaiser Wilhelm II, who insisted on opening a gap in the wall by the historic Jaffa Gate (the gap in the old Ottoman walls is still visible today) so that he could enter on a white horse.[22] The contrast between Jesus, who made his own entry to Jerusalem riding a donkey colt, and the imperious Kaiser had been widely noted at the time.[23] Allenby's piety and modesty were notable by contrast; editorialists and preachers around the country noted the difference, and an apocalyptic thrill ran through the American people.[24] Their historical optimism had been sorely tested by the transmutation of the Age of Hope into an Age of Hate, but the Allied victory in Jerusalem and the promise to give persecuted Jews a chance to build a home in the lands of the Bible pointed to a meaning behind all the madness. God was mysteriously at work behind the noise and thunder of the war; a higher purpose was being fulfilled through these human events. A better world could and would emerge from the terrible slaughter.

The next year, Theodore Roosevelt responded to the revival of the Blackstone Memorial by writing that "there can be no peace worth having" until "the Jews [are] given control of Palestine."[25] The American press went wild. As the *New York American* commented in an editorial entitled "Christianity Has Captured Its Capitol [*sic*], and Jerusalem Is Henceforth for the Jews": "Whatever else is doubtful, it is certainly true that the passage of Jerusalem into the hands of the Allies means the swift establishment of that re-gathered and redeemed Zion for which the world's Jews have dreamed ever since the tribes were scattered in the breaking up of Israel. . . . The Universal Jew, who for centuries has been a religion, not a nation, is to come at last unto his own."[26]

Even after Woodrow Wilson's international agenda was stalled when the Republicans regained control of Congress in 1918, support for the Balfour Declaration remained bipartisan. Support for Zionist aspirations in Palestine quickly became part of the boilerplate foreign policy prescriptions of American politicians in both major political parties. This was not only true of Wilson and the liberal internationalists around him; it was true of the Republicans who opposed him and defeated his League. Indeed, from World War I on, one of the foreign policy ideas that united liberals, conservatives, internationalists, and isolationists in the United States was that the United States should offer diplomatic support to the goal of establishing a Jewish homeland in Palestine. Not only Theodore Roosevelt but his cousins Franklin and Eleanor backed this idea; so did Henry Cabot Lodge, Wilson, arch-isolationist William Borah, Herbert Hoover, and Calvin Coolidge.

Supporting Britain's Balfour Declaration was exactly the kind of distant advocacy that the Blackstone signatories endorsed. The United States would not administer Palestine; it would not send troops to defend the peace there; the American government would send no aid to Jewish emigrants. This was the kind of engagement that even isolationists could applaud, and in any case, as Americans understood the situation, support for the Jewish national home in Palestine matched the ideas that under the Lodge consensus were shaping American policy worldwide.

The Blackstone approach would become the law of the land under the Lodge-Fish Resolution, which Henry Cabot Lodge introduced in the Senate on April 12, 1922. The document, a joint resolution of Congress, read: "Resolved . . . that the United States of America favors the establishment in Palestine of the National Home for the Jewish People, in accordance with the provisions contained in the Declaration of the British Government of November 2, 1917, known as the Balfour Declaration."[27] After some tweaking, it passed by overwhelming majorities—in fact, unanimously in the Senate—and was signed by President Warren Harding on September 21.

The American Jewish community was less united than the Senate when it came to the Zionist agenda. Most of the country's most prosperous and powerful Jews were firmly against what they saw as a foolish and dangerous idea. In 1891, *The New York Times* had been under non-Jewish ownership when it endorsed the Blackstone Memorial; by 1922 it had been sold to a Jewish owner, and it subsequently opposed Zionism.

In 1919, thirty-one of the most influential Jews in America, led by the former ambassador to the Ottoman Empire, Henry Morgenthau, presented a petition to Woodrow Wilson as he left for the Paris Peace Conference requesting him to oppose the Balfour Declaration: "We do not wish to see Palestine, either now or at any time in the future, organized as a Jewish State," they declared.[28] A later edition of the petition signed by almost three hundred prominent American Jews was presented to the American peace commission during the postwar negotiations.[29]

In June of 1918, the Zionist Organization of America had asked each member of Congress for their opinion on Zionism and the Balfour Declaration. Sixty-one senators and 239 congressmen (from forty-three and forty-four states, out of forty-eight, respectively) replied, mostly positively, with few differences in party or region. But one of the few to object was Fiorello La Guardia, at the time a Manhattan congressman. La Guardia, the Jewish-Italian leader who was a leading opponent of immigration restriction and had emerged as a leader in both ethnic communities, wrote, "I do not believe that it is to the interest of the Jews or the world to isolate them or to separate them with an effort to form a distinct and separate nation. While, of course, they are racially one, still the Jews of America, England, France and Italy are no different than their fellow countrymen."[30]

During the Lodge-Fish hearings, the American Jewish community had to be represented by two sets of witnesses, due to the deep split within it. Rabbi David Philipson read into the record an 1897 resolution from the Union of American Hebrew Congregations: "America is our Zion. Here, in the home of religious liberty we have aided in founding this new Zion, the fruition of the beginning laid in the old. The mission of Judaism is spiritual, not political, its aim is not to establish a state, but to spread the truths of religion and humanity throughout the world."[31]

The large majority of the members of Congress who supported Lodge-Fish came from states and districts where there was no significant Jewish vote, and most of the congressmen and senators who voted for the resolution had no expectations of significant Jewish financing for their political campaigns. By and large, rich and well-connected American Jews opposed the Balfour Declaration and the Lodge-Fish Act and would remain distinctly cool to the political agenda of the Zionist movement until World War II was well under way.

To most Americans support for a Jewish homeland in the lands of the Bible looked like the logical application of their general principles on national issues to the unique situation of the Jews. The Jews were a people like other peoples and their natural destiny, which was also their right, was to exercise self-determination in a homeland of their own. Because, uniquely, the Jews were a minority everywhere and a majority nowhere, they needed to build a homeland where they could become the majority and exercise self-determination. Once they had that homeland, they would have a place where they could be safe, there would be no humanitarian case for further Jewish immigration to the United States, and freed from oppression and persecution they could prosper.

This homeland had to be somewhere. Palestine struck most Americans as the natural and obvious choice. It was, historically, the Jewish homeland, and even for Americans who were not particularly religious, the massive weight of the Bible in popular and intellectual culture ensured that this view was widely accepted. That many Americans believed that the return of the Jews to the Holy Land was predicted by the biblical prophets was another reason that such a visionary concept won such ready assent from so many people. Beyond that, in practice, Palestine was the only place to which enough Jews might be willing to go.

That Palestine was inhabited by Arabs struck some Americans, Arab Americans and others, as a problem, but for the majority the obstacle was not seen as insuperable, either morally or practically. Racism played a role in this view; many Americans were not ready at this stage to give equal weight to the wishes and the views of non-European peoples. There was also a cultural distance; just as many Americans today will visit Egypt to see the ruins of ancient Egyptian culture but show no interest whatever in the history and monuments of Islamic times, so most Americans in the 1920s knew little and cared less about what had happened in Palestine between the fall of the last Jewish commonwealth and the fall of the Ottoman Empire. The Jewish connection to ancient Judea was more real to many Americans than the connection of Palestinian Arabs, Muslim or Christian, to the Palestine of the twentieth century. This point of view was obviously one-sided, but it was so deeply implanted in American culture that we cannot be surprised at its predominant influence on the political debate.

There were other, at least somewhat more respectable, reasons behind the general American disposition to overlook the claims of Palestinian Arabs to Palestinian land. Americans at this time saw Palestinian Arabs more as part of a larger Arab nation rather than as a unique people. This cannot be attributed simply to ignorance or bigotry. Exporting ideas like "nation" and "nation-state" from the Atlantic world to the Middle East is no easy task, and many Middle Easterners have fallen into difficulties when using categories derived from western historical experience to describe Middle Eastern realities. In 1917 there were Arabs living in Palestine who identified themselves as members of the Palestinian people. There were others who identified as Arab, or as Syrian, or as Muslim, or as Christian, or as Druze. The strong and vibrant Palestinian national identity that we see today is a product of twentieth-century history, a product above all of the conflict with Zionism, but also of the frustration of many Palestinians with the half-hearted and often self-interested approaches that many Arab leaders took toward the Palestinian movement. That the Palestinians are a young nation who emerged in the twentieth century does not mean that the Palestinians are not a nation or that their national movement is illegitimate; young nations are as legitimate, and sometimes more vigorous, than old ones.

Yet national identity remains a problematic concept. European-based political categories do not always easily translate into Middle East realities. Does "Arab" translate into European political categories as a civilizational or a national word? Does "Arab" as an identity correspond to being "French," to being "Latin," to being "European," to being "Christian," or to something else? These questions are still difficult to answer in the twenty-first century; the answers were even less clear in 1922.

In any case, for many of those Americans engaged enough and aware enough to have opinions on the subject at all, it seemed that to the extent there were two sides to the Palestinian question, it was a contest between Arabs and Jews, not between Jews and a nation of Palestinians. And as Americans saw it, if that was the dispute, then awarding Palestine to Jews seemed like the kind of reasonable compromise that American diplomats supported in similar controversies in other parts of the world.

Americans at the time did not just support Zionism; they supported the creation of independent Arab countries across the vast majority of the territory inhabited by Arabs. Carving out a little sliver for the Jews seemed like the kind of commonsense, compromise solutions to conflicting ethnic claims that was guiding American policy in Europe. The entire Arab nation was going to be liberated from the Ottoman Empire, and under League of Nations mandates would be prepared for independence. Rather than taking something away from Arabs, many Americans at this time felt that their Middle East policy preferences, taken as a whole, would benefit Arabs as much or more than anyone else. Both the Jews and the Arabs would gain, it seemed to many Americans in these years; neither would get all they wanted, but that was a universal problem in the imperial zone. Nobody was going to get 100 percent of the territory they wanted; at 97 percent the Arabs were going to do pretty well.

The Lodge Consensus, Applied

There were two postwar American foreign policy decisions that directly affected Jewish interests, the Johnson-Reed Act that drastically cut Jewish immigration and the Lodge-Fish Resolution in support of the Balfour Declaration. The majority of American Jews opposed both. A vocal Zionist minority was strongly in support of Lodge-Fish, and many other American Jews viewed any increase in Jewish settlement in Palestine as a good thing without embracing the political ambitions of the Zionist movement. But on the whole, right up through World War II, the American Jewish community would have gladly traded Lodge-Fish away in order to repeal Johnson-Reed. Both laws, however, remained on the books, and they would shape American policy toward the Zionist movement and the Jewish people for many years.

Of the two laws, Johnson-Reed, which American Jews overwhelmingly opposed, had more impact on events on the ground in Palestine. Without Johnson-Reed's immigration cap and strict quota system, fewer Polish and German Jews would have been trapped in Europe for Hitler to kill, a thought that must always strike the American conscience with a pang, but many fewer would also have made their way to the swamps and deserts of Palestine. Whether the struggling population of idealistic Zionists could have established their state if the Jewish masses had been free to choose between Palestine and America can never be known. The prewar percentages, however, with only 2 to 3 percent of Jewish emigrants choosing Palestine, strongly suggest that without the restrictive American immigration legislation the Jewish population in Palestine might never have reached numbers large enough to build and maintain an independent state.

This, at least, deserves to be remembered: if "the Jews" ran America, immigration would not have been restricted and Israel would likely not exist. This is part of a more general truth: Zionism only succeeded among Jews as it became clear that the options that most Jews initially preferred—integration into the countries where they lived or, failing that, free immigration into more hospitable places—had failed.

If Johnson-Reed was an unmitigated defeat and even a disaster for American Jews, American Zionists found that the benefits of Lodge-Fish were disappointingly meager. The consensus on the strict limits within which American sympathy for the Zionist movement and other concerns of the Jewish people would operate was stronger and more influential than the consensus that the United States should support the Zionist idea. Americans were prepared to cheer Zionism on in principle, and, in the absence of any serious reasons to the contrary, they were ready to offer diplomatic support to the Jewish settlers. But few Americans would venture beyond these limits. The United States consistently shied away from assuming any direct responsibility for the Zionist cause and refused to provide financial or military assistance to the Zionist pioneers.

Even when it came to diplomatic measures, neither Zionism itself nor the Jewish Question as a whole was a priority for American foreign policy. In the 1920s, concern about antisemitism in the newly independent states created in the imperial zone would not move the United States to effective action to protect the Jews of Eastern and Central Europe. In the 1930s, concern for German and, after 1936, Austrian Jews was not allowed to disrupt normal diplomatic relations with Hitler's Germany. As Arab resistance to Jewish settlement forced the British to reconsider their commitments in Palestine, America's reaction to Britain's retreat was subordinated to the need for good relations with America's most powerful potential ally in an increasingly unpredictable world.

Within these very strict and, from a Zionist standpoint, crippling limits, the consensus around the Blackstone principles was enduring. The horrified reaction of the State Department to the original Blackstone Memorial remained the default institutional response to what seemed to many professional diplomats to be an impractical, unnecessary, and potentially dangerous idea. But as often as the diplomats and their chiefs sought to reverse the Lodge-Fish decision, they faced an unyielding wall of presidential and congressional opposition. Secretary of State Robert Lansing had objected to President Wilson's move to endorse the Balfour Declaration. He was rebuffed. After the passage of Lodge-Fish, chief of the State Department's division of Near Eastern Affairs Allen Dulles wrote that "it is most unfortunate that the thing has come up at all. . . . For it is a species of intervention in the Near Eastern settlement, at a point where we really have no interest at all and where we stir up the very active sensibilities of the Moslem majority to say nothing of the Catholic

Church."[32] Try as they might, however, State Department officials could never get an official statement retreating from the commitment. Indeed, Presidents Coolidge, Hoover, and Franklin Roosevelt all reaffirmed the commitments originally made by Wilson and Harding.

Otherwise, the battles over policy on Jewish issues in the 1920s were mostly over minority rights for Jews in the new countries carved out of the old European empires after World War I. Poland in particular saw controversies and conflict. Jewish groups and others sought to engage American diplomacy on the side of persecuted Jews. The State Department by and large resisted, partly out of the (correct) conviction that given America's limited willingness to back up words with deeds it was a waste of time, energy, and prestige to write pointless diplomatic notes that would largely be ignored. Another factor was antisemitism; a number of diplomats thought that discrimination was a proper and appropriate response to the irritating presence of importunate Jews.

These reactions were typical of the State Department's attitude throughout this period. This was the golden age of the patrician, progressive WASP at the State Department: between the end of the spoils system at the end of the nineteenth century and the reforms that would come in the beginning of the Cold War, the well-educated, upper-crust career officials expected and largely enjoyed a degree of latitude they had not had before and would never have again.

The antisemitism at work in State was mostly the expression of the kind of social prejudice widespread in the era, though some officials went beyond that. The Warsaw embassy in particular was a hotbed of such sentiment; the vice-consul would write in 1923 that "it is true that the Pole hates the Jew. . . . The Jew in business oppresses the Pole to a far greater extent than does the Pole oppress the Jew in a political way."[33] The most infamous diplomat of this type was Assistant Secretary of State Breckinridge Long, who even in the midst of the Holocaust and the Second World War worked to keep visa quotas underfilled (including by giving misleading testimony to Congress), at the estimated cost of 190,000 lives.[34]

As the postwar chaos gradually and slowly subsided, the 1920s became a relatively peaceful era in much of Europe, and despite the Johnson-Reed Act, Jewish immigration was less of an issue in this relatively tranquil time. Many of Europe's Jews were under Soviet rule; conditions gradually worsened for Soviet Jews but they were as effectively silenced as everybody else, and it was in any case impossible for them to leave. While Britain and the United States had closed their doors, Argentina, Brazil, Canada, and elsewhere still had theirs open. Palestine was open to Jewish immigration, too, under the British mandate: between 1924 and 1928, eighty thousand Jews immigrated to Zion.

But as the decade ended, the situation both in Palestine and Europe began to darken. On Friday, August 23, 1929, Muslim Palestinians spilled out of their midday prayers and into the Jewish Quarter of Jerusalem, where they began a riot that became an uprising that lasted into September. One hundred thirty-three Jews were killed and 339 wounded; 116 Arabs died and 232 were wounded.[35] The reactions in the U.S. were diverse. The State Department, represented by the consul general in Jerusalem, blamed the Jews, saying that while the Arabs had started this particular incident, the root cause was "the Zionist's ambition . . . to convert Palestine into . . . a Jewish state."[36]

Zionist sympathizers like New York's Senator Robert Wagner told a radio audience that the "accumulated decay of 2,000 years" had been supplanted by western civilization and standards because of the personal sacrifice of thousands of the best of the Jewish race.

"Is all this to be swept away?" he asked. "Is the noble Jewish dream to be turned into a nightmare by the cowardly dagger of the assassin? The conscience of mankind cries to High Heaven that these shall not come to pass."[37] President Hoover issued words of sympathy, which were echoed by America's Jewish leaders. And nothing was done. The State Department could not persuade the politicians to abandon the Blackstone-Lodge support for the Zionists, nor could the politicians persuade the officials to advocate more strenuously for the cause of the Zionists.

In the 1930s, the combination of the economic depression and the poisonous doctrines of Stalin, Hitler, Spain's Francisco Franco, and Italy's Benito Mussolini created an increasingly dangerous and hostile environment, one in which Jews were particularly vulnerable. The Americans stuck to the Lodge consensus even as its limits imposed higher costs on the Jews: no to immigration, and only token diplomatic responses to oppression abroad. The State Department said little and did less as anti-Jewish laws and policies were imposed not only in Germany but in Poland, Hungary, and other countries. Much of American public opinion sympathized with the plight of Europe's Jews, and a number of politicians protested, but to little avail.

Then, midway through the 1930s, British policy in Palestine changed. The Arab Revolt of 1936–39, partially underwritten with money from Mussolini (because Italy was attempting to undermine British power in the Mediterranean), shocked the British, who now began to fear that their support for a Jewish homeland could drive the Arabs into an alliance with fascist Europe.[38] Fearful that the unrest would weaken their position in Egypt and in other parts of the empire (50 percent of the world's Muslim population was under British rule at the time), the British looked for ways to reduce their commitments to the Zionists under the Mandate for Palestine. A series of commissions and reports led to sharp reductions in Jewish immigration to Palestine after 1935.

These changes came just as Nazi Germany intensified its pressure on German Jews. Beginning with the Nuremberg Laws of 1935, Jews were deprived of more and more legal and economic rights. Civil servants lost their jobs, university professors and schoolteachers were fired, Jewish doctors were prohibited from seeing non-Jewish patients, and Jewish students were barred from most schools. As Hitler's diplomacy incorporated more territory under his control, Jews in the Rhineland, Austria, and Czechoslovakia also came under Nazi rule; many were desperate to leave.

For Jews in the United States, the cascade of disaster abroad led to a harsh education in the limits of their political power in the United States. All efforts to relax immigration quotas or to allow German Jewish refugees to enter the United States met immovable resistance in Congress. As the situation worsened, President Roosevelt convened an international conference at Évian-les-Bains, France, from July 6 to July 15, 1938, to find places for Jewish refugees, but with the United States unwilling to take any additional immigrants, the conference made little progress. Civilized people might find Hitler's increased persecutions distasteful, but as the Australian delegate T. W. White told the assembled delegates: "as we have no real racial problem, we are not desirous of importing one."[39]

Efforts to engage American diplomacy against Nazi persecution also fell short. Still standing by the ideas of the Lodge consensus, most Americans, including most American politicians, were unwilling to get deeply involved in the thankless and futile task of diplomatic representations about minority rights. Furthermore, especially during a depression that saw American unemployment rise to 25 percent, there was little support for economic boycotts against an important trading partner.

As to the question of British restrictions on Jewish immigration into Palestine, yet again the limits of the Blackstone-Lodge approach were clear. President Roosevelt repeatedly reiterated his support for the Balfour Declaration and the Jewish homeland, and gently protested British actions that restricted Jewish immigration, but as the international scene darkened and Britain looked to be facing war with Germany, Roosevelt was unwilling to take actions that would complicate Britain's defense planning or test transatlantic ties.

As far as many American Jews could see, the United States was failing the world's Jews at their hour of crisis. The endorsement of the goal of a Jewish homeland was unaccompanied by any policies that would bring this goal closer. Jews in much of Europe faced much worse persecution than anything Tsars Alexander III or Nicholas II had ever imposed, but it was impossible to stir the American government to action. Franklin Roosevelt reassured Jewish leaders in private of his sympathy with the plight of Europe's Jews, but these kind words failed to lead to the concrete policy changes that could have made a difference.

Huis Clos

With the United States and Palestine essentially closed, the world's Jews began to look elsewhere for refuge from European persecution. The United States had never been the only country to receive Jewish migrants. Jews streamed out of Europe to Brazil, Australia, South Africa, and elsewhere, establishing large diaspora communities in Argentina, Canada, and other New World destinations.

Unfortunately for Jews trapped in Europe, the American turn against immigration was part of a worldwide phenomenon. After World War I, anti-immigrant sentiment intensified in many countries. Even in ethnically diverse nations like Brazil that needed skilled workers, immigration restrictions gained ground. When the Great Depression came, anti-immigrant feeling grew among people worried about job competition and low wages. In 1930–31, Canada responded to the mass unemployment of the Great Depression by reducing its openness to immigration. By the 1930s, just when Jews most needed to leave Europe, there weren't many places left to go. In a bitter irony, Hitler's persecution of the Jews caused the last few doors to slam shut: Mexico in 1937; Argentina in 1938; and Chile, Colombia, Costa Rica, Cuba, Paraguay, and Uruguay in 1939 all tightened their immigration laws, in large part because each feared it would be swamped by an enormous wave of Jews fleeing European persecution.

Only marginal options were left. At the Évian Conference, the Dominican Republic (seeking favorable publicity to offset disturbing stories in the press about mass murders of Haitians illegally settled on the Dominican side of their common border)[40] offered to take up to 100,000 Jews.[41] But the Dominicans lacked the infrastructure to import, much less employ, so many people. In the end, only a thousand Jews settled in the country. Similarly, a few thousand made it to Bolivia,[42] and scattered hundreds to smaller Central American nations. But the places in the New World that could logistically and economically have accommodated a large-scale Jewish migration had shut their gates.

Under these circumstances, to Jews in Europe and Jewish American activists in the U.S., there increasingly appeared only one option left for the persecuted Jews of the Old World: Palestine. The relative handful of Jews who dared the hazards and privations of life among the hostile Arabs, malarial swamps, and barren deserts of Palestine had looked eccentric to many Jews in the first decade of the twentieth century; by the 1930s they looked prescient. The end of the era of mass immigration just as Hitler's persecution of the Jews got under way drove Jews around the world into the arms of the Zionists. Zionism, once dismissed as an irresponsible and impractical dream, began to look like the only political program that offered a pathway, however unlikely, to a secure future for millions of desperate people.

During the 1920s and 1930s, though, it seemed to most American Jewish leaders that easing immigration restrictions for persecuted Jews and pushing the American government to fight harder to uphold the rights of persecuted Jews overseas were more practical goals than to act on the dangerous fantasy of building a Jewish state in the deserts of Palestine. Only the repeated failure of these other efforts even as the condition of Jews overseas became desperate made support for a Jewish homeland in Palestine more attractive to the mainstream leadership of American Jews.

But even then, it would take the shock of World War II and the first reports of Nazi mass murders of eastern Jews to bring the organized American Jewish community into the Zionist camp. America's Jewish leadership would not wholeheartedly embrace Zionism until 1943.

No American leaders, and few world leaders, covered themselves in glory in the years leading up to the Second World War. Even fewer managed to assess and comprehend the magnitude of the horror of the Holocaust, and none intervened in a decisive and timely fashion. What followed was arguably the worst crime in human history, and it was perpetrated concurrently with the bloodiest war of all time. The era during which the Lodge consensus guided American foreign affairs ended in a wave of human suffering that dwarfed even the horrors of World War I. When the Second World War came to an end, Americans were more supportive than ever of the goal of a Jewish state, but they also still favored tight limits on American involvement. It would fall to Harry Truman to balance American sympathy and American restraint as the Jews of Palestine prepared to establish an independent state.

9

American Cyrus

O F ALL THE MEETINGS I ever had with Presidents," Clark Clifford wrote in his memoirs, "this one remains the most vivid."[1]

"That was as rough as a cob," Truman said when it ended.[2]

They were talking about a meeting President Harry Truman convened on May 12, 1948, to reach a decision about the American response to the possibility that the Palestinian Jews would declare the establishment of a new state. Truman staffer Clark Clifford, at the beginning of a long and mostly distinguished career that would include time as an advisor to four presidents and as secretary of defense, responded to a request from the president with a presentation, in the words of the official record of the meeting, "to urge the President to give prompt recognition to the Jewish State after the termination of the [British] mandate on May 15. He said such a move should be taken quickly before the Soviet Union recognized the Jewish State. It would have distinct value in restoring the President's position for support of the partition of Palestine."

As Secretary of State George Marshall later recalled the White House meeting, he said that he

Remarked to the President that, speaking objectively, I could not help but think that the suggestions made by Mr. Clifford were wrong. I thought that to adopt these suggestions would have precisely the opposite effect from that intended by Mr. Clifford. The transparent dodge to win a few votes would not in fact achieve this purpose. The great dignity of the office of the President would be seriously diminished. The counsel offered by Mr. Clifford was based on domestic political considerations, while the problem which confronted us was international. I said bluntly that if the President were to follow Mr.

Clifford's advice and if in the elections I were to vote, I would vote against the President.[3]

Clifford was incensed, recalling later that Marshall spoke "with barely contained rage and more than a hint of self righteousness."[4] Marshall glared at Clifford and acerbically asked why a political advisor was present at a meeting convened to discuss important international questions. Clifford said that State had no policy except to "wait."[5]

Truman abruptly ended the meeting "saying that he was fully aware of the difficulties and dangers in the situation, to say nothing of the political risks involved which he, himself, would run."[6]

"I never saw the General so furious," Truman said to Clifford after Marshall left with his aides. "Suppose we let the dust settle a little and see if we can get this thing turned round."[7]

Two days later the Palestinian Jews adopted a Declaration of Independence for the new Jewish state. Eleven minutes after the declaration took effect, as armies from five Arab states attacked Israel, Truman made his move. After White House and State Department aides met, Marshall had reluctantly agreed that, while he could not support the president's decision, he would not resign over it. With the fear of a devastating crisis in his embattled administration set aside, Truman shocked his own State Department and U.N. delegation (which had spent the whole day urging the United Nations General Assembly to postpone any final decisions about the conflict) by announcing his recognition of Israel as an independent state.[8]

That May 12 White House meeting has fascinated historians and pundits ever since. It has become ground zero for an ongoing debate about whether American interests are better served by working with Israel or by maintaining a distance from it. It's also a central landmark in the debate about whether massive lobbying pressures by American Jews have shaped America's Israel policy. Pro-Israel, pro-Zionist writers, including many American Jews wanting to celebrate the contributions American Jews made to Israeli independence, have developed a mythic history that puts the United States at the center of the story of Israeli independence, and attributes American policy to American Jewish activism. This vision of history is a story of heroes, mostly Jewish, and villains, mostly "Arabists" in the State Department. It is a satisfying story, and it even features a biblical moment of drama, when Eddie

Jacobson, Truman's old Jewish friend and business partner, persuaded the reluctant president to meet the Zionist leader Chaim Weizmann one last, decisive time.[9] That final meeting did the job, the legend has it; from then on American support was assured. Like Queen Esther, who pleads in the Bible with her moody husband, Xerxes, for the life of the Jewish people, Jacobson, an ordinary small businessman from Middle America, persuaded a powerful gentile ruler to support the embattled Jews.

Truman was eager to promote this myth. At a dinner shortly after the end of Truman's presidency, Eddie Jacobson introduced Truman as the man who helped bring Israel into existence. "What do you mean, helped?" was Truman's response. "I am Cyrus! I am Cyrus!" Cyrus was the Persian king who famously gave the exiled Jews permission to return to their homeland and begin the rebuilding of Jerusalem.[10]

Anti-Zionist writers and Planet Vulcan theorists tell a mirror image of this story. The wise State Department experts and patriotic officials like George Marshall did their best to hold Truman to the true path of American national interest, but the incessant pressure and overwhelming financial power of the American Jewish community succeeded in manipulating and bullying a weak president into making the wrong decision. This pattern, they say, has dominated American policymaking on the subject of Israel ever since; the Israel lobby has frustrated one president after another who tried to steer American policy back onto the right path.

These conventional stories, both the pro- and the anti-Israel versions, aren't entirely wrong; myths rarely are. The stories, however, are incomplete, and neither the Zionist nor the anti-Zionist myths can withstand critical scrutiny. Both forms of the myth are America-centric, exaggerating the impact of actions taken by Americans and minimizing the impact of decisions taken elsewhere. They are Jewcentric, failing to put Zionist agitation in proper perspective along with other factors, political and strategic, of more importance to Truman's decision making. They also miss the degree to which Truman's Palestine policy was rooted in his own settled convictions about what should be done. Truman knew what course he wanted to steer, and though contrary winds might force him to make temporary adjustments, he always returned to his original vision. Neither the Zionists nor the anti-Zionists ever quite managed to capture the president; Truman stuck to his guns.

The myths and the misunderstandings that cluster around the American role in Israel's march to independence don't just affect our perceptions of the 1940s. They continue to affect the way policymakers, politicians, pundits, and the public think about U.S.-Israeli relations today. Both in the United States and in the wider world, many, perhaps most, observers continue to underestimate the complexity of U.S.-Israeli relations, to overestimate the influence of American Jews over American policy in the region, and to underestimate the dependence of American policy toward Israel on broader American debates over national strategy as a whole.

To understand the U.S.-Israel relationship clearly, it is necessary to get past both the pro-Zionist and anti-Zionist myths. It is true for example that Harry Truman met with Chaim Weizmann after Eddie Jacobson's intervention ("All right you baldheaded son of a bitch . . . I'll see him"), but the visit's impact on policy was, at most, indirect.[11] The United States government, with Truman's full knowledge and support, continued to urge the Palestinian Jews to defer independence right up to the end. Before the Israelis proclaimed their new state, they voted against a proposal from the Truman administration to postpone it.[12] The new state began with an act of defiance that it intended to repeat; Israel declared its independence as it rejected American advice.

The American debate was never between proponents and opponents of an independent Jewish state. George Marshall, who came close to resigning in frustration over Truman's decision to recognize Israel, was, like Truman, sympathetic to the Jews. He wanted them to succeed, but based on military estimates he was receiving from the CIA, he, like most other military experts at the time, believed that the Jewish cause was doomed to defeat. (Using a cricket metaphor that roughly equates to hitting a home run, British Field Marshal Bernard Montgomery told friends that the Arabs would "knock the Jews for six" if war broke out.)[13] Both Marshall and his State Department colleagues feared that, faced with the prospect of another humanitarian catastrophe for the Jews so soon after World War II, the United States would be caught up in a Jewish-Arab war.

The real American policy debate was never about whether to favor the Arab or the Jewish causes in Palestine. Amin al-Husseini, the Grand Mufti of Jerusalem and the political leader of the Palestinian Arabs, was widely dismissed as a politically incompetent Nazi collaborator and had no significant following in Washington. While there was real human sympathy for Palestinian Arabs on the part of some diplomats and poli-cymakers, many of the State Department officials who opposed support for the Palestinian Jews were, if anything, more hostile to Arab aspira-tions than they were to American Zionists at the time. The State Depart-ment feared that if the Zionists launched a war to build their state, Arab opinion throughout the Middle East would be radicalized. Under those conditions, the client kings and puppet rulers through whom Great Brit-ain controlled the region would fall from power, valuable oil concessions which benefited American as well as British firms could be endangered, and the new rulers would be tempted to align with the Soviet Union.

This was a pro-British and pro-business, not a pro-Arab approach; the State Department wanted the United States to support the British Empire against Arab (and Persian) nationalists in the Middle East. If anything, these were the most orientalist and anti-Arab officials of all, believing that the sleepy peoples of the Near East could be induced to slumber on under British rule if the disturbing noises from Palestine could somehow be suppressed. The American Zionist view, naive and wrongheaded as it proved to be, was actually more pro-Arab than the approach of the mandarins. Many American Zionists hoped that the example of Israeli independence and development would inspire the Arab world to build independent, democratic societies on the Israeli model and saw the weak-ening of British colonial influence in the Middle East as a good thing.

To clear away both the pro-Zionist and anti-Zionist myths that clus-ter so thickly around the critical events of these dramatic times, and to recover a picture of the events of these years which can help us under-stand the choices we face in the contemporary world, the place to start is with understanding the situation and the motives of the man at the center of American foreign policy in these decisive years: Harry Tru-man, one of the most effective foreign policy leaders in American his-tory. Once we step away from the mythmakers, we can begin to see both the accomplishments and the limitations of this extraordinary ordinary man in something like their true form.

The Man from Missouri

The conventional narratives about Harry Truman and Israel are right about one thing: Truman's decisions about Palestine policy were politi-cal. But so were his decisions about the U.N., about NATO, and about the Marshall Plan. They had to be. Truman was a strong man but a weak president. For most of his presidency his ranking in the polls was low, the opposition controlled Congress, and the most powerful figures in his own party distrusted him. Truman never had the freedom to ignore political pressures when making foreign policy choices.

The conventional narratives about Truman's Palestine policy miss two important things: the first is that the political firestorms that regularly raged over American foreign policy during Truman's years in office were much larger and more powerful than anything the Zionist lobby could generate. Even when it came to Palestine policy, the Zionists were only one of several lobbies in the arena; they were never the strongest force that he faced.

The second thing missed is the consistency of Truman's foreign policy approach, to Palestine as well as to more important issues. Somewhat to the surprise of those who knew him only as an undistinguished machine politician from Missouri, in the White House Truman proved to be a man of conviction and consistency. In some ways this reflected both the narrowness of his education and the simplicity of his character. Truman saw a world of timeless truths and classic ideas. His study of history led him to respect and to emulate people who changed the world by the power of their convictions; his stubborn adherence to the truths he knew grounded his foreign policy even as it sometimes infuriated his aides.

At the time, Truman was widely considered a failed president. In early 1952 with the nation caught in the stalemated and deeply unpopular Korean War, Truman's approval rating sank to 22 percent,[14] and he abandoned his quest for a second elected term. But over the years, as historians reflected more deeply about the terrible crises of his era, as some of his policies were vindicated by later experience, and as the passions of the day gradually subsided, historians have come to treat Truman with more respect. He is now considered one of the most successful American presidents, not in the front rank with Washington, Lincoln, and Franklin Roosevelt, but holding his own in the second rank.[15] This is one of the reasons that later generations are sometimes baffled by Truman's foreign policy record; it is hard for us to remember just how weak and incompetent Truman often appeared to his contemporaries, and that makes it difficult to reconstruct the political atmosphere in which he made his decisions.

In his day, political columnists and observers ranging from Walter

Lippmann to I. F. Stone and including Arthur Krock and Drew Pearson saw Truman as a small, misguided man. Intellectuals like Harold Laski and Arthur Schlesinger viewed him with a mix of condescending pity and contempt. His political colleagues for the most part shared the view they expressed to John Chamberlain of *Life* magazine in November 1945: " 'Big' senators of both parties, remembering that Harry Truman was a 'little' senator for practically all his period on the Hill, are now indulging the ancient habit of saying 'I told you so.' They don't want to be quoted directly, for they insist that Harry is their pal. But they manifestly do not fear him, and they will support him only if he happens by chance to be going their way."[16] Three years later, the perception of weakness had only grown. As Krock, the prominent *New York Times* columnist, wrote in 1948, "The President's influence at this writing is weaker than any President's has been in modern American history."[17]

Not since the martyred Lincoln was followed by Andrew Johnson had a man of great stature been succeeded by such an undistinguished person. In many ways Truman was the oddest duck and the biggest misfit to hold the presidency since the end of Johnson's unlamented tenure in 1869. And just as Johnson faced Reconstruction, a task only marginally less difficult than the Civil War, so Truman would face a task only marginally less difficult than fighting and winning World War II: a global reconstruction in the face of some of the gravest foreign policy problems that any statesman in world history had ever faced.

Politically, Truman had two great handicaps, and they were linked. In the first place, he wasn't Franklin Roosevelt, and, in the second place, he was Franklin Roosevelt's successor. He lacked the authority, the self-assurance, the contacts, and the experience that belonged to the most effective political operator who ever lived in the White House. The contrast between the patrician and polished Roosevelt and the scrappy, self-made Missourian who succeeded him could not have been greater. Truman had no college degree. His parents knew little about the wider world. Roosevelt had attended Groton and Harvard, taking extensive European tours in childhood and adolescence, meeting princes and potentates before he was old enough to drink. FDR followed his cousin Theodore's footsteps into government, serving in Teddy's old post as assistant secretary of the navy during World War I. FDR was first nominated for national office (the vice presidency) in 1920, and even as he struggled with polio, he remained in the thick of Democratic politics, ultimately serving as governor of New York, then the most populous and most important state in the union. His unprecedented twelve years in the White House gave him an unrivaled mastery of American politics, greater personal prestige than any American statesman since Thomas Jefferson, a uniquely deep knowledge of the way the American government worked, and an in-depth understanding of the nuances of American policy and politics that no other American president has ever acquired. FDR inspired fear and respect across the federal bureaucracy, and was revered by a generation of Americans for whom he was the towering figure who led the country through the greatest depression and the most dangerous war in its history. Truman was none of the above.

It is sometimes forgotten today, but Truman faced a degree of insubordination in both the military and the State Department that no subsequent president until Donald Trump would experience. There were several reasons the bureaucracies were so willing to defy their nominal master. One was personal: throughout Truman's time in office, he simply did not have the respect of the professional military and diplomats. Truman lacked the charisma, the knowledge, the culture, the ease of manner, and the aristocratic self-confidence that had made Franklin Roosevelt the master of American politics for twelve extraordinary years. He was an uneducated common man in a world of privilege and technocracy, a goose among swans, a mule among thoroughbreds. He would face, and face down, generals still wreathed in the laurels of victory, adored by the nation they had preserved through a terrible war, venerated by their veterans, worshipped by newspapers. His diplomats were for the most part the product of the nation's finest schools; some, like Averell Harriman, came from the nation's richest families; all saw themselves as part of a meritocratic elite, a secular priesthood privy to the arcana of diplomacy and the mysteries of power. When the largely self-educated Truman, who had graduated from the utterly undistinguished Independence High School, argued strategy and history, he argued with people who had read Thucydides in Greek in their teens. His meager accomplishments in two terms in the Senate had failed to impress the leaders of Congress, the national press corps, and the hostesses of Georgetown.

A failure in business whose only success in life came, apparently, from the alacrity with which he responded to the orders of the corrupt Tom Pendergast machine in Missouri, Truman ascended to the presidency lacking the confidence of his party and the respect of his peers. Complicating Truman's task were the circumstances of his nomination to the vice presidency at the 1944 Democratic convention. Henry Wallace, an icon of the party's liberal wing, had been FDR's choice in 1940, and Roosevelt would have been happy to keep Wallace on the ticket in 1944.[18] But party leaders from the conservative South and the pragmatic big city machines worried about Roosevelt's visibly declining health, and about perceptions that the ultraliberal Wallace would hurt the ticket in what was shaping up to be a close presidential race, demanded that Roosevelt dump Wallace for someone less controversial. When Sidney Hillman, the resourceful leader of the CIO labor federation and the most powerful representative of the left wing of organized labor in Democratic politics at the time, signaled that he could accept Truman, the second-term Missouri senator's path to the nomination was open.[19]

FDR made it possible for Truman to replace Wallace; he did not make it easy. Roosevelt wanted to keep the liberals happy even as he shunted Wallace aside. So in a performance that was underhanded even by his Machiavellian standards, FDR gave a weaselly worded statement that many delegates interpreted as an endorsement of Wallace ("I personally would vote for his nomination if I were a delegate to the convention") while he privately signaled a preference for Truman.[20] In the confusion, the liberal delegates at the Chicago convention revolted and the VP nomination went to a floor vote. Wallace led Truman on the first ballot, and it took the persuasive powers of the party bosses to strong-arm enough delegates into selecting Truman.[21] For many Democratic liberals, Truman's elevation to the vice presidency represented a revolt of the conservatives and the party machines against the idealism and liberal leadership that Roosevelt stood for. When Roosevelt died three months into his fourth term of office, nothing had changed their view that Truman could not be trusted to carry out the FDR legacy at home or abroad.

Truman would never forget how fragile his hold on the Democratic Party was. Roosevelt's personal authority and his unparalleled record of political success had not been enough to enable Roosevelt to master the party's barons and interest groups, and southern conservatives had beaten back his effort to "purge" them from the party in 1938. Truman was in a much weaker position than Roosevelt and, much as Lyndon Johnson was haunted by the fear that the Kennedy family and its allies would undermine him, Truman was haunted by the fear that Eleanor

Roosevelt and liberal lions like Wallace would combine to take the Democratic Party out from under him by challenging his legitimacy as the heir to FDR's liberal mantle.

Even if Truman's position had been stronger, the position of the Democratic coalition in 1945 was weak. As Roosevelt's successor, Truman inherited the problems of an administration and a political coalition whose life had been artificially prolonged by the war. Had it not been for Hitler's blitzkrieg across Europe in 1940, it is unlikely that FDR would have sought or obtained a third term. The international crisis of 1940 had become the greatest foreign war in American history by 1944, and once again the wartime emergency allowed Roosevelt to seek and to win an unprecedented fourth term. But the presidential race was again close, and the signs that the country was ready for a change were growing.[22] For the first few months of Truman's presidency, his public support benefited both from sympathy and from the halo effect of V-E Day and V-J Day. With the war over, though, and peacetime problems like inflation and demobilization moving to the fore, the country's desire for political change eroded the administration's support. Truman's approval rating fell from 87 percent in the summer of 1945 to 34 percent in the fall of 1946 as the Republicans swept back into control of Congress.[23] Democrats attributed their losses to Truman's weak leadership.

By 1946, the broad Democratic coalition of Franklin Roosevelt was showing its age. The party had long been split between progressive northern liberals, big-city political machines, and conservative white southerners. The coalition had already begun to fray before World War II, and by the time Truman took office, the fractures were becoming serious. Conservative southern white Democrats had already begun to resist the New Deal, and Eleanor Roosevelt's open sympathy for Black Americans alienated many in a region still committed to upholding white supremacy and Jim Crow. In the North, many urban Democrats, often first- or second-generation immigrants, yearned for a more aggressive social program and a more comprehensive social welfare net than the New Deal offered. Black migrants to the North had voting rights, unlike many of their friends and families in the South. They wanted a stronger federal stance in favor of their rights. The trade unions, newly empowered by Roosevelt-era pro-union legislation, wanted to consolidate their power and extend their control into new industries and new parts of the country.

As northern Democrats moved to the left, the country as a whole was coming to adopt a more conservative stance, led not just by Republicans but also by the southern and pro-business wings of the Democratic Party. In 1948 the party would split into three wings: the regular Democrats under Truman, the conservative Dixiecrats under Strom Thurmond, and the left-wing Progressives under Henry Wallace. The effort to prevent the split, and to hold on to as much of the party as possible, would dominate Truman's political calculations right up through his surprise victory in the 1948 vote.

Economic developments after the war exacerbated the party's problems in 1946. The shift from a war economy to a peacetime economy was never going to be easy and the country was still scarred by the memories of the long Depression that had only really ended with the war. In order to return to something like a "normal" economy, wartime wage and price controls had to be abolished, shortages managed while industrial production shifted from mortars and tanks to civilian goods, government spending had to be reduced to peacetime levels, war contracts terminated, and returning veterans had to be integrated into the job market.

Meanwhile, Truman had to manage the demands of a force that was too strong to ignore and too demanding to appease: organized labor, then at the peak of its power. Working people suffered severely during the Depression and wartime rationing and wage controls fueled their frustration. At the same time, the pro-labor legislation of the New Deal gave labor unions much more power than they had ever enjoyed. Patriotism, assisted by the threat of severe government reprisals, kept organized labor relatively tractable during the war, but with the return of peace the American labor movement was determined to spread its wings and seek fundamental changes in the economic balance of power. Prices inevitably rose as wartime restraints ended and the pent-up demand for new cars, houses, and other goods met the shortages of goods resulting from the delays in conversion from wartime to peacetime production. Inflation made labor all the more determined to seek higher wages, and the result was the greatest outbreak of labor unrest in American history.

Between V-J Day and the end of 1946, millions of workers participated in a series of major strikes that shut down key industries ranging from coal (at a time when coal was the major fuel for the nation's factories, homes, and the freight and passenger trains that were essential to economic activity before the advent of the interstate highway system), steel, railroads, and electricity providers. Coming at a time of rampant shortages and economic uncertainty, the strikes threatened the process of postwar recovery and presented Truman with a painful political dilemma.

The labor movement was an essential part of the Democratic coalition, yet the backlash against the strikers and the threat that some of the strikes posed to a fragile national economy were both very real. Truman saw no choice but to take strong action against striking workers, using the power of the federal government either to force management and labor to a compromise, or in some cases using injunctions and executive orders to break the strikes.[24] One can debate the effect of these measures on the national economy; there is no doubt that they undercut Truman's position in Democratic Party politics.

These were the political realities that continually tested Truman's ability to control his own party and the national agenda. That he survived as long as he did and won a full presidential term in the face of them is a remarkable accomplishment. That he was able to carry out a vigorous foreign policy under the circumstances is extraordinary; few presidents have accomplished so much in such difficult circumstances.

Trouble Abroad

Given his troubles at home, Truman might have wished for a calmer international scene. He didn't get it. From the first day of his presidency as the fires of World War II still raged until he stepped down in the midst of the Korean War, international events would force him, time and time again, to set aside domestic goals and priorities to handle one foreign crisis after another.

The end of the Second World War left much of the world hungry, angry, and insecure. The cities of Japan, China, and most of Europe had been leveled by the most devastating air attacks in the history of warfare. Tens of millions had been killed, tens of millions more driven from their homes, forced into slave labor, or otherwise displaced by the tides of war. States had ceased to function in many places, most currencies were worthless, and trade, agriculture, and industry were prostrate and paralyzed. Food shortages stalked the civilized world. Stalin, it soon became clear, was grimly determined to impose the vicious system of communist rule wherever the Red Army stood. The gulags were stuffed with new prisoners as all those who opposed or might have opposed the Red Terror were hauled off into the living hell of concentration camps far behind what would soon be called the Iron Curtain.

The moral destruction was as bad as the physical. Years of war in both Asia and Europe had broken up families, brutalized millions, and left homeless orphans to fend for themselves in the rubble of great cities. The social capital embodied in churches, schools, and civic institutions had been heavily damaged and in many cases wrecked beyond repair. The veterans and survivors of war were scarred by their experiences. Some of the most glorious monuments humanity had ever produced had been deliberately destroyed. Total war in an age of science and technology resulted in millions of civilian deaths and the systematic destruction of the infrastructure on which the survivors depended. Untold numbers of people had committed atrocities that would scar their consciences forever; millions more had suffered them. Religious and political leadership was often compromised by alliance—however unwilling—with totalitarian power.

The web of world trade, already strained by a decade of Depression, further frayed during the war. Food-growing countries lacked the shipping to export their produce. Food-consuming countries lacked the foreign exchange to buy. Banking and trading systems had fallen apart. Famine threatened much of China and India, to say nothing of Europe and the Middle East. The factories that survived the war could not import the necessary raw materials or secure the needed energy. Shortages made the task of reconstruction extremely difficult. Particular attention had been paid during the war to the destruction of the vital rail networks and the rolling stock that operated on it. From commuter rail systems to the national and international railways needed to move cargo of every kind, rail transport had ground to a halt across Europe and Asia. Mines were flooded, power generators bombed, bridges blown up across the combat zone.

The global political situation was just as bad. The great powers and global empires of earlier times were crippled by the war. The French, British, Belgian, and Dutch colonial empires were suspended between imperial authorities who increasingly lacked the resources or legitimacy to act, and untried, untested nationalist movements just beginning to grapple with tasks of state building and development. China, devastated by a generation of warlordism and the vicious Japanese invasion, was ruined, exhausted, and about to undergo another round of civil war between the communists and the U.S.-supported Kuomintang. British India was moving toward independence even as growing conflict between Hindus and Muslims prefigured partition and the mass murder and flight that accompanied it.

In 1945, no one quite understood what the dynamics of the postwar world would be. Nobody knew whether or how after such horrific crimes Germany and Japan could rejoin the community of nations; Roosevelt advisor Bernard Baruch warned in November 1945 that both might be planning wars of revenge.[25] Great Britain had clearly been damaged by the war, but most British and foreign observers believed that to a large extent, it would recover. The United States, the only major economy to have escaped the physical devastation of the conflict, lacked both the experience and the will for global leadership. American forces had returned home quickly after World War I; most observers believed that the country would once again demobilize and close down the bases it had come to occupy during the war. The Soviet Union, while sustaining immense economic and manpower losses in the brutal fighting on the eastern front, had become the dominant military power on the European mainland as a result of the war. What use the Soviets would make of this position was unknown. Both the Americans and the British hoped that the wartime alliance could continue.

Over everything loomed the specter of the atomic bomb. Developed in the United States (with considerable help from British and exiled German scientists), this powerful weapon disturbed world politics. Initially, the Americans had a monopoly on nuclear weapons, and no one in western governments knew how effective Stalin's espionage was or how close he was to developing a bomb of his own. Humanity was in the early stages of a process that is still going on today: learning to live in the shadow of nuclear destruction.

Trouble at Home

There was bound to be a contentious debate over American foreign policy as the United States shifted from the problems of winning the greatest war in the history of the world to building peace in the midst of the greatest chaos and dislocation the world had ever seen. Just as Democratic liberals continued to support the New Deal policies at home, and believed that it was Truman's duty to honor and extend FDR's domestic policy legacy, they believed that FDR's foreign policy should be preserved and honored abroad.

Eleanor Roosevelt, Franklin's charismatic, passionate, and politically active widow, had seen herself as the guardian of her husband's liberal conscience during their years in the White House. After his death, she became the guardian of his liberal legacy. She had been the most prominent and politically engaged first lady in the history of the United States during her husband's unprecedented twelve years in the presidency. With a syndicated newspaper column appearing six times a week across the country,[26] and a mass following among Democrats and liberals who revered her both for herself and for her association with FDR, she was the most powerful woman in the history of American politics. She was a committed internationalist who felt the horror of war, sympathized deeply with its victims around the world, remembered America's failure to build a peaceful world following World War I, and was determined to ensure a different outcome this time.

For Eleanor Roosevelt, there was no doubt about the foreign policy that the United States should follow after her husband's death: his, as understood by her. The postwar order should rest on two pillars: continued cooperation with the Soviet Union and the development of the United Nations as the principal forum for international politics. The emergence of postcolonial countries offered a great opportunity for the United States to ally with progressive forces around the world, ushering in a new and more peaceful and democratic era in world politics. By resolutely opposing efforts by countries like Britain and France to cling to their empires, by dealing honestly and openly with Stalin, and by offering support to emerging national movements around the world the United States could be true to its principles while building a strong foundation for world peace.

Aligned with Eleanor Roosevelt on these issues was the man who many liberal Democrats believed was Franklin Roosevelt's preferred successor, Henry Wallace. After the end of Wallace's vice presidential term, FDR (who never admitted publicly that he had agreed to replace Wallace with Truman) signaled his continuing respect for Wallace by naming him to the cabinet as commerce secretary.

This yearning for a progressive foreign policy was the vision not only of the former president's widow and former vice president, but of the Democratic liberal establishment, the majority of the nation's religious leaders, leading intellectuals, and the professional upper middle class. The horrors of war, the shock of the atomic bomb, the millennial aspirations that, as we have seen, play such an important role in American life: all combined to impress much of the United States with the conviction that the aftermath of World War II demanded a unique response.

The cascading disasters and crises of the postwar years were so immense, so unprecedented, so complex, and so terrifying that it is difficult for people today to comprehend the psychological and mental state of our ancestors on whose heads the great storm broke. It was not just the vast scale of the starvation and homelessness, the economic disarray, the physical disruption or the anarchic conditions in so much of the world. Something much bigger was at work. The unprecedented horrors of the war, with unspeakable cruelties practiced by Germany and Japan of which the Holocaust was only the most conspicuous, revealed a depravity in the human spirit that seemed to destroy all hope for the kind of gradual amelioration in the human condition that had for two centuries been the mainstay of American and Enlightenment optimism.

The rise of inhuman totalitarianisms in Germany, the Soviet Union, and Japan also delivered a profound shock to believers in the doctrine of progress. The Enlightenment, Americans had long believed, was leading to an inexorable amelioration of the human condition. More wealth and more education would, by all the laws that governed human nature, lead societies to adopt more liberal and more humane forms of government. Societies that rested on free competition and cooperation would, Americans had long held, inevitably triumph over those that restricted human freedom or subjected human economic activity to the rigors of central control. The totalitarian governments of the 1930s made that assumption questionable; that victory over Germany and Japan had only been possible by an alliance with the most murderous and destructive regime of them all was a grim truth that deprived triumph of much of its joy. *Triumph and Tragedy* was the title Winston Churchill would choose for the final volume of his war memoir. While cynics might claim that the tragedy he had in mind was his unexpected general election defeat in the summer of 1945, the title struck most readers as an accurate description of the profoundly disturbing consequences of the bloodiest war ever fought.

At the same time, the detonation of American atomic bombs over Hiroshima and Nagasaki raised the prospect, even the certainty that a third world war would be far more destructive than the second. It was not hard to look into the future and see the overthrow of all civilization and perhaps the annihilation of the human race coming about as the result of the next war.

These shocks felt by policymakers and national leaders echoed and reverberated through the whole of society. The terrible new realities of the human condition were anything but obscure. Everyone could see how Europe and Asia were filled with emaciated and shell-shocked survivors picking through the ruins of their lives in search of their daily bread. Even in sheltered America, millions of soldiers had seen the ferocity of technologically enabled war at first hand. Eyewitness accounts and newsreel footage of Nazi and Japanese atrocities were everywhere. The size and consequences of the nuclear blasts were discussed in full and at length at kitchen tables as much as in cabinet meetings.

Without taking these circumstances into account, it is difficult to understand both the motives and the actions of many American policymakers in the early postwar years. Otherwise intelligent people were willing to believe in Stalin's good intentions and peaceable character less because they loved communism than because an accurate understanding of the evil he represented and the threat that he posed made the world look unendurably grim. Americans clung with such tenacity to the empty shell of the United Nations, imbuing it with unrealistic hopes less because they were stupid than because they could not imagine a future for human beings without an effective international institution that could prevent future wars.

Later generations, who have learned the limits of the United Nations through bitter experience, find it difficult to understand just how intensely so many Americans longed for a truly effective international organization to emerge or how determined they were to give the new organization the chance to succeed. Establishing an effective international organization to prevent war was going to be difficult, but since the alternative was annihilation, the effort had to be made—and it had to succeed. Clearly, reasoned Eleanor Roosevelt, Henry Wallace, and millions of Americans with them, the United States must not only join the United Nations; it must lead the world in supporting it.

In October 1946, the *New York Times* editorial board described the United Nations as "the great adventure in international cooperation that must be the foundation of peace and prosperity," and "the Town Meeting of the World and the conscience of mankind."[27] These views were unrealistic; they were even idiotic given the structure of the United Nations and the condition of the world, but they were to a large degree inevitable under the circumstances of the time. And idiotic or not, they were the settled views of a large section of both the leadership and the base of a political party that Harry Truman led but did not control.

Opposed to this consensus, which dominated the Democratic Party and the internationalist, establishment wing of the Republicans, was an equally irrational and equally unrealistic isolationist school associated with conservative Republicans like Senator Robert Taft of Ohio. This school, which was by and large bitterly opposed to the New Deal's expansion of federal power, believed that the United States should have as little to do as possible with questions of world order. While some Taftians supported membership in the United Nations, they opposed all talk of a global superstate.[28] They mistrusted both the Soviet Union and Great Britain, and believed that other powers were using the gullibility of American liberals to enlist the power of the United States for their own selfish ends. The United States was the strongest power in the world, unique in its possession of nuclear weapons, the greatest oil producer, the greatest industrial power, the most technologically advanced country in the world, the world's greatest producer of food; of course other, weaker nations sought to bend American power to their own purposes. The League of Nations had been a fraud and a disaster; the United Nations was likely to fail whether or not the United States belonged to it. The safest course was for the United States to tend to its own strength at home, secure the Western Hemisphere, and remember George Washington's wise advice against participating in entangling alliances in Europe. Against the Wilsonian liberals, the Jacksonian and Jeffersonian conservatives on the right flank of the Republican Party wanted as limited an American foreign policy as possible. In its way, this approach was as naive about the Soviet danger as the most woolly-minded followers of Eleanor Roosevelt. The belief that the world would somehow stabilize without American engagement was as utopian and impossible as any fantasy that Henry Wallace could conceive.

There was also a third school, which represented the opinion of many of the people in the State Department and the Pentagon. These officials had been close to power under FDR and watched the evolution of Soviet policy in 1944 and 1945 with dismay. One by one, key foreign policy officials like Averell Harriman, George Kennan, and Robert Lovett came to feel the need for a tougher American stance against Stalin. While many in this group remained modestly hopeful about the future of the United Nations, the need to balance the Soviet Union's power was becoming their highest priority, and Great Britain, the strongest remaining non-communist power in the world next to the United States, was seen as an indispensable ally. Including soldiers like Marshall and diplomats like Kennan and Lovett, this group sought to build American alliances with noncommunist Europe in order to limit the power of the Soviet Union. They had chafed as Franklin Roosevelt, in their view, refused to rethink his Soviet policy as Stalin broke one pledge after another in Eastern Europe.[29]

As Truman, whom FDR kept out of the loop on all important foreign policy and war strategy issues even after he was inaugurated as vice president, struggled to find his footing in the hurricane of events following FDR's death, he faced two major problems. The first was his own inexperience. Truman was a newcomer in the world of international diplomacy. He had no idea how to carry on negotiations with foreign leaders. When he meant to sound firm, he would often sound brash. Missteps with the Soviets in particular worried even some of the State Department officials who approved of Truman's tougher stand against Stalin, and helped to promote an image of Truman as a bumbling amateur that would undermine his authority throughout his presidency.

More seriously, Truman gradually came to the view that both the liberal Democratic and conservative Republican approaches to American foreign policy were hopelessly out of touch with the requirements of national strategy. The State Department mandarins were right and the Roosevelt approach to Stalin had to end. The United Nations was a hopeful experiment and Truman would use it as much as he could, but the Soviet veto and the inherent limits on the effectiveness of international institutions constrained its ability to manage the Soviet challenge. To check Stalin's ambitions, the United States would need to work with

European allies. These ideas were anathema to Taftian Republicans. More importantly for Truman, they were also directly opposed to the foreign policy approach that Democratic icons like Wallace and Eleanor Roosevelt wanted him to follow.

The story of Truman's foreign policy is the story of his dogged attempt to keep as much of the Democratic Party as possible with him while he led the country on the path toward a Cold War strategy that, initially at least, most liberal Democrats abhorred.[30] Right up to his upset victory over Thomas Dewey in the 1948 election, most observers thought he would fail. His Cold War policy faced intense and unrelenting opposition from liberal Democrats and New Dealers who saw Truman turning away from the United Nations and diplomacy, away from the wartime alliance with Moscow, away from a program of domestic reform and support of the trade unions, and toward a militarized foreign policy based on global containment. Instead of working with anticolonial nationalists and progressive forces around the world, the United States was collaborating with European colonial powers.

Truman tried to paper over the deepening schism, sometimes resorting to less than candid language. In a diary entry for October 15, 1945, Wallace described a conversation he had with President Truman. "Stalin was a fine man who wanted to do the right thing," Wallace quotes Truman as telling him, to which Wallace responded that "the purpose of Britain was to promote an irreparable break between us and Russia."

"I said Britain's game in international affairs has always been intrigue," Wallace told his diary. "I said Britain may have plenty of excuse for playing the game the way she does; it may fit into her geographical position, but we must not play her game. The president said he agreed."[31]

Cooperation with the U.K. and confrontation with the Soviet Union continued to be unpopular in the United States. George Kennan's Long Telegram on Soviet behavior with its systematic exposition of Stalin's determination to impose dictatorial Soviet rule across Europe electrified official circles in Washington in February 1946,[32] but the Democratic base wasn't interested in anti-Soviet warnings from an elitist State Department. Winston Churchill's Iron Curtain speech, delivered in Fulton, Missouri, on March 5, 1946, as Truman sat in the audience, called for a renewal of the wartime transatlantic relationship in the light of the Soviet threat. This was not yet acceptable to antiwar and anti-British liberal opinion, and despite his enduring personal popularity in the United States, Churchill's remarks about the Soviet Union were attacked by liberals and isolationists alike. Truman had to distance himself from Churchill's call for close cooperation with Britain even as he endorsed Churchill's criticisms of Stalin. Liberal Democrats argued strenuously that Stalin's hostile behavior was driven by his fear of encirclement, and that close U.K.-U.S. cooperation would provoke Moscow and increase the chances of a great power confrontation. To preserve the peace, the United States had to keep its distance from the United Kingdom while working with Stalin wherever it could.

Liberal unhappiness with Truman continued to mount. By September of 1946, when Truman demanded the resignation of Henry Wallace from the cabinet after Wallace refused to stop making dovish foreign policy speeches, leading liberals like Helen Keller and Albert Einstein were becoming harshly critical of the administration and warning that Truman was pushing the country into another world war.[33] After leaving the cabinet, Wallace was invited to edit the then-influential *New Republic*. Cheered on by much of the labor movement and progressive opinion, both *The New Republic* and the other leading liberal publication of the day, *The Nation,* would hurl blasts of criticism at the White House. By 1947, Wallace was ready to organize a third-party presidential campaign to block Truman's reelection. The widespread belief among political observers that Wallace's insurgency would siphon off liberal and progressive votes is why so few people expected Truman to win the 1948 presidential election.

With Wallace in open revolt, Eleanor Roosevelt's importance to the embattled president grew. This did not cause her to rally to Truman. Much as the Kennedys distanced themselves from Lyndon Johnson's presidency, the Roosevelt family grew colder and more distant toward Truman's administration. Franklin Roosevelt's sons would ultimately try to block Truman's quest for the Democratic nomination in 1948.[34] He could not afford to lose Eleanor, too.

Complicating Truman's life in 1945 and early 1946 was the overlap between his liberal and isolationist critics on the questions of military preparedness and relations with Britain. Both liberal internationalists and conservative isolationists favored the rapid demobilization of American forces following Japan's surrender. Liberals wanted an expansive internationalist foreign policy, but they saw a strong American military presence overseas as both wasteful and provocative. Isolationists also wanted American forces to come home, and both liberals and iso-lationists were intensely skeptical of what they saw as cunning British efforts to fool naive Americans into paying the bills for Britain's imperial schemes.

Later in 1946, and more substantively in 1947, the balance in American politics began to change. The evidence that Stalin intended to ignore his Yalta commitments to FDR and impose draconian communist dictator-ships everywhere the Red Army could reach alarmed a growing number of Americans into rethinking the benefits of U.S.-Soviet cooperation. Immigrant communities from countries like Poland and Hungary, along with Catholic religious leaders, reacted to Soviet oppression in Eastern and Central Europe by supporting tougher American policies. Grow-ing evidence that the Western European economies were recovering slowly from the war alarmed American businesses who needed export markets abroad. A number of formerly isolationist Republicans, led by Senator Arthur Vandenberg of Michigan, moved to support Truman administration strategy in Europe; others leapfrogged over the Tru man administration to denounce the State Department as insufficiently alert to the communist menace. The February 1948 communist coup in Czechoslovakia, crushing the last independent political force behind the Iron Curtain, led some liberal Democrats to conclude that the hope of conciliating Stalin through American concessions could no longer be sustained. A split between Henry Wallace and Eleanor Roosevelt began to develop as Wallace became more public in his criticism of Truman and more radical in his politics, and Roosevelt publicly supported the Marshall Plan as Wallace bitterly condemned it.[35] Even as the movement to drop Truman from the Democratic ticket in 1948 gained momentum among liberals, Truman could see a path forward.

Under these circumstances, Truman's approach to Palestine was nec-essarily and appropriately political, but those who see it as a simple exer-cise in ethnic pandering to American Jews miss the drama and meaning of one of the most important episodes in the history of American for-eign policy. President Truman integrated his approach to Palestine into the central political and diplomatic effort of his first term, using his Pal-estine policy to help reconcile American liberals to his shift away from FDR's World War II foreign policy toward the Cold War strategy that would guide the United States for the next forty years.

Truman's Palestine policy was often awkward and at times as "rough as a cob," but in the end it has to be seen as an integral part of one of the most accomplished presidential foreign policy performances in the history of the United States. That one of the most important examples of brilliant presidential leadership in difficult times has been obscured by stale polemics is part of the price America pays for a constricted understanding of the nature and sources of the U.S.-Israel relationship.

10

Cyrus and Britain

THE GREAT ANGLO-AMERICAN STANDOFF over Palestine policy began in July of 1945 when Harry Truman sent what seemed like a reasonable and even a routine request to Winston Churchill that Great Britain allow some of the Jewish displaced persons living in refugee camps across Western Europe to emigrate to Palestine.[1] When the votes in that summer's British general election were counted, Clement Attlee and the Labour Party had replaced Churchill and the Conservatives, so Truman resent his request to the new prime minister.[2] If anything, the change in government should have meant even less trouble for Truman's request; of the two major British political parties, Labour had long been more pro-Zionist than the Conservatives. As recently as May 1945 Labour had restated its support for a Jewish state in Palestine at its party conference; Zionists everywhere rejoiced at the news that Attlee was moving to 10 Downing Street.

From the American side it all seemed very simple. The end of the fighting in Europe left nearly seven million displaced persons (known at the time as "DPs") in the parts of Europe under control of the western Allies,[3] with many more homeless refugees in the devastated East. The Allied forces, already stretched to the limit managing their own logistics and struggling to feed the civilian populations under their control, were faced with all the problems of feeding and sheltering the refugees in the chaotic aftermath of the war. Among these refugees, the Jewish DPs presented some unique problems. While slave laborers and other Nazi victims uprooted by the war could in most cases be repatriated to their homelands, where many had friends and family waiting for them, the Jewish Holocaust survivors often had no place to go. Their former homes had been taken over by newcomers, their property confiscated, and the communities to which they once belonged no longer existed in any meaningful sense.

The issue exploded in American politics in the summer of 1945. At the behest of Acting Secretary of State Joseph Grew, Truman had asked Earl Harrison, Roosevelt's commissioner of immigration and naturalization, to investigate conditions in the DP camps in postwar Europe.[4] Harrison's report was devastating, especially when it came to the conditions facing the Jews:

> Many Jewish displaced persons . . . are living under guard behind barbed-wire fences . . . including some of the most notorious of the concentration camps . . . had no clothing other than their concentration camp garb.

There was more:

> We appear to be treating the Jews as the Nazis treated them except that we do not exterminate them. They are in concentration camps in large numbers under our military guard instead of S.S. troops. One is led to wonder whether the German people, seeing this, are not supposing that we are following or at least condoning Nazi policy.[5]

Moshe Shertok, the political department director of the Jewish Agency, as the communal organization of Palestinian Jews was known at the time, told the British Colonial Office in the summer of 1945 that 100,000 immigration visas were urgently needed,[6] and after Harrison incorporated the figure in his report, the number was adopted in the United States as the immediate goal around which the Zionists and their supporters would rally. Across the United States, appeals from Jewish groups and their allies met with overwhelming public support when the appeals focused on relieving the desperate plight of Holocaust survivors by allowing them to emigrate to Palestine: "the one country on earth that wanted them," as it was said at the time.[7]

Appeals focused on allowing Jewish refugees into the United States met with a cooler reception. The scale of homelessness and displacement after the war strengthened American support for strict limits on immigration; with the memories of the Depression still strong, Americans feared both the economic competition from large numbers of desperate immigrants and the cultural consequences of a wave of migration that, unless controlled, threatened to dwarf all previous episodes of mass migration into the United States. Polls showed 72 percent of the population opposed returning to the pre-1924 open immigration system, and almost as much opposition to special humanitarian quotas to cope with the postwar chaos, whether the beneficiaries of those quotas would be Jewish or not. Under the circumstances, no policymaker could seriously propose immigration to the United States as a significant element in a resolution of the European refugee problem.[8]

Immigration into Palestine appeared to be the only possible alternative to leaving European Jews in displaced persons camps, traumatized and pauperized by the Holocaust. (The deaths of hundreds of Polish Jews in antisemitic riots as they attempted to return home received wide publicity in the West and solidified the perception that there was no place for large populations of Jewish refugees in postwar Europe.) In 1946 and 1947, poll after poll showed over 75 percent of the American public supported the right of Jews to a homeland in Palestine.[9]

American Jews agreed. By November 1945, according to a Roper poll, 80 percent of American Jews supported Jewish statehood in Palestine. Membership in Zionist organizations skyrocketed; hundreds of thousands of American Jews paid dues to organizations ranging from Hadassah to B'nai B'rith, and about a million American Jews were by this point paying dues to the World Zionist Organization or its affiliates. Respected Jewish political and social organizations that had been anti-Zionist also shifted their stance in light of the Holocaust. Institutionally and individually, the bulk of American Jewry had come around.[10]

What became clear to Harry Truman in the summer of 1945 was that American support for the pro-Zionist Blackstone position was stronger than ever, and that the United States had more power to support it than ever before, but that Great Britain was no longer interested in carrying out its commitments to the Jews under the Balfour Declaration. Truman now had to ask himself what priority he should give to the old American Blackstone policy considering his need for a strong and friendly Great Britain as the Soviet threat gradually began to dominate the international scene.

Truman seized on the target of 100,000 visas, and sought to use it as the basis of a policy that he hoped could keep American liberals, Zionist activists, and the British on board. Given the endorsements from the

Jewish Agency and Harrison, the number had credibility among activists. And because it was finite and limited, Truman hoped that the British could ultimately be induced to accept it. But Truman carefully did not go beyond the bare bones. He did not call for an independent Jewish state, nor did he request the 100,000 visas as the first installment of a much larger number.

The public did not think this simple, humanitarian request would be a problem. Just before departing Moscow to become America's ambassador to the U.K., Averell Harriman told his embassy staff in 1946: "England is so weak she must follow our leadership. She will do anything that we insist [upon] and she won't go out on a limb alone."[11] Exactly, thought the public. So where were the visas for the Jewish DPs? What was the holdup?

Saving the Empire

The holdup was that Palestine had suddenly become critical to British postwar planning. Churchill's attachment to the British Empire was well-known, but as the Labour government that succeeded him studied Britain's position in the world and its economic prospects, Attlee and his foreign minister, Ernest Bevin, came to believe that with India leaving the empire, Britain's position in the Middle East was the key not only to Britain's global standing, but to its prosperity at home.

Much as both Attlee and his party wanted to concentrate on domestic affairs, the international situation required Britain's urgent attention. As one of the leading powers in the Allied coalition, Britain had millions of men under arms all over the world. It was charged with a large occupation zone in defeated Germany, and the British quickly discovered that they would have to feed their former enemies and help them find coal to run their factories and heat their homes in the winter if utter chaos and mass death were to be avoided.[12] Moreover, the British Empire still included one fourth of the world's surface and population. Britain was responsible for governing increasingly restive populations across Africa, Asia, and the Middle East. The Japanese had destroyed European colonial power across East and Southeast Asia; Britain found itself trying not only to reestablish order in Japanese-occupied British territories, but also to assist the Dutch and the French.

Behind all this loomed an immense economic problem. Great Britain for decades had depended on its overseas investments to provide the "invisible earnings" that underpinned the British standard of living. Virtually all of these had been sacrificed to win the war. International reserves that had taken three hundred years to accumulate were devoured in the firestorm of the six-year struggle against Nazi Germany. British industry had suffered severely from German bombing. Millions of tons of shipping had been sunk by U-boats. Meanwhile, its major trading partners in Europe were even worse off than Britain was. France and the Low Countries had been looted and occupied by the Nazis. Hundreds of thousands of their best workers had conscripted into forced labor in the Reich. People were starving in what, before 1939, had been among the most prosperous countries in the world.

British planners could see only one way out. Control over the oil resources of the Middle East would provide the United Kingdom with a source of energy that didn't have to be paid for in scarce dollars, and would underwrite British leadership in Europe and the wider world while shoring up the British standard of living. According to the minutes of the cabinet-level Defense Committee, Bevin saw that position as essential: "Without the Middle East and its oil and other potential resources, he saw no hope of our being able to achieve the standard of life at which we were aiming in Great Britain."[13]

Given the new power of nationalist movements in the Arab world as elsewhere, the British understood that they could not hope to control the Middle East in the old imperial way. British power would have to be exercised through relations with friendly Arab governments. The Hashemite kings of Jordan and Iraq, the sheikhs and emirs of the Gulf, and King Farouk of Egypt were willing to work with the British, and it was through good relations with these royals (plus the Shah of Iran) that the British hoped to maintain their position in a changing region.

These pro-British regimes were often weak and vulnerable to public opinion. The British feared that Arab anger over an emerging Jewish state in Palestine would endanger the network of royals and "moderate" politicians who backed continued relations with the U.K. For British policymakers, heartrending as the plight of Jewish displaced persons in the rubble of postwar Europe was, substantial Jewish immigration into Palestine meant the end of Britain's ability to manage its relationships with the Arabs, and the end of Britain's great power status. As the Palestine committee of the Labour government said in its report in September of 1945:

> The Middle East is a region of vital consequence for Britain and the British Empire. It forms the point in the system of communications, by land sea and air which links Britain with India, Australia and the Far East; it is also the Empire's main reservoir of mineral oil. . . . Protection of our vital interests depends, therefore, upon the collaboration which we can obtain from these independent states. . . . Unfortunately the future of Palestine bulks large in all Arab eyes. . . . To enforce any such policy [to which they object] and especially one which lays us open to a charge of breach of faith, is bound seriously to undermine our position and may well lead not only to widespread disturbances . . . but to the withdrawal of cooperation on which our Imperial interests so largely depend.[14]

The relationship with the Arab world was only one of Britain's problems in the Middle East. The Soviet Union clearly had designs on the region, too. The Soviets pressed territorial claims against Turkey, Soviet troops occupied much of northern Iran, and, with the victorious Red Army entrenched across the Balkans, Soviet-aligned communists in Greece posed a serious threat to the ineffective and corrupt government. If Greece fell to the communists, something that seemed more likely than not to many observers, Turkey would be outflanked and would be unable to resist Soviet pressure. With northern Iran, Turkey, and Greece in the Soviet orbit, Britain would be hard put to defend its positions farther south.

Poor and exhausted as Britain was after the war, it committed eighty thousand troops and substantial financial aid to Greece, subsidized Turkey, and warily engaged the Soviet Union over the future of Iran, all in pursuit of this last-ditch imperial strategy.[15] For Attlee's government, these were difficult decisions to make. Not only were the Soviets popular with much of the party's rank and file, but the burden of military spending and foreign aid on an austerity-weary population fell most heavily on Labour voters. The Greek government (corrupt, pro-monarchy, dictatorial, ineffective, and brutal) was deeply unpopular with the left wing of the Labour Party. Yet despite the many misgivings and concerns about costs, the British cabinet believed that living up to Britain's responsibilities in the region was both necessary and right.

THE GREAT COMMITTEE

With American public opinion believing that 100,000 visas for Jewish DPs was a simple and reasonable humanitarian ask, and the British government convinced that admitting that many Jewish immigrants into Palestine would set off a chain of events that could ultimately destroy the most important remaining support of British power, the two governments were headed for a collision that neither Truman nor Attlee wanted. The real question, made sharper by the desperation of the Jewish DPs in Europe, was how to balance the American commitment to the Blackstone approach with its alliance with Britain.

FDR had been the first president to face this dilemma. As you will remember, when Britain responded to the Arab Revolt of 1936–39 by limiting Jewish immigration even as Hitler's attacks on Jews intensified, FDR's policy reflected his assessment that it was more important for the United States to support Britain's position in the Mediterranean than to make a big issue over the immigration restrictions. During the war, it seemed even more obvious that the United States needed to support Britain even if that meant putting Jewish hopes for Palestine on hold. Truman, coming to the Oval Office as the war ground to a close, had to develop a new approach. With the Axis defeated, and the United States emerging from the war a much more powerful state than Great Britain, what priority should the Blackstone approach take in postwar American policy? Should Truman continue to follow Roosevelt, subordinating Palestine to the strategic imperatives of the U.S.-British relationship, or had the time now come when the United States should put its concerns over Palestine front and center in its bilateral relationship with Great Britain?

The State Department and the defense establishment by and large thought that the British relationship should continue to take priority over the Palestine question. From their point of view, the problems of the Jews might be serious, but the confrontation with the Soviet Union, like the earlier confrontation with the Axis, required these concerns to be set aside. The tail should not wag the dog. Truman should do what Roosevelt had done and continue to subordinate his concerns about the

Jewish national home to a global American strategy and its necessary corollary, the British alliance.

Truman himself was torn. Attlee for his part did not want a confrontation with Washington. He could not yield on the visa question without wrecking Britain's only strategy for postwar recovery and independence, but perhaps there was a way to offer the Americans a bargain that both sides could live with. Admitting 100,000 Jews to Palestine would cause problems in Palestine and elsewhere in the Middle East. If resettling the Jews was so important to them, perhaps the Americans would absorb the costs those visas would entail? If additional troops were needed to keep the peace, would the Americans contribute to the peacekeeping force? If the Americans did not want to send troops, would they at least reimburse Britain for the costs that carrying out this American priority would impose on Britain's overstretched defense budget? Or perhaps, once the Americans fully understood how expensive and difficult it would be to resettle Jews in Palestine they would agree with the British that some other solution for the problem of Jewish DPs in Europe needed to be found.

Truman was unlikely to follow Attlee far down this road. In 1945–46 Americans wanted a Jewish homeland in Palestine, but they wanted no part of creating it through military force. Money, especially for the resettlement of refugees, was possible, but liberals and isolationists were utterly opposed to the kind of economic aid that would allow Britain to maintain its Middle East empire on American money. Both the American left and the American right believed Britain had snookered gullible American diplomats into bankrolling its Middle East schemes in the 1920s, and the American people were not going to be fooled twice.

Yet Truman needed British help. Britain was in physical control of Palestine. Unless the United States intended to land the immigrants by force, Britain would have to agree to issue the visas. If Truman was going to get the visas that Americans wanted, he was going to have to negotiate with the U.K.

The gap between London and Washington was wide and deep. At the time of Earl Harrison's visit, Jewish DPs in Europe were being treated on a "national" basis; that is, they were treated like non-Jewish citizens of their countries of origin. Displaced Polish Jews counted as Poles, Bulgarian Jews as Bulgarians, and so on. Harrison took a very American exception to an approach that seemed both natural and right to the British, recommending in his report that "the first and plainest need of these people is a recognition of their actual status and by this I mean their status as Jews. . . . Refusal to recognize the Jews as such has the effect, in this situation, of closing one's eyes to their former and more barbaric persecution."[16]

Not singling out the Jews for special treatment was exactly the way the British believed that the situation ought to be handled. As the Foreign Office put it, "We insistently deny that it is right to segregate persons of Jewish race as such. . . . It has been a cardinal policy hitherto that we regard the nationality factor as the determining one as regards people of Jewish race just as in the case of other racial or religious groups."

For the British, to treat Jewish DPs first and foremost as Jews was to follow Hitler's policy of exclusion. Hitler had denied that Jews could be true Germans, true Frenchmen, true Danes. The British genuinely believed that the best thing to do for the Jews was to reintegrate them into their national societies as quickly as possible. That meant no special treatment in DP camps and it certainly meant no special visas for Palestine. One fought antisemitism by treating Jews like everybody else.

In any case, the British responded to Truman's visa request not with a negative but with a counterproposal that they hoped would avoid an open break with the Americans over Palestine while entangling Washington in an educational discussion that would explain to the Americans why their visa idea was such a bad one. A joint committee would be established, composed of six American and six British members. The committee would study the condition of Jewish DPs in Europe, as well as examine conditions on the ground in Palestine. It would then issue a report with recommendations about what should be done. Truman accepted the proposal, and on November 13, 1945, Ernest Bevin announced the formation of the Anglo-American Committee of Inquiry.

The committee idea was not popular in the United States, and anti-British liberals joined Zionists in denouncing it. Both houses of Congress passed resolutions urging Truman to use America's leverage to permit the free entry of Jews into Palestine.[17] Soon after the joint commission was announced, Truman received a worrying letter from Eleanor Roosevelt:

I am very much distressed that Great Britain has made us take a share in another investigation of the few Jews remaining in Europe. . . .

Great Britain is always anxious to have someone pull her chestnuts out of the fire, and though I am very fond of the British individually and like a great many of them, I object very much to being used by them.[18]

In the letter, Roosevelt explained that she was not a Zionist, and that she well understood the risks involved in sending the Jews to Palestine, given Arab opposition. Nevertheless, in a way that Truman could not ignore, she was indicating an interest in the Palestine issue that would only strengthen as time went on. In February of 1946, she visited Germany (having made a "suggestion" to the army that it invite her over) and saw for herself the misery of the Holocaust survivors and their longing for Palestine. From this point on, the plight of displaced Jews in Europe became one of her central concerns and her nationally syndicated newspaper column would return to it again and again.

The Anglo-American Committee of Inquiry began its work in Washington in early January of 1946 before going on to meetings in London and Palestine. Bevin announced that Britain would implement any unanimous recommendations that the committee made.[19] Truman noted these promises hopefully; perhaps the committee would offer him an easier path forward.

Lend-Lease and Loan Agreements

If the visa issue had been the only problem in Anglo-American relations in the fall of 1945, the two sides might well have found some way to coordinate their approaches to the desperate situation of the Jewish DPs. But Palestine was just one of the issues dividing the two wartime allies, and neither Truman nor Attlee could isolate this issue from the tensions affecting the rest of the bilateral relationship. In the chaotic postwar atmosphere, the international situation was rapidly changing from week to week and month to month, and the assessments in Washington and London of the value of their alliance and the steps necessary to preserve it were changing as well. In 1945, both British and American policymakers significantly underestimated the damage that the war had inflicted on Britain's economic potential and on the health of the empire. In both London and Washington (to say nothing of Paris and Moscow) policymakers thought that Britain was likely to recover fairly quickly from the war and that, while it was unlikely to regain its prewar standing as the lead actor in world politics and the center of gravity of the global economy, it would remain a great power capable of independent action to advance its own interests around the world. Between 1945 and 1948, Washington policymakers were repeatedly changing their basic assessment of the global situation: the danger from the Soviet Union appeared to be steadily increasing, the prospects for economic and political recovery in Western Europe were steadily diminishing, and the chances that Britain would return to a stature approximating its prewar level of international power were steadily shrinking. By 1948 Washington had largely accepted that it needed Britain much more than originally believed, and that Britain was more fragile and in need of greater support if it was to play the role in Europe and the wider world that American interests required.

In 1945, though, all the best people expected Britain to recover from the war. Britain's five largest banks reported their most profitable year in history in 1945, and *The New York Times* reported that their chairmen found "grounds for modified optimism about the future of their institutions as well as of the country in general."[20] They weren't alone; virtually everyone in the early postwar years underestimated the damage the war had done to Britain's capacity to maintain its international system, and observers in Britain and beyond would continually make rosy predictions about how fast and how strong its recovery would be. That optimism led both American and British policymakers into taking steps that, in hindsight, did not look particularly wise.

In the United States, the overestimation of British power strengthened both liberal and conservative opponents of a strong U.S.-British alliance. Liberals thought that a resurgent Great Britain would quickly move to solidify its global empire, where possible using American aid to rebuild its imperial position, and that Britain would seek to draw the U.S. into a reactionary imperialist alliance that would both undermine the U.N. and alienate the Soviet Union. Britain, many liberals believed, wanted a Cold War between the USSR and the U.S. because that would drive the United States into Britain's arms. Many conservatives believed that British power ensured that the USSR could not really threaten American interests. Let London rebuild Europe and worry about containing the Soviet Union in pursuit of its devious imperialistic schemes. The United States could focus on the Western Hemisphere and avoid all the risks and costs associated with global power politics and world order building. Conservative Republicans agreed with liberals that Britain would, however, do everything possible to ensnare the U.S. into supporting its imperial ambitions; they were at this stage as adamantly opposed to postwar U.S. support for Britain as the liberals were.

British leaders, while more aware of and therefore more concerned about the weak economic foundations of British power after the war than their American counterparts, also underestimated the radical decline in British power and prestige still to come. Team Attlee believed that postwar Britain could pursue an active global foreign policy even as it undertook a wholesale transformation of the British economy. Indeed, Attlee and Bevin believed that the two goals were related: that it was only by acting vigorously to uphold the empire that Britain could gain the economic breathing space it required to establish a generous welfare state, nationalize key industries, and institute free health care while expanding educational and social opportunities for the working class. This picture was attractive enough to command widespread support in the U.K. It was largely unworkable in the real world.

The Attlee government was a remarkable one. The British Labour Party had led coalition cabinets before World War II and served in the national unity government during it, but the landslide victory of July 1945 gave Labour its first outright majority in history. The Labour Party of 1945 was much more interested in domestic policy than in foreign affairs. Its ambitious program included the establishment of a national health service, a major expansion of the welfare state, and the nationalization of 20 percent of the economy, including railroads, the coal and steel industries, civil aviation, and the Bank of England. Many of the party's members belonged to the hard left, were deeply suspicious of the United States, and believed that postwar relations with "Uncle Joe" Stalin were the key to European reconstruction and the future of world peace.

The economic problems at home for Britain could not be solved without the reestablishment of some kind of economic normality, but for the first time since the eighteenth century, the British were not the masters of their economic fate. Without support from the United States, Great Britain could scarcely stave off starvation and run its factories, much less achieve the prosperity that Attlee and his colleagues sought to achieve for the long-suffering British working class.

American support proved unexpectedly hard to get. In 1945, American public opinion had not yet realized that one of the consequences of World War II would be that the United States would have to replace Great Britain as the power most responsible for the global economic and security systems. That realization would gradually dawn as Stalin became more threatening and the world situation became more dire in the eighteen months after the war ended, but it wasn't until the spring of 1947 that the real dimensions of America's postwar challenges began to be felt. Until that time, the gap in perceptions between British and American policymakers produced a series of conflicts and controversies that left a lasting bitterness in Britain and contributed to the sharpness of U.S.-U.K. disagreements over Palestine.

The early postwar period was a grim era in transatlantic relations. The British were horrified by a series of American decisions during and after the war. Far from shoring Britain up as a counterweight to the Soviet Union, the American negotiators working on the postwar economic order systematically sought to force Britain to abandon the idea of imperial preference, a way of using tariffs to strengthen the economic ties between different parts of the empire. In 1945 and 1946 the Americans ended Lend-Lease assistance to Britain much more rapidly than the British expected, took a hard line in negotiations for a postwar loan, and swept aside what the British thought was an ironclad agreement over postwar nuclear cooperation.[21] These decisions fed the anti-American, anticapitalist current of opinion in the Labour Party and greatly exacerbated Britain's postwar economic difficulties. Even normally pro-American opinion was dismayed. *The Economist* expressed the general feeling about American policy in December 1945 in a comment on American demands that a postwar loan carry an interest rate for fifty years: "It is aggravating to find that our reward for losing a quarter of our national wealth in the common cause is to pay tribute for half a century to those [the Americans] who have been enriched by the war. . . . Beggars cannot be choosers. But they can by long tradition put a curse on the ambitions of the rich."[22]

The members of the Labour government saw themselves as good guys committed to dismantling the Raj in India and transforming the empire into a commonwealth. The tradition of Liberal imperialism, in which Britain saw itself as a kind of trustee protecting peoples around the world who were unable to defend themselves from more predatory powers and helping them to develop the economic and political foundations of modernity under British auspices, was still strong. As the Labour government saw it, Britain would provide an umbrella of security protection and good governance while laying the foundation for an ultimate transition to independence within the British Commonwealth. Bevin hoped that somehow the British could bolster their Middle East position by siding with "peasants not pashas" and believed that the empire could be a force for good.[23] Additionally, the British were hurt and angered by what they saw as ingratitude. The United States sat out the war between 1939 and 1941 while the British gave everything they had to fight Hitler, saving the world from the Nazi menace at the cost of their economy. Britain, they felt, deserved American sympathy and support thanks to sacrifices made.

London consistently failed to grasp the strength of anti-British feelings in the United States. Americans remembered the aftermath of World War I, when the British pled poverty with respect to their war debts to the United States—even as they spent lavishly on maintaining British rule around the world, and extended their empire in the Middle East. The American consensus of the 1930s, unchanged by the war years, held that devious and unscrupulous British diplomats and bankers exploited American goodwill and naïveté after World War I. This view was particularly strongly held in Congress, and Congress was determined not to be fooled again.

Another problem was that the Labour government program was aggressively socialist, far to the left of the American New Deal. Money is fungible; it looked to many in the United States as if the Labour government would use American aid money to nationalize key industries and to carry out other policies that, antisocialist Americans felt, were likely to retard Britain's economic recovery rather than to help it. Britain had many enemies and few friends in postwar Washington. Liberals despised the British Empire and wanted it destroyed. Conservatives not only loathed the empire, they hated British socialism; they wanted nothing to do with paying the bills for either project.

Ironically, the abrupt aid cutoff, the small size of the loan, and the tough conditions attached to it ultimately had more impact on events in Palestine than any of Truman's decisions about Palestine itself. The British economic crises in 1946 and early 1947, and the grinding impact of postwar austerity on Labour and national morale, all contributed to Britain's decision to turn the Palestine problem over to the United Nations in February 1947. America's harsh financial treatment of Britain after the war meant that Britain could not long bear the high costs of a sustained effort to hold Palestine against the will of its Jewish inhabitants. Had Britain gained more American aid in 1945 and 1946 it would have been better placed to withstand American pressure in 1947 and 1948.

The organized American Jewish community was largely absent from the debate over financial aid to Britain after the war. When Emanuel Celler of New York attempted to block the bill authorizing the British loan, he was soundly defeated.[24] The American decisions that had the most impact on British policy in Palestine would have been exactly what they were if the organized pro-Zionist lobbies had not existed.

One Committee, Two Committees

The Anglo-American Committee produced its report in April 1946. To the chagrin of the British government, and to Truman's great relief, the commission unanimously recommended the immediate settlement of 100,000 Jewish displaced persons in Palestine, and an end to British restrictions on land sales to Jews. Less hopefully from the Zionist point of view, the commission also came out against partition of the territory into two independent states, supported a long-term British role in the territory, and called for the dissolution of armed groups in Palestine, including the Jewish defense forces. For Truman, this looked like vindication. He was giving the Jews and the liberals what they wanted most, the 100,000 visas, but he was doing it without incurring U.S. responsibilities in Palestine and without breaking with Britain. Given the British commitment to accepting unanimous recommendations, Truman hoped for a harmonious end to an unwanted dispute.[25]

He was quickly disillusioned. The Zionists and the British both balked at key aspects of the recommendations. The Zionists could only be induced to offer grudging support of the report by a public endorsement from Truman of the elements in the report that they liked. The British flat out refused to implement the visa recommendations without implementation of the other provisions, including the disarmament of the Jews.[26] Given the determined opposition of the Palestinian Jews to that proposal, enforcing the full report was a recipe for conflict—and the British would expect American support. To commit American troops to

Palestine in order to maintain order while Britain forcibly disarmed the Jewish defense forces was far beyond anything an American president could accept; there was no significant support in either the American government or the population for steps of this kind.

As waves of criticism broke over Truman's head in the American press, the British proposed another committee. The second would review the first set of recommendations and develop plans for their implementation. From London's point of view, this was a reasonable request. Introducing 100,000 Jews into Palestine would set off massive waves of Arab unrest, threatening violence on the scale of the 1936–39 Arab Revolt. (Indeed, the policy changes the commission recommended amounted to a withdrawal of the concessions the Arabs had won in 1939.) The British still wanted what they had wanted from the beginning: either that the United States would allow Britain to manage the Palestine question in its own way and stop nattering on about visas, or that it would provide the military and financial assistance necessary to cover the costs of the policies the Americans preferred. That the United States should choose the policy leaving Britain to bear the economic, military, and political costs of carrying it out did not appeal to anybody in British politics.

The report did nothing to calm the situation on the ground in Palestine. On the contrary. David Ben-Gurion, the political leader of the Palestinian Jews, had authorized attacks on British forces as early as October 1945. On April 25, 1946, Jewish fighters killed seven British soldiers in Tel Aviv. The violence escalated further in June, as Jewish militias blew up ten of the eleven bridges connecting British Palestine to neighboring territories in a show of force. The British struck back, seeking to capture and disarm Jewish fighters. Arrests and acts of terror and reprisal continued to mount.[27] Meanwhile, an effective campaign of illegal immigration into Palestine (with help from many of Stalin's satellites in Eastern Europe who benefited financially from allowing exit and transit rights to Jews in exchange for healthy fees) was contributing to the tensions with the Arabs and would ultimately lead the British into a highly visible and, at times, damaging and embarrassing campaign to force desperate, starving refugees to camps in Cyprus and, when those were filled, back to the European camps.

As the British reneged on their commitment to accept unanimous resolutions and called for more study and more delay, American opinion seethed. Eleanor Roosevelt shared her unhappiness with the public. "There was really no need for a commission of inquiry, but we went along with Great Britain," she wrote in her widely read newspaper column. She underlined the humanitarian case for allowing 100,000 displaced persons to go to Palestine, and rejected Britain's request for American military help in managing the consequences with an airy wave of her hand: "But surely our allied Chiefs of Staff could work out some form of military defense for Palestine which would not mean an increase in manpower."[28]

Through the storms, Truman stuck to his plan to work toward a common Anglo-American approach. Despite the fury of his liberal and Zionist critics at the delay, his options were limited. Tension with Britain over conflicting American and British perceptions and priorities over Palestine was unavoidable, but Truman saw nothing to gain in provoking a full-fledged crisis on the issue. And it is hard to see just how Truman could have forced the U.K. to shift its immigration policy without offering the kind of military and political support that American opinion would reject. Eleanor Roosevelt could gesture vaguely in the direction of miraculous military strategies that would solve Britain's problems without requiring anything other than advice from the United States, but such magical thinking was of no help to Truman.

The second committee was therefore established to study how to implement the recommendations of the first, much to the disgust of American Zionists and Anglo-skeptic liberals. Even this committee was difficult to get under way. Attlee sent Truman a list of forty-three subjects the British wished the new commission to review. Truman responded with his first concrete offer of financial aid in transporting and resettling displaced persons to Palestine, stressing again his need to get the resettlement process started as quickly as possible. Attlee responded by saying that the British could not resettle any refugees until all the unresolved issues had been debated and examined. By now it was June, and the British were about to make Truman's life more difficult still.

On June 12, 1946, Ernest Bevin, who was under continual pressure from the left wing of his own Labour Party for a policy many believed was cravenly pro-American, made a speech at the Labour Party conference that ignited a firestorm in the United States, solidifying liberal opposition to collaboration with the U.K. over Palestine and much else. "There has been the agitation in the United States, and particularly in

New York, for 100,000 Jews to be put into Palestine. I hope I will not be misunderstood in America if I say that this was proposed with the purest of motives. They did not want too many Jews in New York."[29]

Historically speaking, of course, Bevin was not entirely wrong. The American WASP establishment had seen Jewish immigration into Palestine as an alternative to Jewish immigration into the United States since the time of the Blackstone Memorial, and more than a few Christian advocates of the Jewish homeland had made the connection explicit. Nevertheless, in 1946 it was both tactless and wrong to make this charge. Those on the battle lines for Jewish immigration to Palestine in 1946 were liberal humanitarians who, like Eleanor Roosevelt, also favored admitting more refugees to the United States and Jewish activists who were insulted and enraged by the implication that they were serving an antisemitic agenda. The press uproar that followed demonized Bevin as a cynical and imperialistic antisemite; on his next visit to New York the dockworkers' union refused to unload his luggage from the ship.[30] Bevin's ill-chosen remarks combined with Britain's violation of its pledge to accept the unanimous recommendations of the Anglo-American Committee to push American liberal and middle-class opinion away from Britain and toward the increasingly impatient and radicalized Zionist leadership.

Truman continued to push Attlee for the 100,000 visas, tasking Ambassador Averell Harriman with ironing out the practical details, including costs, in talks with British experts. Attlee, in turn, continued to press Truman for military assistance, asking for a member of the Joint Chiefs to meet with the British military to examine the strategic and military implications of the move and its ramifications throughout the Middle East. This was a nonstarter with both Truman and the U.S. military.[31]

Nevertheless, Truman still needed the visas, and he had no good alternative to negotiations with Britain if he was going to get them. He continued to support the joint commission approach, and the new committee of experts issued its report at the end of July. The Morrison-Grady Report, named for the senior British and American officials involved in the meetings, was, from the Zionist perspective, a step back from the Anglo-American Committee report in the spring. The new report by this second commission called for the creation of Jewish, Arab, and international zones in Palestine under British rule, with the Jews receiving only 17 percent of the land. Each community would control its own internal affairs, but Britain would control defense, internal security, and foreign affairs—and the British governor would have veto power over legislation in both Jewish and Arab sectors for five years. One hundred thousand Jews could immigrate in the first year, but the British authority would set immigration limits for subsequent years.[32]

Truman wanted to accept the offer as a basis for American policy, still seeing the 100,000 visas as the key deliverable which would meet his own humanitarian priorities. Since Truman understood that the British could not be forced to produce 100,000 or even 100 visas against their will, his acceptance of the Morrison-Grady recommendations came from what he saw as a realistic appraisal of the balance of forces. He had to persuade the British to move, and since he was unable to give them the military support they named as their price, he had to do what he could to satisfy them on other grounds.

The Morrison-Grady Report exploded in Truman's face. Zionists like the rabbis Abba Hillel Silver and Stephen Wise rejected it out of hand. Liberal senators and congressmen denounced it on the floor of Congress. Even conservative Republicans like Robert Taft attacked the plan as a sellout to the British. Truman kept telling anyone who would listen that "the British control Palestine and there is no way of getting one hundred thousand Jews in there unless they want them in," but no one seemed to be impressed with this logic. In a cabinet meeting devoted to the question of the American response to Morrison-Grady, Truman faced the usual conflicting pressures. Henry Wallace (still, uneasily, secretary of commerce) attacked the plan strongly; from Europe, Secretary of State James Byrnes (who also had presidential ambitions) advised against accepting the proposal. Reluctantly, Truman responded to Attlee that he could not accept the plan.[33]

Meanwhile, the situation in Palestine continued to deteriorate. Violence increased during the summer. In July, bombs planted in the King David Hotel, the headquarters of British administration in Jerusalem, by the Irgun killed ninety-one people, among them Arab, British, and Jewish officials.[34]

Even more ominously from Truman's point of view, the figure of 100,000 refugees came to look increasingly unrealistic. As more Jewish refugees filtered across Europe into the western zone, the number of refugees mounted, their organizations became more effective, and their militancy and their determination grew. A quarter million or more Jewish refugees were now huddled in miserable camps, fed and housed at American expense, and desperate to reach Palestine. The liberal American press focused with growing intensity on the problems of the Jews and the violence in Palestine. Truman was seen as either heartless or incompetent. The left wing of the press and of the Democratic Party continued to believe that the United States confronted the choice between a "reactionary alliance" with imperialist Britain or a "progressive alliance" with Stalin. As Wallace declared in his Madison Square Garden speech that September,

> Certainly we like the British people as individuals. But to make Britain the key to our foreign policy would be, in my opinion, the height of folly. We must not let the reactionary leadership of the Republican party force us into that position. We must not let British balance-of-power manipulations determine whether and when the United States gets into war. . . . We are reckoning with a force which cannot be handled successfully by a "Get tough with Russia" policy. "Getting tough" never bought anything real and lasting—whether for schoolyard bullies or businessmen or world powers. The tougher we get, the tougher the Russians will get. . . . And I believe that we can get cooperation once Russia understands that our primary objective is neither saving the British Empire nor purchasing oil in the Near East with the lives of American soldiers.[35]

Eleanor Roosevelt was becoming more anti-British than ever. In a letter intended for Bevin and Attlee, she wrote in her gentle but implacably unrelenting way that

> I can not bear to think of the Jews of Europe who have spent so many years in concentration camps, behind wire again on Cyprus [where the British were interning illegal Jewish immigrants to Palestine]. Somehow it seems to me that the 100,000 Jews should be let into Palestine and that some real agreement should be reached with the Arabs. Willy-nilly, the feeling grows here that it is [not] just justice which Great Britain is looking for where the Arabs are concerned, but it is that she wishes the friendship in order to get more favorable consideration where oil concessions are concerned.[36]

The camps for refugees, established by the Allies following the war and situated in Germany, Austria, and Italy, offered the sparest of living conditions. Crowded barracks afforded little privacy and the daily diet of bread and soup was hardly appetizing. Eleanor Roosevelt had visited one of the Jewish camps and wrote movingly of a young boy: "He sang for me—a song of his people—a song of freedom. Your heart cried out that there was no freedom—and where was hope, without which human beings cannot live?"[37]

In the fall of 1946, Truman's unpopularity was dragging his party down toward defeat in the midterms. A war-weary public viewed the deteriorating world situation with alarm. The left attacked Truman's tough stance against the Soviets. The right accused the administration of harboring communists and retreating in the face of the communist threat. The Palestine issue brought nothing but frustration, and the American Jewish community, led at this time by the pro–Robert Taft Republican activist Rabbi Silver, attacked the administration at every turn.

"Jesus Christ couldn't please them [the Jews] when he was on earth," said Truman at the end of a particularly frustrating cabinet meeting. "So could anyone expect that I could have any luck?"[38]

GROUND ZERO

While committees considered and diplomats dithered, the future of Palestine was being shaped on the ground as the Jewish inhabitants of Palestine drove steadily toward their longtime goal of an independent state. The British had conquered Palestine from the Ottoman Empire in 1917. Since then a flood of Jewish immigrants had built a proto-state. Describing their program as "another acre, another goat," the Zionists slowly constructed a network of farms, factories, schools, and community institutions as their population grew. By 1945 the Jewish community, with a population of about 650,000, had military forces like the Haganah, the administrative backbone of a civil government, a network of educational and cultural institutions, a communal economy that was integrated and mediated through an effective set of governing institutions and banks, and an embryonic diplomatic service that was capable of representing their interests in the international arena. Thousands of Palestinian Jews had served with the British Army during World War II, gaining military training and experience. The Jewish population of Palestine was highly educated with many scientific and technical specialists, enabling the community, among other things, to develop a sophisticated arms industry from dual-purpose technology and machine tools purchased abroad. At the end of World War II, the Jewish community of Palestine had a health care system, an educational system, local governments, and a range of economic and political institutions that were ready to function as parts of an independent state.[39]

The horrors of the Holocaust served, in the minds of Palestinian Jews above all, to prove that Zionism was the only possible path for the survival of the Jewish people. The Holocaust had not been the work of the Germans alone. In almost every country in occupied Europe, the Nazis had found willing helpers. The Jews had also observed the utter failure of any non-Jewish power to take effective steps to save European Jews from the oncoming disaster. Meanwhile, the poison of Nazi-style anti-semitism had firmly established itself in the Middle East during the war; the leader of the Palestinian Arabs spent the war in German-occupied Europe, among other things recruiting European Muslims to fight for the Third Reich. While the Jews of Palestine were bitterly divided into quarreling parties and political movements, as a people they were united in the belief that they were fighting for their survival. The Jewish people could not survive without a state to protect them and to which they could immigrate when threatened, they believed. Palestine was the only possible place where such a state could arise. The Jews of Palestine approached what they saw as an inevitable showdown with the Arabs in a spirit of careful, thorough, and even ruthless preparation, believing that the survival of their people was at stake.

The Arabs of Palestine were poorly prepared for the coming confrontation. Before 1917 they lived under Ottoman administration, and that empire had provided the basics of government with little input from locals beyond the village and municipal levels. After 1917, except for religious organizations, the British provided the governing structures within which most Arabs lived. The gradual dismantling of the British administrative structure after Britain decided to withdraw would leave the Arabs scrambling to improvise the institutions needed for communal governance beyond the local level. They had taken only limited steps toward developing armed forces of their own, in part because they believed that they could count on the British or, if Britain failed, the nearby Arab powers to protect them.

Although many outside observers—misled both by a fundamentally orientalist and romanticized belief in the warlike reputation of the Arab peoples and an equally prejudiced view that discounted the martial talents of the Jewish people—failed to see it, the Palestinian Jews were coming to believe that, despite their numerical disadvantages, their organizational and technological advantages over the Palestinian Arabs would, under the right circumstances, give them a decisive edge in any military contest between the two peoples. The belief in their military capability stiffened the position of Jewish negotiators with their British counterparts. If the issue was left to the relative strengths of the two local communities in British Palestine, the Jews hoped to impose a solution on the Arabs.

Given the willingness of the Palestinian Jews to stake their fate on war, those who hoped to prevent a conflict needed to offer diplomatic solutions that the Jewish community found attractive. This was a road down which the Arabs did not wish to travel. The Palestinian Arabs were not only confident in their own military strength and that of their fellow Arabs, they believed that the tide of history was moving in their direction. National independence movements were succeeding all over the world. Arab countries like Egypt and Iraq were tearing up old treaties that gave Britain a dominant role. The Palestinians hoped and expected that the British would recognize the Arab majority of Palestine as the legitimate rulers of the country and turn the country over to them. They rejected any and all proposals for confederations, federal structures, Swiss-style cantonal arrangements, and so on—much less the option of partition into two independent states.

Meanwhile, the flashpoint in any negotiation between Arabs and Jews would come over immigration. In July 1946, Ben-Gurion proposed Jewish and Arab entities, each with full control over immigration and settlement policy, but that was as far as the Jewish leadership would or could go. Under duress, Palestinian Jews might temporarily accept a solution short of full independence, but only if they could control immigration into the Jewish parts of any kind of binational confederation.[40] There was simply no way that the Jewish leadership in Palestine could accept a political solution that did not allow the hundreds of thousands of desperate, homeless Holocaust survivors into Palestine. They would choose war, even war at long odds, over immigration restriction; an abandonment of the desperate and stateless Jewish survivors of the Holocaust would be such a fundamental betrayal of Zionist values that it would destroy the cohesion and spirit of the Palestinian Jews.

But immigration was also a do-or-die issue for the Arabs. Given the hundreds of thousands of desperate Jews in Europe (among whom young men of military age were disproportionately represented, as young adults had been better able to survive the rigors of concentration camps and war than children and the old), unrestricted Jewish immigration into Palestine would rapidly change the demographic balance and create an even greater advantage for the Jews. To the Arabs, more Jewish immigration seemed certain to end in the establishment of a Jewish state as the Jewish population grew.

In any case, the Palestinian Arabs, already enraged at the massive Jewish immigration, an influx to which no assembly of Palestinian Arabs had ever consented and that had reshaped much of their country, were utterly opposed to any additional Jewish immigration and would consider no solution that allowed it. The Jews, reeling from the horrors of the Holocaust, burning with the determination to create a secure homeland to prevent any future slaughter, and anguished over the fate of the displaced Jews of Europe, were ready to fight rather than to give up the right of Jewish immigration. The Arabs were determined to fight rather than allow it. Outside negotiators tried to square this circle right up through the outbreak of the Israeli War of Independence, but no formula satisfactory to both sides could be found.

Many, even most, observers missed this at the time, but with hindsight we can see that by 1947 the Jews of Palestine had created an embryonic state whose emergence could only be prevented by the credible threat and perhaps the deployment of clearly superior force by outside powers. There were two possibilities for such a force: it could consist of some combination of Palestinian and other Arab armies, or it could be the army of some outside power. The Americans were unwilling to commit forces to Palestine under any circumstances, and certainly not to suppress the Jews. The Soviets did not have the logistical wherewithal to intervene at this distance from their frontiers, and Soviet intervention in the Middle East would have called forth strong resistance from both the U.S. and the U.K. as the Cold War took shape. The Palestinian Arab cause, then, depended on engaging the British to resist Jewish independence, and, as a backup, on an intervention by neighboring Arab states if the British Army was defeated or went home.

For the Jews, the problem was the opposite. If the British were unwilling to help the Jews gain independence, then the Jews would have to drive the British away, defeat the local Palestinian Arabs, and either prevent or defeat a subsequent intervention by the Arabs. The Palestinian Jews could not defeat the British by force of arms, but they hoped that a combination of military and political measures could persuade the British to withdraw. The Jews of Palestine pursued a two-track approach to neutralize Great Britain: diplomatic efforts sought a compromise with the British that would induce them to withdraw while a guerrilla campaign (the British called it terrorism, not without reason) would raise the price of keeping British forces in Palestine.

Starting in the fall of 1945, military, and in some cases terrorist, resistance by Palestinian Jews to the British presence had begun to impose serious costs on a war-weary U.K. Ultimately, 100,000 British troops would be pinned down in an ugly conflict that was visibly alienating what friends the British had left in the American press. A year after V-E Day, life was still very far from normal in a Britain that continued to ration food and basic consumer goods. One diplomatic effort after another to bring the Arabs and Jews to the peace table foundered on the hopeless issue of migration. The status quo did not look sustainable. In Washington, London, and in Palestine attention began to turn to something that once seemed unthinkable: what should happen in Palestine if the British decided to leave?

Given the unbridgeable gaps between Arab and Jewish demands, beginning in the summer of 1946, the British, the Americans, and the Jews all began to look hard at partitioning the territory into two states. The Arabs continued to reject the concept, insisting on immediate independence for a one-state solution in which the Arabs would rule, the Jews would have minority rights, and all further Jewish immigration would be subject to Arab control.

In the United Kingdom during that summer, Ernest Bevin argued that partition might be the only way out of Britain's difficulties, but Attlee and the military staff still hoped for a solution that would keep Palestine available as a base for British troops.[41] Policymakers tried to bring Arabs and Jews together for talks on some form of confederal solution, but the two communities on the ground in Palestine were united in rejecting it.

In the United States, Truman's frustration over the collapse of Morrison-Grady and the failing negotiations with the U.K. led him to issue a carefully worded statement (timed for maximum political impact on the day before Yom Kippur and just a month before the congressional elections) saying that partition was, in his view, a solution that would be acceptable to American opinion. The statement was carefully hedged; Truman argued that the distance between the Morrison-Grady recommendations and the Jewish Agency's demands was not unbridgeable, and that a reasonable compromise between them was something that could win American support. As is often the case when politicians attempt to please everyone, nobody liked the statement. Truman enraged the British but did not please American Zionists. The Republicans immediately outflanked him, denouncing Truman's closeness to Britain and demanding that he push more aggressively to address the problems of the Jewish DPs. The statement did nothing to stave off the GOP landslide in the November elections, but represented a new stage in the administration's thinking. Truman's preference remained for some kind of confederation of Arab and Jewish provinces under a central government responsible for economic and external affairs, but by the fall of 1946 he was losing faith that the Jews and the Arabs would accept it.[42]

The Palestinian Jews were not prepared to say so publicly, but partition was beginning to look more attractive. Ben-Gurion and some of his colleagues reached the conclusion during the fall of 1946 that their demand for a Jewish state in the whole of Palestine was unrealistic. Arabs were still a majority in the territory at the time, and there was little chance that the Jews could take and hold all of Palestine by military means. Given that reality, a partition of the territory that created a Jewish state seemed preferable to a Morrison-Grady type of confederal solution that forced Jews to accept a de facto partition but left control of immigration in British hands.

The British still hoped to be able to keep bases in Palestine, and so spent the fall in a last attempt to bring the Arabs and the Jews together around some version of the Morrison-Grady compromise that would convert Palestine into a stable platform for British forces. The gap between the Arab and Jewish positions remained too wide to close, though the Arab representatives at a London conference expressed willingness to allow permanent British bases in an independent, Arab-ruled Palestine. On September 20, the Arab states outlined their position in a memorandum. British bases were possible, and Jews legally settled in Palestine could have minority rights, but the Arabs would have the final say over immigration.[43]

By the end of 1946, Britain was running out of options. Holding on to Palestine without agreement with the Jews committed Britain to a long-term, expensive counterinsurgency effort that would deeply and progressively alienate American opinion at a time when good relations with the United States were becoming more vital to Britain's position than ever before. Any effort to conciliate the Jews involved concessions that would inflame the Arab world at a time when Britain's hold on the Middle East remained critical to British imperial strategy.

In the end, however, it was economic weakness rather than American opposition that broke the back of Britain's Palestine strategy and eliminated the British Army as an obstacle to the establishment of a Jewish state. Beginning on January 21, 1947, blizzards and subfreezing temperatures paralyzed transit in Britain with deep snowdrifts blocking both road and rail traffic. In some places it snowed on twenty-six of the twenty-eight days in February. Ferry service to Belgium was suspended due to pack ice on the sea routes.

Coal was used to generate electricity; heat homes, schools, and offices; and power factories. As the freeze tightened its grip, piles of coal assembled for shipping froze solid and could not be transported. The military was called in to try to chip the coal apart. Factories were shut down; radio and television broadcasts were curtailed; power cuts left the British people shivering in the dark. When the snow finally melted in March, floods blocked roads and destroyed houses. Roughly 20 percent of the industries that depended on coal and electricity were forced to shut down, and the slow economic recovery from the war was derailed. The food ration was cut to below wartime levels and unemployment shot up from 400,000 to 2.3 million. One fourth of Britain's sheep population died in the cold, ensuring both meat and wool shortages. Crop production fell by 10 to 20 percent.[44]

The weather disaster was a serious political blow for the Labour government, in part because the controversial nationalization of the British coal mining industry had just taken effect on January 1, only weeks before widening coal shortages spread across the country. *The New York*

Times reported from Sheffield on February 22, "This winter's collapse of industry will be . . . a landmark in Labor's history."[45] Indeed it was, and anger at Prime Minister Attlee, who tried to blame the war, grew more and more intense.

Changes in policy had to be made. Since V-J Day, Ernest Bevin and the military chiefs had been fighting a holding action against cabinet pressure for severe cuts in foreign and defense spending. That fight could no longer be sustained. Between February 14 and February 20 of that year, the cabinet made three fateful decisions: the U.K. would withdraw its support from Greece and Turkey by March 31, it would pull out of India by June of 1948, and it would throw in the towel on Palestine, informing the United Nations of its intention to give up its mandate and to leave the future of the country for the United Nations to decide. The British Army would no longer stand between the Arabs and the Jews of Palestine.[46]

It no longer made sense to pay the price of keeping order in Palestine while hoping for some kind of political solution to emerge. Turning the insoluble and expensive problem of Palestine over to the United Nations offered an attractive way forward. Let Britain's critics in the United States and the United Nations see what they could make of things. British authorities still believed that good relations with the Arab world and access to Middle Eastern oil were necessary to maintain what was left of Great Britain's position as a great power. Freed from its responsibilities to both sides as the mandatory power in Palestine, Britain could concentrate on strengthening its ties to friendly Arab governments. If a Jewish state emerged with American support, Britain could throw as much of the blame as possible onto the United States, and demonstrate to the Arabs where London's sympathies lay.

On February 18, 1947, the British cabinet informed the House of Commons that it would give up its legal authority in Palestine and evacuate its troops by August 1948. In April, Britain asked the General Assembly of the United Nations to convene a special session to consider the future of a territory for which the British Empire would no longer be responsible.[47] Truman had still not received his visas; a new and ultimately even more difficult stage of his Palestine policy was about to begin.

11
===

Cyrus and Stalin

RITAIN'S DECISION TO ABANDON its Palestine mandate was a decisive event in the emergence of a Jewish state. For American foreign policy, and for Harry Truman, however, Britain's simultaneous decision to reduce its commitments to Turkey and Greece was much more consequential for both American politics and world history than anything that happened or could happen in Palestine. The British pullbacks announced in February and March of 1947 launched the most creative and significant period in foreign policy of the Truman administration, and perhaps the most important such era in the history of the United States.

Politically, the news of Britain's intention to reduce its commitments in the Middle East and southeastern Europe helped crystallize a new perception in the United States about the Soviet threat. Signs of Soviet expansionism in the Middle East that both isolationists and liberal internationalists could dismiss as long as they could be perceived as conflicts between Britain and the Soviet Union took on a more threatening complexion if British power was removed from the equation. Was the United States prepared to allow the Soviet Union to impose a communist regime in Greece, cede control of the Dardanelles and the Bosporus to the Soviet navy, and leave Iran exposed to Soviet machinations? It did not take much reflection for many to decide that the time had come for the United States to look to its interests in what suddenly began to look like a very strategic part of the world.

In March, the administration announced that it would come to the aid of Turkey and Greece under the Truman Doctrine, a new principle in American foreign policy under which the United States would support any government against Soviet aggression. The United States for the first time was stepping up to play the great power role that Britain could no longer sustain. Ultimately, the consequences of Britain's withdrawal would lead to the formation of the NATO alliance and the formal adoption of global containment as American foreign policy. In the meantime, the realization that Britain and the other European economies were failing to recover from the war galvanized a new kind of foreign policy initiative from the United States. The State Department's new Policy Planning Staff got to work on the program for European reconstruction and development that would become known as the Marshall Plan; at the Harvard commencement in June, Secretary of State George Marshall would call for the establishment of a massive, American-led project for European reconstruction.

Referring the Palestine problem to the United Nations helped Britain burnish its image in the United States and around the world. Returning its mandate to the United Nations demonstrated what liberal opinion considered a heartening regard for international institutions and the rule of law. This was giving Britain more credit than it deserved. From a British point of view, the decision involved a change of tactics rather than of strategy in the Middle East. Britain's goals of basing its global position on Middle East oil and control of the Suez Canal had not changed, but it now looked to further those goals at a lower cost.

With Britain gaining points from American liberals for the inspired if perhaps slightly cynical decision to give the Palestine issue to the United Nations, even as more people in Washington came to share Britain's concerns about the Soviet threat, the overall entente between Washington and London deepened rapidly in 1947. The announcement of the Marshall Plan also bolstered support for Truman's foreign policy among American liberals. The Marshall Plan separated the increasingly radicalized and erratic Henry Wallace from the more mainstream Eleanor Roosevelt. Wallace, after initially supporting the Marshall Plan, would come to denounce it as an imperialist and even fascist program for the subjugation of Europe.[1] Mrs. Roosevelt hailed it as an act of enlightened statesmanship, in part because the administration blandly and disingenuously declared that nations under communist rule could participate in the plan.[2] This inspired move soothed the delicate consciences of internationalist liberals by making the Marshall Plan look less like a piece of Cold War strategy even as it discomfited Stalin by forcing him to pay the political price of forbidding his European satellite regimes to accept desperately needed credits from the United States.

Thanks in part to the growing evidence of Stalin's ruthlessness and hostility, and thanks in part to Truman's own careful management, during the first half of 1947 he was slowly consolidating his support among moderate liberals even as he continued to strengthen America's anti-Soviet stance—and to deepen its strategic cooperation with Britain. At the same time, the growing perception of a Soviet threat helped the administration to gain support from the Republican-controlled Congress. Managing Mrs. Roosevelt while reaching out to congressional Jacksonians was a difficult balancing act that Truman managed superbly; his success at building a consensus for a more robust foreign policy would restore much of the political authority he lost after the 1946 midterm election, boost his approval ratings throughout 1947, save his endangered nomination for the presidency in 1948, and contribute to his surprise election victory over Thomas Dewey later that year.

As Truman led the most consequential peacetime transformation of American foreign policy in history, he did not need the distraction of more controversy over Palestine. Fortunately, just when his administration most needed a holiday from Palestine, the British decision to refer the issue to the United Nations gave him one. Liberals desperately wanted the U.N. to emerge as the center of international life, and fervently believed that Truman's foreign policy should make support of the United Nations its highest priority. Ethnic and national disputes like the Arab-Jewish dispute in Palestine had been the curse of international life for more than a hundred years and the cause of countless wars. If the United Nations was going to be effective, people reasoned, one of its most important tasks would be to find methods to resolve such disputes peacefully.

Britain's decision to turn the question over to the United Nations gave Truman an excuse to step away from the battle for visas, and he took full advantage of the freedom he had so unexpectedly gained. Between March and October of 1947, Truman could put Palestine on the back burner while the machinery of the United Nations slowly processed the question of the territory's future. During those months, the Truman administration laid the foundation for the Marshall Plan, built a cross-party coalition in favor of a new global role for the United States, and began the reconstruction of American military strength following the postwar demobilization, while devoting less high-level attention to Palestinian matters than at any time until the outbreak of the Korean War. This respite came with a price. Between November 1947 and May 1948, Palestinian issues would erupt once again and plunge American foreign policy into a dangerous crisis, but until that time the administration was happy to set Palestine to one side.

Zionists and their allies hoped that with the Palestine issue going to the United Nations, the United States would lead the global body's deliberations on the matter. That was a challenge Truman badly wanted to avoid; fortunately, liberal ideas about the United Nations offered an escape route. It would be wrong, the administration piously declared, for the United States to prejudge the United Nations process on Palestine by seeking to impose its own vision on the General Assembly. Great powers should not try to dominate the U.N.; the members as a whole must take up the case. The Zionist lobby in the United States seethed, but without broader liberal support Zionist protests carried little weight.

When the United Nations formed yet another committee to study the Palestine issue (UNSCOP, the United Nations Special Committee on Palestine), the United States did not seek to chair it. The U.N. secretary-general, the former Norwegian foreign minister Trygve Lie, appointed the Black American diplomat Ralph Bunche, who left the State Department to join the staff of the fledgling U.N., as special assistant to Victor Hoo, head of the U.N. department charged with trusteeships. Hoo designated Bunche to head an UNSCOP subcommittee charged with drafting its reports.[3] Bunche would go on to win the respect of all sides for his professional skills and impartiality and would later become the first person of African descent to win a Nobel Prize when he was awarded the Peace Prize in 1950 for his work in mediating the cease-fire between Israel and Egypt. Bunche, however, having left the State Department and joined the U.N. civil service, did not represent the Truman administration to the committee, and his independence was one of the qualities for which he was admired worldwide.

Other than Bunche's presence, the United States stayed off the committee completely. The Truman administration was happy to dodge all responsibility for the issue, and, as liberals praised the administration's edifying devotion to the high principles of the U.N. Charter, the Zionist lobby raged in vain.

STALIN AND THE JEWS

Nineteen forty-seven was an important year in Middle East history for many reasons. Perhaps the most significant was that this was the year in which the Soviet Union managed to insert itself as a major factor in the Palestine question. Stalin would play a much more important role in the process that led the Jews to declare and defend their independence than anything Harry Truman did. While neither the Americans, the British, the Arabs, nor the Jews quite understood what was happening, the outlines of the new Soviet initiative began to appear in the spring.

Stalin was an unlikely person to come to the defense of the Zionist movement. The Soviet Union and the Zionists had not had a happy history. Inside the Russian Empire, Zionists and Bolsheviks had been ideological competitors among the empire's Jewish population long before the October Revolution brought Lenin to power. Many Zionists were socialists, and some (though not David Ben-Gurion) sympathized with the Bolshevik movement. The feelings were not reciprocated. Under Moscow's instructions the Communist Party of Palestine was resolutely anti-Zionist in the 1920s and 1930s. After an early thaw, Zionist political activity was ruthlessly suppressed in the Soviet Union.

Beyond that, in the internal political struggles around Stalin's seizure of supreme power in the Soviet Union, many of his enemies were so-called Old Bolsheviks who had been close to Lenin. From Leon Trotsky (born Lev Bronstein) on down, many of these early communist leaders were of Jewish origin. Stalin's purges in the 1930s included a disproportionate number of Jews among their millions of victims. Soon after his short-lived romance with the Jewish state, Stalin would open what, if not cut short by his death, looked to be growing into a full-scale purge aimed principally at Soviet Jews. Yet at the critical time, Joseph Stalin would offer the Jews of Palestine the indispensable support without which they could never have gained the backing of the United Nations or won their war with the Arabs.

The master of the Soviet Union for thirty years, Stalin held his cards close to his chest. Not even his intimates were ever taken fully into his confidence. Nevertheless, Stalin's calculations were usually shrewd if not always well informed, and the circumstances of the Soviet Union in 1947 and 1948 made an alliance, however temporary, with the Zionist movement look attractive. Stalin saw an opportunity to advance several of his foreign policy objectives and, characteristically, he moved rapidly and decisively to take the chance. Later, when a pro-Israel policy no longer served his interests, he washed his hands of the Jewish state with equal determination and ease, throwing many of those who worked with it into the gulags.

The eventful years of 1945–47 brought as much change to Stalin's world and his outlook as they did to the perceptions of policymakers in Washington and London. From Stalin's point of view, the three most important questions about the international system as World War II came to a close were these: Would Washington remain militarily engaged in Europe or, as in 1919, retreat to its hemispheric fortress? Would the United States and Britain remain allied or, as Marxist doctrine seemed to suggest, would the two surviving capitalist powers quarrel over the spoils of Europe, Asia, and the Middle East? Finally, would the continuing economic and political turmoil in Western Europe lead to communist revolutions in western Germany, Italy, and France?

In 1945 and 1946, it looked in the Kremlin as if all three of those questions might be resolved in a positive way. The Americans seemed to be determined to limit their European commitments. U.S. forces demobilized rapidly, and U.S. troop strength in Europe quickly declined. The U.S. Army dropped from eight million on V-J Day to roughly half a million by mid-1948.[4] The election of a Republican Congress in 1946, hostile to Truman and with many anti-interventionist voices, promised an even weaker and less focused American policy. The United States and Great Britain appeared to be quarreling. Additionally, economic conditions continued to worsen across Western Europe. The communist parties of Italy and France, emerging from their roles in the wartime resistance with great prestige, were gaining strength from month to month.

Nineteen forty-seven was a more difficult year. When Washington stepped into the gap left by Britain's withdrawal in Turkey and Greece, proclaimed the Truman Doctrine, and began to develop the Marshall Plan to rebuild Europe, Stalin confronted a new and much less favorable environment. The United States was no longer bent on withdrawal in Europe, and was prepared to make much larger military and economic commitments than Stalin had expected. The promise of large-scale American aid was enticing; even Stalin's puppet governments in Eastern Europe, who between war damage and the problems of socialism were in serious economic trouble, wanted to take part. The new American initiative strengthened the noncommunist parties in Italy and France, and, for the first time since V-E Day, by the fall of 1947 Stalin felt that he was on the defensive in Europe. Late 1947 and 1948 would see Stalin push back, tightening his control over the satellites, pushing political offensives in the West by communist and "popular front" parties, challenging the western allies over the status of Berlin, and stirring up trouble wherever he thought he could distract or divide the adversaries who threatened his position in Europe.

There were, from Stalin's standpoint, some compelling reasons to help the Jews in 1947–48. First, his primary goal in international politics was to prevent the renewal of the Anglo-American alliance that could complicate his plans in Europe, the Middle East, and beyond. During the war, Stalin took every opportunity to drive wedges between Winston Churchill and Franklin Roosevelt. Given the tensions between the United States and Britain over the future of Palestine, it made sense to sharpen the contradictions between the English-speaking powers by raising the temperature in the Jewish-Arab dispute.

Second, 1946 and 1947 had been years of setbacks and retreat for the Soviet Union in the Middle East. Soviet attempts to break through the "northern tier" (Greece, Turkey, Iran) to reach the oil-rich Arab countries had failed. However, Great Britain's hold on the Middle East looked like the weakest link in the chain that the United States and its allies were beginning to forge to contain Stalin's ambitions in Europe and the Mediterranean. Engineering a defeat for Britain and the gaggle of feudal monarchs who supported it might still weaken the West's grip on a region that had fascinated Russian power brokers since the time of Peter the Great. Stalin had no trouble following the train of thought that shaped British strategy in the Middle East: a victory for the Jews in Palestine might alienate the Arabs from Britain and stimulate waves of radical Arab nationalism that the fragile pro-British governments could not contain. If helping the Jews of Palestine could shake or even overturn British power from the Mediterranean to the Persian Gulf, then help the Jews Stalin would.

Third, at a time when world opinion was strongly anti-fascist and anti-Nazi, Jews were much more popular on the left than they have since become. The Jews after all were Hitler's ultimate victims. That popularity began to look like a useful asset as signs of greater American engagement with Europe started to appear in early 1947. Many non-Jewish socialists were deeply concerned about the plight of the Jews. As the British, in pursuit of their imperial ambitions in the Middle East, sought to block Jewish migration to Palestine, communists found a useful way to underline a key point in their propaganda: that capitalist imperialism wasn't all that different from fascism, and that only the communists had the vision and strategy to fight them both. In the special circumstances of 1947 and 1948, support for Zionism could help Stalin's core strategy in Western Europe—to build popular support for communist parties determined to resist their countries' participation in the Marshall Plan and the nascent western alliance.

Finally, there was the potential impact on American politics. Stalin was not pleased by the Truman administration's increasingly energetic and full-throated conduct of what was rapidly becoming the Cold War. We do not know how well Stalin understood American politics, but the efforts of the American Communist Party to put together a left-wing party that would run against Truman were well-known to him.[5] Henry Wallace's decision to run at the head of a party that depended significantly on communist support turned the Progressive Party into a potentially beneficial force from the Kremlin's perspective. As the Democratic Party split into three factions in 1948, Truman's defeat appeared increasingly likely. At this time, many American Jews had strong left-wing sympathies; a solid pro-Zionist stance by Stalin and the American Communist Party would help build support for the Progressive Party among Jews and among other American liberals. Just as support for Zionism could help Stalin build popular front movements in Europe, supporting the Palestinian Jews might help consolidate a left-wing party open to coalitions with communists in the United States, while undermining Truman's hopes for reelection.

Stalin didn't keep a diary, and so we have no way of knowing how each of these factors influenced his thinking in 1947–48. But we do know what he did. On May 14, 1947, as the General Assembly debated the future of Palestine, Stalin's deputy foreign minister Andrei Gromyko stated that, if all efforts to create a joint Arab-Jewish state failed, the Soviet Union would accept partition and an independent Jewish state.[6] This was a bombshell; in the past the Soviets had always denounced the idea of a two-state solution. The next day, the Soviet Union and its satellites voted in favor of the resolution establishing the U.N. Special Committee on Palestine (UNSCOP). Czechoslovakia would be the bloc's representative on the fifteen-member committee charged with determining the future of Palestine.

Two Committees, Three Subcommittees, and a Resolution

UNSCOP, the third high-profile international committee tasked with finding a solution to the Palestine issue in eighteen months, came into existence on May 15, the day following Gromyko's surprise. Eleven nations were represented: Australia, Canada, Czechoslovakia, Guatemala, India, Iran, the Netherlands, Peru, Sweden, Uruguay, and Yugoslavia. For those who believed that the United Nations was the first step to an effective world government, this was a breathtaking accomplishment.[7] Although the great powers had proxies on the committee (both Australia and Canada were members of the British Commonwealth, Yugoslavia was still aligned with the Soviet Union and was unlikely to vote in a way that displeased Stalin, and neither Guatemala nor Uruguay was renowned for defiance of Washington), the membership was broadly representative of the makeup of the world body at the time. By much of the world, and certainly by Mrs. Roosevelt and her wing of the Democratic Party, UNSCOP was seen as the first great test of the ability of the United Nations to function as the supreme arbiter of international disputes. As UNSCOP visited cities in Palestine including Jerusalem, Jaffa, Tel Aviv, Acre, and Tulkaram, the world press followed its progress closely.

The Palestinian Arab leadership doubled down on its tactics of resistance and boycott. Official Arab representatives refused to meet with the UNSCOP delegation in Palestine. In their view, the entire process was illegitimate. The Arab majority had a right to independence; the United Nations had no right to stand between a people and its freedom. The Jews were wiser, and took advantage of every opportunity to win delegates over to their side.

By chance, the visit of the committee coincided with the arrival in Palestinian waters on July 18 of the *Exodus 1947,* a ship carrying more than 4,500 Holocaust survivors hoping to enter Palestine illegally. The British had boarded the ship while it was still in international waters. When the crew and passengers resisted, three people were killed, including an American citizen in the crew who was clubbed to death. Zionist representatives were on board and broadcast live radio accounts of the battle for the ship.[8] The global coverage surrounding the ship's capture was a major publicity victory for the Zionists; the story would become the basis for a best-selling novel by Leon Uris and an Oscar-winning 1960 movie starring Paul Newman. The UNSCOP representatives were in the harbor as British soldiers forcibly placed the unwilling passengers on ships bound back for Europe (in the end, they would be disembarked, again by force, in Germany, in another major publicity disaster for the British). John Stanley Grauel, a Methodist minister and American Christian Zionist, was on board the ship. The horrified UNSCOP members listened to his account of the voyage and were visibly moved. Golda Meir, the future Israeli prime minister, credited Grauel's testimony for persuading the committee to support partition and Jewish statehood. Like William Hechler and William Blackstone, the Reverend John Stanley Grauel gave the Zionist movement a critical boost.[9]

UNSCOP went on to meet with Lebanese and other Arab leaders, including King Abdullah of Transjordan (renamed Jordan in 1949). Convinced, apparently, by Grauel's testimony that the desperation of Jews in Europe should be studied as UNSCOP reviewed the situation in Palestine, a subcommittee visited refugee camps in Europe and interviewed Jewish DPs.[10]

The committee issued its report—or rather its reports—in early September. The eleven members voted unanimously that the mandate over the territory should be terminated. The mandatory system had been originally intended for territories whose populations were deemed not yet "ready" for full independence; there was little question that both the Jewish and the Arab populations of Palestine were ready and eager to govern themselves.

The question that divided the committee was whether the populations could best govern themselves together in one state or separately in two. Given the small size of the territory in question, it seemed clear to all members that some form of cooperation between the two populations was needed. Equally clearly, the bitterness of the struggle between them required a certain degree of separation and autonomy. Three members of the committee (India, Iran, and Yugoslavia) proposed reconciling these two requirements by establishing a binational federal state of Palestine similar in some ways to the Morrison-Grady proposal. Seven committee members (Canada, Czechoslovakia, Guatemala, the Netherlands, Peru, Sweden, and Uruguay) supported a proposal to partition the territory into two independent states in an economic union with Jerusalem under international trusteeship. The eleventh member of the committee, Australia, abstained.[11]

Clearly, it was time for another committee. On September 23, the fourth international Palestine committee was formed: the Ad Hoc Committee on the Palestinian Question. The establishment of this second U.N. committee was a political victory for the Zionists; the Arab states at the U.N. wanted to refer the UNSCOP report to an existing U.N. committee where, they believed, supporters of the majority UNSCOP report would have a harder time moving toward a final decision in favor of partition. The Ad Hoc Committee was charged with assessing the UNSCOP majority and minority reports to develop a practical way forward to implement their recommendations, providing a resolution that the General Assembly could review. The lopsided vote to establish the Ad Hoc Committee (29 in favor, 11 opposed, 16 abstentions) demonstrated that the majority UNSCOP report reflected the views of a majority in the General Assembly. The Ad Hoc Committee in true bureaucratic fashion immediately established three subcommittees: one each to look at how the majority and minority UNSCOP reports could be implemented, and a "conciliation committee" that would try to bring the two sides together. Attention centered on the subcommittee tasked with developing a plan to implement the partition of Palestine into two independent states.[12] That report was completed in November and forwarded to the General Assembly, where the partition resolution would need a two thirds supermajority of all those voting to pass. There were fifty-seven voting members of the United Nations at the time; if every state voted, the resolution would need thirty-eight votes.

For the Truman administration, all this was both good and bad news. It was good news because the liberal internationalists and pro-Zionists (who between them continued to constitute large majorities in national politics generally and especially in the Democratic Party) were generally happy with the results of Truman's passive approach to the Palestine issue. The steady progress toward a positive U.N. decision on the creation of an independent Jewish state thrilled liberals who desperately wanted the United Nations to fulfill its potential as the foundation of a new era of world peace. It was also deeply satisfying to the many Americans who continued to see the Blackstone approach to the Jewish question as reflecting American values and American interests. The United States was employing Blackstone methods to achieve a Blackstone goal; particularly after the Holocaust, millions of Americans approved of the progress being made.

But there was also bad news. In the short term, liberal internationalists, Blackstone believers, and active Zionists rejoiced that a partition resolution was moving through the U.N. But they would judge Truman and his policy based on results. If the resolution failed to pass or, once passed, failed to be implemented on the ground, Truman would have to explain why the most powerful nation on earth was unable to achieve such a small, simple, and, these interlocutors would insist, morally important goal. Worse, from Truman's point of view, was the knowledge that it would not be simply the pro-Zionist lobby whose wrath he needed to fear. The larger and much more influential United Nations lobby, headed by the redoubtable dowager of Dutchess County, now believed that the passage and implementation of the partition resolution would be the acid test of the United Nations' power and relevance. The historicization of the eschaton had reached a dramatic new stage: for American liberals, the establishment of a Jewish state had become identified with humanity's ability to end the cycle of recurring and ever more destructive wars. The cause of Zion fused with the cause of peace, and the cause of peace was the cause of survival.

In early September, the conventional wisdom was that the two thirds supermajority of voting states needed to pass the recommendation was out of reach. The Arab bloc of five states was, of course, opposed, as were non-Arab Muslim states like the newly independent Pakistan. Most observers believed that the USSR, busily building support networks among Arab countries to counter British power in the Middle East, would cast its own three votes (at Stalin's insistence, Belarus and Ukraine had been given votes in the General Assembly) plus that of its Polish satellite against the resolution. (Czechoslovakia was, until the communist coup of February 1948, still seen as at least partially independent of the Soviet Union, and its vote in favor of the majority report was not seen as reflecting Stalin's views.) Britain's hostility to partition was well-known; Australia's abstention on the UNSCOP report suggested that it would follow Britain on the final vote. Given France's concerns about unrest in Muslim Algeria, Paris, too, seemed unlikely to support the UNSCOP report.

Truman was in a difficult position. If a two thirds majority was out of reach, a failed lobbying effort would damage American prestige and American relations with the Arab world to no real purpose. There was also strong opposition inside the government to the majority report, with many officials convinced, correctly as would soon be seen, that the complicated partition resolution could not in fact be implemented as it stood. But to abandon UNSCOP would mean an irrevocable loss of support that would torpedo Truman's reelection hopes. He therefore did what presidents often do in such circumstances, delaying his response as long as possible and splitting the difference as much as he could. On October 11, he announced that the United States would support the UNSCOP majority report in the General Assembly. He made no preparations to round up supporting votes.[13]

Two days later, the situation changed: the Soviet Union announced that it, too, would support the majority report. The conventional wisdom, as it often does, flipped overnight. It was well-known that a number of U.N. members would routinely follow the lead of either the United States or the Soviet Union. Greece, for example, was still fighting a civil war against communist insurgents; it was seen as too dependent on the United States to risk its wrath over a vote in the U.N. Similarly, it would be a very rash or foolhardy Central American republic, or Eastern European Soviet client state, that took an independent course at the United Nations once the superpowers had made their wishes known.

The news that the United States and the Soviet Union agreed on a Palestine policy electrified both Zionists and liberal internationalists across the United States. Zionists rejoiced to see the approach of a Jewish state; liberal internationalists saw, or thought they saw, exactly the future they so desperately wanted as the work of the U.N. brought the great powers together to develop a consensus solution to the kind of problem that, in the past, had frequently led to war. If the United States and the Soviet Union, working through the mechanisms of the U.N., could reach a consensus on an issue as contentious as Palestine, surely they could find other solutions as well.

News of the Soviet switch also came as a relief to Truman. If the partition resolution was going to sail through the General Assembly, Truman could put the Palestine issue back on the back burner where he wanted it. In mid-November, that changed. In the absence of any pressure from the Americans, and quite possibly after conversations with the career

State Department representatives in the U.S. delegation at the U.N. who hoped the resolution would fail, a number of countries that usually followed Washington's line in foreign affairs began to speak out against the resolution. Haiti, Liberia, Cuba, Greece, and the Philippines announced their opposition to partition.[14] It now looked as if the resolution would fail, and that the reason for its failure was the Truman administration's inability to round up enough votes from American allies. This was not a result Truman could live with, and the word from the White House went out to the American delegation at the United Nations telling the diplomats to pull out all the stops to ensure a victory for the resolution. The pressure had its effect, as *Time* magazine dryly reported in its December 8 issue:

> One day Haitian Delegate Antonio Vieux spoke heatedly against partition; two days later he announced shamefacedly that his government had ordered him to switch to yes. Filipino Delegate General Carlos Romulo, on Wednesday, orated against partition and sailed away on the Queen Mary. Saturday a new Filipino delegate flew in from Washington, voted yes. Liberia, which voted no in committee, said yes in the final roll call.[15]

Encouraged by the Zionist leadership in Palestine, Jews around the world reached out to their contacts, though it is not clear how much impact they had. France is said to have made up its mind to vote yes after Chaim Weizmann telephoned former prime minister Leon Blum; others attribute the French vote to threats made by the American financier Bernard Baruch.[16] Both theories seem unlikely. France had enjoyed close relations with the Palestinian Jews dating back to World War II when French authorities in Syria sheltered Jewish terrorists wanted by the British authorities. During the war, Britain was openly scheming to end French rule in Lebanon and Syria. At best, that could lead to a northern Arab federation under pro-British Hashemite rule incorporating Iraq, Transjordan, Syria, and Lebanon. Lord Moyne, the British diplomat who was assassinated by Jewish radicals in Cairo in 1944, seems to have hoped that this confederation would be large enough, and the Arabs would be grateful enough to the British for establishing it, that a Jewish homeland could be incorporated as one of its component parts. In any case, Britain tried, and in 1946 it succeeded, in forcing France out of Syria as it sought to gain favor in the Arab world. Revenge, domestic politics, and humanitarian instincts all pointed Paris toward a pro-Zionist policy, and the French government took every opportunity to punish Britain for its betrayal. It had, for example, allowed the 4,500 Holocaust refugees to board the SS *Exodus 1947* in a French port, and icily refused to allow them to be off-loaded against their will when the British sought to return them to French soil.[17] After Israel achieved its independence, France would become its most important ally, arming Israel, providing it with diplomatic support, and even helping it develop nuclear weapons in defiance of American pressure. The theory that hidden Jewish pressure forced France's partition vote looks Vulcanesque; neither a call from one old friend to another nor a threat from a Jewish American financier seems the best explanation of a policy choice that was entirely consistent with French interests and aligned with settled French policy through many years.[18]

For some it would become an article of faith that the secretive, all-powerful Jewish lobby engineered the vote at the United Nations. Certainly many Jews around the world did their best to promote an outcome that, by this time, most Jews strongly supported. Nevertheless, one wonders how the world's Jews, powerless a decade before to stop the rise of Hitler in Germany, powerless to get the world's countries to oppose Nazi Germany while it was still weak, powerless to stop the Holocaust, powerless to force a war-weakened Great Britain to toe the Zionist line, had suddenly gained the awesome power to manipulate the United Nations behind the scenes. If the world's Jews had this kind of power, why hadn't they used it before? Why even let the question get to the United Nations? Couldn't the all-powerful elders of Zion just call Clement Attlee and read him the riot act? And if the world's Jews hadn't had this power in the past, how had they suddenly become invincible? Who died to make Rothschild king? That such questions have no sensible answer has never bothered Vulcan enthusiasts; reason and evidence are not the wings on which prejudice storms the abyss.

But whatever pressures were applied, and by whom, the General Assembly voted by the necessary two thirds margin to endorse the report of the Ad Hoc Committee, and the partition of Palestine was the official policy of the international community. The outcome was close: 33 nations voted in favor, 13 against, 10 abstained, and one was absent. If Stalin, a man not noted for yielding to outside pressure, Jewish or otherwise, had cast the four votes he controlled against partition, the resolution would have fallen two votes short of the two thirds majority needed.

TRAPPED BY SUCCESS

The United Nations resolution opened a legal path for the establishment of a Jewish state, but the passage of the resolution plunged Truman into one of the most difficult crises of his presidency. On November 29, when the vote was announced, the Arab representatives stormed out of the General Assembly unanimous and unambiguous in their response: the Arab states did not accept the authority of the U.N. to decide the fate of Palestine and they rejected the decision that was taken. Great Britain, still intent on retaining Arab support, announced that while it would evacuate Palestine on schedule and give up its mandate, it would not cooperate with the U.N. on any administrative or security matters pertaining to the partition that did not enjoy the support of both of the communities in Palestine.

This put Truman in an impossible position. With Arab resistance and British noncooperation, the resolution was unworkable, but the liberal internationalists in the United States believed that it was the clear duty of the president of the United States to make the resolution work. They did not know how that could happen, but they knew it was the president's job to make the United Nations effective. Perhaps this meant setting up a U.N. peacekeeping force with Soviet troops; that struck many Democrats as an admirable idea that could advance the cause of peace. Eleanor Roosevelt, for one, saw no problem with a Soviet presence in the Middle East. As she wrote to Truman, "To say that just because Russia might have some soldiers in Palestine on an equal basis with us and all the other nations involved [contributing to a U.N. International Police Force], we would have to mobilize fifty percent for war seems to me complete nonsense and I think it would seem so to most of the people of the United States."[19]

To the officials in the executive branch, this all looked like madness. The State Department, the Pentagon, and the CIA were united in the belief that nothing short of mass American troop deployments could make the resolution work, and that even then the United States could face years of war in the Middle East that would alienate the Arabs, infuriate the American people, interrupt the supply of oil to Europe, and offer a range of enticing opportunities to the Soviet Union.

The State Department turned to George Kennan, then at the height of his power both inside and outside the administration, to review the new situation in the Middle East and develop options for American policy. In preparing his report, Kennan leaned on the advice of Henry Serrano Villard, a career foreign service officer who began his illustrious procession through the ranks of the department as vice-consul in Tehran. In conversations with Kennan, Villard was fearful of Soviet intrusion in Arab states, and also about the possibility of "a Communist dominated Jewish state in Palestine within the next year or two."[20]

The idea of a pro-Soviet Jewish state resonated in the national security bureaucracies in the hothouse atmosphere of 1947–48. Jews in the United States and abroad had long been associated with left-wing and, in enough cases to be noticeable, communist politics. The Palestinian Zionist movement was well to the left of mainstream American or even European politics at this time, and a far-left faction of the movement was pro-Soviet. Cooperation between the Eastern Bloc and the Jewish authorities in promoting a steady stream of illegal immigration from Eastern Europe to Palestine in defiance of British controls had established close links between Jewish officials and the Soviet bloc. American intelligence had evidence, and beyond that common sense suggested, that some number of the Jews arriving in Palestine through this route were Soviet agents.

And there was the case of Shmuel Mikunis, secretary of the Israeli Communist Party. After the war, Mikunis toured all around Eastern Europe, ingratiating himself with various officials including Deputy Premier Joseph Chisinevschi in Romania, leading communists like Władysław Gomułka in Poland, and Milovan Djilas and Marko Ranković in Yugoslavia. Mikunis would remain in Czechoslovakia throughout the spring of 1948, making plans to mobilize and train Eastern European Jewish volunteers. Receiving a telephone call from Georgi Malenkov, Stalin's eventual successor, Mikunis asked if it was within the current international communist policy for him to call a press conference to organize and mobilize Eastern European Jewish youth to fight for Israel. Without hesitating, Malenkov uttered one Russian word *Zakonno* ("It is legal") and the phone went dead.[21]

American officials knew something significant was happening in the field of Soviet-Zionist relations, but did not have all the details. They had reason to worry about the allegiance of some of the Jewish military forces; many in the military leadership of the Palmach, a quasi-independent elite Jewish militia, were sympathetic to Moscow. David Ben-Gurion recognized the danger as well and would fight one of his most difficult political battles to bring the Palmach leadership under state control.[22]

By December 17, Kennan completed a draft paper that began with the consensus view that the U.N. partition resolution was unworkable and outlined two alternative recommendations. The first was that:

> The United States should immediately announce that we have become convinced that the partition of Palestine is impossible of implementation and that the Palestine problem should therefore be referred back to a special session of the General Assembly to meet in a neutral country such as Switzerland. At this session we should propose that a "middle-of-the-road" solution be attempted for which we would endeavor to obtain support from the Arab and Jewish communities of Palestine. If this proved impossible, we should propose a UN trusteeship for Palestine, pending agreement by the Arab and Jewish communities.

The second alternative was more passive:

> The US should take the position that, in view of the manifest impossibility of implementing the partition of Palestine, no steps should be taken to that end. We should oppose sending UN troops to Palestine to enforce partition. We should maintain and enforce our embargo on arms to Palestine and neighboring countries.[23]

Both of these approaches would infuriate both Zionists and pro–United Nations liberals. Kennan, with very little knowledge of, or interest in, the domestic political problems the president faced, was more worried about the potential problems on the ground in the Middle East. On January 20, 1948, Kennan shared his views on Palestine in a top secret report with the wider administration, including Secretary of State Marshall and Undersecretary of State Robert Lovett. The paper set forward the department's view of American interests that were affected by the problem of Palestine: control of the eastern Mediterranean and the Suez Canal; securing Middle Eastern oil supplies, which were necessary to bankroll the Marshall Plan for Europe; and maintenance of stable and friendly relations with the Arab countries, seen as essential in limiting Soviet penetration into the region.

The report dwelt at length on probable Arab reactions to partition:

> The Arabs of Palestine have indicated their determination not to establish a separate government in the Arab area of Palestine designated by the UN, and to boycott all activities of the UN Commission charged with the transfer of authority from the British to the new Arab and Jewish states. Even if partition were economically feasible, the Arab attitude alone renders it improbable that any economic union could be effected between the two new states.

Kennan also feared increasing unrest:

> Strong nationalistic and religious feelings were aroused throughout the Arab world as a result of the UN recommendation on Palestine.... A "jihad" (holy war) against the Jews of Palestine has been proclaimed by Moslem leaders in most of the Arab states and has been joined by Christian leaders in Syria.... Organized large scale opposition by the Arabs is to be expected. Irregular military units are now being organized in Iraq, Syria, Egypt, Transjordan and Saudi Arabia to fight in Palestine.

On the Soviet dimension, Kennan, was adamant:

> The UN decision is favorable to Soviet objectives of sowing dissention and discord in non-communist countries. The partition of Palestine might afford the USSR a pretext on the basis of "self-determination of minorities" to encourage the partition of areas in Iraq, Iran, Turkey and Greece, with a view to setting up separate [Kurdish?] Azerbaijani, Armenian and Macedonian states enjoying the support of the USSR. All in all, there is no way of telling in exactly what manner the USSR will attempt to turn partition to its advantage. It must be assumed,

however, that Moscow will actively endeavor to find some means of exploiting the opportunity.

In conclusion, an alarming portrait is painted:

> So numerous would be the ramifications of mounting Arab ill will, of opening the door to Soviet political or military penetration, and of generally chaotic conditions in Palestine and neighboring countries that the whole structure of peace and security in the Near East and Mediterranean would be directly or indirectly affected with results impossible to predict at this stage in detail but certainly injurious to U.S. interests.

Kennan then makes an argument grounded in domestic politics: "In the U.S., the position of Jews would be gravely undermined as it becomes evident to the public that in supporting a Jewish state in Palestine we were in fact supporting the extreme objectives of political Zionism, to the detriment of overall U.S. security interests."

Given the likelihood of a disastrous outcome in Palestine, Kennan advised the administration to distance itself from the problem: "We should endeavor as far as possible to spread responsibility for the future handling of this question, and to divest ourselves of the imputation of international leadership in the search for a solution to this problem."[24]

When Dean Rusk, acting as director of the recently established Office of United Nations Affairs, criticized the paper's pessimism, Kennan doubled down. Unless the United States somehow dodged responsibility for Palestine, Washington might find itself with a long-term military commitment: "We would finally hold major military and economic responsibility for the indefinite maintenance by armed force of a status quo in Palestine fiercely resented by the bulk of the Arab world. I do not believe that the U.S. public would ever tolerate such a situation."[25] The head of the State Department's Bureau of Near Eastern Affairs (NEA), Loy Henderson, agreed, writing to Rusk on February 6 that "the Palestine Partition Plan is manifestly unworkable. I think that with each passing day our task will be rendered more difficult and that by mid April general chaos will reign in Palestine."[26]

Defense Secretary James Forrestal, the Joint Chiefs of Staff, and the analysts at the CIA all shared deep reservations about the partition plan.

As Forrestal wrote in his diary: "The strategic planning of the Joint Chiefs of Staff had been substantially altered by the Palestine decision. That it had pretty well 'spiked' any consideration of any military operations in the Middle East and had pretty well disposed of the idea that the United States would continue to have access to the Middle East Oil."[27]

The CIA described its misgivings in a report entitled "Possible Developments in Palestine" on February 28:

It is apparent that the partition of Palestine into separate Arab and Jewish states (and an international zone), with economic union between the two states, as recommended by the United Nations General Assembly (UNGA) on 29 November 1947, cannot be implemented. The Arab reaction to the recommendation has been violent, and the Arab refusal to cooperate in any way with the five-nation United Nations Commission will prevent the formation of an Arab state and the organization of economic union. The Arabs will use force to oppose the establishment of a Jewish state and to this end are training troops in Palestine and other Arab [states]. Moreover, the United Kingdom has stated repeatedly that it will take no part in implementing a UN decision not acceptable to both Jews and Arabs. The British have also declared that when the mandate terminates on 15 May, they will not transfer authority to the UN Commission but will merely relinquish that authority, which would then be assumed by the UN. Thus, without Arab and British cooperation, the Commission will be unable to carry out the task assigned to it.[28]

Given these problems, Lovett requested that Kennan's Policy Planning Staff submit a new range of alternative actions that the United States might pursue and their predicted consequences. Three options emerged: a) full support of partition, including the use of arms to enforce it; b) a passive approach, with no further steps either to aid or hinder partition; and c) a reversal of support for partition, instead seeking an Arab-Jewish federated state, perhaps under U.N. trusteeship.

The first option ran counter to the State Department vision of national strategy and there was little public support for sending American troops to Palestine; the second seemed impractical in the light of the intense American domestic interest in the question. Kennan and staff believed that the third option was the only practical choice:

This course of action would encounter strong opposition from the Zionists. It would, however, probably have the support of the Arab States and of world opinion in general. Our prestige in the Middle East would immediately rise and we would regain in large measure our strategically important position in the area. Our national interests would thus be served and our national security strengthened, notwithstanding the disfavor with which such a procedure would be viewed by Zionists [sic] elements.[29]

Truman's position was not an enviable one in early 1948. The political world was largely in favor of partition and looked forward to the rise of a Jewish state under the auspices of the United Nations. The "civil war" in Mandatory Palestine that had broken out on November 30 after the U.N. vote had by January escalated to a full-fledged conflict.[30] And the national security establishment was increasingly and deeply opposed to any American participation in what it saw as a doomed enterprise. Foreign policy professionals denounced Truman as a political panderer, shamelessly mortgaging the American interest to his need for the Jewish vote. Zionists attacked him for doing almost nothing to help the Jewish people in their hour of need. Liberals saw the prestige of the United Nations as being at stake in the crisis, and criticized Truman for inadequate leadership at a historic turning point.

In principle, Truman sympathized with the Zionists and the Jews on humanitarian grounds. In practice, he felt the weight of the arguments emanating from the bureaucracy. With upheavals in Europe and the Soviet pushback against the Marshall Plan raising tensions everywhere and threatening to provoke a real crisis over Berlin, Truman agreed with the bureaucracy's argument that Palestine was a distraction from more critical problems. He also understood that Eleanor Roosevelt's demand that the United States take on the responsibility for carrying out the U.N. resolution entailed unacceptable risks. Yet Truman understood American politics much better than State Department mandarins like George Kennan, and he knew that the policy recommendations emanating from Foggy Bottom were less politically sustainable than the bureaucrats believed.

To make matters worse, 1948 was a presidential election year and Truman's chances for winning the Democratic nomination, much less the November election, hung by a thread. Henry Wallace had already announced a third-party run, threatening to split the Democrats and throw the election to the Republicans. Truman's alleged failure to support the United Nations and the embattled Jews of Palestine figured heavily in his campaign rhetoric.

The steady stream of bad news from Palestine did not help. Not only had fighting between Arabs and Jews broken out almost immediately following the passage of the U.N. resolution, but as the grim winter of 1948 unfolded, the Jews in Palestine were losing the war. Instead of presiding over the birth of a Jewish state, it began to look as if Truman could face a massive humanitarian disaster as hundreds of thousands of Palestinian Jews were driven from their homes.

The winter of 1948 was grim; the spring would be worse.

12

Cyrus Agonistes

OR ANYONE TRYING to make sense out of the historical record, one of the most persistent difficulties involves reconstructing what people at the time believed would happen next. From our privileged perspective in the future, we know how things came out. We know now, for example, that the Jews of Palestine would defeat both the Palestinian Arabs and the subsequent invasion by neighboring states. None of that was obvious to people at the time; indeed, forecasting who will win a particular war, how long a given conflict will last, or how extensive and intensive it will be are tasks at which even the best informed of contemporary observers often fail. Yet forecasts about the course of a particular war, however fallible these prove, are one of the most important pieces of information that policymakers use to analyze their situation and chart their course. Students of history, especially those looking for insights that will make them better foreign policy strategists in their own time, must constantly work to reconstruct the mental pictures and assessments that guided their predecessors.

In the case of Harry Truman and his colleagues, we cannot follow their thought processes in the difficult spring of 1948 without taking the course of events on the ground in Palestine into account. Beginning almost immediately after the results of the U.N. vote on partition were announced, rioting broke out in parts of Palestine as Arabs protested the decision. Over the following days and weeks, the violence continued and intensified. It soon began to look as if the Jews were losing the war.[1]

From December to March, the Jews lost ground. Many of the Jewish settlements were isolated villages, and the roads that connected areas of concentrated Jewish population often ran through territory largely inhabited by Arabs. For political reasons, the Jewish leadership could not follow the advice given by its military commanders to withdraw Jews from scattered outposts and concentrate on the defense of key blocs of territory. As a result, the Jewish forces were spread out across large areas, and much of the Jewish military was tied down by the need to protect communications. Worst of all, the large concentration of Jews in the Jerusalem area was soon cut off and besieged by the Arabs, and the fear that the community would be forced to surrender haunted the Jewish leadership in Palestine and its friends and supporters abroad. In the middle of February, as the situation across Palestine worsened, Ben-Gurion asked the New York representatives of the Jewish Agency to press for the intervention of American or U.N. troops or, at the least, supplies.[2]

The revelation of Jewish weakness highlighted one of Truman's decisions that was controversial at the time but has often been forgotten in retrospect. Immediately after the U.N. vote on partition, the State Department had proposed, and Truman accepted, an embargo on all American arms sales to either side. The arms embargo had been announced on December 5, six days after the vote and five days after fighting started.[3] As many Zionists bitterly pointed out, this amounted to a de facto intervention on the side of the Arabs. The Arabs were well supplied with arms from Great Britain; the Jews had nowhere to turn. Meanwhile American arsenals were bursting with surplus materiel from World War II.

Zionists compared this to events in Spain during its civil war, when the western embargo on arms sales to both sides hurt the Republican side only, as the Fascists were well supplied by Hitler and Mussolini. Even as Jewish outposts fell to Arab attacks, and as the civilian population of Jerusalem endured siege conditions, Truman sided with the State Department; the arms embargo would remain in place until the end of Israel's War of Independence.[4]

For those who believe that "the Jews" were in control of American policy during these critical months, Truman's support for an arms embargo that benefited the Arabs and threatened such dire consequences for Palestinian Jews is hard to explain, especially as the military crisis grew. But Zionist outrage was not the problem that worried Truman most. It was the liberal internationalists that Truman was primarily worried about, and they wanted something much harder to deliver. Eleanor Roosevelt and her allies believed that the United Nations was humanity's only hope to avoid World War III, that Resolution 181 calling for the partition of Palestine was its most important decision to date, and that it was now the job of President Truman to ensure that the U.N. resolution was obeyed. The helplessness of the international community in the face of escalating violence across Palestine threatened to break the credibility of the United Nations. As one observer wrote in the *New York Herald Tribune* in late February,

> The United Nations Security Council is scheduled to take up the Palestine question, and it appears to be the majority view at Lake Success [the early headquarters of the U.N.] that this will mark a turning point in U.N. history. If the Security Council is not able to produce an international force to guarantee Palestine partition, or is not able to take any other action to guarantee partition and at least partially head off the bloody Arab-Jewish war that seems imminent for the Holy Land, then the U.N. will suffer a blow in lost prestige and authority that may mark the beginning of its end.[5]

Meanwhile, the British continued to train and equip Arab armies outside Palestine. With the Palestinian Arabs already gaining the upper hand against the Jews, and the Arab League promising to enter Palestine once the mandate expired, the situation of the Jews—and of the partition plan itself—appeared bleak. Truman's choices looked equally bad. If, as many expected, the Arabs prevailed on the ground, what would happen to the Palestinian Jews? Everyone at this point understood that wars of peoples tended to involve massacres and ethnic cleansing. Where would the Jews go when the time came to flee? To the displaced persons camps in Europe, already teeming with desperate Jews? To the United States, determined to avoid another refugee surge? As the State Department mandarins warning Truman against committing the United States to the implementation of the partition plan argued: if the partition plan meant war, and the Jews lost, the United States and its president would have a political disaster and a humanitarian crisis on their hands.

Unilateral American intervention was militarily and politically impossible. Tensions with the Soviet Union were rising to explosive levels in early 1948. The February coup in Czechoslovakia ended the last hope for some kind of accommodation between Stalin and the West,

communist parties in Italy and France were making their most determined bids for power, and in the spring of 1948 Stalin began to harass
Allied military traffic heading through Soviet-occupied Germany to the
divided city of Berlin.[6]

American forces worldwide were overstretched, and on March 17,
Truman would make one of the most difficult and controversial speeches
of his career, calling on Congress to introduce military conscription.[7] By
summer, when the fighting in Palestine intensified into the Israeli War of
Independence, all available American airpower would be fully engaged
in airlifting supplies to Soviet-blockaded West Berlin. As the military
chiefs made clear to Truman in the spring of 1948, the United States was
seriously overextended and had no military options in Palestine.

What Mrs. Roosevelt and her allies really wanted was the dispatch of
what today we would call U.N. peacekeepers to Palestine, charged with
maintaining order and carrying out the U.N.-mandated partition in an
orderly fashion. Secretary of State George Marshall explained why his
department thought this impossible in closed session testimony before
the Senate Foreign Relations Committee in March. Large military forces
would be required, possibly for a considerable period, to implement
the resolution and maintain peace in Palestine, Marshall told the committee. Thanks to the Soviet position on the Security Council, any UN
involvement "would make substantially certain the use in and around
the Holy Land of large bodies of Russian troops. In the case of Palestine,
the maintenance of such a Soviet force would press down ponderously
on Greece and Turkey, as well as upon the Arabian oil fields, which are
officially held essential to the United States and to the entire European
Recovery Program as well."[8]

In March of 1948, with the Jews of Jerusalem under siege and isolated
settlements cut off around the country even as Arab armies prepared
for war, the internal fighting over Palestine policy in the administration
reached a peak. To many of the career officials, Truman's policy looked
like madness. He had pressed for the impossible U.N. partition resolution
to pass, when simple inaction would have ensured its defeat. He doubled
down on his commitment to the resolution even when it became clear
that, between British and Arab opposition, the resolution could not be
implemented on the ground. He now seemed bent on pursuing a feck-
less, disastrous course at a moment of grave national peril, presumably
because he was pandering to the Jewish vote, that would leave the United

States to face infinitely worse choices in the near future: it could either jeopardize its position in Central Europe by diverting scarce military resources to a military operation in Palestine that would permanently tie the United States down while infuriating the entire Arab world, or the United States could stand by wringing its hands while the Arabs drove the Palestinian Jews into the sea. "Mutinous" is an inadequate word to describe the rage, the sorrow, the horror with which much of the State Department viewed their president's course.

It was against this background that a series of clashes inside the Truman administration took place. The State Department had always believed that the only safe course was to wriggle free from support for the unworkable partition resolution. As May 15, the fateful day on which the British would evacuate their last military force and remove the last obstacle to a major regional conflict, drew near, Foggy Bottom scrambled desperately to separate American policy from the doomed resolution. Officials presented Truman with a draft speech that the chief of the American delegation at the United Nations, Warren Austin, would deliver to the General Assembly, declaring that in view of changing circumstances and the failure to implement the preconditions for a peaceful transfer of power to the two new states, the United States was abandoning the policy of partition, and proposed a United Nations trusteeship while new efforts were made to achieve a solution that both sides could accept.[9]

Truman had very little room to maneuver, and, it appeared, very little time left. He could not fight the substance of the State Department position; if events unfolded as expected, for the sake of the Palestinian Jews some kind of alternative peacekeeping arrangement might well be needed by May. Yet there was one red line Truman did not want to cross. Once again, it was not a Zionist red line; it was a liberal internationalist one. Specifically, it was a line of Eleanor Roosevelt's. Truman could not take the responsibility of abandoning the U.N. resolution as a unilateral American move. That, to Mrs. Roosevelt and to all the Americans who clung tenaciously to their faith in the role of the U.N., would be the unpardonable sin: it would be killing the U.N. and all the hopes it represented.

Between Truman's fury, State Department defensiveness, and a general disposition by everyone involved to avoid taking responsibility for a major policy snafu, what happened next is difficult to assess. Truman and the State Department blamed one another for the chaos, but it appears that Truman gave the department a limited, hedged permission to introduce a trusteeship plan, the U.N. equivalent of the old League of Nations mandate system, so long as the U.N. itself had in some way acknowledged the failure of its partition plan.

For Truman, this approach was the best available option. As long as the U.N. concluded that the partition plan was unworkable first, and called on member states for help in developing a new approach, Truman could claim to be assisting rather than obstructing its work. He could prepare a lifeboat without being accused of wanting to jump ship.

This isn't how it worked out. The State Department either failed to recognize or chose to ignore the importance of Truman's precondition, and while the Security Council had called for a report on the deteriorating situation in Palestine, the U.N. had not yet abandoned the partition plan when Austin announced the change in the American position. It looked to the world, and to American liberals, as if Truman was unilaterally undercutting the United Nations at its hour of greatest need.

Austin's statement set off a firestorm in public opinion, putting liberal internationalists and Zionists on the same page just as the country was digesting Truman's bleak call for a peacetime draft. Truman was furious. Writing to his sister, Mary Jane Truman, on March 21, the president called the State Department officials "striped pants conspirators" who had "completely balled up the Palestine situation."[10]

Then things got even worse: Eleanor Roosevelt wrote Truman to resign her position on the American delegation to the United Nations (her sons, meanwhile, had joined a group of nervous Democrats looking to dump Truman and draft Eisenhower for the 1948 presidential nomination).[11] Mrs. Roosevelt also took to her column to express her bitter disappointment on March 26, 1948, clearly blaming Truman for the crisis at the United Nations:

> I feel that our evident reluctance to accept responsibility and carry out whatever requests the U.N. might make of us, whether of a military or an economic nature, led to increased resistance by the Arabs. They were sure they could have their own way without any consideration of the wishes of the U.N.

The U.N. would have no force unless it was provided by a call on the great nations. And Great Britain was pulling out. This probably meant that we and Russia would be called upon. And our difficulties in Europe made us feel that added difficulties in the Near East would be inevitable if we and the USSR had soldiers and shared responsibility in that region. It might have created an impossible situation.

It looks to me, therefore, as though we have taken the weak course of sacrificing the word we pledged and, in so doing, have weakened the U.N. and prevented it from becoming an instrument to keep peace in the world.[12]

This is the outcome Truman had been struggling for months to avoid: Eleanor Roosevelt was accusing him in public of turning his back on the United Nations. Making things even worse, the day before Austin's statement, at the request of an old friend from St. Louis, Eddie Jacobson, Truman had met with Chaim Weizmann and reassured Weizmann that he remained committed to partition and Jewish independence.

Now, thanks to the State Department's misreading, as he saw it, of his instructions—a misreading that might well have been deliberate sabotage—Truman was taking the kind of political damage that he had struggled for years to avoid. He wrote of his frustration to his brother on March 22: "I think the proper thing to do, and the thing I have been doing, is to do what I think is right and let them all go to hell."[13]

Truman could hardly repudiate Austin in public. For one thing, the trusteeship idea was and remained Truman's policy. Given the vulnerability of Jewish forces on the ground, some form of trusteeship might be the only option that could prevent a ruinous defeat and catastrophe. Truman had been outmaneuvered by his own officials, and both Truman's personal political standing and the administration's prestige at home and abroad were significantly undercut.

In those last two weeks of March, Harry Truman's Palestine policy and his strategy for gaining the Democratic presidential nomination both lay in ruins. Over Europe, over Palestine, over his reelection prospects, dark clouds were gathering. He did not know it then, but the nadir had been reached. Deliverance would come, and from an unexpected quarter. In the spring of 1948, it wasn't Harry Truman who saved the Jews; it was the Jews of Palestine, with an assist from Stalin, who saved Harry Truman.

The "Big Three" at the 1945 Potsdam conference, left to right: Prime Minister Clement Attlee, President Harry Truman, and General Secretary of the Communist Party of the Soviet Union Joseph Stalin would dominate the postwar struggle over the future of Palestine.

Foreign Secretary Ernest Bevin, far right, and Clement Attlee saw the maintenance of British rule over the oil-rich Middle East as the key to Britain's economic survival. Fearing Arab hostility, they opposed resettling Jewish refugees in Palestine.

Eleanor Roosevelt was a liberal icon and firm believer in human rights and in the United Nations. She supported Jewish immigration to Palestine and pressured President Truman to enforce the 1947 U.N. resolution to create Jewish and Arab states in British Palestine.

Led by David Ben-Gurion, the Palestinian Jews were ready to fight for their independence, even if that meant war with Britain.

During his first term as president, Harry Truman struggled to unify the Democrats to oppose the Soviet Union. Henry Wallace, on the right, was seen by liberals as Franklin D. Roosevelt's true heir and opposed the Cold War. He left the Democratic Party to run as a third-party candidate in the 1948 election.

Devastating winter storms in January and February 1947 set off an economic crisis that forced the British cabinet to reduce its military commitments in India and Greece and to return its mandate over Palestine to the United Nations.

Chaim Weizmann testified before the United Nations Special Committee on Palestine (UNSCOP) as Palestinian Jews sought to win the contest for world opinion. Palestinian Arabs boycotted the process.

John Stanley Grauel, a Methodist minister and American Christian Zionist, was on the *Exodus 1947* refugee ship when it was boarded by British forces and turned back from Palestine. Future Israeli prime minister Golda Meir said Grauel's subsequent testimony to the U.N. Special Committee on Palestine persuaded the committee to recommend partition and Jewish statehood.

Joseph Stalin was an unlikely supporter of the Palestinian Jews in 1947 and 1948 as he worked to frustrate American and British policy in the Middle East and Europe.

Following the U.N. vote on partition, violence broke out in Palestine, and as the Jewish community in Jerusalem came under siege, Jewish forces suffered a succession of military reverses. Here, Jewish residents are seen fleeing the Old City through the Zion Gate in May 1948.

George F. Kennan, career diplomat and the first director of Policy Planning at the Department of State, believed that American support for Israeli independence would weaken Britain, strengthen the Soviet Union, and undermine America's position across the Middle East.

Like most western experts, Secretary of State George C. Marshall was convinced that the Palestinian Jews could not win against professional Arab militaries. In May 1948 he warned Jewish Agency representative Moshe Shertok "you are undertaking a grave responsibility."

David Ben-Gurion, standing, reads The Declaration of the Establishment of the State of
Israel on May 14, 1948, to take effect the next day when the British mandate expired.
A portrait of Theodor Herzl hangs on the wall behind him.

Overruling many of his advisers, Harry
Truman immediately issued a de facto
recognition of the new State of Israel. The
State Department's U.N. delegation heard the
news from other delegations while they were
gathering votes to delay partition.

Unknown to the Truman administration,
Ehud Avriel, a close associate of Ben-
Gurion and future Israeli diplomat,
had already negotiated arms purchases
from the communist government
of Czechoslovakia. Czech-made
arms, originally intended for Hitler's
Wehrmacht and sold to Israel with
Stalin's blessing, enabled Israel to win
its War of Independence.

In its early years, Israel was more popular on the American left than on the right. Paul Robeson, standing, was an All-American football player, singer, actor, communist, and Zionist. He helped raise money for the Irgun, a Jewish right-wing militia in Palestine.

Noted civil rights leader Martin Luther King Jr. (shown here with President Lyndon Johnson) was a strong supporter of Israel throughout his career.

Like Senator Bernie Sanders, the American left has increasingly soured on Israel. While supporting Israel's right to exist, Senator Sanders has described the Likud government of Benjamin Netanyahu as "an increasingly intolerant and authoritarian type of racist nationalism," and wrote that the American Israel Public Affairs Committee (AIPAC) provides a platform "for leaders who express bigotry and oppose basic Palestinian rights."

President Dwight Eisenhower, left, with Secretary of State John Foster Dulles, was much more interested in cultivating Egypt's president Gamal Abdel Nasser than he was in a relationship with Israel. Nasser, who was the leading figure in Arab nationalism, seemed to many Americans to embody the future of the Middle East.

Lyndon Johnson in the Oval Office with Clark Clifford (left) and Dean Rusk. Worried about declining liberal support for the Vietnam War, LBJ told American Jewish veterans that he would support Israel if American Jews did more to support the war in Vietnam. Furious Jewish leaders demanded an apology.

Israeli prime minster Golda Meir with President Richard Nixon and Secretary of State Henry Kissinger. Determined to reduce Soviet influence in the Middle East, Nixon and Kissinger laid the foundations of the modern alliance between the U.S. and Israel.

Billy Graham was one of the most consequential religious leaders in American history. The evangelical religious movement he promoted would become central to late-twentieth-century American conservatism and helped make support for Israel a mark of conservative Protestantism.

George W. Bush's mother, Barbara Bush, disapproved of his close relations with Israel and his disdain for Palestinian leader Yasser Arafat, who W. thought was too authoritarian to offer Palestinians a better future. In his second term, Bush pressured Israel heavily in an unsuccessful attempt to broker a peace agreement that he hoped would stabilize the Middle East.

A close relationship with Donald Trump helped Israeli prime minister Benjamin Netanyahu achieve longtime Israeli goals like moving the U.S. embassy to Jerusalem and peace agreements with neighboring Arab countries. But linking Israel this closely with the polarizing Trump led many American liberals, and many American Jews, to become significantly more critical of the Jewish state.

STALIN TO THE RESCUE

By late March, the future of Palestine was a military rather than a political issue. With Jerusalem under siege, the Jews of Palestine desperately needed to change the momentum on the battlefield. More than anything, this was a question of arms. In November 1947, the Yishuv, as the Palestinian Jews were widely known, counted roughly 17,000 rifles, 3,700 submachine guns, 205 machine guns, 775 light machine guns, scarcely over a dozen antitank guns, 750 mortars, and no antiaircraft guns, field guns, communications equipment, or tanks in its arsenals. There were no ships or planes. The Arab armies, on the other hand, had all of these weapons and more.[14] Egypt, Jordan, and Iraq had armies that had been trained and equipped by Great Britain; the Jordanian Arab Legion was staffed by British officers and trained to a high professional standard.

As the various international committees ground out their reports on the question of Palestine, agents of the Haganah, the underground army of the Jewish Agency, scoured the world for weapons, but had met with scant success. (The FBI arrested Haganah agents in the United States who were hoping to make illegal purchases.)[15] Then, on November 30, the day after the U.N. partition vote and the first day of widespread violence between Arabs and Jews across Palestine, a mysterious, well-dressed man knocked on the door of the Paris hotel room occupied by Ehud Avriel, tasked by Ben-Gurion to buy weapons for the Palestinian Jews. As Arnold Krammer tells the story in *The Forgotten Friendship: Israel and the Soviet Bloc, 1947–53*, the well-dressed man came into Avriel's room and

> quickly explained that there was nothing easier than purchasing arms. He produced a factory catalogue and a variety of descriptive folders and, without waiting for comments or questions from the stunned Haganah officials, proceeded through the lists giving explanations and price quotations.... He was Robert Adam Abramovici, Jewish, from Romania. Before the war he had been the Bucharest representative of Ceskoslovenska Zbrojovka Brno, the massive Skoda arms works in Czechoslovakia. He explained to Avriel, who was still awestruck, that he would accompany him to the Skoda factory the following morning, and that they were already expected. He produced two plane tickets from his pocket which he had taken the liberty of

buying on his way to the hotel, shook hands all around, and cordially took his departure. . . .

The Czechs, Avriel soon discovered, were prepared to sell weapons and equipment ordered by the Wehrmacht during the war, but never delivered. The initial contract included 10,000 Mauser P. 18 rifles, 4,500 heavy machine guns and 3 million rounds of ammunition. The Czechs indicated that they were ready and willing to sell other weapons and equipment up to and including Messerschmitt fighters, and even a few Spitfires and Mosquitoes that they had on hand. Communist governments elsewhere in the bloc were willing to allow the Haganah to smuggle the weapons to Palestine using transit routes across Soviet controlled Eastern Europe.[16]

The first shipment of Czech arms, shipped in disguised crates aboard a steamship and hidden under piles of onions, landed in Palestine on April 3, just in time for the launch of Operation Nachson to open a supply line to the besieged Jewish community in Jerusalem. Named for the ancient Hebrew traditionally credited with being the first to step into the Red Sea when Moses parted the waters, the offensive relieved the pressure on Jerusalem and marked a turning point in the war.

By May 15, when the British mandate officially ended, the Jews of Palestine were receiving regular arms deliveries from Czechoslovakia. When Ben-Gurion and his colleagues debated on whether or not to proclaim the Jewish state, they had already received 15,000 rifles, roughly 1,600 machine guns, and 21 million rounds of ammunition. The arms relationship with the Czechs survived the February 1948 communist coup that stripped away the last pretenses of Czech independence, and by May of that year the Israelis, as they would be called after independence was declared, were confident that further shipments were in the pipeline. An air corridor was planned for future arms shipments, and ultimately fighter aircraft (including recognizably German Messerschmitts) would be flown directly to Israeli airfields. With assurances that came from Stalin's closest aides and confidants, and a promise to allow Jewish volunteers to train in Soviet-controlled Europe, the leaders of the Jewish Agency were ready to proclaim the independence of the first Jewish state in Palestine in almost two thousand years.[17]

The first fighter planes from the Czechs arrived within days after Israeli independence was declared.[18] The American response was swift, as the United States persuaded the United Nations Security Council to impose a blanket arms embargo on all the combatant forces on May 29. (Again, the supposedly pliant Truman defied Zionist lobbyists on this point.) Stalin ignored the embargo with his customary ruthlessness, and during the next nine months continuing arms deliveries enabled the Israeli forces to achieve a progressively greater margin of superiority over their Arab opponents—even as Britain's adherence to the U.N. arms embargo left its Arab allies unable to resupply depleted stockpiles of ammunition.[19]

Historians ever since have puzzled over this unique episode in Soviet and Israeli history. After decades of hostility between communists and Zionists, Stalin tilted and tilted hard toward the Zionists just long enough for Israel to win its war of independence. Shortly thereafter, relations between Israel and the Soviet Union returned to the deep freeze, and up until the end of the Cold War, the Soviet Union and its Warsaw Pact allies were among the Jewish state's most resourceful and redoubtable opponents. The Soviets and their East German allies trained and armed terrorist groups who attacked Israeli citizens and territory; supported the intelligence agencies and the military forces of Israel's most radical Arab opponents; and engaged in nonstop disinformation and propaganda against the Jewish state throughout the world.[20]

We've seen that Stalin's hopes of driving a wedge between the United States and Great Britain combined with his interest in using support for the Jews to win friends among non-communist-left parties encouraged him to support the Zionists at the United Nations in 1947. In any case, from Stalin's perspective, the more deeply the United Nations, a forum in which it had a veto on the Security Council and a fair number of votes in the General Assembly, involved itself in Middle East questions, the more influence the Soviet Union could hope to gain in an important part of the world.

There were additional advantages in selling arms. To begin with, the Eastern Bloc countries were in desperate need of hard (western) currency as they struggled to recover from the devastation of the war and to finance a shift from capitalism to Soviet-style socialism. As noted earlier, Soviet satellites had been acquiring foreign currency by allowing Jews to emigrate in exchange for substantial hard currency payments from the Jewish Agency. Shipping this turbulent minority overseas at Jewish expense was an excellent way to subsidize Soviet power while both pacifying the Eastern Bloc and making trouble for the West. By the winter of 1947–48, Stalin was more eager than ever to find money for the satellites. With Western Europe about to benefit from Marshall Plan aid, and with the competition over the future of Europe heating up, Stalin needed to scrounge every dime of hard currency he could get to shore up the socialist economic bloc he was trying to build.

The American offer of Marshall Plan aid to Soviet-controlled countries had, as Truman hoped, done more than turn Eleanor Roosevelt and her allies into supporters of the Marshall Plan. It had also caused problems for Stalin and his allies in Eastern Europe. Czechoslovakia in particular was facing economic troubles as the communists tightened their grip in 1947–48. Access to American dollar credits struck even some Czech communists as an idea to be pursued, and the Soviets had to forbid the Czechs from entering conversations with the West about participating in the plan.

Allowing the Czechs to sell otherwise worthless Nazi surplus weapons to the Jews neatly solved this problem. When the Czechs complained about losing Marshall Plan funding, Stalin's ambassador replied, "You claim that Stalin did not let you join the Marshall Program, but you neglect to mention that he made it possible for you to obtain good dollars from the Israelis, by selling arms which did not even belong to you—for arms that you had already been paid by the Germans—isn't that enough compensation?"[21] The hard-pressed communist government would receive tens of millions of dollars as Israel, often using funds collected by American Jews in the United States, purchased as many weapons as the Czechs were willing to sell.[22]

It seems clear that one of Stalin's goals in making weapons available to the Jews was to further harass and embarrass Great Britain while driving a wedge into its alliance with the United States. Britain, it was clear, still had ambitions in the Middle East, and those ambitions still depended on the weak dynastic regimes aligned with the imperial power. Britain needed to avoid any kind of nationalist awakening in the Arab world. The shock of a long and even a losing war with the Jews would likely undermine the royal and feudal regimes clinging to power under British patronage in Egypt, Iraq, and possibly elsewhere. Any victories the Jews could win against Britain's puppet regimes would weaken those regimes and frustrate Britain's Middle East strategy. It was clear that in a war between Arabs and Jews, Britain would support the Arabs while American public opinion would rally to the Jews. Helping make that war longer and more costly would have struck Stalin as an obvious policy step. To the extent that this was his aim, Stalin's Middle East intervention succeeded. The shock of Arab defeat in the 1948–49 war was the beginning of a crisis that would ultimately sweep the old, pro-British order away. An awakening Arab nationalism turned against the kings who led the Arabs into a humiliating defeat, and against the perfidious foreign master whom they served. Stalin's successors would, as he hoped, find friends and allies among the new wave of nationalistic Arab regimes that spread across much of the region over the next ten years.

Stalin may well have hoped that the war could help the Soviet cause in other, more dramatic ways. Between 1945 and 1948, as Soviet-aligned governments in Eastern Europe had facilitated the movement of Jews to Palestine in defiance of the British immigration controls, a number of communists and Soviet agents had been included. More intriguing still, many senior leaders within the most elite of the Jewish fighting units, the Palmach, which left-wing Israeli historian Tom Segev refers to as "the Haganah's crack military force," were closely associated with the most pro-Soviet of the major Jewish political parties.[23]

During the Spanish Civil War, Moscow-aligned communists had come to dominate the originally noncommunist Republican side, in large part because the Soviet Union was the republic's most significant arms supplier and ensured that groups favorable to the Soviet cause got the best equipment. Something similar might happen in Palestine.

What Stalin did not expect was that the shipments of weapons would turn the military tide at just the moment when Jewish weakness threatened the Truman administration with the complete collapse of its Middle East policy. But that is how things turned out. Thanks to Stalin's intervention, by May, Truman was able to slither out of the cul-de-sac in which he seemed trapped in late March. The contentious White House meeting where Clark Clifford crossed swords with George Marshall was not, as so many pro- and anti-Zionist writers have thought, the moment when Truman put the wishes of the American Jewish community ahead of conventional foreign policy goals. It was the moment when he seized an opportunity to achieve his political and policy objectives at a far lower cost than he had any reason to expect.

THE FIGHT FOR RECOGNITION

In Washington, neither the State Department, the Pentagon, nor the CIA understood Soviet arms shipments were changing the balance of power in Palestine before May 14. Classified CIA briefings continued to predict defeat for the Jews. Seeing no alternative, President Truman spent the two months from mid-March to mid-May following the Palestine policy that the State Department so artfully had foisted on him. The official United States position remained what Warren Austin had announced to the U.N. The partition plan approved by the United Nations the previous November was not working, and that while partition of Palestine into Arab and Jewish states remained an American goal, it was necessary at least in the short term to seek a delay between the British withdrawal and the final resolution of the issue. This delay would take the form of a United Nations trusteeship; if possible, Britain would be persuaded to carry on a while longer; otherwise some other non-Soviet trustee would need to be found, and some sort of peacekeeping police force would have to be assembled. While the trustee maintained the peace, the United Nations would pursue new negotiations between Arabs and Jews to find a partition program or possibly some other solution that both sides could accept.[24]

This was a policy that had very few friends outside the departments of State and Defense. Liberals attacked the retreat from the partition resolution and what they saw as the cavalier treatment afforded to the U.N. American Zionists grimly followed the military news from Palestine and saw the glittering prize of independence slipping away from their grasp, perhaps never to return. Other observers feared that Truman's waffling and inconsistent approach to the issue would end with the United States trapped into maintaining some kind of military presence in Palestine, perhaps to be shot at by both sides.

The American diplomats found little support at the United Nations, where they had called the General Assembly into special session to review the situation in Palestine. The Soviets mocked the Americans for going back on their earlier support for partition, posed as the true friends of the U.N., and stood ready to veto any resolution that would allow the Americans to escape from their embarrassment. The British, enjoying the American discomfiture almost as much as the Soviets, wanted nothing to do with a trusteeship, and in any case now hoped and expected that their client Abdullah of Jordan would annex the portions of Palestine assigned to the Arabs by the partition plan. They also hoped he would conquer the Negev, strengthening his position and theirs.

No country really wanted to be part of a multinational police force in Palestine. Vociferous opposition from both Arabs and Jews meant that the friends of neither side were eager to support the American plan. Many countries, including those who still resented American pressure to vote in favor of the original resolution, felt that a retreat from the partition resolution would be a humiliation for the United Nations. Truman's political support was splintering at home, and the United States was losing prestige at the United Nations with every day the crisis dragged on.

As the end of the mandate approached, American diplomacy grew increasingly desperate. True, the Jews had won some victories since early April, and the military picture was no longer as bleak. But those victories had mostly been won against lightly armed, poorly trained, and badly supplied militias of Palestinian Arabs. With the end of the mandate, the wider war would begin. Already fighters from Jordan's Arab Legion were beginning to intervene in the fighting between Arabs and Jews. Military analysts in both Britain and the United States believed that as professional Arab troops joined the fighting, the overstretched Jewish forces would yield up their recent gains and retreat. A humanitarian crisis would loom, Truman would be blamed for it, and the United States would lack the military forces to stabilize the situation. In a last-minute gesture to get some kind of cease-fire, Truman offered the use of his personal plane for negotiators to travel to the region; nobody wanted to go.[25]

As the clock ran down on the British mandate, Truman's faith in his diplomats was justifiably low. He had taken the advice of the professionals and the experts at the State Department. They told him that they had a practical alternative to the looming disaster of partition. They were wrong; trusteeship was neither practical nor politic. The warring peoples didn't want it; no country would claim it; neither the Security Council nor the General Assembly would endorse it. Truman had let the experts take the wheel, and they had driven the car into a ditch.

What, under these unpromising circumstances, should the United States do? That was the question that the May 12 meeting in the White House with which our account of Truman's Palestine policy began was intended to address. The conventional idea, whether in the pro-Zionist version that a gutsy American president defied the bureaucrats to extend a hand of friendship to our plucky democratic friends in Palestine, or in the anti-Zionist version that a weak president well out of his depth chose political expediency over foreign policy, would shape the way many diplomats and scholars would understand the politics of American Middle East policy for years to come. Yet neither version does justice to Truman or to Marshall, to the situation as they understood it, or to the choices they made.

Marshall is often cast as a determined opponent of the Jewish drive for statehood, but his attitude was ultimately determined by his military judgment. It was not only the CIA that prophesied inevitable defeat for the Jewish forces. Marshall's wartime colleagues in the British military were adamant in their belief that the Jewish cause was hopeless. Four days before the famous meeting with Truman, Marshall met with Moshe Shertok, the foreign representative of the Yishuv. Marshall recalled saying:

> It was extremely dangerous to base long-range policy on temporary military success. There was no doubt but that the Jewish army had gained such temporary success but there was no assurance whatever that in the long-range the tide might not turn against them. I told Mr. Shertok that they were taking a gamble. If the tide did turn adversely and they came running to us for help they should be placed clearly on notice now that there was no warrant to expect help from the United States, which had warned them of the grave risk which they were running.[26]

Marshall, like other observers, had noticed the change in Jewish battlefield performance since early April. But, especially without knowing the causes, how confident could anyone be that this would last? As it happened, on May 13 Kfar Etzion, the most important Jewish outpost on the road south from Jerusalem, fell to an assault involving Jordanian troops after withstanding a siege for four months.[27] Marshall ended the conference by warning Shertok about the likely consequences of the full-scale Arab invasion that would follow a declaration of independence: "What will happen if there's a prolonged invasion? It will weaken you. I have had experience in China. At first there was an easy victory. Now they've been fighting two years and they've lost Manchuria. However, if it turns out that you're right and you will establish the Jewish State, I'll be happy. But you are undertaking a grave responsibility." Shertok was shaken enough by this unsparing analysis by one of the most famous military leaders of the day that he considered advising Ben-Gurion to delay proclaiming the state.[28]

CIA documents make it clear that Marshall and his aides remained uninformed about Stalin's arms shipments, news that presumably Israelis were not eager to share with Americans as Cold War tensions ratcheted up in Europe. By the end of the summer, Israeli forces would have better arms, more ammunition, and a stronger air force than their opponents. The early victories against the Palestinian Arabs were no flash in the pan, as Marshall feared. They were the harbinger of a series of military victories that would leave Israel in control of more territory than the UNSCOP report had assigned to it. With the rapid influx of refugees from Europe (British forces stopped interfering with immigration when the mandate expired), Israel's reservoir of military manpower also grew.

The other factor that the diplomats overlooked was the lack of unity and commitment among the Arab states to a common battle against Israel. Here a kind of orientalism seems to have clouded the otherwise acute analytical powers of State's regional observers. They were so impressed by the unanimity and strength of Arab opposition to the establishment of a Jewish state in Palestine that they overlooked the deep differences in the interests of the Arab states that made their cooperation ineffective. Some Egyptians for example saw Transjordan as a British puppet rather than as an ally against the Jewish interlopers.[29] In Cairo, it seemed absolutely clear that Abdullah was using the war (and the famous Arab Legion, trained and led by British officers and equipped with advanced British military equipment) to seize Palestinian land for himself, and also to advance across the Negev. This meant that the British would have the ability to station forces on the border of the Sinai Desert, posing a long-term threat to the security of a Suez Canal that Egyptian nationalists were already thinking about seizing for themselves. Although no Egyptian would ever say so, an Israeli buffer in the Negev against Britain might suit Egypt's interests better than a Jordanian win.[30]

Other rivalries undercut the power of the Arab "united front" against Israel. Syria feared (correctly) that its Arab allies dreamed of conquering Damascus as well as Jerusalem. Faisal II's grandfather had, before being expelled by the French, once claimed the throne of Syria. Now the French were gone and the new Syrian government, torn between squabbling ethnic and religious groups, was weak.[31] Why not return? During World War II some British officials hinted at supporting Faisal in a bid to take over Vichy-occupied Syria. Might not that dream be revived in the chaos of a war against the Jews? Faisal's brother Abdullah, the emir of Transjordan, was an even nearer and greater worry. And finally, with the partial exception of Jordan, none of the Arab states had the financial strength—or the political and institutional structures—to fight a long war.

All this meant that the Arab opposition to the new state of Israel was much less formidable than Marshall and his aides believed. All along, the State Department "realists" had misread the realities of the Middle East. Partition did mean war (State was right about this and many American Zionists and naive liberals were wrong), but war did not lead to Jewish defeat.

Given that Marshall believed that the push for statehood would lead to a military defeat, it seemed incomprehensible to him that the United States should alienate Arab opinion, further stress its relationship with Great Britain, and distract itself and the world from the looming confrontation with the Soviets in Berlin. His contempt for White House aide Clark Clifford (apparently, he never spoke to him again)[32] and his fury at Truman was less the rage of the frustrated Arabist than the reaction of a man who believed that Truman, at Clifford's prompting, was willing to encourage the Jews into a war that they could not win for the sake of a few headlines and a temporary lift in the polls.

Clifford's argument was, in fact, political, but he was not talking simply about the Jews. As the meeting notes stated, he spoke "to urge the President to give prompt recognition to the Jewish State after the termination of the mandate on May 15. He said such a move should be taken quickly before the Soviet Union recognized the Jewish State. It would have distinct value in restoring the President's position for support of the partition of Palestine." By urging recognition as "restoring the President's position for support of the partition of Palestine," Clifford meant something much more consequential than restoring the president's position among Jews. He meant that this was an opportunity for Truman to regain some of the ground he had lost as a supporter of the U.N. process. What Marshall resented as a narrow political strategy based on cynical ethnic pandering was in fact a political strategy, one aimed at sustaining exactly the foreign policy that, overall, George Marshall and his State Department colleagues believed was essential for the United States.[33]

What Truman and for that matter Clark Clifford understood on May 12 that George Marshall did not was that foreign policy is always a matter of politics. Truman needed authority and power to chart America's course in the Cold War. He could not retain that authority without the support of his own party. The decisive wing of that party, the liberal internationalists and progressives who revered Eleanor Roosevelt and shared her worldview, still believed that helping the United Nations grow into the most important institution in international relations was the key to world peace. George Marshall, Robert Lovett, George Kennan, and for that matter Harry Truman and Clark Clifford, might view this shining faith as akin to a small child's belief in Santa Claus, and they might be correct in doing so, but that was not the point. Without Mrs. Roosevelt and her supporters, there was no future for the Truman administration, no future for George Marshall as secretary of state, and no guarantee that the far-reaching plans for containing the Soviet Union being crafted in George Kennan's Policy Planning office in the State Department would ever be put into play.

Foreign policy is and must be grounded in domestic politics. There may be moments when a national leader must sacrifice his or her own personal political interest to achieve some great national goal, but as a general rule, for a foreign policy to succeed overseas, it must also succeed politically at home. Marshall's job as he understood it was to present the professional views of his department to the president of the United States. Truman's job as he understood it was to reconcile the demands of domestic politics to the requirements of effective foreign policy when that was possible, and to adjudicate between them when it was not.

Clifford's point to Truman was that whatever the United States did, the Palestinian Jews were going to declare their independence in just a few days. The Soviet Union, which had been providing them with continuing support at the United Nations, including opposing the State Department's effort to delay their independence by establishing a new U.N. trusteeship to replace the expiring British mandate, would surely recognize the new state very quickly. That would allow the Soviet Union to claim the credit for supporting U.N. Resolution 181 while the Soviets and all their allies would paint Truman as the man who betrayed it.

If, however, Truman moved faster than the Soviet Union, and recognized the Jewish state before Moscow did, he would be the leader who stood up for 181, the upholder of the United Nations and the international process. American recognition made no difference to what happened or didn't happen in Tel Aviv on May 15; the Jews were going to declare a state. But American recognition made all the difference in how Truman's leadership would be perceived by the American people and by his own party.[34]

Clifford was also right when he said that the State Department did not have a real alternative to propose. The British were leaving and no one else was going to take their place. Jewish independence might be a mistake and might ultimately lead to a humanitarian catastrophe that would create a terrible policy dilemma for the United States, but statehood was going to happen now regardless of what Truman did or didn't do.

Thanks to the State Department, Truman had been left with the political costs of opposing the implementation of 181 without any offsetting benefits. This damage was not just to Truman's domestic political standing. The hasty and undignified American reversal on Palestine had offended many American allies, either because they themselves continued to view the success of the U.N. as an important national interest or because they had only voted for Resolution 181 at American prompting, and were now left looking foolish by the American change of course. The failure of the State Department's diplomacy at the U.N. since March had damaged the prestige of both the United States of America and Truman. Now the State Department had nothing to recommend beyond urging him to look weak and indecisive as events took their course.

There may have been one other factor at work. Truman, it will be remembered, had refused to meet with any Zionist leaders or delegations in March when the policy crisis was at its height. Desperate to arrange a meeting between Chaim Weizmann, the Israeli Zionist leader then visiting the United States, and Truman, American Jewish leaders reached out to Eddie Jacobson to see if he could prevail on his old friend to get Weizmann in to see Truman. Reluctantly, Truman agreed, and Weizmann (ushered into a side entrance to avoid publicity) stopped by the White House the day before Warren Austin announced that the United States no longer supported Resolution 181 at the United Nations.[35] No official record of their meeting exists, and neither Weizmann nor Truman ever gave a full account of what was said.[36] Since after their previous meeting in November of 1947, Truman had instructed the State Department to support the addition of the Negev Desert to the territory to be awarded the Jews at partition,[37] many writers, both pro- and anti-Zionist, have seen the March meeting between the two leaders as equally consequential.

That seems unlikely. As we've noted, Truman's policy did not change after meeting with Weizmann. Following Austin's U.N. speech, the United States continued to oppose partition and support alternatives right up until May 14. Much to their chagrin and embarrassment, the American diplomats at the United Nations would be working the floor in support of a last-ditch mediation proposal right up until the moment when the news that Truman had recognized the state of Israel reached the General Assembly. But there is a case to be made that the meeting with Weizmann affected Truman's, and perhaps also Clark Clifford's, approach to the meeting on May 12.

Weizmann, who had helped usher the Balfour Declaration through the British government in World War I and would serve as the first president of Israel until his death in 1952, had long been associated with the more moderate and conciliatory side of the Zionist movement, believing that good relations with the British and American governments offered the best path to achieving Zionist goals. During World War II his star faded among militant Zionists; a new generation of more radical leaders was ready to pursue more confrontational stances than Weizmann thought were wise. In the first World Zionist Congress held after the Holocaust, Weizmann memorably cautioned his fellow delegates against too rash an approach: "Masada, for all its heroism, was a disaster in our history. It is not our purpose or our right to plunge to destruction in order to bequeath a legend of martyrdom to posterity. Zionism was to mark the end of our glorious deaths and the beginning of a new path leading to life." George Marshall could not have put the risks of independence more cogently, but in the spring of 1948, Weizmann took a different tack.

In that critical time, Weizmann was one of the strongest voices urging Jews to declare their state. While Ben-Gurion had frozen Weizmann out of policymaking in Jewish affairs, he was very much aware of Weizmann's value as a spokesman for the Zionist cause to Anglo-Americans. In March, with Truman and the State Department both adamantly refusing to meet with representatives of the Zionist movement, Weizmann was the only leading Zionist that Truman, reluctantly, agreed to see. There is no doubt that the Zionist leadership wanted Weizmann well prepared for this meeting. It is not clear how much Weizmann knew about the Soviet arms shipments or about the military calculations of the Jewish defense forces, but it seems likely that Ben-Gurion and his associates would have done everything in their power to ensure that Weizmann's message to Truman would strike the right notes. In particular, one expects that Weizmann's message would have stressed that the Jews understood the odds against them, knew that they could not call on the United States for military help, and would not declare independence without believing that they could defend themselves. Truman's confidence in Weizmann's long track record of moderation and sober judgment would have encouraged Truman to believe that the Jewish cause was in better shape than the State Department and Pentagon experts believed. Thanks to Weizmann and, yes, to Eddie Jacobson, Truman seems to have had more confidence than Marshall in the military outlook for the Palestinian Jews during those critical days in May.

At midnight by Tel Aviv time, Israel proclaimed its independence. Eleven minutes later, at 6:11 p.m. Eastern time, Truman extended de facto recognition to the first Jewish state in Palestine since the time of the Maccabees.[38] In a concession to the State Department, protocol was observed. Truman waited to receive a formal request for recognition from the Washington representative of the new government in Tel Aviv, and recognition was de facto, rather than de jure.[39]

It was not Truman's fault that the American delegation at the U.N. was caught unaware by the policy shift. Dean Rusk in the State Department had called Warren Austin a few minutes before the announcement. Austin was so angry at the sudden reversal of policy that he went home without informing his colleagues. The rest of the American delegation only learned about Truman's new policy when the news swept through other delegations.[40]

In a letter written in 1974, Dean Rusk recalled that the General Assembly was in complete pandemonium upon hearing the news. "When I use the word pandemonium," he wrote, "I think I am not exaggerating. I was later told that one of our U.S. Mission staff men literally sat on the lap of the Cuban Delegate to keep him from going to the podium to withdraw Cuba from the United Nations. In any event, about 6:15 I got a call from Secretary Marshall who said, 'Rusk, get up to New York and prevent the

U.S. Delegation from resigning en masse.'" He recounted: "There was a story later that some of Secretary Marshall's friends had told him that he ought to resign because of this incident. He was reported to have replied, 'No, gentlemen, you do not accept a post of this sort and then resign when the man who has the Constitutional authority to make a decision makes one. You may resign at any time for any other reason but not that one.'"[41]

Eleanor Roosevelt, who at Truman's patient urging had withdrawn her March resignation, was still an official member of the American delegation to the U.N. As unaware of the shift as any of her colleagues, she was also enraged by the way the announcement was made. Switching policy this quickly, with no notice to the General Assembly or to the American representatives, struck her as lacking in respect to the institution and to the delegation, herself very much included. Nevertheless, she could not but observe that, awkward as he was, Truman had let the U.N. process take its course and demonstrated his respect for its outcome. She never warmed to him, but she did not join her sons in the "Draft Eisenhower" movement, and though her endorsement of Truman for reelection in 1948 was late, cold, and hedged, it did come.[42]

After so many months of treading carefully, Truman enjoyed the discomfiture of his diplomats. "I was told that to some of the career men of the State Department this announcement came as a surprise. It should not have been if these men had faithfully supported my policy. . . . I wanted to make it plain that the President of the United States, and not the second or third echelon in the State Department, is responsible for making foreign policy."[43]

Truman, despite the obstacles and political headwinds, stuck to his principles and, as he saw it, brought thirty years of bipartisan American foreign policy to a successful conclusion. The Jewish national home was a fact, providing a refuge for persecuted Jews and allowing the United States to see refugees helped without opening its doors to a flood of immigrants. The United States had played its part in the drama through diplomatic means and international institutions only and without sending in troops. Zionist lobbying had not persuaded Truman to advance beyond the Blackstone approach; anti-Zionist lobbying in the State and Defense departments had not persuaded him to abandon it.

The question of Palestine was never the most important issue that Truman faced, and the Zionist lobby was never the most important political force that he took into account. For Truman, Palestine policy was more a means to an end than an end in itself. Keeping the Democratic Party united as he led the country into a Cold War with the Soviet Union was the big goal Truman never lost sight of. Aligning his Palestine policy as far as possible with the liberals who wanted the issue resolved by the United Nations was one of the ways in which he achieved it.

13

The Cold Peace

ARRY TRUMAN'S DE FACTO RECOGNITION of Israel ended one
era in the American relationship, but a generation would pass
before the United States and Israel became aligned. For the
most critical years of Israel's history, when the country was weak and
poor, the United States was more interested in building relationships
with Israel's bitterest Arab opponents than with the Jewish state. Only
after Israel developed nuclear weapons and emerged as a regional superpower did it move to the center of America's diplomatic agenda. Israel
did not grow strong because it had American support. It acquired American support because it had grown strong.

Those who forget this basic fact about the relationship often overestimate America's leverage with Israel and form unrealistic ideas about the
concessions that the United States can extract from Jerusalem. Those
who hope that an end to the U.S.-Israel alliance would cripple the Jewish
state should also take note. Israel, which was not formally designated an
American ally until Ronald Reagan declared Israel a "major non-NATO
ally" in 1987, desperately wanted American military and diplomatic support during its early years. Losing that support would be a serious blow
today, but in a world where Russia, India, China, and Japan all admire
Israeli tech and Israeli military and intelligence capabilities, if abandoned by Washington, Israel would not remain friendless for long.

Just as Truman's policy toward the crisis of British Palestine was
driven by his reading of the international situation as a whole, subsequent American presidents hardly considered Israel policy in a vacuum.
The Cold War was America's overriding strategic concern during the
first forty years of Israeli independence, and the logic of the Cold War as
American policymakers understood it kept the United States and Israel

at arm's length during the 1950s and brought the two countries closer together in the 1970s.

The Cold War forced a massive reassessment and in some ways a reinvention of American foreign policy. World War II left the United States the richest, most powerful, and most widely admired country in the world. Americans had long expected that their day of global preeminence would come. Even before the Revolution, farsighted Americans like Benjamin Franklin had looked at the size and fertility of the American landmass and the dynamism of American society and formed the belief that in the fullness of time the United States would be the greatest power in the world. Now that time had come, but the bed of roses they had expected had somehow turned into a crown of thorns.

The dream had never been just or even principally about power and prestige within the existing state system. Americans had also long dreamed of a decisive victory for American ideas on the stage of world history, a victory that would express itself in the transformation of international politics. After World War II, principles like self-determination swept the world, but not always in forms that simplified the task of American foreign policy. The European empires that Americans had long resented lay humbled in the dust, but the result was a weak Europe and a world unable to resist Soviet power without American help. At the same time, many of the peoples newly emerging from colonial bondage seemed bent on exercising their rights of self-determination under communist leadership.

By 1949, history and geopolitics, which had been moving extraordinarily rapidly and kaleidoscopically since 1945, had begun to settle into the shape they would retain for the next four decades, and Washington policymakers began to come to terms with the long-term implications of the new world situation. Clearly, the ideas and the methods of Lodge-era diplomacy would no longer suffice. It was not enough for the United States to cooperate with central bankers, press for disarmament, preach moral sentiments, and wish our friends well. More active policies, not to mention more dangerous and expensive ones, would be needed to maintain world peace. The illusions of the "One World" liberals would also have to be set aside. Good intentions and high hopes would not make the United Nations an effective substitute for American power in the postwar world.

In confronting this stark new reality, Americans were driven by both their hopes and their fears. American culture is fundamentally an optimistic culture. The American experience for more than three centuries was one of material and social progress. An entrepreneurial, forward-looking people set in a rich continent, most Americans have been drawn to optimistic readings of history and of the human potential for improvement. In the eighteenth and nineteenth centuries, this cultural optimism was reflected in the development of a benign vision of a peaceful and gradual transformation of human history in a new kind of progressive march to a utopian future. As we've seen, many Americans came to believe, either as a religious idea or as a secular vision, that the gradual improvement of economic and social conditions that they saw taking place around them would culminate in a universal reign of peace. Liberal Christians interpreted this through the lens of scripture, arguing that human progress would eventually lead to the peaceful return of Christ and the establishment of a millennial kingdom. For secular thinkers, visions of the utopian future looked to a democratic world in which the nations of the world would renounce war, embrace democracy, and cooperate to establish universal equality and prosperity.

We've already seen how the dissolution of the great eastern empires in Europe and the Middle East began to challenge the habitual optimism of American opinion in the nineteenth century. Economic development, the spread of education, and the rise of democracy were not turning the imperial zone into a paradise of liberal enlightenment. Vicious ethnic, religious, and nationalistic rivalries erupted in succession, and, to the accompaniment of ethnic cleansings and genocides, a series of escalating wars boiled out of the region, progressively forcing American engagement and culminating in the Second World War.

The struggle of the American mind to reconcile what looked to be the catastrophic arc of world history into a series of escalating and ultimately exterminatory wars with the national faith in liberal values was a difficult one. It became more difficult as American power grew even while the world itself seemed to be lurching closer to final destruction. Two events at the end of World War II crystallized the feeling of unease into what would remain a bedrock perception in the United States.

On July 22, 1944, Soviet troops liberated the Majdanek concentration camp near Lublin, Poland. The Nazi guards were not prepared for the speed of the Soviet advance, and they were unable to destroy the evidence of what had taken place there. Majdanek had not primarily been an extermination center like Auschwitz or Treblinka. It was a forced labor camp for Polish Jews temporarily spared from extermination, although it sometimes served as a killing site when other facilities were not available. Something like 100,000 Jews and a smaller number of Poles had been imprisoned or murdered in the camp between its construction in 1941 and its liberation.[1] Shocked at what they saw there, Soviet commanders quickly contacted higher authorities, and journalists and photographers were brought in to share the information with the world.[2]

There had been many reports about Nazi extermination camps, and by 1943 most people in both Germany and the West knew at least something about the murder of the Jews and other atrocities under Hitler's rule. Abstract knowledge, however, is one thing, but the photographs of stacked corpses, rows of skulls, mounds of shoes, emaciated survivors, piles of human hair, and other grisly relics of systematized murder reverberated across the world and forced a new reckoning with the bleak realities of human nature for many people in the United States. Over the next nine months as Allied troops slowly overcame the resistance of the Reich's defenders, the horrors of more camps were gradually uncovered and progressively revealed to the world. Evil, pure, cold, and calculating, had taken its seat in the most advanced and enlightened culture in Europe, and the revelation of what had been done seared the conscience but also challenged the fundamental assumptions of what, for most Americans, was their basic outlook on life.

The outpouring of detailed evidence about German crimes, the Holocaust above all, but also the fiendish atrocities committed by so many hundreds of thousands of German soldiers and officials from Occupied France to the Soviet Union, scarred the American conscience in ways that still affect us today. There were other atrocities in that terrible age, the homicidal madness and twisted hate the Japanese manifested in their drive across China, the everyday brutality of Stalinist rule—but the German crimes left a deeper impression on the American mind. Next to Britain, Germany was the nation to which Americans felt closest. Only the British Isles (Ireland included) had contributed more immigrants to the United States than Germany.[3]

For most Americans of the mid-twentieth century, the moral collapse of Germany was something that Americans couldn't explain away by attributing it to some alleged defect of race. Germany was a white,

Protestant, European culture of the highest level. Many of the Protestant churches of Germany had close associations with leading American denominations and thinkers, and those churches, for the most part,
had followed Hitler into hell with little or no resistance. If Germany, the
land of Bach, Beethoven, Goethe, and Kant, could fall in this way, what
did this mean for liberal hopes about enlightenment, progress, and the
ultimate destiny of the human race? What prospect was there for the
kind of peaceful, liberal world Americans hoped so desperately to build?
Was there some ineradicable horror at the heart of human nature, some
depraved hunger for power and for death that all the education, all the
enlightenment in the world could never fully uproot?

The second event of those momentous years that still shakes the
foundations of our world was America's use of nuclear weapons against
Japan in August 1945. The bombs were part of a massive air offensive
against Japanese cities that killed hundreds of thousands of civilians in
the closing months of the Pacific War,[4] and they transformed the human
condition in ways we still struggle to grasp and to cope with today.

The historicization of the eschaton, the migration of the concept of
the end of the world from the realm of myth to the realm of politics, had,
as we've seen, long been a factor in Americans' understanding of their
country and its world role. With the explosion in Hiroshima, the end of
the world entered the realm of politics and policy in a new and much
more terrifying way. As the outlandish concept of "mutually assured
destruction" entrenched itself as a pillar of American strategic thought,
the end of the world was no longer a purely speculative concept. In think
tanks, in university seminars, in military planning sessions, American
defense intellectuals and officials were integrating the possibility of a
nuclear holocaust into their scenario planning. And it was not only officials and military planners who grappled with these realities. As the two
superpowers developed missiles capable of striking targets thousands
of miles away with nuclear weapons delivered at supersonic speeds, the
reality that humanity could now drive itself into extinction percolated
into the consciousness of ordinary people across the planet.

That the Holocaust and the attack on Hiroshima came almost simultaneously at the conclusion of the most terrible war humanity had ever
fought helped drive the horror home around the world. The capacity for
evil revealed in the Holocaust combined with the capacity for destruction revealed by the explosion at Hiroshima opened up a prospect that

few could contemplate calmly and that none could ignore. Seventy years later, the shock of these events has not faded, and we still struggle to manage their consequences.

The near-simultaneous eruption of absolute evil and the emergence of an absolute power of destruction into human history transformed the nature of politics and international relations. Avoiding a recurrence of the genocidal madness and unspeakable cruelty of the Hitler movement, and avoiding nuclear suicide, would from the 1940s come to be basic tasks that policymakers and political movements would put at the center of their missions. The United States was becoming a global power at a uniquely dire moment in the history of the human race.

THE AMERICAN MISSION

Facing these terrifying truths, the vast majority of Americans believed this situation called them to lead. Belief in some kind of singular world role had always been an element in American thought. From the Puritan beginning, through the Revolution and Civil War periods, Americans had always believed that what was happening in their country would, in due course, play a decisive role in world events.

The United States had always been a more outward-looking nation than isolationists wanted it to be, or remembered it as being. American business and American missionaries had been active in the Middle East, South and East Asia, Africa, and Latin America from the early days of the republic. American universities began admitting students from the non-European, non-Atlantic world in the 1850s. American forces had been stationed in the South Pacific and the Mediterranean from the early decades of the nineteenth century. Well before the Spanish-American War, American forces had been engaged in military action on every continent except Australia and Antarctica.[5]

The global engagement of the United States had not been the private preserve of elites. Appalachian backwoodsmen dug ginseng root for the China trade.[6] Semiliterate sailors served on whaling ships. In a time when more than half of all Americans earned their living from farms, the export trade was vital to farm prices.[7] Thomas Jefferson's embargo of Britain and France led to bankruptcies across the American farming economy; Britain's repeal of the Corn Laws opened up a rich export market that helped fuel westward expansion.

Missionary activity, which involved both religious proselytization and what we would now think of as development work and human rights advocacy, also brought millions of ordinary Americans into the sphere of international activity and awareness. Black American congregations raised money for mission work in Africa.[8] Small churches across rural America regularly raised money for missions abroad. Through letters and publications and from lectures by missionaries home on fundraising trips, millions of Americans followed the progress of Christianity and modernization from China to Peru. Women played an outsized role in this movement. Barred from many professions, from political careers, and from pastoring churches or leading denominational bodies, women found opportunities in the foreign mission field to lead big-budget organizations, acquire and use professional skills at home and abroad, and chart an independent course as single women took up foreign mission careers.[9]

The soldiers, missionaries, educators, and merchants who had pioneered America's global engagement and the national strategists who, from the time of George Washington forward, had looked to the moment when the United States would be the most powerful nation on earth saw their vision fulfilled after World War II. But America's transition to world leadership was far more epochal and far more challenging than anyone had expected. The United States had been summoned to take the lead in a global battle for the survival of freedom and the human race itself. The experience of confronting, first, the horrifically evil and brutal empires of Axis Germany and Japan, and then of leading the battle against the Stalinist and Maoist empires of institutionalized mass murder and human repression, left a deep imprint on Americans of the time. The United States might not be perfect, but its enemies appeared to be about as close to pure evil as any political systems had ever been. A nation long steeped in a Christian and Protestant worldview could not interpret these events other than through the prism of a divine calling and mission. The historicization of the eschaton led, among Americans, to an Americanization of history. Given the reality of American power and its centrality to international politics in what looked like the climactic stages of the human story, many Americans began to think of history as something that America made and was responsible for. It was America's job to save the planet by sound policy, wise leadership, and, when no better way could be found, by the courageous use of necessary force.

As Americans tried to think this mission through, they saw two inter-connected efforts: a political and military strategy aimed at containing communism, and a global agenda that would transform the free world. They hoped to eliminate the specter of great power war among noncom-munist countries even as they worked to contain the Soviet Union with-out direct conflict, and they adopted a mix of policies to achieve that. One was to build on the lessons of the Marshall Plan, and to embark on a quest for development for the postcolonial countries emerging from the wreckage of the old empires. Another was to develop a network of security partnerships, economic institutions, political institutions, and a body of international law that would reduce the probability of war. The Americans hoped that a network of interlocking institutions, a surge in economic growth promoting interdependent prosperity, a legal basis for international life ultimately expressed in the United Nations and similar institutions, and a set of enduring military commitments and alliances backed ultimately by the strength and commitment of the United States would stave off the nightmare of nuclear war and open a path to the future for the world.

It was clear to American policymakers in the early Cold War era that these goals required a much greater investment of American money, political effort, and military power than the nation had ever before expended in time of peace. After all, the goal was to transform the world, to stop the series of ever-more-destructive great power wars that threatened to exterminate humankind. Given that none of the postwar allied states could withstand the Soviet Union on its own, this meant that American security commitments had to be extended. Given the interconnected nature of economic prosperity with the fight against communism and the struggle for stability, the guarantees had to go beyond military security. It was up to the United States, the only country with the resources for such a task, to provide the framework for postwar recovery and long-term prosperity.

The new forms of American guarantees and support for both devel-oped and developing allies in the Cold War differ so much from the Lodge consensus and what had come before it as to amount to a new dispensation. Under the Lodge consensus, Americans minimized their military and financial commitments abroad. That approach would not work in the Cold War. To nations that were willing to join in resisting the spread of communist totalitarianism, America offered to do whatever it took to defend its allies. This would include bearing any price, be it in money or blood, to keep the allies independent. Like wealthy colleges who accept students without regard to their financial circumstances, committing to provide whatever scholarship aid students require, America offered a "needs blind" alliance; countries like South Korea that needed a lot of help would get whatever they needed—as long as they did their part. Countries that needed less would get less. And while America always had a preference for liberalism, capitalism, and democracy, it was willing to work with any form of government—from social democracies to authoritarian dictatorships—that was willing to resist the bigger enemy.

Beyond that, in order to reestablish the kind of open global trading system that the British Empire had fostered at its height, the United States undertook to provide various global public goods. The American navy would ensure the security of the world's sea lanes. The United States would provide the bulk of the financing for the International Monetary Fund (IMF) and the World Bank. The United States, despite its long-standing commitment to industrial protection, would open its markets, in many cases on a nonreciprocal basis, to other countries.

The implications of these immense changes in policy took many years to work themselves out. When Harry Truman announced the Truman Doctrine as the British withdrew from Turkey and Greece, he did not foresee the full consequences of America's new international stance. He did not, for example, understand that as the United States extended protection to countries threatened by the Soviet Union but who hated one another, American diplomats would be committed to years of shuttle diplomacy and cat herding as they attempted to keep Greeks and Turks, Koreans and Japanese, Indians and Pakistanis, Argentines and Brazilians, Malaysians and Indonesians, Saudis and (before 1979) Iranians, and, of course, Arabs and Israelis, from letting their mutual rivalries and distrust spill over into actions that would disrupt the Pax Americana. That 2,700,000 American troops would serve in Vietnam (the largest number at any given time was 549,500 in 1968),[10] that there would still be U.S. military bases in both Europe and Japan seventy years after World War II and a generation after the fall of the Soviet Union, that the American navy would be undertaking Freedom of Navigation Operations in the South China Sea to protect Philippine claims to offshore waters—none of this, of course, was in Truman's mind in 1947 when he initiated the change in American diplomacy.

In the early years of the new dispensation, the Truman administration tried to limit the geographic scope of its increasingly open-ended commitments. The immediate focus of America's containment policy was restricted to Western Europe, Japan, and the southern perimeter of the Soviet empire (Turkey, Greece, Iran). Countries in these key areas would benefit from essentially unlimited American guarantees, with all the economic and military assistance they required up to the use of nuclear weapons. Events and the logic of world politics would force both Truman and his successors to extend the new dispensation to more and more places. When on June 25, 1950, North Korean troops backed by both Mao's China and Stalin's USSR invaded South Korea, they were offering a direct challenge to the security of Japan. The result was a demonstration of just how open-ended America's new foreign policy could be.

At the peak of the Korean War, the United States committed 327,000 troops and would spend $388 billion fighting the war.[11] In 1952, the U.S. spent 4.2 percent of its GDP on the Korean War, and 13.2 percent on defense in general.[12] Thirty-six thousand, five hundred and seventy-four Americans died in theater, while 103,284 were wounded.[13] The U.S. also marshaled a global coalition of fifteen other U.N. member states, and armed and equipped both South Korea and many of the allied states. President Eisenhower even threatened explicitly to use nuclear weapons, both to secure a cease-fire and to protect it against violation.[14] The verdict was clear: America was willing to hold up its end of the bargain to the uttermost.

During the Eisenhower and Kennedy administrations, the increasingly globalized conflict spread throughout the world, and over the next few decades almost all of Africa, Southeast Asia, Latin America, and the Middle East was touched in some way by this conflict. By the 1970s, the Soviet Union had established itself as a major power in the Middle East. This extension of the Cold War rivalry into Israel's neighborhood would transform American-Israeli relations much as it transformed relations with other countries around the world.

The overall arc of American engagement with the world during the Cold War was set very early on. In the years and decades that followed World War II, Americans built on these foundations to create an extraordinary network of public, nonprofit, and corporate institutions and initiatives that form the foundation of global society even today. The American military, intelligence, and diplomatic services became larger by orders of magnitude and engaged on a profound level with other governments and societies around the world. American corporations led in the creation of the multinational enterprise that came to dominate the postwar international economy. American agricultural and industrial scientists and engineers played a major role in the economic development of dozens of countries. American experts helped many postcolonial countries construct states, and American universities played an increasing role in providing the training for the people who would run them. Mission groups, whose presence and impact in the postwar era grew substantially (despite setbacks like their expulsion from China),[15] were joined by secular NGOs on an increasing basis. Health care, women's rights, fights for press freedom, the rule of law, and political democracy—U.S.-based and U.S.-funded NGOs led the way in the development of new kinds of civil society organizations.

At home, Americans created a vastly expanded infrastructure to train the specialists who would work on these projects. Old academic disciplines like anthropology and sociology were transformed; new disciplines like regional studies and development economics were created.

Americans no longer dominate the vast activities of this global civil society the way they did in the 1940s and 1950s. As Europe recovered from the war and as postcolonial countries began to generate their own ideas and institutions, the nature of international life changed in many ways. Yet the ever larger and ever more complex structure of international institutions and civil society continued along many of the lines that came out of the initial U.S.-based burst of creative activity in the decade following World War II.

This enormous burst of creative and, in large part, constructive statesmanship and activism was not, of course, a purely philanthropic program. Americans hoped above all to ensure their own security, survival, and prosperity by adopting this program. And they were no more secure against the temptations of using their power to obtain advantageous agreements than anybody else. Nevertheless, to large majorities of Americans in the postwar decades, it appeared that America's self-interests were bound up in the general interests of humanity and that the United States would best serve itself by seeking its own future in the promotion of harmony and prosperity abroad. This did not, at first, imply any special concern for the struggling nation of Israel.

ARM'S LENGTH

The first era in U.S.-Israel relations was a cold and distant one. During the summer of 1948 American officials began to understand the Soviet bloc's role in Israel's military successes. Not only was Israel getting Soviet bloc arms, and providing in exchange hard currency that helped the Czechoslovakian Communist Party solidify its power. It was also violating the United Nations arms embargo.[16] The hundreds of thousands of Palestinians fleeing advancing Israeli forces created another humanitarian disaster in a world still suffering the aftereffects of the Second World War. Public opinion in the Arab world was enraged both by the failure of the Arab states to defeat the Zionist upstarts in 1948–49 and by the plight of Arab Palestinian refugees.[17] The warnings of State Department and CIA opponents of Israeli independence all seemed to be coming true.

Having opposed Israel's declaration of independence up until the last minute, American policy shifted toward one of trying to limit Israel's military gains. The Israelis, who had only accepted the boundaries of the U.N. partition plan with reluctance, had no intention of abiding by them once the Arabs went to war. Between May of 1948 and the final cease-fire in 1949, Washington backed proposals to stop the fighting, allow Palestinian refugees to return to their homes, and reduce Israel's territorial gains.[18]

The coolness between the two countries did not end quickly. Under President Dwight Eisenhower, the quest for an alliance with Egypt dominated American regional policy. During the critical early years of Israeli independence, Washington policymakers believed that Egypt was the key to the Middle East and that good relations with Arab nationalists and military rulers offered greater promise for American Cold War strategy than an alliance with Israel. Even if Kennan and Marshall lost the battle over partition and recognition, their perspective on Israel dominated official thinking in Washington. The United States, it was widely believed, could not enjoy close relations with both Israel and the

Arab world, and the Arab world was almost infinitely more important to American security and prosperity than the tiny Jewish state.

President Eisenhower and his secretary of state, John Foster Dulles, built their Middle East policy around an effort to form anti-Soviet alliances with Turkey, Iran, Egypt, Pakistan, and Iraq. The countries fell in line relatively easily, except for Egypt, which was more elusive.[19] Developing a strong relationship with Gamal Abdel Nasser's Egypt would remain, on and off, an important American goal until the Kennedy administration regretfully abandoned it.

The intellectual case for this policy looked compelling at the time. Once the Marshall Plan and the NATO alliance had limited communism's spread in Europe, the Middle East looked to be the soft underbelly of the West. As the weakest point in the chain of states the West was attempting to construct around the Soviet Union and as a strategically vital artery of communications and a base for airpower to be used against Moscow, the Middle East, judged policymakers, was both vital to American security and vulnerable to communist penetration.

Oil, as always, played a significant role in American calculations. The Middle East offered the only possible source for the oil that Europe's Marshall Plan–fueled economic recovery would require. As American oil imports gradually rose through the 1950s,[20] American oil companies needed to maintain and if possible expand their role in Middle Eastern energy production, and American policymakers were forced to pay increasing attention to the security of the nation's oil supply.

Although its energy resources were minimal, Egypt's large population, cultural influence, relative political cohesion, and location (home of the Suez Canal) made Egypt the most important of the Arab countries from the Washington policy perspective. The Egyptian revolution that overthrew the ineffectual British ally King Farouk and ultimately brought Nasser to power pointed toward a new future for the region. The Middle East was full of British-aligned monarchies and sheikhdoms. Americans, convinced that most of these regimes were doomed to fall, wanted to ensure that British colonialism was not equated in Arab minds with the United States.[21] American strategists felt that events in Egypt could determine the direction of postcolonial regimes not only in the Middle East but throughout the developing world.

The world was a dangerous place in the 1950s. Even as the success of the Marshall Plan led to a stabilization of Western Europe, the emergence of new and often fragile and underdeveloped states across the rest of the world created opportunities for communist advances. New, postcolonial states struggled to establish control over their territory and to develop the institutions that would cement order and lay the foundations for development. For American foreign policy, these new nations were both an opportunity and a threat. On the positive side, Americans believed that with American technical assistance, development advice, and foreign aid, these new countries could develop and become strong American allies. Understanding that nationalism was the strongest political force in many emerging states, Americans wanted to win the nationalists over. Often, this involved working with the professional military in civilian states or with army officers who seized power either as part of independence struggles or soon thereafter.

The military forces of foreign countries, many American strategists and academics believed at this time, could play a critical role in the development of their societies. Unlike the old feudal and aristocratic elites from the premodern period, military officers had often been educated in technical subjects in military academies organized along western lines, and believed in the development of strong nation-states. The idea was that the military would be the agent of technocratic modernization, breaking the stranglehold of feudal landlords through land reform, building infrastructure for urbanization and industrialization, and promoting social reforms like universal education that would diminish the appeal of communism while accelerating the pace of economic development.

America had a lot to offer modernizing foreign officers: professional training with the United States armed forces, increasingly recognized as the best equipped and best trained forces in the world; military assistance including weapons that were as glamorous as they were powerful; and a range of development programs, technical assistance, and loans and grants. Many newly independent states perceived themselves as choosing between capitalist and socialist growth models. The United States desperately wanted to keep these states out of Moscow's orbit and it hoped that the military establishments in the developing world—often the strongest and most dynamic institutions in postcolonial governments still struggling to establish themselves—would be drawn into an America-supported and capitalist modernization paradigm.

Americans at this time saw their ability to work with nationalist modernizers as a crucial advantage in the competition with European colonial powers as well as with the Soviet and Chinese communists. French, British, Dutch, and Belgian rule, however indirect and light by the end of World War II, especially compared with Soviet rule of its own territories, was almost infinitely galling to nationalists of every description. Local rulers who continued to cooperate with the colonial powers looked like quislings to many nationalists, and one of the reasons Americans disliked colonial rule at this time was the concern that, even if the colonial power preserved order for the time being, its rule alienated the best elements in a rising people, and could force patriots into alliance with communists. The Arab world, particularly the non-oil-producing countries, was comparatively much more advanced with respect to Asia in the early 1950s than it is now; Egypt had one of the largest stock markets in the developing world and its location close to Europe made it look like one of the postcolonial countries heading for success.[22] Britain and France were hated through much of the Arab world. During the 1950s France would be fighting a brutal colonial war in a vain attempt to maintain its hold on Algeria. For Nasser, Britain, the former colonial power in Egypt, still in control of the Suez Canal, was the great enemy. To build up an anti-Soviet coalition in the Arab world, the United States needed to demonstrate to Nasser and other Arab nationalists that it was possible to overthrow imperialism without reaching out to Moscow. At the same time, Americans understood that drawing a strong contrast between the virtuous, freedom-loving United States and the scheming imperialist powers could be helpful to American oil companies in the ongoing regional competition.

An alliance with Nasser and his fellow Arab nationalists was so clearly desirable that the Eisenhower administration went to great lengths and paid a heavy price to build bridges to Cairo. Prior to the Suez Crisis, the United States offered Nasser arms, food, and a willingness to fund the construction of the Aswan Dam. In 1956, Eisenhower forced France, Britain, and Israel to return the Suez Canal and the Sinai to Egyptian control after their joint invasion. This was not only an open break with Israel; it was a dramatic rupture with two of America's most important allies at the height of the Cold War.

In addition to diplomatic support, the Americans offered cold, hard cash. In 1955, the year before the Suez Crisis, Eisenhower and Congress gave Egypt $506 million in economic aid. In the Kennedy administration, as fears of the Soviet influence in the Middle East increased, aid reached $1.3 billion in 1962. A similar pattern emerged as Americans worried more about Soviet designs on the region. From 1950 to 1958, U.S. aid to Iran climbed from $103 million to over $1 billion, making it the largest recipient of American aid in the Middle East between 1946 and 1976.

Aid to Israel, by contrast, was minimal, and with the exception of $6 million in loans and grants was largely restricted to humanitarian assistance as Israel resettled hundreds of thousands of refugees from Europe and the Arab world.[23] On a per capita basis, total humanitarian and economic aid to Israel was roughly comparable to the aid the United States gave Palestinians through the United Nations Relief and Works Agency for Palestine Refugees in the Near East (UNRWA).[24] As long as building a close relationship with Nasser's Egypt was the primary goal of America's Middle East policy, keeping Israel at arm's length was seen as a vital American concern.

Ultimately the policy of conciliating Nasser failed. Nasser chose the Soviet Union over the United States as his principal source of arms and foreign credit, and he refused to moderate his foreign policy in order to improve relations with Washington. The problem was that Washington's vision for the Middle East and Nasser's ambitions did not mesh. Nasser believed that the Arab people should be united into one state, and that this state, combining the oil resources of the Gulf with the populations of countries like Syria and Egypt, would become a great global force. The Arabs, led of course by Egypt and Nasser himself, would in his vision rise from European and Turkish colonialism to reestablish the place among the world's leading powers they had enjoyed in the early centuries of the Islamic era.

The United States opposed this intoxicating vision. For reasons that had nothing to do with Israeli interests, the Eisenhower administration and its successors did not want a Greater Egypt or a United Arab Republic that would conquer or cow the oil sheikhdoms and dominate the region's oil resources. The Eisenhower and Kennedy administrations were prepared to support Nasser's efforts to build up Egypt as one Arab state among many, but they opposed his pan-Arab ideas and were unwilling to underwrite his effort to become the hegemonic power in the oil-rich Middle East. For Nasser, the hegemonic ambitions were the whole point.

By the end of his time in office, Eisenhower had largely given up on Nasser, but the end of the American effort to engage came in the 1960s as a result of Nasser's continuing attempts to extend his power across the Arab world. In 1958, Syria and Egypt were united in the United Arab Republic under Nasser's leadership in what was hailed by some and feared by others as the first step in the formation of a pan-Arab power. The Egypt-Syria union broke up in 1961 when conservative business interests in Syria supported a coup to prevent Egyptian officials from nationalizing Syrian business, but the break with Syria did not end Nasser's dreams. In 1962, in a move that eventually attracted Soviet support, Nasser sent thousands of troops across the Red Sea to Yemen in support of a coup by military officers against that country's British-aligned monarchy. In 1963, anti-Nasser governments in Syria and Iraq were both overthrown. On April 17 of that year, Iraq, Syria, and Egypt called for the establishment of a new, tripartite United Arab Republic. They also began to push the overthrow of the king of Jordan so that a "free" Jordan could join the emerging Arab union.[25]

As was often the case, grandiose rhetoric about Arab unity and undying friendship proved hollow; the military officers who led the coups in Syria and Iraq soon became Nasser's bitter rivals. Nevertheless, by the time Lyndon Johnson succeeded Kennedy, the option of basing America's regional policy on an understanding with Nasser no longer looked realistic.

RESPECT

As policymakers contemplated the ruin of America's Nasser policy, the rise of Israel was impossible to ignore. Much to the surprise of everyone, Israeli leaders very much included, the relatively poor and weak Israel of the late 1940s quickly grew into a significant military power. The Suez Crisis of 1956 might have ended in humiliation for Britain and France, but it was impossible to miss the reality that Israeli forces inflicted a notable defeat on the Egyptian army before international intervention brought an end to the combat. Meanwhile, Israeli scientists (with French help in the crucial early stages) were making rapid progress on the development of nuclear weapons.[26] Only the United States, the Soviet Union, Britain, and France had nuclear weapons in 1960. That a state of just over two million inhabitants, surrounded by enemies and with extremely limited natural resources, could accomplish a technological feat which taxed the ability of the great powers was as shocking as it was impressive. It also boded poorly for efforts to prevent the spread of nuclear weapons.

Power speaks to power. As Israel became a stronger country with more freedom of action in a region of vital interest to the United States, American presidents had more reasons to want to influence Israeli policy. Left to its own devices, Israel could destabilize the Middle East by preemptive attacks on its neighbors. Fear of Israel's growing military might could make Arab regimes more eager for high-tech weapons sales from the Soviet Union. Fear of those weapons would make Israeli attacks more likely. In a worst-case scenario, the Israeli nuclear program, Americans feared, could set off a regional nuclear arms race. This, unsurprisingly, was a destructive cycle that the United States wished to avoid.

At the same time, Israel's growing capacities could also assist the United States in blocking the Soviet Union and frustrating the ambitions of aspiring hegemons like Nasser. Thanks to the mass expulsions of Jews from Arab lands in the 1950s and the rapid development of intelligence capabilities in a country fighting for survival, Israel had unmatched intelligence about the region.[27] Israel also proved quietly useful to the anti-Nasser forces in Yemen.[28] American policy in the Middle East needed to take this new reality on board.

The first major sale of an American weapons system to Israel illustrates the mix of concerns shaping American policy in the Kennedy years. During Kennedy's short presidency the world went to the brink of nuclear war between the superpowers twice: during the Berlin Crisis of 1961 and again in the Cuban Missile Crisis of October 1962. The Limited Test Ban Treaty of 1963 ended atmospheric tests of nuclear weapons at a time when the Soviets had recently tested a 50-megaton bomb (more than 3,300 times more powerful than the bomb dropped on Hiroshima) in the atmosphere. Stopping the spread of nuclear weapons was one of Kennedy's most important objectives, and the Israeli program was one of the world's most advanced nuclear efforts.

Kennedy was willing to go to the mat with Israeli leaders to get regular American inspections of the Dimona complex to ensure that Israel didn't have a nuclear weapons program. Ben-Gurion was equally determined to press forward with the nuclear program that, he believed, would be Israel's ultimate safeguard.[29]

Pressuring Israel could not just be a matter of sticks. Carrots would also be needed. Reassuring Israel that the United States was unequivocally committed to its security was, Kennedy believed, the best and perhaps the only way to persuade Israel to give up its quest for nuclear weapons. Arms sales would reduce Israeli fears and build their confidence in American guarantees and commitments. For Kennedy, arms sales to Israel flowed very naturally out of his desire to modify Israeli behavior. To block Israel's nuclear program, Kennedy would mix threats and offers of aid, as well as flattery and kind words. Kennedy was the first president to use the term "special relationship" to describe U.S.-Israel relations, explicitly comparing it to the U.S.-U.K. relationship in a conversation with Golda Meir, then Israeli foreign minister.[30]

Had Kennedy lived, it is likely he would have continued to oppose the Israeli nuclear program, but he would probably not have stopped it. At the time of Kennedy's death, a flood of Soviet arms to radical Arab regimes was unsettling both Israel and the conservative Arab states. The Middle East was becoming more complicated: Israel was more powerful and the Soviet Union was expanding its footprint. What some called the "Arab Cold War" between radicals like Nasser and the monarchies was intensifying and becoming more of a concern for the United States.

During Lyndon Johnson's administration, Middle East matters were on the back burner as U.S. attention shifted to the Vietnam War, America's largest and costliest military effort since World War II. Not even the 1967 Six-Day War, when Israel crushed the military forces of Egypt, Syria, and Jordan in a spectacular sequence of air strikes and ground attacks, could divert official American attention for long from the conflict in Asia. Increasingly frustrated by liberal opposition to the war that was consuming his presidency, in September 1966 Johnson reportedly told Malcolm Tarlov, the head of Jewish War Veterans, that American Jews would receive a better hearing about Israel if they openly and strongly supported his Vietnam policy.[31] Enough American Jewish leaders were outraged by the comments that the president was forced to issue a grudging and guarded walk-back.[32] American Jews were among the most enthusiastic supporters of Johnson's Great Society programs, but a large majority refused then, as before and after, to privilege Israeli interests over their own convictions about American foreign policy.

The ease with which Israel defeated threatening Arab armies in 1967 shocked most of the world, but not Washington. The American intelligence agencies that in 1948 had warned Truman about Jewish Palestine's incipient demise reassured Johnson that in less than two decades, the Israeli military had become strong enough to pummel any combination of Arab powers. This time they were right, and when Israel responded to an Egyptian naval blockade and escalating threats by launching surprise preemptive air strikes, Israel conquered the Golan Heights, Sinai Peninsula, and West Bank of the Jordan River in six days.[33] The radical Arab rulers in Syria and Egypt proved no more effective at crushing Israel than their more conservative predecessors. Jordan, whose British-trained, led, and armed troops put up the most effective resistance against Israel in 1948–49, retreated ignominiously from the West Bank as Israeli forces overran positions in Jerusalem and its vicinity that Jordanians had successfully defended two decades earlier.

Although the Six-Day War only revealed to all what many American decision makers had already recognized, it changed Israel's position in world opinion. To many American Christians, Israel's seemingly miraculous victory and Jerusalem's reunification seemed to confirm some of the most cherished tenets of their faith. Even in the midst of turmoil at home and wars abroad, God had preserved his people, who had triumphed over their adversaries yet again against what, to lay observers, seemed to be miraculous odds.

At the same time, the western left's sympathy for Israel began to erode following its dramatic military victory. Instead of creating a trade unionist's paradise on the Mediterranean, the Jewish state had become a military juggernaut. When Israeli prime minister Golda Meir contemplated preemptive attacks against Egypt and Syria in the tense lead-up to the 1973 Yom Kippur War, National Security Advisor Henry Kissinger warned her that most other nations would condemn Israel even though they had turned a blind eye to similar tactics in 1967. David could seize any weapons that came to hand; Goliath had to show more restraint.[34]

Israel's victory opened the door for deeper cooperation between Jerusalem and Washington. The United States replaced France as Israel's greatest weapons supplier after consummating a deal for 150 military aircraft.[35] But it took a different administration to create a functional alliance between the United States and Israel.

14

Alignment

THE STATE OF ISRAEL was born out of a great storm of crashing empires, clashing nationalisms, and the emergence of a new world system based on the hostile rivalry of nuclear superpowers. It took another storm to bring Israel and the United States into strategic alignment. The United States rebounded so robustly from the crisis of the 1970s that even those who lived through those years can forget how disorientating and terrifying the tempest actually was. Defeat followed dishonor and failure followed shock during five years of crisis as the Bretton Woods monetary system collapsed, the Vietnam War ended in humiliating defeat and humanitarian tragedy, a wild burst of inflation fueled by exploding energy prices challenged the prosperity of the American middle class, and a series of scandals ranging from the revelations of CIA skullduggery to Watergate undermined Americans' faith in the health of their institutions and the righteousness of their state.

As we've seen, the chaos and confusion of world events in the late 1940s made the rationale behind Truman's Israel policy difficult to follow, and Vulcanist conjectures about Truman's policies took root at the time and have flourished ever since. Those conjectures and the pro- and anti-Zionist myths that they nurtured have helped obscure our understanding of one of the most consequential eras in the history of American statecraft.

A similar confusion attended the birth of what would ultimately grow into an alliance between the United States and the Jewish state. It is not hard to see why. The sudden rise in the power and wealth of the oil-producing Arab states was the most dramatic development of the 1970s. Israel was not so well placed. As Golda Meir observed in 1973, Moses had led the children of Israel through the Middle East for forty years only to bring them to the one place in the region with no oil.[1] It seemed obvious to many people at the time that the natural choice for American foreign policy was to distance itself from Israel to gain favor with the Arabs—and indeed, at the time of the 1973 Yom Kippur War, the United States became the object of an oil boycott by Arab states precisely because of its support for the Jewish state. All the world needed Arab oil and hoped for Arab investments; why, except for Vulcanist influence, would the United States cozy up to Israel at a time like this?

Cozy, however, America did. The 1970s were the years in which Israel, previously banned from purchasing American arms, moved toward its future status as the largest single recipient of American military aid. These were the years in which AIPAC, previously a sleepy organization with little presence or power, ballooned to become a large and professionally staffed lobbying organization. These were the years in which the United States moved to the center stage of Middle East peacemaking, as Presidents Nixon, Gerald Ford, and Jimmy Carter made peace between Israel and its neighbors a major diplomatic objective. And these were also the years when a campaign to support the right of Soviet Jews to emigrate to Israel disrupted America's pursuit of détente with Moscow.

Many observers believed that the United States was assuming even heavier burdens for the benefit of Israel. American aid to Egypt soared during the 1970s as Egypt moved from launching a war against Israel in 1973 to becoming the first Arab nation to sign a comprehensive peace treaty with the Jewish state just six years later. From the standpoint of Vulcanist analysis, there could be only one reason for this turn of events. The implacably powerful Israel lobby was forcing huge Egyptian aid packages through Congress as a bribe to keep Egypt on the peace train. To add up the full cost of our new Israeli friendship, these analysts insisted, one must total up the cost of the ill will pro-Israel policies generated in the Arab world, the money we lavished on direct aid to Israel, and the multibillion-dollar multiyear cost of the Egyptian "peace bribe."

Only occult Jewish influence could account for such a dramatic shift in America's orbit, many reasoned, and with Henry Kissinger, a Jewish refugee from Nazi Germany, serving as secretary of state, the influence of "the Jews" on American foreign policy seemed obvious. But the Vulcanist analysis was, as usual, superficial. Far from undermining the American position in the Middle East, the alignment with Israel helped Nixon and his successors displace the Soviet Union and solidify America's position in the Middle East just as the region's resources and growing financial power became critical to America's power worldwide.

To understand the Nixon-Kissinger Israel policy we must step back briefly to take account of the national, global, and regional context in which the key decisions were taken. At home, American society was even more bitterly divided in the late 1960s than it would become half a century later. The long era of post–World War II prosperity was challenged as foreign competition began to eat into the profit margins of American manufacturers and slow the growth of blue-collar living standards. The "stagflation" of the 1970s, fed by the energy crises of the decade as well as by imprudent Vietnam era fiscal policy, saw the first serious decline in middle-class economic expectations since the Depression. The early stages of the feminist and gay rights movements were leading Americans to question their basic moral values and the structure of the family. The use of marijuana, LSD, and opiates exploded across an alienated younger generation even as old moral certainties and taboos collapsed. The civil rights movement forced Americans to confront the continuing legacy of American racism, and racial tensions regularly erupted late in the 1960s in staggering episodes of urban violence that, in the case of the 1967 riot in Detroit, could not be suppressed without the dispatch of regular army troops.

The still raging Vietnam War—fought by an army of draftees, with an American death toll ten times that of George W. Bush's Iraq War—embittered American politics and drove millions of young people into antiwar activism. Revelations of atrocities committed by American forces and of deceit on the part of American political and military authorities touched off firestorms in public opinion. A generation of American military and civilian leadership was scarred by the experience of the war and of the ensuing defeat—the first unambiguous military defeat in a serious war since the founding of the American republic. Richard Nixon had not started the war, although he shared the intellectual and political assumptions that made it look necessary to the Kennedy and Johnson administrations that waged it, nor was he responsible for the strategic and political choices that left the United States irretrievably entangled in an unwinnable war. But on taking office, he was not only confronted with an intractable military and diplomatic problem in Indochina; he was faced with a multifaceted crisis of American foreign policy for which no simple solution existed.

To begin with, the economic foundations of the postwar order looked increasingly unsustainable. As American leaders scrambled to stabilize the international economy after World War II, they erected a set of institutions that reflected the conditions of the late 1940s in which the United States held more than half the world's gold reserves, contained half the world's manufacturing capacity, and was the world's only nuclear weapons state, the largest producer of agricultural goods, the largest producer of energy, and, by an almost infinite degree, the largest and richest consumer market in the world.[2] America's postwar goal was to reduce rather than perpetuate this dangerous and unsustainable pre-eminence. Unless other countries could recover from the war and regain their prosperity, the United States would have no foreign customers for its products, no strong military allies in the struggle with communism, and the poverty and misery of postwar Europe would make communism appealing to the peoples of the region. To avoid this outcome, the United States would open its markets to foreign goods on a nonreciprocal basis to encourage global recovery while promoting American aid and investment abroad, maintaining a stable system of exchange rates, and bearing a disproportionate share of the burden of the common defense.

By 1969 the global economic picture had radically changed. Led by West Germany and Japan, defeated enemies and impoverished allies had come roaring back. European countries and Japan were running large trade surpluses with the United States, with the resulting balance of payments deficits placing an increasingly unsustainable pressure on the $35 an ounce fixed price of gold that underpinned the Bretton Woods currency system.[3] America's newly vigorous allies resented what they saw as a heavy-handed and outmoded form of American dominance in free world (as the anticommunist coalition in the Cold War was often known) policymaking. The Vietnam War and the evidence of American divisions at home had undercut their respect for American leadership and stability; the American alliance system could no longer be managed in the old, quasi-proconsular way.

Meanwhile, the military underpinnings of containment were failing. The American strategy to contain the Soviet Union and its communist ideology revolved around two sometimes competing and sometimes complementary approaches. One, championed by the Eisenhower administration as a way of reducing both the risks and costs of the Cold War, was the so-called massive retaliation approach. The Soviet Union and its allies were put on notice that attacks on the status quo could result in an annihilating wave of nuclear retaliation. This allowed President Eisenhower to pass eight years in the White House during which the Soviet Union was largely contained without involving American forces in a war, but it also had drawbacks that the military strategists who rallied to John F. Kennedy's 1960 presidential campaign were not slow to identify.

Massive retaliation might be a useful tool in its way, but it increased the risk of what Secretary of State John Foster Dulles infelicitously called "brinkmanship," in which threats of nuclear war became a standard diplomatic tool in American policy. This policy of periodically invoking the prospect of a civilization-ending conflict tested the outer limits of morality, was deeply unsettling to American and allied public opinion, and was not suitable for every problem that the expansion of communism presented to the United States. What, for example, did massive retaliation offer as a response to a communist-backed guerrilla insurgency in a small postcolonial state? One could hardly threaten the Soviet Union with nuclear destruction, a destruction that would necessarily lead to great losses in the United States as the Soviets retaliated in turn, over the occupation of a provincial capital in Laos by a communist militia. The United States needed policy options for smaller challenges, or it risked helplessness in the face of communist expansion in the postcolonial world.

The Kennedy administration's response had been to emphasize a variety of military and civilian responses to the potential range of threats. Development aid and democracy promotion would reduce the appeal of communist ideology in key countries. The CIA would provide training, information, and sometimes more direct if less respectable assistance to local anticommunist forces. And on the military side, Americans would enhance the capacity of local forces and increase America's counterinsurgency capabilities through new specialized military units like the Green Berets. Flexible response, as this family of new approaches was known, would, proponents hoped, calm the international scene and reduce the need for Dulles-style brinkmanship even as it enabled the United States to contain the communist threat more effectively than before.

The problem for the incoming Nixon administration was that both strategies appeared to have failed. Massive retaliation, in addition to its other disadvantages, suffered a crippling blow as the Soviet Union's nuclear arsenal approached strategic parity with the United States. Through the 1950s the United States had a significantly greater nuclear arsenal than its Soviet rival; by the 1970s that advantage had largely disappeared. In a world of strategic nuclear parity, the threat of massive retaliation lost credibility. Nuclear weapons might deter a Soviet strike against the United States or its treaty allies but could not credibly deter against less dramatic forms of Soviet adventurism.

The Vietnam experience made flexible response equally problematic. The full arsenal of tactics in the flexible response textbook had been used in Vietnam. Economic development, governance reform, military training, and intelligence cooperation in counterinsurgency operations followed by massive direct American military intervention had all failed to halt the communist advance. Worse, from the standpoint of committed Cold Warriors, the political consequences of the Vietnam failure inside the United States ensured that Congress would resist U.S. participation in Vietnam-style counterinsurgency campaigns anywhere in the world.

Yet even as the tools in their anticommunist tool kit lost their utility, American policymakers in the early 1970s worried about a new wave of communist and far-left advances around the world. In Latin America, the government of Chilean Marxist president Salvador Allende was, despite its narrow electoral base, pursuing a radical transformation of the Chilean economy and society. The fall of Saigon ensured communist victories in the smaller countries of Indochina. In the Middle East, the Soviet Union had emerged as the paymaster and arms supplier of Egypt, Syria, and Iraq, and seemed poised to extend its reach across the region. The Soviet Union and its Cuban proxies were increasingly engaged in guerrilla wars across sub-Saharan Africa.

It was all about to get worse. As Henry Kissinger recalls, early on President Nixon sent him to consult with George Shultz. "You don't know anything about economics," Nixon told Kissinger. "So go talk to Shultz about what's going on."

Then serving as secretary of labor before moving on to head the Office of Management and Budget and ultimately the Treasury Department under Nixon, Shultz had some disturbing information. The oil market, he said, was due to explode. Demand was rising faster than supply, and the American dependence on imported oil from the Middle East was steadily increasing as domestic production stagnated.[4]

The first oil price shock came in 1973. As the Watergate crisis crippled Richard Nixon's political authority at home, the price of oil tripled in six months. An Arab oil boycott to retaliate against the United States for supporting Israel in its 1973 October War against Egypt and Syria highlighted America's new dependency on the Middle East even as policymakers around the world struggled to adapt to a new world of energy shortages and skyrocketing prices. New wealth surged into the oil-producing Arab states and managing both the geopolitical and the economic consequences of a historic wealth transfer from energy-consuming to energy-producing countries would become one of America's highest priorities in the troubled 1970s. For decades to come the Middle East would figure prominently in American foreign policy—and in American politics at home.

Crises came thick and fast in those years at a pace Americans would not experience again until the Trump and Biden years. The 1973 war between Israel, Egypt, and Syria began on October 6 and ended October 25. The infamous "Saturday night massacre," in which the attorney general of the United States and his deputy resigned rather than carry out Richard Nixon's order to fire the Watergate special prosecutor Archibald Cox, occurred on October 20.[5]

Political leaders in addition to Nixon tumbled like ninepins across the world of the western alliance in 1974. A spy scandal forced West German chancellor Willy Brandt to resign.[6] After nine days in office his interim successor was replaced by Helmut Schmidt.[7] Not to be outdone, France also had three leaders in 1974 as Georges Pompidou died in office, Senate president Alain Poher briefly filled in,[8] and Valéry Giscard d'Estaing was elected to succeed him.[9] In normally staid Britain, a February election led to the first hung Parliament since the 1930s and a second election after eight months produced a weak Labour government.[10] In Japan, a scandal forced the resignation of the powerful and popular prime minister Kakuei Tanaka.[11] When Turkey invaded Cyprus and defeated a government backed by the ruling junta in Greece, the Greek military government fell after seven years in power.[12] In Portugal, the long-established Estado Novo dictatorship was overthrown in a military coup.[13] In this context, the comprehensive and humiliating 1975 defeat of America's allies in Indochina appeared to mark an important stage in the irreversible decline of American power.

Behind the scenes, however, the American revival was already under way. Within a decade, the United States had regained its political balance at home, laid the groundwork for a generation of global economic expansion, restored its alliances, and embarked on the path that led to the defeat of the Soviet Union, leading to a period of American predominance matched only by the height of American power after World War II.

These extraordinary developments constitute one of the defining achievements in the history of American statecraft but have not yet received their just due. Partly because the disgrace of Watergate justly taints Nixon's legacy, partly because episodes like the murderous Chilean coup of September 1973 cast a moral shadow over American choices in those years, and partly because the passions unleashed by the Vietnam War would forever shape the memory and the intellectual approaches of the generation of scholars who came of age in that era, the great American revival receives less attention than it deserves. That is not only unjust to the memory of those involved; it deprives later generations of an understanding of a complex episode in the history of American power whose lessons, positive and negative, provide insights into the wellsprings of success in American foreign policy that we cannot safely ignore.

Understood in its proper historical context, the U.S-Israel alignment was a central element of the establishment of a new, America-based regional order in the Middle East, and that regional order in turn was one of a series of readjustments and realignments that both grew from and facilitated the revival of American power. We shall briefly describe the Nixonian order that, under the leadership of Henry Kissinger with substantial support from George Shultz, emerged from the Nixon-Ford era before looking at how the new U.S.-Israel relationship bolstered the new system in the Middle East and beyond.

Two basic ideas underpinned the foreign policy of the Nixon-Ford era. The first was that some American commitments had become unsustainable. The war in Indochina could not be won. The Bretton Woods monetary system, with its fixed exchange rate regime and the dollar's peg to a fixed price in gold, was no longer viable. The United States could not stand on the front lines against communism and Soviet power in every country and every region of the world. American foreign policy was going to have to adjust to the new circumstances, and that meant abandoning some commitments. In addition to retreating from economic commitments like Bretton Woods, and open-ended military commitments to clients in places like Indochina, America would have to scale back its ideological and humanitarian goals as well. Rigid and moralistic anticommunism on the John Foster Dulles model could no longer be the basis for American Cold War strategy. The opening to China and the pursuit of détente with the Soviet Union demonstrated a more pragmatic approach toward communist regimes. Détente with Leonid Brezhnev's authoritarian Soviet Union was a bitter pill for many Americans to swallow; in many ways the Nixon-Kissinger outreach to a communist China, then at the height of the murderous frenzy of the Cultural Revolution, was a more shocking departure from the moral foundations of American postwar policy.

Subsequent historians have generally forgiven Nixon and Kissinger for their realist approaches to the communist powers of the 1970s. Their pragmatism receives less indulgence when it comes to Nixon's penchant for overlooking the crimes and shortcomings of American allies, whether it was support for Pakistan in its futile and vicious war against Bangladeshi independence; for the military dictatorships in Latin American countries like Brazil, Argentina, and Pinochet's Chile; or American tolerance for dictatorial regional allies ranging from the Shah of Iran to the junta in Greece.

Historians and moralists will long debate the merits of these decisions, but to Nixon and Kissinger the retreat from ideological anticommunism and from a human rights agenda in the noncommunist world were both necessary elements in a strategy of fitting American commitments to American resources. The American ship of state was caught in a dangerous storm; unnecessary baggage had to be thrown overboard.

The Nixon policy was less of a retreat than a rebalancing. The United States needed to adapt, but the country was not in decline. The success of the American-led international order at promoting the recovery and revival of so many other countries might mean a decline in relative American power. But it also meant that the international system on which American power ultimately rested was stronger than ever before and that American allies were more capable and more deeply aligned with the United States. By sloughing off outdated commitments and attitudes, Washington could position itself to take advantage of the growing strength of an international system that put the United States firmly at the center of world events.

Germany and Japan were no longer jealous rivals seeking to overturn the international system. They were increasingly zealous upholders of a system that offered them unprecedented economic opportunities while ensuring their safety. If the United States was no longer, to use President Kennedy's phrase, prepared to "pay any price, bear any burden, meet any hardship" to protect freedom around the world, other countries were increasingly ready and willing to step up to the task. The American world system could stabilize, develop, and grow even as the burdens the system imposed were more broadly distributed among the states large and small, rich and poor, who benefited from the American order.

At the same time, American policy in important regional theaters shifted to reflect what was called the Nixon Doctrine. As Nixon explained it to a group of reporters in a 1969 press briefing in Guam, "As far as the problems of internal security are concerned, as far as the problems of military defense, except for the threat of a major power involving nuclear weapons, the United States is going to encourage and has a right to expect that this problem will be increasingly handled by, and the responsibility for it taken by, the Asian nations themselves."[14] The same approach would guide Nixon's approach to the Middle East and Latin America.

The new policies were largely successful in limiting communist advances, although the consequences for human rights and other less tangible American concerns were sometimes dire. In Latin America, military governments in Chile, Argentina, and Brazil harshly suppressed leftist movements in those key countries; the focus of radical left-wing politics in the Americas shifted away from the principal economies to tiny, resource-poor countries like Nicaragua and El Salvador. In Asia, where the bloody suppression of the Indonesian Communist Party in the 1960s had eliminated the greatest communist threat outside Indochina, the early stages of the "Asian miracle" made communist ideology less attractive and significantly enhanced the value of aligning with the United States and its top regional ally Japan.

It was in the Middle East where the new strategy of working with regional partners to block Soviet influence would face its sternest tests and achieve its most important results. Even as the oil shortages and price increases put the Middle East at the center of global politics, the Nixon-Kissinger policies would result in the marginalization of the Soviet Union and the establishment of a regional order broadly compatible with American interests. That result in turn enhanced American power and prestige around the world. At a time when world politics revolved around energy, and when the oil-producing countries became major markets for arms sales, big infrastructure projects, and other big-ticket items even as their balance of payments surpluses made them vital players in global finance, the United States would be uniquely influential in the Persian Gulf and beyond. The Nixon strategy would survive the fall of the Shah of Iran, initially a more important regional partner for the United States than Israel or any of the Arab countries, to establish an era of American supremacy in the Middle East that endured into the twenty-first century.

This is the context out of which the U.S.-Israel alignment emerged, and far from being an obstacle to the close working relationship the United States formed with critical regional partners like Egypt and Saudi Arabia, the relationship with Israel was a cornerstone of the new edifice of American power rising in the Middle East.

THE RIDDLE AND THE SPHINX

Oil and the domestic and international consequences of the shift in production and pricing power to the Organization of the Petroleum Exporting Countries (OPEC) put the Middle East at the center of American politics and foreign policy in the 1970s. As far back as 1859 with Edwin Drake's oil well in Titusville, Pennsylvania, the United States had become the first country to harness the power of oil to industry and transport in a major way, and for almost a century the United States largely dominated the burgeoning oil industry.[15] Even as domestic demand grew, American production largely kept up through the end of World War II, and as late as the early 1960s the United States only imported about 1 million barrels of oil a day. However, domestic production peaked in 1970 and began a slow but seemingly inexorable decline. In 1950 American fields produced 5.9 million barrels per day of petroleum while the U.S. economy consumed 6.5 million. As the U.S.

approached its peak production in 1970 with 10 million barrels per day, the U.S. net imports of petroleum products reached 1.2 million barrels per day and spiked to 4.7 million by 1975.[16]

The consequences of this shift became clear in 1973 when the Arab members of OPEC announced an embargo on oil shipments to the United States and the Netherlands along with a drastic cut in production. It was only lifted in March of the following year after the first disengagement agreement between Israel and Egypt enabled American negotiators to persuade their Arab counterparts that good faith progress toward full Israeli withdrawal was being made.[17]

During the embargo, oil spiked from $3 to $12 a barrel; it had risen $1 in total over the preceding twenty years.[18] Gas prices rose from 36 cents a gallon at the pump in 1972 to 53 cents in 1974—at a time when the average American car could travel less than fourteen miles on a gallon of gas while vans and pickup trucks averaged only 10.3 miles to the gallon.[19] A shaken government fumbled the policy response, and high prices were soon exacerbated by a serious national fuel shortage. All over America, drivers fumed for hours in long lines to buy high-priced gas. To cope with the problem, authorities imposed rationing, banned odd or even numbered license plates from shopping for fuel on certain days of the week, and imposed a national speed limit of 55 miles an hour.[20]

The rise of OPEC was that rare international event whose consequences directly and visibly affected the situation of every family in the United States. At a time when the median American household had an annual income of $12,050,[21] a homeowner who had paid $400 for heat in 1972 was paying $800 by 1975. The State of Oregon banned Christmas lights in 1973 to conserve electricity. Consumers around the country were disconnected for failure to pay their mounting utility bills.[22] While rising heating prices also had to do with complex government price regulations in place at the time, many Americans blamed everything on the Arabs. One of the earliest beneficiaries was Israel: in December 1973, Gallup found that 54 percent of Americans sympathized more with Israel than with the Arabs, up 7 percent over an October poll.[23]

It was the biggest shock to the American economy and to the functioning of American society since World War II. The impact of the crisis would ripple through the global and American economies for the next decade. A global recession, ruinous inflation, and high unemployment shook the western world. A massive debt crisis in Latin America brought on both by the shock of higher energy prices and the frantic efforts of the banking system to find borrowers to help absorb the large cash balances of Arab clients plunged Latin America into a decade-long era of stagnation and retrenchment, and came close to toppling the American financial system. High energy prices meant that consumer discretionary income declined, denting demand even as the rising interest rates brought on by rising fuel prices stunted business investment. Even after the OPEC embargo was lifted, energy prices continued to rise and rose again after the fall of the Shah in 1979. Not until the mid-1980s would the American economy fully recover, and the stagnation in real wages for blue-collar Americans that began in the 1970s would last for decades to come.

International financial markets were much less sophisticated in the 1970s than they have since become. The massive flows of money into the coffers of the petrostates appeared to threaten both the financial stability and the economic prosperity of the industrialized world. Recycling the dollar surpluses of the oil producers became a major concern of American treasury secretaries and Federal Reserve officials. Unless the newly rich countries of OPEC could be persuaded to buy American products and to reinvest their holdings in American securities and American banks, the consequences for the American economy, and the world's, looked grim.

The immense wealth pouring into the Middle East also made regional security a more pressing issue. In 1969 the situation was not bright. Great Britain and France, the two western powers with the most important ties to the Arab world, had lost most of their influence in the region. The French began the 1960s by accepting defeat in the Algerian War of Independence; in the following years French power and influence continued to wane from Syria to Morocco. In 1968 the British announced that they would withdraw their remaining forces from the Persian Gulf and "East of Suez" by 1971; in 1969 the pro-western King Idris was overthrown in Libya and the Qaddafi era began. The Soviet Union had enjoyed a close relationship with Egypt, largest and most powerful of the Arab states, since the 1950s. As pro-western regimes toppled in countries like Syria and Iraq, the new rulers turned to the Soviets for arms and aid. Now, as new oil wealth coursed through the region, the USSR seemed well placed to increase its influence.

Under these conditions, American policymakers saw few alternatives.

The United States would somehow have to marginalize the Soviet Union in the Middle East even as it developed close and intimate partnerships with as many of the newly rich oil producers as possible. It would have to ensure the security of the oil producers (and the waters around them), whether against external powers like the Soviet Union or jealous regional rivals, so that no single power had the ability to interrupt the oil flow. It would have to persuade OPEC to use its pricing power wisely and moderately, keeping the price of oil below levels that would put the economies of the United States and its allies under unbearable stress. And it would have to ensure that American businesses and American banks were the privileged and preferred business partners of the newly rich Arabs, and that American diplomats had the necessary access and influence to ensure that American business got the lion's share of the orders, contracts, and investments that would soon be pouring out of the Arab world.

That would not be an easy task under any circumstances, but the existence of the Jewish state further complicated the picture. After the 1967 war, Israel was in a strong but unstable situation. It was militarily supreme, diplomatically isolated, and, as an oil-importing economy, economically exposed. Having fought three wars with Arab states since 1948, Israel could not help viewing the huge transfers of wealth to the Arab world with deep alarm. Besides the conventional military superiority that it had demonstrated in both 1956 and 1967, Israel had become a nuclear weapons state by 1969. If Israel, reduced to the last extremity, were to use nuclear weapons in self-defense, the human, political, and economic consequences would be catastrophic for the United States and the world. Equally worrying, if Israel continually flaunted its nuclear arsenal to intimidate enemies and reassure its own population, the political pressure on neighboring states to develop nuclear weapons of their own would become irresistible. The United States did not want a destabilizing nuclear arms race in the region—especially as oil wealth would endow Arab countries with the economic resources needed for nuclear programs. Reopening the Suez Canal was another important American objective that required cooperation from Israel. Since 1967 Israeli forces had occupied the east bank of the Canal, and shipping from the Middle East had to detour around the Cape of Good Hope to reach Europe or the Americas.

American objectives in the region could not be met unless Israel felt secure—but how could a policy of reassuring Israel be squared with a policy of drawing closer to the Arabs? This was the riddle confronting American policymakers in the early 1970s; fortunately for Washington, the land of the Sphinx would produce a man who found the way forward for the United States, the conservative Arab countries, and the Jewish state.

The story of Anwar Sadat's decision to shift Egyptian foreign policy from its Nasser-era pan-Arabist, anti-American, and anti-Israel orientation has been told and told well, most recently in Martin Indyk's *Master of the Game: Henry Kissinger and the Art of Middle East Diplomacy*. There is no need to revisit the details of that story here, but Sadat's visionary recasting of Egypt's regional role led to a transformation of the American role in the Middle East.

Essentially, as Sadat contemplated the ruins of Nasser's foreign policy following the catastrophe of the 1967 war, he reached a set of conclusions that would revolutionize the politics of the Middle East. The first and most fundamental of these was that the national interest of Egypt needed to guide Egyptian foreign policy, rather than the pursuit of a pan-Arab union that Egypt could not achieve, that no other Arab state really wanted, and that kept Egypt tied to a destructive radical and anti-Israel agenda. What Egypt most needed was the return of the territory in the Sinai that Israel seized in 1967. First and foremost that meant an Israeli withdrawal from the Suez Canal so that Egypt could reopen the canal and begin collecting the substantial fees from passing ships. Beyond that it meant recovering national dignity and honor by regaining every inch of lost territory and shifting from the Soviet Union to the United States as a source of military, economic, and technical aid.

These were difficult changes to make. For almost twenty years under Nasser's leadership, Egyptians had been dazzled by the idea of a pan-Arab revival that would unite the Arab world under Egypt's leadership, transform living standards through the wonders of a planned economy, and avenge the humiliations of 1948–49 and 1956 by defeating the hated "Zionist entity." Now Anwar Sadat needed to accustom the Egyptian people to less ambitious but more achievable goals. To consolidate his authority to depart so radically from Nasser's agenda, Sadat needed concrete achievements that would bolster his prestige. Complacency had made the Israeli military units on the east bank of the canal careless and sloppy. Sadat saw a historic opportunity to establish his leadership by attacking the Israelis. The first step toward peace would be war.

The Yom Kippur or October War of 1973, when Syria and Egypt attacked Israel on October 6, was the largest and to date the last of the four international conflicts between Israel and neighboring Arab states. It was also the most successful from the Egyptian point of view, ending with Egyptian forces holding, if tenuously, on to gains in Israeli-held territory on the east bank of the Suez Canal before the heavy fighting ended with a cease-fire on October 28.

The war was largely confined to the Sinai and the Golan Heights, the territory Israeli forces seized during the 1967 war. On both fronts, Egypt and Syria achieved significant initial successes, with Egyptian forces crossing the Suez Canal and penetrating several miles into the Sinai, and Syrian tanks moving well into Israeli-occupied territory on the Golan Heights.

With heavy losses of both men and matériel (an estimated four hundred tanks on the Suez front alone), Israeli forces managed first to stabilize both fronts in three days of heavy fighting.[24] On October 11, Israeli forces crossed the 1967 cease-fire line into Syria proper. Jordanian and Iraqi forces advanced to support Syria (though Jordan conspicuously did not seek to reopen fighting along its own cease-fire line with Israel on the Jordan River), but against resurgent Israeli air and ground power they accomplished little. Eager to demonstrate their continuing military superiority, Israeli forces pushed through Syrian defenses to within twenty miles of Damascus even as Israeli planes struck at a variety of targets deep inside Syria. Having advanced significantly beyond the 1967 lines, Israeli forces halted and, although exchanges of fire would continue into December, once Syria accepted a U.N. Security Council cease-fire resolution on October 22, the war in the north was essentially over.[25]

Events in the Sinai followed a similar pattern. After stabilizing the situation on the east bank of the Canal, Israeli forces crossed the canal on October 15 and established an Israeli bridgehead on the west bank. The U.N. cease-fire was slow to take hold on this southern front as well, with sporadic fighting continuing through January 1974. Embattled Egyptian forces held on to a strip of territory on the east bank of the Canal, while on the west bank the Israelis had reached positions just thirty miles from Cairo.[26] Palestinian and Kuwaiti military units had

fought with the Egyptian armies, but like the Jordanian and Iraqi interventions in the north, their participation had more political than military significance.[27]

The events on the battlefields of the October War were dramatic
enough, but politics and diplomacy had as much to do with the war's
outcome as events on the ground, and the consequences of the war for
American foreign policy were much more important than the relatively
modest, limited, and ultimately ephemeral territorial changes brought
about in the fighting. Soviet influence and prestige suffered blows from
which they never recovered. Egypt moved decisively from Nasser's pan-
Arabism to Sadat's Egypt First policy. The United States came out of the
fighting more deeply and publicly aligned with both Israel and Egypt
than ever before and established as the arbiter of the Middle East.

For Egypt also, the war was a strategic success. Anwar Sadat's victory, however limited and partial, was solid enough to silence his critics.
The United States would now engage directly with Israel to negotiate
successive withdrawals from occupied Egyptian territory. The Suez
Canal would reopen in 1975. In 1979 Sadat would secure the return of
every inch of occupied Egyptian territory—as of the time of writing, an
accomplishment that neither Jordan nor Syria can match.

The idea that a reluctant Sadat was only lured into supporting Israel
by an American "peace bribe" represents a fusion of Vulcanist and orientalist reasoning. In this view, agency is something that westerners and
Jews have; Arabs, operating on passion alone, hate Israel with a pure
and fiery hatred. They do not reason, they do not calculate, they do not
develop visions of their political and national interests that lead to any
stance short of blind and eternal enmity toward the Zionist interlopers
in their midst.

This was not the thinking behind the 2020 Abraham Accords; it was
not how Anwar Sadat's mind worked. Far from being pushed into his
peace policy by American pressure and "bribes," Sadat was committed
enough to his approach to wreck Jimmy Carter's 1978 Middle East policy
to reach his goal.

Jimmy Carter had his foreign policy victories in the White House—
like the negotiation and ratification of the Panama Canal Treaty that
returned control of the Canal to Panama—but the Middle East did not
bring him success. In 1978, Carter drew back from the Nixon-era policy
of promoting a bilateral Egyptian-Israeli peace. Carter wanted a general

peace that would lead to an Israeli withdrawal not only from the Sinai, but also from the Golan Heights and the West Bank. To this end, he sought to convene a peace conference of all the interested countries and, in pursuit of a better relationship with Moscow, he invited the Soviets to attend.

Sadat understood that this approach would torpedo his foreign policy, giving the Syrians, Palestinians, and Soviets a veto over the return of Egyptian territory. The single most dramatic act of diplomacy in the history of the modern Middle East, Sadat's flight to Jerusalem and address to the Knesset, was Sadat's riposte.

It worked, as the Israelis shared Sadat's visceral opposition to the Carter agenda. The Israelis and the Egyptians moved forward on their peace agenda despite Carter's skepticism, and in the end, Carter was forced to abandon his own approach and jump on Sadat's bandwagon. Far from being bribed by the Americans to make peace with Israel, the Egyptians forced the Americans to get out of the way so that they could conclude the deal.

═══

To return to 1973, the October War could not have come at a worse time for the Nixon administration. On September 11, General Augusto Pinochet overthrew the democratically elected government of President Salvador Allende in a bloody coup that initiated a savage wave of repression against the Chilean left—with many then and later suspecting the United States of direct involvement in the coup. On October 5, Vice President Spiro Agnew decided to enter plea bargaining over allegations of corrupt behavior dating from his years in Maryland government. On October 9, as the military crisis in the Middle East was at its height, Agnew met with Richard Nixon to announce that he had decided to plead guilty and to resign.[28]

Simultaneously, the Watergate investigation was undermining Nixon's own position. The U.S. Court of Appeals ruled on October 12 that Nixon had to turn over potentially incriminating tapes to the Federal District Court. On Wednesday, October 17, OPEC announced an oil boycott of the United States because of its support for Israel in the war.[29] That Saturday night witnessed the "Saturday Night Massacre," and the firestorm ignited by these events led to the start of the impeachment inquiry in the House of Representatives. Nixon's political fortunes would never recover.

Despite these distractions, the United States was heavily involved in all the stages of the war. When worried Israelis contacted the United States with information that another war might be imminent, the Americans were as we've seen unambiguous in their response: Israel could not again do what it did in 1967 and launch a preemptive strike. Kissinger was crystal clear with Israeli prime minister Golda Meir: if Israel launched a war, the United States would feel no obligation to come to its aid.

As the news of Syrian and Egyptian successes came in from the battle-fields on October 8 and 9, Israeli leaders worried about the sustainability of their position. Military equipment and supplies were being consumed at an unsustainable rate. On October 8 air force commander General Benny Peled warned that Israeli airpower would be exhausted in a week without resupply. Defense Minister Moshe Dayan warned that the time had come to prepare Israel's nuclear weapons and, in what was likely a signal to the United States, Israeli missiles were prepared for launch.[30] On October 9 Israeli ambassador Simcha Dinitz warned Kissinger that Israel might lose the war.[31]

As Israel stabilized the battlefronts and prepared counteroffensives, the question of supply still dominated the bilateral U.S.-Israeli conversa-tion. The battlefield progress was consuming Israeli ammunition and equipment at a ferocious pace. Golda Meir wanted to fly to the United States to ask for supplies in person. That plea was rejected, but the pres-sure on the United States to act was rising.[32]

It was not always clear who could speak for the United States. On October 11, when 10 Downing Street called to set up an urgent call about the Middle East situation between Prime Minister Edward Heath and President Nixon, Kissinger asked his deputy Brent Scowcroft whether the call could be postponed. "Can we tell them no?" Kissinger asked. "When I talked to the president he was loaded."[33]

Meanwhile the war in the Middle East was threatening to draw in the superpowers. The Soviet Union, seizing an opportunity to rebuild ties with Egypt and to consolidate its role in the Middle East, launched a major airlift of military supplies to Egypt, Syria, and Iraq on October 9. Soviet technicians and military advisors were working closely with the

Syrian military, and Soviet warships were authorized to fire on Israeli ships and planes approaching Soviet vessels and convoys.[34]

Confronted with a Soviet airlift, Washington decided on October 13 to launch a full-scale airlift of its own. A victory for the Soviet Union and its clients in the critical Middle East was unacceptable. The superpower crisis deepened dramatically on October 24 when, as a U.N.-brokered cease-fire appeared to be breaking down, American sensors detected nuclear weapons on Soviet ships passing through the Dardanelles from the Black Sea toward the Mediterranean. The House of Representatives had announced the beginning of impeachment proceedings against Nixon earlier that day; Nixon had gone to sleep following another heavy night of drinking as his top aides debated the American response. The decision was taken to raise the American global nuclear alert level to DEFCON III, one step below warning that nuclear war was imminent. The 82nd Airborne was placed on alert, three warships were dispatched to the combat theater, and seventy-five nuclear bombers were recalled from Guam to be available for action in the European and Middle East theaters.[35]

It was a very unpromising start, but the war ended by creating a series of opportunities that American diplomacy would go on to exploit. In the first place, thanks in part to strong American pressure to force Israel to terminate its counteroffensive while Egypt still held some Sinai territory on the east bank of the canal and without destroying the Egyptian military units in place there, Sadat could claim a victory against Israel. The prestige of that victory would enable him to go further to liquidate the Nasser legacy and won him support for the difficult decisions ahead. In the second place, with the Soviets discredited by the failure of their clients and of their resupply efforts, the United States emerged as the dominant superpower in the region, enjoying a unique and privileged position as the one power that could promote the diplomatic processes through which both Arabs and Israelis could reach their objectives. The Egyptians knew that their hopes of Israeli disengagement and withdrawal from Sinai depended on America's willingness and ability to broker agreements between Jerusalem and Cairo. The Syrians, now desperate to negotiate an Israeli withdrawal from its advanced positions on the outskirts of Damascus, similarly understood that their longtime Soviet patron was worse than useless to them.

Over the next three years until Jimmy Carter's victory over Nixon's successor, Gerald Ford, brought an end to Kissinger's time in government, Kissinger would engage in what became known as "shuttle diplomacy," brokering disengagement and withdrawal agreements between Arabs and Israelis that calmed the region while securing, first, an end to the oil embargo and, second, a deepening of American ties with both sides. A special American relationship with Israel facilitated both the expulsion of the Soviet Union from the Middle East and the establishment of much closer relations between the United States and the Arab world.

Selling Arms

As is often the case in American foreign policy, it was more difficult for Nixon and his successors to win domestic support for their foreign policy initiatives than to hammer out agreements with foreign leaders. There were excellent foreign policy reasons for building deeper relations with the Arab world following the rise of OPEC. But this was a policy that many Americans loathed in the early 1970s.

Americans have always hated monopolists who abuse their power to overcharge customers. The Arab role in jacking up the world oil price struck many Americans as an exercise in unadulterated and unjustifiable greed. The Arab countries and, by extension, the Islamic world became associated in many American minds with treachery. This image would be reinforced many times over in subsequent years and would help shape the public response to the attacks of 9/11 and many other events. Americans may not be given to massive demonstrations and flag burnings to show their dislike of foreign countries, but from the 1970s forward both the Arabs, and then the Iranians after the fall of the Shah, entered the American imagination as villains.

The energy crisis helped to drive a revival of populist nationalism in 1970s America. These populists, often middle- and lower-middle-class working people whose tight budgets did not leave much room for price increases and whose lifestyles depended heavily on the automobile, were seriously affected by the oil price hikes. Explicitly tying their embargo to U.S. policy on Israel, OPEC countries looked like a cabal of unprincipled and cowardly blackmailers. Unable to beat the Israelis on the battlefield, the sneaky Arabs were now trying to use underhanded economic methods to undermine a brave little country and to cow the United States. One can argue whether this view of the case was entirely fair to the Arabs, but that was hardly the point politically. To most Americans, the Gulf states were backward (Saudi Arabia and North Yemen only abolished slavery in 1962; Oman abolished it in 1970),[36] bigoted (banning or persecuting non-Muslim religions), and dictatorial with little or no concern for human rights. American policies aimed at appeasing OPEC infuriated millions of Americans who felt the consequences of the oil shock at the gas pump, in their utility bills, in the inflation that increasingly dogged the American economy in these years, and in the job losses and wage stagnation as high oil prices took their toll. The hours Americans spent waiting in line to buy overpriced gas provided ample opportunities to reflect on just how they felt about the oil sheikhs.

Populist nationalists (or Jacksonians) were enraged by Arab actions and were dismayed by any signs of pusillanimous complaisance whether from business, Washington policymakers, or European allies. Standing up to Arab blackmail became a moral test for Jacksonian America. Politicians seen as knuckling under to the Arabs or trying to appease them were considered cowards. When the Iranians seized the American embassy and took diplomats hostage, the earlier fury at the oil price rises exploded into a bonfire of rage. More than anything else, President Carter's failure to handle the consequences of the energy shocks and the Iran hostage crisis to the satisfaction of Jacksonian America led to the election of Ronald Reagan and a dramatic new turn in American foreign policy.

Washington policymakers could not indulge in such rage. Ensuring that the huge dollar surpluses accumulated by OPEC states were handled in ways that supported rather than eroded the U.S.-led financial system was a vital American interest. This involved persuading the oil sheikhs to recycle their petrodollar surpluses through a still-shaky post–Bretton Woods global financial system, to purchase enough American-made goods and services to limit the damage of the growing oil import bills to the American balance of payments deficit—a central preoccupation of economic policymakers in these years—and to invest their new wealth in American securities and companies. On the security side, at a time when the United States was attempting to reduce its global defense responsibilities, Washington needed to ensure that the Persian Gulf remained open to commerce and that neither the USSR nor any hostile regional state acquired the ability to shut off the flow of oil to world, and American, markets.

Promoting American exports to the newly rich Gulf states became a high priority at a time when financial experts saw trade deficits as dangerously destabilizing. The export drive took strange turns and a gold rush atmosphere developed as Americans flocked to the Gulf. Much of the new Gulf wealth disappeared into a world populated by corrupt officials, shady con artists, embezzlers, and Ponzi schemes. The Arabs had more money than they knew what to do with; America teemed with consultants ready and willing to help them solve this terrible problem.

It quickly became evident that arms sales, already a growing business, would be a major component of the new relationship between the oil-rich Gulf states and the United States. Arms sales allowed Americans to court the traditional Arab monarchies and increase the collective defense capacities of America's alliance system, while also ensuring that the Gulf petrostates poured billions of dollars back into the U.S. A steady, large scale flow of advanced American weapons would deter the Soviets, assure the Arabs that the United States was committed to their defense, alleviate American balance of payment problems, and cement ties between the American and Gulf militaries.

Selling vast quantities of arms to the oil-rich Arabs was an obvious and appealing solution to many of America's strategic worries in the Middle East at a time when not many alternative policies could be found. But the policy had its opponents both in the United States and abroad. At home, it wasn't just that selling arms to hated Arab despots was distasteful to American public opinion. Most of the governments that the United States wanted to arm—Egypt and the Gulf monarchies, the Shah—were exactly the kind of corrupt and dictatorial regimes that American public opinion had wearied of supporting. Tens of thousands of Americans died in Vietnam to defend a military dictatorship and its political cronies, and $839 billion had disappeared in the jungles of Vietnam.[37] Now the Nixon administration and its heirs would have to call for more American support for the oil sheikhs and dictators of the Middle East.

=====

And there was Israel. At a time when Americans were seething with rage at Arab oil policies, selling Arab states enough weapons to attack

Israel was a policy that no American Congress would accept. American public opinion was not going to tolerate a policy that weakened Israel's ability to defend itself against the newly rich Arabs. Arms sales needed congressional approval; that approval would not be forthcoming if the sales undermined Israel's security.

But concern about Israel's attitude toward wholesale weapons sales to the Arabs was not just about the sentiments of American voters. The oil shock was not just an economic shock to western consumers; it was a geopolitical shock to Israel. Suddenly the Arab world was awash in cash. While Israel's relationships with the more conservative Gulf sheikhdoms had never been as bad as those with the radical Arab states, there could be no denying the reality that hundreds of billions of dollars in new Arab oil wealth would have political and military consequences. Countries including France and Britain, less important in the Middle East than they used to be, still had deep ties with the Arab world. Those countries would be even more eager than the United States to sell arms into the Gulf and win investments and business partnerships from it. How might that change their political attitudes toward Israel, and what weapons would they be willing to sell to Arab states for both financial and political reasons? Beyond that, the United States wanted to ensure that American firms got the lion's share of the contracts and opportunities opening up in the oil states. While British and French and others' arms companies could compete with the United States on individual weapons systems, overall the American defense industry offered the widest selection of technologically advanced weapons.[38] If the United States wanted to secure the high ground in the competition for influence among western powers, it would need to offer weapons in quantities and at a level of quality that would relegate European competitors to the second tier.

But the prospect of large weapons sales to the Arab world could set off a regional war. The Israelis prepared to strike Egypt after the Czech arms sale of 1955 threatened to tip the military balance. Would they now sit patiently with their hands folded as foreign weapons streamed into the Middle East, potentially giving Arab countries the edge they needed to attack Israel again?

The answer seemed obvious: the way to stop Israel from fighting a preemptive war was to ensure that arms sales to the Arabs did not worsen Israel's military position. The United States would have to arm

Israel. This approach might seem cynical, with the United States pushing an arms race on both Arabs and Israelis in the Middle East, but at
a time of a balance of payments crisis and job-destroying recessions,
most American policymakers were willing to overlook such concerns.
There was, however, a problem. Israel, while no longer living the hand-
to-mouth life of its early years, did not have large deposits of oil with
which to pay multibillion-dollar arms import bills every year. If the
United States planned a vast expansion of weapons sales to the Arab
world, Israel would be saddled with crippling debts if it tried to match
the purchases that the Saudis, the Kuwaitis, and others might choose to
make. Making matters worse, Israel would not just need to match Saudi
Arabia or Kuwait dollar for dollar to maintain the military balance.
Israel would need to acquire enough weapons to offset the combined
purchases of the Arab states.

Forcing Israel to choose between bankrupting itself in an arms race
and launching a preemptive war to protect itself against a looming Arab
superiority in conventional weapons was an unsustainable policy in the
American Congress, and it could only lead to disaster in the Middle
East. This was a fact whose implications were not lost on American arms
manufacturers, worried about finding new markets to fill up their order
books with the end of the Vietnam War reducing the Pentagon's weapons purchases.

The implications were clear if paradoxical: if the United States wanted
to sell more weapons to the Arab nations, it would have to deepen its
relationship with Israel.

In 1979, both Egypt and Israel became still more important when the
Shah of Iran, America's key regional ally, fell from power and the Islamic
Republic was born. Long the greatest beneficiary of American aid in the
region, Iran now became Washington's most implacable regional enemy.
Relations deteriorated through 1979 until radical Iranian students seized
sixty-six American diplomats and other personnel in the American
embassy in November.[39] Iran had been the cornerstone of American
efforts to keep the Soviet Union from establishing itself in the region.
Now, that bulwark gone, the Gulf monarchies were horrified and American regional strategy was left in a state of near-total disarray. To make
matters worse, the Soviets invaded neighboring Afghanistan, the first
direct intervention by the USSR outside of its Warsaw Pact sphere of
influence since the 1940s.[40]

Israel now emerged as Iran's replacement in American strategic thinking, and the effect of this shift on American aid levels to Israel was momentous. In 1965, Israel had received $391 million, compared to $645 million for Iran and $619 million for Egypt. In 1979, after Israel signed the Camp David Accords with Egypt, Israel received $14.1 billion in aid, and it received on average more than $5.5 billion annually for the next decade.[41] The United States was not only helping Israel match the arms buildup in the Gulf, but it was also supporting the Israeli military to balance the new threat of Iran. Alignment was turning into alliance.

The fall of the Shah and the rise of Ronald Reagan to the presidency on a tide of Jacksonian sentiment cemented the new arrangement. There were still quarrels, as when the increasingly visible pro-Israel lobbying group the American Israel Public Affairs Committee (AIPAC) led an all-out effort to stop the sale of advanced AWACS planes to Saudi Arabia.[42] That attempt failed and did not disrupt the tacit alliance linking Israel, the Gulf Arabs, oil companies, arms sales companies, the Pentagon, the State Department, and pro-Israel Americans in support of a pattern of diplomatic, military, and economic ties among them.

The closest the understanding behind this long-standing policy has come to a formal expression is the concept known as QME, or qualitative military edge. Under this doctrine the United States ensures that Israel will always have the capabilities to deter and defeat hostile neighbors in conventional military battle. Reagan, who increased American annual aid to Israel to the $3 billion level (over $7 billion in 2019 dollars), was the first U.S. president to endorse QME publicly.[43] It has been U.S. policy since the 1980s and was enshrined into law by large bipartisan majorities in the Democrat-controlled Congress of 2008.[44]

QME has lasted this long because it benefits so many parties. The Israelis, of course, gain an important guarantee for their security as well as long-term institutional links with American arms and tech companies. The conservative Arab states, who do not fear attacks from Israel but who worry about other warlike states in the region, have long understood that Israeli strength helps secure their own independence. The arrangement also ensures that Arab states get access to very large quantities of extremely good American weapons, and whenever the Israelis get access to a new U.S. weapons system, the Arabs can upgrade their own arsenals to the next highest level.

For American arms manufacturers and the Pentagon, it is difficult to think of a better arrangement. American arms companies have large export markets, helping them to generate the research and development funding that preserves America's technological advantages. Even long-suffering American taxpayers benefit as the costs of development of new weapons systems get spread over more units, helping to control the costs that the Pentagon pays for its own arms supplies and helping to preserve the technological edge on which American security ultimately depends.

One can debate the wisdom of steadily shipping arms of growing sophistication and power to a very unstable part of the world, and one can debate the morality of arming nondemocratic governments and their security services to the teeth, but from a realist perspective the American policy of large arms sales to the oil-producing countries along with the aid necessary to help Israel maintain its QME has, since the 1970s, served on balance to reduce tensions between the countries of the region and to draw key countries closer to the United States even as their influence in world affairs increased. The development of America's special relationship with Israel enabled the special relationship with the Arab oil producers without which the American political, economic, and foreign policy revival from the crisis of the early 1970s could not have taken place.

The formative years of the special relationship also witnessed the rise of some of the basic elements of the American political landscape around the Israel alliance. The 1970s and early 1980s saw the transformation of AIPAC into a significant Washington presence, the rise of Jacksonian and evangelical Zionism, and the establishment of a strong bipartisan coalition in support of the alliance. Before the 1973 war, AIPAC had one lobbyist on its staff; by 1981, its budget had increased sixfold and it had a team of specialists working the halls of Congress.[45] AIPAC's strength was not the cause of the new relationship. Neither President Nixon nor Secretary of State Kissinger made the key decisions of October 1973 with AIPAC or any other lobbying group in mind. Those decisions were driven by their perception of American interests in the most dangerous superpower crisis since the Cuban Missile Crisis eleven years earlier. Given the broad public sympathy for Israel and the intense public antipathy toward the Arab oil producers, AIPAC's reputation as a defender of Israeli interests could be, and was, used by presidents more to neutralize opposition to arms sales to the Arabs. Just as the relationship with Israel enabled rather than disrupted the American relationship with the Arabs, the presence of AIPAC in the political and policy process facilitated rather than distorted or hindered the construction of the new framework for the promotion of American interests in the Middle East.

Like many other partnerships the U.S. formed during the Cold War, the relationships that the United States forged in the Middle East during and after the 1973 war proved durable, outliving the Soviet Union. From the beginning, these relationships with Israel, Egypt, and the Gulf monarchies, have been controversial in American politics. Whether because of Israeli policies toward the Palestinians, Saudi support for radical Islamism, or the repressive nature of Egyptian governance, significant sectors of American public opinion have repeatedly criticized all of these partnerships. They still do, but the relationships, tested and frayed, remain important factors in Middle East policies half a century later.

Over time, all three sides profited substantially from the relationship. Egypt recovered all the territory lost in 1967 and benefited from close and supportive relations with the United States. The Gulf Arabs enjoyed American protection, most spectacularly during the 1991 Gulf War when the United States led a global coalition to roll back Saddam Hussein's occupation of Kuwait. And as for the United States, between the benefits of expelling the Soviet Union and those of becoming the paramount power in the Middle East at the time when the region's oil resources made it the central factor in global economics, it benefited most of all.

For some Vulcanists, the question of why the oil companies failed to stop the development of the U.S.-Israel entente remains perplexing. Oil, after all, had become the most important substance in the world, and Arab goodwill was key to obtaining it. That the United States paid the price of an oil embargo for its support of Israel in the 1973 war was bad enough; that it would repeatedly test the limits of Arab tolerance by continuing to support the Jewish state for decades to come seemed clear evidence of Planet Vulcan's power.

Oil executives and politicians who were close to them—like the Bush family and other members of the Republican establishment—did promote close relations with the Arab world and realized that too close or too public an American embrace of Israel could cause problems in the Middle East. These tensions often erupted into policy battles between "pro-Arab" and "pro-Israel" officials and policymakers both inside and outside of government. However, in part because they understood the complex but compelling logic behind the American approach to both sides embedded in Kissingerian diplomacy, and in part because the nature of the relationship of American oil companies to Arab governments had changed since the 1950s, their concerns were more nuanced than many outsiders understood.

In the 1940s and 1950s, American oil companies enjoyed a set of privileges in Arab oil-producing countries that they very much wanted to maintain. The contracts between foreign oil companies and national governments reflected the unequal bargaining power of multinational, western-backed oil companies and weak, inexperienced governments in the Middle East. The oil companies ran their businesses as they liked, were fully in control of pricing and production decisions, and received the lion's share of the profits.

The connection between an "Arabist" position on Israel and the desire to maintain control over Arab oil resources had a long history behind it. The so-called pro-Arab British diplomats who opposed the Zionists in the 1940s were as we've seen far less interested in the Palestinian cause than in preserving British power in the region. Many British officials in the area developed a genuine love of Arab culture and sympathy with the Arab people, but hardheaded calculations of the national interest, like Attlee's belief that control over Arab oil was necessary to fund the rise in living standards of the British working class that Labour had been elected to achieve, were what drove British policy.

The American relationship with the Arab world had never been quite this controlling, but the colonial origins of the economic relationship between oil-producing countries and western oil companies shaped an economic relationship of profound and unequal benefit to the companies. Such a one-sided relationship is rarely secure, and both diplomats and corporate executives feared that the slightest outbreak of anti-Americanism or nationalism in oil-producing countries could result in the termination of their privileged arrangements.

The rise of OPEC was part of a process through which these quasi-colonial arrangements gave way to arrangements that put host governments in the driver's seat. Between 1971, when Algeria nationalized its (French-owned) oil industry,[46] and 1980, when Saudi Arabia bought out the remaining privately held foreign share of the Arabian-American Oil Company (Aramco),[47] the economic relationship between the Arab states and foreign investors was revolutionized. Under the new conditions, Middle Eastern operations became less profitable for the oil majors, but also less fraught.[48] American companies needed less help from diplomats to defend their interests and the Arab governments were less inclined to let politics interfere with a relationship that paid handsomely in both security and economic terms.

It was still in the interest of the oil companies for the United States to maintain good relations with Arab oil producers, but from an oil company point of view the world was becoming flatter. There were no super profits to protect in the Arab world, and while access to Arab production, and operating agreements with nationalized oil companies, provided a steady stream of both product and income, a barrel of Saudi or Kuwaiti oil was no longer more valuable to an American oil company than a barrel produced elsewhere. Indeed, the price shocks of the 1970s led to a new boom in exploration around the world. Mobilizing American technology to exploit offshore resources or to prospect for new oilfields in more welcoming countries might produce less oil but more profit for American firms while reducing their dependence on special political relationships with Arab rulers.

The "Arabist" case in Washington was less urgently seconded by oil executives fearful that Washington missteps on Israel would cost them billions in nationalized assets. Oil companies, banks, arms manufacturers, and other corporate interests who wanted access to the immense wealth flooding into the Arab world in the 1970s continued to press for pro-Arab policies, but because mutual benefit played a greater role in these relationships, business advocacy was more measured and its position more flexible. Ultimately, the new American posture in the Middle East was consensual. Oil companies, AIPAC and its allies, and the Israeli and Arab governments might try to push at the edges of the consensus, but the overall framework of American policy was one that all interested parties, and American public opinion at large, could accept.

Solomon's Temple

Thanks in substantial part to its successes in the Middle East, Kissingerian diplomacy during the Nixon-Ford years had stopped the disintegration of the American world position and begun the work of recovery. But in the view of many Americans in both parties, the work of reconstruction was not yet done. The abandonment of principled anticommunism, and behind that the national commitment to human rights and a transformative global agenda, did not sit well.

In the minds of many Americans, the United States remained a providential nation. The ideals of the liberal enlightenment were not merely ethical aspirations; they were part of the glue that held a diverse society together, and without some kind of adherence to these popular ideals the American government was felt to be lacking an essential element of political legitimacy.

The competition with the Soviet Union had never been, these Americans felt, just a soulless battle for power, a clash of imperial ambitions like the wars of the Assyrians against Babylon. The Cold War was a continuation of the American mission to stand for something positive in the world and to share the precious legacy of freedom with peoples all over the earth.

Paradoxically, the success of Nixonian diplomacy on the ground led to increased dissatisfaction with its apparently amoral or even immoral approach to world politics. Shell-shocked by multiple crises at home and abroad, Americans in the early 1970s seemed ready to accept the various moral and political sacrifices Nixonian policy entailed. But as the crisis faded and feelings of normalcy returned, the mood of the country changed.

A cynic might say that Americans did not just want foreign policies that worked. They also wanted foreign policies that made them feel good about themselves. Others would say that Americans wanted foreign policies that addressed their values as well as their interests. In any case, a growing hunger for a return to a more ideological, values-driven foreign policy made itself felt on both the right and the left. The right, represented by conservative Republicans like Ronald Reagan, wanted a return to anticommunism as a moral anchor for American policy. On the left, liberal Democrats including Jimmy Carter wanted the United States to bring a concern for human rights into the center of policymaking.

In the Hebrew scriptures we read that the national hero King David wanted to complete his reign by building a temple for God in Jerusalem. But this was not to be. God told David, "Thou shalt not build an house for my name, because thou hast been a man of war, and hast shed blood." The glory of building the Temple would be reserved for a successor whose hands were clean.

The reconstruction of the holy temple of human rights in American foreign policy would similarly be reserved for Nixon's successors. Under Gerald Ford, aides Richard Cheney and Donald Rumsfeld worked together to reduce Kissinger's policy influence and return the U.S. to a more hostile posture toward the USSR. President Jimmy Carter sought to put human rights at the center of policymaking, but the fall of the Shah and the Soviet occupation of Afghanistan frustrated his attempts to set American foreign policy on a new direction. The task of temple building ultimately fell to Ronald Reagan, whose administration incorporated a tough anti-Soviet stance with a human rights posture that brought great pressure to bear on the South African apartheid regime and helped promote democratic transitions among American allies like South Korea and the Philippines. Far from weakening American foreign policy, the incorporation of human rights and principled anticommunism in the 1980s would contribute significantly to the processes which destroyed the appeal of Soviet ideology in much of the world, weakened the Soviet hold on its European satellite states, and ultimately undermined Soviet ideology at home.

The story of the "refuseniks," Jews whose application for exit visas were rejected by Soviet authorities, played a significant role in the creation and implementation of a post-Nixonian foreign policy in the United States. In 1974 both houses of Congress voted overwhelmingly to incorporate the Jackson-Vanik Amendment in the U.S. Trade Act of that year; the amendment restricted American trade with nonmarket economies that limited the right of Jews to emigrate. This amendment, which seriously disrupted the Nixon-Kissinger policy of détente with the Soviet Union and would bedevil U.S.-Soviet relations for many years, was widely seen as yet another example of occult Jewish power in the United States. Israel would clearly be a chief beneficiary of any flow of Jewish emigrants from the Soviet Union, so only Jewish power could explain why the United States would antagonize a nuclear superpower, anger the Arabs (who had been opposing Jewish immigration since the time of the Balfour Declaration), and forgo profitable trade deals to make life easier for the Jewish state.

The story of Jews under Soviet rule is a complex one. The antisemitism of imperial Russian policy under Alexander III and Nicholas II had embittered Jews in Russia and around the world and, as we've seen, led to mass Jewish migration from the Russian Empire, primarily though not exclusively into the United States. At a time when

American Jews possessed very little political or economic power in the United States, American indignation at barbarous and violent Russian antisemitism culminated in the abrogation of a Russian-American trade agreement[49]—an early example of civil society pressure leading the American government to impose economic sanctions on a foreign government. Brutal pogroms and official antisemitism were among the reasons why so many Americans welcomed the February Revolution that overthrew Nicholas II in 1917 and contributed to the sympathy with which many initially regarded the Bolshevik Revolution later that year.

In its initial stages the Soviet government appeared to offer some sympathy to local Jews. Soviet nationality policy encouraged the cultural life of minorities, and the secular, scientific orientation of the new government offered many Jews more opportunity and better education than the old regime. One must never forget that with all its faults, the Soviet government protected its Jewish citizens to the best of its abilities against Nazi invaders during the 1941–45 war and it was Soviet forces who liberated the extermination camps where the mass of the killing of European Jews took place.

Nevertheless, the Soviet Union was no utopia for the Jews. Religious Jews faced the same repression that the officially atheist regime turned against all forms of belief and organization that challenged however indirectly the totalitarian demands of the Soviet state. Under Stalin, Jewish communists were targeted for repression and murder precisely because of their links to once revered Bolshevik heroes like Leon Trotsky. The popular antisemitism that was such an engrained feature of life in the pre-Soviet Russian Empire did not disappear with the Revolution, and over time gradually made itself felt in the Communist Party.

Stalin's brief but consequential honeymoon with Israel filled Soviet Jews with excitement, but their enthusiasm for Ben-Gurion's new state contributed to communist doubts about Jewish loyalty. In the last months of his life, Stalin appeared to be planning a major new purge that would have hit "rootless cosmopolites" particularly hard. Saved by Stalin's death and the following thaws in the climate of Soviet repression, Jews like many other Soviet citizens enjoyed more breathing space during Nikita Khrushchev's time in power. In the Brezhnev years, however, Jews were once again targeted and their opportunities for education and advancement were sharply restricted. A nationalities quota system had the impact of reducing Jewish student enrollment in Moscow (where the best and most prestigious Soviet schools were located) by 50 percent. Jewish scientists faced targeted discrimination. Emigration from a stagnant, repressive, antireligious, and antisemitic society looked attractive to growing numbers of Soviet Jews.

The modern era of Jewish emigration from the Soviet Union began when Premier Alexei Kosygin issued a statement in 1966 saying that Soviet citizens would be permitted to emigrate in cases where this would facilitate family reunions. Israel's victory in the Six-Day War encouraged Jews to seek permission to emigrate; 2,000 permits were issued in 1969, and Soviet Jews began to organize around the issue and seek permits in much larger numbers. Thirteen thousand would be allowed to leave in 1971. During the American debate over ratification of the SALT I treaty and the peak of détente, 31,000 Jews received exit visas. Soviet authorities retaliated against what they saw as the unacceptable interference of the Jackson-Vanik Amendment by cracking down severely on emigration. A second wave of emigration peaked with 51,000 permits in 1979, but it was not until the fall of the Soviet Union that the floodgates opened, with roughly one million post-Soviet immigrants reaching Israel, not all of them halachically Jewish.[50]

Before the fall of the Soviet Union, many more Jews (and members of other ethnic minorities like the Volga Germans) petitioned for exit visas than received them. Those whose petitions were denied, either because a ceiling limited the overall number of exit visas permitted at a particular time, because authorities believed that a particular individual had knowledge too valuable or too sensitive to be permitted to leave, or because local officials arbitrarily chose to deny the request, became known as refuseniks. They, and those whose requests had been accepted but were waiting for their turn to leave, were regarded as enemies and traitors by many officials and faced retaliation of many kinds. The refuseniks, often fighting intense government repression, organized, wrote petitions, and sought to attract international attention to their plight.

In past generations, the victims of Soviet oppression had often failed to attract significant sympathy or help in the West. In part this was due to the romantic notions many westerners, especially but not only on the political left, cherished about the Soviet Union. Communism enjoyed an intellectual vogue in much of the West when, during the Depression, capitalism appeared to be failing. While Stalin's agreement to partition

Poland with Hitler in 1939 disillusioned many, the heroism of the Red Army during World War II and the prominent role that communists played in the various European resistance movements during the war helped restore the mystique. Episodes like the suppression of the Hungarian Revolt in 1956, the construction of the Berlin Wall in 1961, and the crushing of the 1968 Prague Spring furthered the process of disillusionment, however, and by the 1970s there was little sympathy for the repressive, sclerotic, and bureaucratic Soviet communist model among serious Western observers.

For American Democrats, reeling from George McGovern's landslide defeat in 1972 and still scarred by the catastrophic failure of Kennedy-Johnson foreign policy in Vietnam, the plight of the refuseniks was a heaven-sent opportunity to unite the party while attacking Nixon's alleged soft line toward the Soviet Union. For conservative Republicans, the refusenik cause was a banner that could rally the party's anticommunist base against what, to hardliners, appeared to be Nixon's sellout of anticommunist principle.

It was in vain that Kissinger and his allies warned that Jackson-Vanik would derail détente and lead to reductions in the number of exit visas awarded to Soviet Jews. Liberal Democrats believed Kissinger was as wrong about this as, in their view, he was wrong about so much else. Conservative Republicans thought he was correct, but since their goal was to use Jackson-Vanik to derail détente they pressed ahead regardless.

In the end, while the Jackson-Vanik Amendment frustrated advocates of Kissingerian détente by reinserting an unfinessable human rights component into the bilateral relationship with the Soviet Union and, as Kissinger warned, slowed the rate of Jewish emigration from the USSR, its ultimate effect on American foreign policy was to strengthen the hands of Washington policymakers. The perception that the United States stood for something might have been a luxury that Washington could not afford in 1970, but a recovering America needed to regain the moral high ground. Embracing the cause of the refuseniks as part of a broader human rights strategy primarily directed at undermining the legitimacy of communist rule in Europe was one of the ways Americans signaled the growing revival of American strength and purpose that marked the recovery from the crisis of the early 1970s.

The revival of American self-confidence and the return of ideology to American foreign policy associated with the pro-refusenik movement was not an unmitigated good in subsequent years. As we shall see, with the end of the Cold War, ideological overconfidence would lead the United States into a series of unsustainable and unrealistic expectations and commitments.

In American foreign policy debates, realists and idealists both like to see themselves as expressing radically different worldviews. Realists scoff that idealists are naive; idealists despise realists as moral defectives too stupid to grasp the many ways in which ideas and values ultimately drive history. The history of the 1970s suggests that the relationship between the two approaches can be symbiotic. Without the success of Kissingerian realpolitik in the 1970s the return of ideology and human rights that characterized the Carter and Reagan years—and that metastasized into fantasies of liberal world order building after the Soviet collapse—might never have occurred. Without a firm grounding in realpolitik, the idealism of the Carter years, and the grand projects of the post–Cold War era, were doomed to fail.

The art of American statecraft lies less in choosing between idealism and realism than in judiciously blending them together.

15

The Great Miscalculation

I WARNED READERS in the first chapter of this book that Israel occupies a continent in the American mind—and that telling the story of the relationship would involve an exploratory journey into the heart of that continent. Already our journey has taken us into topics like theology and cultural history that foreign policy studies often try to avoid. As the story approaches the present, the connections between America's Israel policy and the inner life of the American people play an ever more decisive and ever more surprising role both in the story of America's Israel policy and in the story of American domestic politics.

From George H. W. Bush's campaign to drive Saddam Hussein out of Kuwait to the Abraham Accords signed while Donald Trump was in the White House, events in the Middle East were more central to American politics than at any other time in our history. At the same time, events ranging from the evangelical religious revivals of the 1990s to the attacks of 9/11 put the Middle East and Israel into the heart of America's escalating culture wars and internal debates. To complicate matters even further, the post–Cold War years brought a torrent of economic and social changes that precipitated something like an identity crisis in the United States as long-accepted narratives about America's place in the world came under attack. Debates over Israel policy in these years both reflected and helped to shape a profound internal debate taking place in a nation that was no longer certain of its role in world history or the value of its inherited institutions and beliefs. We cannot really understand American policy toward Israel in this era if we do not see how the ideas that shape American perceptions of Israel, ideas that also shape America's perceptions of itself, were changing as the United States struggled to navigate the unexpectedly choppy waters of the post–Cold War world.

Understanding American politics and perceptions in these years also matters because to a degree not seen since the 1920s and 1930s, the post–Cold War decades were a time when American foreign policy was based on ideas about the state of the country and the state of the world that turned out not to be true. The American foreign policy consensus of the era was, like the 1920s and 1930s Lodge consensus before it, based on heroic assumptions about the power of liberal ideology more in accordance with American wishes than with external facts. The old foreign policy establishment, mostly based among prominent East Coast banks, newspapers, law firms, and organizations like the Council on Foreign Relations, had changed profoundly since Lodge's day. The new American foreign policy universe—a loose group that included journalists, academics, activists, community and civil society leaders, leaders in the world of business and labor as well as career officials in the vast national security complex and elected officials—had never been as large, as diverse, as well traveled or as credentialed as it had become by the end of the Cold War. It would only grow larger, better credentialed, and more diverse in the years that followed.

But despite all these advantages, with some notable individual exceptions the broad group of Americans who concerned themselves with guiding the country's foreign policy was not very good at understanding either the state of American society or the state of the post–Cold War world. The gap between the world as these Americans conceived it and the world as it was seemed relatively narrow in the 1990s, but as time went by the gap between the intellectual basis of American foreign policy and the forces driving world events would widen until American foreign policy became increasingly controversial at home even as it became less successful overseas.

What can fairly be called the Great Miscalculation would have a profound impact on American politics and American foreign policy. While the miscalculation only occasionally involved Israel policy directly (for example, by promoting the persistent illusion that an Israeli-Palestinian peace agreement was just one more summit away), the consequences of a fundamentally misguided American national strategy, and a national self-perception increasingly dissociated from reality, would inevitably affect American policy in Israel and in the Middle East more broadly.

This complex and frustrating post–Cold War era is also the time in American history when Israel policy loomed largest, both in American foreign policy and in American politics at home. The thirty years after the end of the Cold War saw the rise and fall of the Israeli-Palestinian peace process. These years also witnessed both the eruption of the Middle East into the center of American foreign policy after 9/11, and the subsequent shift in American foreign policy priorities to the Indo-Pacific.

As the U.S.-Israel cooperation intensified the alliance became more controversial. Prominent scholars and advocates of "realist" foreign policy blamed Israel and its American supporters for a series of disastrous foreign policy steps in the Middle East, even as public support for Israel reached all-time highs. These were also years in which the politics of Israel policy changed dramatically in the United States. Support for Israel had once been a left-wing, internationalist cause in the United States; by the Trump years Israel's most vociferous and uncritical advocates were on the right, while left-wing Democrats and groups like Human Rights Watch had become some of Israel's most dedicated critics.

Americans were, to use a phrase that Joseph Stalin made famous in 1930, "dizzy with success"[1] after the fall of the Berlin Wall. Many agreed that the end of the Cold War and the collapse of the Soviet Union meant what Francis Fukuyama called the "end of history." They believed, for the most part, that the unipolar moment in world politics that followed the USSR's demise could be converted into a lasting democratic peace around the world. American power deployed in the service of a rules-based international order could secure vital American and western security and economic interests at minimal risk and with low costs. Opening the system to rising powers like China and India would improve economic outcomes for all countries, integrate the new powers into not just the structures but also the values of the American system, and promote rising standards of living around the world.

These policies, American elites generally felt, would not just promote a peaceful world, they would enhance the prosperity of the American people. In what some called "a great moderation," on economic issues Democrats were moving right and Republicans were moving left. The chief instrument of social progress, leading Americans believed, was the rapid growth facilitated by a deregulated economy and a dynamic financial sector. What was good for Wall Street, with relatively few exceptions, was good for the country. And what was good for the country was good for the world. While the parties differed on the details, they agreed that on the whole only modest interventions would be required to make the United States a more just society. Racial inequality was believed to be on the road to extinction. While social problems remained, progress was possible without wrenching changes to the status quo.

The first two decades of the new century, however, witnessed a series of shocks to the optimism and confidence of post–Cold War era triumphalism. Beginning with the 9/11 attacks in 2001, continuing with the unhappy wars in Afghanistan and Iraq and the financial crisis of 2007–09, world events diverged from the path many Americans once confidently assumed they would take. As the global wave of democratization subsided and went into reverse, as Russia and China moved increasingly aggressively to counter American power, as automation and losses to foreign competition created new problems for the American middle class, and as the Covid-19 pandemic stunned the world and sent the global economy spiraling into its sharpest contraction on record, the gap between the future that the American establishment had expected and prepared for and the future that had actually arrived gradually became too wide to ignore.

Over time these developments led to an erosion of political support for post–Cold War global policy, a rise in antiestablishment political movements on the right and the left, and to a rupture in the previously dominant Sun Belt coalition that broke the continuity of Republican Party leadership and policy. The rise of a socialist left and an ultranationalist right were disquieting signs that many Americans had lost faith in the American economic and political system.

Disenchantment came in waves. When Bill Clinton left office in 2001, many Americans still felt as if they were inhabiting a unipolar moment at the end of history. That changed with the shocks of the George W. Bush years, but many Americans believed that if only Bush could be replaced, the world would return to the calmer conditions of the 1990s. Barack Obama swept into office on a tsunami of optimism and his supporters confidently expected that a new approach to foreign policy would bring back happier times.

By the time the Obama administration ended, these hopes had largely faded away. Donald Trump was elected in large part because he appeared to represent the kind of deep change in both domestic policy ("Drain the Swamp!") and foreign affairs ("America First!") that many Americans had come to believe was required. With the swamp still undrained and the world less stable than ever, by 2020 many Americans were wondering if the problems of the United States, much less those of the world system, could ever be solved.

———

The end of the Cold War left American policymakers and their colleagues in the European Union and Japan committed to a set of ideas that proved to be less than satisfactory as guides to the future.

First, they believed that the wrinkles had been smoothed out of capitalism, that the institutions and ideas that were generally accepted among the financial and business elite of the day would serve as adequate guides into the future, and that the global capitalist system they were building was adequately protected against the great economic storms that had marked the preceding three hundred years of capitalist development, sometimes with catastrophic social and geopolitical consequences. They were wrong, and the global financial crisis of 2007–09 shook the United States and its order-building efforts to their foundations.

Second, they believed that the social and economic system that took shape in the Atlantic world and Japan after World War II represented the culmination of the historical process, that the prosperity and social harmony of the postwar era were permanent and unassailable, and that no further serious political or economic challenges would threaten the institutional foundations of the so-called developed world. They were wrong about this, and rising resentment over income inequality and other economic conditions would progressively undermine the ability of political leaders in the United States to carry out the domestic and foreign policies they believed that the times demanded.

Third, they believed that the economic and political model that had taken shape in the Atlantic world was easily exportable—to Russia, to China, to the Middle East, to South Asia and around the world. They did not believe that culture really mattered all that much. People everywhere wanted more or less the same things, and the laws of economics were the same all over. Now that the best policies were known, and the technical skill to apply them was becoming common all over the world, progress would be rapid, and nobody would ever want to go back. They were wrong. There were large parts of the world where the model did not work as advertised, and within a generation of the triumph of 1990, the world would once again be filled with those who believed that the American model would never and perhaps should never work for them.

Fourth, they believed that the identity wars were over. Nationalism and religious fanaticism, they believed, would quickly fade away in the postmodern, post-historical, and post–Cold War world. It was the old Age of Hope all over again. As their nineteenth-century predecessors had done, Americans at the end of the Cold War failed to grasp the power of identity politics and the drive for cultural recognition. As in the nineteenth century, rapid and far-reaching social, political, and technological changes brought on by the advance of capitalism would combine with the resentments and hatreds that seethed in much of the world to create a much more dangerous international environment than optimistic Americans expected.

Finally, as a result of all of these errors of analysis and judgment, America's elite opinionmakers and foreign policy gurus fundamentally misread the international position of the United States. They seriously underestimated the difficulties in their path and did not understand just how ambitious their goal of global transformation was. They believed, like the proponents of the Lodge consensus, that Americans could steer world history in their preferred direction on the cheap.

As a result, the United States and its principal allies set off on a noble and hopeful adventure in the early 1990s. Hamiltonians believed that the time had come at last when the United States could build a truly global economic order that would ensure both American prosperity and world peace. Wilsonians believed that the time had come at last when tyranny and oppression could be banished from the world. The United States and its allies could overthrow the customs of many generations to bring equal rights to women and sexual minorities, replace personalistic, premodern forms of government with sleekly modern legal-bureaucratic structures, engineer transitions to democracy, and impose a model of international relations that was deeply grounded in Euro-American history on countries like China, Russia, India, and Pakistan without a lot of trouble. Along the way, we could stop global warming, religious persecution, poverty, and war.

Incredible as it may appear in hindsight, most of America's foreign policy makers and commentators sincerely and passionately believed that all this could be achieved without a lot of hard work. There was no need to mobilize public opinion behind this ambitious program of global transformation. The job did not require a major arms buildup, huge foreign aid budgets, or massive American military commitments around the world. Indeed, even as Americans undertook the most far-reaching and challenging program of global transformation in the history of the human race, they debated how best to use the "peace dividend"—the anticipated savings that would come from cutting defense, foreign aid, and public diplomacy budgets after the demise of the Soviet Union.

What makes this pandemic of hubris at least partially explicable is that the end of the Cold War seemed like part of a larger story. From 1945 to 1990 the world seemed to be finding its footing. Societies first in the West and then in much of the rest of the world progressively mastered the art of managing the problems of industrial society. The bitter class struggle that defined European politics from the time of Marx to the end of World War II softened into a political competition between center-left social democrats who accepted the basic assumptions of capitalist society and center-right parties that accepted the basic features of the welfare state. Big business, big labor, and big government learned to negotiate with one another. Across the world of NATO and Japan, most workers were assured of stable employment, rising wages, and opportunity for their children. Inherited problems from the frenzied industrialization of the past were gradually being addressed. The air and water in the great cities of the West began to clear. The gates of higher education opened to the children of the working class. Old scourges like child labor and dangerous working conditions faded into memory.

The end of the Soviet Union, it did not seem unreasonable to suppose, would accelerate this benign trend toward global prosperity and peace. If Americans and their allies had the vision and the courage to seize the opportunity before them, the world could move to what people called a "post-historical" state of abundance and peace.

Even in hindsight, with so many of the ambitious plans of the early 1990s in disarray, and the enticing illusions of the era now painfully exposed, it is impossible to write off thirty years of American and western foreign policy based on this vision as a total failure. The post–Cold War world order gave unprecedented economic opportunities to billions of people in Asia, Africa, and Latin America. Living standards rose, life expectancies increased, and medical emergencies like the HIV-AIDS pandemic met with an effective response unthinkable in past times. More children survived the diseases of infancy and fewer people lived in the presence of chronic hunger and famine. Yet despite some of the most dramatic economic progress in the history of the world, both America and the world seemed less secure and less stable a generation after the Cold War than in those halcyon days when the Berlin Wall had fallen and history was thought to be over.

What so many Americans and others missed in those years was that the interlude of relatively stable social and political life that character-ized the post–World War II decades was moving toward a close as the twentieth century neared its end. This was not only because the growing competition from low-wage manufacturing economies undercut wages and union power in the advanced industrial democracies. The Informa-tion Revolution was going to be at least as disruptive, as transformative, and as challenging as the Industrial Revolution itself had been. Just as the Industrial Revolution had shaken every society on earth to its core, transforming the most powerful and embedded institutions and bring-ing waves of political and social revolutions in its train, so the Informa-tion Revolution would test the foundations of the social and political order in countries around the world, the United States of America very much included.

The American leadership class was not blind to the existence of the Information Revolution. Indeed in 1990 information technology was already triggering massive economic and social changes in the United States and beyond, and more change clearly lay ahead. But this change would, the American establishment generally assumed, reinforce the foundations of American stability at home and power abroad, not chal-lenge them. After all, the collapse of the Soviet Union was driven in large part by the inability of the Soviet system to adjust to the requirements of the Information Age. What Americans and many others missed was the degree to which the Information Revolution would challenge and even reverse what many political scientists and economists, to say nothing of policymakers, considered one of the most fundamental features of the modernization process: convergence.

The Industrial Revolution had been an era of convergence. As coun-tries around the world mastered the secrets of industrial production, they tended to converge toward similar bureaucratic and economic models, and cultural and religious differences tended to fade into the background. This process accelerated dramatically after World War II as more and more postcolonial states were learning the secrets of industrial development. The export-oriented economic growth model based on exports of light consumer industrial products from low-wage, loosely regulated economies into the rich consumer markets of the industrialized global North ignited extraordinary growth across much of East and Southeast Asia. Over time, economies like those of Taiwan, South Korea, Vietnam, and mainland China followed the Japanese path.

Most development economists and political scientists who studied these phenomena in the 1980s and 1990s believed that the process would continue indefinitely and that as Asian laggards like Bangladesh and Pakistan jumped on the light manufacturing conveyor belt to prosperity, the earlier adopters would continue to advance toward higher value-added manufacturing and higher levels of prosperity and peace. Meanwhile, countries in Africa, Latin America, and the Arab world could and would jump onto the prosperity train, and all these countries would ultimately achieve western-style affluence. As these countries prospered, they would achieve the kind of social stability that characterized the advanced industrial democracies after World War II. That stability in turn would promote the peaceful democratization of emerging economies (as happened in places like Taiwan and South Korea), and the stable new democratic governments springing up around the world would eagerly sign up to be "responsible stakeholders" in a peaceful and democratic world order.

This vision of global progress and gradual, voluntary convergence was the foundation on which Americans and not only Americans thought the twenty-first century would rest. It was a beautiful dream, but history had other plans.

Like the Industrial Revolution before it, the Information Revolution would arrive on the wings of a storm. Waves of economic and social disruption would test the stability of the advanced industrial democracies as old industries disappeared or fled offshore, as manufacturing and clerical jobs disappeared, as tensions over migration grew, and as a threatening new great power rose in the Far East. Those same waves washing across the postcolonial world would undermine the forces powering their social and political convergence with the West.

It is important to grasp three large facts that became more evident and more disruptive in the three decades following the fall of the Berlin Wall. The first was that instead of becoming more manageable and tractable and turning toward the kind of global liberal order Americans hoped to build, the world beyond America's borders was becoming a more geopolitically competitive and less liberal place. The second of these inconvenient truths, as former vice president Al Gore might have called them, was that American society, which many at home and abroad believed to be the solid rock on which a permanent global economic and political order could safely be founded, revealed previously unsuspected fissures and cracks. Far from stabilizing the rest of the world, American society lost much of its unity and élan. The third bitter reality was that the sense of existential danger and apocalyptic potential that briefly faded when the terrifying nuclear standoff between the two hostile Cold War superpowers came to an end would gradually return even as it shifted its shape.

These three disagreeable truths were not of course the only features of the post–Cold War era, but over time they exerted an increasingly powerful and, for the most part, baleful influence over American foreign policy worldwide. They would also elevate the importance of the U.S.-Israel relationship in the minds of many Americans, and the relationship would become more fraught, more visible, and perhaps also more mysterious than ever before. These three inconvenient realities put American foreign policy onto increasingly dangerous terrain.

The Return of Great Power Rivalry

As the Cold War drew to a close, political leaders and intellectuals from Seattle to the Saarland thought that they were witnessing the end of the great power rivalries of the past. Now that communism was thoroughly discredited by the Soviet Union's ignominious collapse, the United States and its prosperous allies dominated the world, and other countries would need to become like them to enjoy the prosperity and power they had. Countries who rejected the path of democratic industrial democracy would remain backward and weak—too weak to challenge the world system taking root around them.

There would still be rivalries and jostling between countries, much as the nations of the European Union continued to advance their national interests within the framework of common European institutions, but the nature of international competition would change. We would not see a new Wilhelm II or Napoleon seeking dominance, and the days of powerful antiliberal and antidemocratic empires like both tsarist Russia and the Soviet Union were past. Giving credence to this line of thought was the behavior of both Russia and China in the years immediately following the fall of the Soviet Union. Russia in the early years of the Boris Yeltsin presidency appeared to be introducing both political and economic reforms to convert itself into a western country. China, too, despite its continued emphasis on one-party communist rule, appeared to be borrowing as much from the West as it could absorb. Whether it was the African National Congress (ANC) seeking advice from the IMF and the World Bank as it took power in South Africa, or Brazil and Argentina embracing liberal economic ideas, the world seemed to be heading Washington's way.

International politics took on a new and more peaceful aspect. Saddam Hussein's 1990 invasion of Kuwait triggered the greatest display of global unity in the history of the world as Russia supported a resolution at the Security Council to reverse Saddam's invasion under America's lead.[2] Rogue states like North Korea and Iraq might defy the international consensus, but these were small, economically marginal powers. The storms of the twentieth century seemed to have burned themselves out, and the world appeared to be embracing the wisdom of the American Way.

The world, as it turned out, was a more complicated place than the architects of the post–Cold War order understood. The post–Cold War economic paradigm of free trade, deregulation, and financial deregulation, sometimes called the Washington Consensus, did not last. Too many countries were unwilling or unable to adopt it, and in those that tried, political resistance and unexpected economic upheavals often yielded results very different from those the textbooks predicted.

After a lost decade of floundering as it experimented with western-style "shock therapy" and privatization, the Kremlin turned to former KGB officer Vladimir Putin to employ more traditional Russian means to grapple with the new economic order. Putin would not turn Russia into an economic superpower, nor could he match Washington in conventional military power, but he succeeded brilliantly at returning Russia to the world stage as a significant force. Putin's Russia did not offer the kind of comprehensive ideological challenge to western ideas that Soviet communism developed, but his Russia was unbendingly hostile to the kind of order that Washington sought to build. His ability to perceive western weakness and to act on it allowed him to stage the most dramatic revisions to the map of Europe since World War II, end NATO's eastern expansion, and exploit the divisions within the European Union on a scale few in the West had foreseen.

Although economic weakness placed limits on Putin's power, he was able to harness the power of the Information Revolution to his national ambitions. Russia is not a vital cog in global manufacturing, nor has it created a Wall Street or Silicon Valley on the Volga, but the Russians have developed some of the most advanced cyber capabilities in the world and have become masters at exploiting global financial markets, employing dark money networks, and at using information warfare to disorient, divide, and in many cases defeat their opponents.

The other great power that rose to challenge the American vision of a post–Cold War order was of course the People's Republic of China. Defying the American belief that political liberalization would necessarily follow economic modernization, China would ultimately strengthen the stranglehold of the Chinese Communist Party on national life even as its economy exploded in size and sophistication.

Russia and China did not see eye-to-eye on every issue, but both governments see Washington's vision of post–Cold War order as a mortal threat to their regimes and as a strategic threat to their national power. Some in both countries fear that democratic reforms would lead to the kind of collapse that the Soviet Union experienced under Mikhail Gorbachev, followed by the weakness, misery, and national humiliation Russia suffered under Yeltsin. They fear that their countries are neither ready for nor suited to western institutions, and that efforts to introduce them would have catastrophic results. More pragmatically, leading figures in both governments do not believe that their personal wealth and power would survive the transition away from the political status quo.

As both countries took stock of the changed 1990s world, they were initially unsure how to respond. Over time, however, as China's economy surged and as Putin consolidated the power of his new state, they began to test the limits of American and western power. The West, convinced of the superiority of its political and economic models, failed to take the two Eurasian giants seriously for many years, giving them both the opportunity they needed to prepare for the competition that, unlike the West, they were certain was on the way.

The return of traditional great power competition to world politics did not happen all at once. In the 1990s, Russia and China appeared relatively quiescent and compliant. In the 2000s, as the United States bogged down in Iraq and Afghanistan and as the European Union struggled with the consequences of its poorly designed currency union, the Eurasian giants began to reassess. Beginning with the 2008 Russian attack on Georgia, which fell between the Fannie Mae bailout and the collapse of Lehman Brothers when an exhausted and unpopular George W. Bush administration was struggling with the greatest American financial crisis since the Great Depression,[3] Russia moved to a policy of open defiance and contestation against what westerners considered the most sacred tenets of the "rules-based international order." China, which interpreted the financial crisis to mean that American economic power was entering an era of decline, abandoned the "peaceful rise" policy of Deng Xiaoping to assert its status as a rising superpower around the world. Aligned rather than allied, the Eurasian powers brought complementary strengths and focuses to the game of thrones. Neither the Bush, Obama, nor Trump administrations managed to develop an effective counterstrategy, leaving a sense of failure and drift to take hold in the United States.

The sense that the country's foreign policy was adrift, and that other powers were pushing successfully against American designs, would contribute to the crisis of confidence within the United States that, a few short decades after the triumphant end of the Cold War, left many Americans wondering whether their basic institutions were strong enough to survive.

American Transformation

The series of disruptions that shook American society between 1990 and 2021 were as unexpected as they were, for many, unwelcome. Since World War II the United States had built the largest and most prosperous middle-class society the world had ever seen. The majority of Americans owned their own homes.[4] Two successive generations had seen their living standards rise far beyond what their parents had known, and the next generation was expected to see more of the same. I call this the "blue model" economy and society because of its abiding popularity in "blue state" and "blue city" America: a highly regulated system of economic and political order based on a mature industrial economy in a liberal political system.

In the United States and in many other "advanced industrial democracies," as these countries were known at the time, it seemed that the historic problems of capitalism had been solved once and for all. Competent, independent central banks and sophisticated financial regulation had eliminated the financial crises and panics that periodically cast the capitalist world into turmoil from the times of the seventeenth-century boom and bust known historically as the Dutch Tulip Bubble to the Great Depression.

For working people, this mid-century system offered stable employment, reasonable wages, and the opportunity for social mobility. While women and minorities experienced systematic discrimination in education and employment, for white males—along with the women and children who depended on a white male breadwinner—the new system represented a significant advance over Depression and prewar-era conditions. The unprecedented productivity of America's vast industrial capacity, greatly expanded during World War II and largely converted to civilian production after 1945, produced a cornucopia of consumer goods that made life-changing products like cars, television sets, washing machines, and dishwashers affordable for a growing proportion of the public. The expansion of the road and highway network opened the possibility of suburban home ownership to blue-collar as well as white-collar workers; the 1950s saw millions of Americans who grew up in crowded cities, often in slums, move their young families to leafy suburbs.[5]

At the time, most Americans believed that this system of organized industrial capitalism represented the final point of human social evolution. The future, they believed, would bring more of the same. Over time, as labor productivity rose and technology advanced, real wages would continue to rise, and the quality of consumer products would improve, but the fundamental features of this elegant social model would not change. Intellectuals bemoaned the conformity that seemed to be overtaking American life, and radicals grumbled about the emptiness of a society organized around the production and marketing of an endless succession of consumer goods, but these problems were much less distressing to the average person than the poverty and insecurity that they remembered from the Depression.

This was the American example that inspired imitators around the world. The American model appeared to demonstrate that capitalism plus democracy led to mass prosperity and deep social stability. Both during and after the Cold War, it was this model of a developed industrial society that Americans sought to export. In the 1950s the successful adaptation of liberal democratic capitalism across Western Europe and Japan anchored the western alliances and blocked the expansionist dreams of Stalin and his heirs. In the 1980s the success of East Asian countries that built advanced industrial societies of their own increased American confidence that a bright new era in world history was well under way.

The end of the Cold War, however, did not usher in the era of tranquil progress for which so many hoped. Capitalism is a revolutionary social and economic force and it does not stop being revolutionary merely because some members of a capitalist society would like to get off the train. At the end of the Cold War, fundamental changes, many directly rooted in the Information Revolution, were transforming American society and would upend assumptions and challenge institutions that many Americans thought were solidly planted. The foundations of the post-1945 economic system were already beginning to totter by 1990, and the golden age of the American middle class was drawing toward a close even as the nation's intellectuals and politicians celebrated the victory of American capitalism over the Soviet Union.

Nostalgia is myopic; the blue model society of the 1950s and 1960s was far from the utopia that later generations sometimes imagine it to be. Americans born into the twenty-first century for all its problems would be horrified if transported back to this supposed middle-class paradise. Filthy air and bad food, shoddy and unsafe gas-guzzling cars, clunky phones and bad service, tiny houses, sclerotic bureaucracies, inflexibly hierarchical workplaces, racism and xenophobia at levels inconceivable in a later time, stultifying social conformity, stifling oppression of women and their talents, openly expressed hatred and contempt for sexual minorities: it was not, by later standards, a model to emulate. Yet at the time blue model America was the wonder of the world, and the shining example of American success that it offered was the foundation not only of American world power but of the domestic stability and political coherence of the United States itself.

Americans often attributed the country's global "soft power" to what they saw as its compelling moral example. Our dedication to human freedom, our inspiring record of international leadership, the self-evident excellence of our political institutions: these are, many otherwise quite intelligent and sensible people believe, the vital foundations of American power around the world and the reasons why other countries have so often been willing to work with us and follow our lead.

To travel and engage with people around the world is to learn that others do not see Americans in quite these flattering terms. Our ideals may be inspiring, but being human, we betray them as often as other people do. Other people note our betrayals and think harder about them than we do. As for international leadership, while our thoughts often turn to such triumphs as the Marshall Plan, others around the world find less-inspiring episodes in American history to be equally compelling. Our institutions, however satisfying we find them, can seem quaint, funny, or even barbarous to people grounded in different cultural and political traditions.

The primary foundation of American soft power after World War II and again at the end of the Cold War was something more basic: success. America won the major international conflicts of the twentieth century, and mastered the challenges of the Industrial Revolution to create the kind of stable, prosperous, powerful society that people all over the world wanted to live in. American institutions and ideas were appealing in large part because they appeared to work. People listened to American economic, agricultural, medical, and industrial experts and consultants because they wanted their own societies to be as prosperous and stable as America was, and they studied American business methods because they wanted to build corporations as global, as innovative, as large, and as profitable as the American-based multinationals. People might resent American arrogance, repudiate American racism, recoil from the vulgarity of American culture, reject American hypocrisy, and mock American pomposity—but they wanted what America had. The cow might be smelly, but the milk was sweet.

As the Soviet empire imploded and American military and economic prestige reached new highs, it appeared to many around the world that the way forward for your country was to align with America politically and to adapt its economic and social model to your own situation as best you could. This in turn encouraged the American foreign policy universe to believe that its goal of transforming the world into something like America's image could be achieved with relatively low levels of cost and risk. Rather than imposing a model, one was assisting a movement.

The gradual decline in American soft power as the American model ran into trouble was one of the principal factors turning American foreign policy from a merry summer ramble to a grim winter slog after the Cold War, but the growing difficulties of blue model society would have an even more profound, and equally unexpected, impact on American domestic order. The perception of American success and American progress wasn't just politically important in the sense that happy voters tend to support centrist parties and stable policies. It wasn't just important because prosperity helped legitimize the social order and marginalize radicals who might otherwise seek massive change. It was important because of the role that American success played in the construction of American identity in the twentieth century. That so many Americans embraced the idea that the gradual development of a (relatively) egalitarian and prosperous America based on the adherence to principles which had all along been part of the country's cultural DNA helped unite a complex society around a common vision. The success of the blue social model was not just a piece of American history; it had become a building block of American identity. The gradual decay of blue model American society would eventually produce a profound crisis of American identity and ideology that is now the most important issue in American life.

All national identities are to some degree arbitrary and artificial, and the United States, unusually large, unusually diverse, and unusually young among the great nations is no exception to this rule. As a child growing up in the Carolinas in the 1950s and 1960s, I lived among people who were Americans the way French people are French. That is, we were Americans because we lived in America. We knew as a historical fact that our ancestors had come from other parts of the world, but no living members of our families had any memory of living anywhere but America or being anything but American. The America we knew was diverse: some Americans were white and some were Black, most but not all belonged to various Protestant denominations, and there were clear differences of accent, class, and culture even among whites. Southern whites also thought of themselves as southerners, very different from Yankees, who were also American, but who we were not particularly encouraged to like. However, when outsiders—Germans, Japanese, or Russian communists—attacked in one way or another the United States, they attacked all of us and we would stand together against them.

It was not until I came north for my higher education that I learned that there were people who experienced their American identity in ideological terms. For them, America was defined as a set of ideas about democracy, liberty, equality, and the rule of law. I believed then and still believe all these years later in those ideas, but neither then nor now does it seem to me that my identity or anyone else's as an American rests on accepting these or indeed any ideas. To me, a person is an American because either by choice or by birth they are citizens of the American republic and therefore members of the American people.

But solid and self-evident as this conviction is for me, I have learned that the other, more ideological approach to American identity is as deeply grounded for many people I like and admire as mine is for me. American identity means different things to different people.

In the eighteenth and nineteenth centuries, many white Americans experienced their identity in the ways I did as a child. They were "American" because of who they were, not because of how they thought. People were aware that Americans generally thought in different ways from Europeans and others, but those differences were not seen as constitutive of American identity.

The development of an ideological vision—that those who accepted a certain set of ideas were "true Americans" while those who rejected them were "un-American" even if they were legal citizens—was the product of both a nativist suspicion of Roman Catholic immigrants, primarily Irish, in the mid-nineteenth century and attempts by said Catholic immigrants to demonstrate that their religious beliefs did not preclude an acceptance of the main articles of what came to be known as the American creed. The construction of an ideological American identity served both to integrate and to police immigrants. "Good" immigrants bought into the American creed; "bad" ones didn't, and could be deported, as in the post–World War I Red Scare, or marginalized, as in the McCarthy era. That Congress convened the House Un-American Activities Committee is a sign of how important the creedal nature of American identity had become.

In substance, being American in this creedal sense meant assent to the principles of the Declaration of Independence, the institutions established by the Constitution, and to the ethics (though not the specific doctrines) of Judeo-Christian religion. The Pledge of Allegiance, "I pledge allegiance to the flag of the United States of American, and to the republic for which it stands, one nation, indivisible, with liberty and justice for all," was seen as the American creed. (The words "under God" were added in the 1950s to underline the distinction between atheistic communists and good Americans.)[6]

The construction of a creedal identity was particularly important to groups whose integration into American society was otherwise questionable or controversial. It not only meant that Catholics, Jews, and Black Americans could lay claim to full membership in the American nation on the basis of the creed, it was a creed which seemed to cover all the basics to the old majority population while being broad and inclusive enough so that most (though never all) members of these groups could, with whatever reservations they may have had, generally subscribe to it.

The challenges of assimilating the waves of immigration culminating in the Great Wave of 1880–1924 made creedal nationalism more important than ever. Orthodox Greeks, Catholic Sicilians, Russian Jews, and Syrian Arab Christians did not have a lot in common with each other or with the "old stock" of mostly Anglo-Protestant settlers already ensconced in the United States. It was not just that they came from cultural and religious backgrounds far removed from the old American mainstream. The America into which they came—increasingly urban and industrial—was very different from the agrarian republic into which the earlier settlers had come. For new immigrants, it was increasingly difficult to see themselves in the portraits of silk-stockinged Anglo Founders in tricorn hats; for "old stock" Americans, it was also difficult to see the exotic newcomers and the bustling smoky cities in which they lived as recognizably related to a past that seemed more idyllic as it receded from living memory. As the European Great Wave subsided during World War I and was curtailed by the Johnson-Reed Act of 1924, the Black American Great Migration filled the vacant workstations of bustling factories across the North, and for the first time since Reconstruction a large, enfranchised Black population began to make its presence felt. "Blood and soil nationalism" could not cover this multitude. Developing a national identity strong enough to command enthusiastic adherence and elastic enough to cover the extraordinary diversity of this newly assembled multitude was a task that preoccupied American thinkers and social activists from the 1880s through the 1960s. The long pause in immigration, the national ordeals of the Depression and World War II, and, not least, the broadly shared prosperity of postwar, blue model America appeared to have answered the anxious petition of the Episcopal prayer book and fashioned "into one united people the multitudes brought hither out of many kindreds and tongues."[7]

Creedal nationalism was and had to be progressive—not in a partisan or narrow way, but in the broad sense that an American idea that could hold the allegiance of its citizens had to be forward looking. America in the first half of the twentieth century was more affluent than any large country in the world, but it was a profoundly unequal society, and not only for people from racial minority groups. Life for working-class families could be and often was bitterly hard: long hours, unsafe working conditions, dismal and crowded living conditions, brutal policing, polluted water and air, poor-quality and often contaminated food. Social mobility existed, but for people from ethnic groups whose physical appearance or cultural habits differed widely from what "old stock" Americans considered "normal," opportunities were limited and discrimination was both common and legal. Single women faced both social prejudice and low pay. Asian Americans, whose numbers remained limited at this time due to race-based immigration discrimination well antedating Johnson-Reed, faced extraordinary barriers in many states and met with suspicion almost everywhere. The majority of Black Americans still living in the old Confederacy suffered under Jim Crow laws,[8] while those who came north faced popular prejudice, unsympathetic teachers, hostile law enforcement as well as discrimination in housing, employment, and pay.

An American creed that could mean something to these Americans could not be a triumphalist celebration of the status quo any more than it could simply be the mythologization of an imagined past. The American creed needed to point to a better, fairer future. America was a place that had high ideals, and gradually approached them over time. For "old stock" Americans, this vision acknowledged the value of American heritage, but the vital principle of that heritage that made it valuable was its openness to progress and change. That was, like any historical myth, something of a cosmetic simplification of a complicated reality, but it rang true to enough people that it helped the country maintain a sense of continuity and groundedness even as it underwent massive social and demographic change.

Many of the problems of American identity seemed to sort themselves out after World War II. Second- and third-generation Americans descended from the Great Wave immigrants both assimilated into American material and cultural life and faced declining levels of discrimination. The 1950s and 1960s were the decades in which white Catholics, as well as Jews, saw their full entry into American life, and racial minorities experienced a significant opening. The election of John Fitzgerald Kennedy to the White House demonstrated to Catholics that they were equal members of the body politic—and reassured WASPs that American Catholics were pillars of, rather than dangers to, the American way of life.

The great postwar wave of middle-class prosperity helped cement the loyalty of the descendants of the Great Wave to the American system both because that prosperity demonstrated that the system worked and because the transition from ethnically homogeneous urban neighborhoods to intermixed suburbs broke up old ethnic enclaves and institutions and propelled the suburbanites into a new and more purely American pattern of life. The children of these suburban residents attended school with one another, worked at the same factories or offices, and intermarried. Families that were Polish on one side and Italian on the other were much more American than they were anything else. The rising tide of mid-century prosperity was the background against which a new American identity emerged, one suited to the multiethnic, largely Catholic character of the tens of millions of immigrants attracted to the United States by the booming factories of the Industrial Revolution. For most of them, the American Dream of secure prosperity and self-respect had become a reality. They believed in an America that they saw.

This was an America of fusion and convergence. It was not only that any differences in status and opportunity between "old stock" Americans and the descendants of the Great Wave were fading away. It was more broadly that the differences between classes were also fading. In 1900 the difference between the working class and the professional middle class was an unbridgeable chasm. The classes wore different clothes, ate different foods, lived in very different environments, got their information from different sources, and American class differences in speech were almost as marked as in the U.K.

Rising incomes, suburbanization, and the homogenizing effects of mass advertising and mass media changed all that. America's stratified class society simplified during the twentieth century. At the fringes were the plutocrats and the marginalized poor. In between, the working class, middle class, and administrative professional elite merged into the vast American "middle class." This class was not homogeneous; people spoke of lower middle (blue-collar factory workers), middle middle (post office workers, police and firefighters, K–12 teachers, and lower-level office employees), and upper middle (middle- and upper-level managers, doctors, professors, lawyers, and other "professional" workers) strata. Nevertheless, most Americans thought they lived in a relatively open and equal society, that this openness and equality were the natural consequence of American values, and that further progress would bring more leveling up and more fusion.

It was the context of convergence that gave so many hope that the deepest wound in American society might also heal. If different religious, ethnic, and regional groups could come together in an increasingly equal, prosperous, and homogeneous union, could not this assimilative principle in American life also bring Black America into its field of operation? There were signs of hope. As the white South lost some of its regional distinctiveness, southern whites clung to their ancient racial prejudices less obsessively than before. The barriers that once blocked the advancement of Irish, Italian, Asian, and Jewish Americans had fallen or were visibly melting. Would not the passage of more time extend this dynamic to Black Americans, and was not the collapse of Jim Crow and the passage of civil rights laws evidence that this was in fact happening? Beyond this, the rising tide of working-class prosperity that had brought American blue-collar workers to living standards that were the envy of the world would surely in due course elevate Black living standards as well. Here, too, there was evidence. Black wages and incomes rose dramatically after World War II.[9] The magic of the American Way was visibly working.

The progressive disintegration of blue model America under the blows of the Information Revolution and the globalization to which that revolution gave birth is the most important driver of American domestic politics and foreign policy today. But our concern here is the U.S.-Israel relationship, and we must restrict our focus to the aspects of these unexpected and disturbing social changes that most directly affected the domestic politics around that relationship, the fears and hopes that shaped the actions of American policymakers during this era, and the consequences of those policies in the Middle East and beyond.

The post-1990 developments in American life most relevant to our subject were the gradual loss of faith among many (by no means all) Americans in the ideological form of American identity that dominated the post–World War II generation, and the consequent splintering of American politics, culture, and identity that gradually appeared. As the sun set, the stars and the planets stepped out onstage, and not all of the planets were benign.

What happened was that a failure of convergence led to a crisis of creed and that, in turn, led to an identity crisis as more Americans doubted whether the mid-century vision of a diverse nation united around a set of values was possible or even desirable.

The failure of convergence was, first and foremost, a failure of class convergence. A mix of deindustrialization, the decline of clerical work, global competition, and other factors undermined the power of the (private sector) labor movement and saw a long stagnation and in some cases serious decline of blue-collar wages and living standards. The upper middle class, on the other hand, the professional and administrative elites, prospered. Those differences were magnified by the entry of more women into the professional workforce. Upper-middle-class families often had two six-figure incomes, and the gap between college and noncollege workers continued to widen.

The term "working class" came back into wider usage as these differences widened and as studies showed declining social mobility between classes in American life. After 2000, America in some ways started to look more like the America of 1900 with deep and easily visible class differences.

As economic inequality increased and social mobility became more difficult, the consequences for racial politics in the United States were profound. While there had long been a vibrant Black middle class, and while Black access to professional and managerial jobs widened significantly after the civil rights era, most Black Americans were in the lower economic strata of the postwar middle class. When high-wage manufacturing jobs began to disappear, and blue-collar wages generally stagnated or fell, Blacks were disproportionately affected by the widening class divide.

Worse, systemic racism in the pre–civil rights era had excluded many Black families from the most important engine of American middle-class wealth development: housing. Black borrowers suffered mortgage discrimination and Black homebuyers were often excluded from all but a handful of neighborhoods. For millions of American blue-collar families, buying affordable homes in suburbs on thirty-year mortgages at low fixed rates, often subsidized by G.I. benefits as well as generous tax deductions for interest and tax payments, served both as a wealth generator and as an introduction to the principles of investment and finance. As housing prices rose over time, homebuying families reaped substantial profits, adding to their growing equity as they paid down their mortgages. By 1989, American households owned $4.7 trillion worth of real estate,[10] and homeownership was 40 percent of the total worth of middle-class families.[11] In the second quarter of 2019, the rate of Black homeownership fell to 40.6 percent, its lowest since 1970, two years after the passage of the 1968 Fair Housing Act.[12]

Adjusting for inflation, the average middle-class Black household in 1968 had $6,674 in wealth compared to $70,786 for the average middle-class white household. In 2016 those numbers stood at $13,024 and $149,703, respectively.[13] Black households also inherited less wealth than white households, with 10 percent of Black households receiving an inheritance at an average level of $100,000 in 2019, compared to 30 percent of white households at an average level of $195,500.[14]

The failure to achieve something like equality of income and status was not just a Black problem. The failure undercut the perceived legitimacy of the American system. As long as Americans believed that racism was a legacy from the past that the country was progressively overcoming, awareness of the stain of racism could be squared with a faith in America's ultimate goodness and success. But what if the country wasn't leaving racism behind? If the United States was not ultimately an inclusive society but if, as some maintained, racism was so deeply encoded in the country's DNA that it could not be eradicated, what made the couns the meaning of common citizenship in

The American creed was more than a
prosperous country and a nice place to
colonial era had seen their country as
oying its hour on the historical stage.
tial nation, a nation whose destiny it
a new and higher kind of life. The
leas that defined the American Way
shores and it was America's special
oles to the world. Like the ancient
been entrusted with a providen-
human race. By defeating fascism
tury, by creating a society of mass
ng from a past of discrimination
f national existence, America was

What if American providential
n the egotism of white suprem-
ras a kind of fever dream from
ing to awake?
national creed wasn't true was
mericans were falling behind
ty to rise, and if Black Amer-
legacies of slavery and Jim
eration, it was reasonable to
t something anymore. And,
an?
American identity and the
ects of a new Great Wave
ite terms than the immi-
he 1965 Hart-Celler Act,
nber of new immigrants,
d encouraged migration
imbers of immigrants,
ls in their countries of
ited States, many more
i cities and metropoli-

ned alien
merican

, though,
he process
ed signifi-

ion of the
and anar-
ration con-
lly the first
tates added
. The exten-
ible growth
shut of the

ns and social
Wave These
migration is
major demo-
ade the post–
n the elite had

the shape and
ore difficult for
rly in the twen-
ans that it was
omers, to make
nited States was
troversial a cen-
out the value of
values be foisted

istence and even
ial stress arising
of confidence in
t as a whole. This
ome development

tan areas. As in the year 1900, an urban working class that see
and perhaps ideologically or socially dangerous to significant
subcultures was a growing presence in American life.

The successful incorporation of the Great Wave migrant
led to historical amnesia about how difficult and contentious t
was—or how patchy it was as Asian and Latin migrants fac
cantly greater barriers to acceptance and integration.

Also missing from the historical memory was a recogni
political consequences of the Great Wave: a rise of socialist
chist movements among immigrants facing the shock of mig
tributed to the emergence of a nativist backlash and eventua
Red Scare. Limited economic opportunities in the United S
to these tensions and to the recent migrants' disillusionment
sive history of violent suppression, mob action, and irresis
of the anti-immigrant consensus that led to the slamming
nation's doors was all but forgotten.

The new Great Wave saw a return of many of the tensio
and economic conflicts that characterized the first Great
were going to be disruptive and difficult in any case—in
beneficial but never stress free—but the combination of
graphic shifts with the economic and social changes m
Cold War era a far more tumultuous time than many i
expected.

That the new immigrant wave came at a time when
value of American identity was hotly contested made it m
Americans to think about questions like assimilation. Ea
tieth century, it seemed obvious to "old stock" Americ
the duty of public institutions to "Americanize" newc
them fit and eager participants in the mission that the U
appointed to carry out. That point of view was more con
tury later; if native-born Americans were ambivalent a
their inherited ideas and institutions, why should these
on newcomers?

The widening income and class disparities, the per
widening of the racial gap, and the cultural and so
from a new Great Wave gradually opened up a crisis
the national creed and, therefore, the American proje
could not have been a more unexpected and unwel

for an establishment that essentially took the health and unity of its country for granted. While many countries were experiencing political difficulties as the Information Revolution swept across the world, America's unique role in the international system made the stability and success of the American project of vital interest to people everywhere— and meant that the consequences of political failure in the United States would be incalculably large.

The thirty years that followed the Cold War saw the United States travel from the smug sense of success and self-confidence that followed the Soviet collapse to an era of questioning, conflict, and doubt. The growing disorder at home came as the world situation also darkened. In 1990 the United States seemed effortlessly dominant; by 2020 it faced hostile opponents in a tumultuous world. It is essential for the American elite, like elites anywhere, to be able to explain events to the public at large in ways that maintain public confidence in, and support for, the country's direction. An elite must be able to justify and legitimate its privileges while effectively making the case either for the justice of existing social arrangements or for the wisdom of, and prospects for, reform efforts currently under way. Unfortunately, even as the American situation became more difficult and the world situation became more challenging, the American leadership class—among Democrats and Republicans alike—was becoming less able to fulfill this vital and necessary role. Part of the reason for this was that the relationship between the establishment and the polity had changed drastically over the course of several decades.

After World War II the American elite transformed from a small group, predominantly from a relatively narrow stratum of long-established families based largely in the Northeast, to a much larger group of administrators, managers, and researchers. This new elite was demographically and geographically more diverse than the old establishment and in its early decades more representative of class distribution in the United States. Rapid upward mobility meant that many members of the new establishment had blue-collar backgrounds. For members of the "new elite," understanding the outlooks and concerns of the working class was intuitive because they had come from it.

But the social and economic forces that were separating the classes in American life meant that the social distance between the upper middle class and the rest of the country expanded as income stratification and sharp divides in educational opportunities grew. And while many Americans outside the elite bubble struggled to achieve or maintain a middle-class living standard, and the industrial working class suffered a long and painful decline, the post-1990 era on the whole was a time of unprecedented and even glorious opportunity for America's upper middle class.

There were exceptions. Journalists were almost as hard hit as steelworkers as the internet disrupted the media oligopolies and business models on which the profession rested. Academics, except for a dwindling minority who still enjoyed the advantages of limited teaching loads and lifetime tenure, faced an increasingly precarious future as an oversupply of aspirants flooded the market and colleges staffed more positions with poorly paid, insecure adjunct teachers.

But on the whole, the burgeoning American upper middle class of professionals like bankers, lawyers, doctors, tech engineers, and consultants enjoyed a boom as long lived and as intoxicating as the postwar prosperity for the country as a whole. For these Americans, the problems of the lower middle class looked like sad but necessary shifts to respond to the ultimately healthy forces of globalization. They were for the most part only dimly aware of the growing discontent and alienation that, in due course, would power political movements as diverse as the Tea Party, Occupy Wall Street, the 2016 Trump campaign, the Bernie Sanders movement, and Black Lives Matter. Living in class-segregated suburbs, attending hothouse colleges with students mostly from homes and families like their own, the American elite increasingly shared all the characteristics of an aristocracy—with the exception in too many cases of a sense of noblesse oblige. Feeling that their accomplishments were the result of "merit" and hard work, they felt entitled to the widening income gap that separated them from the slackers and losers who occupied the lower rungs on the American ladder.

Meanwhile, more and more Americans were questioning institutions and ideas that their predecessors had seen as essential building blocks of American life. Rising levels of education and affluence, combined with the heightening of the endemic individualism of American society due to the increasing impact of an advertisement-rich consumer society, led many Americans to reject traditional social norms. Questions related to gender identity, sexual mores, and family structure had already appeared during the Cold War, but their impact on society grew dramatically in the 1990s and beyond. As previously unthinkable concepts like gay marriage gained widespread acceptance, and trans activists and others sought to push the shift in mores beyond the comfort zone of many, the impact on American politics went beyond the division of the country into factions in the "culture wars."

If the western civilization in which America was rooted was not only irredeemably racist but entirely patriarchal, homophobic, and transphobic to boot, and if the Judeo-Christian morality at the foundation of traditional American values was little more than an assemblage of false and even harmful ideas, what exactly was the American creed? Was there enough of a "there" there to hold a political society together, or should Americans forge a new identity around a struggle to free themselves from the wreckage of the old one?

The widening gap between traditional values and contemporary practices caused political rifts in many countries. But the fact that for many Americans their sense of national identity came from adherence to a common creed meant that the culture wars found across the western world divided Americans more profoundly and potentially more dangerously than people in many other countries.

Belief in progress was getting harder to sustain, and that waning belief would contribute to another of the problems dogging the footsteps of those charged with the shaping of American foreign policy.

Steering the Apocalypse

In AD 1000, fears that the milestone date would mark the end of the world and the return of Christ are said to have swept across the medieval world. One thousand years later, as a second millennium approached, there was a similar round of foreboding, this time directed at the prospect that due to programming oversights, older computer devices would be unable to read the date in a new century, leading to a massively catastrophic global computer crash. The first millennial panic was good for church institutions, who received rich gifts and bequests from those hoping to square their accounts. The second was a gold mine for computer consultants. The best available records suggest that neither the church nor the consultants returned any funds when the predicted apocalypse failed to appear. But if the Y2K bug* did not bring the world to a juddering halt, apocalyptic concerns would play a large and growing role after the end of the Cold War.

We've seen how the historicization of the eschaton, the movement of the concept of the end of history and even the end of the world from the realms of mythology and religion to the realms of politics and statecraft, has been shaping world history from the Enlightenment onward, and how central the idea that America has a unique role to play in this historical drama has been to the construction of American identity. We've also noted an unexpected consequence of historicization. The idea that the human condition could be fundamentally changed through social progress and political action was originally seen as a secularizing force in world affairs. If human beings could either create utopia or destroy life on earth through their own actions, why spend a lot of time thinking about God?

In practice, however, things worked out differently. As the question of the survival of human civilization and the human race entered the realm of politics, politics became more intense, more confrontational, and more infused with moral and religious values. The historicization of the eschaton leads to the mythologization of politics, as ordinary political debates transform into arguments about the construction of utopias or the avoidance of massive catastrophe.

The twentieth century marked a new stage in the history of humanity's encounter with the idea of apocalypse. From the Enlightenment forward, people believed that the historical and political processes they saw unfolding around them were leading to a fundamental change in the conditions of human existence as significant as those that various religious traditions had long predicted. In the twentieth century, more and more people came to believe that this great change was no longer something that would appear at some distant point in the future. Apocalypse was happening around us.

For communists, the Russian Revolution was the moment when the world transitioned from a time of anticipation and preparation to the apocalyptic era in which the great climax of world history was happening before their eyes. Soviet ideology held that the Soviet Union was a kind of living apocalypse, the great embodiment of a revolutionary

---

* Y2K = Year Two Thousand

movement designed to transform the human race and to end war and injustice forever. To study the apocalypse, communists read the morning news.

The nuclear explosions at Hiroshima and Nagasaki meant that humanity as a whole now lived in what can fairly be called an age of apocalypse. The Cold War was a new kind of conflict. With both sides building enough nuclear weapons and intercontinental missiles to annihilate not only the adversary but the whole human race, the potential for political misjudgments to have apocalyptic consequences had never felt more real. But that was not all. Neither of the great parties to the Cold War was what could be called an ordinary great power.

Both of the antagonists saw themselves as the agent of rival programs for bringing history to a successful conclusion. The Soviets believed that Leninism was the magic formula that would end war and establish universal prosperity forever. The Americans believed that liberal capitalist democracy was the magic bullet. Each saw the other as a rival faith whose precepts would lead to destruction. The Cold War was a religious conflict between secular states, fought under the shadow of the apocalypse, over conflicting visions of the path to utopia.

The apocalyptic nature of the Cold War is one reason that so many Americans interpreted their victory as the final vindication of the American Way and the beginning of a new era of universal freedom and peace. The apparent end of the long nuclear nightmare of the Cold War combined with the disappearance of the most formidable antagonist to liberal society to make a heady brew, and the American establishment drank the cup to the dregs. Future generations who had not lived under the shadow of the nuclear standoff, when serious, well-informed people understood that nuclear annihilation could happen by accident—if, for example, Soviet or American radar systems confused a flock of geese with a sneak missile attack, unleashing a retaliatory strike in response— cannot fully grasp how sweet the world suddenly seemed when that threat was removed.

However, the end of the Cold War did not end the age of apocalypse. If the specter of nuclear war faded in the 1990s, other visions of human suicide began to appear. The most prominent was the specter of climate change. The uncontrolled emission of carbon dioxide and other greenhouse gasses through human industrial and agricultural activity threatened to unleash a climate cascade. Warming temperatures, an effect expected to be especially marked near the poles, would melt the vast polar icecaps, leading to rapid and disastrous flooding as sea levels rose and cities and coastal areas sank beneath the waves. Vast areas of the tropics would become too hot for human habitation or for agriculture. Rivers would dry up as glaciers melted, and hundreds of millions of people would be on the march from their devastated homelands in search of subsistence. Some foresaw what climate scientist James Hansen called a "Venus syndrome" as feedback loops led to temperature increases that made the planet uninhabitable.[15] Others foresaw wars of survival leading ultimately to a nuclear holocaust on an exhausted, dying planet.

Climate change was only one in a series of existential threats that captured the imagination of the twenty-first century. The terror attacks of 9/11 raised the specter of a nondeterrable nuclear threat. If nonstate actors ranging from terrorists to blackmailers managed to acquire nuclear weapons, they could detonate a bomb without there being a homeland or government against which the aggrieved party could retaliate. The almost simultaneous anthrax attacks of the fall of 2001 demonstrated another peril. The steady progress of biology raised the possibility that biological warfare, either by a state or by a terror organization, could wreak untold havoc on the world. The 2020 Covid-19 pandemic showed what even a relatively mild contagious disease could accomplish in an unprepared world. As the century unfolded, what new and artificial horrors could be engineered in untraceable labs?

The internet, which had first appeared to many as a harmless phenomenon promoting the free exchange of ideas and information, quickly took on a more sinister aspect. Cyberwar offered new scenarios of attacks that paralyzed a country's electrical grid, opened the floodgates of its dams, or wiped out its financial system. The marriage of information technology and totalitarian social control seemed to be consummated in China, where an all-seeing state looked determined to use the power of electronic surveillance to impose the kind of control over its citizens that no king, no religious dictatorship of the past, had ever been able to acquire. Applied ruthlessly in Tibet and Xinjiang, the new instruments of total social control demonstrated that the fall of Soviet communism had not exhausted the ability of human society to produce monstrous tyrannies capable of the most horrifying crimes.

The nuclear specter, meanwhile, never really disappeared as nuclear proliferation continued to dominate both popular and elite concerns about American foreign policy. The North Korean nuclear program was one of the thorniest policy issues that presidents from Bill Clinton to Joe Biden had to face. Millions of Americans supported George W. Bush's invasion of Iraq because they believed that Saddam Hussein had a nuclear program that might provide terrorists with nuclear weapons. The controversy over how best to deal with the Iranian nuclear program was one of the most bitter partisan issues in the debates of the Obama and Trump administrations. The intensification of great power competition made nuclear arms talks with Russia a major issue in American politics and diplomacy. And China's rapidly growing nuclear arsenal suggested that the nuclear balance of terror was about to return to the center stage of both world politics and the human imagination. The apocalyptic specter could not be wished away.

======

During the Cold War, the task of American foreign policy had been threefold: to defeat the Soviet Union, to avoid a catastrophic nuclear war, and, among the nations of what in those times was called the "Free World" of noncommunist countries, to further the construction of the peaceful international order which most American liberals believed would usher in an age of universal peace and abundance.

After the Cold War, American foreign policy makers initially thought that their lives had become much easier. They could concentrate on peaceful order building in a world without opponents. Yet the task was still herculean; the Soviet heresy had fallen to the wayside, and now the American faith would have to deliver. The alternative futures for humanity were as stark as ever. On one side a utopian future of freedom, abundance, and peace beckoned invitingly. On the other, a dystopian world of eco-catastrophe, conflict, and, quite possibly, the extinction of the human race sulphurously loomed. Was the human race headed toward a "hot" apocalypse of eco-catastrophe, nuclear holocaust, or some other hideous culmination, or were we on track toward a "cool" apocalypse of gradual progress toward a world of freedom and peace? Policymakers and national leaders had a new task in the twenty-first century: managing apocalypse.

The idea that America was on the path that would lead, not only locally but ultimately globally, toward a gloriously cool apocalypse had been central to American thought and identity since the eighteenth century. This view of the future corresponds both to the theological position in Christianity known as "postmillennialism" and to the secular, liberal ideas associated with the so-called Whig Narrative of peaceful and gradual progress. It was a fundamental element of the American creed that emerged in the twentieth century around which post–Great Wave America was able to unite.

The successful conclusion of the Cold War seemed to confirm that this vision of history was correct, as was the providential nation thesis that gave the United States a starring role in the historical drama. In sixty years, the United States had played a critical role in the destruction of fascism, ended generations of bitter class conflict in the West by building an affluent middle-class society, and defeated a nuclear superpower adversary through the power of its ideas and capacity for innovation—while also laying the foundations for unprecedented waves of economic prosperity and democratic governance across much of the world. The dragon was dead and the princess was saved; that is how many Americans interpreted the fall of the Soviet Union. Elites noted that it was their wise leadership that had brought about this grand result and faced the future with renewed confidence in their own capabilities, and with an assumption that these dramatic successes would teach the rest of the country to follow their lead in the future.

But American culture is complicated, and the expectation of a hot apocalypse also has a place in it. In Christian theology, the belief that the apocalypse will be a hot one—that divine wrath will destroy the world before divine mercy rebuilds it on a new and better foundation—is known as "premillennialism." In secular politics, this view is associated with those who believe the status quo is so unjust or dysfunctional that only a great and cleansing catastrophe can bring about the kind of change that people need. In the twentieth century, Bolsheviks were Marxists who believed in a hot, revolutionary road to the utopian workers' state while more moderate socialists hoped for a cooler, gentler road to the workers' utopia through gradual reform. Belief in a hot apocalypse has often been strongest among the marginalized, the dispossessed, and the alienated.

The twentieth century, with its string of historical catastrophes stretching from World War I through the rise of communism and fascism, World War II, the Holocaust, Hiroshima, the upheavals associated with both the rise and the fall of European colonialism, and the terrifying nuclear standoff of the Cold War, saw a global surge in fears that a hot apocalypse was at hand. The establishment of an apparently stable and prosperous democratic order in the advanced industrial democracies after World War II calmed these concerns for many people, supporting faith in a cool apocalypse, and of course the peaceful end of the Cold War greatly strengthened that faith.

However, to an extent that few realized at the time, this confidence was fragile. As the post–World War II stable social order showed signs of decay, as the global political scene darkened, and as fears of climate change grew, hot apocalypse scenarios seemed more compelling to more people. People animated by a strong belief that the technocracy and the political establishment were failing and that under their leadership the world was slouching closer to some kind of existential crisis, are not reliable supporters of centrist, moderate political movements. The sense in much of the Islamic world that its institutions and leaders were failing and that hostile powers opposed to Islam were in charge of the world provided a powerful boost to apocalyptic cults and radical Islamist movements. Populist movements in Europe drew strength from the growing sense that the EU was unable to cope with problems ranging from economic growth to mass migration from the south and east. And in the United States itself, growing dissatisfaction with economic and social conditions, along with disenchantment with a globalist foreign policy that was costing more and providing less than many Americans felt they had been promised, helped stimulate the rise of anti-establishment populism among both Democrats and Republicans.

From visions of apocalypse to thoughts of the Middle East is always a short road in Abrahamic cultures. In much of the Islamic world, the seemingly inexorable rise of Israel and the progressive marginalization of Palestinians contributed to the sense of civilizational and religious crisis out of which radical Islamist movements grew. In much of Europe and for many Americans, what they saw as Israel's defiance of international law seemed to pose a serious threat to the establishment of the liberal, rules-based order on which they placed their hopes for a quiet, cool, and liberal apocalypse. And among many other Americans, attacks against the United States by radical jihadi terrorists animated by a hatred of Israel and of America as Israel's ally appeared to confirm their intuitions that the biblically prophesied hot apocalypse was well on its way.

More than ever before, America's Israel policy after the Cold War would struggle to reconcile the convictions of differing American political movements about the national interest in the Middle East with the consequences of passionate internal debates about the nature of American identity, the role of the United States in the world, and the state of the human condition. From the relatively sunny days of the 1990s when the Arab-Israeli peace process dominated American policymaking through the consequences and aftermath of the George W. Bush administration's "war on terror" in the region through the messy efforts of both the Obama and Trump administrations to reduce American commitments in the Middle East as the country turned its attention to the Indo-Pacific, America's Israel policy would continue to occupy a uniquely important symbolic role in American politics.

The "Middle East peace process," as the tangle of diplomatic activity around the Israeli-Palestinian conflict is frequently called, was the most sustained and most expensive single diplomatic effort in the history of the United States. In the 1990s, advocates of the peace process saw Middle East peace as a critical task for the new world order. Previous generations of Americans saw the United Nations as the only way to prevent a nuclear war and Palestine's partition as the first test of the new peace; their successors saw Israel-Palestine negotiations as the most visible sign that peaceful negotiations could stop global violence, spread democratic values, and keep the apocalypse cool.

16

The Great MacGuffin and
the Quest for the Holy Grail

THE MIDDLE EAST PEACE PROCESS is a more remarkable thing than we frequently take it to be. Historians often marvel at the complex negotiations resulting in the Peace of Westphalia that ended the Thirty Years' War. The Middle East peace process has not only lasted longer, cost more, and involved more meetings among more diplomats than the Westphalian negotiations—the Middle East peace process has lasted longer than the Thirty Years' War.

Harry Truman was the first American president to try to make peace between Israel and the Arab world, and the formula he proposed—Israeli concessions on land, the return of some Palestinian refugees, and development funding for everyone—prefigured seventy years of similar proposals from his successors.

Peace negotiations gained momentum with the end of the Cold War, when American policymakers vigorously pursued the dream of a comprehensive Middle East settlement that had eluded them for decades. This renewed effort marked the entrance of the Palestinians into the negotiations at the time of the 1991 Madrid Conference in the George H. W. Bush administration. Under George W. Bush, the establishment of a Palestinian state on the West Bank and Gaza was recognized as a key goal of the negotiations. Yet despite the attention of several presidents and the indefatigable efforts of hordes of diplomats and policy thinkers, the most significant progress toward peace in the region was not the fruit of American labors.

During President Bill Clinton's administration, a limited Israeli-Palestinian agreement made the goal of peace seem closer than ever.

Secret negotiations between the Palestine Liberation Organization (PLO) and Israel, conducted without American involvement just like Anwar Sadat's visit to Jerusalem, culminated in the signing of the first of the Oslo Accords at the White House in 1993. Israel recognized the PLO "as the representative of the Palestinian people" and Yasser Arafat, on behalf of the PLO, recognized "the right of the State of Israel to exist in peace and security" and renounced "the use of terrorism and other acts of violence."[1] A year later Jordan would sign a peace treaty of its own with Israel, following Egypt's 1978 agreement to become the second of Israel's neighbors to withdraw from the conflict. Following another Israeli-Palestinian agreement in Cairo, the Palestinian Authority (PA) was formally established in July of 1994. The process continued with the signing of Oslo II in 1995, which established areas of limited PA rule.

As was the case for Jimmy Carter, Bill Clinton got a significant peace agreement, but the deeper and broader peace he desired eluded him. Progress slowed after Oslo II and the assassination of Israeli prime minister Yitzhak Rabin by a radical Israeli opponent of the peace process, but under heavy pressure from the Clinton administration the Israelis and Palestinians signed the 1998 Wye River Memorandum. Benjamin Netanyahu's government fell from power shortly after the agreement, but after a delay for elections, the new Israeli prime minister, Ehud Barak, returned to the process, stepping up the pace of diplomacy as the clock began to run out for the Clinton administration. After consultations with Barak, Clinton proposed the "Clinton Parameters" to Arafat, but at this point both Clinton and Barak were about to exit from power. In the United States, Clinton's successor, George W. Bush, was at this early stage less interested in the peace process than he would become later, and Barak's successor, opposition leader Ariel Sharon, was elected in part because many Israeli voters were uncomfortable with Barak's perceived willingness to concede "too much" to the Palestinians. This feeling was particularly strong because the Second Intifada (a wave of violence engulfing both Israel and the Palestinian territories that would last through 2005 and lead to approximately three thousand deaths) was raging at the time. The Taba Summit, which was meant to conclude negotiations over the Clinton Parameters, began the day after George W. Bush's inauguration and concluded six days later after the Barak government ended talks to prepare for the general election scheduled in February. Sharon's government did not resume talks after his victory.

After initially hesitating to enter into the process, George W. Bush tried to democratize and reform Palestine to make peace more attainable. He introduced his initiative to resolve the conflict, the Roadmap for Peace, in 2002 by calling for a two-state solution. The Roadmap wasn't published until April 2003, a month after Mahmoud Abbas was appointed prime minister. Despite President Bush's personal intervention and the announcement of cease-fires from multiple Palestinian factions, violence flared, reform efforts failed, and the expansion of Israeli settlements in the Occupied Territories continued. By the end of 2003, it was clear that the terms of Phase I of the Roadmap had not been met. Three months after Arafat's death in 2004, Abbas and Sharon managed to negotiate a formal end to the Second Intifada at the Sharm El Sheikh Summit on February 8, 2005. Both sides expressed their commitment to the Roadmap for Peace. Efforts to restart negotiations led to the Annapolis Conference in November of 2007. Although Israeli representative and then–prime minister Ehud Olmert stated that he and Abbas were close to a deal, no agreement was reached. The Roadmap for Peace was largely shelved following the Bush administration's close.

Early in the Obama administration, Israeli prime minister Netanyahu expressed a conditional openness to the creation of a Palestinian state, but negotiators made little progress before the expiration of Netanyahu's ten-month freeze on settlement construction and expansion in the Occupied Territories. Peace talks resumed in 2013 with Secretary of State John Kerry meeting with Abbas and Netanyahu individually dozens of times over the course of months. Direct negotiations fell apart shortly after the deadline to establish an outline for an agreement expired in April of 2014. The gaps between the sides narrowed in subsequent discussions, but no real agreement was reached. Donald Trump's victory in the 2016 presidential election put Obama-era negotiating approaches on ice.[2]

Like some of his predecessors, Donald Trump benefited from decisions made by other leaders to get a new round of peace agreements. He sought to advance Israeli-Arab peace agreements whether or not the Palestinians were engaged and to deepen U.S.-Israeli cooperation with little regard for Palestinian sentiment. In a highly symbolic move, Trump shifted the American embassy from Tel Aviv to Jerusalem in 2018, and recognized the Golan Heights as part of Israel in 2019. In 2020's Abraham Accords, the United Arab Emirates and Bahrain became the first

Arab countries since Jordan to normalize relations with Israel. Sudan and Morocco would follow suit, marking the biggest shift in the political dynamics of the Arab-Israeli conflict in decades. Peace between Israelis and Palestinians, however, seemed farther away than ever.

———

In all the years of American independence, no foreign territorial dispute anywhere in the world has occupied this much American official attention for this amount of time nor been covered so avidly in the American press. Yet this heroic American perseverance has not been crowned with the desired success. President after president developed a strategy to capture the Holy Grail of American diplomacy, but the goal of Israeli-Palestinian peace eluded them all.

That peace agreement may have looked to successive presidents like the Holy Grail, the ultimate trophy whose acquisition would secure their place in history, but it was also something Alfred Hitchcock called a MacGuffin—an object whose intrinsic importance was dwarfed by events that it set in motion. There are many other international problems of equal or greater consequence for American interests than the Israeli-Palestinian conflict, but none of them received this kind of attention. The Indian-Pakistani dispute over Kashmir, a dispute that regularly brings two nuclear powers into conflict and which has acquired increasing significance as Pakistan aligns more with China and India draws nearer to the United States, is part of an ongoing dispute that has produced more refugees than the Israeli-Palestinian dispute and cost up to one hundred times as many lives. Yet this conflict has never engaged as much American attention as the smaller and arguably less consequential struggle in the Middle East. During the peak years of the peace process, which roughly coincided with the administration of President Bill Clinton, the United States appears to have devoted more attention to Israeli-Palestinian affairs than to the failure of Russian democracy, the Taliban's conquest of Afghanistan, the nuclear programs of Iraq, Syria, Iran, and North Korea, or the rise of China.

Between 1990 and 2001, American presidents and secretaries of state visited Israel and the Palestinian territories a combined total of seventy-five times. There were many more undisclosed meetings between high-ranking American officials and their Israeli and Palestinian counterparts, as well as an incalculable number of meetings between lower-level diplomatic officers from all parties involved in negotiations. No foreign country has ever received this level of sustained American attention and in fact no great power in world history has ever dedicated this much attention to a territorial dispute between two very small peoples thousands of miles from its frontiers.

The Americans were not the only outsiders transfixed by the conflict. At the United Nations, not only the secretary-general but the General Assembly, the Security Council, UNESCO, and the United Nations Human Rights Council sought to influence the course of negotiations. The Arab League and the Organization of Islamic Cooperation regularly weighed in, as did the European Union. The Quartet composed of the United Nations, the European Union, the United States, and Russia occasionally made an appearance.

Beyond these official bodies, a host of civil society and advocacy organizations around the world sought to influence the peace process. From the Council on Foreign Relations to the World Economic Forum at Davos, the world's most prestigious talking shops held program after program on virtually every aspect of the peace process. Academic and public-facing journals ran an endless procession of articles from current and former diplomats, politicians, journalists, and scholars about what was or wasn't happening, who was or wasn't responsible, and how the negotiations should or shouldn't end. University professors on campuses around the world taught courses on the peace process. Students demonstrated and held sit-ins; activists organized social movements; terrorists detonated bombs; pundits pontificated; editors opined; cable news guests debated; and political candidates grandstanded for votes.

Discussion of the peace process was often both polarized and moralistic. For some, the question of American policy toward this struggle was simple. Whose case, Israeli or Palestinian, is most deserving? Once that is ascertained, many assume, America's course must be clear: to support the case of the party judged to be in the right so that justice can be done. America's peace process diplomacy is then judged by whether it serves the cause a particular observer has determined to be the just one.

Others seek to assign blame for the failure of the peace process to the intransigence of one side or the other. Were the Israelis or the Palestinians truly sincere about peace? Should Israel have made more concessions? Should Arafat have signed on the dotted line?

As the process ground along but hopes of peace diminished, many began to ask where the effort went wrong. Was it the assassination of Yitzhak Rabin? Did Clinton move too slowly at some points, too quickly at others? Should George W. Bush have reached out to Yasser Arafat on taking office? Was Bush wrong to promote the elections that gave Gaza to Hamas? Did Obama take too hard a line on settlements in the first months of his administration? Should he have taken a harder line in the closing years of his second term?

Others debate the style of American engagement. Should the United States act as a neutral broker, or should it favor one side—and if so, on what grounds should that choice be made?

And as always when questions involving Jewish interests and the Jewish state come up, the Vulcanists shamble onstage, blinking owlishly, muttering about "the Benjamins" and looking for signs that "the Jews" have once again worked their dark magic on American foreign policy to further some sinister plot.

The place to start in seeking to understand the Great MacGuffin is to ask why so many American presidents in the post–Cold War era found pursuing Middle East peace such a compelling pursuit, and why so many foreign powers participated in the quest. That will make it easier to see why the process has, so far, failed to bring peace, and to grasp the importance of this failure for subsequent events in the Middle East and beyond.

Peace at Home, Peace Abroad

Some rushed to embrace it, some struggled to resist, but ultimately all the post–Cold War American presidents from George H. W. Bush to Joe Biden found themselves engaged in the quest for an Israeli-Palestinian peace agreement. What drew them in was hardly the power of the Jewish lobby; both Israelis and American Jews were at times deeply skeptical about the value of extended negotiations that would legitimize and finance their Palestinian opponents while giving them a place at the featured table of world politics. More than one president launched into the process more in the hope of constraining Israel than of empowering it.

What drew them in was what made Middle East diplomacy so important to Harry Truman. Involvement in the Middle East, however frustrating at times, was unavoidable considering both the domestic and international demands on American presidents. Given that, working to find some kind of compromise that could satisfy both Arabs and Israelis was not just the path of least resistance; it was a way for presidents, as Truman had done, to mobilize support for unrelated policy goals at home and abroad.

And there was, of course, always the prospect of a success that would offer global acclaim, prestigious awards, and a secure niche for one's statue in the Temple of Fame.

The end of the Cold War found presidents looking for ways to get Americans to engage with foreign policy and support the military and civil costs of a global strategy. This was not easy to do. The project of building the liberal global order that captured elite imaginations in the post–Cold War period enjoyed only limited support in the public at large, and most Clinton-era order-building initiatives ranging from military actions in the Balkans to admitting China into the WTO faced significant opposition. The problem was particularly acute in the Middle East. Saddam Hussein's 1990 attack on Kuwait highlighted the danger to key countries there, but the Gulf states—widely perceived among the public at large as price-gouging monopolists, religious extremists, and antisemitic America-haters—were not the kind of allies most Americans really wanted to help.

Engaging in the quest for Middle East peace helped build a constituency for a global foreign policy. American public opinion liked peace and it liked Israel. Negotiating with Israel's neighbors to help make Israel safe, while reducing the chances of war in a region still vitally important to the nation's oil supply, struck many American voters as an excellent use of a president's time and reassured them that his foreign policy comported with their personal values and goals. An initiative to make Israel secure was much more popular than an agenda of selling arms to Arab despots in the Middle East while embarking globally on a series of nation- and culture-building missions that many Americans didn't think would work and that others didn't think were important.

The peace process also served as a way for presidents to adjust their policies to the political needs of the moment. Presidential trips to the Middle East almost always led to favorable press coverage, underlining the difference between a president and the lesser mortals who competed against him politically. Presidents could also use the process to engage supporters. A small shift toward reducing pressure on Israel would bring applause from some quarters; an equally small shift to ratchet the pressure up would win applause from others.

———

Beyond the short-term problems of alliance management lay much more difficult, long-term questions about the future of the region. What if anything could the United States do to ensure that when, as most American policymakers believed was inevitable, the authoritarian regimes of the region finally crumbled their successors would be favorably disposed toward the United States? Here the lesson of Iran was unforgettable. The United States had enjoyed a long and mutually beneficial relationship with the Shah of Iran, only to see this regional powerhouse turn bitterly anti-American when the Shah finally fell. One needed to manage the alliances of today without foreclosing the possibility of good relations with successor regimes in the future.

Promoting the Israeli-Palestinian peace process seemed to work in both time scales. In the short term, the peace process was as superb a tool for alliance management abroad as it was useful for political management at home. When American policy seemed to favor Israel, or when Israelis behaved in ways Arab public opinion found unbearably provocative, the peace process offered a diplomatic safety valve. Arab rulers were often torn between a clear-eyed view that cooperation with the United States was essential for regime, and even national, security and an equally strong understanding that public opinion in the Arab world could only be pushed so far and that both the United States and Israel were and remained deeply unpopular with the Arab public at large.

The peace process provided a handy framework for both Arab leaders and American presidents to manage this tension. Arab rulers could respond to public indignation by pressing the Americans to take a stronger stand in the ongoing peace negotiations. If nothing else, this took some of the political heat off American regional allies—good in and of itself from Washington's point of view. And if more action seemed necessary, the United States could and sometimes did consciously shape its approach to the peace process in ways that demonstrated a responsiveness to Arab concerns. George H. W. Bush initiated the post–Cold War peace process to fulfill promises he made to Mikhail Gorbachev as he assembled the coalition against Saddam Hussein in the Gulf War.[3] His son would return, somewhat reluctantly, to the peace process as a way to help manage the political fallout from the Iraq War. President Obama would engage with the peace process as a way of demonstrating his, and America's, interest in promoting reconciliation between the United States and the Islamic and Arab worlds.

Meanwhile, the existence of the peace process and America's dominant role within it served both to highlight and to strengthen America's uniquely powerful role in the Middle East. It was clear that the United States and only the United States had at least some ability to persuade Israel to modify its policies toward the Palestinians or to offer more generous peace plans. That meant that other countries seeking to influence Israel needed to come to the United States. The drama around the peace process, the succession of high-profile negotiations and summits that marked its course, and the rapt attention with which European and Arab media followed every twist and turn in the saga continuously drove home the reality that the United States was in a league of its own and that virtually every country in the world sought to be its ally.

For American policymakers, the peace process was not just a tool for handling the inevitable tensions as the United States worked to keep its restive regional partners onside. It also offered a path to the kind of democratic and social progress that Americans believed was the best way to make the Middle East both stable and pro-American in the longer term.

The heady atmosphere of the early 1990s as tyrannies fell and democracy surged around the world deepened the sense among American policymakers that the only way to safeguard American interests in the Middle East was to promote pacification, modernization, and democratization across the Middle East. This was not a new idea; the American diplomats, aid officials, NGO workers, consultants, and financiers who promoted a transformational agenda in the post–Cold War Middle East were following one of the most consistent impulses in the history of American foreign policy.

American policymakers and civil society leaders in the early 1990s were as certain as their predecessors had been for two centuries that liberal principles and liberal order would be good for the Middle East. With all of the confidence of their missionary forebears, Americans turned to the region intending to foster a liberal order on the models of the United States and Europe. Economic freedom, globalization, and reforms to dismantle the costly systems of state subsidies and corruption would bring prosperity. Freedom of speech and political rights would detoxify public life and produce regimes that governed in the interest of the people. Full and equal rights for women and minorities, whether sexual, ethnic, or religious, would solidify democracy and create a culture of tolerant diversity. These internal reforms within states would change the relations between states. A long-lasting peace would gradually descend on the region as borders opened and trade grew. Those who resisted the change would soon be economically and therefore militarily outstripped by those who embraced it. As this became obvious, leaders of all nations would hurry to get on the bandwagon leading the Middle East into the post-historical future.

All this might take some time, and there would be those who did not see reason on this issue right away. This is where American power and American influence would come in. We would keep the peace until the peace could keep itself. Bad actors like Saddam Hussein and the ayatollahs of Iran would be prevented from disturbing their neighbors while the process of development produced the green shoots of liberal order.

There was another issue. The fight against nuclear weapons proliferation had been an important American priority since the 1940s. Thanks in part to the willingness of Pakistani scientist A. Q. Khan and his colleagues to sell their knowledge to aspiring nuclear powers and in part to North Korea's proliferation activities, the growing danger of a nuclear arms race in the Middle East kept American strategists awake at night.[4]

If the Middle East was going to become part of the liberal world order Americans hoped to build, the Israelis and the Palestinians would have to make peace. The Israeli-Palestinian dispute had for too long kept the region in turmoil. It was the excuse that dictators used to justify their arms buildups and their imposition of military rule. Popular fury over Israeli occupation of Palestinian land was a weapon used to keep moderate democrats from power, and to bolster religious extremists. Producing peace between the Palestinians and the Israelis was a key step on the road to a stable and modernizing Middle East—and a long step toward heading off a regional arms race.

Ending the Israeli-Palestinian conflict had other advantages for America's post–Cold War strategy. Demonstrating the ability of new world order diplomacy backed by American military might to blunt identity conflicts would reduce the chances for war worldwide. What would demonstrate this more clearly than overcoming the Arab-Israeli divide? If a dispute this intractable, this explosive, could be solved, then there was hope for every frozen or intermittent conflict, including Taiwan vs. China and India vs. Pakistan. Peace in the Middle East would help cement the peace of the world.

THE PROBLEM OF PEACE

In the heady "post-historical" years after the Cold War, Americans debated how we could create Middle East peace. In the grimmer 2020s the more common question is why did the peace process fail? There are battalions of writers who make very eloquent and convincing cases that the peace-loving Palestinians were cynically thwarted by brutal Israelis and weak-kneed Americans at every turn. Many others assemble massive piles of documentation and long chains of logic to demonstrate that Israel has repeatedly made extremely generous offers, only to be spurned by Palestinians too radical or too cowardly to accept. There are more debates on the American side about who made the great mistake so that the Holy Grail was so frequently glimpsed but never quite caught. The partisans and allies of various presidents write defending the strategies used; advisors and critics argue that more firmness with Israel here or a tougher stand against Palestinians there would have done the trick. Should President X have launched his peace process effort in his first months in office? Had President Z listened to the advice of Aide Q instead of Aide P would everything have worked out? Aide Q has written a book saying that this is certainly true; Aide P has written a book saying that thanks to that infernal busybody Aide Q, President Z was never able to implement Aide P's brilliant policy advice.

This is an interesting debate in its way, but the premise is unconvincing. British and American leaders have been trying to get the Jews and Arabs of the Holy Land to agree on a solution for a century now, and the list of rejected solutions is a long one. One-state solutions, two-state solutions, international trusteeships, a regional federation under Jordanian leadership: many ingenious ideas, and even more ingenious variations, have been proposed one after another—and nothing has worked. If one peace negotiation fails, perhaps we blame the negotiator. If two or three fail, we might stick with that theory, though perhaps with less confidence. But if dozens of negotiations stretching back over a century have all failed to get an agreement, perhaps there is something structural at work.

Two factors seem to be involved. The first is that the type of peace the Americans tried to create was particularly difficult to foster. If the aim of the Middle East peace negotiations were simply to stop the killing, the road to an agreement would be fairly straightforward. That kind of peace is already here. Most of the time, Israelis and Palestinians are not actually shooting at one another, and even Hamas has talked about negotiating a "hudna," a long-term cease-fire that would suspend the conflict for some specified time without settling the underlying issues. This is what "peace" has meant in much of history for much of the time. But it is not what the western world has meant by peace since the end of World War II. This is not the end of history. This is not liberal order.

With the end of the Cold War fueling their optimism, Americans weren't just trying to arrange cease-fires. In the order Americans and others wanted to build after 1990, peace was something deeper, richer, and more binding than it had been in Westphalian Europe. Peace after the Cold War was meant to be thick: a deep interstate relationship that involved economic integration and a liberal security order.

The second other principal reason the peace process failed is that the Israeli-Palestinian dispute is genuinely hard to resolve. It is the most charismatic conflict in the world, one that engages the attention and excites the emotions of people all over the planet. It is not just another conflict between squabbling tribes over a few stony acres. It's a conflict that engages some of the most volatile and emotional issues of our times and each dimension of the conflict increases the difficulty of resolving it.

At the most obvious level, the Israeli-Palestinian conflict is simply one more dreary, intractable ethno-nationalist conflict like the ones that wrecked the old Russian, Austro-Hungarian, and Ottoman empires, and that have frustrated and perplexed diplomats for the last two hundred years.

There have been dozens of these conflicts since the Spanish rose against occupying French troops during the Napoleonic Wars, and they don't often end well. They are, for one thing, zero sum. Kosovo cannot be both part of Serbia and an independent republic. Nagorno-Karabakh must either be part of Armenia or part of Azerbaijan. Crimea is either part of Ukraine or part of Russia.

Worse, these conflicts almost always engage whole peoples. Each side passionately and sometimes fanatically believes in the justice of its own cause. Territorial compromise feels immoral to many people on both sides of the conflict, and the two sides do not agree on a common set of principles and facts that could allow the dispute to be settled on the basis of a common standard of justice or law.

Because compromise is so difficult, horrors like ethnic cleansing and genocide have played a greater role than one would like in the resolution of these disputes. There is no longer a German minority problem in the Czech Sudetenland because the Czechs drove the Germans out after World War II. The problem of the Greek and Turkish minorities in Turkey and Greece has been largely "solved" in much the same way. The Israelis and Palestinians who fantasize about driving their opponents out of the territory they want are following a well-worn road.

The other common approach to these disputes involves the imposition of an unshakable order by a determined power that neither ethnic group feels able to contest. While the Soviet Union stood, the Armenians, Azeris, Georgians, Ossetians, Abkhazians, and others lived peacefully side by side in the Soviet Caucasus. While Josip Broz Tito ruled Yugoslavia, the rival national groups in that country accepted the status quo and got on with their lives.

To the degree that the Israeli-Palestinian conflict is a classic ethnonational conflict, it is difficult to solve. But this conflict is even less tractable. From a Palestinian point of view, this is not just a typical ethnic quarrel. The Jews are not just aggressive neighbors; they are, many Palestinians feel, illegitimate immigrants. While Jews have continuously lived in Palestine since biblical times, the migration that led to Israeli independence was a product of modern times—and it was imposed on the native population by an imperial power.

The combination of imperial rule and large-scale nineteenth- and twentieth-century labor migration changed the demographic makeup of a number of countries around the world. The British encouraged wholesale migration of Chinese into what is now Malaysia and Singapore. British India sent workers and merchants to destinations ranging from British-ruled East Africa to British colonies in the Caribbean and South Pacific. In many cases the tensions between the native populations of those countries and the migrants of the imperial period remain flashpoints to this day.

These immigrants are rejected not just because they are foreign. They are rejected because their presence is both a consequence and a reminder of the humiliation of imperial rule. The demand to expel the "illegitimate" foreigners often plays a major role in the struggle against imperial rule. Tensions between native and immigrant groups frequently persist for generations and in many countries post-independence regimes have either discriminated against the descendants of migrants or expelled them. The expulsions of long-settled Greeks from Nasserite Egypt, of Indians from newly independent East African nations, the genocidal violence and ethnic cleansing directed against the Rohingya of Burma (many of whose ancestors migrated from British India in the days of the Raj): these all came about in reaction to episodes of imperially licensed or encouraged migration. For Palestinians who do not accept the legitimacy of Britain's seizure of Palestine in World War I, the Balfour Declaration and the subsequent immigration of hundreds of thousands of Jews represents a historical crime.

This sentiment has legs. Some of the strongest support for the Palestinian cause is found in countries like South Africa, Malaysia, and Algeria where struggles against the consequences of imperial migration have been central to political life.

This brings us to a third level of the Israeli-Palestinian dispute: the degree to which it reflects the politics of decolonization and national liberation. The Palestinians were fighting, as they saw it, for exactly the same thing Indian, Egyptian, Algerian, Nigerian, and Indonesian liberation movements were fighting for. They wanted to rule themselves in their own land in their own way. They still do.

The perception of the Palestinian struggle as a conventional national liberation movement grounded in anti-imperialism and a rejection of western hegemony is widespread today, not only among Palestinians. That is how the Palestinian cause is still seen in much of the world: as one of a handful of national liberation movements not yet crowned with success. That ensures the Palestinians of deep sympathy and solidarity far beyond the confines of the Arab world.

Additionally, the Israeli-Palestinian dispute is widely seen as part of an ongoing struggle between Christianity and Islam. While the image of the Crusades is often invoked in this context, wars of religion have played a greater role in the more recent history of the lands that once belonged to the Ottoman, Russian, and Austro-Hungarian empires. Imperial Russia was as hostile an environment for Muslims as it was for Jews; roughly two million Muslims fled tsarist repression in Russia and the Caucasus for the Ottoman Empire in the decades before World War I—about the same as the number of Jews who fled Russia in those years. From the Greek Revolt of 1821 to the allied occupation of Constantinople in 1918, Ottoman defeats were interpreted by both Ottoman and western sources as defeats for "Islam" at the hands of an ascendant "Christendom." Catholic missionaries followed French arms into Algeria and Lebanon; Muslims and Jews fled or were expelled from their homes as the Orthodox Christian peoples of the Balkans threw off the Ottoman yoke.

From the Caucasus through the Balkans and across the Middle East, conflict between Christianity and Islam is not some relic of the Middle Ages. The last two centuries, from an Islamic point of view, saw a series of Christian conquests and serial invasions of the Ottoman and Persian empires. That the British sponsored the Zionists in their early days and that the Americans embraced them as they became powerful underlines the association of the Zionists with the Christian West. The injustice that Palestinians experience, deprived of their land and of the dignity of national independence, exemplifies and symbolizes the injustices that many Muslims in the Arab Middle East and beyond see encoded into the existing world order.

Caught up in this charismatic conflict, the Palestinians have become a kind of representative nationality, one whose experience resonates around the world. At one level, their situation evokes the plight of indigenous peoples worldwide who have lost their homes to a tide of foreign, usually western, colonization and conquest. At another, the Palestinians represent all those treated unfairly or left behind in the contemporary world. Their plight is emblematic of those who feel born into the "loser" nations—kept out of the wealthy precincts of the "advanced countries" by walls, fences, and identity papers.

The talismanic role of the Israeli-Palestinian struggle in the global political imagination made the conflict difficult and perhaps impossible to resolve by conventional means, but it also made solving that conflict look irresistibly attractive to a generation of American leaders eager both to establish and to legitimize the post-historical liberal order they hoped would secure the peace after the Cold War. Just as Solomon established his wisdom by adroitly adjudicating tangled disputes, America would establish its world order by resolving this most difficult and intractable of disputes. We would pull the sword out of the stone; we would capture the Holy Grail.

The American-led peace process after the Cold War was the center-piece of the American effort to replace the historical rivalries and preoccupations of the Middle East with the kind of liberal order Americans had promoted in Western Europe after World War II and hoped to extend globally following the Cold War. Americans wanted a Middle East composed of liberal democracies enjoying a thick peace, and the establishment of a lasting peace between Israelis and Palestinians would, many Americans felt, both symbolize and ensure the establishment of liberal order in a critical part of the world.

This ambitious design did not fail because a particular Israeli leader or Palestinian leader failed to endorse a particular proposal or take a particular step at a particular time. Fundamentally, the plan failed because the United States did not have the power, the wisdom, or the will to impose it. At the end of the day, neither the Israelis nor the Palestinians shared the American faith in liberal order, and the accumulating failures of American policy in the region eroded any faith the two peoples might have had in American wisdom and reliability. In Arthurian legend, the Holy Grail could only be achieved by a knight who combined a pure heart with perfect faith and superhuman strength. Uncle Sam, sadly, was not quite the man for the job.

The Glittering Grail

In late 2000, President Bill Clinton led the peace process to what remains its high-water point when he put forward what became known as the Clinton Parameters for a final settlement to the conflict. Under those parameters, the Palestinians would receive all of Gaza, 97 percent of the West Bank, with territorial compensation elsewhere for the 3 percent (mostly densely populated Jewish settlements near Jerusalem) of West Bank territory that Israel would keep. East Jerusalem would be the capital of the Palestinian state, the Palestinian diaspora would have a "right of return" to the Palestinian state (though not to Israel), there would be an elevated train or highway connecting Gaza and the West Bank over Israeli territory, and the new state would receive $30 billion in aid. Arafat refused to sign on.[5]

"I am a failure," Clinton told Arafat. "And you have made me one."[6]

The peace process has not entirely failed. It provided a framework for limited Palestinian self-governance; it managed and limited the conflict for many years; and it helped to secure American power in a crucial region of the world in the aftermath of the Cold War. It helped the Palestinians move into the diplomatic mainstream, immensely assisted their fundraising, and kept their cause in the public eye. For Israelis, the peace process bought them some time to consolidate the settlement blocs near the Green Line (the line of demarcation between Arab and Israeli control at the end of the 1948–49 war) that they most wanted to integrate into Israel proper, reduced violence on both sides of the Green Line, and defused some international criticism against their treatment of the Palestinians.

But if the American effort to mediate an Israeli-Palestinian peace did not utterly fail, it fell far short of success. The Palestinians did not get the land, and the Israelis did not get their peace, and in many ways the two parties seemed further apart in 2022 than in 1990.

Too often in the course of this long series of negotiations, the Americans seemed more interested in selling peace than either the Israelis or the Palestinians were in buying it. Rather than helping the two sides reach an accommodation that both wanted but that neither could reach without help, American diplomacy often involved attempting to bribe, intimidate, or cajole both sides into accepting positions that neither side on the ground really liked, but that the Americans believed could pave the road to peace.

As American diplomats sought to keep the peace process moving forward, they made some unpleasant discoveries. The first was that steering the peace process was like riding a bicycle; if you weren't making progress the bicycle would wobble and ultimately crash. But that wasn't all. The closer negotiators came to the final-stage negotiations, the more difficult progress became—the road turned narrower, rockier, steeper, and more pitted with potholes the nearer one came to the goal.

The second was that neither the Israelis nor the Palestinians really believed in the liberal order the Americans were trying to promote. At best, they thought it was a naive American dream with little relevance in the real world; at worst, they saw it as a dangerous delusion. Israelis and Palestinians have complicated political cultures, and there are many different points of view among both groups of people, but for sometimes similar and sometimes different reasons, both cultures have a lot of skepticism about the idea of liberal order. Added to that skepticism were serious and well-grounded concerns about whether the Americans are wise enough and committed enough to the long, arduous, and quite possibly bloody task of creating and defending that order in the years and decades to come. The more both Israelis and Palestinians saw of American policies in the Middle East, the graver those doubts grew.

ISRAEL AND LIBERAL ORDER

The single most important thing about Israel that most Americans do not understand is that the Jewish state was founded on a reasonable and historically justified skepticism about the ability of liberal order to protect Jews. American liberals in particular long believed that Israel was the firstborn offspring of the United Nations, and that a nation that owed its existence to the international community and liberal values should live by the values which gave it life. That is a beautiful story, but if Stalin had not made a mockery of the arms embargos first imposed by the U.S. and then by the U.N., there would likely be no State of Israel today.

The profoundly ambivalent relationship between liberalism and Zionism goes back to Herzl's time. In nineteenth-century Europe, liberal, assimilationist Jews argued that the triumph of enlightened values would allow Jews to live in dignity and security. The Zionist movement insisted this faith in the power of liberal order was a fatal mistake. Liberalism cannot save the Jews, Herzl taught, international institutions cannot save the Jews, democracy cannot save the Jews, good intentions cannot save the Jews. Only the sovereign power of a Jewish state offers the Jews hope for survival. For many Israeli Jews today, Herzl's view makes more sense than ever.

Liberalism remains, many Israelis believe, too weak and too wedded to magical thinking for a nation like Israel to trust. And weak as liberalism is inside countries, the utter uselessness of liberal principles in international life is much worse. How has the "rules-based international order" worked out for victims of the Syrian civil war? How safe are the Rohingya? The Uighurs? The Tibetans?

Many Israelis believe that if the Jewish state had relied on the "international community" for its survival, it would have perished long ago. The United Nations voted for the partition of Palestine and the creation of a Jewish state but didn't lift a finger to enforce it. Only Stalin's willingness to defy the arms embargo brought victory to the Jews. The United Nations charter declares that member states must respect the territorial integrity of other states. This has never been enforced on Israel's behalf—not when Britain and the United States schemed to force Israel to give up the Negev in the early 1950s,[7] not when Arab neighbors gave aid to terrorists seeking to attack Jewish targets in Israel and beyond, not when Arab countries and, later, Iran regularly announced their intention to destroy Israel and drive its citizens into the sea.[8] The United States promised Israel in 1957 that it would protect Israel's ability to use the Straits of Tiran if Israel returned the Sinai to Egypt.[9] To enforce that commitment, U.N. troops were dispatched to the Straits. In 1967, Nasser ordered those troops to leave. They obeyed. When Israelis asked Washington to honor its promises and prevent Nasser from blocking Israeli sea traffic, the United States was too preoccupied with the Vietnam War to respond. The U.N. was equally passive.[10]

For a nation of refugees, many still in shock from the Holocaust and many others from the shock of expulsion or exile from the Arab majority nations of the Middle East, the lesson could not be clearer. Israel could only count on itself.

The international community's failures in the 1967 crisis were not Israel's only experience with the weakness of liberal order. UNIFIL (United Nations Interim Force in Lebanon) troops have been solemnly tasked by the Security Council to establish a zone on the Lebanese side of the border where the only armed forces would be UNIFIL itself and the regular Lebanese army.[11] UNIFIL continues to patrol, yet somehow this area has become one of the most heavily armed terrorist zones on the planet, bristling with tens of thousands of missiles that somehow slipped past the no doubt eagle-eyed and incorruptible UNIFIL guardians of the peace.[12] The "international community" remains placid and calm unless a prospect of Israeli military action against the peaceful Hezbollah missile sites that dot the graceful hills disturbs the tranquil and liberal order that UNIFIL so respectably provides.

Think, Israelis say, of the Muslims of Bosnia, who trusted in the protection of U.N. peacekeepers in Srebenica. They were massacred by the Serbs and while many world leaders wept beautiful tears on television, the Bosnian victims stayed dead.[13] All this, many Israelis feel, proves that Herzl was right: if the Jewish people entrust their survival to liberal institutions and liberal ideas, they will die.

American Jews and Israeli Jews are often deeply divided over the value of liberal order. American Jews are, by and large, people for whom Herzl was wrong. The liberal principles of American society opened the path for Jewish integration of a depth and scale that Europe had never seen. Since the nineteenth century, many American Jews have felt that the United States, founded on Enlightenment principles and religious freedom, had much more to offer its Jewish citizens than any Jewish state in Palestine ever could. This history has helped make American Jews one of the most deeply and seriously liberal communities in the United States.

While Israelis are not monolithic on this or any other subject, large numbers reject the optimism of their American cousins. Many Israelis who grew up in the former Soviet Union, particularly those who left after 1990, brought the deep-seated Russian cynicism about the West's liberal values with them. They no more believe in the inevitable triumph of liberal principles than does Vladimir Putin. Russian history teaches lessons similar to Herzl's: we live in a hard world, and power is the language in which countries speak to each other.

The difference in political orientation between American and Israeli Jews is not just confined to the peace process or to Palestinian issues. During the refusenik era, when Israeli and American Jews were united in their support for Soviet Jews seeking to emigrate to Israel, a yawning gap opened between the two communities. Not all the Jews who wanted to get out of the Soviet Union, it soon became evident, wanted to go to Israel. Many wanted to come to the United States. Many other Soviet Jews didn't want to go anywhere at all; they just wanted to practice their religion freely in the USSR.

The American Jewish community by and large instinctively supported all of the choices of all of these Jews. American Jews wanted aid to go to refuseniks awaiting exit permits whatever country they wanted to reach. And they responded to pleas by Soviet Jews for religious freedom by working with Americans of all faiths and no faith to pressure the Soviet Union to provide freedom of religion for all of its citizens, not just the Jews.

The Israeli government had a narrower focus. It was only interested in the Jews who wanted to come to Israel. Jews wanting to emigrate to America or other countries were on their own. As for pressuring the Soviet Union to allow religious freedom for people of all faiths, or even only for Jews, this was not a diplomatic burden the Israeli government, which had enough problems with a Soviet government actively supporting Palestinian terrorism, wanted to bear.[14] American Jews in a position of relative security fixed on universal principles; Israeli Jews relentlessly focusing on what Israel in their view needed to survive: the tension between these two approaches to Jewish ethics and priorities continues to this day.

In any case, the plurality of Israeli Jews today who trace their ancestry to the Middle East and the old Ottoman Empire rather than to Western Europe[15] are also deeply skeptical about the prospects for liberal order in the Middle East. Rooted in the Arab world and speaking and reading Arabic, these Israelis often believe that they understand the Arabs better than American intellectuals. A more democratic Middle East, many of them believe, will be more radical and more antisemitic than a Middle East of cautious kings and embattled dictators. Why, they sometimes ask, do so many westerners believe that a surge of populism in the West might lead to fascist identity politics and white nationalism, while Middle East populism would inevitably lead to social democracy and brotherly love?

These different political outlooks lead to very different assessments about what the peace process can accomplish. Americans, including many American Jews, tend to think that an end to the conflict is possible, and argue that Israelis should be more willing to "take risks for peace." Many Israelis approach the question of Palestinian statehood with a long laundry list of things that could go wrong. Americans counter by pointing out the risks and costs of a continuing conflict.

Herzl's attitude toward liberalism was complex. He did not believe that European liberalism could save the Jews, but he appreciated the beauty of liberal values and wanted the Jewish state, once its existential concerns had been addressed, to be politically liberal.[16] For much of the history of Jewish Palestine and Israel, the dominant Zionist parties were democratic socialist parties economically well to the left not only of most American liberals but of most European social democrats as well. These parties were economically socialist but politically liberal, combining support for a substantial government role in a tightly regulated economy with a strong emphasis on political and intellectual freedom.

Democratic and liberal values shaped Israel's political development, and many Israelis continue to believe that preserving and extending this liberal heritage is a noble and necessary project. Equal treatment for Israel's minority Arab population and as generous an approach to the Palestinians as consistent with Israeli security strike liberal Zionists as consistent with Israel's founding values and their understanding of Jewish ethics.

These Israelis would like to meet the Americans and for that matter the Palestinians halfway, partly out of conviction, partly because they see the U.S. as Israel's best friend and want to promote American power and prestige, and partly because they know that a more forthcoming stance on peace issues helps Israeli diplomacy in much of Europe and strengthens relations with the largely liberal American Jewish community. Liberal Zionists of this kind, generally the descendants of Jews with European roots, once dominated Israeli politics and are still powerful in some important Israeli institutions. Since the 1970s, however, their political fortunes have been ebbing, and the weakness of liberal Zionist political parties has been one reason that the American-sponsored peace process has lost momentum over the years.

On the right, many Israelis share the convictions of Ze'ev Jabotinsky, founder of the Revisionist Zionism that inspired Menachem Begin and the Likud movement. The Revisionists believed that territorial expansion to the Jordan River offered Israel better security than any foreign-brokered peace agreement. The "pragmatic" wing of the Likud movement, including Benjamin Netanyahu, the longest-serving prime minister in Israeli history, was more willing to meet the Americans partway than other branches of the movement, but to Netanyahu's right there were many Israelis who made no secret of their desire for territorial expansion and their opposition to Palestinian statehood. Religious Zionists who believe in a divine mandate for Jews to reoccupy all the lands promised to Abraham in the Bible are joined by secular Zionists arguing that the original mission of the Zionist movement was to reclaim the historical homeland of the Jews. This homeland was centered in what is now the West Bank rather than on the coastal plains where most Israelis live today. Hebron and Jericho, these Zionists argue, were more important to the project of a Jewish return than Tel Aviv.

These arguments horrify most American Jews and American liberals, as well as many liberal Zionists. It is not just that continued construction of Israeli settlements in the West Bank offends Arab and European opinion and can involve serious injustice to Palestinians with preexisting claims. The greater fear is that Israeli annexation of the West Bank combined with continuing Arab population growth will lead to a situation in which Israel must either cease to be Jewish or stop being democratic. The question here is not whether Israel can entrust its security to the false promises of a weak and flawed liberal international order; it is whether Herzl's dream of a liberal Zionist state can be realized.

There are counterclaims that pro-annexation Israelis make about the future demography of a united West Bank/Israel, but the real problem for the peace process is the widespread sense that the status quo works reasonably well for Israel, that a Palestinian state—which might end up being controlled by Hamas rather than Fatah—cannot be trusted to keep its agreements, and that the kind of deep regional peace and liberal order Americans want to build is unrealistic. Over time, Israeli enthusiasm for the peace process has waned, reflecting broader social and political trends in Israeli society, growing disarray in the Arab world, and diminishing confidence both in the wisdom of American foreign policy and the depth of Washington's commitment to the future of the region.

Palestinians and Liberal Order

The Palestinian relationship to the American drive for a compromise peace and a liberal order is as complex as the Israeli one. Like many Israelis, large numbers of Palestinians find both the geography and the liberal ideology of the kind of peace Americans want far less attractive than most Americans do.

Americans and many others who don't follow the peace process closely sometimes think that the chief beneficiaries of any peace agreement will be the Palestinians and assume that the Palestinian objective in peace talks is to get an agreement as quickly as possible. They would have a state of their own; the Israeli occupation would come to an end, and the Palestinian people would be able to put the unhappy past behind them and get on with the business of building a prosperous future.

While it is certainly true that the Palestinians can expect some substantial benefits from an agreement on the two-state solution, making peace with Israel is anything but a cost-free exercise for the Palestinian leadership. Given the disparity in power between the two sides, even with the help of outside mediators the Palestinians cannot negotiate on an equal basis with the Israelis, and so long as that power disparity continues the terms of any realistic agreement must inevitably fall far short of what most Palestinians believe justice demands.

To secure a small, poor share of a land most Palestinians believe is rightfully theirs, the Palestinians would have to cede all claims to the great majority of British Palestine, including virtually all of the best agricultural land, ports, and transportation networks. Of the two states, the Palestinian one would be by far the weaker and the poorer, with disarmament provisions in the treaty that would make it a second-class nation permanently. An "independent" Palestine would be hobbled with a long list of restrictions and prohibitions that no Palestinian government could legally terminate. The new state, semi-sovereign in important respects, may well have to accept the long-term presence of foreign troops on its soil in the interest of Israel's security. It could probably not exercise full control over its airspace. This is not national independence wrested victoriously from a defeated oppressor; it is an acceptance of a truncated independence on enemy terms.

To many Palestinians, this looks more like surrender than victory. It looks like the acceptance of a kind of rump Palestine, a shrunken state economically and militarily dependent on Israel. That does not mean that there are not a significant number of Palestinians who would welcome or at least accept a two-state solution on these terms. Palestinian society is not monolithic; it includes a wide range of political and religious views. Many Palestinians, especially on the West Bank, would accept and some would welcome a two-state solution based roughly on the 1949 lines. Others, especially in Gaza and among the displaced refugee communities in countries like Syria and Lebanon, would hold out for more. Many, on the West Bank and beyond, might accept the two-state solution for now, but like many Irish nationalists after the partition of 1921 would continue to hope, to work, and even to fight for more.

Beyond this, like Zionism, the Palestinian national movement is built to some degree on a rejection of the ideal of western order to which Americans seek to convert the Middle East. In the Palestinian case, the rejection is literal: the 1947 United Nations resolution partitioning British Palestine was seen by Americans like Eleanor Roosevelt as a cornerstone of their efforts to build a liberal order. The Palestinians and other Arabs who rejected this resolution did so on the basis of an important principle. The British had no legitimate rights in Palestine, they said.

Britain conquered the country from the Ottomans, but the Balfour Declaration had no moral standing whatever. How can you give away someone else's home? The Balfour Declaration was illegitimate, the League of Nations was an imperialist club with no moral right to assign mandates, and the United Nations had no more right to partition Palestine than to, for example, demand the partition of Britain.

The rejection of the partition, in this view, is not the petulant stance of a selfish and childish people. It is the mature and thoughtful repudiation of western imperialism. Liberalism, seen as reproducing the power relationships—and legitimizing the decisions—of the imperial powers cannot be the basis for a legitimate and just global order. This is not a view restricted to Arabs and Palestinians but is a common view in postcolonial countries where the phrase "liberal world order" has a more sinister meaning than American diplomats would like it to have.

It was resistance to liberalism and not just to Zionism that made the Palestinians a people. Following the defeats of 1948–49, it was the spirit of resistance and rejection that shaped a Palestinian national movement in the refugee camps. The world wanted to forget them. Arab leaders sought to control and use them. But the Palestinians refused. They resisted, they persisted, they fought with every weapon they could find, including terror when nothing better came to hand, and they ultimately succeeded in forcing the world to acknowledge their existence and, however partially, the justice of their cause.

The experience of dispossession and occupation along with generations of living in refugee camps shaped the political consciousness of the Palestinians. It was not an easy school and the people that came out of it are strong. The explosive anger and hatred seething in parts of the Palestinian community, the feelings that drive teenagers to attack Israeli citizens with knives, come out of a long and painful history. Even for the many Palestinians who neither commit violence nor condone the murder of Israeli civilians, the idea that resistance is the foundation of Palestinian identity is evidently and obviously true.

To accept the kind of shrunken, dependent Palestinian semi-state on offer today and to give up the struggle would not just mean the renunciation of resistance as a tool for the future. It confesses the futility of Palestinian resistance in the past. If the two-state solution is the best choice the Palestinians have today, it means that the Palestinian national movement has been wrong on virtually every major decision since the

1930s. If the Palestinians had accepted the 1937 Peel Commission plan, they would hold much more territory and better territory than they can get today. The 1946 Morrison-Grady proposal was not as good as the Peel Commission Report, but it was better than either of the two partition plans discussed at the United Nations in 1947. And those plans offered more land and better land to the Palestinians than the Arabs held when the 1949 armistice ended the war.

Is the Nakba, the disaster that overwhelmed the Arab Palestinians when hundreds of thousands fled or were expelled from their homes during Israel's war for independence, the result of the political blindness and incompetence of the Palestinian leadership in the 1940s? Should the stateless Palestinians and refugees scattered across the diaspora blame the bad decisions of Palestinian leaders for the upheaval that scattered them to the four winds? Has the net result of a century of Palestinian resistance been a century of misery for the Palestinian people culminating in an ignominious surrender on worse terms than they could have gotten thirty, fifty, or one hundred years ago?

The leaders of the Palestinian Authority, who derive their legitimacy from the decades of heroic struggle and suffering, cannot repudiate the legacy of Palestinian resistance without chopping down the tree in which they perch. To build a rump Palestinian state while rejecting the founding myths and ideology of the Palestinian people is a difficult task, but this is what the American-led peace process requires Palestinian leaders to attempt. It is not perhaps as surprising as some think that Yasser Arafat only entered the process under duress and ultimately declined to take up the task.

For Palestinians who would live in this new country, there is another problem with the two-state solution. The Palestinian state will be small and poor; how will it be governed?

Here, many Palestinians thought they detected a certain western hypocrisy. Both Israelis and Americans find themselves talking about the need for a "Palestinian partner for peace." What exactly did they mean when they said that?

Yasser Arafat was not a moral monster like Hitler, Stalin, or Mao. He was not even a thug like Saddam Hussein. He was a sincere Palestinian nationalist, but his nationalism was shaped by the harsh realities of the post–World War II liberation struggles. He knew the price of power in the world of feuding Palestinian militias in exile; niceties like press freedom and democratic elections never stood high among his priorities. If the PLO had to embrace terror to achieve its objectives, so be it. He could launch wars and murder rivals. Westerners might deplore these characteristics, but if he had signed a peace agreement with Israel they would have overlooked these problems just as they overlook the secret police and lack of civil liberties in many other Arab countries. The presidents of Egypt and the kings of Jordan enjoyed stable relationships with the United States and Israel in part because however deplorable the methods, their security services kept the peace. Arafat's Palestine could expect a similar indulgence.

A new Palestinian state would probably not have an easy birth. There are powerful armed factions like Hamas and Palestinian Islamic Jihad who will not accept any agreement with Israel and who will regard any Palestinian government that signs such a treaty as illegal. They will feel no scruples whatever about continuing the armed struggle with Israel and, as has been demonstrated many times in the past, they also stand ready to launch an armed struggle against any Palestinian government that signs such a treaty.

More, there are powerful governments that would support these factions with money and arms. In past times, Iraq and Syria would have certainly armed radical Palestinian rejectionists. Today, Iran certainly, and quite possibly Turkey, would do the same. Given that there are hundreds of thousands of Palestinians in countries like Jordan, Syria, and Lebanon for whom the establishment of a rump Palestinian state on the West Bank and Gaza would offer very little, and given that the widespread poverty and misery in Gaza would linger for many years under even the best-case scenarios for independence, foreigners seeking to stir the pot by recruiting disaffected Palestinians into radical and rejectionist organizations would have no shortage of potential recruits. As happened in Ireland, the independence of Palestine would likely begin with a vicious civil war.

The Israelis, Americans, and Europeans who thought that Arafat could be the "partner for peace" that Israel needed did not mean that they thought he was an idealistic dreamer whose love of peace and nonviolence would enable Palestinian society to transcend its difficult past. They meant that they thought he had the combination of political charisma and brutal ruthlessness needed to crush his Palestinian opponents by any means necessary.

The establishment of a truncated state with limited powers under a corrupt and brutal dictatorship fighting a dirty guerrilla war might have been the best choice the Palestinians had in the 1990s, but for many Palestinian intellectuals and observers, it was not a particularly attractive culmination to a hundred years of struggle.

Another factor that tended to undercut the enthusiasm of ordinary Palestinians for the two-state solution as envisioned by the Oslo Accords was a not unnatural nor unreasonable fear that the new Palestinian state would be as kleptocratic and developmentally ineffective as so many Arab states have been. Under the circumstances of the 1990s, this was a reasonable prediction. The Palestinian Authority was already demonstrating the mix of state failure and kleptocratic initiative so familiar from other countries in the region and beyond. The West, it is clear to any Palestinian or indeed to any Arab, was willing to ignore or even collude with the corruption of Arab governments seen as useful on security grounds; an Arafat government struggling to keep Palestine quiet to uphold the regional peace would be seen as important in just that way.

As for the lavish offers of foreign aid from Europe, the Gulf Arabs, and even the United States for a future Palestinian state, many Palestinians viewed them with cynicism. First, the Palestinian experience is that donors are much quicker to make pledges than to pay them. Second, the United States has been sending billions in aid to Egypt since the 1970s. Has poverty been eliminated in Egypt?

This does not mean that Palestinian public opinion preferred Israeli occupation to Palestinian self-government, or that Palestinians did not resent continued Israeli settlement building on the West Bank and what they saw as a reluctance to give Palestinians more control over more territory. Nor does it mean that all Palestinians were pessimistic about what life would be like under home rule. Indeed, leaders like Salam Fayyad worked seriously and effectively to improve Palestinian governance and lay the foundations for a future state. Even so, Palestinians were less invested in the kind of peace Washington wanted than many sympathetic Americans believed, and the prospects for peace were dimmer than successive American presidents and secretaries of state quite understood.

A peace treaty with Israel did not mean to Palestinians what the peace treaty with Britain meant to Americans in 1783. It was the ratification of a historic defeat and while, from a pragmatic point of view, it might have been (was, in my opinion) by far the best option Palestinians had in the 1990s, it was anything but the peace of their dreams. When war instead of peace came out of the Middle East on 9/11, the prospects for liberal order and a calm, democratic post-historical world began to dim, and for many people around the world, a much darker future began to look probable.

Middle East peacemaking was practically more difficult and morally more complicated than it looked and not even the talented and knowledgeable American diplomats who dedicated decades of their lives to the quest could ever quite capture the luminous Grail that hovered perpetually just beyond reach.

The Unsettling

Rivaled only by the question of the future of Jerusalem, the question of the steadily expanding numbers of Jewish settlements established in the territories conquered from Jordan and Syria in 1967 was the most vexed and perplexing issue for diplomats seeking an end to the dispute.

By 2019, the number of Jewish Israeli citizens living in East Jerusalem and the West Bank had reached 670,000. About 560,000 of these lived in a set of densely populated developments, primarily in the neighborhood of Jerusalem, or otherwise close to the Green Line marking the position of forces at the time of the 1949 armistice.[17] Smaller groups of settlers lived on the Golan Heights or at strategic points in the Jordan River valley where their presence was seen as helping to stabilize boundaries with neighboring states. The remainder were scattered across the West Bank, sometimes on isolated hilltops, sometimes on previously empty land, sometimes in the midst of Palestinian cities such as Hebron. Some settlers were drawn by lower home prices and subsidized financing. Some were attracted for religious or national reasons.

Different settlements had different statuses under Israeli law. Israel had annexed the parts of Jerusalem formerly under Jordanian control in 1967, and the Golan Heights (de facto) in 1981. While most countries considered all Israeli settlements beyond the Green Line illegal, Israeli law saw no difference between new housing developments in East Jerusalem and new suburbs of Tel Aviv. Many Jewish settlements in the West

Bank were legally recognized by Israeli authorities. Some were in a gray zone where enterprising settlers built homes without government permission. Others have been declared illegal under Israeli law, and a few have even been demolished.

From the standpoint of diplomats trying to shepherd the peace process, settlements are a continuing source of trouble. The largest settlements, close to Jerusalem and the Green Line, are paradoxically the least problematic. Since the 1990s negotiators have assumed that Israel would keep all or most of these settlements in any final peace agreement, compensating the Palestinians with cessions of an equivalent amount of land elsewhere along the frontier.

It is the settlements deeper inside the future Palestinian state, and the possible expansion of settlement activity into additional areas near Jerusalem, that create the most significant problems for peace negotiators.

The expansion of settlements alarms and embitters Palestinian opinion, raising increasing questions over time about the viability of any Palestinian state. Those questions become particularly acute in the neighborhood of Jerusalem, where certain proposed Jewish housing developments would block Palestinian access to what most Palestinians expect will be part of their future capital. The presence of settlers exacerbates the tensions, the injustices, and the inconveniences of the occupation and generates a steady stream of violent incidents that erodes any trust between the two national communities and keeps tensions high. The reality that disputes between the two communities are settled by Israeli courts and sometimes by Israeli military authorities creates, at the least, a perception of systemic injustice that angers Palestinians and attracts global sympathy to their cause. What under other circumstances would be routine questions of land ownership, water rights, building permits, and infrastructure investment can trigger intercommunal violence and flare up into international incidents overnight.

Support for settlements, while not universal, is strong enough in Israeli politics that putting real and lasting limits on settlement expansion tests the authority and undermines the power of even the strongest Israeli leaders. Israeli support for settlements falls into three groups. There are the pragmatists who support the settlements in or near the Green Line aimed at improving the defensibility of Israel's frontiers, and who see settlements more generally as a bargaining chip that may push Palestinians toward an agreement out of the fear that the longer they wait, the worse their final frontiers will be. Another group sees settlements as an extension of the original work of the Zionist movement. For them, the West Bank, not the coastal plain, is the Hebrew heartland. This is where the ancient kingdoms of Israel and Judah stood, and if the aim of the Jewish national movement is to erect an independent Jewish commonwealth on the original homeland of the Jewish people, that movement has not accomplished its mission until the heartland is once again part of the Jewish state. The third group of religiously motivated settlers believes that in establishing Jewish settlements in the ancient heartland they are fulfilling a divine mandate and in some cases they do not recognize the authority of any government, including the Israeli government, to tell Jews where they may or may not live in the divinely Promised Land.

As the number and density of Israeli settlements have grown over the years, the issue has become simultaneously harder to solve and more consequential for the health of the peace process. From the Palestinian side, the inability of their negotiators to stop a process that humiliates and enrages public opinion while, increasingly, making the establishment of a geographically contiguous and economically viable Palestinian state less likely contributes to growing public skepticism about the Palestinian leadership and about the possibility of a peaceful compromise with Israel.

From the Israeli side, fighting settlements has never been an easy political task, and few politicians want to order troops to force unwilling settlers from their homes in order to please the Palestinians or even the Americans. The larger the settlements grow, the greater this reluctance becomes. As more voters either live on the West Bank or have friends and relatives who do, the higher rise the political costs of curtailing new settlements and withdrawing from old ones.

For both sides, settlements make a compromise peace seem less likely and less attractive. Palestinians do not believe Israelis will give up enough settlements and territory to fulfill even their minimum demands for statehood. Some Israelis see less and less advantage in giving up flourishing towns and alienating large numbers of voters in exchange for what they fear will be empty promises of peace and coexistence from the Palestinian side.

American diplomats would find themselves repeatedly caught between Palestinian demands for partial or total settlement freezes as a condition for entering serious peace talks and Israeli politicians unwilling to take on powerful domestic forces. Over time, as both sides dug in on their settlement positions and American prestige and authority gradually declined, it became progressively more difficult and ultimately impossible for American diplomacy to manage this contentious issue.

PARTICIPATION TROPHIES

Decades of focused American advocacy failed to end the conflict, but the diplomatic efforts were not entirely in vain. As an exercise in diplomatic staging and conflict management the peace process was an American triumph. Even without a final agreement, the peace process reduced American risks in the region at very low cost; dramatized and furthered American primacy in world politics; facilitated the task of alliance management as the Americans continued to support the triple entente of Washington, Israel, and the conservative Arab states; ended Palestinian engagement in international and regional (as opposed to anti-Israel) terrorism; maximized American and presidential flexibility; and turned what could have been a source of weakness and vulnerability at home and abroad for American presidents into a formidable source of political advantage.

While American power was essential to make the peace process the center of Middle East diplomacy for such an extended period, the peace process worked so well for the United States in large part because so many other states in the region and beyond benefited from it. For Israel, a process under American sponsorship helped it manage its relations with Europe without risk of being pressured into unacceptable concessions. Both Israelis and leaders of conservative Arab states like Saudi Arabia, Egypt, and Kuwait appreciated the way that the Oslo Accords and the peace process drew the leading armed factions into a political process and increased the leverage of conservative Arabs and western funders over the movement as a whole.

Managing the Palestinian movement was a longtime headache for the Arab states. The movement's popularity with Arab public opinion meant that Arab leaders could not act openly against it, but the Palestinian leadership had never been an easy partner, fighting wars against both the Jordanian and Lebanese governments when headquartered in those countries and aligning itself with radical forces in the Arab world that challenged the status quo.[18] The PLO's support for Saddam Hussein after his 1990 conquest of Kuwait marked a low point in relations between the Gulf States and the Palestinian movement. Angry and alarmed at what they saw as an unprincipled and undeserved betrayal, the Gulf states expelled more than 300,000 Palestinian expatriates—roughly half the number of Palestinians forced out of Israel in the 1948–49 war. "What Kuwait did to the Palestinian people is worse than what has been done by Israel to Palestinians in the occupied territories," said Arafat—who had only himself to blame for the disaster.[19] It was not in the interest of these governments to destroy the Palestinian movement or to be seen as its enemies. But neither was it in their interest to support a truly independent Palestinian movement.

Europeans also had a Palestinian problem. For twenty years some Palestinian organizations and individuals had been a major force in terror attacks worldwide, operating in networks that enjoyed funding and state sponsorship from countries like East Germany and Syria, ultimately backed by the Soviet Union. As Palestinians pursued Israeli targets through Europe, horrific violence—like the Black September attacks on Israeli athletes at the Munich Olympics—exploded across a continent struggling with indigenous terror movements of its own.

The peace process soon became a golden cage for the Palestinian movement. With financial aid from Europe, rich Arab countries, and the United States pouring in, Arafat and his successors could build patronage networks and reward loyal supporters with government jobs. That made the Palestinian Authority a formidable political force in the Occupied Territories, and ensured significant wealth for the movement's elite, but dependence on foreign paymasters also limited Palestinian freedom of action. The Palestinian Authority could not walk away from the peace process without alienating key backers, and it could not walk back its recognition of Israel without inflicting massive economic hardship on its most loyal supporters. At the same time, as the movement's once fiery activists settled into a comfortable middle age on their civil service salaries from the Palestinian Authority with children to educate and bills to pay, the movement's moral authority began to erode among Palestinians and the Arab world at large.

From very early on, the peace process became a flourishing cottage industry for both Israelis and Palestinians. Both sides could and did trade their willingness to participate in the process or to make concessions for aid. The Palestinians, with fewer resources and fewer cards to play, in particular benefited from the largesse. Shortly after the famous handshake between Yitzhak Rabin and Yasser Arafat on the White House lawn, an international consortium of donors pledged $2.4 billion in aid to the Palestinians, $500 million of which would come from the United States.[20] As one American official later described it, "international assistance" should "build a peace constituency among the Palestinians."[21]

The PA was and at the time of writing remains dependent on foreign aid to cover its core expenses. According to World Bank figures, between 1994 and 2018, the PA received $38 billion in aid, and this accounted on average for 30 percent of the PA's expenses in each year. Additionally, so-called clearance revenue, tax revenues and other payments collected by Israeli authorities and handed over to the Palestinians, accounted for more than half of the PA budget during much of this time.[22]

For Americans in particular, this was an excellent bargain. The payments kept the PA, however reluctantly at times, committed to a peace process that was one of the most helpful instruments of American foreign policy, and for their own diplomatic and political purposes, the Europeans and the Gulf Arabs were helping to pay the bills to support a diplomatic structure that bolstered American power and advanced key American goals.

Meanwhile, Arab and European leaders could always win political points at home by criticizing America's allegedly one-sided support for Israel in the negotiations. American presidents could take these criticisms in stride as they changed nothing and, if anything, helped American presidents at home by boosting their "pro-Israel" credentials.

For Palestinians, the peace process was a mixed blessing. As the weakest party in the negotiations, Palestinians consistently had less control over the agenda and direction of the peace process, received the least benefits, and paid the highest price for participating. This was partly reflected in the structure: the price of admission for the Palestinians was something they had always rejected—recognizing Israel as a legitimate state without the establishment or recognition of a state of their own. Palestinian participation in such an unsatisfactory but unavoidable process was so difficult for Palestinians that the movement split, with Hamas rejecting the peace process entirely and setting up a rival government in Gaza.

But ultimately Arafat's wing of the Palestinian movement—flat broke after the fall of the Soviet Union and its break with the Gulf Arabs over the Gulf War—had little choice. The ability to set up an administration in waiting in the Occupied Territories and to put thousands of faithful supporters on a secure payroll was too attractive to pass up. Beyond that, the transition from pariah status into the world of respectable diplomacy was hard to resist. Ambivalent, divided, and suspicious, the Palestinians came to the table.

The Israelis were also conflicted. The Zionist and religious hardliners most committed to the idea of expanding the Israeli state across the West Bank to the Jordan River saw the peace process as dangerous from the start. For other Israelis, by giving formal standing to the Palestinians and creating an arena for face-to-face negotiations, the process could potentially expose Israel to orchestrated pressure from the United States and other powers to accept a territorial solution short of Israeli wishes.

Yet at the same time, the peace process forced Yasser Arafat to recognize the existence of the Jewish state and facilitated a steady deepening of relationships between Israel and conservative Arab states. It also provided a forum for holding Palestinians at least somewhat accountable for terror attacks against civilians. Israel could toughen or loosen its stance in the talks based on Palestinian behavior, and open Palestinian violations of commitments made in the peace negotiations could be used to pressure foreign governments to reduce or suspend aid to the PA.

Additionally, a substantial result of the onset of negotiations was to give the PA responsibility for security in Palestinian population centers, a responsibility that inevitably led to joint antiterror efforts, reduced the pressure on Israelis to carry out these efforts alone, and created many points of contact for the Israeli government deep into the Palestinian movement. Finally, Israel (like the Palestinians) could and did use the reality that the outside powers valued the peace process more than the insiders to leverage "compensation for compliance" deals. The peace process was worth a lot of money to various governments around the world; like the Palestinians, Israel could and did charge accordingly.

17

Right Nation

THE CLINTON-ERA PEACE PROCESS collapsed in January 2001. In September 2001, the attacks on the World Trade Center and the Pentagon opened an era in which questions of war and peace in the Middle East preoccupied Americans as never before. As the wars in Afghanistan and Iraq saw hundreds of thousands of American troops engaged in bitter combat across the region while Americans nervously awaited new terror attacks, debates over the wars and over Middle East strategy dominated American politics.

Inevitably, the relationship between the United States and Israel came under close scrutiny in the course of these debates, and both supporters and opponents of the relationship grew more passionate and engaged. For some Americans, the relationship was a contributing factor that led Al-Qaeda to attack the United States and distancing the country from Israel was a necessary step in preventing a long and bitter war between the United States and much of the Islamic world. For others, the attacks of 9/11 demonstrated the importance of the alliance as never before. Those who hated Israel hated the United States as well, and the best and fastest way to prevail in what some called "the long war" against terror was to work more closely than ever with our closest ally in the Middle East.

The twenty-first-century debates over Israel policy were new in another way. From the 1940s through the 1970s, American liberals and leftists had ordinarily been supportive of Israel, while conservatives and Republicans were often more critical. By this century, as noted earlier, the two sides had largely changed places. While no American political party is monolithic and many shades of opinion could be found in both parties, on the whole Republicans and conservatives had now become

Israel's most full-throated and least critical supporters, while opinions among Democrats were increasingly mixed.

The deep connection between Israel and the American right is unique. In no other country has a profound emotional and ideological connection between Israel and traditionalist conservatives, free market conservatives, and nationalist conservatives become a major political force. Yet in the United States, the bond with Israel has not only been a hallmark of most conservative political action for more than a generation; the bond has been a common tie that helped hold the fractious conservative coalition together.

From the beginning, the American right's embrace of Israel was problematic for the largely liberal and Democratic majority of American Jews. Fifteen hundred years of grim history in Europe had taught Jews that popular Christianity was often twisted into antisemitism. The ugly history of nineteenth- and twentieth-century Europe had shown that populist nationalism could also turn toward Jew hatred. The anti-welfare-state, antisocialist ideas that inspired Ronald Reagan struck a large majority of American Jews as both mean-spirited and wrongheaded.

While Herzl had predicted that a Jewish state would be able to overcome antisemitism in other countries and form useful connections with them, the emerging alliance between Israel and the American right was not what he had in mind. Herzl expected that the emigration of Jews from other countries to Israel would gradually eliminate antisemitism, and that formerly antisemitic parties and politicians would learn to treat the Jewish state as just another factor in world politics.[1]

What happened on the American right was not that. What drew the American right to Israel was not the perceived normalcy of the Jewish people and state but their perceived uniqueness, whether as a focus of God's intervention in history or as the focus of bitter, irrational hatred by groups who often also hated the United States and its capitalist economy and, as some would put it, its settler state ethos and cowboy culture.

For the Republican Party to fall in love with Israel, the eastern Republican establishment had to fall. In the 1950s, the American establishment looked much as it had since the Civil War: overwhelmingly Republican, overwhelmingly white, overwhelmingly Protestant or culturally Protestant, overwhelmingly based in the great cities of the Northeast and the Middle West, with an enclave along the Pacific coast stretching from Seattle to San Francisco. The banks, manufacturing companies, stock and commodity exchanges, universities, publishers, foundations, and law firms based in these cities dominated both Republican Party politics and national life. While the streets of the great cities, and increasingly their city halls, teemed with Irish and Great Wave immigrants, the boards of directors who ran both the for-profit corporations and the nonprofit foundations, hospitals, and universities were drawn almost entirely from "old stock" Americans.

The domination of this American establishment was not only ethnic and racial. It was regional. The Civil War had brought both the abolition of slavery and the victory of northern industrial capitalism over the slave-based commodity capitalism of the South, and the domination of the urban manufacturing economy of the North over southern and midwestern farmers. Southern white resistance succeeded in installing a racial hierarchy and Jim Crow laws across the former Confederacy, but for many years it was unable to challenge the ability of the victorious Northeast to make economic and trade policy that favored industry over agriculture, cities over the countryside, Wall Street over Main Street, and the North over the South. Southern and midwestern farmers and local businesses united to fight the hard money, pro-monopoly Republican power structure, but for the first fifty years after the Civil War their occasional political victories did little to weaken the entrenched economic and cultural power of what came to be called the eastern establishment.

Beginning with the upheavals of the 1960s, the power of the eastern establishment in the Republican Party would gradually weaken. This did not mean a new era of nonhierarchical politics was developing in the United States. The American establishment was not lying on its deathbed; it was undergoing a metamorphosis. Over time, this process would yield a new, socially liberal multiethnic American establishment based largely in the Democratic Party. This new incarnation of the American establishment would dominate the universities, foundations, publishing houses, museums, cultural institutions, broadcasters, and corporate boards almost as effectively as the old incarnation, but it would gradually drop the Republican affiliation, the Protestant religious character, and the ethnic and racial exclusivity of its predecessor. The protean new American establishment would bring Silicon Valley, Wall Street, the Ivy League, and Hollywood into a powerful and fateful alignment.

This shift worked itself out over several decades, and was often generational: the sons and daughters of liberal Republicans became socially liberal, fiscally conservative Democrats. As the base of the Republican Party became more socially conservative and more demonstrably (some would say, obstreperously) Christian, the elite shift away from the GOP accelerated. By the start of the twenty-first century, what was left of the WASP establishment was largely Democratic; the Hamptons, Nantucket, Martha's Vineyard, and Cape Cod became, at least during August, among the most Democratic places in the country. A liberal Republican establishment continued to exist, but its power in the Republican Party continued to dwindle.

Rebirth of a Nation

The so-called Reagan Revolution was one of the most unexpected developments in American political history. The once marginalized right, a collection of fringe figures espousing what most American intellectuals and political activists regarded as discarded, discredited ideas, roared back from Barry Goldwater's landslide defeat in 1964 to wrench American history into a new direction. Power shifted regionally in the United States as well in these years, from the Rust Belt North of declining factories and crime-ridden, fiscally strapped cities to the Sun Belt that stretched from modernizing and growing southern cities like Charlotte and Atlanta to the prosperous landscapes of Southern California. For the South, in particular, it was a heady time. A new generation of southern Republican leaders like Georgia's Newt Gingrich made the audacious claim that the South was no longer America's problem region, backward, bigoted, and blighted, but was now a modern, forward-looking place, leading the United States as a whole toward a brighter future.

Israel was part of the glue that held the Sun Belt coalition together and was encoded into the ideological DNA of the Republican Party from the Reagan era through the Trump years. The connections were often missed by those who saw the New Right primarily in terms of its economic agenda. How and why a program of deregulation and smaller government at home meshed with support for a small and in the 1970s still semisocialist country thousands of miles away was not immediately obvious. But the connections, though indirect, were strong. The Sun

Belt Republican coalition was both unlikely and inherently unstable. Pious evangelicals, honky-tonking southern good ol' boys, blue-collar midwestern Catholics, and elite neoconservative policy intellectuals were not naturally drawn toward one another.

Support for Israel helped unite Southern California with the old South, creating the Sun Belt alliance that dominated American politics for a generation. It helped to enlist often skeptical Jacksonian populists in support of an economic and social program and a foreign policy vision that would propel the United States to victory in the Cold War and shape a generation of Republican policy at home and abroad.

———

"In Your Heart You Know He's Right" was the slogan for Barry Goldwater's 1964 presidential campaign. "In your guts you know he's nuts," responded the Democrats,[2] and most voters sided with them as Goldwater lost the presidency in the largest popular vote landslide since FDR defeated Alf Landon in 1936. By 1980, when Goldwater's political heir Ronald Reagan took up the New Right banner against President Jimmy Carter, somehow those same ideas had moved to the mainstream. From 1980 through 2008, when then-Senator Barack Obama defeated another Arizona senator in the Goldwater-Reagan tradition, the New Right was the dominant force in American politics. Even when, as from 1993 to 2001, Democrats controlled the White House, they found it necessary to co-opt rather than oppose key New Right themes. As president, Bill Clinton balanced the federal budget, reformed welfare to encourage recipients to reenter the labor market by limiting benefits, and passed some of the toughest crime legislation in American history.

The New Right challenged the political orthodoxies of New Deal America; as a movement largely grounded in the ex-Confederate states, it also shook the balance of power in regional politics. The South has not, historically speaking, been America's trendsetter. It has more often been the exception than the rule, more stepchild than favorite son. It was not all that obvious even in hindsight how what since before the Civil War had been seen as the most backward region of the country emerged in the 1970s to set the national agenda, how the most Democratic region of the country reshaped the Republican Party in its image, how a region that still venerated the "Lost Cause" of the Confederacy revived full-throated American nationalism, how the least developed, most agrarian, and most anticapitalist American region midwifed the greatest extension of global financial capitalism in the history of the world, and why the most inward-turning and anti-imperialist region of the country supported a global American foreign policy of enormous ambition and idealism for thirty years.

It was not, however, the South as a whole or even the white South as a whole that brought this about. Those responsible for the transformation, first of the South and then of the country, were the heirs of the New South pragmatic southern progressives who tried to steer a middle course between agrarian populists and Bourbon Democrats—whose ranks included many plantation owners and other members of the pre-war southern elite—to promote modernization and development in a backward and impoverished region.

═══

When American historians look at the post World War II history of the American South, the civil rights movement fills center stage, as it should. The discipline, focus, and moral leadership of southern Blacks astonished the region, the nation, and the world. It was not just that leaders like Martin Luther King Jr. made eloquent speeches or stood for uplifting principles. It was the patient courage and human dignity of people in all walks of life who insisted on their rights under God and the Constitution. Southern Blacks stood up to insidious economic pressure and outrageous violence. They could not be cowed; they would not stoop to the violence and vandalism of their opponents. That America could produce a people and a movement of this grace and strength is one of our greatest national accomplishments; that we needed such a movement is one of our great national shames.

But the civil rights movement was not the only thing that was happening in the post-1945 South. Even as the Black South began to see some of its long-deferred hopes move toward fruition, pro-business white moderates were also reaping the rewards of decades of work.

The end of Reconstruction left southern whites divided into two large political camps and one small one: Bourbon Democrats, agrarian populists, and New South modernizers. The Bourbons had little interest in improving conditions for either poor Blacks or poor whites. While remaining under the Democratic umbrella the Bourbons were conservatives, supporting the gold standard and opposing all forms of business regulation. They were more interested in preserving their own privileged status than in building up either the region or the country as a whole.[3]

Opposed to the Bourbons were agrarian populists, small farmers in many cases who wanted cheap money and tough regulations on railroads, banks, and other companies seen as exploiting them. In some cases, white southern populists made alliances across racial lines with Black southerners against Bourbon rule, but such alliances were mostly short-lived and always vulnerable to race-baiting politicians ready to exploit prejudice for political gain.[4]

A much smaller third force also existed. These so-called New South supporters were the closest thing the South had to the Progressive movement in the North. Like the Bourbons, men like North Carolina's Josephus Daniels and South Carolina's James Byrnes were frankly and fully pro-capitalist. But unlike the Bourbons, they wanted to transform the southern status quo—to promote public education, to invest in infrastructure, improve public health, and otherwise bring the South into the twentieth century. It was largely due to their efforts that school attendance finally became compulsory throughout the South, that state bureaucracies were at least partially professionalized, and that various progressive "good governance" reforms were introduced. At times they supported the regulation of nonsouthern companies like railroads and banks, but they wanted taxes and regulations to remain low overall.[5]

While the Bourbons were happy with the racial status quo, believing that poor whites could always be manipulated into supporting Bourbon policies as long as the race card was available, the New South Democrats were on the whole embarrassed by the suffocating consequences of entrenched southern racial attitudes and sought to downplay the race issue. They supported segregation in the aftermath of Reconstruction because they believed that an ordered, administered system would reduce the outbreaks of violence that disfigured the South and made it unattractive to investors. It was also a concession to the reality that the Bourbon Democrats could always checkmate attempts to provide public services like schools unless the mass of white voters felt that first, Blacks and whites would not mix in the schools and, second, that funds collected from white taxpayers would be spent primarily on white people.

The three-cornered fight for supremacy between Bourbons, populists, and New South progressives was perhaps more bitter—and was certainly harder for outsiders to follow—because the post-Reconstruction South had shifted to a one-party system that was quite peculiar in other ways. Not only were most Blacks excluded from voting, but poll taxes and other factors discouraged poor white voting as well. This opaque system produced results that often confounded outsiders, but over time some patterns emerged. There was a premium on outsize personalities and sometimes outrageous political behavior. Electoral corruption was widespread and routine, with ballot box stuffing common. Loyalties were often tribal. Once one candidate played the race card, it was hard for competitors not to follow suit.

Through it all, New South progressives continued to pursue what we would now call a regional development strategy, and over time it began to pay off. The idea was to attract northern industry and investment to the South. To achieve this, the South would need to build better railroads and, later, highways and airports. It needed cheap and reliable electric power, partly to run factories and partly to make air-conditioning—a technology that would change the arc of southern history almost as dramatically as the cotton gin—widely available. It would need to achieve basic universal literacy and improve public health. And it would need to be competitive on costs, offering lower wages, lower taxes, and less burdensome regulation than states in the North.

As late as the 1930s, the southern states were desperately poor. In 1940, the per capita state income in Mississippi, the poorest state in the union, was $212 per year—20 percent of the figure in wealthy Delaware.[6] In 1940, 15 percent of Arkansas residents had a high school diploma, less than half the percentage in California, Massachusetts, and the District of Columbia.[7] While more than half of young people between sixteen and twenty living in western states were enrolled in school in 1940, fewer than a third of young people in Kentucky, North Carolina, Maryland, Virginia, Georgia, and South Carolina stayed in school after age sixteen.[8] While Blacks were at the bottom of the economic ladder across the South, poor whites lagged well behind the rest of the country as well. Unpainted cabins without running water or plumbing were still relatively common sights into the 1950s and 1960s in some areas; chain gangs of convicts still toiled on the roads. Prevailing wages were considerably lower across the South. In textiles, the lowest paid category of industrial employment, southern workers earned 18 percent less in the South than their northern counterparts before World War II.[9] This was an improvement from 1922, when Alabama textile workers earned 21 cents an hour compared to 40.9 cents an hour in Massachusetts,[10] but stark wage differentials remained, and skilled factory and industrial jobs remained scarce across the South.

The New South strategy had already begun to enjoy both economic and political success in the late nineteenth century, but it took the New Deal, World War II, and the Cold War buildup to bring the South closer to parity with the rest of the country. Federal spending played a critical role; long-serving southern Democrats controlled key committees in Congress and ensured that the South had its fair share and more of any available money.

Thanks to New Deal projects like the Tennessee Valley Authority, the South was able to power the factories and military bases needed for World War II. Waves of new factories propelled urbanization across the region. The Interstate Highway System linked southern cities with each other and with the national market. The G.I. Bill jolted sleepy southern universities into new life. Cheap Veterans Administration loans gave the rising generation of white southerners access to modern housing. (Shamefully, Black veterans were only able to use G.I. Bill money in underfunded and less developed all-Black institutions, and were generally unable to find bankers willing to lend them money for housing.) With space program facilities dotting the South in Cape Canaveral, Florida, Huntsville, Alabama, Houston, Texas, and elsewhere; with nuclear facilities in Georgia and South Carolina; bustling navy yards and giant military bases including Fort Bragg, Fort Benning, and Fort Hood, the South teemed with federal facilities hosting everyone from rocket scientists to GIs undergoing basic training.

The waves of prosperity that flooded across the South helped solidify the political appeal of the moderates over both the populists and the Bourbons. As more southerners moved off the farms, and the sharecropper system disappeared, agrarian populism seemed less relevant. And working for good wages in an air-conditioned factory did not seem like exploitation to people who had grown up in rural or small-town homes without electricity or piped water.

The greatest challenge moderate leaders faced was the civil rights movement, and the most emotional issue was school integration. The Supreme Court's unanimous 1954 *Brown v. Board of Education* decision declared segregated school systems inherently unconstitutional and ordered the integration of public schools across the country. Moderates, who had long understood that southern racial politics were, if nothing else, "bad for business," did their best to temporize and find ways to avoid scenes like the violent mobs in cities like Little Rock and Birmingham, Alabama. However, white opposition to integrated schools was so strong that several states made plans to close all of their public schools rather than integrate. Some went so far as to repeal state constitutional provisions that required the state to provide free public education for their children.

At first, moderates were unable to make much headway against the public reaction. Over time, however, cooler heads began to prevail. By the 1950s, most white southerners understood how important northern investment was to their future. Major corporations were increasingly reluctant to operate segregated facilities. Northern managers and their families did not want to be transferred to cities where mobs of angry white people spat and screamed at small children on their way to school. Cities like Birmingham and Selma, Alabama, where the violent resistance to peaceful civil rights activism was particularly brutal, received worldwide publicity that community and civic leaders elsewhere were determined to avoid. Quietly, in city after city and town after town, white moderates were able to marginalize the extremists, and move with Black leaders toward local progress.

As consequential for southern politics as the civil rights cases, the 1964 Warren Court decision in *Reynolds v. Sims* and subsequent cases radically recast power at the state level. Previously, state laws and constitutions magnified the power of rural voters by allowing and in some cases mandating radically unequal representation. Alabama's state constitution, for example, allocated one state representative to each county regardless of population.[11] The reapportionment of state legislatures that followed these decisions shifted the balance of power in southern politics permanently toward the cities and growing suburbs, away from the most conservative rural districts.

Between the economic prosperity and urbanization that New South policies had brought to the South, the evident practicality of the moderates' approach to the civil rights movement, and the shift in political strength that followed the "one man one vote" decisions, the New South was more dominant in southern politics than ever before. Throwback populists like Alabama governor George Wallace still existed, but by the end of the 1960s the American South was firmly on the road if not to true racial reconciliation and justice, at least to formal racial equality and was fully invested in the idea that maintaining a "competitive" business climate was the high road to prosperity for all.

═══

Meanwhile, even as New South thinking triumphed in the old Confederacy, another kind of New South was rising in the West. California today is a blue state, but the red California of the Reagan years was a cornerstone of the new American right. Orange County was a citadel of Republican power, and the Southland, as Californians affectionately called the southern third of the state, was home to conservative institutions like Pepperdine University and the Bible Institute of Los Angeles (known today as Biola), and gave rise to such distinctive American religious forms as the suburban megachurch. Many of the country's most conservative politicians hailed from this part of California, where a vibrant aerospace industry provided stable, well-paid jobs to the children and grandchildren of the Okies and other migrants who brought southern culture, southern religion, and southern politics with them.

Energy was to the Southwest what cotton had once been to the South: a basic commodity on whose production and sale the whole region depended. Vast oil deposits across the Southwest extended from the Gulf of Mexico to Los Angeles. Historically, the founders of the southwestern oil industry were refugees from the rise of Standard Oil in the Northeast. As the Rockefeller colossus used its monopoly and political power to squeeze rivals, wildcatters and independents left the oilfields of Pennsylvania and Ohio for the Southwest.[12] There, the rich oilfields of these still remote regions allowed them to create companies strong enough to remain independent from northeastern banks and oil companies, and they laid the foundations for a Sun Belt establishment that rejected the liberal politics and liberal religion of the establishment Rockefeller Republicans.[13]

Like the South, the Southwest was a major beneficiary of federal infrastructure investment and defense spending from the Depression into the Cold War. Huge irrigation projects supported the expansion of agriculture and the rise of new cities. Electricity generated by facilities like the Hoover Dam provided power for air-conditioning and factory operations. With the United States engaged in three major Pacific wars between 1941 and 1971, an enormous aerospace and national defense complex grew up in the Southwest.

Los Angeles, already the global dream factory thanks to its dominance of the film industry, helped pioneer a new kind of urban civilization based on the car and the freeway rather than subways and commuter trains. Caught up in this tsunami of prosperity, the Okies and other Depression era migrants could hardly believe the golden dream of California living that unfolded around them.

But like their southern peers, the entrepreneurs and business leaders of the Sun Belt came from a tradition of laissez-faire economic thinking. Combining the individualism of the West with the self-reliance and self-confidence of newly successful entrepreneurs, the southwestern elite saw no contradiction between a pro-free-market stance and a heavy reliance on government-funded public works and infrastructure. Without the South's bitter heritage of defeat and resentment, they still had a healthy suspicion of northeastern banks and corporate giants. For the most part, they viewed labor unions as a threat to their competitiveness, and resented what they saw as the heavy hand of federal regulation.

What this meant in politics was that from the 1950s forward Sun Belt and southern entrepreneurs and politicians were drawn toward the Republican Party, seen as more business friendly than the Democrats, but opposed the dominance of the eastern establishment within it. In the late 1940s Richard Nixon's rise into national politics based on his investigation of establishment hero and Soviet spy Alger Hiss was an early sign that new political forces were rising in California. Arizona senator Barry Goldwater's 1964 victory over New York governor and Standard Oil heir Nelson Rockefeller in his quest for the GOP presidential nomination was funded in part by J. Howard Pew, who had moved to Texas with his father to escape the suffocating power of the Rockefeller clan.[14] Goldwater may have failed nationally, but he was the first Republican to carry the Deep South since the end of Reconstruction. The Sun Belt coalition had arrived.

The difficult economic conditions of the 1970s offered an opening to an insurgent political coalition, but the existence of an opportunity is no guarantee of success. Sun Belt Republicans learned from the Goldwater defeat that Goldwater's opposition to key civil rights legislation turned many suburban and northern Republican voters away. Goldwater's opposition was on constitutional not racial grounds, but the lesson seemed clear: no political force that set itself against legal equality between the races could compete at the national level. This was not just true for liberal Republicans and independents in the North. The Southwest was not as racially polarized as the old South, and states like California would remain out of reach for a party that was "too Southern" on race.

A regional agenda grounded in a distinctive regional subculture and speaking to the economic priorities of an underdeveloped part of the country could not easily appeal to voters in the nation at large. To make Sun Belt Republicanism the dominant political force during thirty turbulent years, its architects had to keep the white South on board without compromising the GOP's appeal west of the Mississippi and north of the Mason-Dixon line.

Both parts of the task were difficult. When the dust settled after Nixon and Reagan had brought the white South into the Republican Party, the old divisions between Bourbons, populists, and New South party factions remained. When former Alabama governor and arch-segregationist George Wallace ran as a third-party candidate in 1968 against Hubert Humphrey and Richard Nixon, he won five southern states. Men like future speaker of the house Newt Gingrich articulated the longtime antiregulation, antilabor, small government, and balanced budget message of conservative pro-business white southerners. But not all southern whites shared these values. To win, Sun Belt Republicanism would have to feel like the old South to supporters in places like Georgia and Alabama while looking modern and national to voters in places like Alaska and Maine.

The answer was to wrap the coalition in red, white, and blue. Overall, the New Right was a movement of what one could call "hyper-Americanism," a vision that elevated and intensified selected elements of American culture and history into a dynamic and theatrical political movement. Individualistic capitalism, Christianity, and unabashed and unrestrained American patriotism were the foundation on which Sun Belt Republicanism set up its shop. Sun Belt Republicanism offered visions of economic progress, American civic religion, and American identity that were attractive on both sides of the Mason-Dixon line and on both banks of the Mississippi.

In each of these dimensions Sun Belt Republicans made a similar case: that New Deal ideology had fallen away from "true" American beliefs and values, and that what needed to happen was a return from the failing values of post–New Deal America to the solid, enduring verities on which the nation had been founded.

The overregulated crony capitalism of the New Deal state was failing because it had fallen away from the true American capitalist system of free competition. American foreign policy was too full of self-doubt and muddled thinking. Victory in the Cold War required self-confident and courageous thinking, not the timid nostrums of State Department cookie pushers. Above all, the nation was experiencing a social and a values crisis because the liberal Christianity of the Protestant establishment was too tepid and uninspiring to keep America close to God.

What America needed to escape from the dismal social and economic conditions of the 1970s, the New Right insisted, was a revival. To restore American dynamism, the country would have to return to the values that made it great in the first place.

As it happened, the 1980s seemed to demonstrate the validity of this approach. By unshackling capitalism from the chains of mid-century regulation, Americans opened up a new era of economic growth and technological progress. By prosecuting the Cold War more vigorously, the Reagan administration pushed the Soviet Union and its communist empire toward ignominious collapse. And those who called for a return to the "old-time religion" of salvationist Christianity were rewarded with the greatest religious revival in American history, a revival that spread well beyond the boundaries of the United States and helped to bind the South, the Southwest, and much of the Middle West into a new majority coalition in American culture as well as politics.

The economics was the easy part. As they watched factories close and opportunities shrink, the idea of "competitiveness" appealed to many voters. America needed a new model for industrial policy and the Sun Belt had one ready to hand. The rising prosperity of the Sun Belt states was so evident that hundreds of thousands of Rust Belt residents were packing their bags to build new lives in Sun Belt cities from Charlotte, North Carolina, through the rapidly growing Fort Worth–Dallas metroplex and Phoenix into Los Angeles and San Diego. Whatever the Sun Belt had, it seemed to be working. Why not give it a try?

But people do not live by bread alone. The New Right needed more than an economic policy agenda. Sun Belt Republicanism needed to renew the American spirit as well as the American economy. To do so, it drew on the religious and cultural history of the South, tempered by the experiences of the Southwest, to offer a new kind of civil religion and patriotic vision that, for a time, united the white South, strengthened the Sun Belt coalition, and appealed to many middle- and working-class Americans around the country.

There were two complementary elements to the new platform for American life that the Sun Belt proposed. First, the religious movement exemplified by the ministry of post–World War II evangelicals like Billy Graham sought to renew the American spirit through a religious revival. Second, the patriotic synthesis of Ronald Reagan linked Jacksonian populist nationalism to an expansive vision of American power and ideals that united much of the country behind the foreign policy vision of the Sun Belt right.

Israel played a central role in both the religious and the patriotic projects of the New Right. As a fulfillment of biblical prophecy in a dark hour for the human race, the return of the Jews to the Holy Land and their seemingly miraculous victories over larger and richer enemies helped empower the preaching of a generation of American evangelists. As an example of a nation blessed by God overcoming its enemies through the strength of its values, Israel was a powerful symbol of the role of America in the world that animated the Reagan right.

Israel worked in Sun Belt politics like the bronze serpent that Moses raised in the desert. Those who gazed on it were healed, and the higher it was exalted, the more widely the blessings flowed. None of this came from Planet Vulcan; to understand the sources and significance of Israel in Sun Belt Republicanism, we need to look in a different direction. Sun Belt Republicanism's deeply rooted support for Israel owes much more to Planet Billy Graham and Planet Andrew Jackson than to the efforts or the sentiments of American Jews.

Located for the most part in so-called flyover country, these two planets are relatively unknown to the foreign policy pundits and policymakers who cluster along the Acela corridor from Boston to Washington. That is unfortunate. The views of evangelical Christians and populist nationalists are often decisive in the political struggles around American foreign policy. But anyone who wants to understand the role that Israel plays in American life must venture beyond Acelaland into the mysterious recesses of *l'Amérique profonde*.

The World of Billy Graham

America was not just facing economic and foreign policy crises in the 1970s. It was facing a spiritual crisis. The loss of the Vietnam War challenged long-held beliefs about America's invincibility. The manner in which it was fought undermined confidence in America's virtue as well. The civil rights movement was forcing a long, deep look into the American past. Many Americans who had long assumed that their country was a beacon of hope and a tower of liberty first began to wrestle with the role of slavery and racial injustice in American history.

At the same time, the irrepressible conflict between the individualism fostered by a consumer society and the discipline required to maintain traditional social structures erupted in the 1970s. The feminist movement and the early stirrings of what would grow into the movement for lesbian and gay recognition and rights raised basic questions about family life. More and more women wanted to work outside the home, and as cheap and reliable birth control became widely available, both men and women saw less need for traditional marriage. The "cultural contradictions of capitalism" as outlined by sociologist Daniel Bell were on full display as Americans attempted to negotiate a growing divide between their inherited values and their lived experience.[15]

The sense of insecurity about the ideological and institutional foundations of American life deepened the persistent underlying fears about the fragility of human civilization that never ceased troubling Americans who lived under the shadows of the Cold War and a nuclear holocaust. The idea that the rise of the United States was part of a global movement toward the establishment of a peaceful and prosperous world, toward the culmination of human history in abundance and liberty, was not just a comforting story Americans liked to tell themselves. It was one of the crucial beliefs that held the country together. What if that wasn't true? What if the cool apocalypse of the American Dream was an illusion, and that illusion was beginning to dissolve?

In a country with deep Christian roots like the United States, a social crisis of this depth and intensity inevitably had repercussions in the world of religion. So-called mainline Protestant denominations had long dominated American cultural and intellectual life. They were increasingly under pressure as the descendants of Catholic and Jewish Great

Wave immigrants rose to positions of leadership in politics and culture. The upheavals of the 1970s would further disrupt what remained of the cultural hegemony of the mainline churches even as their membership began a sustained generational decline. By the twenty-first century the social influence and financial heft of some of the most important institutions in American life had largely faded away. Intellectually, demographically, and financially, mainline Protestantism had plunged into a steep decline which left these churches unable to play their traditional role at the center of both spiritual and intellectual life in the United States.

American Catholics were not ready to step into the void; Roman Catholicism in the United States, as in much of the West, was confronting a set of theological and vocational challenges in the wake of the Second Vatican Council. With nuns, priests, and brothers leaving their orders and in some cases the Church,[16] American Catholics were preoccupied by internal organizational problems and were not in a position to replace mainline Protestantism at the ethical and religious center of American culture.

Led by Billy Graham, a North Carolina–born Southern Baptist minister who became the greatest revivalist and preacher on American soil since George Whitefield's triumphal eighteenth-century career at the height of the Great Awakening, a movement of Sun Belt Christianity rose to fill the void left by the decline of mainline Protestantism. Graham and his fellow evangelicals, as they called themselves, united the Sun Belt behind a specific version of Protestant Christianity that both reaffirmed key elements of classic southern Protestant religion and reshaped southern religion into a force that could have a national and indeed international impact.

"Evangelical" is one of the many words in our cultural vocabulary that can mean many different things. The word comes from ancient Greek, where it literally means "good news." The early Christians spoke of their message of divine redemption as "the good news." In English, the word "gospel" comes from Anglo-Saxon roots meaning "good news." Martin Luther used the term "evangelical" to describe his theology in order to underline what he believed to be its close connection to the original message proclaimed by Jesus's original followers. "Evangelical" is still used as a synonym for Lutheran denominations and theological ideas, and Lutheran churches continue to use the term (written with a capital "E") as part of their official denominational names.

The term was appropriated by a group of American conservative Protestants who founded the National Association of Evangelicals in 1942 to describe an approach to Christianity that was conservative in doctrine but much more open to engagement with contemporary scholarship and politics than the self-described fundamentalists who dominated the world of conservative Protestantism at the time. Over the next fifteen years Carl F. H. Henry, Billy Graham, and Harold Ockenga helped define a new approach built around six key beliefs: that although human beings are made in God's image, the consequences of sin have so twisted and ruined human nature that without divine grace human beings cannot lead good lives or approach God; that the sacrifice of Jesus Christ on the cross and his subsequent resurrection from the dead have opened a path, the only path, by which human beings can recover from a condition of spiritual failure and death through accepting Jesus Christ as their personal savior in a process known as being "born again"; that the Holy Spirit acts in the lives of those who have accepted Christ to enlighten and improve them; that the Bible was directly inspired by God and is the supreme authority for believers on matters of faith and morals; that it is a religious duty to share one's faith with nonbelievers; and finally that Christians should engage in the intellectual and political life of their times.

The new synthesis highlighted some elements of classic conservative southern Protestantism and downplayed some of the most important and distinctive elements in the southern fundamentalism that previously dominated both the states of the old Confederacy and the new Southwest. The new evangelicals reiterated their absolute faith in the infallibility and divine inspiration of the Bible, but for the most part downplayed ideas like the "Young Earth" version of anti-Darwinism which held on the basis of biblical calculations that the universe was only about six thousand years old. They broke with the theological defense of segregation and racial inequality. They dropped the denominational hostility and rivalry that was once a primary feature of southern and conservative religious culture. They dropped the bitter anti-Catholicism that had long been a mainstay of conservative Protestantism. They also accepted the Pentecostal movement into the fold.

These were radical steps. Most of them would have been impossible a decade before the war—or would have been so divisive that they would have split the white South rather than uniting it. Billy Graham invited

Catholics to share the platform with him at public meetings and included Catholic clergy among the counselors to whom those who came forward to make "decisions for Christ" at his revival services were referred—a step that was as controversial at the time as his 1953 decision to reject racial segregation at his revival meetings.[17] Graham's efforts to act as a bridge between the old South and the Northern establishment forced him to strike a difficult balance. While he preached against racism, he did not support the passage of the Civil Rights Act. As it was, there were some significant figures who did not go along with the new thinking, but Graham and his associates were gradually able to marginalize them, in part because of the impact of Graham's success in the pulpit, in part because the younger generation of conservative American Christians preferred the new ideas.

In retrospect, the critical insight that Graham and his associates brought to American religion was that the deepest divide in contemporary American Christianity was not the line between Protestants and Catholics. It was not between believers in infant baptism and believers in adult baptism. It was not between Pentecostal and charismatic Christians and those who regarded with skepticism and suspicion such characteristic phenomena of the Pentecostals as "speaking in tongues." It was not even between conservatives and liberals or "fundamentalists" and "modernists." To oversimplify a complex distinction, the great divide was between "ethical Christianity," the belief that the moral teachings of Jesus Christ and his followers are the core of Christian faith, and "salvationist Christianity," the belief that the core of Christianity is the miraculous salvation of believers through Christ's suffering and death.

During sixty years in the national spotlight, Billy Graham's preaching returned over and over again to a few basic ideas: that without God no human political creed or movement could solve the world's problems; that the only way forward was for individuals to repent of their sin, accept Christ as their savior, and begin a new life; that God was supernaturally at work in history and that the terrifying developments in the political and international spheres reflected his long prophesied judgment on the failures of humanity.

It worked. Graham's message caught fire, and the evangelical movement not only became the most visible expression of conservative Protestantism in American life for the next sixty years, but a transformative force in American culture and politics. This evangelical surge came just as the mainline Protestant churches (often more liberal both theologically and politically) were losing members in what amounted to a mass defection. Between 1965 and 2012, membership in the United Church of Christ and the Episcopal Church declined roughly 50 percent, while the American Methodist church saw a decline of 33 percent. Meanwhile, evangelical churches saw a membership explosion. The Assemblies of God (for our purposes, Pentecostals are part of the evangelical world) grew by 430 percent, and the Southern Baptist denomination grew by 46 percent. From 1965 to 2013, the Evangelical Free Church of America's membership increased 750 percent.[18]

Graham's breakthrough onto the national scene came in 1949, when the still unknown thirty-three-year-old preacher opened a revival meeting in downtown Los Angeles two days after Harry Truman announced that the Soviet Union had just detonated a nuclear bomb. Graham's message of apocalypse and judgment struck a chord in the City of Angels. As celebrities made decisions for Christ at Graham's rallies and William Randolph Hearst publicized the new preacher, local print and broadcast media rushed to cover the phenomenon.[19] The then prominent and influential newsweeklies *Time* and *Life* ran stories about him, and the crowds grew.[20] Graham's message highlighted two themes: the imminence of apocalypse as demonstrated by the Soviet threat, and the traditional message of salvationist Christianity that the only way to save your soul and save the human race was to accept the miracle of redemption through the love of Jesus Christ.

For the first time since Clarence Darrow and H. L. Mencken turned the elderly fundamentalist William Jennings Bryan into a national laughingstock at the Scopes Trial over evolution in Tennessee, salvationist Christianity had a spokesman whose message commanded the attention and the respect of Americans in all sections of the country and from many different cultural and religious backgrounds. And Graham's evangelical synthesis meshed with the emerging religious culture of Southern California. The defensive mindset of embattled southern fundamentalism, the entanglement with populist and left-wing economics, the ugly racism carrying over at times into theology: the baggage of the old South had no place in the rapturously sunny Californian Southland.

That the rise of this evangelical movement contributes in some way to increased American support for Israel is well known, but the dynamics behind the relationship are not widely grasped. Those who say American policy is pro-Israel because evangelicals are strong have missed at least half of the story. It is less that Israel is strong in American politics because of evangelical support than that the existence of Israel helped evangelical religion become a major force in American life. For hundreds of millions of evangelical and Pentecostal Christians in the United States and beyond, the rise of Israel is seen to prove the truth of salvationist Christianity in the real world.

The return of the Jews to the Holy Land and the establishment against all odds of a powerful Jewish state in the deserts of Palestine strikes many people as a concrete demonstration of the essential truths of the Christian religion. God exists; he drives history; he performs miracles in real time; God's word in the Bible is true.

In the United States, the focus by salvationist Christians on Israel acted as a weapon against skeptics and, perhaps especially, ethical Christians. It solidified the claim of contemporary evangelicals to religious authenticity in the light of American Protestant history. Historically, it helped marginalize those within the world of American salvationist Christianity who preferred the pre-Graham fundamentalism to the evangelicalism that overshadowed it. Israel energized evangelical Christianity, it reaffirmed core evangelical beliefs, it drew converts, and it marginalized opponents on the theological and cultural right.

The existence of Israel has given a tremendous boost to the credibility of a variety of speculative interpretations of biblical prophecies about the end of the world among some believers, but it did more to focus than to create a sense of apocalyptic expectancy among Christians at large. In an era like ours, dominated by apocalyptic forebodings, it does not take a Jewish state to make many people feel as if the end of the world is at hand.

Evangelicals were if anything more worried about the end of the world than most. They tend to be skeptical about the effectiveness and even the goodwill of the secular bureaucrats and the weak international institutions that, for liberal Christians and secular progressives, are humanity's best hope against the dangers around us.

It was not just the survival and the return of the Jews that caught evangelical attention. It was that all the right people hated them. Jew-hatred was, for salvationist preachers, confirmation of a central Christian doctrine: the depravity of the unredeemed. Fallen man, classic Christianity teaches, is not innocent; the power of sin causes people actively and spontaneously to hate God and the signs of his presence.

Evangelicals look at what seems to be the obsessive and compulsive attention of the United Nations to condemnations of and attacks on Israel, often made by countries whose human rights record is far more atrocious than anything Israel can be accused of, and see evidence of the unreasoning hatred against the things of God that evangelical doctrine teaches them to expect among the unsaved. The fire and fury of hate that surrounds the Jewish people, the irrational but seemingly immortal foulness of antisemitic conspiracy theories from fascists, communists, radical Muslims, and secular post-Christians simply confirms the evangelical idea that fallen humanity hates Israel because the existence of the Chosen People is a standing rebuke to those who deafen their ears to God's call.

The religious importance of Israel to American salvationist Christians was personal as well as global. Not even the most dedicated believers remain free from all doubt. Am I really saved from my sins? Am I wasting my time praying to an imaginary sky god? Is death the end of all things? Will my prayers be answered? Will I see my loved ones again? Does the Creator of the Universe care about my happiness and well-being?

For the hundreds and thousands of questions and doubts that surface in the minds of religious people, the existence and the prosperity of Israel provided reassurance and relief. That they regarded the country whose existence provided such comfort and solace with affection should not come as a surprise. Millions of American Christians were warmly attached to the Jewish state, not as a result of television news, newspaper reports, or social media posts, but because it seemed to them that the existence of Israel made their lives more meaningful and their beliefs more secure.

There was another important relationship between Zionism and evangelical religion. From the Reformation forward, a high regard for the Bible has been a hallmark of Protestantism, but through much of the twentieth century the historical accuracy of the Bible came under sustained attack by modernist scholars and archaeologists. Both the Old and New Testaments, critics said, were filled with legendary accounts.

They were written long past the times they purported to describe. The scribes who copied the manuscripts were prone to error. The declining authority of scripture was one of the principal intellectual drivers of the retreat of salvationist Christianity among the educated and professional classes.

Zionism had little interest in the New Testament, but many Israelis believed that the legitimacy of the Zionist project depended on a defense of the historical accuracy of the Hebrew scriptures. Those, after all, were the documents that demonstrated the presence of the Jewish people in the Holy Land. If the Old Testament was a tissue of fabrications and legends, if David and Solomon had never existed, if Judaism was a cultural fabrication of the Hellenistic period, if the story of Abraham was a pious fable, what business did modern Jews have in a land that had never really been theirs?

Both evangelical Christians and Zionist Jews, including secular as well as religious Jews, wanted to demonstrate the historicity of the Hebrew Bible and the accuracy of its text, and Zionist Jews moved enthusiastically into the field of "biblical archaeology." Using the Bible as a guide, they fanned out across the land to discover signs of ancient Jewish inhabitants as well as, where possible, establishing the historical accuracy of biblical accounts. These archaeologists, like many of their counterparts in a time when nationalists around the world sought to demonstrate the glories of their culture and the legitimacy of their territorial claims through the study of the physical remains of the past, had an agenda, but they were professionally trained, and their discoveries were reported on in the media and analyzed in scientific journals.

American evangelicals and conservative mainline Protestants received the results of these efforts like manna from heaven. The first Dead Sea Scrolls, ancient Jewish documents dating from before the time of Christ, hidden away in caves and preserved for two millennia by the arid conditions of the Judean desert, were dramatically unveiled in a Jerusalem press conference in 1948. The first scrolls were found by Bedouins; Eleazar Lipa Sukenik, head of archaeology at Hebrew University, bought three of them and an intensive search over the next decade uncovered many more, ranging from large scrolls to tiny fragments.[21] Patiently assembled, the material would ultimately provide rich insights into the religious and political conditions of ancient Judea, and do much to resolve doubts over the integrity of the received biblical text.

That would not be all. Sukenik's son Yigael Yadin had served as head of operations for the Jewish forces in the War of Independence, but returned to archaeology after his military career. Yadin led excavations in Hazor and announced what he believed were gates built by King Solomon and evidence that supported the biblical account of Joshua's campaigns.[22] Yadin's interpretations, like much in the field of archaeology, were and remain controversial, but these and other excavations provided conservative Protestant preachers and apologists with important evidence for their claims about the Bible.

Biblical archaeology continues to play a significant role today both in Zionist politics and evangelical apologetics. Following the Israeli conquest of the Old City of Jerusalem in 1967, Israeli archaeologists began to examine the neighborhood of the ancient temple, finding evidence of the biblical "First Temple" that existed before the Babylonian conquest.[23] In 2005, excavators found what they claimed was the palace of the pre-Babylonian Jewish kings, and objects found at the site have been linked to people named in the biblical book of Jeremiah.[24] For Zionists, these discoveries offer support for Jewish claims to Jerusalem; for conservative Protestants, they offer evidence of the antiquity and the accuracy of the Bible itself.

Given these realities, the rapid growth of pro-Israel political movements like CUFI (Christians United for Israel) is not hard to explain.[25] But there was another benefit to evangelicals in a close association with Israel. The growing fascination with Israel among salvationist Christians tended to weaken what remained of the elements in the fundamentalist movement who resented and would, if they could, resist the hegemony of evangelicals whose orthodoxy and authenticity they felt they had reason to doubt.

Forward-thinking evangelicals like Billy Graham and Carl Henry faced significant opposition from more conservative, often economically more populist and racially more polarizing figures. Both in the old South and across the Sun Belt, it was necessary for the new pro-business, New South sensibility in religion and culture to marginalize the old populist and fundamentalist culture. Bringing a focus on Israel to the front of the Christian agenda served this purpose well.

The old fundamentalism had always had a strong populist streak. This was partly about class; the post-bellum South had a socially stratified denominational hierarchy. Presbyterians and Episcopalians were at the top, with Methodists close behind. Baptists, the majority faith among much of the white (and Black) South, might sometimes occupy a less exalted social position, especially in the older cities and towns of the region, but were highly differentiated among themselves. Further down came the Pentecostals, often referred to disparagingly by higher and drier religious denominations as "Holy Rollers."

In general, the further down one was in the social scale, the more fundamentalist one's doctrine and the more rigid one's lifestyle. Episcopalians and Presbyterians drank freely ("Wherever three or four are gathered together, there is always a fifth" as people used to say about Episcopalians), danced, and, while mostly supernatural and salvationist in their understanding of Christianity, were much readier to accommodate elements of modernist thought and biblical criticism than other southern Christians. Methodists were generally expected to dance decorously and to drink less if at all, and Baptists and Pentecostals were opposed to drinking, dancing, and in many cases to tobacco and the use of cosmetics. ("You can't go to Heaven/With your powder and your paint/'Cause it makes you look/Like what you ain't," as an old southern gospel song put it.)

The evangelical movement was anything but monolithic, but socially and ideologically it was much closer to the pro-business and racially moderate sensibilities of the New South than to the populism and identity politics often found among poor and less educated whites. One could say that evangelicals were the New South at prayer, and the triumph in the South of evangelicalism was in part about the recasting of old class and cultural differences within the white South.

White southern populism on the other hand was associated with fundamentalism in religion, and the populists' suspicions of big business, in particular finance, were very much a part of the message of many fundamentalist preachers. Like William Jennings Bryan, many fundamentalists saw themselves in a battle with both Charles Darwin and Wall Street. For some, the failure of evangelicals to attack "Romanism" with sufficient vigor, to make a biblical case for segregation, or to make the fight for Prohibition a central element of their political engagement were signs of creeping liberalism and moral cowardice.

Southern politicians who appealed to this constituency embraced political and economic messages sharply at variance with the pro-business attitudes of New South developers and industrialists. Early in

Graham's career, preachers like Gerald K. Smith, a notorious antisemite as well as a supporter of Louisiana's arch-populist governor Huey Long, still claimed a significant following.

For evangelicals, pointing to the rise of Israel as a proof of biblical prophetic truth offered an opportunity to burnish their credentials as true Bible-believing salvationist Christians while making open anti-semitism a mark of Cain in the Christian church. Billy Graham might not, as some fundamentalists wished he would, preach about how the dinosaurs went extinct in Noah's Flood, but when he preached that God was working a miracle that was on the front page of every newspaper in the world it was hard not to accept him as a Bible-believing Christian. And it was hard to keep the flames of antisemitic conspiracy theories burning brightly when the conspicuous success of the Zionist project was a principal pillar of the case for Christian faith.

For American evangelicals, the rise of Israel was good news.

It was also good news for American Jacksonians.

THE OTHER NEW SOUTH

The Sun Belt coalition united two New Souths: the pro-business, urban, and suburban political coalition that came to dominate politics across much of the old Confederacy in the post–civil rights era, and the politi-cally and religiously conservative Southwest, made up of Southern Cali-fornia, Arizona, Texas, and Oklahoma. (In fact, the Sun Belt coalition stretched farther than this—it also included the Mountain West where, as in Southern California, the political culture managed to reconcile the region's dependence on federal infrastructure and subsidy programs with a fiercely individualistic and pro-business ethos.)

Beyond both of these, and critical to the success of the Sun Belt coali-tion under both Ronald Reagan and the Bush family, was what can fairly be called a third New South. Blue-collar white workers in the Middle West, called Reagan Democrats in the 1980s, had been, like most south-ern whites, loyal supporters of the New Deal before transferring their allegiance to Ronald Reagan in 1980. The North's Reagan Democrats came in two basic types. One was made up of descendants of white southern migrants drawn to the Middle West since the nineteenth cen-tury, first by fertile farmland and then by the factory jobs of new mega-cities like Chicago and Detroit. These migrants gave a strong southern flavor to southern Ohio and Illinois along with much of Indiana and were found in and around the declining manufacturing hubs as well as in rural areas.

The other big group among Reagan Democrats were blue-collar and rural white voters with roots in the waves of European migration to the region between the Civil War and the Johnson-Reed Act. Many were Catholic; most had been reliably Democratic voters at least through the 1960s. The economic turmoil of the 1970s hit these voters hard. Prices for gasoline and home heating skyrocketed; inflation eroded savings; factory closures destroyed jobs, drove home prices down, and eroded the tax bases of local governments facing unprecedented strains.

What came to be called the culture wars also had a role to play. As late as the 1960s, the consensus morality of the American establishment was fairly close to traditional morality as taught by both Catholic and Protestant churches. Secular American society condemned sex outside marriage, homosexual activity, and (in middle-class circles) divorce. Those taboos began to weaken as early as the 1950s when the wide availability of antibiotics turned syphilis from a horrifying fatal disease into an inconvenience and the individualism and hedonism intrinsic to a consumer society began to change attitudes especially among young people. The advent of oral contraception in the 1960s and the popularization of feminist ideas widened the gap between traditional values and the dominant values of American society. After *Roe v. Wade* and the rise of what was at the time known as gay liberation, the gap would widen into a chasm that half a century later remains a prominent feature in American life.

As the Democratic Party increasingly defined itself as a party open to the latest new perspectives on human sexuality and related issues, the gap between tradition-minded northern Catholics and the Democratic establishment widened. Like southern evangelicals, this once loyal Democratic constituency was increasingly drawn to the social conservatism of Sun Belt Republicanism. Here, too, the Graham reconstruction of southern religion helped. By working with Catholic clergy at his revivals, and by stressing the common salvationist theology that traditional Catholics and evangelicals shared, Graham and the new breed of evangelical preachers and activists laid the foundation for an ecumenism of the right that would include conservative Protestants, Catholics, and Orthodox Jews who supported traditional moral teachings against the post-1960s values revolution.

I've written about the Jacksonian school of American foreign policy in *Special Providence: American Foreign Policy and How It Changed the World* and I made mention of it earlier in these pages. America's Jacksonian heritage is a complex but powerful set of values, perceptions, and associations originally found among the poor Protestant Scots-Irish who arrived late in the colonial period and settled in the less fertile uplands and mountainous areas of the southern and Middle-Atlantic colonies. Jacksonian culture has been the largest single element in the formation of non-elite white culture in the United States.

Originally a nativist and anti-Catholic subculture that flourished on the frontier, twentieth-century Jacksonianism evolved to attract the multiethnic, multiconfessional white working class of the Middle West. The newer "Crabgrass Jacksonians" share some basic beliefs, attitudes, and interests with the old Jacksonians. In domestic politics, Jacksonians tend to be suspicious of the federal government, resistant to the claims of the progressive and bureaucratic state, but strongly committed to government transfers and entitlements believed primarily to be protecting middle-class Americans.

Jacksonians mix conservative and liberal beliefs in ways that frequently confound those unfamiliar with this most distinctive and widespread of American subcultures. They are both populist and instinctively egalitarian; the Jacksonian belief that all working members of the folk community are equal in dignity and rights to everyone else was, historically, a cornerstone of American democracy. Yet at the same time, Jacksonian tribal feeling has at times been a major support of Jim Crow legislation, the exclusion of Chinese immigrants, the rise of the KKK, and other dark episodes in American history. Like Andrew Jackson himself, Jacksonians express some of the highest and lowest elements in the American character.

Jacksonians' expectations of politicians tend to be low and their engagement with politics can be erratic, but when Jacksonians find a charismatic leader in troubled times, they can exhibit great loyalty and persistence. In quite different ways, George Washington, Thomas Jefferson, Andrew Jackson, Abraham Lincoln, both Roosevelts, Jack Kennedy, and Ronald Reagan all found ways to engage Jacksonian America.

Bill Clinton owes much of his political success to his fluent command, increasingly rare among American elites, of Jacksonian language and ideology. Later in the twenty-first century, Jacksonians would prove to be the most committed and persistent elements in Donald Trump's political coalition.

While many American policymakers think of foreign policy in terms of opportunities—creating a global order, spreading human rights, promoting democracy, fostering economic development—Jacksonians take a more realist, even tribal approach. They are much more motivated by dangers and threats. Jacksonians are suspicious of free trade agreements and of human rights crusades. They would far rather fight a war for oil than a war to build democracy in West Kleptostan. They can tolerate foreign dictators quite well—as long as those dictators don't challenge or threaten the United States. Partly because so many Jacksonians have military experience, Jacksonians are not in awe of the military establishment. They know very well that the Pentagon wastes money and plans poorly. While successful generals can become Jacksonian heroes, staff officers and Pentagon administrators in gold braid do not necessarily command much admiration. Even so, Jacksonians believe that national defense is the most important reason we have a national government and are willing to support a large defense establishment.

Historically, Jacksonians are sometimes an irresistible force in American politics, and sometimes an immovable object. After triggering events like Pearl Harbor and 9/11, Jacksonian America demanded vigorous and even harsh action against those responsible. At other times, Jacksonian resistance can block overseas deployments and scuttle treaties. When Jacksonians are fully roused, as they were after Pearl Harbor or early in the Cold War, they become a dominant political force, and no president or Congress can disregard their views. At other times, and on many issues, Jacksonians tune out the noises coming from the political system which proceeds by and large as if they didn't exist.

Jacksonians look at world events very differently from most American and European policy experts and foreign policy professionals. Jacksonians are not great believers in just war theory or in a robust role for international law. In any war, Jacksonians believe in using all the available force to win; Sherman's March to the Sea is an excellent example of Jacksonian ideas of warfare at work. In wars against "dishonorable opponents," like the Japanese in World War II who, Jacksonians believed, carried out a dishonorable "sneak attack" at Pearl Harbor and then went on to mistreat American prisoners of war, Jacksonians believe in taking off the gloves. With full-throated Jacksonian approval, Japan was subjected to the most extensive and brutal bombing campaign in human history, with total casualties in the hundreds of thousands in the six months between March 1945 and the end of the war.[26]

Jacksonian attitudes in foreign policy contain what can look like an odd and troubling mix of Manichaean dichotomies and realist beliefs. Jacksonians are deeply skeptical about attempts to build a liberal international order based on human rights and democracy. They have little faith in international institutions and believe that many foreign countries are incapable, at least for now, of establishing democratic governments and prosperous market societies. They think about foreign affairs in terms of threats and security questions, as I said, and they have more confidence in the Pentagon on the whole than in the State Department or USAID. In the early years of Israel's existence, when it was perceived as the weak darling of internationalists, Jacksonians were neither interested nor impressed. Over time, their attitudes toward Israel changed and this would have important consequences for the Republican Party and for the politics of Israel policy in the United States.

JACKSONIAN ZION

Strength is the foundation of the Jacksonian affinity for Israel. Jacksonians admire strength. They can be romantic retrospectively about past heroes and they admire courage against the odds and last stands. But they prefer winners to the "beautiful losers" favored by more sentimental observers of international politics. Israel's triumph in the Six-Day War while the United States was struggling in the quagmires of Vietnam first drew the attention of Jacksonian America to the Jewish state. The refusal of the Arabs to make peace afterward, and the adoption of terrorist tactics by some Palestinians, heightened what Jacksonians saw as a contrast between a strong and upstanding nation and, again from their particular and partial point of view, what they saw as its cowardly, incompetent, and treacherous opponents.

It is not just Israeli strength that appeals to Jacksonian America. It is Israel's approach to power. This can be hard for people not raised in a Jacksonian milieu to understand: some of the very things that make

Israel most unpopular around the world actually make Jacksonians respect Israel more.

Jacksonian beliefs about war, for example, mesh well with some of Israel's more controversial policies. When Hamas or Islamic Jihad fighters send a few rockets from Gaza into Israel, and Israel occasionally retaliates with its air force and tanks, much of the world is appalled by what it sees as a "disproportionate" Israeli response. Overreacting to a provocation is, many feel, as bad as launching the original attack. This is not how many Israelis feel, and American Jacksonians agree.

For Jacksonian America, the most logical and appropriate response to a terrorist attack is a massive response that breaks the will and the ability of the enemy to resume hostilities. While one should try to avoid civilian casualties if possible, the original aggressor bears all the guilt for all the deaths caused in the ensuing conflict. When American Jacksonians see Israelis launching massive attacks on Gaza and talking about trying to break Hamas in response to rocket attacks, the Jacksonians support the effort and wish Israel well. Far from agreeing with European and other critics of Israel's response, Jacksonians wish that more of the NATO allies shared what they see as the refreshingly honest and realistic approach to war that the Israelis have. They believe that if more countries had the courage and determination of the Israelis, there would be many fewer terrorists and the world would have more peace.

Jacksonians see no problems with the controversial American prison for captured enemy combatants established at Guantánamo during the Bush administration. Similarly, they are comfortable with Israeli actions on the West Bank that many find unacceptable. Jacksonians tend to support strong and even harsh measures against terrorists, and they think the job of American presidents is to protect the American people regardless of what squeamish human rights lawyers think about the methods employed. While Israel's actual policies are often more restrained than Jacksonians would like, and its military is far more concerned about legality than the average American Jacksonian would be in a similar situation, nevertheless Israel's clear determination to defend its people and its military resonates deeply with Jacksonian ideas about how a country should defend itself.

A strong U.S.-Israel alliance appeals to most Jacksonians in part because they like Israel and admire its approach to world politics, but Jacksonians instinctively think in "America First" terms and their support for an alliance ultimately depends on their views of whether they think an alliance with Israel is good for the United States. Where Wilsonians look for common values in choosing allies, Jacksonians look for allies with similar interests, and by interests Jacksonians mean primarily enemies. Believing as they do that fear is the most important factor in international relations, Jacksonians look for allies who can help the United States overcome the enemies it fears. Believing as they do that nations do not act altruistically, Jacksonians look for countries who fear the same enemies that the United States fears and, ideally, fear them more than we do. That fear, and their eagerness to win American help against their enemies, will keep allies helpful and loyal. Jacksonians also look for evidence that an ally or potential ally is committed to its own security. They do not think it is America's place to provide free guarantees to foreign countries that refuse to invest in their own defense. America's help should go to those who are prepared to earn it.

From this standpoint, Israel appears to be an exemplary ally. The United States and Israel share so many enemies that anti-U.S. signs can often be found at anti-Israel rallies and that those most prominently associated with the cry of "Death to America!" will often also be found shouting "Death to Israel!"

Ever since the oil embargos and the seizure of American diplomatic hostages during the Iranian Revolution, Jacksonian America has mostly seen the Muslim Middle East as dominated by the hatred of America and everything it stands for. The wars in the Gulf, the long-standing hostility of the Iranian regime, and the attacks of 9/11 further strengthened this impression.

The rise of the threat of Middle East terrorism has made Israel's position seem even more sympathetic to Jacksonians. To Jacksonians deeply concerned about what they believe to be serious and long-term threats from the Middle East, Israel looks like a good ally to have, if only because Israel's geographical position and relations with militant Islam put it even more firmly in the crosshairs than the United States. Israel needs American help in what is ultimately a war of survival, and so Americans can count on Israel being there through thick and thin. Rather than wanting to distance themselves from Israel in the hope that this will deflect the terrorists' wrath from the United States, Jacksonians see Israel's regional unpopularity as an asset because it ensures that Israel is fully committed to the common cause. Beyond that, Jacksonians do not believe that it is either prudent or wise to let fear of your enemies make you abandon your friends. This, in their view, is cowardly and dishonorable behavior that signals weakness and invites attack.

Israel's enemies have always, despite their best efforts, been Israel's most helpful friends. It may not be rational in the sense that non-Jacksonians understand the meaning of the word, but every time a violent mob burns American and Israeli flags side by side in the Islamic world, every time a United Nations office issues what to Jacksonian ears sounds like a grotesquely one-sided condemnation of Israel for behaving exactly as Jacksonians under enemy fire would behave, every time a suicide bomber kills innocent people out of a twisted and fanatical belief, every time a village of Christians flees their ancestral homes in terror, American Jacksonians become less interested in the case against the Jewish state and more eager to deepen our alliance with it.

Finally, Israel holds up its end of the bargain when it comes to defending itself. While rich countries like Germany reject any and all American requests to pay an appropriate share of NATO's costs, Israel invests in excellent military forces and is not afraid to use them. In 2020, Israel spent 5.6 percent of its GDP on defense, compared to 2.2 percent in Britain, 2.1 percent in France, 1.4 percent in Germany, and 3.7 percent in the United States.[27] For many Jacksonians, Israel is a better, more trustworthy, and more useful ally than most of the NATO countries. While both Germany and Japan have had major American bases on their soil since World War II, the American military presence in Israel is minimal. Israel does more, many Jacksonians feel, and asks less, than many of the American allies that coast on American security guarantees while criticizing both Israel and the United States nonstop.

The alliance with Israel, far from looking like a strategic liability to Jacksonians, looks like a source of strength and prestige. One advantage, in the Jacksonian mind, is the signal Israel's success sends about the wisdom of alliances with America. Israel is a small country that (until recent oil and gas discoveries changed the picture somewhat) had few natural resources and a much smaller population than many of its enemies. Criticized by Europe, ostracized by the Muslim world, Israel has only one true friend in the world—and look at how well Israel is doing. It is prosperous, extremely well armed and well integrated into global financial markets. The message to other countries: there is only one country in the world whose friendship you need. If the United States is your ally, even if everyone else turns against you, life will go well. Jacksonians believe that this perception around the world will help keep America safe.

Similarly, ever since the United States became Israel's principal arms supplier during the Cold War, Israel's wars and confrontations with its neighbors have served to showcase the superiority of American technology and weapons. When Israel's American-supplied arsenal overmasters its rivals in conventional warfare, governments all over the world get two messages. First, you want to have the kind of relationship with the Americans in which you can buy their top-shelf hardware, and second, you do not want the Americans so annoyed with you that they sell the really powerful gear to your opponents.

Finally, Jacksonians have come to see Israel as a kind of symbolic surrogate of the United States. Their view of Israeli Jews—as a Chosen People with a unique message, embattled in a hostile world by the enemies of God, united against hostile outsiders in an unbreakable unity of kith and kin—applies the ideas that Bible-reading Protestant Christians in the British Isles and the American colonies once held about the ancient Hebrews to the Jews of today. It is easy for scholars and skeptics to take issue with this vision, but its roots are deeply implanted in American culture.

As Israel has gone from strength to strength it has become a kind of talisman for many American Jacksonians. Recent generations have seen Jacksonian America undergo a series of shocks and challenges. The civil rights movement undermined long-held ideas about the nature of American society and forced Jacksonians to confront some of its historical demons. A culture and belief system shaped in a rural, ethnically homogeneous America had to adapt to life in multiethnic suburbs. Feminism and the gay rights movement forced Jacksonians to take another look at the relationship of their traditional social values and assumptions to the individualism that Jacksonian culture cherishes. As Jacksonian America struggles to make its peace with a host of new forces and new ideas, signs of continuity with the past are welcome. The modern Israeli success story appears to vindicate both Jacksonian principles and biblical religion; there is a balm in Gilead that soothes the wounded soul.

Apocalypse, admiration, alliance, identification: these pillars of the relationship between Israel and Jacksonian America would only deepen after the attacks of 9/11. With Jacksonian and evangelical support more critical than ever to a Republican president, George W. Bush would struggle to integrate the convictions of his base into a strategic response to terrorism. Both his successes and his failures would reflect the unexpected tensions of a twenty-first century that did not appear to be following an American script.

18

Apocalypse Now:
Israel Policy Under George W. Bush

ow's the first Jewish president doing?" Barbara Bush acidly greeted her son on a telephone call after he gave a 2002 speech demanding that the Palestinians break with Yasser Arafat's leadership.[1] George W. Bush interpreted that comment as an expression of both parents' disapproval at his rupture with the conventional approach to the peace process.

Israel policy would create discomfort in both the Bush family and the Republican Party during the George W. Bush presidency. As the heir to the most successful American political dynasty since the heyday of the Adams family, the younger Bush was rooted in the history and networks of the old establishment. The Bush dynasty like much of that establishment had deep ties with the oil industry and, consequentially, with countries in the Middle East that went back in some cases for generations. But in the party over which the younger Bush presided the remnants of the establishment were fighting a long rearguard action against Ronald Reagan's Sun Belt coalition, and strong support for Israel was, as we've seen, one of the bonds holding the rising coalition together.

Texas, the most important state in the Sun Belt as California shifted to blue, presented a particularly complicated picture. As a leading player in the global hydrocarbon industry, Texas was a major focus of Gulf Arab investment, and links between Texas businesses and universities and the Arab world were strong. Yet pro-Israel sentiment was deeply embedded in Texas's religious and political culture. After 9/11, the administration scrambled, not always successfully, to respond to the challenge of Middle East–based religious terrorism in ways that at times disappointed and baffled both wings of the Republican Party.

Grounded in the older Republican tradition, the George H. W. Bush administration sought to avoid the costs in the Arab and Islamic world of any perceived excessive American support of Israel. That traditional caution was reinforced by the international politics of the 1991 Gulf War. To hold the international coalition against Saddam Hussein's conquest of Kuwait together, the first Bush administration made large promises to Gorbachev and took pains to demonstrate its sympathy for the Arab and Palestinian viewpoints.[2] When the Bush 41 administration tried to pressure Israel to halt West Bank and Gaza settlement construction by suspending loan guarantees for relocating Soviet Jews in 1991, the move was bitterly criticized by pro-Israel groups in the United States[3] and assisted Bill Clinton's successful attempt to oust the elder Bush.

Yet while the old GOP establishment—which included many of George H. W. Bush's associates—was still influential and represented by Colin Powell and, as was assumed at the time, by Dick Cheney, Donald Rumsfeld, and George Shultz protegée Condoleezza Rice in W's administration, the younger Bush was personally and politically much more attuned to Israel and its American supporters. The center of gravity in Republican politics had continued to move south and west since the elder Bush's term in office, and the next generation of the Bush family, despite its continuing habit of returning to the Northeast for prep school and summer vacations, was more closely connected to Sun Belt conservatism than the elder Bush had ever been. George W. had risen to national prominence as governor of Texas; his brother Jeb was elected governor of Florida. Immersed in a milieu where Christian Zionism and a symbolic identification of the Israeli and American causes were powerful cultural influences, W came to the White House with a much stronger emotional connection to Israel than any Republican president except Ronald Reagan—and unlike Reagan, who had a visceral dislike of Ariel Sharon, Bush admired the man who would dominate the Israeli political scene in the years following 9/11.[4] Trying to balance his pro-Israel instincts with his deeply felt sense of the country's energy interests in the treacherous circumstances following the 9/11 attacks would test his political skills—and not just with his mother.

To this day, George W. Bush is one of the most misunderstood of modern American presidents. The Bush administration came at a time when the inadequacies of America's post–Cold War vision of the world were leading the country's leadership into an intellectual and strategic quagmire, but many of the country's opinion leaders and policymakers were still committed to a naive reading of the prospects for liberal order. It was easier and more soothing to blame the shortcomings of Bush policies (and there were many shortcomings to blame) for the growing disarray than to take stock of the challenges that were disrupting the hoped-for transition to a peaceful, democratic, and post-historical world.

Beyond this, the Bush presidency both helped to cause, and suffered from, a dramatic intensification of the political polarization that marked the Clinton years leading both supporters and opponents to interpret events in hyper-partisan ways. For some, George W. Bush was courageously defending the United States against the gravest of dangers; for others, he was a crazed, incompetent warmonger and a danger to American democracy. That polarization would continue to deepen and intensify during the Obama and Trump administrations, making a clear-sighted and dispassionate view of the Bush years difficult to achieve.

Add to these factors the rapid dramatic shifts in both strategy and tone that marked the Bush administration's response to changing conditions, the centrality of the poorly understood Middle East to American policy following the attacks of 9/11, and the simplistic and polarizing nature of the American debate over Israel policy and it is, perhaps, not hard to see why Americans have struggled to come to terms with both the achievements and the shortcomings of this momentous presidency.

Bush's reputation as a strongly pro-Israel president was already well established before the 9/11 terror attacks. His problems with the foreign policy establishment began when he turned a deaf ear to pleas from European allies and the old Republican establishment to launch a major diplomatic effort to calm Israeli-Palestinian relations early in his term.[5] The Second Intifada was believed in much of the Arab world and beyond to have been triggered by Ariel Sharon's controversial decision in 2000 to take a walk through the Haram al-Sharif, the area containing the Dome of the Rock and the Al-Aqsa mosque in the Old City of Jerusalem.[6] The violence in the Holy Land, with daily reports of clashes between Israeli security forces and Palestinian demonstrators, inflamed public opinion against both Israel and the United States across the Arab world and in much of Europe.

This was precisely the kind of situation that the foreign policy establishment believed it was Washington's job to manage—and Sharon's apparent role in creating it demonstrated why, in their view, Israel was a strategic liability for the United States and needed to be held at arm's length. Experienced Washington hands wise in the complications of the Middle East might not believe that a peace process begun under such unpromising conditions might actually create peace, but they appreciated the international benefits Washington reaped by at least appearing to engage. Secretary of State Colin Powell was ready and eager to set forth on a new round of diplomacy. In the opening months of the new administration, Powell and many senior figures in both Democratic and Republican wings of the Washington foreign policy establishment were baffled by 43's reluctance to take what they saw as a natural, necessary, and virtually risk-free step.

Bush's decision to remain aloof from peace talks was hailed by some and deplored by others as reflecting a robust pro-Israel stance. Bush's strong and heartfelt condemnations of terrorism as well as his emerging personal rapport with Prime Minister Sharon—widely seen as a hardliner's hardliner—further cemented the impression that the new American president was either from conviction or opportunism determined to drive American foreign policy toward a relentlessly pro-Israel posture. Bush's response to the 9/11 attacks would further entrench this view.

The Shock of 9/11

The September 11, 2001, terrorist attacks on the World Trade Center and the Pentagon dramatically if temporarily increased the importance of the Middle East in American policy and politics. For roughly a dozen years following those attacks, the Middle East would be the central focus of American foreign policy, and both President Bush and President Obama would feel that their presidencies could not succeed unless voters were confident that they were reducing the threat to Americans of fanatical religious terrorism.

Overall, America's Middle East policy between 9/11 and the end of the Trump presidency can be divided into two eras. Between 2001 and the collapse of the Arab Spring movements for democracy in many Middle

Eastern countries, the United States would pursue a transformational strategy in the Middle East. While the Bush and Obama administrations differed sharply over tactics, they agreed that the best, and in the long run the only, way to address the specter of religious violence was to eliminate the "root causes" of the radical ideology that inspired it. The lack of political freedom in much of the Middle East combined with the failure of most countries in the region to provide rising living standards and good jobs for young people made radical ideology attractive, and as long as those conditions persisted, terror groups would find support. To stop the terror, we needed to address the social conditions that caused it.

That this vast transformation seemed possible reflected the post–Cold War optimism of the American establishment. If history was over, and the tide of western-style modernization was rolling across the world, it could as easily roll across the Middle East as anywhere else. In 2001 leading Americans for the most part still believed that China was moving toward liberal democracy, that democracy was becoming stronger in Latin America and sub-Saharan Africa, and that Russian backsliding was a temporary phenomenon with no lessons and few consequences for the rest of the world. The Middle East was an anomalous region, the only place on earth where economic and political liberalism were failing to advance. After 9/11, that needed to change.

As President Bush wrote in his memoirs, "For most of the Cold War, America's priority in the Middle East was stability. . . . After 9/11, I decided that the stability we had been promoting was a mirage. The focus of the freedom agenda would be the Middle East."[7] This implied a major change in American objectives and in the resources needed to achieve them. After 9/11, practically unlimited resources were available to the Bush administration for the purpose of preventing new attacks, and the Bush administration began to take stock of the policy changes that needed to happen.

The old stability agenda presumed close and enduring cooperation with conservative Arab allies like Egypt, Saudi Arabia, and the other Gulf states. This had been the mainstay of Republican thinking about the Middle East since World War II. The younger Bush, however, was prepared to break away. A freedom agenda would inevitably be interpreted as a threat by those regimes, as none of them saw democratic transitions as either possible or desirable. Indeed, it appeared that the conservative regimes deliberately suppressed liberal political movements while allowing more space to Islamist parties, then fended off American calls for reform by pointing to the "Islamist radicals" who were likely to benefit from any changes in power.

The other dimension of the transformation agenda involved reducing the sense among many Muslims that the United States specifically, and the Christian and post-Christian West more generally, was their enemy. This was a daunting task, and both George W. Bush and Barack Obama believed that the unresolved Palestinian issue needed to be addressed if the United States and the Middle East were to build a better relationship.

The transformation agenda was not a success. By the end of Obama's first term, Americans were no longer confident that we knew how to eliminate poverty and dictatorship in the Middle East, and the mood of the country shifted. As year followed year with no successful repetition of the 9/11 attacks, and as the importance of Middle East oil to the American economy gradually declined, American priorities began to shift away from the Middle East toward the Indo-Pacific theater in world politics, where China appeared to be emerging as the new great power rival to the United States. In Obama's second term and under President Trump, policymakers sought to extricate the U.S. from the Middle East as much as possible. The Obama team thought that this could best be accomplished by reaching out to Iran. The Trump team thought that building on existing alliances with Israel and the Gulf Arab states offered a faster and safer way to reduce commitments—but both administrations were looking to scale back American involvement.

The move to reduce America's Middle East commitments intersected with an increasing sense among many Americans that the entire post-1945 framework of American foreign policy needed a rethink. Here again, despite their enormous differences in ideology, character, and political style, Obama and Trump seemed to converge. Both displayed impatience with traditional allies who were playing Uncle Sam as a sucker. Both believed that the United States could no longer afford the kind of global leadership that had characterized the last seventy years. Both believed that American foreign policy could and should change fundamentally in the twenty-first century; both were willing to ignore established conventions and consider approaches that "The Blob," as Obama aide Ben Rhodes characterized the Washington foreign policy establishment, had firmly rejected since the time of President Truman.[8]

That two such radically different leaders supported by such radically different constituencies were both willing to challenge long-standing foreign policy orthodoxy is a sign of just how weak the post-historical consensus had become.

═════

That era of disillusionment and disengagement lay in the future as the George W. Bush administration grappled with the consequences of the 9/11 terror attacks. In the immediate aftermath of the attacks, the vast majority of Americans experienced a wave of unity and solidarity, but such moments rarely last. As the wars in Afghanistan and Iraq saw hundreds of thousands of American troops engaged in bloody combat across the region while Americans nervously awaited new terror attacks, debates over the wars and over Middle East strategy more broadly inevitably brought Israel policy under the spotlight.

As the Iraq War turned into a quagmire and the weapons of mass destruction the administration had used to make the case for war failed to appear, the American Middle East debate became more bitter still. That Bush was a minority president, whose disputed election involved a controversial Supreme Court decision over votes in Florida, a state governed by Jeb Bush, was momentarily forgotten in the emotional outpouring that followed 9/11. But as more Americans questioned the decision to invade Iraq, and the vicious guerrilla struggle led to an indefinite prolongation of an American combat role, resentment over the contested election fused with anger over the war to further inflame a national political climate already stressed by the partisan warfare of the Clinton years. With an assist from the developing power of social media, Americans got their first taste of the ugly polarization that would mark their politics in the early decades of the new century, and the question of Israel policy was inevitably drawn into the melee.

While Israel policy itself was never at the center of American debates over how to respond to the threat of terror after 9/11, those debates had large implications for America's Israel policy—and the importance of Israel in American culture, among both supporters and opponents, helped to make those debates more bitter. In the end, polarization over Middle East policy would continue from the Bush and Obama administrations into the Trump years, drawing from and feeding the growing rancor and divisions in American society as a whole. With the wisdom of hindsight one can say that at least some of this rancor was due to the sad truth that neither of the principal strategic camps into which American society and the American foreign policy machine divided after 9/11 offered a genuinely workable approach to a new and quite difficult problem in foreign affairs.

The 9/11 attacks confronted the country with new and urgent but also deeply perplexing foreign policy problems. That an attack on this scale could be mounted by, essentially, a private organization forced Americans to reevaluate the nature of strategic threats and of such concepts as deterrence. If transnational terrorists secured a nuclear bomb, deterrence might well not work with them. If a nuclear attack comes from a state, you at least know where to retaliate. But what if it comes from an elusive organization whose agents are everywhere but has no homeland or capital city? And the United States had invested hundreds of billions, even trillions, of dollars in building up its capabilities to defeat state-led forces in conventional warfare. Did these attacks mean that much of that investment was now obsolete?

Within weeks of the 9/11 attacks, as toxic smoke still poured from the rubble of the World Trade Center and Manhattan struggled to restore transit services, packages with weapons-grade anthrax began to appear at news organizations and political offices.[9] Were the anthrax attacks related to the hijackings? In any case, they heightened the American sense of new risks and dangers and raised the specter of chemical and biological attacks with, potentially, even greater consequences than anything seen on 9/11.

Questions proliferated. Was radical Islamism an emerging new ideological challenge to liberal capitalist democracy? Just how far into the world of Islam did this theology of hate extend? Was it a fringe movement like the radical and sometimes violent sectarian movements that emerge in Christianity from time to time or was it closer to the Islamic mainstream? Was it the inevitable result of the intersection of the poverty and corrupt dictatorships found through so much of the Islamic world with a civilizational and religious rage at centuries of humiliation at the hands of the at least nominally Christian West? Or were the violent radicals, as they claimed, the "true face" of Islam, the most authentic form of a religion that counted more than one billion adherents around the world? Was the Saudi Wahabi state to blame for this fanatical band providing vast sums of money in the form of both public and private funding for radical preachers around the world?

There were other questions as well. The attacks of 9/11 came at a time of rapid population growth in the Islamic world, and at a time of growing migration by Muslims to the advanced industrial democracies.[10] Did these migrants and their children pose a security threat to western countries? Were Muslims assimilable? Should Americans and Europeans worry about a "fifth column" of terror sympathizers at home? Were the prisons producing new terrorists?

In the aftermath of the attacks, it was difficult to assess how much danger movements like Al-Qaeda posed to the United States and western democracies at home, and to vital American interests (especially to the security of the oil states) abroad. And how did one defend against an ideological movement that spread through propaganda and civil society? Was a defensive strategy even possible? How could one "harden" enough targets in the West to keep the public secure? Did this involve Israeli levels of domestic security, guarding against gunmen and suicide bombers in every mall, hijackers on every plane, dirty nuclear bombs on every container ship?

Assuming that while the contest was in part a military and security problem it was at its core an ideological one, how could the non-Muslim West address the challenge at its roots? How does western liberalism win the fight against Islamist fanaticism? Presumably this meant trying to find allies in the Muslim world, but who were they? Were they the military dictators and traditional monarchs who had long experience of maintaining public order in these turbulent countries, or were those repressive regimes part of the problem? Were we in trouble because for too long we had supported authoritarian regimes for the sake of stability, or were these regimes with all their faults our only bulwark against something much worse?

And if we were to turn away from the status quo regimes, to whom should we turn next? There were the pro-western, well-educated liberals who seemed entirely at home with western ideas and political forms, but were they too weak, too inexperienced, and too isolated from mass opinion to replace the old monarchs and dictators? Then there were the "democratic Islamists" like those associated with the Muslim Brotherhood in Egypt and their ideological soulmate Recep Tayyip Erdoğan in

Turkey. Were these true moderates who, if empowered, could marginal-ize the real radicals by offering a genuinely Islamic but also democratic and effective form of governance? Were they wolves in sheep's clothing, who once in power would impose dictatorships of their own, and who would use their new power to promote an expansionist and narrow form of Islamist ideology?

Or what about Iran? While Iran billed itself as a revolutionary Islamist power, it was Shi'a, and the new extremists were Sunni. Could the enemy of my enemy be my friend? Could Iran be a partner in the struggle against Al-Qaeda and its associates, and if so, what kind of partner and on what terms?

Finally, there was the question of Israel. Was Israel an important asset, given its military and intelligence capabilities and its long experi-ence with terrorists based in Arab Muslim societies, or would even the appearance of closer U.S.-Israel cooperation inflame public opinion in the Islamic world and simply make Al-Qaeda and other similar groups more attractive? Or, as the George H. W. Bush administration had done in the 1991 Gulf War, was there a way to offset the consequences of an Israeli alliance by adroit management and peace diplomacy? In American politics there was an additional question: Did the 9/11 attacks "prove" that Israeli hardliners were justified in their tough and distrust-ful stance and that one could not really make peace with Islamist fanat-ics, or did the attacks "prove" that hardline, uncompromising policies simply stoked the fires of hate, leading to more conflict and more danger down the road? Would the United States need to force Israel to change its ways or, failing that, to separate itself from the impenitent and pro-vocative Jewish state?

Over time, some of these questions have found at least temporary and partial answers, but the problem of radical and violent groups emerging from the culture of Islamism remains a serious concern for American defense and foreign policy more than two decades after 9/11. While no single attack has killed as many people or inflicted a psychological shock as great as those attacks, the United States and many other countries have dedicated significant resources to a struggle that has by no means come to an end.

Given the stakes and the complexity of the problem, the debate over how to respond to 9/11 would have been intensely conducted under any circumstances. As it happened, the debate exposed many of the cultural and ideological rifts in American society that would do so much to shape the contentious politics of coming years.

If the West needed to wage an ideological war against this movement of fanatics, it needed at least a rough sketch of what the West stood for. During the Cold War it had been relatively easy for the Truman and Eisenhower administrations to develop a generic American ideology that could more or less mesh with European ideas about what the West was all about. But the West had become much more fragmented since the 1950s. Did the American consensus on human rights, for example, include or exclude the rights of sexual minorities?

In the United States, these questions exacerbated rising tensions between cultural liberals and conservatives at a time of rapid social change. Social conservatives tended to feel that Americans should respond to the new danger by returning to their cultural and religious roots to find the unity required to defeat the new enemy. Social liberals read the situation quite differently. It was time for America to reach out, to demonstrate its openness to individual Muslims and to Islam as a faith. At the same time, the attacks were an urgent warning that Americans needed to purge themselves from the elements of racism and western imperialism so sadly prevalent in traditional American culture and so firmly rooted in the biases derived from the nation's Christian and European roots.

Those debates played into and exacerbated a growing polarization around the question of world order that had been almost invisible to the establishment. Many American salvationist Christians reject the idea that human effort can build a stable and peaceful world order. More than this, they believe that the final catastrophe will be triggered by precisely what the cosmopolitan technocrats and world order engineers are trying to accomplish: the establishment of a peaceful world order through human means with neither reference nor deference to the God of the Bible in whose hands lies the true fate of the human race.

"Millennial polarization," as one can call political divisions that reflect the impact of conflicting "end of history" scenarios, had begun well before 9/11. While the post–Cold War American establishment considered its commitment to a liberal, secular world-order-building project benign and noncontroversial, many Americans saw these activities in more sinister terms.

In the evangelical world, the 1990s saw the publication of the first volumes of the sixteen-volume series of Left Behind novels by Tim LaHaye and Jerry B. Jenkins, a series whose sales around the world have reached approximately 80 million copies.[11] These novels, grounded in a version of the premillennialist theology that has been one of the sources of Christian Zionism since the mid-nineteenth century, tell of a "global community" under the leadership of the secretary-general of the United Nations who is ultimately revealed as the Antichrist. In short order, the forces of globalism overthrow the American government, ban any form of Christianity that doesn't hew to progressive orthodoxies, destroy the free market economy, and institute a global dictatorship that quickly degenerates into satanic totalitarianism.

The success of these novels—and many similar works by other authors—should not be taken as evidence that their readers fully or even partially accepted their specific outline of Christian theology. But it was or should have been clear to the national political establishment that a substantial portion of the American people were deeply suspicious of what looked superficially like a consensus American policy.

Believers, secular and religious, in a cool and peaceful end of history are fundamentally optimistic about the direction of the world. Humanity is on the road to solving its deepest problems, or at least under the right management, it can be. Globalization in particular is part of the benign revolution that is making humanity less tribal and less backward. New ideas about morality and about gender are part of a kind of ongoing, progressive revelation about how people ought to live together. The spirit of the age can be trusted, human reason is creating a better future, our institutions—while needing reform and improvement—are taking us in a good direction, and the state itself is a positive force for change.

The hot millennialist position was historically more prevalent among those who felt marginalized by the dominant culture and ethos of the country. Those who did not trust or accept the conventional wisdom of the American establishment saw a hot apocalypse coming, one in which the righteousness of God would strip away the vanities and burn off the corruption of the smug and the powerful. Hot millennialism was popular in both the Black and the white South, among poor farmers, immigrants, and the urban dispossessed. It was not always religious; belief that a socialist revolution must destroy the bourgeoisie is the secular equivalent of a hot biblical apocalypse. Redemption comes only after the cleansing and purifying fire.

One characteristic of apocalyptic eras like ours is that ideas about the final destiny of the human race become politically relevant. If the apocalypse seems very far away, differences of opinion about how the apocalypse will unfold when and if it arrives have little political salience. In eras like ours of intruding apocalypse, when the culmination of history seems near at hand, the difference between hot and cool millennial viewpoints can become a determining factor in the way many people understand current events and serves increasingly to shape political affiliations. After the 9/11 attacks the importance of this division to the course of American politics and foreign policy in the twenty-first century is difficult to overstate.

During the Cold War, cool and hot millennialism were both well integrated into the political consensus. Cool millennialists saw the American-led free world as a step toward the creation of a peaceful and progressive world order; hot millennialists saw the Soviet Union as an atheistic power attempting to impose an anti-Christian order on the world. That such a power existed focused the fears and apocalyptic forebodings of many Graham-era evangelicals; that it was America's opponent legitimated American foreign policy, including its world-order-building aspects, in their eyes. The end of the Cold War meant the end of that consensus, and the consequences of its gradual unraveling continue to be felt.

Hot and cool millennialists responded to the shock of 9/11 in very different ways. Those looking to a cool millennium of orderly progress and developing world order interpreted the attack as a call both to intensify and reconfigure America's order-building efforts. The existence of the pathology that led to such hatred needed to be dealt with, and the United States would have to double down on efforts to create a democratic and liberal order in the Middle East in order to get the process of benign historical transformation back on track. That the attacks were on the United States, that the attackers expressed hatred for western values and policies, and that the attackers came from undemocratic, religiously repressive societies where poverty and inequality were rife, confirmed the confidence that what the world needed was more America, and what America needed to do to meet the challenge was to become . . .

more American: to live up to its values more consistently and to press its transformation agenda with more energy and force—while becoming more culturally sensitive to the specific challenges of building liberal order in the Middle East.

Hot millennium evangelicals also interpreted the attacks as bolstering their worldview. The attacks on the United States by Israel-hating, Christianity-hating, America-hating religious fanatics confirmed their view of history as following the trajectory of biblical prophecy. The vaunted peace process of the secular globalists had collapsed into chaos and war; instead of a liberal world order we were moving into an era of religious conflict of unpredictable dimensions. That Al-Qaeda hated the United States both because it rejected Islam and because it supported Israel made the conflict look like a religious conflict to many Americans—and simultaneously reinforced their belief that in this apocalyptic age, Israel stands at the center of world history and that those who hate Israel are at war with God.

The events of 2001 reinforced this identification of the Israeli, American, and divine causes. The summer of 2001 saw a wave of suicide bomb attacks across Israel as the violence of the Second Intifada surged. Twenty-one people were killed at the Dolphinarium nightclub in Tel Aviv in June. As attacks, mostly from Hamas with some from a group calling itself Islamic Jihad, swept across Israel and the Palestinian Territories, many Palestinians celebrated the suicide bomb as a Palestinian tactic that could force the Israelis to come to terms. Two attacks on September 9 had left seventeen dead and three wounded; further attacks would continue through the fall. Israel and the United States were, it felt to many Americans, under attack from the same forces.[12] We needed to stand together.

From the Bush administration's point of view, Israel was a policy asset as well as a political one. As the U.S. rushed frantically to upgrade security, Israel was the country that had the most experience. Israel had the know-how and in many cases the contacts and sources that could accelerate the buildup of American intelligence capabilities and the integration of overseas and domestic intelligence that was Washington's most urgent priority in the aftermath of the attacks.

For many Americans, the attacks seemed to demonstrate that the process of the intrusion of the apocalypse into daily life had taken another lurch forward, and that the hot apocalypse toward which we were headed had a distinctively biblical shape to it. Russia might not be targeting the United States with nuclear missiles, but radical terrorists were actively looking to wreak as much havoc in America as possible. Would the next wave of attackers detonate a dirty bomb (an explosive device intended to scatter radioactive material) in an American city? Would they unleash bioweapons to bring on a plague? The existential fears of the Cold War era returned as Americans from President Bush on down worried about the potentially devastating consequences of anti-Christian, anti-Israel, and anti-American terror groups gaining access to weapons of mass destruction.

The New Prudence and the Iraq War

Contrary to some media speculation at the time, neither President Bush nor the circle of senior officials around him saw 9/11 as the opening scene of a Tim LaHaye apocalyptic novel. Bush was not expecting a Rapture, a Great Tribulation, or the arrival of the Antichrist at the podium of the U.N. Nor did Bush hand over control of American foreign policy to a cabal of pro-Israel neoconservatives who ordered the invasion of Iraq to satisfy the elders of Zion.

But the increasingly apocalyptic tenor of the times did play a role in the decision that would define the Bush presidency more than any other. Bush believed, as did Vice President Cheney and other key policymakers, that the potential that terror groups like Al-Qaeda could obtain chemical, biological, or nuclear weapons of mass destruction had changed the rules of world politics.[13] Rational state actors, we had learned during the Cold War and our long coexistence with the Soviet Union and its nuclear arsenal, could be deterred from the use of such weapons by the sure and certain threat of an annihilating response. The "balance of terror," as Canadian statesman Lester Pearson called the resulting standoff, had kept the peace; no American or Soviet leader would order a nuclear strike that would provoke an equally devastating riposte. The balance of terror might have been a permanent Sword of Damocles hanging over the head of the human race, but it was a terror one could live with.[14]

The events of 9/11 changed those rules. If a nonstate actor like Al-Qaeda, neither attached to nor responsible for any particular nation or place, could paralyze America's biggest city, disrupt air travel worldwide, and send the American economy into a sharp but brief recession, what was the meaning of deterrence? And while nonstate actors were unlikely to develop nuclear weapons programs of their own, the existence of an undeterrable third party offered nuclear-armed states a way to attack the United States without necessarily facing retaliation. What would prevent a country like Iran, Iraq (assuming that Saddam Hussein had nuclear weapons), or Pakistan from surreptitiously passing nuclear weapons to a terror group for use against the United States? Clearly, nonproliferation had moved to the front burner and the acquisition of nuclear weapons by "rogue states" was so dangerous that the United States might need to go to war to prevent this from happening.

In a less challenging time, as during the Gulf War, the United States aimed to guard a status quo that was both favorable and complex. Although strong action and leadership were sometimes necessary, the best course for the United States was to exercise international leadership more like the board chair of a successful corporation than like an entrepreneur launching a start-up. Faced with an international crisis, an American president should assemble a consensus, work carefully with allies, weigh options carefully, and pursue limited rather than revolutionary objectives. A reputation for sound judgment was an important asset for U.S. power and should not lightly be hazarded.

That strategy, Bush and his closest advisors believed, had to change in the wake of 9/11. Facing the literally apocalyptic threat of a new age of terrorists armed with the deadliest chemical, biological, and nuclear weapons that the human mind has created to date, they believed the danger of inaction was greater than the danger of moving too fast. The United States would not only have to step up its monitoring of terror groups around the world. It would have to focus on hostile states developing or possibly developing weapons of mass destruction, and when a state appeared to be engaged in WMD production even as it developed relationships with terror groups, the United States might need to move quickly.

That decision would almost certainly have to be taken in the absence of incontrovertible proof that such activities were taking place. In the past, American intelligence had been blindsided by the Indian nuclear program. It was only after the fact that Americans discovered the full scope of the proliferation activities carried out by Pakistan. The Bush administration would be surprised in 2003 to discover the full extent of Libyan nuclear activity, and in 2007 the Israelis would destroy a Syrian reactor built with North Korean assistance as part of a nuclear weapons program.[15]

Further, the threshold was lower for a dirty bomb. The nightmare that Al-Qaeda or a similar group could put a dirty bomb on a container ship that destroyed the downtown of a major city haunted officials.

True prudence, Bush officials reasoned, might under these circumstances require launching a war against a country whose nuclear program was in the gray zone—where we did not know exactly how far the program had progressed or indeed whether the program was real or merely nominal. And if such a war were to be launched, the half measures of the Gulf War could no longer be tolerated: the war would need to be fought to its end, the offending regime overturned, and a new government established under conditions that ensured against a repetition of the danger.

Initially popular in a country still reeling from the shock of 9/11, the 2003 invasion of Iraq would dominate the rest of Bush's presidency.[16] In its initial stages, the war unified the Sun Belt coalition behind the president, but over time the war in Iraq became a millstone around the neck of both the president and his party. The occupation of Iraq transformed into a guerrilla war that, for most of the remaining years of the president's time in office, the United States seemed unable to win. Investigations on the ground did not bear out the sensational charges about Iraq's WMD program that Secretary of State Powell presented to the United Nations in order to make the case for the war.[17] That critical and deeply embarrassing failure undermined faith in the competence or, among many, in the good faith of an administration that appeared to have gotten the country into a major war by mistake. Increasingly in Bush's second term, the administration adopted a strategy of democracy promotion in the Middle East that ran counter to the Jacksonian and Jeffersonian approaches to foreign affairs that were gaining traction among the Republican base—as well as confounded many in the traditional GOP establishment.[18]

The war in Iraq would have many consequences in American politics. In the long run, it would accelerate the breakup of the Sun Belt Republican coalition and open the door to Donald Trump's presidential candidacy. In the short term, the war would reshape both the Israel policy of the Bush presidency and the national debate over the relationship with Israel.

ISRAEL POLICY AND THE IRAQ WAR

It was not immediately obvious that the Iraq War was a strategic and political disaster for Israel. Saddam had been a principal funder of Palestinian terrorism, and his fall was a serious blow to Yasser Arafat. His overthrow, moreover, dealt a final blow to the pan-Arab nationalism that once, under the leadership of men like Egypt's Nasser, had been Israel's deadliest foe. However, by 2003 pan-Arabism was yesterday's worry, and there were others waiting in the wings ready to take over his role as a terrorism funder.

Strategically, while Saddam was a committed enemy of the Jewish state, the collapse of his regime (as many critics of the invasion had pointed out in advance) shattered the balance of power in the Persian Gulf and elevated Iran. With more than double Iraq's population (66 million to 23 million in 2000), four times its territory, more than twice its GDP, a more advanced technological base, and a more capable state structure, Iran was a much more formidable opponent to Israel than Saddam could ever be. Iran and Iraq were bitter foes; the 1980–88 war between them devastated both economies and led to approximately half a million deaths. The destruction of Saddam, and the resulting removal of a much weakened Iraq from the regional power balance, was a disaster not only for Israel but even for the conservative Gulf monarchies that cordially hated the man who invaded Kuwait.

It was worse. Saddam's regime was more than a personal dictatorship. It represented the power of Iraq's Sunni minority over a large and restive Shi'a majority. While Arab nationalism, and an age-old antipathy against Persians, were obstacles to the extension of Iranian influence in Iraq, the deep religious and cultural ties between Iraqi and Iranian Shi'a offered Iran many channels into the power structures of the emerging post-Saddam Iraq. In the wake of the invasion, Iran would create what opponents called a "Shi'a Crescent" stretching from Baghdad to Beirut, confronting Israel with one of the most dangerous challenges in its short but eventful history.

If the war empowered Israel's most dangerous opponent, it also weakened Jerusalem's closest friend. As the Iraq War dragged on and lost popularity in the United States, the American appetite for Middle East engagement contracted. American alliances in both Europe and the Arab world were affected by the war's widening unpopularity abroad, and, until the Surge of 2007–08 improved American military fortunes on the ground, the perception that the United States was unable to deal effectively with the Iraqi insurgency dented American credibility. As Iran grew more powerful, America's willingness to confront it militarily declined.

Politically, the Iraq War also damaged Israel's position inside the United States. The war stimulated the rise of isolationist sentiment on both the left and the right and gave prominence to the views of intellectuals and activists who opposed the U.S.-Israel alliance as part of a larger program of wanting to reduce American commitments overseas. These "realist restrainers," representing a resurgence of the Jeffersonian school in American foreign policy, would breathe new life into anti-Israel politics in the United States even as the deepening polarization of American political life that followed the devolution of the Iraq War into an unpopular quagmire created a new audience for anti-Israel policy arguments. Because a number of the neoconservative supporters of the Iraq War were American Jews, the idea that the unpopular war had been foisted on the United States by Israel and a Jewish led, all-powerful "Israel lobby" whose loyalty was at best doubtful and dual began to spread in the United States and abroad. Not all of the realist restrainers by any means were Vulcanists, and the ideas themselves were neither antisemitic nor even anti-Zionist, but the fallout from the Iraq War would offer Vulcanism around the world a favorable medium for growth.

The new anti-Israel sentiment repeated some of the same arguments that State Department Arabists had been making continuously since the Truman administration, but there was an important difference. Arabists historically supported a far-reaching American foreign policy. They wanted a strong American presence in the Middle East. They opposed a close relationship with Israel because in their view this relationship complicated the essential task of building the strong relations with Arab states that could secure America's Middle East position for the long run.

The realist restrainers of the post-9/11 era opposed both Israeli and Arab alliances. They saw the American presence in the Middle East as a whole as a liability and believed that reducing the American exposure to its conflicts and rivalries was essential to American security. This point of view found support mostly outside the foreign policy establishment and remained deeply unpopular within it. Among politicians and the wider public, however, the idea of realist restraint would only gain credibility as the shortcomings of the post–Cold War globalist consensus became more visible.

By the time a political term has become commonplace among academics, policymakers, and journalists, it has almost invariably lost any definite meaning. In the field of foreign affairs, the term "realist" is such a term; nobody hearing the term can be confident of understanding exactly what meaning its user intends to convey.

Long before the Iraq War, the term "realist" became a catch-all label for different people with quite different perspectives on foreign policy in the United States, but the term "realist restrainer" describes a growing group who opposed what they saw as excessive interventionism in American foreign policy after the Cold War and objected to the underlying premise that the establishment of a liberal world order was the proper or even a possible goal for American national strategy.

The essence of the realist restrainer position was to oppose the global ambitions of post–Cold War American foreign policy and to promote a less ambitious American agenda in keeping with a less expansive and ideological vision of the national interest. The adherents were a mixed group. They included paleo-conservative isolationists like Pat Buchanan, who also believed that U.S. intervention in World War II had been a mistake. They included left-wing critics of American society who believed that the American commitment to a global capitalist system was both a moral disaster and a political obscenity. They included distinguished political scientists and foreign policy commentators who saw globalist foreign policy leading into one absurdity and misadventure after another. And they included a growing chorus of those who objected both to the conceptualization of the "global war on terror" the Bush administration had proclaimed, and to the strategy, especially the war in Iraq, that had been chosen to fight it.

The 9/11 attacks first further marginalized restrainers as a wave of Jacksonian-tinctured patriotism surged across the country, but when the problems of the Iraq War multiplied, the realist restrainer position became much more influential. The core critiques that the restrainers were making about post–Cold War foreign policy began to resonate. American overreach, hubris, overreliance on military measures: to many Americans this looked like an accurate description of the Bush foreign policy. One of the consequences of the Iraq War was the revival of a mass base for opposition to military interventions overseas. In the Bush years, given the Republican tendency to support a Republican president, the antiwar movement seemed, like the antiwar movement of the Vietnam era, to be an expression of the left. But the disillusionment not just with the war in Iraq but with the intense global engagement that post-1990 American grand strategy entailed was if anything more pronounced in the Republican base than among Democrats.

For the realist restrainers, the U.S.-Israel alliance was a problem disguised as a solution. There were no significant foreign policy problems that the alliance helped solve, while there were some significant problems that it either caused or made worse. Most restrainers rejected the extreme, isolationist idea that the United States had no interests in the Middle East but saw those interests in limited and realist terms: maintaining access to Middle Eastern oil, preventing hostile powers from controlling the oil flow. These interests, restrainers like Andrew Bacevich argued, could be safeguarded without an extensive American presence in the region. America's true role was to be an offshore balancer in the Middle East, assembling coalitions if needed to prevent a single power from inside or outside the region seizing control. To this end, a long-term alliance with any country, and especially one as widely disliked as Israel, was a mistake, and simply drew the United States further into quarrels that were not its own.

The 9/11 attacks struck these analysts as the tragic result of excessive American involvement in the region. The long alliance with the Saudis (an alliance that, unlike classic Arabists, realist restrainers deplored) had made the United States a target for those whose principal quarrels were with Middle Eastern governments. The long alliance with Israel made the United States a natural target for the enemies of the Jewish state. For the United States to respond to 9/11 by deepening its entanglements in the region was exactly the wrong step.

Worse, the excessive U.S. focus on the Middle East was distracting the country from more serious problems around the world. Some might point to Latin America, some to China, others still to problems like global public health and climate change, but for the United States to devote immense resources to a conflict that our own poor policy choices had done so much to ignite was to heap folly on folly.

The alliance with Israel looks particularly costly from this perspective. Israel has no oil, and as the experience of the 1991 Gulf War shows, when the United States went to great lengths to keep Israel out of the war, it contributed less than nothing to America's ability to defend Arab allies. Worse, since the alliance is such an affront to Arab opinion, the United States finds itself having to offset the negative impact of the Israeli alliance in the Arab world by making a host of concessions to Arab states, as well as involving ourselves in such time-consuming and (from the standpoint of true American interests) irrelevant sideshows as the endless and fruitless Israeli-Palestinian peace process.

This list of the real-world costs of a useless alliance only scratches the surface of the realist restrainer objections to the U.S.-Israel relationship. In the politics of American foreign policy, realists of all stripes oppose distortions that, in their view, "idealism" imposes on American policymaking. This takes two forms. One is the more familiar set of realist objections to the perceived illusions of "liberal internationalism," progressive pacifism, and the whole catalog of what realists think of as the magical thinking endemic to American culture. Woodrow Wilson bleating about the League of Nations, Henry Wallace mooning sentimentally about winning over Stalin by earning his trust, Jimmy Carter moralizing on the subject of human rights, but also George W. Bush preaching democracy promotion: realists want to cleanse the American foreign policy system of such foolish illusions.

But conventional liberal idealism is just a symptom of the real problem that worries realists and, in their view, creates so many disasters in American policy. The belief that America is a providential nation with a set of duties and obligations in the world that transcend the limited objectives of realist foreign policymaking is, realists believe, dead wrong. For America to succeed in the world, Americans must abandon the idea that America has to promote democracy, human rights, stop war, and promote any number of other good causes through alliances and interventions abroad. If we wish to inspire the world, we should improve our society at home.

Trying to reform the world or to build a "liberal world order" for that matter will be counterproductive, the argument runs. These ideals, however inspiring they may be on their own, leave the United States and the world less well off than they would otherwise be by creating unnecessary enemies, avoidable crises, and an endless series of unwinnable wars for the United States. You try to make the world safe for liberal democracy and human rights—and you end up operating the Abu

Ghraib prison in Iraq while spending your blood and your treasure in an unwinnable war.

From this perspective, the U.S.-Israel alliance is just the outward manifestation of a dangerous cultural construct that empowers the worst kind of idealistic foreign policy in American life. The national fascination with Israel is a shackle that doesn't just chain the United States to a set of bad policies in the Middle East. It is a shackle that chains America to the whole dangerous set of illusions about the nature of history and our place in the world that led the U.S. into one disastrous overreach after another.

Liberal internationalists for the most part hated Bush and hated his approach to the war on terror. But realists could see a connection that escaped both liberal internationalists and Bush-supporting neoconservatives. America's foreign policy for both groups was and had to be about more than just ensuring American security and promoting conventional economic interests. America was a transformational power and it could only be true to itself by embracing a revolutionary global agenda.

The realist restrainers believed that America needed to be disenchanted to flourish, and that the idea that there was or should be a special relationship between the United States and Israel was high on the list of fantasies that needed to go.

This position does not necessarily lead to Vulcanism, and there are many realist restrainers who avoid the pitfall of blaming American Jews for foreign policy choices of which they disapprove. Yet for some realist restrainers there were compelling reasons to look into the question of the "Israel lobby." The alliance was, they believed, so obviously and radically against the American national interest that some explanation was required to show why American policymakers kept returning to it. The Iraq War of 2003 crystallized these concerns for many observers, some of whom would argue that Israel, acting with the support of American neoconservatives, inveigled the United States into the war.

This charge was widespread among foreign and, to a lesser extent, American opponents of the Iraq War, but over time it has lost credibility outside the most fervent centers of anti-Zionist sentiment. The surge in support for this idea was partly due to the prominence of neoconservative thinkers both in the Bush administration and among the supporters of the 2003 invasion. Neoconservatism embraces a highly ideologized vision of America in the world that is toxic for realists. Neoconservatism combines Wilsonian universalism with muscular unilateralism in ways that maximize the use of American power in the service of goals that realists consider unachievable, irrelevant, or both. It is liberal internationalism without the brake pedal that reliance on multilateral institutions provides. That so many prominent neoconservatives were both Jewish and ardently pro-Israel, and that neoconservative ideology struck so many realists as obviously absurd, could engender a suspicion in some minds that neoconservative ideology was constructed more to justify support for Israel ("the only democracy in the Middle East") than as a sincere worldview.

Vulcanism appealed to some realist restrainers for another reason. Realism in foreign policy comes in many varieties. In some of its forms, realist doctrine maintains that domestic politics are largely irrelevant to the foreign policy choices that states make. The international system, with its ruthlessly competitive nature and the constant jockeying of states for advantage, dictates the kinds of choices governments can embrace. While liberal theories of international relations emphasize the role of domestic politics in foreign policy, realist theories are more likely to compare states to billiard balls on a pool table. Nobody cares what the billiard ball thinks or feels; it is knocked into motion by external forces and goes where it is pushed.

Yet if that picture is true—and it is easy to make strong arguments in its favor—what do we make of the American tendencies that realists so strongly deplore? The United States, it appears, is less predictable and well behaved than your average respectable billiard ball. Instead of waiting patiently until it is knocked into motion and then moving swiftly in a direct line toward some economic or geopolitical goal, it spontaneously leaps into erratic motion, now pursuing democracy promotion in Belarus, now supporting women's empowerment in Ghana.

One way to address the problem is to make the point that great powers have more flexibility than small ones. Belgium and Sri Lanka must follow the iron laws of the pool table, but a superpower like the United States can afford to indulge its emotions and expend its energy on relatively minor issues.

But after 9/11, that approach came under pressure. For realist restrainers, the Bush administration's response to those attacks was a series of dangerously misguided blunders. Spending more money than realists think useful on women's empowerment programs in Ghana may be easy to explain; but what happens when the American reaction to the central issue of the day—terrorism after 9/11—is fundamentally distorted by weird ideological ideas so that the U.S. simultaneously embraces what realists would consider a crazy-pants doctrine of Middle East democratization and launches a foolishly conceived invasion and poorly executed occupation of Iraq? What happens when the billiard ball leaps five feet from the surface of the pool table, rotates in the air, and starts singing "Bill Bailey Won't You Please Come Home"? How, exactly, was this response dictated by the structural realities of the international system?

This is more than a test of American foreign policy. It is an intellectual test of realism's ability to explain international events. If a great power like the U.S. is guided by illusions and ideology into hugely counterproductive policies at a moment of grave crisis, then the more structural forms of realist theory have some explaining to do.

The answer had to satisfy two criteria. In the first place, it had to explain why the United States was flouting all the "rules" of realist behavior. But the goal was to defend realist theory not to refute it, so the answer could not be to concede that liberal theorists are right and that domestic political struggles routinely drive foreign policy choices. The Iraq War needed to be the exception that proved the rule. Domestic politics might have been responsible for the Iraq War, but this had to be a very rare case.

The "Israel lobby" might be responsible for the Iraq War, but one had to be careful. To say that the "Israel lobby" was simply one of many lobbies all jostling in Washington to influence policy, all subject to more or less the same political dynamics, some more successful than others, is to destroy the intellectual position the theorists sought to defend. To make the theory work, the Israel lobby must be a uniquely powerful force with no real rivals or peers.

One could work oneself into this contorted position on purely theoretical grounds without any antisemitic or even anti-Zionist intent, but the idea that Jews and their allies exercise unique power over governments where Jewish interests are concerned has always been a cornerstone of antisemitism. The Israel lobby thesis electrified antisemites around the world as it appeared to place the authority of well-known academics behind one of the oldest, ugliest, and silliest conspiracy theories in the world.[19]

While those who believe "the Jews" are responsible for everything from the weather to speculative attacks on the currencies of Muslim-majority countries continue to uphold the view that "the Jews" also gave the Iraq War to the world, this view has, as noted earlier, gradually lost currency outside the fever swamps. The disastrous consequences of the Iraq War for Israeli interests and the evident Israeli skepticism for the idea that an American-led democratic transition in the Muslim Middle East would pave the way to Arab-Israeli peace agreements eroded the credibility of the core argument. It was not "the Jews" and their Benjamins-motivated hirelings who made the billiard ball jump; the ball has a mind of its own.

Bush, the Palestinians, and the Return of the Peace Process

The specific reason that Barbara Bush tartly addressed her son as the first Jewish president was her skepticism about George Bush's 2002 decision to break off relations with Yasser Arafat and to make further U.S. participation in the peace process contingent on a change in Palestinian leadership.[20] Next to the invasion of Iraq, this decision was, from the point of view of both European and American foreign policy establishments, the most shocking act of the Bush presidency.

Arafat's position as leader of the Palestinian national movement had long been the cornerstone of the Middle East peace process. The PLO chairman was directly or indirectly responsible for scores of hijackings and terror attacks around the world. Palestinian finances were murky in every way, but not so murky as to disguise the reality that for Arafat the distinction between the public purse of the Palestinian movement and the private purse of the Arafat family was shifting and vague. That he could speak of peace at an international conference in the morning and give the go-ahead for a suicide attack on a civilian target in the afternoon was a secret from no one.

Arafat was, in addition to everything else, a man of great charm and charisma. But it was ruthlessness and cleverness linked to an extraordinary political intuition that enabled him to build Fatah into the dominant organization in Palestinian politics, frustrate efforts from various Arab rulers to capture the Palestinian movement and turn it to their own ends, to survive one catastrophic defeat after another, fend off all rivals within the movement, and ultimately to create such an effective mix of terrorist army and political movement that he was able to impose himself on both Israel and the United States as the only possible interlocutor for peace.

For professional diplomats and policymakers, Arafat was one of many leaders of the emerging postcolonial world whose legitimacy came from the gun barrel rather than the ballot box. Such figures often had connections with terrorist movements in the past, and many continued to maintain power by arts darker than the mere mastery of Robert's Rules of Order. They regularly made large if irregular deposits in shady banks, and more than a few corporate executives knew how to maintain their goodwill.

When, after the 2002 capture of the *Karine A,* a ship carrying weapons from Iran to Gaza (then under Arafat's control), George Bush branded Arafat a terrorist and refused to have any further dealings with him, it was Bush's behavior more than Arafat's that shocked international opinion. For Bush, the incident demonstrated Arafat's unsuitability as a peace partner. Bush could not negotiate with Osama bin Laden; he could not ask Sharon to negotiate with Arafat.

As Bush looked at the operations of the Palestinian Authority, the entity that many hoped would one day become the nucleus of the future Palestinian state, he saw an organization that was incapable of governing democratically or competently. At a time when disgust with bad Arab governments around the region was driving thousands of young people toward radical ideologies and terror movements, the Palestinian Authority looked to be as inept, corrupt, and unfree as any existing Arab government—and it was already promoting terrorism through the suicide bombings that were the principal element of Palestinian resistance in the Second Intifada.[21]

Everything that Bush believed told him that a government of this nature could never produce the kind of stability required for a successful peace with Israel; that Arafat either could not or would not change course; and that the Palestinian people therefore both needed and deserved new leadership democratically chosen.

At the time, the Israelis were building what they called a security barrier to block Palestinians from crossing into Israel proper, given that this was how suicide bombers were entering the country. The barrier—which

Palestinians referred to as the Wall—snaked across the West Bank, sometimes separating Palestinian communities and cutting villagers off from the farmlands their families had cultivated for generations.

The barrier was the subject of widespread concern around the world, often portrayed as an illegal Israeli land grab, an infringement of Palestinian rights, and an instance of the inherent cruelty and inhumanity of the occupation. To these charges Israelis replied that the barrier was the only way to stop suicide bomb attacks, and that other countries faced with the same problem would take similar measures.[22]

The Bush administration, in a move that was popular with pro-Israel American Jacksonians and others, supported Sharon's construction of the barrier even as it asked Israelis to show as much concern as possible for the Palestinians whose lives the barrier was disrupting. To break off relations with Arafat while endorsing Sharon's wall seemed to be the very definition of one-sided pro-Israel policy. To those who sympathized with the Palestinian cause, it was a brutally unfair policy; to those who believed that only by building bridges to the Arab world could the United States blunt the appeal of terrorism and radical religious ideology, it seemed an act of suicidal self-harm.

That Bush was simultaneously endorsing the creation of a Palestinian state as the goal of U.S. policy (a position that went significantly further than anything his predecessors had said) did nothing to reduce the impression that his policies were blindly pro-Israel. His support for the goal of a Palestinian state was so conditional and so hedged about with demands for reform (reforms that, however noble considered abstractly, seasoned observers of national liberation movements considered arbitrary, unreasonable, and, in the real world, impossible to achieve) that it seemed a lot less impressive than the concrete steps the United States was taking that strengthened the Israeli position.

This is not an unreasonable summary of the consequences of Bush's position in the 2003–05 period, but Bush and his associates saw themselves as rebuilding the peace process on a more stable foundation rather than demolishing it, and their ideas about Palestinian political reform reflected their wider optimism about the possibilities for democratic transitions across the Middle East. The shock of 9/11 had not extinguished the heady optimism of the 1990s; in the minds of many liberal internationalists and neoconservatives alike, democracy was still on the march worldwide, and it was both racist and Islamophobic to believe that the democratic enlightenment would fail to illuminate the Middle East. Bush's forays into Palestinian state building, such as supporting reformist prime minister Salam Fayyad late in his second term, were part of this effort.

The worldly, cynical, and pessimistic European diplomats who believed that the Middle East was doomed to remain indefinitely under a mix of demagogic dictators like Saddam and Qaddafi, bigoted mullahs in Iran, corrupt monarchies in other countries were on the wrong side of history. A new wind was blowing; the times they were a-changing.

In this ill-grounded optimism, President Bush and his advisors were tragically and destructively wrong, but they were not wrong about everything. The Obama administration in its turn would fall victim to the same ideologically driven American optimism when it embraced the Arab Spring. Obama appointee Samantha Power and Bush appointee Condoleezza Rice were not far apart in their thinking. The times had in fact changed since the 1970s. The old systems were failing and were seen to be failing by peoples all over the Middle East. From Algeria to Pakistan, public discontent was rising, governing structures were becoming less effective, and the status quo was becoming less sustainable.

Moreover, they were right to see that the question of Palestinian governance was of critical importance to the prospect of peace between Israelis and Palestinians. Peace would not last unless the new state was willing and able to crack down on the minority of Palestinians who could not accept the compromises that a negotiated peace must inevitably bring. The Palestinians were not strong enough to impose the peace that Palestinian opinion truly wanted on Israel; the new state would have to be strong enough to enforce an unsatisfactory peace. There would be no right of return to Israeli-held territory. Jerusalem would at best be divided, with the Palestinians receiving the smaller portion. Inevitably, in a society where the idea of resistance to Zionism was the touchstone of legitimacy, a minority of Palestinians would reject the new state while others would see it as, at best, a first, halting step toward the Greater Palestine of their dreams.

None of this was unique to the Palestinians or represented some psychological disorder in the Palestinian political psyche. This is the absolutely normal and near-universal course of nationalist politics. German and Italian nationalism in the nineteenth century, French desire for revenge after the peace of 1871, Balkan feuds then and now, Irish rejection of the Partition, Russia's dream today of restoring its former boundaries, mainland China's hunger for Taiwan—these political passions are, however regrettable in their consequences, normal and natural in human politics.

But if peace between Israelis and Palestinians was to last, it would be the inevitable task of Palestine's rulers to prevent hotheaded nationalists from carrying out acts of violence against either Israeli or Palestinian targets. The Palestinian government would unavoidably become the enforcer of a peace that favored Israeli over Palestinian interests.

Worse, outside actors would certainly be willing to fund rejectionist Palestinian splinter movements. The Soviet Union had supported Palestinian terrorism in its heyday; every major country in the region had a history of supporting rival Palestinian factions. The government of a Palestinian state would have to have the means and the will to crush nationalist Palestinians supported, armed, and trained by foreign states.

The rise of political Islamism added another complication. Many Islamists believed that it was immoral to cede Islamic land to non-Islamic states, and that this prohibition grew stronger in the case of sacred sites like those in Jerusalem. The rise of Hamas in Palestinian politics coincided with the perception that Fatah was becoming too "soft" with Israel; there are more radical parties competing with Hamas, should it falter in its rejectionism.

The Arafat-centered peace process, as we've seen, depended on the idea that Arafat was a competent enough thug that he could manage these problems once he made peace with Israel. He could develop a Palestinian secret police force as competent and as ruthless as the security forces of Egypt, Syria, or Saddam's Iraq. In exchange for the wealth he could extract and the prestige he would incur from heading a Palestinian state, Arafat would impose an unpopular peace.

Bush's decision to demand a change in Palestinian leadership reflected a moral discomfort with what he saw as a devil's bargain with an aspiring autocrat, a conviction that Arafat was too wedded to terrorism to keep his word and play the part envisioned for him by the conventional peace process, and the realization that the durability of peace—in Palestine as well as in other countries in the region—could not be separated from the question of governance. A poorly governed Palestine would be a nursery for terror, just as poor governance across the region had contributed to the rise of Al-Qaeda.

The new Palestinian state could not base its legitimacy on the ideology of resistance to Zionism. More radical movements could always outflank a governing party committed to a peace deal that renounced key Palestinian objectives. Nor could the new state base itself on its adherence to Islam. It would have to find other sources of legitimacy, and these could only be "modern" sources like economic competence and participatory governance. For peace between Israel and Palestine to endure, Palestinians would have to prefer the prosperity and freedom that statehood brought to the emotional rewards of resistance or the siren song of fundamentalism.

Clearly, the Bush team reasoned, a democratic transition in Palestine—assisted and enabled by the United States and its allies— was the first step toward an enduring peace. Introduce democracy into Palestinian politics and allow civil society to flourish, and the dynamic would shift from resistance to achievement. Hamas could no longer compete for office by promises to drive the Jews into the sea; it would have to learn to fix potholes and manage the trash. Economic cooperation with Israel would bring greater prosperity; parties who embraced such policies—and who did a good job in administering government services—would defeat parties who stood in the way of the economic interests of the Palestinian people.

Bush and Rice did not see themselves as breaking the Middle East peace process by excluding Arafat. They saw themselves as reforming the peace process, outlining a "roadmap" (as their plan for Palestinian statehood was called) that, unlike President Clinton's strategy, might actually work. They did not see themselves as choosing between Israel and Palestine, but as offering both sides a way out of their dilemma.

This grand design suffered from the same fatal flaw as their overall project for a "Greater Middle East" of democratic and modernizing states. It was beautiful in theory, unrealizable on the map. In language that became popular in the next administration, the "arc of history" might bend toward justice in the long run, but it did not run to a schedule on which American policymakers could prudently rely. It is one thing to hail the rainbow as a sign of God's continuing care for humanity in a troubled world; it is another to expect to fund one's retirement with the pot of gold at the end of it.

In the end, the Bush-era peace process had no better success than the Clintonian one. American aid to the Palestinian Authority did result in some improvements in the effectiveness of its security forces, but once Hamas stunned Washington by winning the 2006 Palestinian elections, the prospect of a democratic peace between Palestinians and Israelis faded away.[23] The Palestinians who wanted a peace agreement on the available terms were too weak to agree. The Palestinians who opposed the agreement were too strong to ignore. The Israelis, accurately reading the politics on the Palestinian side, were too skeptical about the value and longevity of any agreement to make the additional concessions that might have made a compromise peace easier for moderate Palestinians to sell. Neither American promises nor threats could move either side past its red lines.

————

Although Bush's courageous and correct decision to launch the Surge in Iraq offered hope of a better future for Iraq by the end of his second term, and, as noted above, his success in preventing new major attacks on American soil was a significant achievement, it is hard to consider his overall record a success. An administration that began in a period of optimism and unchallenged American power left office with the Middle East inflamed, China ready to step up its campaign against the American-led world order, Russia hostile and resurgent, and the American economy mired in the worst financial crisis since the Great Depression.

What nobody expected was that when his successor left office eight years later, the financial crisis would have been resolved, but the geopolitical situation would become more dangerous than ever. The foundations of the post–Cold War order were coming unglued and the problems of American foreign policy did not flow from the ways in which Bush's vision of the world differed from those of Bill Clinton and Barack Obama. All three leaders had misread the nature of the post–Cold War world and the state of American society, and their failures in Middle East peacemaking reflected the widening gap between the world Americans wanted to live in and the planet they actually inhabited.

19

Israel and the Exceptional American Left

I T FELT TO MANY AMERICANS that the millennium was heating up in the closing months of the George W. Bush administration. A devastating financial crisis had badly shaken a country still reeling from the shock of 9/11, worried about new terror attacks, and fighting wars in Afghanistan and Iraq.[1] Putin's invasion of Georgia in the summer of 2008 was the first concrete sign that the post–Cold War "holiday from history" might be coming to an end.[2] The economy continued to hemorrhage middle-class jobs. The polarization unleashed by the Iraq War continued to divide the country. Many Americans, mostly but not all liberals, felt that the country had lost its way.

Against this background, Barack Obama's election struck many Americans as an extraordinary moment of hope. That an America so embattled and challenged could look forward in optimism appeared to many observers at home and abroad as an eloquent testimony to the underlying strengths of American society. It seemed that the election, not only of the first Black president, but of a man who was equally at home in the seminar room or on the basketball court, and gifted with the ability to represent the ideas and aspirations of his political constituency with a dignity and grace given to only a few American presidents, marked a notable return to the promise of the post–Cold War era. The millennium was turning cool again as "No Drama Obama" took the wheel.

No American president had had this kind of charismatic impact since John Fitzgerald Kennedy, and in many ways Obama can be called the "Black Kennedy." Just as the ascent of Jack Kennedy signaled the triumph of Catholic and Irish (and, by extension, other descendants of the Great Wave immigrants, including American Jews), so Obama's election was felt by many to represent a decisive turn in the long and sorry story of American race relations.

But Kennedy's election was not just a triumph of integration. It had been a triumph of assimilation. Kennedy's message for the New England WASPs who had once viewed the surge of Irish and Catholic immigrants as a threat to American identity and values was blissfully reassuring. America's first Catholic president might have an Irish surname and attend Roman masses, but his heart was on the Charles, not the Tiber. His aides and associates weren't disreputable South Boston ward heelers; they were Harvard men like McGeorge Bundy and John Kenneth Galbraith. JFK was a miracle that only America could produce: an Anglophile Irishman ready to take his place among fellow Brahmins in the New England elite.

Barack Obama was called to a similar but even more talismanic role in American life. The racial divide was an even older and deeper chasm than the gap between the "old stock" and Great Wave immigrants had been. From the 1960s on, American liberalism had made racial equality its most important single domestic policy priority. The Civil Rights and Voting Rights Acts of the 1960s, the Great Society's extension of the welfare state, and a generation of work to desegregate schools and housing and to decrease discrimination in employment and education through a broad range of affirmative action movements had shaped the Democratic agenda for half a century. Obama's election was a sign that these monumental labors were having an effect. The color line was not what it was.

Moreover, Obama was in his own way as reassuring a figure as JFK. His long attendance at Jeremiah Wright's church seemed to have had as little impact on Barack Obama as JFK's membership in the Catholic Church had on the earlier president. Like Kennedy, Obama was a product of elite institutions steeped in the New England ethos. Kennedy attended Choate before Harvard; Obama's elite high school in Hawaii, Punahou, had been founded in 1841 by Congregationalist missionaries from New England and is sometimes called the Andover of the Pacific. While slightly to the left of his domestic rivals on domestic policy issues in the 2008 primary campaign, Obama was clearly as much a part of the Democratic Party mainstream in his era as JFK had been in his and, like Kennedy, Obama would choose many of his close advisors from the heart of the American establishment.

The meaning of Obama's victory seemed both intoxicating and clear: America still worked. The liberal ideas and values of the American democratic tradition were strong enough to overcome even the racial divide, and those same ideas were so universal and appealing that, as members of once excluded groups fought their way into national leadership, they would rally to those American ideals.

Sadly, these hopeful expectations would remain unfulfilled. This was to some degree inevitable. No president, no human being could fulfill all the expectations that some Obama supporters hung on their champion. At home, the record was disappointing. As the recovery from the Great Recession—real but for many agonizingly slow and incomplete—continued, inequality grew, good blue-collar jobs continued to disappear, and a devastating epidemic of drug abuse and addiction sent life expectancy for working-class white men into a steep decline.[3] Poor housing policy both before and after the financial crisis destroyed much of the wealth of the Black middle class and put millions of non-Black Americans under great stress as well.

The economic crisis of Black America—laid bare in statistics that showed no diminishment in the "wealth gap" between Black and white families since the end of the civil rights movement—raised the disturbing prospect that half a century of liberal policy had failed to reduce the racial divide.[4] Racial resentment among both Blacks and working-class whites was on the rise during the Obama years.[5]

Internationally, the Obama years were also challenging. When President Obama turned the White House over to Donald Trump in 2017, the United States would be more hated and despised in a Middle East that was more inflamed than in 2009. During those eight years, Russia and China would emerge as bitter and determined opponents of the United States and inflict a series of setbacks on the Obama administration that eroded its authority at home and abroad. President Obama's most important diplomatic victories, the nuclear weapons agreement with Iran, known as the JCPOA (Joint Comprehensive Plan of Action), and the Paris Climate Accords did not have enough backing in American politics to be enshrined in treaties that the Senate would ratify, and so remained vulnerable and weak.

Despite the many differences between them, George W. Bush and

Barack Obama both saw their terms in office disrupted by events at home and abroad that did not fulfill the expectations they brought with them. Russia's and China's hostility, and their ability to find chinks in America's armor stunned Obama as much as the ability of Iraqi guerrillas to turn Iraq into a quagmire and consume the political capital of his administration had shocked Bush. In the Middle East, Obama's hopes of fostering democratic transitions turned out to be as ill-founded as Bush's had been.

That such very different presidents as Bush and Obama presided over years of increasing American political polarization, declining perceived economic well-being, and foreign policy frustration is a phenomenon that deserves more attention than it receives. Like the American leadership class as a whole, the two presidents were profoundly mistaken about the forces reshaping the world. The well-meaning presidents of the era between the two world wars had similarly launched international initiatives to secure world peace and stabilize the global economy. Those hopeful initiatives foundered against realities leaders did not anticipate and could not understand. Like their Lodge-era predecessors, America's leaders in the post–Cold War era brought the conventional ideas of their generation to the task of statecraft. Neither Bush's earnest Sun Belt Republicanism nor Obama's sleek and stylish neoliberalism proved adequate to the domestic and foreign challenges of the day. The world had become a darker and more dangerous place under their leadership even as growing swaths of the American population felt increasingly alienated from both parties and the political establishment.

======

No premonitions of future trouble blighted the jubilant dawn of the Obama years, particularly for the more liberal wing of the Democratic Party drawn to him by his early and steadfast opposition to the Iraq War. Most of the Democratic leadership had, with whatever qualms, endorsed George W. Bush's decision to invade Iraq. For some it was political calculation based on the national mood in the post-9/11 era; for others, it was based on instincts for engagement and a forward-leaning American posture formed during the Cold War and heightened by the post–Cold War successes of President George H. W. Bush in the Gulf War and of President Bill Clinton's interventions in the Balkans.

The Iraq War dissenters reflected many different points of view. Some remembered the Vietnam War and had consistently opposed American military interventions in subsequent years. Some were aligned with the realist restrainers and wanted a less global, less ideological, and less ambitious foreign policy for the United States. Some saw the Iraq War as part of an overmilitarized and Islamophobic response to unrest in the Middle East and hoped for a more creative, diplomatic, and sympathetic American engagement under President Obama.

At one time, the election of a liberal Democrat would have been good news for Israel. By 2008 the picture had altered. A reflexive sympathy for Zionism was no longer standard equipment for the American left, and doubts about the justice of Israeli policies on the West Bank and Gaza were widespread among Democrats and liberals, including many liberal Jews. A new and more critical perspective on Israel had put down roots among many American liberals and progressives, and this perspective, shared by the incoming president in his characteristically cautious and cerebral way, would influence the deliberations of his incoming team.

Yet those who hoped for a revolution in American policy toward Israel would be disappointed. Israeli settlements in the Palestinian territories would continue to expand, there would be no progress toward the establishment of a Palestinian state, and Israel would receive the largest aid package in its history from Obama. For Vulcanists, this was just one more proof that "the Jews" were too powerful for any American politician to oppose. As usual, the truth was more interesting and more enlightening. On the one hand, the evolution of the American left's views of Zionism was as complicated and, in its way, as unique and exceptional a story as developments on the right. And on the other hand, the course of Obama-era Israel policy, like that of so many of his predecessors, had as much or more to do with the power of Israel on the ground in the Middle East as with the actions of any domestic lobby.

Israel and the Left

When I lecture and teach about Israel policy to student audiences, many are genuinely astonished to learn that during the earlier decades of its existence, Israel was more popular on the left than on the right, and more popular in Europe than in the United States. Young Europeans in particular are often shocked by a forgotten chapter in their own history.

Europeans have not always been prominent among Israel's critics.

At a time when many American Republicans and conservatives wanted little to do with Israel, Britain, West Germany, and France were providing arms and diplomatic help to the impoverished and endangered new state. At the time of the 1967 war, 55 percent of British respondents and 59 percent of those in France backed the Israelis; only 2 percent in either country supported the Arab cause.[6] That spring, a Gallup poll found that 38 percent of Americans viewed Israelis more favorably than they viewed the Palestinians. As usual, this dwarfed the percentage that favored the Palestinians (3 percent), but most respondents weren't engaged on either side.

British newspapers across the spectrum, including *The Guardian*, *The Times,* and *The Economist,* ran pro-Israel editorials. In France, prominent left-wingers like Jean-Paul Sartre, Simone de Beauvoir, and Pablo Picasso led a chorus of marquee-name intellectuals in support of Israel's position.[7] Thirty thousand French citizens gathered in front of the Israeli embassy in Paris to offer replacement labor so that more Israelis could fight at the front.[8] In Bonn, West Germany's Cold War capital, the Israeli embassy was besieged with offers of help, including military volunteers.

Middle East wars can still bring large crowds of students and protesters to Israeli embassies across Europe today, but their view of Israel has dramatically changed. The shift in European opinion from enthusiasm to reserve and then at times hostility toward Israel is sometimes portrayed in the United States as a consequence of immigration from the Islamic world and the return of old-fashioned European antisemitism. While both migration and resurgent antisemitism are part of the story, the shift in European opinion toward Israel cannot be reduced to these causes.

═══

As we've seen, the relationship between philo-Semitic politics and the European left has deep roots dating back to the struggle against absolute monarchies and clerical rule. This long-standing alliance emerged strengthened and renewed following the tragedies and horrors of the Third Reich and the world war it launched. In the late 1940s and early 1950s, to be pro-Jewish was to be antifascist. In addition to reflecting a sincere and widely felt horror at Nazi crimes, sympathy for the Jews was a stick with which the postwar European left could happily beat the (traditionally more clerical and antisemitic) right. Also appalled by Nazi crimes, and determined to demonstrate their own repudiation of fascism, members of the postwar Christian Democratic and centrist parties competed with the left to show their affinity for Zionism and their concern for the victims of the Holocaust.[9]

In the United States, pro-Israel sentiment was also strongest on the left. To be pro-Israel was to embrace a foreign policy vision that owed much to the liberals who had pushed Truman to support the Zionists after World War II. The pro-Arab foreign policy supported by State Department mandarins and embraced by the Eisenhower administration for much of its tenure did not just offend American liberals because it was bad for Israel. They hated John Foster Dulles's approach to the Cold War because the United States ended up backing undemocratic and even antidemocratic forces all over the world. The Middle East was just one example, 1950s liberals felt, of an American foreign policy that had lost its moral bearings.

Toadying to absolute monarchies in the Middle East in order to prevent the nationalization of American oil companies in the region struck many liberals as a grotesque abandonment of important American principles and a symbol of excessive corporate influence over our foreign policy. At the same time, the whole strategy of aligning the United States with "modernizing" military rulers seemed a betrayal of American principles. American liberals did not like American support for repressive military regimes in Europe, Latin America, and Asia, and they didn't like it in the Middle East either. They wanted an anticommunist strategy that relied on alliances with democrats, not on dubious arrangements with fascists like Spain's Francisco Franco. Israel was exactly the kind of social democracy that many American liberals believed should be our preferred partners in the Cold War.

It is largely forgotten today, but for much of its history Israel was one of the most socialist countries in the democratic world. This was not just a question of the famous kibbutzim or collective farms that were long a leading force in Israeli agriculture. Histadrut, a labor union headed by future prime minister David Ben-Gurion after 1921, owned many of the largest enterprises in Israel, including the country's largest bank and shipping company. In Israel the workers actually did own the means of production. That a country this socialist could be both dynamic and democratic was an immense source of pride to democratic socialists across the West, and helped the left defend itself against conservative attacks. Democratic socialists across Europe and in the United States looked to Israel as a role model and source of new thinking and policy ideas.

The open antisemitism of the Arab world at the time, expressed not just in rhetoric but including the repression and expulsion of its Jewish citizens, underlined the connection for many liberals between Arab opposition to Israel and the traditional antisemitism of the European right. Support for Israel was seen as a moral duty and a test of character. American liberals responded to the 1967 war with much of the enthusiasm of their European peers. Liberal icon John Kenneth Galbraith said on the television show *Meet the Press* that he would "absolutely" support direct intervention on Israel's behalf. One of the only two senators to vote against the Gulf of Tonkin Resolution used to justify the American war in Vietnam, Senator Wayne Morse, advocated using the U.S. Navy to break Nasser's blockade.[10]

From the 1940s well into the 1970s support for Israel was a leftist cause in the United States. Liberal icons like Eleanor Roosevelt, Martin Luther King Jr., and Adlai Stevenson were the most visible pro-Israel faces to many Americans at that time.[11] Paul Robeson, a prominent Black member of the Communist Party of the United States and a leading musician of the day, performed at a benefit concert for the Irgun, the right-wing, more radical Zionist movement out of which today's Likud Party ultimately grew.[12] Groups like Peter, Paul and Mary included songs from Israeli kibbutzim in the folk festivals that served as meeting places for iconoclastic young people in the 1950s and 1960s.

The civil rights movement was a hotbed of pro-Zionist sentiment. Black leaders like King were strong, consistent, and engaged supporters of Israel and of U.S. support for it. Black civil rights leader Bayard Rustin, the organizer of the 1963 March on Washington, a Quaker and longtime activist for nonviolence and pacifism, supported placing an ad in *The New York Times* in 1970 calling for the U.S. to sell Israel "the full number of jet aircraft it has requested."[13] In 1975, BASIC (Black Americans to Support Israel Committee) published a full-page ad in *The New York Times* attacking the U.N.'s "Zionism is racism" resolution. The ad cited an article by Rustin and was cosigned by several hundred prominent Black Americans, including Congressman Charles Rangel, union leaders, King's widow, Coretta Scott King, author Ralph Ellison, and civil rights activist Rosa Parks.[14]

Neither in Europe nor in the United States did the problems of the Palestinian refugees engage the conscience of the left in the ways they did in later years. There were a number of reasons for this, some better than others. For many years after World War II, the world was filled with refugees. Israel itself was a majority-refugee nation in the early years, including both European refugees from Nazism and Middle Eastern refugees from Arab persecution. German politicians had to deal with the millions of Germans expelled from Poland and the Sudetenland after the war; for decades German politics would be troubled by the "refugee lobby" with its demands for a right of return and the inheritability of refugee status.[15]

In the early postwar decades the epidemic of violence, ethnic cleansing, and murder continued. Up to two million Hindus and Muslims were killed and more than 10 million refugees were displaced during the communal violence that accompanied the partition of British India.[16] After Burma achieved independence, some 300,000 South Asians, many of whose families had lived in Burma for generations, were forced from their homes and businesses.[17] Hundreds of thousands of Jews were expelled or fled from Arab and Muslim countries following Israel's war of independence. Egypt also expelled tens of thousands of Greeks and other foreigners who had made cities like Alexandria and Cairo cosmopolitan centers while Egypt was effectively under British control. Wave after wave of desperate refugees fled advancing communist control, from Iron Curtain countries in the 1940s and 1950s, from Cuba in the 1960s, and from Indochina following the fall of Saigon in 1975. Over ten thousand Greeks were forced out of Istanbul in 1964.[18] The Turkish invasion of Cyprus in 1974 sent 150,000 panicky Greeks fleeing south to lands still under Greek Cypriot control; about fifty thousand Turkish Cypriots had to flee to the north.

In the midst of this chaos and carnage, the plight of the Palestinians did not command as much attention as would later be the case. Many in the West and on the left did not initially think of the Palestinians as a separate people. They were seen as part of the Arab people, a people with large territories and many states to which refugees could turn for new homes. The Germans expelled from Poland went to Germany; the Greeks expelled from Istanbul went to Greece. The Jews the Arabs expelled were resettled in Israel. Why could the Arabs expelled by the Israelis not go to other Arab lands for a fresh start? One can blame orientalism, racism, imperialism, or simply the sheer complexity of the issues and the history involved, but the idea that this was a conflict between Israelis and Palestinians rather than between Israelis and Arabs took many years to impress itself on western minds.

After the 1967 war, the Palestinians became more visible on both sides of the Atlantic, and the occupation of Palestinian territory by Israeli forces would gradually change the way the left in both Europe and the United States saw the conflict. As other refugee problems in the world gradually faded, and as Israel integrated the Jewish refugees from the Arab world, the problems of the Palestinians, both the refugees in the Arab world and those under occupation, began to look both more unique and more shocking. Jews, meanwhile, were looking less like hapless victims of persecution and more like oppressors.

The rise of the political right in Israel also had its effect on the way the Euro-American left saw Israel. Beginning in 1977 when Menachem Begin led the Likud Party to its first election victory, the balance of power in Israeli politics gradually shifted to the right. In subsequent decades Likud and its allies moved toward a combination of free market deregulation in the Israeli economy and a more nationalistic and expansionist agenda when it came to relations with the Palestinians. The western left generally saw this shift through the prism of the rise of Thatcher and Reagan, and this made the shift to sympathy with the Palestinians, seen as victims of Israel's rightward turn, a natural development. In some cases, many on the left, with real heartache and pain, began to turn away from their former support for Israel.

Another force pulling the European left away from its early support of Israel was the influence of what can be called the hard left. As the ideological and military front lines of the Cold War shifted from the heart of Europe into what was then called the Third World, there were many European leftists who actively sympathized with communist and anti-capitalist movements in countries like Cuba, Angola, and Vietnam.[19] As the American alliance with Israel began to develop in the 1970s and the U.S.-Soviet rivalry came to play a larger role in Middle East politics, Arab leaders like Syria's Hafez al-Assad, Iraq's Saddam Hussein, and even Libya's deeply eccentric Muammar Qaddafi became more popular on the more radical fringes of the European left. Israel began to look more and more like an avatar of American capitalism in the Middle East, and an increasingly strident anti-Zionism began to emerge as a hallmark of hardcore left-wing movements across the democratic West. To reject their predecessors' Zionism became a way for student radicals in what Europeans called the "68 generation"—after the protests and upheavals of 1968—to demonstrate their rejection of what they saw as the colonial mindset of the older generation. A strong anti-Zionism that did not always stop short of sympathy for groups engaging in terrorism became a hallmark of the more radical groupings on the far fringes of the European left.

Driving the shift in European attitudes toward Israel was a revolution in European attitudes toward colonialism, nationalism, and national power. Historically, nationalism and social democracy had been joined at the hip. Nationalism created a bond between people speaking the same language and sharing a cultural heritage, and this sense of common identity and mutual obligation created the political basis for the welfare states of the twentieth century. The relatively small and homogeneous Scandinavian countries offered an example of how successfully social democracy could create stable mass prosperity under favorable conditions, but the idea that the ethnic nation state could serve as the incubator for democratic and progressive governance emerged in the nineteenth century and remained central to European politics during much of the twentieth century. This was the political culture and worldview out of which Herzlian Zionism grew, and the socialist ideals that shaped the Yishuv and the early decades of Israeli independence continued to reflect what one might call the progressive nationalism of European social democracy.

The split in the socialist movement between pro-Soviet communists and anti-Soviet social democrats was, among other things, driven by nationalism. The pro-Soviet parties committed themselves to an internationalist standpoint, often refusing to support their national governments in World War I and supporting revolutions during and after the war. More moderate socialists remained committed both to the nation-state and to democratic and parliamentary politics.

The relationship between nationalism and progressive ideology was, however, more complicated than it looked, and over time the European understanding of the relationship between the two forces would change.

By the end of the twentieth century, nationalism would look to many Europeans like a dangerous relic of a toxic past. Many factors supported this evolution in European thought and the result was a growing moral gap between Zionism and progressive European sensibilities. History did not operate in quite the same way in the United States, with the result that the revised and more critical liberal approach to Zionism that gradually gained ground among American Democrats was both super-ficially similar to and profoundly different from the dominant approach in Europe.

Before 1939, Europe had been a continent of assertive nation-states and world powers. That began to change after World War II. As Euro-peans gradually began to adjust to a world in which no European state other than the Soviet Union could claim to be a major world power, and as they contemplated the disasters that conflicts between European nations had brought about, nationalism was increasingly rejected as a backward, destructive, and atavistic force.

For most of the last sixty years, the construction of what would become the European Union was the most important project of Euro-pean politics, and as the process gained momentum it created a new kind of European political sensibility. Nationalism, from this new Euro-pean perspective, was a backward and dangerous force (in Europe at least; nationalism in the postcolonial world was still highly regarded). Nineteenth-century nationalism had not only led European countries into the imperial ventures that in retrospect shamed them; it led Europe into one hideous war after the next. For the future, cooperation, respect for international institutions, reconciliation with neighboring nations, and the pooling of sovereignty were the values on which civilization had to be built.

To the new European sensibility, Israel, as a nationalist state edg-ing toward the annexation of "unredeemed" national territory, grad-ually came to look less like the state of fellow traveling cosmopolites than like a practitioner—indeed, an embodiment—of exactly the kind of nationalism and realpolitik that right-thinking Europeans believed had poisoned their past and would be a threat to their common future. Transcending national rivalries to build a cosmopolitan order became the ethical foundation of European politics; for Israel to use its supe-rior military power to create settlements on occupied territory struck European sensibilities as exactly the kind of irresponsible and unjust national self-assertion that led Europe into calamity. Every European country had to give up irredentist claims on its neighbors; why could not the Israelis leave the West Bank alone?

Attitudes toward hard power also divided Israel from its old allies on the European left. Europeans who came of age during or before World War II had the habit of command. They had reached maturity in countries that were world powers. Winston Churchill was born when Britain was the greatest power in the world. Charles de Gaulle, Konrad Adenauer, Alcide De Gasperi, and the whole older generation had come to maturity in the age of European empire when Britain, France, Germany, and Italy ranked among the great powers. They had played the game of thrones on a world scale and understood realpolitik as well as any Caesar. They had not given up their power easily or willingly. In the 1950s and early 1960s, the British and the French had fought a series of colonial wars—often with the support of the democratic left parties. The British Labour Party tried to preserve the British Empire in the Middle East, and French socialists supported their country's efforts to keep its colonies in Indochina and, especially, North Africa.

Then came the generational shift. Robert Schuman, revered as a founding father of a united Europe, died in 1963. He was followed two years later by Churchill. In 1967 it was the turn of Adenauer, one of the greatest statesmen in the long history of Germany. De Gaulle retired from public life in 1969 and died in 1970. The successor generation had grown up in a very different world. Their life experiences reflected Europe's reduced, post–World War I circumstances, the Depression, and the horrors of the Second World War.

As the end of empire came to look both inevitable and, in economic terms, unimportant, the moral calculus changed. As the British, the French, the Italians, the Belgians, and the Dutch retreated from empire, and the Germans reflected on the horror and misery that came from their own ventures in Weltpolitik, Europeans increasingly recoiled from the moral and military costs of power seeking. Among other things, this meant that they tended both to see Israel's experiences wielding power through the unhappy lens of their own recent colonial history and to embrace idealistic views of world politics that put Israeli behavior in a particularly harsh light.

This shift also led many Europeans, and especially those on the political left, to look with anguish and horror on the left's often enthusiastic support for imperialist policies in the past. That so many of Europe's center-left parties embraced vicious colonial wars in the Middle East and elsewhere led to a generational and ideological rift. The postwar generation that erupted on the European scene in the student revolts of 1968 looked back on their parents' complicity in the Algerian, Indonesian, and Indochinese wars of the 1940s and 1950s with contempt. As the Israelis began to plant settlements in the West Bank and Gaza, apparent similarities between Israeli behavior and the discredited policies of European imperialism were impossible to ignore. Even for more moderate figures who accepted the existence of Israel within the cease-fire lines of 1949, any effort to expand those frontiers looked like the kind of settler colonialism that the French, for example, had practiced in Algeria. That the French policy of supporting Israel in the 1950s was largely driven by a common opposition to Arab nationalism further stained Israel's reputation in the eyes of the new generation of the postcolonial European left. Israelis gradually morphed in the mind of the European left from victims of fascism desperately seeking refuge to avatars of European colonialism, sharing the guilt of Europe's long and often cruel domination of the global south.

After the end of the Cold War, much of the European left signed up enthusiastically to build a post-nationalist and even post-historical union. By leaving nationalism and realpolitik behind, the European Union could be a new kind of power in a new kind of world. The attraction of its values, the wealth of its consumer market, and the power of its example would transform Europe's neighborhood. Turkey, Russia, Ukraine, and Egypt might never join the EU, but they would increasingly share its values and outlook, and their foreign policy would become increasingly peaceful.

From this standpoint, Israel was a problem. Its constant resort to "disproportionate" force in retaliation against attacks, the nonstop provocations of its settlement policy, and its insistence on the Jewish nature of the state were not just affronts to Europe's values. They were threats to Europe's peace. Israeli policies were encouraging Islamism and jihadi terror across the Middle East, creating obstacles in the path of both the economic and the social development of the region, and ultimately endangering Europe itself.

For Europeans coming to terms with large populations of immigrant Muslims, this was not just a foreign policy problem. Europe's new inhabitants were alienated from western culture and western values at least in part because of the West's long record of support for Zionism, a cause that many Middle Eastern migrants viscerally loathed and regarded as perverse and unjust. As the number of migrants from predominantly Muslim countries in Europe grew, the danger that Israeli policies seen as provocative would inflame tensions and promote terrorism in Europe itself grew with it.

Many Israeli Jews dissented from Europe's post-historical project as vehemently as their ancestors had done from the order-building efforts of Holy Roman emperors and popes. From a Zionist point of view, the EU dream of a post-nationalist, post-historical world of tolerant and enlightened societies dwelling peacefully together looked like a beautiful fantasy, not a solid foundation on which to build the future of the Jewish people. Not only did European dreams of a universal, values-based peace look naive to a nation in arms and educated in the school of Herzl; it also did not appear as if this beautiful new Europe could protect its surviving Jewish minority.

This was not only a matter of attacks on Jews and Jewish institutions by migrants. The rise of nationalist and populist parties, including the Golden Dawn in Greece and the AfD in Germany, provided evidence that antisemitism among other Europeans had not disappeared after 1945. The willingness of so many European governments to engage with Iran, despite the frequent bloodcurdling threats from its leaders to annihilate Israel, reinforced a suspicion among many Israelis that Herzl's warnings about reliance on "enlightened" Europeans were correct. The post-historical utopia Europeans hoped to build would not be a safe or a welcoming place for Jews.

AMERICA'S EXCEPTIONAL LEFT

The shift in attitudes toward Israel was not uniform in Europe. In Germany, political criticism of Israel always had to be balanced with a sense of historical responsibility. In the Netherlands and Denmark, historically philo-Semitic influences continued to make themselves felt. And there were differences between more moderate voices and more radical ones everywhere. Attitudes toward Israel became a kind of marker: the more radical one's politics in general, the more radical one's position against Zionism—and, for that matter, the more critical one was of the United States and capitalism generally.

While the American left generally moved in the same direction as the European left, it tended to move later, more slowly, and not as far. There were groups on the left who shared the full-throated anti-Zionist convictions of some in Europe, but they long remained smaller and less influential in the American Democratic Party than similar groups across the EU.

Americans who shared the visceral anti-Israel bias of politicians like Britain's Jeremy Corbyn existed, but they were marginal political figures. Barack Obama, Hillary Clinton, and Joe Biden were all significantly more pro-Israel than any European major party leaders on the left, and although their pro-Israel stands were often controversial, they paid no significant political price either in their party or with voters at large for advocating a close and supportive relationship with the Jewish state, in spite of occasional disagreements.

This difference existed even though many Americans on the center-left shared some of the perceptions, values, and ideas that gradually turned the European left against Israel. Whether it was the suffering of the Palestinians, increasingly conspicuous as other refugee populations were resettled and absorbed, the injustices of military occupation, the perception that a more forthcoming approach by Israeli negotiators would lead to a peace settlement, or the belief that old-fashioned nationalism needed to be left behind in order to build a better world, American liberals saw and were troubled by the same Middle Eastern events as their Europeans peers. But the American left stands on cultural and political foundations that are significantly different from those of Europe, and the relationship between the American left and the Jewish state has, so far at least, not broken down in quite the same way that the European-Israeli relationship has.

For Vulcanists, the reason was the obvious and traditional one: the American left was less anti-Zionist than the left in other countries because of the financial and media power of the usual suspects. Clearly, the only possible explanation for the inability of anti-Israel activists to dominate the mainstream Democratic Party had to be that American Jews were deploying their massive financial resources to frustrate what would otherwise be the natural and inevitable course of American politics.

There were, of course, Jews in the Democratic Party and Jews on the left. The shift away from Israel was not universally or immediately popular among the large percentage of the American Jewish population whose natural political affiliations are on the left. Some pro-Israel Jews abandoned the left over what they saw as a dangerous anti-Zionist turn. Ronald Reagan's pro-Israel stance, and the popularity of Israel among Sun Belt Republicans more widely, attracted some formerly Democratic Jews to the GOP. Other pro-Israel Jewish Democrats like former Connecticut senator Joe Lieberman felt increasingly marginalized by the party's shift.

Meanwhile, Black Democrats were sometimes among the progressive voices pushing for a faster shift to a more critical and pro-Palestinian stance on Israel policy. The split over Israel policy was part of a split between Blacks and Jews rooted in mutual grievances dating back to the civil rights era when emerging Black student leaders rose up against what they saw as the overly cautious and moderate stances of an older generation of activists and leaders—many of whom happened to be Jewish. At the same time, American Jews whose financial contributions supported the civil rights movement in its early years and who took real risks to support Black rights felt cast aside and disrespected by the new and more militant leaders.

Beginning with Malcolm X, the fiery speaker and charismatic leader who emerged from the Nation of Islam to help define and popularize a vision of Black empowerment more radical and confrontational than King's approach, a new generation of Black leaders began to see closer similarities between the Palestinian and Black causes. In the 1940s, at a time when antisemitic attitudes in the United States were near their all-time peak, American Jews and American Blacks both faced conspicuous hostility and overt discrimination. By the end of the 1960s, American Jews had had much more success working their way into the mainstream, while for the majority of American Blacks, economic marginalization and social exclusion remained. As the U.S.-Israeli alliance deepened, and as large numbers of American Jews continued a highly visible ascent into the upper reaches of American life, both philo-Semitism and Zionism gradually lost standing on the left.

Although Israel policy was neither the root cause of nor the most burning issue in the tensions that arose between some Black and some Jewish leaders and communities in the 1960s and later, the impression that more centrist Jewish Democrats were opposing efforts by more progressive Black Democrats to change America's Middle East policy contributed to the wave of Vulcanist political analysis on the left. The narrative that big-money Jewish donors placed limits on the political direction of Democratic Middle East policy was widely accepted in some circles, but while pro-Israel Jewish Democrats were never shy about making their sentiments clear, and while Barack Obama, like Harry Truman, grew weary at times of the indefatigable ardor with which pro-Zionist Democrats made their case, in the Obama administration as well as in the Truman years, Israel policy reflected a sophisticated and complex response to a wide range of political and strategic considerations.

In his memoir of his first term, President Obama described both the deep roots of his personal engagement with Israel and his concerns about Israeli policies. He learned about the Holocaust, an "unconscionable catastrophe," from his mother, and about the biblical Exodus in grade school. American Jewish authors like Saul Bellow and Philip Roth helped shape his literary imagination with their stories of outsiders trying to find a place in America. The predominantly liberal politics of American Jews, the influence of Jewish thinkers like Martin Buber on Martin Luther King Jr., and the friendship and support that Obama found among Jewish neighbors and friends in Chicago all created a sense of attachment and fellowship that is not easily broken.

As Obama writes, "I believed there was an essential bond between the Black and the Jewish experiences" and all this "made me fiercely protective of the right of the Jewish people to have a state of their own."

The values that led him to feel connected to American Jews and to the right of the Jewish people to live peacefully in a Jewish state also led him to care about the rights and needs of Palestinians, including the right to self-determination in a state of their own. Obama, whose friends included prominent American Palestinians as well as American Jews, saw the evils and injustice of occupation as keenly as his contemporaries on the European left, but this sense was always related to an instinctive sense that the Zionist case was at bottom legitimate.[20]

Obama's approach to the question reflected mainstream Democratic priorities and concerns and, as in President Truman's case, he consistently sought to make Middle East policy on the basis of his convictions about the national interest. And unlike Truman, Obama was and remained popular among American Jews. In 2008, no ethnic or racial group in the United States except Blacks voted for Obama in higher percentages than American Jews, and four years later he still held 69 percent of the Jewish vote.[21]

For many liberal Jews, the young senator from Illinois was a figure of extraordinary promise and hope. They shared the hope that he would reverse the post Reagan direction of American politics, which veered away from the more liberal ideas that dominated American politics from FDR to Jimmy Carter. It was partly that his commitment to the idea of an America that needed deep and continuing reform to live up to its values matched their own vision of the United States. And it was partly that his vision of Israel policy and his idea about the future of U.S.-Israel relations resonated deeply with their own cherished views. Indeed, during the Obama administration, many of the voices in the White House and the political community urging the president to take a tougher stand against Israeli settlement policies, to defy Israeli pressure on negotiations with Iran, and to press Israel to make more concessions to the Palestinians for the sake of peace, were Jewish.

For such Jews among Obama's supporters, as well as many other Democrats, the issue wasn't whether American policy should be pro-Israel or anti-Israel. The question was whether Israel and the United States would benefit more from a policy of "tough love" than from a policy which they saw as abetting shortsighted views of Israeli interests. They wanted to press Israel on Palestinian issues to clear the path for a Palestinian state in the belief that this would allow Israel to remain both a Jewish and a democratic state, and because they believed that the establishment of a Palestinian state would improve Israel's security and enhance Israel's standing worldwide.

＝＝＝

A more useful way to think about the differences between American Democrats and their international counterparts on Israel policy focuses on more powerful political and cultural forces than the alleged power and allegedly fanatical Zionism of American Jews. Israel policy, after all, is not the only political issue on which American Democrats have chosen a unique path compared to other center left parties in the western world.

American Democrats were historically more sympathetic to organized religion and, in particular, the Catholic Church than most European social democratic parties—a difference that would be difficult to attribute to the influence of American Jews. It is a commonplace observation that by European standards the American Democratic Party has been something of a center-right party. Just as Israeli socialists were to the left of European socialists during the 1950s and 1960s, American Democrats were well to their right during the same era. If, as views on the left globally have generally turned against Israel, American Democrats take a more moderate view than Europeans do, we should not be surprised—nor should we attribute the difference to Jewish string-pullers behind the curtains. It is more profitable if we look at how their very different historical experiences led American liberals to a unique view of Israel than if we join the Vulcanists in searching for the hidden Jewish hand.

While twentieth-century history made European social democrats and liberals sensitive to the limits of national power and skeptical of its potential for good, American liberals took very different lessons from the history of their times. The lesson most Americans drew from the most destructive war in world history was that the way to avoid a repetition was to extend the protection and projection of American power globally to lay the foundation of world order. Despite episodes of protest against national policy since—the Vietnam and Iraq wars, for example—the left in America has remained broadly pro-government and even pro-national defense.

The twentieth century felt very different depending on which side of the Atlantic you were on. Neither world war scarred the United States as deeply as both scarred Europe. American casualties in World War I were relatively light. Casualties were greater in World War II, but in both conflicts the United States escaped invasion and occupation and the two wars combined killed fewer Americans and left a lighter impress on the American memory than our own Civil War. The American generation that came of age in World War II and afterward had the experience of achieving progressive, liberal goals through the exercise of national power. These were the years of Marshall Plan aid, ambitious development plans and foreign aid programs around the world, and, of course, of deep engagement in the Cold War against a foe that noncommunist American leftists saw as both dangerous and evil.

The Cold War liberals of the era, led by figures like Arthur Schlesinger

Jr. and Reinhold Niebuhr, had made a decisive break with what they later felt was the hothouse naïveté of their youthful ideals. The horrors of World War II taught them the fallacy of trusting paper schemes like the Kellogg-Briand Pact to bring world peace, and the harsh necessities of the Cold War taught them the need to break eggs in order to make omelets. Fighting the evil of the Soviet Union often meant compromising with evils elsewhere, just as fighting Hitler had required the support of Stalin. The United States needed allies in the Middle East, and none of the available candidates was morally perfect. Israel, warts and all, was less problematic as an ally than the pet dictators and bigoted monarchs favored by State Department Arabists and the Eisenhower administration.

American liberals were more comfortable than their European counterparts with a tough, strong Israel that sometimes needed to behave ruthlessly to defend itself. Even in the post-Vietnam era, American liberals remained engaged with power, and perceived Israel pragmatically as well as moralistically. Its moral credentials might become questionable, but its growing regional power made it an increasingly valuable and indeed indispensable ally in the volatile Middle East.

The American left is intellectually, politically, and culturally complex. It is a river with many tributaries. There is a social democratic left that is culturally and politically close to the mainstream of European social democracy. There is a hard left grounded in Marxist thought, and often influenced by the experiences of the Latin American left. There are various forms of identity and gender politics, in some cases reflecting the demographic weight and cultural experiences of a fifty-year period of mass migration to the United States from all over the world. There is a religious left bent on making the United States a more just society in accordance with its religious convictions. There is a technocratic, modernizing left grounded in the Progressive movement of the early twentieth century. There is an environmental left focused above all on climate change. These currents interact with one another, sometimes cooperatively and sometimes competitively, and they rise and fall in strength and salience depending on events.

But the largest tributary in the river and the most important current in the American left is an inheritance from the nineteenth century: the providential nationalism that sees the United States as an avatar of a new kind of political and social existence with a world mission to spread democratic and egalitarian values. American democracy, America as a country where ordinary people could live in reasonable affluence and full equality before the law, America as a country that welcomed immigrants from around the world—these have always been important values for the American left. Whether it is to defend those values against internal or external threats, or to build a better society on these foundations, generations of American political activism on the left have looked to that vision, however imperfectly realized, of a shining city on the hill—and tried to build it.

These perceptions strengthened and confirmed American liberals in their traditional belief in the value and importance of a strong federal government. From the time of Lincoln onward, Black Americans have looked to the central government to protect their rights. From the Progressive Era onward, backers of a strong welfare state and economic regulation have usually considered Washington a better place to get a hearing than state capitals. In the U.S., progressive ideas are most frequently identified with the power of the nation-state, and American liberals have often appealed to national sentiment to promote goals like civil rights and help for the poor. More than that, the ideal of a common national citizenship has been a cornerstone for efforts aimed at including minority groups and immigrant groups into full economic and political rights.

In Europe, the concept of nationalism was almost universally linked to a specific ethnic, cultural, and, often, confessional identity. In the United States, nationalism has been a more dynamic and wide-ranging concept. As we've seen, the "denominational nation" idea that emerged from the seventeenth century, in which many confessional groups could be part of a single Protestant nation, set the American approach to nationalism on a different path. In the eighteenth century, American national identity was erected not only on the basis of religious pluralism, but also out of the preexisting colonial identities. An "American" was a Methodist, a Congregationalist, or a freethinker; she was also a New Yorker, a Virginian, or a Pennsylvanian. In the nineteenth century, the increasing ethnic diversity of the American nation was addressed by extending the denominational model to "national origin." Irish-Americans, Swedish-Americans, Jewish-Americans, Italian-Americans could all find a place under the American flag.

In American history, nationalism became the rallying cry of those who believed in widening the circle of participation in political and cultural life. It was, Frederick Douglass argued, un-American to deny Americans of African descent their right to the flag and the citizenship that it represented. It was, new immigrants argued, un-American to deny them their equal rights. It was un-American to intern American citizens of Japanese origin during World War II.

Nationalism was not the problem that American liberals attempted to solve. It was one of the tools they needed to address the religious, ethnic, and racial bigotry that disfigured American society. Solving these problems required *more* America, not less. The more Americans believed in their common identity and citizenship, the more acceptance minority groups would find. "America the beautiful" remains an ideal for many American liberals, who grow misty-eyed on the Fourth of July, feel a lump in their throats when they visit the Lincoln Memorial, and who see the suffragist, labor, and civil rights movements as embodiments of an American spirit that should be honored and emulated today.

Given the deep appeal of these views among American Democrats, the view on the European left that "nationalism" must inevitably lead to irredentism, aggression, chauvinism, and war resonates weakly if at all with many ordinary American left-leaning voters. This is not because—or only because—some Americans are naive and idealistic about international affairs. Nor is it because the American people are essentially satisfied with their current boundaries and lack any sense that American nationalism must pick fights with the neighbors. It is because for most Americans, their concept of nationalism has been harnessed into a moral framework by the belief that America has a unique role in world history and its success as a nation is connected to whether it fulfills the responsibilities of its world historical mission.

We saw early on that Americans' awareness in the eighteenth and nineteenth centuries that their country was destined, if it held together, to play a pivotal part in world history was an important ingredient in the emerging American identity. To some observers, the idea that one's country has an important part to play in world history sounds like the height of arrogance and chauvinism. In the American case that has sometimes been true, but the concept of a special American destiny has often served to set moral limits on American behavior. It has also served to deepen the bond of unity among Americans at home, and to give what might have been a somewhat nebulous sense of common identity and citizenship a much more practical focus. When Lincoln said in the Gettysburg Address that the American Civil War was a war to save democracy worldwide ("Now we are engaged in a great civil war, testing whether that nation, *or any nation* so conceived and so dedicated, can long endure") he was drawing on this sense of America's global importance to strengthen the nation's commitment. He was not saying that America had a right to rule the world or to expand its frontiers at will; his idea of America's providential role acted as a check on chauvinistic ideas and pointed toward an American destiny that involved the peaceful coexistence with many other states.

For much of the American left and the electoral base of the Democratic Party, the idea that America had a providential role to fulfill in the dissemination of political enlightenment was as useful at home as abroad. How could the United States fulfill its global role if it did not abolish slavery, give women the vote, repeal bans against Asian immigration, end discrimination against minority groups, attack poverty, and offer a decent social safety net? A long line of American reformers used these arguments—at the same time that they used the idea of a common national identity and citizenship—to unite disparate and sometimes suspicious voters from many different cultural and ethnic backgrounds into the Democratic coalition that brought the New Deal and the Great Society into being. These arguments would be deployed once again as American liberals attacked the Trump administration for abandoning, as they saw it, the values that were an essential part of America's world role.

Many Americans on the left do not think "America" is all about conquest, domination, or racism, and they do not feel a tension between wishing America well and wishing other countries prosperity and success. They certainly feel that America sometimes behaves foolishly or even selfishly, and they know that not all Americans share their view of the world. They do not think America is perfect, and many of them have had searing firsthand experiences with racist, sexist, or otherwise oppressive teachers, bosses, or institutions. They know that life in America is often unfair to the little guy, and they look for political leaders who can do something about it. Whether it is a single-payer health care system or a wealth tax, they are willing to consider political and economic changes that horrify many conservatives—in the name of further perfecting the American union. If America falls short it is not because our ideals are flawed but because we have failed to live up to them. Liberals aren't less American than conservatives or others in this view; from their perspective they are more American than their opponents, and that is a good thing.

═══

Events in the twentieth century deepened the liberal faith in a unique American destiny. Franklin Roosevelt's legacy to the Democratic Party in both peace and war reflected his deep immersion in the culture and values of providential American nationalism. For FDR, the belief that the United States had a great role and a great responsibility in world affairs was too obvious to need to be defended. That its global role rested on the traditions of political and economic freedom that undergirded the American system was self-evident, and this faith animates his wartime speeches and statements from the fireside chats to the Atlantic Charter. Care for the poor and for the integration of immigrants and minorities was also fundamental to his vision of the nation and of the responsibilities of the federal government. And if his leadership on issues like civil rights, and his acquiescence in the internment of Japanese Americans during World War II, failed to live up to his lofty rhetoric, Roosevelt never seems to have lost the faith that he was leading the nation toward a place from which, in the future, it could reach the goal of liberty and justice for all its citizens. He did not think that America had reached the end of the road of human progress, but rather that America was on that road and that American leadership was necessary to help the whole world reach that road, and that it was his job to lead America further down that road.

Internationally, the United States played a critical role in the defeat of fascism. It then went on to press for the establishment of the United Nations and, thanks to Eleanor Roosevelt, it succeeded in introducing the Universal Declaration of Human Rights. Faced with the danger of a totalitarian Soviet Union armed with nuclear weapons, the United States responded by building a democratic alliance of western nations. The Marshall Plan, widely hailed as one of the most visionary and effective exercises in foreign policy in the history of the world, not only consolidated democracy in Europe, it set former enemy nations on the road toward what would become the European Union.

Further afield, the United States did its best to accelerate the process of decolonization, and American economists, health specialists, and aid workers spread around the world to help the new nations achieve prosperity, democracy, and stability. That these efforts did not always succeed, and that when retrograde Republicans like the despised John Foster Dulles were in charge, American foreign policy did not always live up to liberal ideals, did not, liberals felt, diminish America's historical role. Failures and limitations were a sign that liberals needed to try harder.

Comparing the second half of the twentieth century when the United States exercised a leading world role with the earlier decades when it limited its role, American liberals felt sure that American leadership was good for the world. When the Cold War between two nuclear superpowers ended peacefully with the collapse of the Soviet Union, and Americans along with their allies moved to expand the world of prosperous democracy from the West into the Warsaw Pact world and beyond, the sense of a special American vocation only deepened. Facing unprecedented evils and navigating an era of nuclear terror the likes of which had never been seen before, the providential nation brought the world through to a safe harbor.

The gap between American liberals who embraced this perspective and Israel was real, but it was not nearly as wide as the gap between Israel and the European left. Israel's behavior, especially with respect to the Palestinians, might be problematic for the American center-left, but its Zionist ideology was not. For many on the American left, the cause of Zionism was viewed through the same lens as any other national struggle. The plight of the Jews was treated in the same way any other human rights or refugee crisis would be.

For decades, the Soviet Jewry Movement enjoyed widespread support from the left in the United States, among Jews and gentiles alike. The Jackson-Vanik amendment that threatened to frustrate Kissinger's efforts at détente is named for two Democrats. Human rights advocates as well as pro-Israel groups like AIPAC supported emigration for Jews in the Soviet bloc throughout much of the Cold War. The refusenik issue kept the American Jewish community united in its support for Zionism and Israel through the twentieth century, even as denunciations of Israel's treatment of the Palestinians became more and more frequent on the left. Even into the twenty-first century, when it came to the right of persecuted Jews to emigrate to Israel—or to the right of Israel to defend itself against attack—many Democrats remained instinctively supportive of the Jewish state. Israeli providential nationalism made a certain intuitive sense to American providential nationalists, and the belief that the revival of the Jewish people was part of the globally liberating mission of the American nation had deep roots among American progressives.

The uniquely American answer to the Jewish Question continued to influence the way American liberals understood the Israeli-Palestinian conflict. The European idea that Jewish identity was religious or racial rather than "national" made Zionism look like either a theocratic or a racial program. To Americans, liberal or conservative, the idea that Jews were a national group and that American Jews could be proud of a Jewish national identity while being fully integrated into the American nation made Zionism look like a natural and normal exercise of the right of self-determination. From this perspective, the conflict between Israelis and Palestinians was not a conflict between racist or theocratic colonizers and a non-European people struggling against imperialism. It was a tragic conflict between two rights: the right of the Jewish people to a national home and the right of the Palestinian people to the same.

One should also note the role of liberal Protestant religious groups from so-called mainline denominations in the gradual shift of liberal and leftist Americans away from a pro-Israel stance. Providential nationalism has played a particularly significant role in American liberal Protestantism. That tradition, whose adherents dominated the American establishment for most of the century following the Civil War, acknowledges the inherent tension between the natural affection people have for their homeland and Christianity's more universal mission. Providential nationalism largely resolves that tension: if the larger purpose of the United States is to advance universal values that are drawn from the Christian tradition, then love of country is a natural complement to religion, not a competitor. Most though not all saw support for Zionism as consistent with their support for other liberal international causes ranging from the liberation of the classical nations of antiquity to national self-determination for Poles, Czechs, and other nations of the imperial zone to the breakup of the European colonial empires. Liberal Protestants were often at the forefront of these movements.

Other crosscurrents within liberal Protestantism have complicated its relationship with Zionism. Some, like Reinhold Niebuhr, were strong advocates of the Jewish state for secular and humanitarian reasons while rejecting the literal interpretations of biblical prophecy widely embraced by Christian Zionists like William Blackstone. Many, however, had opposed the Zionist movement from its beginnings. Connected to Arab Christians, and sympathetic to the cause of Arab nationalism, Protestant leaders like Oberlin president Henry Churchill King and businessman and philanthropist Charles Richard Crane saw the Zionist dream as a nightmare for Middle East Christians and Muslims alike. At Woodrow Wilson's request, King and Crane traveled across former Ottoman territories to discern what the inhabitants sought from the Versailles Peace Conference. Their report was strongly anti-Zionist, and described the strong opposition of the majority of residents in the region to the Balfour Declaration.[22] These sentiments never disappeared, influencing men like John Foster Dulles and contributing to a tradition of pro-Arab engagement in denominations as varied as the Quakers, Presbyterians, and Episcopalians.

In the 1920s and 1930s, the natural home for liberal Protestants was in the Republican Party, but during the 1960s the mainline churches tended to move toward the Democratic Party and, at a somewhat slower pace, the views of their members moved toward the left. Closer culturally and even theologically to Reform Judaism than to some evangelical and Pentecostal movements, mainline churches have grown increasingly critical of Israeli policies toward the Palestinians.

Yet consistent and fervent as their criticism of Israel sometimes becomes, precisely because of their liberal theological roots, mainline Christians remember the long history of Christian antisemitism. They are generally careful to put their criticisms of Israeli conduct in the context of continuing goodwill toward the Jewish people and, especially, to American Jews. The effect is both to increase the amount and to limit the content of anti-Israel sentiment among liberals and Democrats.

Beyond that, American liberals were still responsible for conducting the foreign policy of a global superpower. They understood the sometimes ugly compromises that power necessarily involves in international affairs, and even as they struggled to elevate the moral tone of world politics they knew that American foreign policy could not be reduced to a set of simple moral rules. That perspective made it easier for them to understand, if not always to accept, the realism and hard-power calculations informing Israeli policies toward the Palestinians. It also put perceived Israeli misbehavior in context. Even at its worst, Israel was not the most difficult or hardheaded foreign power with which the United States needed to engage.

For all these reasons, the Democratic Party remained a much more pro-Israel party than many center-left parties in Europe. That orientation would be tested in the next twenty years as America grew more polarized, the prospects for peace between Israelis and Palestinians faded, and as doubts about providential nationalism grew among some Democrats. Yet the relationship endured. After a year that saw bitter battles between the Obama administration and Republicans in Congress over the Iran nuclear deal and over a GOP-organized speech by Prime Minister Benjamin Netanyahu to Congress that angered many of President Obama's allies, 53 percent of Democrats in a Gallup poll at the end of February 2016 reported that they sympathized more with Israel than with the Palestinians.[23] When Senator Joe Biden handily defeated Senator Bernie Sanders for the Democratic presidential nomination four years later, the wing of the party most closely associated with confidence in American values, appreciation for the difficult realities of power politics, and continuing if sometimes critical sympathy for Zionism seemed poised to control American foreign policy in a new Democratic administration.

Even so, the ground continued to shift. As the economic, political, and military shocks of the twenty-first century reverberated across American politics, Democrats increasingly questioned the assumptions behind the Rooseveltian liberalism that still broadly informed the party. Was America becoming a more equal and a more just society? Was America really a beacon of freedom to the world, an example that others should imitate—or was it time for Americans to start learning from others? And if America was not leading the world toward a better future, in what sense could American nationalism be justified? Was American nationalism even justifiable from a moral point of view?

These were normal and natural, even unavoidable questions given the economic and social pressures of the day, but the effect was to drive a wedge between Rooseveltian Democrats and an active if not always united or organized post-Rooseveltian left. Some were motivated primarily by a sense of identity politics, believing that, for example, racism was so foundational to American identity that any form of American nationalism was essentially a form of "white nationalism." For others, the resistance of flag-waving populists on the right on global governance issues ranging from climate change to the International Criminal Court demonstrated the incompatibility of any form of nationalism, American nationalism included, with the deep global cooperation increasingly required to address critical twenty-first-century issues.

It was out of this complex of ideas and associations that Democratic views of Israel policy developed, and the Obama administration would retain widespread popularity with American Jews, among others, as it sought to build an Israel policy on this basis—even when those policies led to direct conflicts with the government of Israeli prime minister Benjamin Netanyahu.

20

Cool Hands, Hot World

WHEN PRESIDENT BARACK OBAMA entered the White House in January 2009, the world and the nation were in disarray. An economy in crisis, a revanchist Russia occupying parts of Georgian territory, wars in Afghanistan and Iraq: it was beginning to look as if the end of the Cold War might not have ushered in a post-historical liberal millennium of peace and democracy after all. Could it be that history with all its tyranny and bloodshed was shambling back onto the stage?

The incoming Obama administration's answer to that question was a resounding No. George W. Bush had misled the nation into unnecessary wars, and the laxly regulated economy favored by Sun Belt Republicans and conservative Democrats had crashed, but those errors could be reversed. With the right policies and the right leader, the economy could be restored, peace and democracy could flourish, America's own sins of racism and problems of inequality could be addressed, climate change could be countered. Coolheaded technocratic skill informed by the values of providential progressive nationalism could undo the errors of the Bush administration and bend the arc of history back onto its proper course.

The new administration embraced a complicated and even paradoxical approach to foreign policy. In part, the Obama administration accepted the realist restrainer critique of Bush-era policy. Under Bush, the United States had both overextended and overmilitarized its international commitments. A sensible foreign policy would involve a certain amount of retrenchment.

But at the same time, many in the new administration believed that fighting climate change, moving toward the abolition of nuclear weapons, and the promotion of human rights were objectives that the United States could not afford to ignore. To achieve these ambitious goals would require a significant expansion of American commitments and an even deeper entanglement in a complex world situation.

The balance between realist restraint and Wilsonian ambition would shift during the Obama administration as the limits to American power weighed more heavily on White House thinking, but the tension between an essentially realist strategy and the determined pursuit of transformational goals would endure. This gap between the outsized goals Americans wanted to achieve and the limited means they were willing to employ was, of course, the characteristic and bipartisan problem of post-historical consensus foreign policy—as it had been for the Lodge consensus almost a century before. This new consensus was built on the belief that the arc of history was a double rainbow; technological progress and liberal order arched across the heavens on parallel tracks. And like its predecessors, the Obama administration would address any discrepancies between its hopeful projections and the actual state of the world with the traditional American tool of magical thinking: basing American national strategy on unrealistic assumptions about the short-term transformational power of American ideals.

That said, the global strategy that the Obama administration put forward was more realist than the aggressive democracy promotion of George W. Bush's second term and more modest than many of the administration's critics were prepared to acknowledge, and it had more than a little in common with the strategy Richard Nixon and Henry Kissinger employed to wind down American commitments.

Nixon and Kissinger combined withdrawal from Indochina, détente with the Soviet Union, the abandonment of Bretton Woods, and the outreach to China to put American policy on a more sustainable footing. President Obama hoped to combine a reduction in America's Middle East presence and commitments with a better relationship with Russia, an increased focus on global governance issues like disarmament and climate change, and a "pivot to Asia" to better balance American commitments with American interests.

It was a clear design and success would have brought significant benefits to the United States. But things did not go as planned. Vladimir Putin saw more advantages in scoring points against the Americans than in reaching an arrangement with them. The "pivot to Asia" had such a modest military component that it did more to reinforce than to counter the Chinese belief that the United States was locked in an irreversible process of decline. The global governance objectives attracted too little support at home and too much opposition abroad to achieve the hoped-for success. And developing a coherent strategy for reducing American commitments in the Middle East proved much harder on the ground and more contentious in American politics than perhaps the administration had expected—a not uncommon problem when foreign policy conceptions move from the briefing books into the real world.

On its realist restrainer side, the administration seemed ready to accept and even to celebrate the end of unipolarity and the arrival of a new, multipolar world. But on its aspirational, Wilsonian side, the administration appeared to believe that the ideals that inspired American liberals were driving world history.

This conviction is easily caricatured, but there are reasons why serious people with long experience in international affairs embrace a Wilsonian stance. They argue that Wilsonian principles will not prevail because they are morally beautiful or because people are basically good but because they reflect realities to which political leaders must ultimately conform.

Reflecting on the consequences of nuclear weapons for international politics can help us appreciate the power of this idea. By all the logic of geopolitical thinking, the United States and the Soviet Union should have settled their differences in the traditional way: a great power war. That never happened in forty years of bitter global rivalry because both sides understood that a nuclear war between them was not just immoral but pointless. Self-interest not idealism kept American presidents and Soviet leaders from pushing the button. More than that, the existence of nuclear weapons and the impossibility of great power war led the two sides into disarmament talks and drove them to manage their conflict peacefully.

Wilsonians observe that nuclear weapons are only one of the means by which technological progress is gradually and progressively imposing a new kind of logic on geopolitics. As the world becomes more advanced technologically and integrated economically, the reality of interdependence will force national governments toward new forms of cooperation whether they like it or not. Problems like climate change, pandemics, financial regulation, and cybersecurity cannot be solved by national governments acting alone. Those problems are so important, and the consequences of failing to address them adequately are so grave, that regardless of culture, ideology, and geopolitical rivalries, liberal internationalists believe, countries have no choice but to work together on them.

The necessity of deepening cooperation across a growing number of issues changes the nature of geopolitical rivalry just as the existence of nuclear weapons imposed a new shape on the U.S.-Soviet rivalry and kept the Cold War cold. Different countries will continue to compete, but that competition will take place in a framework increasingly defined by the common interests that no country can afford to ignore. Those interests, liberal internationalist ideology maintains, will drive even bitter geopolitical rivals into long-term arrangements and binding institutions, and that development in turn will further limit the scope and intensity of their competition.

Confusion often creeps in, and creep it did in the Obama administration, whenever American liberals conflate the forces driving countries into more far-reaching and durable forms of international cooperation with the hoped-for triumph of the values and ideals that American liberals care most about. In practice, things aren't that simple.

If the United States, Russia, and China among others must cooperate to address urgent problems, that does not necessarily mean that Russia and China must convert their political systems to match the United States. Quite possibly, in order to achieve the necessary cooperation, the United States might have to accept their illiberal regimes as legitimate and permanent partners—as co-pillars of a world order that would be something other than liberal. This might not simply involve an "authoritarian carve-out" that accepted that foreign great powers could maintain their own systems at home. It might well require an acceptance of spheres of interest beyond their frontiers. Perhaps ideological competition is one of the forms of international competition that must be discarded if humanity is to survive.

President Richard Nixon's foreign policy of détente with the Soviet Union and opening to Maoist China was based on the belief that the United States did not have the ability to produce a global liberal order, and that compromises would have to be made. Those compromises were moral and ideological as well as geopolitical, and in the interests of its global strategy the Nixon administration moderated its criticism of the rampant suppression of dissenters in the Soviet Union and the unspeakable cruelties of China's Cultural Revolution. In Nixon's judgment, the United States needed an orderly world more than it needed a liberal order.

The intellectual essence of the post-historical consensus was a firm conviction that the processes of globalization and liberalization were connected. The same forces that drove the great powers toward closer cooperation on issues like climate change were also driving them toward ideological convergence around liberal values.

In some ways the Obama administration had a more sophisticated view of world politics than its immediate predecessors. It understood that the cultural arrogance inherent in Euro-Atlantic societies and the resentment of that arrogance by nonwestern countries were significant factors in international life. The administration hoped that the president's life story and racial background would help bridge this divide, and also believed that less American chest-thumping about their exceptionalism and more reliance on patient diplomacy would smooth the path of the emergent world order.

Like most Americans (and certainly like the Bush administration that preceded it), the Obama administration overestimated the role that admiration for American ideology plays in global attitudes toward the United States. Because it was so firmly convinced that American ideas are both universally valid and universally shared, the administration failed to grasp the degree to which America's "soft power" was tied less to admiration for the inspirational qualities of American values than to perceptions of American economic success and military prowess.

Conventional liberal opinion in the United States drew a sharp distinction between "hard power," usually military, and "soft power" approaches grounded in ideology, values, and the promotion of international institutions and the liberal world order. Hard power was seen as likely to lead to confrontational relations with other countries, while a greater reliance on soft power would lead to a more peaceful international system and wider support for American initiatives. Hard power was about win-lose international competition, while soft power, seeking win-win solutions, was more likely to lead to consensus and cooperation. For the Obama administration, therefore, rebalancing American foreign policy away from hard power toward the promotion of values and norms would lead to more harmonious relations with other powers even as the United States would make more progress on promoting its democratic values.

This is not how Beijing and Moscow saw matters. America's moral and political support for "color revolutions" (democratic revolutions in previously authoritarian countries) looked like a dangerous and relentless policy of ideological aggression aimed ultimately at overthrowing Putin in Moscow and the Chinese Communist Party in Beijing. Promoting a "liberal world order" and human rights might seem innocent and peaceful to American liberals, but this soft power diplomacy both attacked the legitimacy of nonliberal governments and attempted to restrict their sovereign independence in a web of liberal norms and law-driven international institutions.

America's opponents, even though they saw what they considered an ambitious ideological offensive aimed at destabilizing and endangering them, still noted that the Obama administration was largely unprepared to withstand any pushback. Washington might welcome an anti-Russian revolution in Ukraine and hail the new government's desire to turn toward the West, but neither the United States nor the European Union was prepared for a vigorous Russian response.

The Obama administration was slow to understand both the degree of Chinese and Russian opposition and the dramatic growth in their ability to frustrate American designs. Whether occupying Crimea, dispatching troops to Syria, or building artificial islands in the South China Sea, the two adversarial powers consistently wrong-footed the Obama administration, eroding the prestige and influence of the administration and of the United States as a whole. Rather than witnessing a return to the post–Cold War democratic euphoria, the Obama years would see a further decline in the power of liberal ideology—within the United States as well as globally—and the return of full-fledged geopolitical competition between the United States and an emerging, revisionist, and illiberal Sino-Russian entente.

It was the unhappy fate of the Obama administration to take office at a time when the optimistic post-historical consensus encountered a rising tide of illiberalism in world politics. Faced with political and intellectual challenges for which it was largely unprepared, the administration would oscillate between engagement and retreat.

THE UNICORN HUNT

The Middle East, President Obama and his team believed, was not America's highest priority for the long or even medium term, but initially at least no region of the world mattered more to the Obama strategy. It was his early, eloquent, and unceasing opposition to the Iraq War that made the young Illinois senator a national figure, and that record contributed mightily to his ability to mobilize liberal Democrats against what had once appeared to be the inevitable 2008 nomination of Hillary Clinton as the Democratic presidential candidate. Obama also understood that, despite qualms among some human rights activists in the Democratic coalition, his administration needed to remain vigilant against terrorism. Successful terrorist attacks emerging from the Middle East or clearly linked to groups operating there had the potential to turn the political climate back to the incandescent conditions of the first eighteen months after 9/11, a development that might well prove fatal to the Obama presidency and to any hopes of setting American foreign policy on what the incoming president considered a more sustainable and sensible path.

The Bush administration might have left the Middle East in a chaotic condition and awash in anti-American sentiment, but the Obama team saw some hopeful signs in 2009. Bush's policies had been so unpopular in the Arab world that any kind of change would buy goodwill. And Obama's biography and race made him, potentially, a much more attractive figure in the region than other presidents had been. Add to this Obama's genuine understanding of some of the grievances that formerly colonized peoples and people of color felt toward the West, and it seemed possible, even likely, that the new president could calm the relationship between the United States and the Arab world.

Even better, it appeared that a reaction to terrorism among moderate Islamist political forces offered the possibility of a dramatic new opening. In Iraq, the courageous leadership of the Ayatollah Ali al-Sistani contributed decisively to the establishment of a weak but real democratic system in that troubled country. Recep Tayyip Erdoğan, then prime minister of Turkey, seemed to be pointing the way to "democratic Islamism." Many figures in the Muslim Brotherhood also spoke of reaching Islamist goals through democratic methods.[1] For American liberals, this appeared to be a welcome reprise of the Cold War dynamic in which social democrats, who supported many ideals claimed by communist parties but shunned their calls for violent revolution and the installation of autocratic regimes, became indispensable allies. The Muslim Brotherhood and its allies, many hoped, would promote democratization and blunt the appeal of radical groups like Al-Qaeda in much the same way. Iranian exiles and expatriates described a generation of moderates yearning to end the confrontation with the West if only the United States would open the door. To take advantage of this opportunity, American foreign policy should have focused on creating conditions in which the more democratically minded elements in Islamic society, religious and secular, could partner with the United States to remake the region.

To reach a position in which this kind of outreach was possible, the United States needed to shift its approach on some important regional issues. In the first place, to appeal to moderate Muslim opinion the United States would need to achieve something on the Palestinian issue. Israeli policies on settlements and intransigence in negotiations, the Obama administration believed, were not just bad for Israel (endangering its future status as a Jewish and democratic state by preventing the emergence of a Palestinian state on the Occupied Territories), but so exacerbated the feelings of Arab Muslims that radical anti-Americanism prospered among them and even moderates would not or could not side with an American government seen as too indulgent toward Israel.[2]

But the relationship with Israel was only part of the American problem in the Middle East. America's cozy relationships with Arab monarchs and dictatorships also needed to change. These so-called American allies were the chief obstacle to democratic progress in the Middle East. Their secret police relentlessly suppressed all democratic opposition, and America's long-standing alliance with these rulers helped them cling to power.[3]

In effect, the Obama administration saw Israel the way John Foster Dulles and the Arabists saw it and saw the Arab leaders the way Eleanor Roosevelt and the pro-Israel liberals saw them. Like the Arabists, the Obama administration thought that the Israeli alliance made the natural and necessary warm U.S. relationship with other Muslim Middle East countries more difficult if not impossible and carried a heavy cost that the U.S. needed to work to offset. And like the pro-Israel liberals in the 1940s, an important group of officials in the Obama administration thought that the existing monarchies and autocracies of the Arab world were about to be swept away by rising democratic tides, and that basing American policy on close alliances with nondemocratic Middle East governments was immoral, shortsighted, and costly.

There were two new elements in the Obama approach. First, while both the Arabists and the Cold War liberals had seen the Middle East as a critical theater for American world policy and wanted to entrench the United States more deeply in it, the Obama administration accepted the realist restrainer view that the United States was overextended and needed to reduce its commitments and entanglements in the Middle East. Second, the Obama administration embraced the idea, increasingly dominant among Democratic liberals in general and liberal American Jews in particular, that what Israel needed from the United States was tough love. To permit Israel to drift toward settlement and annexation policies that made the two-state solution impossible was to undermine Israel, not to support it. The United States needed to rescue Israel from itself.

Yet dissolving the special relationship was not part of Obama's agenda. Obama's approach to Israel was more sophisticated and realistic as well as more sympathetic than the prescriptions of many realist restrainer policy intellectuals because it acknowledged the power of political facts. The deep American political attachment to Israel, still strongly felt in both parties, was a reality that Obama was ready to accept, even as he sought to limit the constraints this attachment imposed on American policymaking.

Some of the perceptions shaping the Obama administration's approach had the merit of being true, but building an effective or even a coherent foreign policy on this basis proved unexpectedly hard. Showing tough love to the Arabs by pushing democratic reforms on monarchies and dictatorships might be moral, but it would not smooth relationships with Arab governments. To offer Israel tough love on the occupation might serve Israeli and American interests better in the long run than the alternative but would lead to difficult relations and policy clashes from day one. And to appeal to both Arab and Israeli governments to support American positions and assist American projects when the prospect of a reduction of American commitments in the region undermined American influence was not an easy lift.

The plan was to begin by reaching out to Arab and Muslim public opinion directly with a new message about the relationship between the United States and Islam. President Obama's eloquent speeches in Cairo and Ankara launched this process,[4] and despite his courageous defense of American support for Israel's right to exist, the speeches, and the new president, were warmly received.

But the applause faded away, and the next steps were not clear. Ironically, and tragically, while the Obama administration was initially more cautious than its immediate predecessor about the prospects for a democratic transformation of the Middle East, the intoxicating excitement of the series of protests and upheavals known collectively if misleadingly as the Arab Spring would persuade the administration to discard its caution and reserve. The idea that the region was on the verge of a liberal political transformation was a dazzling daydream produced by an American policy community intoxicated on liberal ideology and post-historical triumphalism. Bill Clinton, George W. Bush, and, despite his skepticism, Barack Obama were all influenced by this optimism, their appointees and advisors perhaps even more so. It was an age of miracles when magical dancing democracy unicorns would appear in country after country, shattering autocracies and installing democratic and pro-American regimes. Perhaps the next manifestation of democracy unicorns would take place in the Middle East.

The vision of a transformed Middle East that haunted post–Cold War American thinking had two fundamental problems. In the first place, it was impossible to achieve—there was simply no short- or even medium-term prospect for the kind of transformation Americans sought. Second, poorly conceived efforts to promote democratic change weakened American alliances, reduced American prestige, and scrambled what order the Middle East had managed to cobble together.

President Obama understood that American assistance for democratic and opposition movements in the Arab world was inevitably constrained. Washington's ability and willingness to support democracy movements always had to be conditioned and limited by the pressing need to do business with the governments in power. Bahrain, where a Sunni dynasty ruled a predominantly Shi'a population, was not a very democratic country, but it was the site of an American base that the Obama administration did not wish to close. The United States government did not want to see the Kingdom of Jordan destabilized in any way.

Regardless of how many Palestinians voted for Hamas, its authorities in Gaza were hated and detested not only by Israel, but by Egypt, the Palestinian Authority, and most of the Gulf monarchies. American policy could not long ignore facts as powerful as these.

If the constraints on American support were one factor limiting the potential for a Middle East transition to liberal order, the limits of Middle East democracy movements were another. The democratic moderate Islamists for whose sake the administration was pursuing this challenging policy mix were either unwilling (as in the case of Turkey's Erdoğan) or unable (as in the case of Egypt's Muslim Brotherhood) to do in the Middle East what democratic socialists had done in Cold War Europe. This does not mean that democracy has no future in the Middle East. But the democratic and proto-democratic forces at work in the region were not strong enough or well developed enough to steer the region toward the kind of order Americans hoped to see. There were fewer unicorns than optimistic American policymakers expected, and the unicorns that did exist were clumsier dancers and less magical than the ambitious American timetable required.

The Unicorns Miss the Bus

The Arab Spring, as the 2011 wave of pro-reform demonstrations and movements stretching from Morocco to Iraq became known, seemed to vindicate those in the American government who believed that American foreign policy should work for the establishment of democratic governance across the Middle East.

When protests exploded in Cairo, more credulous and less seasoned western observers, tragically including a number of prominent White House staffers, were exhilarated beyond measure by pro-democracy demonstrations. Here was the democratic revolution Wilsonian foreign policy aimed to promote, and it was breaking out in the very city where Obama launched his policy of outreach and reconciliation with moderate Arab opinion. The arc of history was bending at last! The United States needed to break with Egyptian president Hosni Mubarak and support Egypt's emerging democracy before it was too late.

More experienced and knowledgeable aides and observers, including the secretaries of state and defense, were more cautious, but the enthusiasm of the younger folks prevailed with the normally skeptical president, and with high hopes that the Democracy Train was making a Cairo stop, the United States used its influence to force Mubarak out.[5]

Events failed to follow the American script. Egypt's liberals were politically isolated and organizationally weak. The largest opposition force in the country, the Muslim Brotherhood, broke earlier pledges to refrain from offering a candidate in the presidential race and ran the undistinguished Mohamed Morsi for the presidency.[6] Morsi was elected, but between the ineptitude of the Muslim Brotherhood, the resistance of the Egyptian bureaucracy, and the hostility of the military, the government floundered. Tourists fled, both foreign and Egyptian investors sent their money to safer havens, and the economy stumbled toward collapse. In 2013, mass demonstrations against the failing Morsi government swept the country leading to a military coup with, initially at least, broad popular support.[7]

What the unicorn spotters had missed was the historical and political context around the Egyptian events. Egypt has been a military republic since Gamal Abdel Nasser and the Egyptian military leaders aligned with him overthrew the pro-British King Farouk in 1952. During those seventy years, Egypt has been ruled by a succession of powerful presidents, all coming from the military. There are reasons why this is the case. Fundamentally, while Egyptian liberals and the business community dislike the corruption, stagnation, and repression that accompany military government, they prefer military rule to the risks of majoritarian and populist governance that, they fear, will inevitably be heavily influenced by conservative interpretations of Islamic ideas.

The Egyptian military was not happy with Hosni Mubarak in 2011. Mubarak was promoting his second son, Gamal Mubarak, as his successor, much as Syrian president Hafez al-Assad groomed his son as his political heir. This was a direct threat to the basis of the Egyptian status quo, and to the interests of those in and around the military who expected to benefit when the time came to replace Mubarak with another military figure. A republic whose presidency is hereditary can no longer be called a republic, and the Egyptian military did not welcome the conversion of the Egyptian state into the dynastic possession of the Mubarak family.

Egyptian security forces did not refrain from crushing the democracy demonstrations because they thought an irresistible tide of democracy was sweeping their country. The military let the protests continue as a way of forcing Mubarak to abandon his dynastic ambitions.

Over the following months, the military seems to have explored what might be called the Pakistan model of military governance in which real power would remain in the hands of the generals while civilian politicians managed the daily business of government and took the blame when scapegoats were required. This kind of fraudulent pseudo-democracy was the only real alternative in Egypt to the historical Nasser model, but Morsi and the Muslim Brotherhood were both unwilling to play the inglorious role this scenario offered them and unable to capture and hold real power on their own.

As the ineptitude of the Morsi government became increasingly evident, the liberal and business preference for military rule over Islamism reasserted itself. As the passive resistance of the civil service bureaucracy combined with capital flight driven by jumpy investors threatened the stability and even the solvency of the national economy, the government could do little but wring its hands as its popularity waned. When the time was right, military authorities overthrew the elected government, drove the Muslim Brotherhood underground, and imposed the most severe crackdown on civil liberties in modern Egyptian history. Abdel Fattah el-Sisi, a career military officer who had served as head of Egyptian intelligence and was defense minister at the time of the coup against Morsi, was elected to the presidency in a vote conducted under strict limits by the post-coup government as much of the country hoped that stability even at the cost of political oppression might improve their economic conditions.[8] The old military republic was back in business.

═══

American policy during this period dismayed and alienated virtually every political tendency and every ally in the Middle East. The unceremonious dumping of President Mubarak, a longtime American ally who more than once had provided critical assistance to the United States, horrified and appalled Gulf rulers. The United States was a reliable ally until you needed help, they concluded, but when you needed help most, the Americans would betray you without a qualm.

American policies during the Egyptian crisis brought no discernible benefits to the United States or to anyone else. The cause of democracy was not advanced. The Egyptian political opposition had less space under el-Sisi than ever before. America's reputation was significantly degraded as the weakness of the intellectual foundations and the ineptitude of the practitioners of American-style democracy promotion were indecorously revealed. But if the United States lost points with autocrats and the protectors of the status quo, did its role in the Egyptian Arab Spring at least win it points with the democrats?

Sadly, the answer here, too, is no. Many in the Muslim Brotherhood blamed America's weak support and dithering, to say nothing of its failure to offer robust opposition to the anti-Morsi coup, for the failure of their experiment. That after all its talk about democracy Washington ended by accepting if not loving the coup only demonstrated to Muslim Brotherhood activists and other moderate Islamists how weak the United States was and how untrustworthy its support.

Reinforcing the disagreeable impression Obama's Egypt policy left across the region was the shortsighted and destructive Libyan intervention. The Egyptian "revolution" of January 2011 came as Libya, long ruled by the erratic Muammar Qaddafi, was about to descend into a state of civil war. In February, protests escalated into rebellion and in March, with Libyan government forces on the offensive and Qaddafi uttering bloodcurdling threats against the population of rebel-controlled cities, the United States, Britain, and France obtained a resolution from the U.N. Security Council authorizing operations to protect civilians and a NATO air campaign got under way.[9] Under NATO air cover rebel forces rallied, and Qaddafi fled the capital of Tripoli in August and was killed two months later.[10]

To the more optimistic officials in the Obama administration, this initially looked like a triumph for international law and the campaign to transform the Middle East. The American-led multilateral world order was working. NATO and the United Nations were preventing mass civilian atrocities. An evil despot had met a just reward and a new, more representative government appeared to be taking shape in Libya. The idea that grave abuses of human rights could justify international intervention had gained credibility, strengthening the framework of international law. Russia and China had abstained on the Security Council resolution authorizing force, allowing the resolution to pass and suggesting to hopeful internationalists that with sufficient patience and wise diplomacy those powers could still become responsible stakehold-ers in a world order built around American ideas.[11]

The disillusionment process was gradual but thorough. The National Transition Council, created in Benghazi in February 2011, handed power over to an elected government in August of 2012, but militias contin-ued to fight for control of much of the country. The collapse of central-ized control allowed various militias, warlords, and radical Islamists to seize the weaponry stockpiled over decades by the Qaddafi government. Libyan weapons and fighters would spread across northern Africa, into the Sahel and beyond, fueling substantial increases in civil conflict and jihadi violence well beyond Libya's frontiers. Inside the country, the prospect of controlling Libya's rich hydrocarbon resources drew neigh-boring countries like Egypt, Algeria, Italy, and France as well as more distant powers including Qatar, the UAE, Turkey, and Russia into the conflict.

The devolution of Libya into a continual state of civil war and the increasingly thuggish behavior of every participant in the conflict made it progressively harder to see the NATO intervention as either a human-itarian or a democratization success. Further consequences unfolded as the instability spread from Libya across the region. Desperate Afri-cans streamed across Libya's unpatrolled frontiers for the coast where they hoped to board ships for Europe. Libyan warlords were not slow to capitalize on the opportunity represented by hundreds of thousands of migrants. Between people-smuggling operations and extortion schemes (migrants were held in work camps and beaten and tortured while beg-ging their relatives over cell phones to send ransoms), post-NATO Libya became the locus for what were some of the most horrific abuses taking place on the planet.[12]

On September 11, 2012, an armed attack on the U.S. diplomatic mis-sion in Benghazi and a CIA facility nearby led to a firefight whose casu-alties included Christopher Stevens, the American ambassador to Libya, along with foreign service and CIA employees and contractors.[13] The attack set off a political firestorm in the United States, and while Repub-lican allegations of wrongdoing against senior administration officials ultimately fell short, it was clear following Benghazi that neither democ-racy nor liberal order was coming to the Middle East anytime soon.

For eleven years since the 9/11 attacks, two American presidents had built Middle East policy around the idea that the United States could best defend itself from terror attacks by engineering a political and economic transformation of the Middle East. In 2012 that era was coming to an end.

The disaster in Libya would shape the American response to the Syria crisis in ways that lost all the ground gained by the administration's earlier attempts to build bridges to the Sunni world. The spectacle of American passivity regarding Syria when confronted with the greatest human catastrophe in the Middle East in living memory, and the appearance that American policy was tilting toward Shi'a Iran when the Sunni world felt beleaguered as never before, blanketed the region in a toxic cloud of suspicion and hate.

Past supporters of the place of values in foreign policy—for example FDR and Ronald Reagan's secretary of state George Shultz—had been able to combine rights advocacy with effective power diplomacy. This was an accomplishment that, for different reasons, neither President Obama nor his Republican predecessor were able to match. In Washington, the result was frustration as democratic transformations failed to appear or, as in Iraq where democratic institutions took hold, their impact fell well short of Washington's hopes. In the region and in the wider world, the result was a precipitous and continuing loss of confidence in the United States. Viewed from the region, whether from Cairo, Damascus, Tehran, Riyadh, or Jerusalem, the United States looked less formidable, less wise, less dependable, and less competent in 2012 than in 2001. This unhappy trend has continued up through the time in 2022 that I write these words.

The Unicorns Go Under the Bus

In its second term, the Obama administration carried out a momentous and even a historic shift in America's Middle East policy. Since the Truman administration, American engagement in the Middle East had steadily deepened. The strategic requirements of the Cold War, the growing importance of Middle East oil, and, after 9/11, the threat of fanatical terror attacks led successive American presidents to devote an ever-increasing share of attention and resources to the region.

That long-established pattern changed in President Obama's second term and his successors would follow his lead. From the death of

Ambassador Stevens in 2012 to the present day, the dominant theme in America's Middle East policy has been to reduce our regional footprint to the greatest degree compatible with American security. The more visionary goals associated with George W. Bush and President Obama's first term have been set aside. Since 2012, the United States has been more interested in reducing its commitments than in transforming the region.

The disappointing results of American democracy promotion played an important role in persuading President Obama to shift his focus, but it is misleading to think of the decision to pivot away from the Middle East as solely a consequence of failure.

Both Obama and Trump saw something else. In part, they agreed that the rise of China meant that the United States needed to turn its attention away from the Middle East toward the Indo-Pacific. But while so many high-profile American initiatives in the region had been failing spectacularly, some less obvious but highly successful policies were creating new realities that significantly enhanced the American position. Not for the first time, American soldiers, scientists, and entrepreneurs were renewing the country's strength even as intellectuals, political leaders, and diplomats failed to comprehend the forces at work.

The first success was against the jihadi terror threat. Since 9/11, American counterintelligence and counterterror operations had become far more effective. Fanatical terror attacks remained a concern, and occasional "lone wolf" attacks succeeded, but in the twenty years following 9/11 no attack on a similar scale had succeeded against the United States. The increased sophistication and power of drones added another formidable weapon to the American arsenal, a weapon that could be guided remotely by "pilots" sitting comfortably in facilities back in the United States.

The second success was connected to the first. Continuing advances in the development of the electronic battlefield and information warfare allowed a very small American presence to make an enormous difference in the fighting ability of a motivated force. Their ability to link local forces to the torrents of information coursing through American intelligence, targeting, and surveillance systems meant that a very light American footprint could turn the tide of battle on the ground. When the resurgence of radical Islamism in the ISIS revolt against Syria and Iraq briefly drew attention in the United States toward the horrors of fanaticism, only a modest American military presence sufficed to help turn the tide against the "Caliphate."

Third, after the disaster of the failed attempt to rescue the American diplomats held hostage by Iranian revolutionaries following the fall of the Shah, the military vowed to give future presidents better tools for future emergencies. That would require enhancing the training of Special Forces to new levels of effectiveness as well as developing better and more reliable equipment for action in challenging environments. The operation that resulted in the death of Osama bin Laden demonstrated the success of these efforts.

Finally, the Obama and later the Trump and Biden administrations would reap the rewards of yet another major American policy success with its roots in the 1970s. The energy crises of the 1970s made a deep impression on the American public. It was bad enough that sudden swings in a manipulated oil market could plunge the United States into years of stagflation (high unemployment, high interest rates, and high inflation); it was worse that shortfalls in foreign production could force the United States to ration energy supplies.

The shock led to a range of initiatives in government, the academy, and the private sector. Fuel efficiency standards for cars were increased, and new requirements for energy efficiency in appliances and industrial processes were introduced. Long before concerns about climate change, Americans invested in renewable energy sources like solar power, wind power, and ethanol to reduce dependence on imported fuel. Every American household and enterprise looked for ways to cut fuel consumption. Well before climate change activism began to reshape the politics of energy, the American economy was beginning to decouple from hydrocarbons in response to the high prices and political uncertainties associated with Middle East oil supplies.

A second set of initiatives aimed to diversify the nation's oil supply. Some of this involved a search for new domestic sources of oil—in Alaska, in deep water wells in the Gulf of Mexico, and in other remote locations. But the search was also worldwide. Deep water technology developed in the United States could be used off the coast of West Africa and elsewhere; over time, the dependence of the United States on Middle East oil steadily declined.

Finally, the government, universities, and private energy companies sought to unlock previously unavailable energy resources. The most prominent of these were known as shale oil and gas. New techniques of drilling collectively known as "fracking" were developed and first in a trickle and then in a flood, new sources of energy began to flow.[14] American domestic oil production fell as low as four million barrels a day in 2008. By the time President Obama left office production was at 8.88 million barrels per day and still rising. In 2019, domestic American production would reach 13 million barrels a day, well above the production of Saudi Arabia.[15]

In environmental terms these new techniques could be problematic, unleashing earthquakes in some places and leading to groundwater contamination in others. And for climate activists, who previously believed that the inevitable exhaustion of the world's fossil fuel resources would help drive the transition to renewable energy, the news that the world's fossil fuel reserves were vastly greater than expected was a deeply unwelcome development.

Nevertheless, from the standpoint of American foreign policy, the country's new energy wealth was a game changer. OPEC could no longer threaten the United States with an energy boycott. Better still from a foreign policy standpoint, the shift in pricing power from OPEC to North America (Canada had even larger reserves of unconventional hydrocarbons than the United States) meant that the global oil market was less sensitive to political developments in the Middle East. In the past, at a time of tight supplies, any sign of instability or conflict in the Middle East could set oil prices soaring worldwide. As long as this was true, American foreign policy was in a sense glued to the Middle East; American presidents could not ignore regional instability for fear of the economic upheaval that could result. Thanks to shale oil and gas, American foreign policy was less closely tied to the region.

There were other benefits as well. The surge in American oil production represented a significant transfer of income away from OPEC producers and Russia to oil consumers worldwide and especially to the United States. Putin's Russia was a less formidable adversary when oil was at $50 a barrel than at $150. At structurally lower oil prices, Iran had less money for foreign adventures and Saudi Arabia needed to think more about domestic economic development and less about funding radical mosques around the world.

———

When President Obama saw that his Middle East policies of reconciliation and engagement had ground to a halt, he had an option that none of his predecessors had enjoyed. He could significantly reduce the American footprint in the Middle East without abandoning vital American economic and security interests. In the second phase of Obama Middle East policy, the goals of Arab democratization and Sunni outreach were largely set to one side as the administration's attention shifted to the effort to extricate the United States from an inhospitable arena.

In 2004 George W. Bush called the overthrow of Saddam Hussein a "catastrophic success."[16] By contrast, President Obama's second term in the Middle East was a successful catastrophe. On the ground in the Middle East, the second phase of Obama policy would be a succession of failures and setbacks without precedent in American diplomatic history. By the end of his administration many Middle Easterners were longing for the good old days of George W. Bush. Alienated allies, weakened order, mass death and displacement on a scale that eclipsed the Iraq War, and displaced Palestinians on the greatest scale since 1948–49; not since World War I had the Middle East seen this kind of destruction. As American prestige, favorability, and credibility dropped in most of the region, a hostile Russia reestablished itself as a Middle East power for the first time since the Cold War.

Yet in American politics President Obama's Middle East policy was a success. The administration not only achieved its primary diplomatic objective, the negotiation of a nuclear agreement with Iran, it also rolled over determined opposition by the allegedly omnipotent Israel lobby. And although no previous president feuded so often or so publicly with Israel, like so many of his predecessors, President Obama was able to use Israel policy to unify and energize his own supporters.

In fact, the administration's new goal of extricating the United States from unrewarding and expensive conflicts in the Middle East was more politically popular at home than the old policy of regional transformation. With terrorism fading into the rearview mirror as an urgent danger in many American minds and with the wars in Afghanistan and Iraq looking more pointless and less brilliantly strategized as time went on, Americans were ready to move on. With the Republican establishment still pinned to a defense of Bush administration war policy, Obama's evident desire to disengage was more popular than neoconservative calls to stay the course.

As President Obama and the new secretary of state, John Kerry, looked at their options, they saw two major problems that limited American freedom of action: the danger to American security posed by the Iranian drive for nuclear weapons, and the constraints and obligations flowing from the American commitments to, and support for, the Jewish state. The two were related, in that the Iranian nuclear program represented the only real threat to Israeli security. If that threat could be addressed, then concern for Israel's security would diminish as a factor in American politics, allowing the United States to reduce its engagement with the Middle East without a bruising domestic battle over Israel policy.

The focus on a nuclear agreement with Iran was understandable. As the Obama administration looked to reduce America's exposure to new conflicts in the Middle East, Iran's quest for nuclear weapons was a contingency, perhaps the only contingency, that could force the United States into another war. Concern over this issue wasn't a new preoccupation for the second term. During the 2008 campaign, Obama had been criticized for saying that he was willing to meet the Iranians without preconditions,[17] but the desire to find a diplomatic alternative to war with Iran was a long-standing and, frankly, justifiable concern. Such a war would almost certainly be bloodier, more expensive, and more prolonged than the Iraq War, and the potential for an endless cycle of insurgencies by Iran and its proxies inside and outside the country was a strategic and political nightmare. The consequences at home and on the Democratic Party of a third unpopular Middle East war would be almost equally grave and would certainly doom any hopes the Obama administration had for enacting a wave of progressive reforms.

To make matters worse, the United States could easily lose control of events. As Iran approached the threshold of nuclear capability, Israel or possibly one of the Arab countries could launch preemptive attacks on Iran, setting off a spiral of retaliation that would draw the United States into an escalating conflict.

There were other reasons that made the goal of a nuclear agreement with Iran attractive. A successful Iranian nuclear test would likely set off a "proliferation cascade" as neighboring countries including Saudi Arabia, the UAE, and Turkey developed bombs of their own. Such a cascade would effectively end any real hope of stopping the spread of nuclear weapons. This was a development that any American administration would view as a grave danger. For President Obama, for whom nuclear disarmament was a primary long-term goal,[18] the specter of a proliferation cascade in the volatile Middle East was unacceptable.

Iran was already a disruptive power in the region. While thanks to deterrence it would be extremely unlikely to use nuclear weapons, its ownership of these weapons would deter the United States and other countries from retaliating against Iran and its proxies. The need to establish a security umbrella capable of protecting shipping in the Gulf and important allies (like Saudi Arabia) from a nuclear Iran would drive the United States into a much deeper engagement in the region, one likely to feature a perpetual cycle of crisis and retaliation.

Finally, some in the administration believed that a nuclear agreement with Iran could be the first step toward a genuine U.S.-Iranian détente. Based on encounters with Iranian diplomats and well-connected members of the Iranian diaspora, there was a widespread belief among American liberals that the "real" Iran—a complex, cosmopolitan, tolerant, and pro-Western society—was being held back by a diminishing reactionary group of regime loyalists and hardliners. The confrontation with the United States empowered the hardliners, and the sanctions against Iran gave great economic power to the government and its hardline allies. If the United States could bring the hostility to an end, Iranian society would begin to thaw, the hardliners would retreat, and this vibrant and sophisticated society could finally emerge. In that case the United States could reduce its commitments and presence in the Middle East even as the region became more stable, more peaceful, and, who knows, perhaps more democratic. The magical dancing democracy unicorns might have proven inconveniently elusive in the Sunni Arab world, but there was no shortage of optimists in the administration who heard the heavenly hoofbeats echo across the stony mountains of Iran.

Improving relations with Iran had been high on the incoming Obama administration's wish list in 2009, and when protests broke out across Iran following charges that its 2009 presidential election had been fraudulent, the Obama administration refrained from supporting the demonstrations, or criticizing Iran for the harsh measures taken to suppress them. This silence, and accompanying attempts to establish a dialogue, initially met with a hostile response, but by 2012 secret talks between Iranian and American officials had begun.[19] The quest to negotiate an agreement with Iran that would eliminate or at least postpone the development of Iranian nuclear weapons and then to get that agreement through a skeptical Congress would become the defining Middle East initiative of the second Obama term.

The search for this agreement would define the Obama second term with major implications for U.S. relations with the Sunni Arab states and with Israel. On the one hand, fear that the United States was tilting away from its old regional allies to reach an understanding with Iran helped drive Arab-Israeli reconciliation that would lead ultimately to the Abraham Accords between Israel and a number of Arab states during the Trump years. On the other hand, the Israeli-Palestinian peace process, already fading during the first Obama term, flickered and died during the second, a casualty of the new turn in American foreign policy.

THE DEATH OF THE PEACE PROCESS

In the ambitious first term, reviving the Israeli-Palestinian peace process had been one of President Obama's top priorities. Signaling a new, more sympathetic stance on Palestinian aspirations was both popular with Obama's liberal political base and a vital component of his strategy to reset the relationship between the United States and the Islamic world. On his second full day in office, President Obama attended a State Department ceremony where newly minted Secretary of State Hillary Clinton introduced former senator George Mitchell as the administration's special envoy for Middle East peace.[20]

The new envoy got to work immediately, and within months Israelis and Palestinians were communicating through U.S. officials. This was not, yet, direct negotiations between Israelis and Palestinians, but the administration could argue that progress was being made. The next month, Prime Minister Benjamin Netanyahu gave a speech at Bar-Ilan University outside Tel Aviv in which he declared support for the creation of a demilitarized Palestinian state.[21]

In November the process took another step forward as Israel announced a ten-month partial settlement freeze. For the Palestinians, however, this was not enough, as Netanyahu's freeze excluded new construction in East Jerusalem and Israel had not accepted the 1949 ceasefire line as the basis for negotiations on the boundary between Israel and the Palestinian state. The United States continued to press both sides to resume direct talks, but the freeze had almost expired by the time the two sides finally met in September 2010. Progress was desultory, and nobody was surprised when Israel refused to extend the construction freeze and the Palestinians refused to continue direct talks without it.[22]

Even by the standards of past failed negotiations, the 2009–10 talks were uninspiring, failing to reach the intensity of the Olmert-Abbas talks during the Bush presidency, to say nothing of the Arafat-Barak negotiations under Clinton's sponsorship. Many things had changed between the dramatic Clinton era talks and the anticlimactic negotiations of the Obama years. Israeli politics had moved to the right, in part because many Israelis no longer believed that the Palestinian leadership could ever accept or enforce an agreement that the Israelis could live with.

On top of all this, by 2010 Israel had become a much more secure, powerful, and self-confident country. Palestinian violence had been essentially contained. The intifadas had failed, the Wall effectively stopped suicide bombers and other terrorists from entering Israel proper, and the hostility between Hamas in Gaza and Fatah in the West Bank kept the Palestinian movement divided. Jerusalem's cooperation with neighboring Arab states had never been stronger. Israel's investment in tech was beginning to pay off and Israel's economy continued to power ahead.

Under these circumstances, the expectation that the United States could wring large concessions from Israel to jump-start a peace process was as unrealistic as the belief that the United States could promote a democratic transition across the Middle East. That the Obama administration failed either to anticipate or to accommodate this fact of life did not promote respect for the intellectual acuity of American policymakers in either Jerusalem or the region at large.

For different reasons, the situation among Palestinians was equally unfavorable. If the Israelis were too strong to feel the need for concessions, the Palestinians were too weak to bear the political costs of what, from the standpoint either of Islamist or secular Palestinian nationalism, was certain to be an imperfect and unsatisfactory peace. The Hamas takeover of Gaza in 2007 left the Palestinian movement divided, and no Palestinian leader or organization had the power or the legitimacy to sign a peace agreement that would, at best, be little better than the agreement Arafat had rejected in 2001.

By the start of his second term, President Obama seemed to have grasped the changing dynamics around the disintegrating peace process, but overcame his skepticism to allow Secretary of State John Kerry to embark on one last quest for the Grail in 2013.[23] Whether Washington was trying to transform the Middle East or to reduce its commitments there, settling the Israeli-Palestinian dispute retained its allure.

Given that nothing could be done to break the alliance with Israel, the question was how to manage the relationship to minimize its potential to keep the United States tied to the conflicts and concerns of a region it wished to escape. There were two key problems. One, as noted, was the prospect of a war between Iran and Israel. Such a war would be a nightmare for both countries and could embroil the United States. And if Iran should get a nuclear weapon, the potential for escalation could not be ruled out.

There was also the problem of the Palestinians. The Obama administration might have deferred its hopes for solving the problem of religious fanaticism by transforming the Middle East, but establishing a Palestinian state through a negotiated agreement with Israel would still be good for the United States—and the cost of yet another attempt would not be high.

Sympathy for Palestinians trapped under occupation was one factor in the administration's continued engagement in peace process diplomacy, but hardly the only or even the leading one. For Washington, the unresolved Palestinian question posed a political problem, a diplomatic problem, and a Zionist problem. From a political standpoint, the unresolved conflict meant a continuing series of Palestinian-Israeli disputes that would force the administration to stand either with Jerusalem or with the Palestinian Authority in Ramallah. To side with Jerusalem would enrage progressives; to side with Ramallah risked angering centrists and offered opportunities for Republicans to attack the president's popularity among voters at large.

In diplomacy, Israeli-Palestinian controversies continually led to disputes in venues ranging from the United Nations Security Council to the International Criminal Court. As Israel's chief international supporter, the United States found itself continually forced to expend energy and political capital managing these various issues. From President Obama's standpoint, the United States had too much real work to do in the world of international institutions to be continually at odds with key part-ners in Europe and beyond over disputes about Israel. In December 2016, as the clock ran down on his second term, Obama would order the American delegation not to veto a U.N. Security Council resolution condemning Israeli settlements on the West Bank and in East Jerusalem as illegal.[24]

On the positive side, for President Obama and many of his associates and supporters, liberating Israel from the moral and political burdens of occupation and establishing a Palestinian state was the best and perhaps the only way to ensure that Zionism could achieve its historic goal: the establishment of a democratic Jewish state at peace with its neighbors. President Obama did not expect Kerry to succeed, and he was unwilling to plunge himself into the process with the enthusiasm of his prede-cessors, but on balance the domestic political calculus seemed to favor another round of talks.

As the driving force behind the second term peace process, Secre-tary Kerry relied on the traditional ham-and-eggs negotiating pattern: if only we had some ham, then we could have ham and eggs once we get some eggs. Like generations of negotiators wrestling over the decades with this intractable problem, the Americans would attempt to push the Israelis toward positions that they would then press the Palestinians to accept, and repeat the same process in reverse, hoping eventually to get the two sides to meet somewhere in the middle. During the nine months of the Kerry-led peace process, he would meet more than one hundred times with Netanyahu and Mahmoud Abbas. The process collapsed with little to show for this effort, an ignominious setback that revealed just how far American prestige in the Middle East had fallen from the 1990s.[25]

The Kerry process was not wholly barren. In the opinion of Mar-tin Indyk, who served as President Obama's special Middle East envoy in the second term, Netanyahu eventually responded to intense American efforts by moving into what Indyk called a "zone of poten-tial agreement"—that is, within a range of positions with which, in the Americans' opinion, the Palestinians could work.[26] Netanyahu, after much poking and prodding, was ready to offer something that at least looked like ham. But the process of getting Netanyahu to these positions was so difficult and drawn out and involved so many steps on his part that angered Palestinian opinion (like issuing permits for settlement expansion), that by the time Netanyahu had moved, the Palestinians were no longer interested. As the clock wound down on the nine-month negotiation period, Kerry tried for one last late-night meeting with Abbas. Aides responded that Abbas was tired and preferred to go to bed. Despite continued frantic American efforts to get an agreement for an extension of the negotiations, the Palestinians crossed an Israeli red line by opening national unity talks with Hamas, and the Israelis announced the negotiations at an end.[27]

With that failure, the long post–Cold War American effort to broker an agreement between Israelis and Palestinians essentially came to an end. Indyk, who worked with presidents from Bill Clinton through Barack Obama, published an essay in *The Wall Street Journal* in January 2020 declaring that although "Arab-Israeli peacemaking has captivated me for my entire professional life . . . the task is now clearly hopeless."[28]

Strikingly, many in the administration seemed unaware of the damage American policy failures around the region had done to their country's prestige and to the reputation of its policy class for analytic competence. After the string of American Middle East fiascos commencing with the disastrous Iraq War and continuing under Obama with one failed call after another, nobody thought the Americans understood the region particularly well or had a coherent policy for addressing its problems. Like many others around the world at this point, both Israelis and Palestinians tended to regard the United States as a very large beast with a very small brain—an impression that the subsequent Trump administration would do little to erase.

The Middle East was not the only topic over which the gulf between American assumptions and global reality was widening. The sunny assumptions of Clintonian America about the course of post–Cold War history were looking less plausible. The framework of international law, deep peace, and sustained multilateral cooperation that Americans expected to deepen and develop was beginning to fray and the Obama administration appeared unable to reverse the trend. The Obama administration's steady shift toward a Middle East strategy of disengagement looked to regional observers like another step in the disorienting American retreat from its post–Cold War effort to build a new world order.

Yet even as their behavior telegraphed a belief that liberal order was retreating from the Middle East, the Americans continued to push both

Israelis and Palestinians toward a peace that only made sense in the context of that order. For Palestinians, accepting demilitarization only made sense if treaties and legal agreements could be relied on to protect their small and weak state. Otherwise they would be giving up legal and territorial claims against Israel in exchange for a state that would only exist on Israeli sufferance—which is to say, the degree to which Israel felt constrained by the wishes of the "international community."

For the Israelis, the chief advantage of an agreement with the Palestinians wasn't physical security. They had achieved that already. It also wasn't in opening doors to the Arabs. Those doors were opening on their own, in part because regional perceptions of American softness on Iran were driving Arabs and Israelis together in self-defense. The value of a peace deal to Israel was to end the Palestinian use of international institutions to harass the Jewish state at the U.N. and to bring actions against it in forums like the World Court. This was more nuisance than existential threat, and if such institutions were losing clout as the American-sponsored world order grew less robust, the price Israel was willing to pay for peace would only decline.

For both sides, the value of a peace agreement was directly connected to the probability that the quest for world order would succeed. As China and Russia began to challenge the American-led order, and as the Americans themselves despaired of imposing it in the Middle East, Israelis and Palestinians alike grew less interested in the kind of peace the Americans hoped to promote.

By 2013, while the professionalism and knowledge of many experienced American diplomats continued to impress many regional observers, neither Israelis nor Palestinians had much intellectual respect for America's political leadership. The inability of senior American officials to understand just how ineffectual their own track record of poor decisions made them appear only further undercut their authority. Unable to pacify Iraq, unable to promote democracy in Egypt, unable to secure Libya, and capable only of grandiose rhetoric over the Syrian crisis that they signally failed to back up, America's senior leaders did not inspire great confidence among either Israelis or Palestinians.

Kerry lectured his interlocutors tirelessly about what their true interests were. "You Palestinians can never get the f***ing big picture," Susan Rice admonished the chief Palestinian negotiator Saeb Erekat. At a White House meeting on March 17, 2014, Obama tried to persuade

Abbas to sign on the dotted line, telling him "Don't quibble with this detail or that detail. The occupation will end. You will get a Palestinian state. You will never have an administration as committed to that as this one."

Abbas, who had heard exactly this kind of logic from American presidents in the past, was unimpressed. The day before, Kerry had asked him to accept another delay in the release of the next tranche of Palestinian prisoners to take the pressure off the Israelis. For Abbas, this was decisive. As Ben Birnbaum and Amir Tibon reported in *The New Republic,* this was the moment Abbas tuned the Americans out. Abbas would later tell people that if the Americans can't convince Israel to give me twenty-six prisoners, how will they ever get them to give me East Jerusalem?[29]

Abbas was right and Obama was wrong. The gaps between the two sides were not going to close on Obama's watch and Abbas and Erekat, to say nothing of Netanyahu, saw the big picture much better than the Americans did at this point. Besides failing to grasp their own drastically diminished authority and prestige, Obama officials failed to grasp the changing nature of Israeli society and the implications of those changes for American peace diplomacy.

The more liberal wing of the Israeli political establishment was rooted in the "Ashkenazi ascendancy" that dominated Israel in the early decades of independence as thoroughly as WASPs had dominated American life a hundred years before. But over time a mix of Sephardic and Russian immigrants along with the rapidly growing ultra-Orthodox and Hasidic populations began to challenge the old largely secular and western-minded elite. It was the surge of these groups that drove Israel's shift to the right in economics and in security policy. The old Israeli establishment held on in institutions like the judiciary, the universities, and certain institutions in the security field, but its members were increasingly alienated from the less polished, less western, less liberal, more religious, and more Middle Eastern country into which Israel was changing. In an Israeli form of identity politics, right-leaning voters, resenting what they saw as discrimination and contempt from the establishment, banded together behind leaders like Menachem Begin and Netanyahu. These leaders were less open to American ideas and less vulnerable to American pressure than their predecessors had been. The Russian, Sephardic, and ultra-Orthodox voters who supported them did not for the most part share the feelings of guilt about the Palestinians that haunted the old Israeli establishment. Their knowledge of Arab culture, language, and attitude left them contemptuous of what they saw as fuzzy-minded Americans spouting foolish platitudes about the Arab world.

Israel's coalition of the ascendant scoffed at the idea of a peaceful world order based on international institutions—like the reflexively anti-Israel United Nations—and shared Herzl's belief that to trust in the power of liberal ideas and political movements was to condemn the Jewish people to extinction. Having watched the Americans chase magical dancing democracy unicorns across the Middle East, these Israelis were increasingly contemptuous of America's ability to build, defend, or even recognize a liberal world order. There was certainly no question of making territorial concessions in exchange for American security guarantees.

They had even less respect for the opinions of American Jews. Themselves often victims or the children of refugees from Arab discrimination and persecution, they felt they owed the world and the Palestinians no apologies. When, as they saw it, pampered and affluent American Jews who had never held a gun, patrolled a Palestinian street, or crouched in the basement with their families as Palestinian missiles soared overhead lectured Israelis on where their boundaries should be, right-leaning Israelis did not stand abashed.

Neither Kerry nor Obama seems to have understood how their own personal unpopularity in Israel changed the politics of peace among Israelis. As Russian and ex-Soviet Jews watched Putin run rings around Obama on the international stage, as Mizrahi Jews from the Muslim Middle East heard the Americans echoing the flabby liberal rhetoric of a condescending Israeli establishment that despised them, and as all Israelis saw American Middle East policy floundering from one miserable mishap to the next, association with the Americans became toxic. Right-wing politicians saw no reason to conceal their disdain for the Americans and their process; on the contrary, attacking Kerry in particular brought political dividends. Defense Minister Moshe Ya'alon would mock what he saw as American naïveté, messianic delusions, and arrogance to journalists. The only thing that will save Israel, he was quoted as saying, "is for John Kerry to win his Nobel Prize and leave us alone."[30] That these criticisms were unfair did not lessen their effect.

Increasingly, some of the key arguments the Americans used to convince Israelis to move toward a two-state solution were losing traction. The most important was that high Palestinian birthrates meant that in the near future Jews would become a minority in the land between the Jordan River and the Mediterranean. Many younger Palestinians were giving up on a separate Palestinian state and demanding to join Israel as citizens with equal rights. Unless a Palestinian state could be established, Israelis would face the choice between setting up an "apartheid" state that denied the Arab majority full democratic rights or watching the Jewish character of Israel disappear as Arabs took over the Knesset.

The demographic argument does not play as well among serious Zionists as many well-intentioned outsiders assume. In the 1930s and 1940s, Arabs heavily outnumbered Jews. The Jewish minority faced constant pressure from both the Arab majority and Great Britain to accept minority status in a single state. If the tiny, impoverished and almost friendless Yishuv could reject a one state solution then surely a nuclear-armed regional superpower with technological capabilities envied and desired by the whole world could define its frontiers and chart its political course at least as successfully.

The demographic outlook is also changing. Arab birthrates have been falling and Jewish birthrates rising for most of this century. In 2015 for the first time, inside Israel, the Jewish and Arab fertility rates (at 3.1 children per woman) were equal. Driven partly though not entirely by high fertility rates among Israeli settlers and ultra-Orthodox Jews, Jewish fertility rates have continued to climb.[31] Palestinian fertility rates appear to be declining in line with trends seen elsewhere in the Arab world.

Another reason many Israelis worry less about numbers than many Americans would like them to is that when Gaza is excluded from the boundaries of a future Israeli-Arab state, the demographic outlook changes significantly. Subtract the approximately 2.1 million Gazans from the 6.8 million Palestinians who live between the Jordan River and the Mediterranean[32] and the numbers are less formidable.

Americans might argue that Israel would be required to incorporate Gaza or face condemnation as an apartheid state, but it is difficult to see Hamas demanding annexation by a state whose existence it refuses to recognize. The legal picture is murky. Plans by some Israelis to annex much if not all of the West Bank while excluding what would be an archipelago of Palestinian-inhabited areas raise troubling moral and practical questions. However, there are no precedents in international law for requiring a country to annex territory that it has never legally owned and from which it wishes to withdraw.

Others on the Israeli right contest both the reported numbers of Palestinians in the territories and the migration and fertility rate statistics on which they are based, offering estimates of the total Palestinian population well below those from official sources. Such numbers lack credibility with most demography experts, but there are large political constituencies in Israel who accept them—and those Israeli audiences did not trust the American politicians and Jewish leaders offering a different message.[33]

Beyond this, while some observers cite diminishing support for the two-state solution among Palestinians as a sign of heightened militancy, close observers of the Palestinian scene will privately offer a more nuanced opinion. When right-wing Israeli politician Avigdor Liberman proposed that the so-called Triangle, a group of villages on the Israeli side of the 1949 cease-fire line containing between 10 and 15 percent of the Arab population of Israel, be ceded to a Palestinian state in exchange for Israeli settlement blocs in the West Bank, Triangle residents angrily rejected the idea.[34] This was more a vote of no confidence in the Palestinian leadership and the prospects of a Palestinian state than a declaration of love for Israel.

Rising Palestinian skepticism about the value of the two-state solution represents heightened radicalization for some.[35] For others it represents demobilization, indifference, or perhaps despair. For still others it is a pragmatic calculation. In any case, American diplomats seeking to persuade Israelis to make painful compromises in Jerusalem and elsewhere by invoking the specter of an Arab majority in Israel were less persuasive to many Israelis than they hoped.

Finally, in part because important Arab states were as angered and bemused by Obama-era American policy in the Middle East as the Israelis, it was clear to informed Israelis long before the Abraham Accords of the Trump years that Israel was becoming less regionally isolated than ever before. Unable to trust American resolve or negotiating skills when it came to Iran, and eager to expand intelligence cooperation against the Muslim Brotherhood, including Hamas, Israel's Arab neighbors increasingly saw the Jewish state as an indispensable strategic and security partner.

When Obama negotiators warned that failure to fall in line with the Kerry peace initiative would isolate Israel, Israeli officials felt that once again the Americans had lost touch with key regional dynamics. Even as Israeli settlements on the West Bank grew, Arab governments drew closer to Israel, and their impatience with the Palestinians was becoming more visible. As the Obama administration shifted from a policy of reconciliation with the Arab world to one of bridge-building with Iran, many Arabs interpreted the seeming inaction and passivity of American policy in Syria as a historic betrayal. Public opinion in the Arab world, appalled at the bloodletting in Libya and Syria (and shocked by America's lack of any kind of positive agenda for these critical regional problems), became more tolerant of the faults of their current rulers and less willing to support dangerous movements for political change. Nobody wanted to be Syria or Libya, and everyone could see how worthless American support had been to the Egyptian democracy movement.

In a world in which Russia and Iran were prepared to brutalize Syria back into obedience to the Assad dynasty, the fate of the West Bank seemed less significant than ever before. And Israel and its Arab neighbors increasingly saw America's new Iran policy as their gravest security threat.

The new constellation of forces debuted during the Gaza War in the summer of 2014, just after the last flickering flames of the Kerry process went out. Following a series of mutual provocations and retaliations, the Israel Defense Forces (IDF) launched massive air strikes into Gaza. Israeli ground forces moved into Gaza after ten days of air strikes and missile launches. As negotiations for an end to the shooting dragged on in the usual way, it became clear that Egypt, Fatah, Saudi Arabia, and the United Arab Emirates were quietly supporting the Israeli position in the hope that Hamas would be hit as hard as possible. American negotiators were siding with Turkey and Qatar to end the fighting more quickly, a result likely to reduce the death toll at the cost of offering Hamas a result it could spin as a victory.[36]

For Israelis one lesson seemed obvious. In a shooting conflict that saw Israelis firing on Palestinian cities, the heavyweight powers of the Arab world were backing Israel—against the United States. Unintentionally and unwittingly the Obama administration had achieved a goal that had eluded generations of American diplomats: it had laid the foundation for the integration of Israel into the Middle East.

Rolling Over the "Lobby"

Of President Obama's two Middle East initiatives in the second term, negotiating the nuclear agreement with Iran was far more important to him than the Kerry peace process. Like many American liberals, Obama believed that American foreign policy had been too militarized for too long. Diplomacy was a frustrating pursuit and the solutions it produced were often partial and messy, but war had a greater downside.

Signing the JCPOA nuclear agreement with Iran, however, led to an all-out struggle between President Obama and AIPAC and its allies— the so-called Israel lobby. Despite the lobby's reputation for almost infinite power and cunning, President Obama defeated it hands down.

As the struggle commenced, the odds did not appear to favor the president. The JCPOA was not just unpopular with AIPAC; it was broadly unpopular with the public at large. A University of Maryland poll in September 2015 found a 52 percent majority supporting the agreement, but this was something of an outlier. A Quinnipiac poll found 55 percent opposed, and a CNN-ORC poll found 52 percent of respondents wanting Congress to reject the agreement.[37] Pew found that support for the agreement was actually falling as the congressional vote approached.[38] In the end, majorities in both houses of Congress voted against the agreement, but under the terms negotiated with the White House, the agreement could only be blocked with a supermajority. Four Democratic senators joined with the entire Republican caucus, but opponents fell two votes short of the sixty-vote threshold required to block the deal.

The defeat, one of a number of high-profile defeats that the Israel lobby has sustained going back to the 1950s, was due to many factors. One was partisanship. Just as Republicans were ready to support Eisenhower against Britain, France, and Israel over the Suez Crisis, Democrats, Jewish Democrats very much included, rallied behind President Obama. The polls showed a sharp partisan split over the Iran deal, with Republicans opposing the deal and most Democrats supporting it.

Another was presidential leadership. When Ronald Reagan beat back massive opposition to sell five advanced E-3 AWACS aircraft to Saudi

Arabia, he faced a similar array of hostile political forces. AIPAC and its allies had sprung into action. Israel was public in its opposition, the polling was terrible, and many members of his own party were concerned.[39] The Reagan administration, however, was convinced of the necessity of the sale (at the time, part of the largest single arms sale in American history), and the president and his aides were indefatigable in working Congress and the public. In the end, they prevailed.[40]

The Obama administration was equally committed to the Iran deal, and from the president on down the lobbying was intense. Knowing that the key to victory was preventing Democratic defections, the president personally contacted 125 Democratic senators and representatives between July and September 2015, many repeatedly, sometimes calling between rounds of golf on Martha's Vineyard. As CNN reported, "The lobbying effort to back the deal was far more targeted and relentless than the public push and advertising campaigns aimed at scuttling it, according to lawmakers in both parties."[41]

The point is not just that the Israel lobby lost the battle over the JCPOA. It had lost important battles before and no doubt will lose more in the future. What is more significant is that in this high-profile fight with AIPAC and its allies on a matter of the gravest importance to Israel, American Jews continued to support President Obama through the controversy. A Social Science Research Solutions poll of American Jews found that Jews were more supportive of the Iran deal than the population at large, even though almost half of American Jews believed that the agreement made Israel less safe.[42] President Obama fought, and won, more policy battles with Israel than any of his predecessors. Next to Bill Clinton, he was the most popular president in modern times among American Jews.

There seem to be two reasons for this. The first is that Israel policy is not the most important issue for many American Jews. A 2012 poll by the Public Religion Research Institute found that only 4 percent of American Jews named "Israel" as the most important factor in determining their vote.[43] A poll for the American Jewish Committee found that 7.2 percent of Jewish voters identified "U.S.-Israel relations" as their most important voting priority. Only 25.9 percent of the AJC sample identified U.S.-Israel relations as one of the three most important issues.[44]

The second reason is that President Obama's approach to Israel and the Middle East broadly reflected the values and ideas of large numbers of American Jews. Many of Obama's close friends and advisors were Jewish. At one point in the Kerry negotiations, Palestinians noted that his diplomatic team was overwhelmingly Jewish; *The New Republic* compared it to "a Bar Mitzvah guest list."[45] Israeli Jews and American Jews have moved in very different directions in recent decades, and the debate among Jews in both countries reflected those divisions.

Those political divisions would only deepen as Donald Trump embarked on the most disruptive administration in American history.

American Crisis and the Fate of the Jewish People

PRESIDENT OBAMA'S CORE GOAL had been to make the millennium cool again by lowering the temperature of global and domestic politics and showing the power of carefully crafted, liberal technocratic policy to master the stresses of the twenty-first century. Abroad, the failure to respond effectively to Russia's conquest of the Crimea, invasion of the Donbas region of Ukraine, and deployment in Syria combined with Washington's inability to find an effective counter to China's relentless militarization of the South China Sea left Americans—and others—feeling insecure in a world suddenly dominated by geopolitical great power competition. The victory of the liberal world order that every American president since the end of the Cold War had tried to build no longer seemed assured, or perhaps even possible. At home, on a scale not seen since the 1930s, Americans were questioning the durability and even the value of basic American ideas and institutions. Gone was the old optimism that American values were transforming Russia. By 2016 many Americans feared that autocracy was on the march worldwide and that Russian disinformation had grown powerful enough to imperil American democracy at home.

The gap between the post-historical world Americans expected and the turbulent, crisis-ridden planet they actually inhabited had become impossible to ignore, and by 2016 growing numbers of Americans were moving away both from the post-historical consensus and from the political establishment that had for so long embraced it. At the same time, unhappiness with the state of the domestic economy,[1] rising racial tensions,[2] and fears that long-standing American values were on the decline intersected with the rise of social media to create an overwhelming sense of crisis and frustration.

This, it soon became clear, was more than a policy crisis. It was an identity crisis. If the mid-century model of an American economy built on the growing success and stability of a mass middle class no longer worked, what kind of society was the United States? If sixty years after the civil rights movement achieved the legislative victories of the 1960s Blacks still suffered systemic discrimination and violence, could liberal capitalism ever hope to address the deep injustices in American life? If the United States was not erecting a liberal and democratic world order that would promote the prosperity of the American people while ending the era of great power war and preventing a nuclear holocaust, what should American foreign policy be about? And if the United States could no longer see itself as a providential nation with a global mission, what did it mean to be an American?

As the post-historical foreign policy consensus lost political traction, alternative ideas—like Trump's "America First" policy, the neo-isolationist prescriptions of the realist restrainers, and the anticapitalist ideas that inspired the Bernie Sanders movement—sought to fill the void. These ideas all had implications for Israel policy, and the Israel policy debate would become an arena in which both the old post-historical establishment and those who sought to replace it dueled for advantage.

As a result, even as virtually all parties to the American debate agreed that the Middle East was becoming a less crucial arena for American foreign policy, the salience of Israel policy in American politics was undiminished. And as American politics became more polarized overall, attitudes toward Israel became more tribal, intensifying Republican support for and identification with the Jewish state, while cooling pro-Israel ardor among many Democrats.

Trump was in many ways a unique figure, but while the substance of his Israel policy was new, he followed a well-established precedent of using Israel policy to unite and energize his supporters. It's therefore useful to examine Trump's Israel policy in the light of his overall political approach, and to look at how the deepening crisis of American identity intensified the Israel debate and posed troubling new challenges not only for America's approach to the Middle East but for the position of American Jews at home.

Trump and the Crisis of Sun Belt Republicanism

Getting to grips with the Trump presidency is a trying task. Trump was such a unique and controversial figure that both his achievements and his failures defy conventional analysis. Petty, hotheaded, undisciplined, mendacious, erratic, and egocentric, he frequently sabotaged his own policy goals by the simultaneous pursuit of conflicting agendas. His presidency was more productive of polarization than of enduring success. Yet with all his many shortcomings, he understood some important truths about international politics and the state of the world that eluded his establishment critics. To millions of Americans, he was like the little boy who dared to cry out that the emperor had no clothes—that the American elite had lost its way and had no answers for the problems of the United States, much less for those of the world beyond our frontiers. This was a message that Americans were ready to hear in 2016, nowhere more than in the GOP, where the core ideas of Sun Belt Republicanism—optimism, laissez-faire conservatism, free trade, and a vigorous promotion of American values abroad and at home—were losing their hold for reasons that many Republican politicians failed to understand.

American conservative intellectuals and political elites spent a lot of time in the Obama years chiding liberal intellectuals and politicians for being out of touch, but the Republican establishment, both intellectual and political, were the ones to suffer defenestration as Trump stole the Republican Party out from under them in 2016. Through four tumultuous years in office, even as his poll ratings remained below those of most presidents,[3] he steadily intensified his hold on the party. Not even his 2020 reelection defeat could loosen his grip, not as of this writing (early 2022).

As he took over the party, Trump broke with Republican orthodoxy across the board. There was not much in Trump's policy mix, foreign or domestic, that Sun Belt Republicans like James Baker, George Shultz, or Ronald Reagan would have recognized. The ideological fervor of Reagan's global anticommunist crusade found few echoes in the Trump years. Free trade, robust support of American alliances, steadfast belief in promoting American values, and the commitment to the establishment of a world order seen to enhance American power and support

American economic interests—none of these had their place in Trump's policies. For Trump, the world order was no longer something a victorious America sought to promote around the world; it was a web of obligations and restrictions that threatened American sovereignty.

Israel policy, however, was different. Even as he sought to reduce the American footprint in the Middle East he offered Israel the kind of unstinting support that the Jewish state had never previously received. During his four years in office, he would move the American embassy to Jerusalem,[4] offer Israel uncritical support in its contest with Iran, drop U.S. legal objections to Israeli settlements on the West Bank,[5] recognize the Israeli annexation of the Golan Heights,[6] offer symbolic recognition of Israeli claims to Jerusalem by allowing American citizens born in Jerusalem to list "Israel" as their birthplace in their passports,[7] and do everything in his power to promote the Abraham Accords normalizing relations between Israel and Arab countries including the UAE, Bahrain, Sudan, and Morocco.[8]

While a handful of Jewish donors, most notably Sheldon Adelson, provided significant financial support to the Trump campaign, the goal of Trump's Israel policy was not to placate American Jews. Had he sought Jewish support, he would have followed a much more conventional Middle East policy. Trump used Israel policy to seal the bonds that united him to his base: the predominantly white, predominantly working-class and lower-middle-class voters in the South and Middle West who put him in the White House. By the time of Donald Trump's election, the facade of evangelical unity had worn thin, and the term "evangelical" no longer described a coherent group. While figures in the twentieth century like Billy Graham were able to use their influence to pull disparate groups together to form an evangelical base, by 2020 this group had splintered once more. We've seen the role that support for Israel played in knitting the Sun Belt coalition together, bringing economic and religious populists into the alignment with pro-market and pro-business leaders that made the Republican Party a formidable force in American politics for forty years. What Trump understood, and his Republican opponents did not, was that the Sun Belt synthesis that bound pro-business southern and southwestern economic and social elites into a bloc with blue-collar populists in the South and Middle West was ripe for disruption—and that Israel policy was one of the instruments that would allow him to break the old coalition and remake the Republican Party in his image.

======

Sun Belt Republicanism was showing its age by 2016. After California, once crucial to Sun Belt Republican success, turned blue in 1992, the center of gravity in Republican politics would gradually shift to the South, and within the South the optimistic, pro-business ideology historically associated with New South progressivism would lose ground to a reviving populist movement that was deeply skeptical of key tenets of Sun Belt policy ranging from free trade, fiscal restraint, and easy immigration to the aggressive promotion of democracy around the world. Beyond the South, ethnic blue-collar workers in the Rust Belt, the "Reagan Democrats" of the 1980s, also moved away from Sun Belt Republicanism to antiestablishment populism.

Economics was one of the factors driving the shift. As we've seen, the swift rise in southern living standards in the decades following World War II helped put New South progressives firmly in control of southern politics and transformed the place of the South in American life. Southern economic success drew new residents and increased southern strength in Congress and the electoral college. Detroit was hemorrhaging automobile jobs while a wave of both foreign and domestic investment into Alabama, Tennessee, and South Carolina was reshaping the American car industry.[9] The traditional pro-business agenda of New South leaders (attracting outside capital by creating a low-tax, low-regulation business environment with weak labor unions) was packaged as a "competitiveness agenda" and won increasing favor outside the South as Rust Belt states scrambled to reinvent themselves.

As early as the 1990s, this began to change. Manufacturing jobs were no longer leaving the North for the South.[10] They were leaving the North and the South for the rest of the world.[11] Meanwhile companies like Walmart, though headquartered in the South, were undermining the small retail sector across the country, adding small businesses to the list of economic losers. As the region's economic prospects eroded, the appeal of appeasing northerners and their liberal sentiments dwindled as well. Factory closures, foreign competition, and the destruction of locally owned retail outlets led many southerners and blue-collar midwesterners to question the New South economic story and to look back to their populist roots.

The growing gap between the incomes and opportunities available to working- and lower-middle-class white families and the burgeoning affluence of the upper middle class[12] promoted a return to the politics of class. The old fissure between poor whites and the white gentry, a primary driver of southern politics in the century that followed Reconstruction, had been papered over in the second half of the twentieth century. It now reopened with a vengeance, ripping the pro-business consensus behind Sun Belt Republicanism apart in ways that conventional GOP leaders and thinkers, most of whom assumed that the Reagan synthesis provided an unshakable foundation beneath the modern Republican Party, were unprepared to diagnose or to repair.

Migration was another factor. Mass migration into the United States essentially came to an end in 1925 and resumed as we've seen in 1968 when the Hart-Celler Act went into effect.[13] By 2010, immigration had returned to levels last seen at the peak of the Great Wave, and the percentage of foreign-born American residents was near an all-time high. The new wave was significantly more geographically and culturally diverse than the Great Wave, with fewer European migrants and more from Asia, Africa, and Latin America than in the past. More, the new wave came at a time when the South was booming.[14] The Great Wave had passed the impoverished South by, and southern states had relatively little experience with migration. The booming South of the post–Cold War period was much more attractive, and states like Texas, Georgia, Florida, Virginia, and the Carolinas were home to more immigrants from more places than ever before.

The anti-immigration populist backlash caught the Republican political establishment by surprise. The mythologization of the Great Wave immigrant experience and the cult of the melting pot blinded the American leadership to the inevitable cultural and social stress that attends great waves of immigration. Trump intuited the importance of the topic and, with supporters of the old Republican pro-immigrant consensus unable to reach skeptical voters on the issue, was able to make it an important part of his political program.

Similarly, the return of race to the center of American politics helped pull the Sun Belt coalition apart. The post–civil rights movement racial settlement hoped to ease and ultimately end racial tensions in the United

States by offering Blacks an end to formal segregation and full voting rights along with efforts to equalize opportunity in education, employment, and housing. At the same time, tough laws on crime and stringent mandatory sentencing guidelines addressed the concerns of those troubled by the rising crime rates of the era.

By the twenty-first century, this settlement was showing its age. Though some hoped that the election of Barack Obama would herald a new era of racial concord, the economic consequences of the financial crisis and the long-term stagnation in blue-collar wages combined with other forces to undo Black economic progress, and as we've seen the wealth gap between Black and non-Black households in the United States steadily refused to narrow.[15] Against this background, civil rights activists pushed for more affirmative action, fought the mass imprisonment of Blacks, and made the denial of voting rights to felons a potent political issue. Urban policing returned as a flash point in national politics after high-profile incidents of police violence ignited the Black Lives Matter movement. Historic inequities had continued to go unaddressed since the civil rights era. While the South acknowledged this to a degree, in the twenty-first century the northern establishment's drift to the left far outpaced the South's evolution. Relitigating the issue on the national level exacerbated the tension between the regions.

A return of Black identity politics along with the growing political mobilization of new immigrant groups helped promote a surge in what some called "white nationalism." Just as the Great Wave and the Black Great Migration to the North helped touch off the Klan revival of the 1920s and the wave of race riots that followed World War I, racial tensions rose in the twenty-first century.

The post–civil rights movement race settlement, while it lasted, had allowed Sun Belt Republicans to sidestep this explosive issue. As that settlement eroded and questions of race and identity gained political saliency, corporate America leaned into the issue, using support for causes like the BLM movement to broadcast its virtue to the northern establishment and the world more broadly. Understanding the South's (and much of rural America's) cultural isolation from big business, populists were able to once again play the race card against the more moderate and pro-business Republican establishment. One could no longer take the full George Wallace approach ("I'll never be out-[n-worded] again," he vowed after losing an election to a less scrupulous race demagogue),[16] but there were many ways to let racially anxious voters know that one understood their concerns.

Many grassroots Republican voters were also dissatisfied with the party's failure to make progress on cultural issues. Republican president after Republican president took office promising to turn the tide in the culture wars. Yet *Roe v. Wade* was still the law of the land, gay marriage was now legal everywhere in the United States, and a new movement in support of trans rights was beginning to make serious headway. On each of these issues, academia, corporate America, and mainstream media seemed united against the cultural sensibilities of Republican voters. As the gap between the establishment and white southern public opinion widened, New South political leaders faced a credibility crisis. What was the point, socially conservative voters asked, of a "conservative" party that failed to address such fundamental issues?

The fall of red California and the long series of defeats in the culture wars changed the mood of many American conservatives. Ronald Reagan had been known for his untroubled confidence in the vitality of American life and his sunny optimism about the American future. Optimism historically had not been a frequent visitor to Dixie, where the pessimism born of military defeat and zero-sum race and class polarization gave white southerners a more checkered and perhaps more insightful vision of the human prospect. The long post–World War II boom had eroded that pessimism and converted much of the bustling New South to a boisterous optimism in the Reagan era. But that optimistic outlook began to dim in the 1990s. In Southern California, once the Promised Land for migrating southerners, Republicans watched a demographic shift turn the state an ever deeper blue. The 1980s and 1990s would witness the decline of the aerospace industries that once provided well-paid employment for Southern Californians.[17] By 2016 Southern California conservatives had become much more pessimistic about the future of the United States. As fears that inexorable demographic change would produce a national permanent Democratic majority, as had seemingly happened in California, spread through Republican circles, American conservatism became angrier and less optimistic. This was a mood that Trump, like populists generally, found easy to exploit.

We've seen how the religious synthesis of Billy Graham and his associates enabled the rise of a new form of individualistic American Protestantism, self-consciously orthodox over and against the perceived theological errors of modernists, but significantly more open than the old fundamentalists to cooperation across denominational boundaries. On issues like opposition to abortion and support of religious freedom, Graham evangelicals and conservative Roman Catholics were able to establish durable political coalitions that reinforced the Republican Party. The new evangelical consensus also helped bridge the socioeconomic divide between the more socially elite conservative denominations and the more populist religious currents previously associated with the fundamentalist movement.

By 2016, however, like the Sun Belt coalition as a whole, the Graham synthesis was showing its age. After the national religious revivals of the late twentieth century, American Protestantism faced an era of reconsideration and consolidation. The generation of preachers who followed Graham and the other figures of the revival years did not match the stature of their predecessors. As so often in the American past, the children of those converted in a great revival were less religiously engaged than their parents.

The widening socioeconomic gap in American life was reflected in the widening fissures in American conservative Protestantism. Educated, upper-middle-class Christians were drawn to forms of Christian belief that minimized the gaps between them and their more secular colleagues and neighbors. Educated upper-middle-class congregations attempted to accommodate contemporary political and cultural sensibilities where possible without abandoning key pillars of orthodox Protestant belief. These churchgoers would often resist Trump's populist appeal, much as their grandparents and great-grandparents had disdained populists like South Carolina's "Pitchfork" Ben Tillman and Louisiana's Huey Long.

Trump's support among conservative Protestants would come from congregations that had more in common with pre-Graham fundamentalism, as well as Pentecostals, the increasing numbers of nondenomination evangelical churches, and the so-called Prosperity Gospel preachers. Profoundly alienated from the rapidly changing American mainstream, these believers often interpreted contemporary American events through the lens of biblical prophecy. Apocalyptic speculation has been a prominent feature of Christianity for most of the past two millennia, and American Christianity is no different. Although groups like the Millerites have never attracted the majority of the American faithful, some of the most dynamic movements, like modern Pentecostalism, prominently feature the End of Days. Over the past two centuries, the specific details of their envisioned scenario have changed, but there are some broad continuities. Generally, they have believed that the Antichrist, a charismatic individual of uniquely evil intent, would gain control of one or more significant forces in global affairs and lead a worldwide attack on Jews and Christians before a final battle occurs in modern Israel. Sometimes individuals like Adolf Hitler were identified as a potential Antichrist; in other circumstances, powerful forces like Communism or international bodies like the United Nations or the European Union appeared to be the perfect springboard to propel him to power. The forced imposition of a secular morality at variance with classic Christian teachings would accompany his rise and faithful Christians would face persecution as the Antichrist's hour approached. Although usually a minority viewpoint within American Christianity, these beliefs overlap with Jacksonian distrust for centralized authority and international institutions and have a powerful impact on American politics.

For many adherents of these beliefs, the twenty-first century has been full of dark forebodings. The fall of American democracy and the submergence of American sovereignty in an anti-Christian transnational government had long figured in their apocalyptic scenarios. For such believers, it was easy to see American efforts to create a "new world order" as attempts to install the kind of anti-Christian world dictatorship that would herald the Last Days. As the beliefs of many secular Americans diverged ever more dramatically from inherited Christian morality, and as LBGTQ activists sought to label the restatement of classic Christian doctrine on these topics as a form of hate speech, it appeared to conservative Protestants that the kingdom of the Antichrist was well on its way.

As the usual liberal prescription for good governance in American life moved to embrace the enforcement of gay and trans rights, gun control, and a greater role for international governance to fight such problems as climate change, the split between Christians looking to accommodate the new approach while remaining faithful to historic Protestant orthodoxy and those who felt called to resist widened. The resisters tended to embrace Trump, in some cases as the lesser of two evils, but often as a divinely appointed champion, however imperfect, sent to defend the American church in its hour of need.

Just as the coalition of populist and New South progressives that Barry Goldwater and Ronald Reagan had forged into the Sun Belt Republican Party was breaking up under the accumulated stresses of the twenty-first century, so the coalition of populist and conservative Christians that Billy Graham and his colleagues united under the banner of evangelicalism was dissolving.

Declining support for neoconservative foreign policy prescriptions among rank-and-file Republicans also helped Trump. Jacksonians had supported the Afghan and Iraq wars for simple reasons. When the Taliban government in Afghanistan refused to hand Osama bin Laden over to the United States, Jacksonians wanted to punish the Taliban and capture bin Laden. On Iraq, they believed George W. Bush's claim that Saddam Hussein was building nuclear weapons and had a relationship with terrorists. They saw the Iraq War as a necessary act of self-defense. But when American forces failed to find the level of WMD production they expected in Iraq, and when both wars turned into long counterinsurgency campaigns without clearly defined victory conditions in support of corrupt governments, Jacksonians felt betrayed. Jacksonian America believes in democracy and schooling for girls, but it does not believe in fighting wars thousands of miles from the United States to promote them. By 2016, Jacksonians had lost faith in the foreign policy judgment of the Republican leadership, and many returned, with a vengeance, to the view that the United States should remain aloof from foreign wars and messy political interventions unless directly attacked.

Jacksonian America had never accepted the post-historical consensus and its grand plans for world order. The isolationism against which the Clinton administration had struggled went, temporarily, into abeyance following the 9/11 attacks. But with the terror threat fading and the wars inconclusive, and with internal polarization growing, Jacksonians wanted less and less to do with conventional Republican foreign policy. They still scorned Democratic talk about multilateralism and international institutions, but they no longer saw establishment Republicans as trustworthy opponents of the Democratic agenda at home or abroad.

The power of these sentiments in Republican politics was amplified by a surge of neo-isolationist sentiment exemplified by politicians like Kentucky senator Rand Paul. Often aligned with realist restrainers, sometimes making common cause with the anti-interventionist left, and particularly strong among younger generations for whom the Cold War was ancient history, the neo-isolationists railed against the global alliances and commitments that the old Republican establishment believed were the foundation of American security.

By 2016, millions of GOP voters were ready to strike out in a new direction. Donald Trump was in the right place at the right time.

Israel Policy and the Trump Coalition

From his entry into presidential politics through his post-presidential political career, the overthrow of the Republican establishment and the reconstruction of the GOP as a party of populist nationalism tightly bound to his personal brand were the principal focus points of Donald Trump's political activity. The success of these efforts made Trump a transformational figure in American political history. Despite his reputation for indiscipline and impulsiveness, to a remarkable degree Trump consistently shaped his rhetoric and policies across the range of foreign and domestic policy to mobilize the political constituency that enabled him to master the Republican Party. Trump used Israel policy, as he used trade policy, China policy, migration policy, and many others to communicate with his base. Trump's foreign policy approach troubled American relations with important allies and was often counterproductive in policy terms. It contributed to the mobilization among Trump opponents that enabled Democrats to take control of both branches of Congress and the White House between the House elections in 2018 and the Georgia Senate runoff elections in 2021. It was, however, a success in making Trump the most powerful figure in Republican politics since Ronald Reagan, with a hold on his party that survived his 2020 defeat.

Both Israel and Middle East policy were of particular importance to a candidate bent on challenging the Republican establishment in 2016. Israel remained popular with populist Republicans and both Iran and jihadi terror were hated and feared, but the party base decisively rejected George W. Bush's transformational Middle East policies and the neoconservative political ideas behind them. More than that, a critical mass of ordinary voters in the Republican Party had lost faith in the post-historical consensus and the globalist policy agenda that came with it. Neither in the Middle East nor anywhere else did a majority of grassroots Republicans support a policy of global transformation in the service of a cosmopolitan post-nationalist agenda they saw as a threat to their values and traditional beliefs.

The Middle East offered Trump rich opportunities. While foreign policy generally was of little interest to many of the voters Trump wanted to reach, Israel retained its talismanic power. Both religious and nonreligious southerners and Republicans generally cared more about Israel than about almost any other foreign country. Additionally, the region had changed in ways that offered genuine opportunities for American policy that Trump's establishment rivals had not perceived. While unconventional Trump interventions on topics like trade policy and relations with NATO allies often had mixed or poor consequences, the results of his Middle East policies, however controversial in the region or among his opponents, led to dramatic headlines and diplomatic developments that looked like historic successes to his base.

Trump would use Middle East policy to communicate three important ideas to his base: that he could and would deliver results that establishment Republicans only talked about, that he rejected the cosmopolitan globalism of the post-historical consensus, and that his unconventional foreign policy methods could simultaneously confront American enemies and reduce American commitments around the world.

Throughout his campaign and administration, Trump took care to distinguish himself from what his supporters considered the insincere conservatism of the establishment GOP. On issues like the barrier along the Mexican frontier, Trump would struggle desperately to show progress. On Supreme Court appointments, where conservative activists had been frequently disappointed by the moderate voting records of past Republican-appointed justices like Chief Justice John Roberts and Associate Justices John Paul Stevens, David Souter, and Sandra Day O'Connor, Trump took great pains to distinguish himself by appointing justices more likely to support conservative constitutional ideas.

Middle East policy offered Trump an additional and important opportunity to separate himself from what some called "conservative squishes," and hypocritical politicians across the spectrum. Israel had proclaimed Jerusalem as its capital in 1949, even as the cease-fire line left the city divided.[18] The United States, out of concern for Arab opinion, rejected both Israeli and Jordanian attempts to define Jerusalem as a political capital. (In the Jordanian case, the Arab-occupied Old City and East Jerusalem was to become the "second capital" of the kingdom that from 1948 to 1967 controlled the West Bank.)[19] The American embassy to Israel was established in the coastal city of Tel Aviv.

Candidate Bill Clinton attacked George H. W. Bush for failing to recognize Jerusalem as Israel's capital during the 1992 election, but once in office let the matter rest. In 1995, both houses of Congress passed, and President Clinton signed, the Jerusalem Embassy Act, ordering the American embassy moved to Jerusalem within five years. Clinton left the embassy in place for the rest of his term. In the 2000 election, George W. Bush attacked the Clinton-Gore administration for failing to move the embassy. Eight years later, the embassy remained in Tel Aviv. And candidate Barack Obama called Jerusalem the "capital of Israel,"[20] but the American embassy remained where it was as Obama, like Clinton and Bush, signed waivers every six months to delay implementation of the 1995 law.[21]

For Trump, this situation was a perfect opportunity. The election season rhetoric about moving the embassy, and the passage of a law that was never implemented, showed the American political system at its most demagogic and cynical. Politicians routinely whipped up the voters when they needed their votes, then routinely disregarded some of their wishes once safely in office. That ostensibly conservative and pro-Israel Republicans connived at this charade with Democrats like Clinton and Obama made the Trump case: establishment Republicans viewed their conservative backers as stupid cattle to be manipulated at will.

Moving the embassy was, for Trump, a no-brainer. In December 2017, he formally recognized Jerusalem as the capital of Israel (without specifying the boundaries of Israeli Jerusalem or changing the American position on the holy sites in the Old City),[22] and the new embassy opened in May 2018 on the seventieth anniversary of the Israeli declaration of independence. John Hagee, leader of the powerful pro-Israel evangelical group CUFI (Christians United for Israel), gave the benediction.[23] The American consulate in Jerusalem, previously a freestanding unit that managed American relations with the Palestinians, was folded into the regular diplomatic structure under the authority of the American ambassador to Israel.[24]

Whatever the long-term consequences of the shift, in the short term it was a clear political victory for Trump. Nine of eleven former U.S. ambassadors to Israel warned against the embassy move and Middle East experts and commentators prophesied that the move would set off another intifada and wreck American relations with the Arab governments.[25] When none of this happened, Trump had tightened his hold on his political base, further discredited his establishment Republican rivals, and produced another piece of evidence for his naked emperor polemic—that the settled establishment foreign policy consensus was blind to major changes taking place in the world.

Trump approached other questions involving Israel in much the same spirit. Recognizing Israel's annexation of the Golan Heights, downgrading relations with the Palestinians, abandoning the old-fashioned peace process in the interest of an approach more compatible with the views of the Israeli right, and indicating that the United States might recognize the legality of Israeli settlements on the West Bank and back further annexations all worked to highlight the differences between Trump and the establishment Republicans.

Additionally, making Israel policy a linchpin of his approach to foreign affairs helped limit the impact of radical hard-right voices who hoped to hijack the Trump movement. Throughout his presidency Trump had a difficult relationship with those whose alt-right populism went considerably further than anything he was ready to espouse. Alt-right events like the infamous tiki torch march in Charlottesville, Virginia, pushed Trump into difficult choices. If he accepted their support, he alienated center and center-right voters who liked much of Trump's populist agenda but were revolted by open racism and antisemitism and concerned about the radicalism springing up on the far right. But if he repudiated the far-right groups too openly he risked provoking an organized movement to his right that could cause him significant political problems.

Support for Israel proved to be a useful wedge issue for Trump. There are individual exceptions, but the further one travels out toward the alt-right political fringe, the more common and the more virulent antisemitism tends to become. The conspiratorial mindset that dominates this section of American politics has no immunity against the antisemitic tropes that have animated past far-right movements in the United States and elsewhere. But antisemitism of this virulent type is repugnant to most of the American right; Trump's firm embrace of Israel consolidated his conservative support and made it more difficult for the alt-right to pressure him.

The second dimension of Trump's Israel policy also helped solidify his connection with his base—and to reach out beyond his core constituency to attract other voters who rejected the cosmopolitan globalism that, many believed, was distorting American foreign policy. The reaction against the post–Cold War strategy of building a liberal world order had been gaining force on the right since disillusion with George W. Bush's idealistic Middle East policy began to set in. Jacksonian America did not think global democracy was possible, did not think it was America's business to promote it, and rejected the idea that American sovereignty should be bound and contained in a web of multinational institutions and international law.

For many years liberal internationalists and neoconservatives failed to grasp the political force of these sentiments. The Brexit vote in the U.K. and Trump's 2016 election demonstrated the power of this electoral force, but many still underestimate its potential impact in the United States and beyond. The new populism was not simply the product of economic dissatisfaction. It drew much of its power from the growing gulf between the American corporate and political establishment that emerged in the post–Cold War era and large sections of the American public for whom the priorities and the values of that multicultural, cosmopolitan, and post-Christian establishment were fundamentally alien.

The popular demand to be ruled by people who share one's values, mores, language, and culture has been the strongest single political force around the world in the last two hundred years. Under the label of "nationalism" it disrupted and destroyed the multicultural empires that dominated Eastern Europe and the Middle East in the nineteenth century. Under the label of "anticolonialism" it smashed the European empires that, as recently as a century ago, held most of Asia and Africa in subjection. Under the label of "anticommunism" it broke the Soviet Union into its constituent republics. Under the label of "populism" it has seen traditional elites displaced by indigenous political movements in parts of Latin America, taken Britain out of the European Union, may well take Scotland out of the United Kingdom, and imposed the Trump presidency on the United States.

It is not always a wise or a prudent force. From the nineteenth century on, the larger and more cosmopolitan entities disrupted by the forces of identity politics were often both better governed and more economically viable than the smaller states that replaced them. From the standpoint of pure economic rationality, the successor states of the Austro-Hungarian Empire, the British Raj of South Asia, the Yugoslav Federation, and the Soviet Union would have been significantly better off had those multinational states reformed rather than disintegrated.

Very often, the new leadership that comes with these movements is less effective and even less honest than the leaders it displaces. Bolivia's Evo Morales was a poor administrator. Zimbabwe's Robert Mugabe was a historically bad ruler. Algeria has not been particularly well governed since independence. Some of the republics into which Tito's Yugoslavia disintegrated were shambolically administered and fell under the control of criminal gangs.

Yet these disadvantages have not diminished the perceived value of self-governance. The demand for self-government is different from and often stronger than the demand for good governance. Few Uzbeks or Azeris wish to return to the Soviet Union. A certain nostalgia for the old empires may quietly persist among certain families or circles in the former European colonies, but with all the corruption and state failure that some postcolonial countries have experienced, there is a remarkable scarcity of petitions seeking the old colonial masters' return. First-time Trump voters largely stayed loyal in 2020 despite evidence that the Covid response was mishandled; support for Brexit held up in the U.K. even as trade disputes flared with the EU.

Trump's political appeal depended ultimately on the kind of us-versus-them politics that drove nationalist, anticolonial, and populist movements to victory in so much of the world, and that continues to reverberate widely today. Enough Americans had become sufficiently alienated from national elite culture and policy that they felt increasingly like the colonial subjects of an imperial regime. Trump's political genius, or perhaps his luck, lay in his ability both to perceive that the United States had reached this grim state and to mobilize this alienation into a movement.

However, his position is more complicated than, say, that of the African anticolonialists who were able to translate victory over the colonial ruler into lifetime tenure in power. Many Americans may feel that the globalist elite is for all intents and purposes a group of alien overlords whose rule must be overthrown, but many others do not. America is a land of many cultures, and many Americans regard Trump and his white, conservative, and populist supporters as hostile and alien interlopers. In America, identity politics cuts in more than one direction. American identity is contested, and the Confederate flags sometimes seen at Trump rallies underlined the degree to which Trump's movement represented a slice of America rather than the nation as a whole.

In this way, Trump's position—and problem—was similar to that of other populist nationalist figures in countries where gaps existed between the "official opinion" of an established elite and the "common-sense" opinions and emotions of a large share of the public. Recep Tayyip Erdoğan in Turkey, appealing to the Islamic values and folk culture of Turks who dissented from the Kemalist secularism of the entrenched Turkish elite, Narendra Modi in India appealing to Hindu nationalist sentiment against the entrenched secularism and soft socialism of the Congress Party establishment, and Benjamin Netanyahu in Israel were similarly situated. These leaders were engaged in a permanent quest for issues that drew the line between the cosmopolitan values of the hated elite and the "true" values and sentiments of the nation in a way that maximized the breadth and the intensity of their public support.

It was in this context that Trump saw Israel policy as a major opportunity. As we've seen, the idea of a special relationship with the Jewish people and the Jewish state is a thread that runs through American history and is closely associated with ideas of American exceptionalism and providential nationalism at the core of American ideology.

Making unwavering support of Israel a major element of his public stance offered Trump a chance to advance his claim to represent the "true" America against its false-hearted foes at home and abroad while underlining his polemical case against the cosmopolitan globalists and their nefarious allies at the U.N. and elsewhere.

Trump's pro-Israel stance also sought to pin his opponents to the most unpopular aspects of the "cosmopolitan globalism" of the American establishment and the international Davoisie. Israel is frequently targeted by international institutions like the United Nations Human Rights Council for actions, real or alleged, against the Palestinians. To most Americans, this has always looked like antisemitism, and this perception has gone far to delegitimize these institutions in American opinion. This perception reminds many Americans that their nation is different from other nations, and reminds them of why they want to preserve those differences.

By claiming a uniquely strong affiliation with Israel, Trump was wrapping himself in the American flag in a way calculated to expand the appeal of his populist movement and to reinforce the identification of his political opponents with the least popular aspect of the globalist, multilateralist agenda.

Finally, Trump's pro-Israel policies helped him develop a strategy for the Middle East as a whole that satisfied the hawkish instincts of his Jacksonian supporters without alienating the neo-isolationist wing of the Trump coalition.

Trump's foreign policy was so unconventional and, as his critics noted, so disorderly, that many mainstream critics could find no coherence in it and saw it as a mass of slogans and impulses. These critics were not wholly wrong, but, obscured as it often was by Trump's own inconsistent behavior and restless opportunism, the warring factions in his administration, and the entrenched resistance of a bureaucracy that fundamentally rejected the Trumpian approach, Trump did possess and in his unique way sought to impose a strategic vision for American foreign policy.

The post-historical consensus Trump came to disrupt was essentially a synthesis of Wilsonian and Hamiltonian ideas about world order. Hamiltonians had long seen the possibility that the advantages of trade could create a world order based on mutual economic interest, and that promoting that kind of order would advance American security and prosperity. Wilsonians do not entirely dissent from this view but argue that no world order could long endure—or would be worth having—that did not ultimately rest on the protection of human rights within countries and the rule of law in relations between them. The post-historical consensus blended these two viewpoints for an era of unipolar American power.

From both personal conviction and political necessity, Trump was at war against the post-historical consensus. He did not share its optimism about world prospects in the post–Cold War era. He instinctively distrusted international institutions and believed that there was, at most, a very limited role for rule-driven institutions and law in the affairs of sovereign states. Alliances like NATO which presupposed a permanent pool of shared interests binding its members together from generation to generation struck him as unrealistic and he simply did not believe that the goal of American foreign policy was to create an international political system that one day might limit, condition, and ultimately replace American sovereignty. He did not accept the fundamental Hamiltonian axiom that trade, at least potentially, offered an opportunity to replace the win-lose dynamic of traditional state competition with a win-win dynamic based on mutual economic advantage. Trade, for Trump, was win-lose.

His base largely agreed, and voter disenchantment with post-historical foreign policy was one of the driving forces behind Trump's rise. But in office, Trump would need to do more than recycle criticisms of the foreign policies of the recent past. He would need to replace those policies with new ideas and new methods that his political supporters would see as responsive to their concerns.

That was not easy to do. Trump's base was united in its critique of post-historical foreign policy whether neoliberal or neoconservative, but it was deeply divided over what should come next. One large group of Trump supporters belonged to the Jacksonian school in American foreign policy. While opposed to ideological crusades and grandiose schemes for world order, they believed in a strong national defense and believed that the United States needed to act vigorously around the world where its interests or the interests of its true allies were involved.

Many Trump supporters, however, were Jeffersonian neo-isolationists. They believed that the United States was woefully overextended and that so-called allies, especially in NATO, were playing Uncle Sam for a sucker. In 1947 Europe might have been so weak that American support was required to hold Stalin at bay, but by 2016 the wealthy, selfish countries of the European Union were rich enough to take care of themselves. Jeffersonian neo-isolationists wanted the United States to define its interests as narrowly as possible, to withdraw from contested theaters like the Middle East, to scale back and even to eliminate the American commitment to Europe, and to avoid military engagement wherever possible.

Trump's political fortunes depended on keeping both wings of his coalition active and engaged, and if possible, he preferred to avoid making choices that decisively aligned him with one wing to the exclusion of the other. With regard to Europe, both the Jeffersonian neo-isolationists and the Jacksonian hawks were angry at what they saw as freeloading behavior by wealthy NATO allies like Germany who refused, as many Americans saw it, to take serious responsibility for their own defense while stiffing America on trade, and Trump-era policy was consistently cold to NATO as well as to the human rights and climate change agendas popular among many Western Europeans.

On China policy, Trump came to a different place. China was an issue that united Jacksonians behind the need for forward defense and a tougher foreign policy, while it divided the neo-isolationists. Some of them believed that the China threat was being hyped and did not see the need for serious American commitments in the Far East, but many others believed that the rise of a hostile communist superpower in Asia was one of the rare cases that justified significant American efforts far from our shores. Trump would pursue a consistently hawkish policy toward China, but, in part with an eye to the neo-isolationist wing of his base, he would accompany that hostility with efforts to get American allies like South Korea and Japan to increase their contributions to the joint defense, and with a confrontational stance on trade. The policy mix looked inconsistent and self-defeating to most professionals in the field, but the audience Trump most hoped to impress saw a consistent effort to conduct American policy along what they perceived as a commonsense basis.

The Middle East was a world theater that divided the Trump base. Jacksonian hawks loved Israel and believed that American honor and interest were engaged in the defense of the Jewish state against its enemies. They also hated Iran, a legacy of the constant hostility of the Islamic Republic against the United States from the time of the seizure of American diplomats during the 1979 Revolution, refreshed by Iran's support for Shi'a militants involved in attacks on American personnel in Iraq after the 2003 invasion. If Jacksonian America had one enemy on earth, it was the Islamic Republic of Iran.

Neo-isolationists were not so sure, and their opposition mattered to Trump. Of the relative handful of Republicans in the foreign policy world who sided with Trump—and who did not sign Never Trump letters pledging their undying hostility to Trump during the 2016 race for the GOP nomination—many were critics of the neoconservative orthodoxy of the Republican establishment. Most paleoconservatives had dissented from the Iraq War and their critique of Bush administration policy in the Middle East only intensified as that administration lost its way. They were suspicious of Israel's influence in the Republican Party and in some circles were not universally free from Vulcanist conspiracy thinking.

Yet in part because it was Obama's policy and in part because the Iran deal struck so many Republicans as an unsatisfactory agreement, opposition to the deal was one of the points that united Republicans across the divides separating Trumpers and Never-Trumpers, Jacksonians and Jeffersonians. Trump made opposition to the Iran deal an important part of his campaign and observed that anti-Iran and anti-JCPOA rhetoric evoked rapturous applause from those who attended his rallies. Given that the problem of Iran dominated international politics in the Middle East as well as in Washington, it was inevitable that Iran policy would be the leading issue in Middle East policy during Trump's tenure. The approach he found did not "solve" the Iranian problem on his abbreviated watch, and critics argued that a U.S.-Iran war might have been inevitable in a second Trump term, but Trump's Iran policy kept Republicans enthusiastically united, burnished his pro-Israel credentials without alienating his neo-isolationist supporters, demonstrated the extent of American power in dramatic fashion as European countries were unable to evade Trump's unilateral sanctions, caused even some of his critics to acknowledge that the Obama administration had underestimated its leverage over Iran, and promoted the Arab-Israeli reconciliation that stands as one of the most notable accomplishments of his controversial career.

The key to Trump's Iran policy was the ability to leverage two assets: the unique American ability to give unilateral sanctions global effect by denying the use of the American banking system to sanctions violators, and the sense of existential fear that Iran's relentless march toward regional hegemony and nuclear weapons created among Israelis and Arabs alike. The power of American sanctions allowed Trump to enforce his unpopular views of Iran on restive allies in Europe and elsewhere without spending American money or using American troops. The Gulf Arabs' hatred of Iran combined with Israel's formidable military and intelligence power meant that American proxies could deliver credible threats of force without direct U.S. commitments or involvement.

For Trump, this was close to an ideal policy mix, and it served as a demonstration of the kind of American foreign policy he would like to see. While NATO allies like Germany, Italy, and France were at most half-hearted supporters of anti-Russian policy in Eastern Europe, Middle East allies and above all Israel were more concerned about Iran than the Americans were. Like Britain and the Soviet Union before the United States entered World War II, the message from the Middle East allies was, give us the tools and we will finish the job! Trump could be a cheap hawk and, one suspects, hoped that even in a worst-case scenario it would be Israeli planes and troops that would act to destroy Iran's nuclear capabilities—with the help of American bunker-busting bombs and anything else the Israelis might need.

Trump could argue to isolationists that he was sloughing off responsibility for Iran to local allies as the United States headed for the exits in the Middle East. And he could argue to Jacksonians and other pro-Israel supporters that he was absolutely committed to ensuring that Israel had everything it needed to defend itself, and that it would receive unstinting American support.

Meanwhile, the prospect of a diminishing American presence in the region combined with changing calculations among most of the Gulf states to force the long-hidden relationship between Israel and much of the Arab world out into the open. Looking at Iran, looking at the likelihood that their energy wealth would diminish as American fracking and the global turn away from fossil fuels undercut the oil business, a number of Arab countries concluded that the old mix of public hostility and quiet cooperation with Israel was no longer enough.

Geopolitically speaking, the Arabs and the Israelis were turning into strategic allies. If the United States was going to withdraw from the Middle East, Russia, Turkey, and Iran would immediately contest the succession. Nobody trusted Russia and neither Israel nor the Gulf states would do well if Turkey or Iran emerged as a regional hegemon. In the view of Egypt and most Gulf states, the Palestinian issue was small potatoes compared to the urgent need to build an Arab-Israeli alliance to prevent the submergence of the Arab world under a renewed Ottoman or Persian empire. That alliance would need to be diplomatic and military, and it would need to operate in Washington and Europe.

It would also need to be economic. The oil wealth coursing through the Gulf states had, for a time, concealed the economic failure of the

Arab world. The glittering skyscrapers of Dubai, the Arabian playboys coursing through the casinos and fleshpots of Europe, the financial flows surging through world markets—these were all linked to oil. As the populations of the Gulf countries inexorably rose, the underlying weakness of Arab economies began to drive policy. Economic development was clearly the priority of the century, and Israel was a natural and even necessary partner for the kind of Arab revival that the security and independence of the Gulf, of Egypt, and of Lebanon would require.

The shock of the 1967 war revealed the bankruptcy of the rejectionist Arab approach to the Jewish state, but the oil boom that soon followed allowed many in the Arab world to avoid drawing the necessary conclusions about the future of Israel in the region. Fifty years later, reality could no longer be avoided. Israel was part of the region, like it or not, and the independence of the Arab world depended on reaching a realistic and even a close relationship with the "Zionist entity."

Here Trump reaped what he did not sow, although Trump administration officials worked diligently to finalize the agreements and to recruit additional members to the new Middle East peace club. The United Arab Emirates, Bahrain, Sudan, and Morocco all agreed to normalize relations with Israel during the closing weeks of his presidency. The cascade of agreements were historic in themselves, an unprecedented wave of neighboring states accepting normal relations with Israel. As significant, perhaps, was that Bahrain was widely believed to have Saudi backing for this step. Nothing remotely similar had happened in all the anxious years of American peace diplomacy in the region, and Donald Trump had broken every rule of conventional Middle East diplomacy without derailing the process. Trump's policy did not create the conditions that drove the Arab-Israeli rapprochement, but the steady progress in Arab-Israeli relations on his watch meant, among other things, that Trump's decisions like the shift of the embassy did not result in the catastrophes his opponents confidently and repeatedly predicted. On Israel and Middle East policy Trump looked to his base like a winner, and his perceived success there lent support to the belief of his supporters that his approach to American foreign policy works better than the old establishment approach even as it challenges establishment myths.

THE AMERICAN QUESTION
AND THE JUDEO-AMERICAN ENTANGLEMENT

The Covid-19 pandemic, together with the strength of the continuing opposition to Donald Trump's form of populist identity politics, denied him a second term in the White House. Populist leaders in other countries had been able to assert government control over the press, weaken the independence of the judiciary, or pass draconian security legislation that crippled their opponents' ability to compete in electoral politics. Thanks to the strength of American institutions and to the continuing commitment of a large American majority to the foundations of their political order, these options were not available to President Trump. The unswerving loyalty of the military to constitutional governance, the fierce independence and principled approach of both liberal and conservative judges to their legal responsibilities as well as the narrow base of Trump's electoral support meant that Trump, even if he tried, could not become an American Putin. That road remained closed.

Trump could, however, retain his commanding position in the Republican Party, and the grievances and anger that brought him into the White House did not disappear when he left. From his seaside Florida retreat of Mar-a-Lago, transformed into an American Elba after his defeat, Trump continued to challenge the legitimacy of his successor and to stoke his followers' rage at what Trump, in the face of a growing accumulation of evidence to the contrary, much of it compiled by Republican election officials, insisted was the "stolen" election of 2020.

Joe Biden was swept into office as his promises to restore the prosperity and peace of the post-historical era appealed to voters weary of the Sturm und Drang of the Trump years. It is still much too soon to tell whether and to what extent he will succeed. The new president and his team are seasoned professionals who are deeply committed to their vision and mission; it would be a mistake to underestimate either their ingenuity or their tenacity. Yet the forces that frustrated the Obama presidency are, if anything, stronger and more entrenched in the 2020s than they were in the last decade. China and Russia are more settled and resolute in their hostility to the U.S.-based world order, the fissures among America's alliances are deeper and harder to close, and public confidence in post-historical foreign policy has by no means been restored.

Between the pandemic, the eruption of the Black Lives Matter movement, and the hotly contested presidential election, 2020 was the most dramatic year in American politics since 1968, and momentous cultural, political, and economic changes were set in motion that would test the strength of American institutions and the resilience of American social order in the years to come. Yet even among these upheavals, the quantum entanglement between the Jewish people, the Jewish state, and the United States was as strong, and as relevant to American politics as ever before.

That entanglement dates back to the earliest moments of the American story. It deepened as both Protestant theologians and Enlightenment visionaries looked to the Restoration of the Jews as a consequence of the same forces shaping the American people and their republic.

The entanglement tightened during the late nineteenth century and continued into the Cold War. During those years, Americans discovered that the identity wars of the far-off imperial zone, the region dominated by the Russian, Ottoman, and Austro-Hungarian empires, were impossible to ignore. The nationalism that shattered the imperial zone created a global geopolitical crisis that ultimately produced two world wars and the Cold War that dominated the twentieth century and transformed America's place in the world. It also stimulated the Great Wave of migrants that challenged, enriched, and reshaped American society in ways that still engage us today.

The revolutionary transformation of the imperial zone was itself both product and sign of another revolution that was also upending American life. The Industrial Revolution disrupted the agrarian and mostly rural republic the Founders knew and replaced it with the kind of predominantly urban and deeply unequal society that many of the Founders believed was incompatible with the republican values they professed. The crowded, smoky cities of this industrial America teemed with Great Wave immigrants rooted in cultures and grounded in religions that "old stock" Americans considered outlandish at best, subversive at worst. Old political ideologies had to be discarded and new ones developed for the challenges at home, even as Americans recalibrated their ideas about foreign policy to accommodate the uneven process that would culminate in America's post–World War II assumption of world leadership in a dangerous new era dominated by fears of a nuclear holocaust.

The Jewish people were caught up in the same maelstrom. The Great Wave brought more than two million Jews to the United States, turning the American Jewish community from a numerically insignificant presence to a community making major contributions to science, culture, and business across American life. The Zionist movement was both the Jewish face of the new nationalist movements that broke up the imperial zone and a desperate effort to secure the survival of the Jewish people from the forces the nationalist movements unleashed.

As Americans grappled with the interlocking crises at home and abroad, the Jewish people kept stepping onto center stage. Domestically, mass Jewish immigration was one of the most prominent aspects of the Great Wave, challenging America's image of their nation as a "Christian culture." The old denominational model of American identity, in which Americans with different religious, ethnic, and geographical backgrounds could participate in a common national citizenship and culture without renouncing their other loyalties, was severely challenged during the Great Wave and the xenophobic reaction that accompanied it. Was the United States less antisemitic than other Euro-Atlantic cultures only because it had contained a relative handful of Jewish residents before the Great Wave began, or was the liberal nationalism of the United States sufficiently flexible and resilient to flourish under twentieth-century conditions?

Abroad, the struggle of the Jewish people to survive the surging anti semitism of the era and to establish a refuge in Palestine engaged the sympathies of many Americans and also served to test, many felt, the ability of the international system Americans tried to build to protect the rights and security of small peoples as well as to test American ideas about the direction of history and the nature of progress.

For many, though by no means for all, Americans, including American Jews, the lesson of the twentieth century seemed to be that America worked. The framework of American society inherited from the past produced a society that was flexible enough to accommodate the strains and stresses of the Industrial Revolution, and dynamic and productive enough to win the two world wars and establish the model for advanced industrial democracy that captured the world's imagination and won the Cold War. The Great Wave was accommodated, the civil rights movement pointed toward a resolution of America's racial injustices, a new social order based on mass consumption and mass production generated mass affluence, American diplomacy helped produce, or was seen to help produce, a Jewish state in the Middle East, and Americans felt that even as the world changed on an unprecedented scale, somehow their core institutions and values had powered them through to a new synthesis.

Although we cannot know whether the twenty-first century will confirm the lasting value and power of America's values and the contributions they can make to the world, the parallels between the contemporary situation and the crises of the past are striking. As the information revolution upends the economy, as the ideologies of the last century no longer seem to work, the stable post–World War II domestic order is breaking up. As a new Great Wave of immigration heralds a new period of cultural and demographic change, Americans are discovering that problems once thought to be the concern of less fortunate, less exceptional lands must be addressed at home even as comfortable assumptions about American identity demand to be reassessed.

Internationally, the geopolitical challenges to the post–Cold War American order threaten to test the limits of the post-historical foreign policy consensus as cruelly as the activities of Germany, Italy, and Japan demonstrated the shortcomings of the Lodge consensus back in the 1930s. Today as in the 1930s, the foreign policies Americans are prepared to support do not seem capable of producing the results they require, and it remains to be seen just how much more dangerous the international situation becomes before Americans and their allies summon the imagination and the will that the world crisis demands. While it takes greater prophetic powers than I possess to predict how American democracy and foreign policy will fare in the coming years, it is easier to see that the Jewish people will be caught up in the coming events in ways that keep the Judeo-American entanglement strong.

═══

Domestically, one of the most potent and divisive questions in American life today is, as it was a century ago, whether the denominational model of American identity can accommodate the needs of an increasingly diverse society. The old model of American identity, in which Americans with different religious, ethnic, and geographical backgrounds could participate in a common national citizenship and culture without renouncing their other loyalties, was tested almost to destruction during the Great Wave and the xenophobic reaction that accompanied it. Could "hyphenated Americans" be real Americans? One hundred years ago, with Asians largely excluded by discriminatory laws, the question was, on the one hand, whether "old stock" Americans were or could become tolerant and open-minded enough to accept masses of Catholics, Eastern Orthodox, and Jewish immigrants as equal members of American society and, on the other hand, whether the immigrants wanted to integrate into American society, as opposed to the practice in their homelands where different religious and ethnic groups lived largely separated lives.

Today the question is partly about race and partly about migration. The failure of sixty years of post–civil rights era policy to eliminate the consequences of slavery and segregation led many to question whether that old denominational model, and the liberal providential nationalism associated with it, had simply been part of a fundamentally racist social order whose purpose had been to suppress Blacks. Was a common "whiteness" the secret sauce that allowed American majority society to welcome wave after wave of white migrants, while relentlessly holding native Blacks back? With racial protests on a scale not seen since the 1960s sweeping the country in the early 2020s, many Americans had come to believe that a sense of national identity and of the nation's global mission that could tolerate so much racial privilege and discrimination for so long would no longer suffice. The hard right, on the other hand, saw American identity connected to the maintenance of a white demographic majority in the United States. White nationalist groups, some willing to countenance violence, began to organize in opposition to what they feared was an establishment conspiracy to destroy the supposed values of "white America" and to "replace" the current majority with, allegedly, more biddable nonwhites.

With migration, the question was one our predecessors would easily recognize. The new immigrants are coming at such a rate, and from so many countries whose cultural and religious traditions are so different from those of the United States, that many wonder whether these immigrants will follow the patterns of the past. Some fear and some hope that the new immigrants will embrace a more social, less individualistic economic and political position that will shift American politics permanently toward the left. Immigrants from Mexico and Central America, largely because their numbers have been so great, and from the Muslim world, because of the perceived gap between Islamic and traditional American values, have been the objects of particular hostility.

Overall, American Jews have been, if anything, more welcoming toward immigrants, and more concerned about the consequences of racism than the public at large. This in part reflects specific Jewish values and experiences, including memories of the hostility experienced by earlier groups of Jewish immigrants and shame at the American refusal to admit many victims of the Nazis. It also reflects the reality that American Jews largely skew left in voting behavior and on a range of social issues. Given this, it is perhaps not surprising to see criticism of the patriotic bona fides of American Jews coming from the far right. However, American Jews have also come under attack from the left. American Jews, say some, are "white Jews" invested in the perpetuation of an oppressive system that benefits them.

Many on the hard left and hard right also see Zionism as illegitimate. For opponents from the hard right, American Jews who support Israel are doing so out of "dual loyalty," and cannot be trusted to prefer America's interest to Israel's. Proud Boy leader Kyle Chapman vowed that "we will confront the Zionist criminals who wish to destroy our civilization."[26] Alex Jones, whose hard-right InfoWars site averaged almost 1.4 million visits a day before being "deplatformed" (and which continued to receive more than 700,000 daily visits after YouTube and Facebook banned it), said that "the Jews" "run Uber, they run the health care, they're going to scam you, they're going to hurt you," and promised to expose "the Jewish mafia" allegedly ruling the world in alliance with other nefarious groups.[27]

For many on the hard left, Israel is an example of an apartheid state and "settler state colonialism." American Jews who support Israel, or who oppose movements like BDS (Boycott, Divest, Sanction) Israel are siding with the forces of evil and oppression and cannot be accepted or respected by the left. As the prominent activist Linda Sarsour put it in a 2017 interview, "It just doesn't make any sense for someone to say, 'Is there room for people who support the state of Israel and do not criticize it in the movement?' There can't be in feminism. You either stand up for the rights of all women, including Palestinians, or none. There's just no way around it."[28] The 2016 platform of the Black Lives Matter movement asserts that Israel is worse than an apartheid state, and Americans who support a close relationship with Israel are guilty, too: "The US justifies and advances the global war on terror via its alliance with Israel and is complicit in the genocide taking place against the Palestinian people."[29]

The result is sobering. While not all of the hard right or the hard left is antisemitic, political movements that embrace a racialized vision of American identity are frequently hotbeds of anti-Jewish conspiracy theories. As the center erodes, and more radical political voices move from the internet to the world of electoral politics, the crudest antisemitic slanders are slithering into public discourse. In 2018 a Democratic councilmember in Washington, D.C., charged that the Rothschild banking family controlled the weather;[30] in the same year a Republican representative from Georgia alleged that Rothschild-funded space lasers were responsible for California wildfires.[31]

It remains the case that the health of American society can be measured by the degree to which the ignorant hatreds behind statements like these are ashamed to show their face in the public square. Conversely, the radicalization and polarization of post–post-historical American politics is the gravest threat to the integration of American Jews since the 1940s, and at the time these words were written, antisemitic violence in the United States has reached the highest levels ever reported.

Adding to the spotlight on Jewish Americans will be the continuing prominence of the Jewish state in world affairs. From the first meetings of the World Zionist Organization, the Zionist movement and the state the Zionists ultimately built have attracted more than their share of attention and comment, both favorable and unfavorable. There are no signs that Israel will lose its place in the limelight. Despite the Abraham Accords and peace at last with most of its Arab neighbors, Israel remains a flashpoint in world politics and the Israeli-Palestinian conflict will for the foreseeable future engage the passions and loyalties of people all over the world.

In addition to the sheer drama of what by any standard is one of the most remarkable national stories in the history of the world, the controversies that swirl around the Jewish state touch on some of the most sensitive and inflammable issues in the contemporary world. Israel's stubborn defense of its national sovereignty, from its insistence on building a nuclear arsenal to its ongoing confrontations with international organizations ranging from UNESCO to the European Union, attracts the ire of "cosmopolitan globalists" and the warmth of nationalists all over the world. The perception that Israel is a white European settler state encamped on land stolen from brown Palestinians may be crude and superficial, but it is widespread enough to make the Israeli-Palestinian struggle intensely relevant to billions of people in post-colonial societies around the world. Similarly, the sense that Zionism represents an attack on the integrity and dignity of the Islamic and/or the Arab world ensures that Israel retains an object of irresistible interest wherever Arabic is spoken, or the Koran is invoked. Behind all this, the reality that both the Holy Land and the fate of the Jews are bound up with theological ideas about the end of the world for billions of believing Muslims and Christians will, in an era when apocalypse often feels more likely than not, ensure that news about Israel continues to find massive audiences around the world. The continuing global importance, symbolic and otherwise, of Israel in turn will increase the attention paid to it in the United States, and the importance that Israel has in American politics will, as in the last seventy years, further stoke the global fascination with the Jewish state.

For both Israelis and Palestinians, two peoples whose fates have become intertwined in ways that neither side wanted or foresaw, this means that their private quarrel must be fought out in the glare of global publicity. Politicians all over the world will comment; legislatures will pass resolutions; students will demonstrate; historians will drone on; and, worst of all, demagogues will sensationalize and further inflame a conflict that is already dangerously hot. Whether it is an Iran looking to legitimize its aspirations for a wider role in the Sunni Middle East, Russia looking to further reinsert itself in an important world theater, or China looking to build its international profile, outside powers will find ways to turn the conflict to their own advantage.

For Jews, this is the modern form of an ancient problem. The Jewish people have sometimes benefited from, and more often suffered under, the fascinated gentile gaze since the Pyramids were young. For the Palestinians, global fame has been a more recent experience, purchased at the cost of an unwanted Jewish presence on land that their great-grandfathers never doubted was legitimately theirs.

Now the Jews and the Palestinians are stuck with each other, and stuck with their position on the global center stage. That entanglement has in turn drawn the Americans in; the future of the Palestinians has become as much a domestic political question in the United States as the future of the Jews used to be.

It remains my hope that Palestinians and Jews find ways to make this entanglement work better for both sides, as it remains my conviction that the creation of a Palestinian state will move both sides closer to a mutually acceptable accommodation. In the meantime, Israel will continue to occupy its continent in the American mind, with both supporters and opponents of a U.S.-Israel alliance putting considerably more energy into their lobbying than a purely objective assessment of the national interest would support. Many observers in the United States and beyond will attribute this intense focus on Israel to the hidden hand, the Benjamins, or to the space lasers, of American Jews. But the driving forces behind Americans' fascination with Israel originate outside the American Jewish community and are among the most powerful forces in American life. Anyone seeking to analyze American foreign policy or to reform it needs to come to grips with them.

Policy advice has a short shelf life, and my goal here has not been to change readers' minds about what America's Middle East policies should be. Instead, at a time when the assumptions behind a generation of American global and regional policy have been found badly wanting, I have tried to shine a useful light on the relationship between the ways Americans think about the world and the approaches they develop to act in it. I believe this is an essential step in developing new concepts for American national strategy in a new era. I can only hope that my readers agree.

Acknowledgments

During the more than a decade of thought, research, and writing that I have worked on this book I have benefited from the wisdom and insights of countless people. I can only hope that anyone whom I inadvertently omit will accept my apology along with my profound thanks.

I must first acknowledge my debt to those who have supported my work over the years. Bard College under the inspired leadership of Leon Botstein has been my academic home for almost two decades and my colleagues and students there have taught me more than they know. Research on this book began while I was at the Council on Foreign Relations, where I benefited from the wise counsel and thoughtful suggestions of Les Gelb, Richard Haass, and Jim Lindsay. At the invitation of Charles Davidson and Francis Fukuyama I was able to pursue my interest in American Middle East policy while writing for *The American Interest,* where I was fortunate enough to learn from Adam Garfinkle. I do not know which is more remarkable: Adam's depth of knowledge about the Middle East or the generosity with which he shares that knowledge with colleagues.

Five years ago, I accepted Ken Weinstein's invitation to move to Washington and work at Hudson Institute. First Ken and now his successor John Walters have fostered an atmosphere of intellectual freedom and rigorous debate that makes Hudson an extraordinary base for scholarship and policy work. I am grateful to Walter Stern and Sarah Stern for their leadership of Hudson, and to Ravenel Curry for supporting my work there. Many of my Hudson colleagues, including Doug Feith, Hillel Fradkin, Tod Lindberg, Ron Radosh, Peter Rough, and Nina Shea have provided thoughtful and detailed feedback on the manuscript that has made the book much stronger and better.

In addition to my colleagues at Hudson, other friends and colleagues have provided excellent edits and suggestions that have sharpened my thoughts and improved the manuscript and I thank Elliott Abrams, Allen Adler, Mustafa Akyol, Richard Aldous, Daniel Beilman, Roger Berkowitz, Hal Brands, Steven A. Cook, Sadanand Dhume, Nicholas Eberstadt, Mark Fisch, Samuel Goldman, Yossi Klein Halevi, Shadi Hamid, Husain Haqqani, Hussein Ibish, Martin Indyk, Henry Kissinger, Damir Marusic, Gerald McDermott, Michelle Murray, Henry Nau, Michael Oren, Danielle Pletka, Ken Pollack, Dalibor Rohac, Dennis Ross, Karl Rove, Kori Schake, Allison Stanger, Matthew Avery Sutton, Shibley Telhami, and Paul Wolfowitz.

This book would have been much harder to produce without a world-class team. Geri Thoma has been an invaluable agent for many years. My long-suffering and endlessly patient editor Jonathan Segal provided his usual insightful comments and thoughtful edits. Sarah Perrin and the team at Knopf have been tremendously helpful. I have worked with many researchers on this project, but three in particular stand out: the brilliant Gabe Perlman, whose keen insights and extraordinary research skills helped get the project off to a serious start; the peerless George Bogden, who helped me reconceptualize the book midway through; and finally the indispensable Mike Watson, without whose mastery of the many themes and subjects in the manuscript the book might never have been finished. In addition, Jake Barnett, Andrew Bernard, Nick Clairmont, Harry Zieve Cohen, Nick Gallagher, Eitan Goldstein, Lauren Gottlieb Lockshin, Grady Nixon, Dion Pierre, and Jeremy Stern have all helped, as has a small army of research interns over the years.

Without the love and support of a close and growing family, my life would be poorer and, I suspect, my books would be worse. Christopher Mead, my oldest friend and most faithful reader, gave the manuscript a close and careful edit. I am, as always, grateful for his friendship and help.

The responsibility for any remaining errors of fact or analysis is, of course, mine.

Notes

1. The Mystery of Zion

1. Alexander Pope, "The Dunciad, Book III," *The Complete Poetical Works,* ed. Henry W. Boynton (Houghton, Mifflin & Co., 1903), 169–72.
2. Alan John Percivale Taylor, *Bismarck: The Man and the Statesman* (Vintage, 1967), 115.
3. Michael B. Oren, *Power, Faith, and Fantasy: America in the Middle East, 1776 to the Present* (W. W. Norton, 2007), 442.
4. Noah Lewin-Epstein and Yinon Cohen, "Ethnic Origin and Identity in the Jewish Population of Israel," *Journal of Ethnic and Migration Studies* (June 2018), 9.
5. Oren, *Power, Faith, and Fantasy,* 91–95.
6. Lawrence Davidson, "The Past as Prelude: Zionism and the Betrayal of American Democratic Principles, 1917–48," *Journal of Palestine Studies* 31, no. 3 (2002): 25.
7. Jay Walz, "Iran's Shah Leads a 'White Revolution,'" *New York Times,* October 27, 1963.
8. Nicholas Kristof, "Unfit for Democracy?," *New York Times,* February 26, 2011.
9. Roger Cohen, "My Libya, Your Libya, Our Libya," *New York Times,* April 30, 2011.
10. Editorial Board, "Turkey's Leadership," *New York Times,* September 20, 2011.
11. Fred Kaplan, "The Benefits of Butting Out," *Slate,* October 11, 2021.
12. Oren, *Power, Faith, and Fantasy,* 158–66.
13. Dennis Ross, *Doomed to Succeed: The U.S.-Israel Relationship from Truman to Obama* (Farrar, Straus & Giroux, 2016), 64–65.
14. Adam Garfinkle, *Jewcentricity: Why the Jews Are Praised, Blamed, and Used to Explain Just About Everything* (Wiley, 2009).

2. The Quest for Planet Vulcan

1. Thomas Levenson, *The Hunt for Vulcan* (Random House, 2016), 33–41.
2. Richard Baum and William Sheehan, *In Search of Planet Vulcan* (Basic Books, 1997), 145–55.
3. Ibid., 196–210.

4. Ibid., 216.

5. Mike DeBonis and Rachael Bade, "Rep. Omar Apologizes After House Democratic Leadership Condemns Her Comments as 'Anti-Semitic Tropes,'" *Washington Post,* February 11, 2019.

6. John W. Finney, "Chairman of Joint Chiefs Regrets Remarks on Jews," *New York Times,* November 14, 1974.

7. Howard Kurtz, "Pat Buchanan: The Jewish Question," *Washington Post,* September 20, 1990.

8. Eric Fingerhut, "Farrakhan: 'Israeli lobby' Controls U.S. Government," *Jewish Telegraphic Agency,* March 31, 2009.

9. "Fulbright: Israel Controls Senate," *Jewish Telegraphic Agency,* April 17, 1973.

10. Thomas Babington Macaulay, *The History of England from the Accession of James II,* vol. 3 (J. B. Lippincott & Company, 1879), 446.

11. Dean Acheson, *Present at the Creation: My Years in the State Department* (W. W. Norton, 1987), 375.

12. Library of Congress, "Alaska Purchase Treaty: Primary Documents in American History."

13. Stephen Walt, "I Don't Mean to Say I Told You So, But . . ." *Foreign Policy,* February 8, 2010.

14. "AARP Membership," AARP, https://www.aarp.org.

15. Mark J. Perry, "Looking Back at the Remarkable History of the Nobel Prize from 1901–2020 Using Maps, Charts, and Tables," *American Enterprise Institute,* October 12, 2020.

16. "A Portrait of Jewish Americans," Pew Research Center, October 1, 2013.

17. "Nonprofit Explorer: American Israel Public Affairs Committee," ProPublica.

18. "Your Career At AIPAC," AIPAC, https://www.aipac.org/careers.

19. Frank Newport, "American Jews, Politics and Israel," Gallup, August 27, 2019.

20. Eitan Hersh and Brian Schaffner, "The GOP's Jewish Donors Are Abandoning Trump," *FiveThirtyEight,* September 21, 2016.

21. Gil Troy, "The Jewish Vote: Political Power and Identity in US Elections," The Ruderman Program for American Jewish Studies, September 2016.

22. David Philipson, *Centenary Papers and Others* (Ark Publishing Company, 1919), 26.

23. Howard M. Sachar, *A History of the Jews in America* (Vintage, 1993), 246–51.

24. Connie De Boer, "The Polls: Attitudes Toward the Arab-Israeli Conflict," *The Public Opinion Quarterly* 47, no. 1 (1983): 123.

25. George Lardner Jr. and Michael Dobbs, "New Tapes Reveal Depth of Nixon's Anti-Semitism," *Washington Post,* October 6, 1999.

3. A Knock at the Door

1. David Ohana, *The Shaping of Israeli Identity: Myth, Memory and Trauma* (Taylor & Francis, 2014), 7.

2. Shlomo Avineri, *Theodor Herzl and the Foundation of the Jewish State* (Phoenix, 2014), 52.

3. Todd M. Endelman, "Disraeli's Jewishness Reconsidered," *Modern Judaism* 5, no. 2 (1985): 109–23.

4. Avineri, *Theodor Herzl and the Foundation of the Jewish State,* 27.

5. Ibid., 31, 35.

6. "'Admission of Jews to Rights of Citizenship,' 27 September 1791," *Liberté, Egalité, Fraternité: Exploring the French Revolution,* https://revolution.chnm .org/d/287.

7. Avineri, *Theodor Herzl and the Foundation of the Jewish State,* 43.

8. Ibid., 57–58.

9. Theodor Herzl, *The Complete Diaries of Theodor Herzl* (Herzl Press and Thomas Yoseloff, 1960), 5.

10. Ernst Pawel, *The Labyrinth of Exile: A Life of Theodor Herzl* (Farrar, Straus & Giroux, 2011), 152–53, 487.

11. Jacques Kornberg, *Theodor Herzl: From Assimilation to Zionism* (Indiana University Press, 1993), 52.

12. Pawel, *The Labyrinth of Exile,* 137–38.

13. Howard M. Sachar, *A History of the Jews in America* (Vintage, 1993), 117–18.

14. Léo Abram Errera, *The Russian Jews: Extermination or Emancipation?* (David Nutt, 1894), 18.

15. Sachar, *A History of the Jews in America,* 120–21, 130–31.

16. Avineri, *Theodor Herzl and the Foundation of the Jewish State,* 37–42, 51.

17. Ibid., 66.

18. Richard S. Geehr, *Karl Lueger: Mayor of Fin de Siècle Vienna* (Wayne State University Press, 1990), 91.

19. Avineri, *Theodor Herzl and the Foundation of the Jewish State,* 111–14.

20. Theodore Herzl, *Altneuland,* 350.

21. Avineri, *Theodor Herzl and the Foundation of the Jewish State,* 258.

22. Herzl, *The Complete Diaries of Theodor Herzl,* 308.

23. Ibid., 310.

24. Shalom Goldman, *Zeal for Zion: Christians, Jews, and the Idea of the Promised Land* (University of North Carolina Press, 2009), 109.

25. Albert M. Hyamson, "British Projects for the Restoration of Jews to Palestine," *Publications of the American Jewish Historical Society* 26 (1918): 139–40.

26. Thomas Parnell Bach, "Throne and Altar: Halle Pietism and the Hohenzollerns. A Contribution to the History of Church State Relations in Eighteenth-Century Brandenburg-Prussia" (diss., Syracuse University, 2005).

27. Jill Storm, "Culture and Exchange: The Jews of Königsberg, 1700–1820" (diss., Washington University in St. Louis, 2010), 51.

28. Richard L. Gawthrop, *Pietism and the Making of Eighteenth-Century Prussia* (Cambridge University Press, 1993), 61, 122.

29. Barbara Tuchman, *Bible and Sword: England and Palestine from the Bronze Age to Balfour* (New York University Press, 1956), 162–65.

30. Goldman, *Zeal for Zion,* 106–7.

31. Herzl, *The Complete Diaries of Theodor Herzl,* 310.

32. Ibid., 311–13.

33. Ibid., 333–40.

34. Ibid., 352.

35. Ibid., 436.
36. Ibid., 656.
37. Norman Domeier, *The Eulenburg Affair: A Cultural History of Politics in the German Empire* (Camden House, 2015), 173–74.
38. John C. G. Röhl, *The Kaiser and His Court: Wilhelm II and the Government of Germany* (Cambridge University Press, 1996), 54.
39. Domeier, *The Eulenburg Affair*, 174–75.
40. Herzl, *The Complete Diaries of Theodor Herzl*, 660–64.
41. Ibid., 701.
42. Goldman, *Zeal for Zion*, 114.
43. Herzl, *The Complete Diaries of Theodor Herzl*, 735.
44. Ibid., 743.
45. Ibid., 720.
46. Ibid., 741.
47. Ibid., 756.
48. Domeier, *The Eulenburg Affair*, 177–78.

4. George Washington and the Jews

1. Samuel Goldman, *God's Country: Christian Zionism in America* (University of Pennsylvania Press, 2018), 34.
2. Peter Grose, *Israel in the Mind of America* (Alfred A. Knopf, 1983), 37–41.
3. Goldman, *God's Country*, 65–68.
4. Philippa Byrne, "Why Were the Jews Expelled from England in 1290?," Faculty of History, University of Oxford, 2017.
5. "7.3 The Prioress' Prologue and Tale," Harvard's Geoffrey Chaucer website, 586–634.
6. "From George Washington to the Hebrew Congregation in Newport, Rhode Island, 18 August 1790," *Founders Online*, National Archives. Punctuation has been lightly edited: I have inserted a period after the phrase "immunities of citizenship."
7. Howard M. Sachar, *A History of the Jews in America* (Vintage, 1993), 26–31.
8. Stefan Rohrbacher, "The Charge of Deicide: An Anti-Jewish Motif in Medieval Christian Art," *Journal of Medieval History* 17, no. 4 (1991).
9. E. Ray Canterbery, *Harry S. Truman: The Economics of a Populist President* (World Scientific Publishing Company, 2014), 17.
10. Goldman, *God's Country*, 21.
11. Ibid., 13–14.
12. Gerald R. McDermott, ed., *The New Christian Zionism: Fresh Perspectives on Israel and the Land* (InterVarsity Academic, 2016), 59–60.
13. Jonathan Edwards, *The Works of Jonathan Edwards*, Vol. 5: *Apocalyptic Writings*, ed. Stephen J. Stein (Yale University Press, 1977), 134.
14. Goldman, *God's Country*, 23–25.
15. McDermott, ed., *The New Christian Zionism*, 65.
16. John Milton, *Paradise Regained*, Book III, l, 433–40.
17. David Hackett Fischer, *Albion's Seed: Four British Folkways in America* (Oxford University Press, 1989), 616.

18. Todd Gitlin and Liel Leibovitz, *The Chosen Peoples: America, Israel, and the Ordeals of Divine Election* (Simon & Schuster, 2010), 66.
19. Donald S. Lutz, "The Relative Influence of European Writers on Late Eighteenth-Century American Political Thought," *The American Political Science Review* 78, no. 1 (1984): 192.
20. Grose, *Israel in the Mind of America*, 5.
21. "From Thomas Jefferson to William Short, 4 August 1820," *Founders Online*, National Archives.
22. "From Haven to Home: 350 Years of Jewish Life in America—1800s," Library of Congress.
23. J. H. Hollander, "Some Unpublished Material Relating to Dr. Jacob Lumbrozo, Of Maryland," *Publications of the American Jewish Historical Society* 1 (1893): 26–28.
24. Leonard Dinnerstein, *Antisemitism in America* (Oxford University Press, 1995), 10.
25. Barbara Tuchman, *Bible and Sword: England and Palestine from the Bronze Age to Balfour* (New York University Press, 1956), 114.

5. THE "END OF HISTORY" AND THE AMERICAN MIND

1. Peter Grose, *Israel in the Mind of America* (Alfred A. Knopf, 1983), 31.
2. Amos Elon, *Herzl* (Holt, Rinehart & Winston, 1975), 11, 33.
3. "A Century of Immigration, 1820–1924," in "From Haven to Home: 350 Years of Jewish Life in America," Library of Congress.
4. Grose, *Israel in the Mind of America*, 24.
5. Ibid., 30.
6. Steven R. Weisman, *The Chosen Wars: How Judaism Became an American Religion* (Simon & Schuster, 2018), 146.
7. Robert Kagan, *Dangerous Nation* (Alfred A. Knopf, 2006), 40, 49.
8. Ibid., 15, 40–41.
9. Eran Shalev, *Rome Reborn on Western Shores: Historical Imagination and the Creation of the American Republic* (University of Virginia Press, 2009), 28–33.
10. Max Savelle, *Seeds of Liberty: The Genesis of the American Mind* (Alfred A. Knopf, 1948), 84–85.
11. Michael B. Oren, *Power, Faith, and Fantasy: America in the Middle East, 1776 to the Present* (W. W. Norton, 2007), 109.
12. Kagan, *Dangerous Nation*, 255.
13. Walter Russell Mead, *Special Providence: American Foreign Policy and How It Changed the World* (Routledge, 2002), 164.
14. William Ewart Gladstone, *Two Letters to the Earl of Aberdeen, on the State Prosecutions of the Neapolitan Government* (John Murray, 1851), 9.
15. Oren, *Power, Faith, and Fantasy*, 158–59; Barbara Tuchman, *Bible and Sword: England and Palestine from the Bronze Age to Balfour* (New York University Press, 1956), 159.
16. Oren, *Power, Faith, and Fantasy*, 46.
17. Ibid., 257–58.

18. Tuchman, *Bible and Sword*, 158–65.

19. Ibid., 152–55.

20. Ibid., 177–79.

21. Ibid., 190.

22. Nakum Sokolow, *History of Zionism, 1600–1918* (Longmans, Green & Co., 1919), 123.

23. Tuchman, *Bible and Sword*, 141.

24. "From John Adams to Mordecai M. Noah, 15 March 1819," *Founders Online*, National Archives.

25. Grose, *Israel in the Mind of America*, 8–9.

26. Lester I. Vogel, *To See a Promised Land: Americans and the Holy Land in the Nineteenth Century* (Pennsylvania State University Press, 1993), 99–104.

27. Ibid., 129–59.

28. Grose, *Israel in the Mind of America*, 10–11, 25.

29. Susan Nance, "The Ottoman Empire and the American Flag: Patriotic Travel Before the Age of Package Tours, 1830–1870," *Journal of Tourism History* 1, no. 1 (2009): 16.

30. Vogel, *To See a Promised Land*, 41–42, 54–56.

31. Oren, *Power, Faith, and Fantasy*, 359.

32. Vogel, *To See a Promised Land*, 44–46.

33. Oren, *Power, Faith, and Fantasy*, 249–50.

34. Burke O. Long, *Imagining the Holy Land: Maps, Models and Fantasy Travels* (Indiana University Press, 2002), 28.

35. Mark Twain and Daniel Morley McKeithan (compiler), *Travelling with the Innocents Abroad: Mark Twain's Original Reports from Europe and the Holy Land* (University of Oklahoma Press, 2012).

36. Vogel, *To See a Promised Land*, 72.

37. Ibid., 105–6.

38. "The American Colony in Palestine," *New-York Daily Tribune*, November 2, 1867.

39. Oren, *Power, Faith, and Fantasy*, 223.

40. Samuel Goldman, *God's Country: Christian Zionism in America* (University of Pennsylvania Press, 2018), 57–58.

41. Kagan, *Dangerous Nation*, 157–59.

42. Henry Kissinger, *World Order* (Penguin, 2014), 67.

43. Otto Pflanze, "Nationalism in Europe, 1848–1871," *The Review of Politics* 28, no. 2 (April 1966): 129.

44. Grose, *Israel in the Mind of America*, 31.

45. Kagan, *Dangerous Nation*, 286–87.

46. Ibid., 159.

47. Ibid.

48. Andrei S. Markovits, *Uncouth Nation: Why Europe Dislikes America* (Princeton University Press, 2007), 53.

49. Sir Leslie Stephen, ed., *Dictionary of National Biography*, vol. 19, *Finch–Forman* (Macmillan, 1889), 20–21.

50. Cecil Roth, "The Jews in the English Universities," *Miscellanies (Jewish Historical Society of England)*, vol. 4 (1942), 113.

51. Nancy Fitch, "Mass Culture, Mass Parliamentary Politics, and Modern Anti-

Semitism: The Dreyfus Affair in Rural France," *The American Historical Review* 97, no. 1 (February 1992): 73–74.

52. Markovits, *Uncouth Nation*, 53.

6. MAELSTROM

1. Sonja Weinberg, *Pogroms and Riots: German Press Responses to Anti-Jewish Violence in Germany and Russia (1881–1882)* (Peter Lang, 2010), 71–72; Hannah Pakula, *An Uncommon Woman: The Empress Frederick: Daughter of Queen Victoria, Wife of the Crown Prince of Prussia, Mother of Kaiser Wilhelm* (Simon & Schuster, 1995), 394–95.

2. Edvard Radzinsky, trans. Antonina Bouis, *Alexander II: The Last Great Tsar* (Free Press, 2005), 104, 144.

3. M. Şükrü Hanioğlu, *A Brief History of the Late Ottoman Empire* (Princeton University Press, 2008), 123–26.

4. Howard M. Sachar, *A History of the Jews in America* (Vintage, 1993), 117–18.

5. Mark Vishniak, "Antisemitism in Tsarist Russia," in *Essays on Antisemitism*, ed. Koppel S. Pinson (Conference on Jewish Relations, 1942), 97.

6. Henry L. Feingold, *Zion in America: The Jewish Experience from Colonial Times to the Present* (Dover, 2002), 119–20.

7. François Ruegg and Rudolf Poledna, *Interculturalism and Discrimination in Romania: Policies, Practices, Identities and Representations* (Lit, 2006), 50.

8. Michal Oren-Nordheim and Ruth Kark, *Jerusalem and Its Environs: Quarters, Neighborhoods, Villages, 1800–1948* (Wayne State University Press, 2001), 28.

9. Lauren Markoe, "Iraqi Jewish Archive to Go on the Road," *Religion News Service*, September 5, 2014.

10. *The Jewish Encyclopedia: A Descriptive Record of the History, Religion, Literature, and Customs of the Jewish People from the Earliest Times to the Present Day* (Funk & Wagnalls Company, 1901), 531–32.

11. David A. Hollinger, *Protestants Abroad: How Missionaries Tried to Change the World but Changed America* (Princeton University Press, 2017), 6.

12. Michael C. LeMay, *U.S. Immigration Policy, Ethnicity, and Religion in American History* (ABC-CLIO, 2018), 93.

13. Abby Budiman, "Key Findings About U.S. Immigrants," *Pew Research Center*, August 20, 2020.

14. Charles Abram Ellwood, *Sociology and Modern Social Problems* (American Book Company, 1910), 173–74.

15. Michael C. LeMay, *Guarding the Gates: Immigration and National Security* (Praeger Security International, 2006), 71.

16. William Paul Dillingham, *Statistical Review of Immigration, 1820–1910* (U.S. Government Printing Office, 1911), 12.

17. Sachar, *A History of the Jews in America*, 117.

18. Alan M. Kraut, "Immigration, Ethnicity, and the Pandemic," *Public Health Reports* 125, Supplement 3 (2010): 124, 130.

19. Feingold, *Zion in America*, 120.

20. Ken Drexler, "Homestead Act: Primary Documents in American History," Library of Congress, December 3, 2020.

21. Greg Bradsher, "How the West Was Settled: The 150-Year-Old Homestead Act Lured Americans Looking for a New Life and New Opportunities," *Prologue: The Journal of the National Archives* 44, no. 4 (Winter 2012): 27.

22. U.S. Census Bureau, "Urban and Rural Population, Metropolitan Districts; Center of Population," 1930 Census, vol. 2, 8.

23. Meagan Flynn, "New Orleans to Apologize for Lynching of 11 Italians in 1891, Among Worst in American History," *Washington Post,* April 1, 2019.

24. Sachar, *A History of the Jews in America,* 300–307.

7. Great Decisions

1. Thomas C. Leonard, *Illiberal Reformers: Race, Eugenics, and American Economics in the Progressive Era* (Princeton University Press, 2016), 144–45, 155–57, 162–67.

2. Ibid., 125–26, 142–45.

3. National Park Service, "A Distant Shore."

4. Leonard, *Illiberal Reformers,* 143.

5. Committee on Immigration, *Immigrants in Industries Part 1: Bituminous Coal Mining,* vol. 2 (U.S. Government Printing Office, 1911), 11.

6. Howard M. Sachar, *A History of the Jews in America* (Vintage, 1993), 320.

7. Ibid., 322–24.

8. U. S. Bureau of the Census, *Historical Statistics of the United States, 1789–1945* (1949), 33.

9. American Jewish Community, *The American Jewish Year Book,* vol. 29 (The Jewish Publication Society of America, 1927–1928), 232.

10. Leonard Dinnerstein, *Antisemitism in America* (Oxford University Press, 1995), 10–14.

11. Sachar, *A History of the Jews in America,* 38–42, 72.

12. Increase Mather, *The mystery of Israel's salvation, explained and applyed* (1669), 174–76.

13. "Friday 25th of August 1780," *Founders Online,* National Archives.

14. Adam D. Mendelsohn, *Jews and the Civil War: A Reader* (NYU Press, 2011), 149.

15. *Niles Weekly Register* 37 (September 1829–March 1830), 214; *Niles Weekly Register* 49 (September 1835–March 1836), 41.

16. Lydia Maria Child, *Letters from New York* (C. S. Francis & Company, 1844), 45.

17. Frederic Cople Jaher, *Scapegoat in the New Wilderness: The Origins and Rise of Anti-Semitism in America* (Harvard University Press, 1994), 226.

18. George G. Foster, *New York by Gas-Light and Other Urban Sketches* (University of California Press, 1990), 128.

19. Jaher, *Scapegoat in the New Wilderness,* 229.

20. "Belmont's Confederate Bonds," *Chicago Tribune,* October 16, 1864.

21. Ron Chernow, *Grant* (Penguin, 2017), 233–36.

22. Jaher, *Scapegoat in the New Wilderness,* 227.

23. Dinnerstein, *Antisemitism in America,* 55–56.

24. Ibid., 36–39.

25. Sachar, *A History of the Jews in America,* 98.
26. Dinnerstein, *Antisemitism in America,* 70–72.
27. Sachar, *A History of the Jews in America,* 29–33, 327–33.
28. *The Menorah* 21 (July–December 1896): 102.
29. Dinnerstein, *Antisemitism in America,* 72.
30. Theodore A. Bingham, "Foreign Criminals in New York," *The North American Review* 188, no. 634 (1908): 383.
31. Dinnerstein, *Antisemitism in America,* 97.
32. Max Nordau, *Max Nordau to His People: A Summons and a Challenge,* ed. B. Netanyahu (Nordau Zionist Society, 1941), 66.
33. Shlomo Avineri, *The Making of Modern Zionism: The Intellectual Origins of the Jewish State* (Basic Books, 1981).
34. Nordau, *Max Nordau to His People,* 66.
35. Joseph L. Grabill, *Protestant Diplomacy and the Near East: Missionary Influence on American Policy, 1810–1927* (University of Minnesota Press, 1971), 159, 180–83, 200.

8. BLACKSTONE AND LODGE

1. Samuel Goldman, *God's Country: Christian Zionism in America* (University of Pennsylvania Press, 2018), 65.
2. Michael B. Oren, *Power, Faith, and Fantasy: America in the Middle East, 1776 to the Present* (W. W. Norton, 2007), 278.
3. Rose Eveleth, "Peruse the Weird Medical History of Every Single U.S. President," *Smithsonian Magazine,* December 12, 2013.
4. George Marsden, *Understanding Fundamentalism and Evangelicalism* (Wm. B. Eerdmans, 1991), 22; George Thomas Kurian and Mark A. Lamport, with a foreword by Martin E. Marty, *Encyclopedia of Christianity in the United States,* Vol. 5 (Rowman & Littlefield, 2016), 279–80.
5. Marsden, *Understanding Fundamentalism and Evangelicalism,* 21.
6. Stanley Gundry, *Love Them In: The Proclamation Theology of D. L. Moody* (Moody Press, 1976), 10.
7. "1891 Blackstone Memorial," Wheaton College Billy Graham Center Archives, 3–4, 6–13.
8. Ibid., 6–7.
9. Goldman, *God's Country,* 93; Marnin Feinstein, *American Zionism, 1884–1904* (Herzl Press, 1965), 57.
10. "1891 Blackstone Memorial," Wheaton College Billy Graham Center Archives, 1.
11. Ibid., 1–2.
12. Michael D. Evans, *The American Prophecies: Ancient Scriptures Reveal Our Nation's Future* (Warner Books, 2004); Paul C. Merkley, *The Politics of Christian Zionism: 1891–1948* (Routledge, 1998), 69.
13. Louis Dembitz Brandeis and Melvin L. Urofsky, *Letters of Louis D. Brandeis, vol. 4, 1916–1921* (SUNY Press, 1975), 196; Robert O. Smith, *More Desired than Our Owne Salvation: The Roots of Christian Zionism* (Oxford University Press,

2013), 168; "Joint Resolution Favoring the Establishment in Palestine of a National Home for the Jewish People," Statutes at Large, 67th Congress, Session 2 (1921–1922), Chapter 372, September 21, 1922.

14. "Aliens Act, 1905," UK Public General Acts, Chapter 13, August 11, 1905.

15. "Aliens Bill," House of Commons Debate, vol. 149, § 1281–86, July 19, 1905.

16. Oren, *Power, Faith, and Fantasy*, 360.

17. Ibid., 362.

18. Merkley, *The Politics of Christian Zionism*, 69.

19. "The American Expeditionary Forces," Library of Congress.

20. Oren, *Power, Faith, and Fantasy*, 362.

21. David B. Green, "1917: General Allenby Shows How a 'Moral Man' Conquers Jerusalem," *Haaretz*, December 10, 2014.

22. Ibid.

23. James Barr, *Setting the Desert on Fire: T. E. Lawrence and Britain's Secret War in Arabia, 1916–1918* (W. W. Norton, 2009), 214.

24. Ibid.

25. Oren, *Power, Faith, and Fantasy*, 359.

26. Charles Israel Goldblatt, "The Impact of the Balfour Declaration in America," *American Jewish Historical Quarterly* 57, no. 4 (June 1968): 463.

27. *Statutes of the United States of America Passed at the Second Session of the Sixty-Seventh Congress* (U.S. Government Printing Office, 1922), 1012.

28. "Protest to Wilson Against Zionist State," *New York Times*, March 5, 1919.

29. Oren, *Power, Faith, and Fantasy*, 383–84; Selig Adler, "The Palestine Question in the Wilson Era," *Jewish Social Studies* 10, no. 4 (October 1948): 312; Thomas A. Kolsky, *Jews Against Zionism: The American Council for Judaism, 1942–1948* (Temple University Press, 1990), 31; Menachem Mor, *Eretz Israel, Israel, and the Jewish Diaspora Mutual Relations* (University Press of America, 1991), 133.

30. Reuben Fink, *The American War Congress and Zionism: Statements by Members of the American War Congress on the Jewish National Movement* (Zionist Organization of America, 1919), 165.

31. Jonathan D. Sarna, "Converts to Zionism in the American Reform Movement," in Shmuel Almog, Jehuda Reinharz, and Anita Shapira, eds., *Zionism and Religion* (Brandeis University Press, 1998), 189.

32. Robert L. MacDonald, "'A Land Without a People for a People Without a Land': Civilizing Mission and American Support For Zionism, 1880s–1929" (diss., Bowling Green State University, 2012), 283.

33. Peter Grose, *Israel in the Mind of America* (Alfred A. Knopf, 1983), 95.

34. Joseph Tovares (Director), "Breckinridge Long (1881–1958)," *America and the Holocaust* (PBS documentary).

35. Martin Kolinsky, "Premeditation in the Palestine Disturbances of August 1929?," *Middle Eastern Studies* 26, no. 1 (1990): 18.

36. Oren, *Power, Faith, and Fantasy*, 425; Khaled Elgindy, *Blind Spot: America and the Palestinians, from Balfour to Trump* (Brookings Institution Press, 2019), 28; Lawrence Davidson, "Competing Responses to the 1929 Arab Uprising in Palestine: The Zionist Press Versus the State Department," *Middle East Policy* 5, no. 2 (May 1997): 102.

37. "Wagner Says Arabs Planned 'Murders,'" *New York Times*, September 2, 1929.

38. Nir Arielli, "Italian Involvement in the Arab Revolt in Palestine, 1936–1939," *British Journal of Middle Eastern Studies* 35, no. 2 (August 2008): 187–90.

39. Peter Hoffmann, *Carl Goerdeler and the Jewish Question, 1933–1942* (Cambridge University Press, 2011), 73.

40. Marlon Bishop and Tatiana Fernandez, "80 Years On, Dominicans and Haitians Revisit Painful Memories of Parsley Massacre," *NPR*, October 7, 2017.

41. "80 Years Ago: An International Conference to Discuss Jewish Refugees Ends in Failure," USC Shoah Foundation, June 29, 2018.

42. "Refuge in Latin America," United States Holocaust Memorial Museum.

9. American Cyrus

1. Clark Clifford, *Counsel to the President: A Memoir* (Random House, 1991), 3.

2. David McCullough, *Truman* (Simon & Schuster, 1992), 617.

3. "Memorandum of Conversation, by Secretary of State," *Foreign Relations of the United States, 1948*, Volume V, Part 2, The Near East, South Asia, and Africa, 975.

4. Clifford, *Counsel to the President*, 12–13.

5. "Editorial Note," *Foreign Relations of the United States, 1948*, Volume V, Part 2, 976.

6. "Memorandum of Conversation, by Secretary of State," *Foreign Relations of the United States, 1948*, Volume 5, Part 2, 976.

7. Clifford, *Counsel to the President*, 15.

8. Michael B. Oren, *Power, Faith, and Fantasy: America in the Middle East, 1776 to the Present* (W. W. Norton, 2007), 499; McCullough, *Truman*, 618.

9. "Edward Jacobson Papers," Harry S. Truman Presidential Library and Museum.

10. John B. Judis, *Genesis: Truman, American Jews, and the Origins of the Arab/Israeli Conflict* (Farrar, Straus & Giroux, 2014), 349.

11. McCullough, *Truman*, 607–8.

12. Evan M. Wilson, *A Calculated Risk: The U.S. Decision to Recognize Israel* (Clerisy Press, 2008), 269; Oren, *Power, Faith, and Fantasy*, 497.

13. S. J. Goldsmith, "New Montgomery Pro-Israel Stand," *Detroit Jewish News*, June 26, 1964.

14. "Presidential Approval Ratings—Gallup Historical Statistics and Trends," *Gallup*.

15. "Presidential Historians Survey 2017: Total Scores/Overall Rankings," C-SPAN; Arthur M. Schlesinger Jr., "Rating the Presidents: Washington to Clinton," *Political Science Quarterly* 112, no. 2 (Summer 1997): 183.

16. John Chamberlain, "Truman's Troubles: Washington Has Begun to Turn Against Him," *Life*, November 26, 1945.

17. Arthur Krock, "Prestige of President Is Vital Problem Now," *New York Times*, April 4, 1948.

18. McCullough, *Truman*, 302.

19. Jeff Greenfield, "The Year the Veepstakes Really Mattered," *Politico Magazine*, July 10, 2016; McCullough, *Truman*, 306, 311.

20. McCullough, *Truman*, 303–10.

21. Ibid., 319.

22. David Leip, "1944 Presidential General Election Results," *Atlas of Presidential Elections.*
23. "Presidential Approval Ratings—Gallup Historical Statistics and Trends," *Gallup*; McCullough, *Truman,* 523.
24. McCullough, *Truman,* 503.
25. Winfred Mallon, "Baruch Predicts Plot for New War: Germans and Japanese Will Strive Through Science to Devise Means," *New York Times,* November 2, 1945.
26. "My Day," George Washington University Columbian College of Arts & Sciences Eleanor Roosevelt Papers Project.
27. Editorial, "The Task of the Assembly," *New York Times,* October 23, 1946.
28. Geoffrey Matthews, "Robert A. Taft, The Constitution and American Foreign Policy, 1939–53," *Journal of Contemporary History* 17, no. 3 (July 1982): 507–19.
29. Robert L. Beisner, "Patterns of Peril: Dean Acheson Joins the Cold Warriors, 1945–46," *Diplomatic History* 20, no. 3 (1996): 324.
30. Hamby, "Henry A. Wallace, the Liberals, and Soviet-American Relations," 167.
31. John C. Culver and John Hyde, *American Dreamer: A Life of Henry A. Wallace* (W. W. Norton; reprint, 2001), 404–5.
32. McCullough, *Truman,* 490–91.
33. Ibid., 517.
34. Ibid., 612.
35. Joseph P. Lash, *Eleanor: The Years Alone* (W. W. Norton, 1972), 82.

10. Cyrus and Britain

1. "President Truman to Prime Minister Churchill," *Foreign Relations of the United States, 1945,* Document 1344.
2. "President Truman to the British Prime Minister (Attlee)," *Foreign Relations of the United States, 1945,* Document 867N.01/8–3145.
3. "DPs: Millions of Displaced Persons Stream Across Europe to Their Homes," *Life,* July 30, 1945, 13.
4. Michael J. Cohen, *Truman and Israel* (University of California Press, 1990), 111.
5. Earl G. Harrison, *Report of Earl G. Harrison,* 1, 2, 7, https://www.eisenhow erlibrary.gov/sites/default/files/research/online-documents/holocaust/report-harrison.pdf.
6. Monty Noam Penkower, "The Earl Harrison Report: Its Genesis and Its Significance," *The American Jewish Archives Journal* 68, no. 1 (2016): 22.
7. Michael J. Cohen, *Palestine and the Great Powers, 1945–1948* (Princeton University Press, 2014), 60–61; Cohen, *Truman and Israel,* 122–23.
8. Cohen, *Truman and Israel,* 113.
9. Howard M. Sachar, *A History of the Jews in America* (Vintage, 1993), 595.
10. Ibid., 592.
11. William Averell Harriman and Elie Abel, *Special Envoy to Churchill and Stalin, 1941–1946* (Random House, 1975), 531.
12. Derek Leebaert, *Grand Improvisation: America Confronts the British Superpower, 1945–1957* (Farrar, Straus & Giroux, 2018), 29–30.

13. Alan Bullock, *Ernest Bevin: Foreign Secretary, 1945–1951* (W. W. Norton, 1983), 359.
14. Ibid., 170–71.
15. Ibid., 221.
16. Harrison, *Report of Earl G. Harrison*, 1, 3.
17. Associated Press, "House Votes Plea on Open Palestine; Senate-Passed Resolution Is Approved, Calling for Appeal for British Action," *New York Times*, December 19, 1945.
18. Joseph P. Lash, *Eleanor: The Years Alone* (W. W. Norton, 1972), 105.
19. Herbert Feis, *The Birth of Israel: The Tousled Diplomatic Bed* (W. W. Norton, 1969), 25.
20. "Britain's Big Banks Review Best Year; Optimistic About Future, They Voice Some Concern About Government Controls," *New York Times*, January 22, 1946.
21. Randall Bennett Woods, *A Changing of the Guard: Anglo American Relations, 1941–1946* (University of North Carolina Press, 1990), 313–16; *Atomic Energy Act of 1946 (McMahon Act)*, Public Law 585, 79th Congress.
22. Thomas G. Paterson, *On Every Front: The Making and the Unmaking of the Cold War* (W. W. Norton, 1993), 77; Bullock, *Ernest Bevin*, 203.
23. Leebaert, *Grand Improvisation*, 59–63.
24. *Congressional Record*, 79th Congress, 2nd Session, vol. 92, part 7, 8915–16.
25. Harry S. Truman, *Memoirs by Harry S. Truman*, vol. 2, *Years of Trial and Hope* (Signet, 1965), 175.
26. Cohen, *Palestine and the Great Powers*, 107–13.
27. Ibid., 68–71, 79–83.
28. Eleanor Roosevelt, "June 22, 1946," *My Day*.
29. Robert J. Donovan, *Conflict and Crisis: The Presidency of Harry S. Truman, 1945–1948* (University of Missouri Press, 1996), 317.
30. Bullock, *Ernest Bevin*, 333.
31. Cohen, *Palestine and the Great Powers*, 121–22.
32. Donovan, *Conflict and Crisis*, 318–19.
33. Ronald Radosh and Allis Radosh, *A Safe Haven: Harry S. Truman and the Founding of Israel* (HarperCollins, 2009), 177–79.
34. Benny Morris, *1948: A History of the First Arab-Israeli War* (Yale University Press, 2008), 35.
35. Henry Wallace, "Madison Square Garden Speech," September 12, 1946.
36. Lash, *Eleanor*, 109.
37. Eleanor Roosevelt, "February 16, 1946," *My Day*.
38. Alonzo L. Hamby, *Man of the People: A Life of Harry S. Truman* (Oxford University Press, 1995), 407.
39. Morris, *1948*, 83–84.
40. Cohen, *Palestine and the Great Powers*, 139.
41. Bullock, *Ernest Bevin*, 294–96.
42. Cohen, *Palestine and the Great Powers*, 163.
43. Ibid., 191–200.
44. J. Bradford De Long and Barry Eichengreen, "The Marshall Plan: History's Most Successful Structural Adjustment Program," in *Postwar Economic*

Reconstruction and Lessons for the East Today, ed. Rudiger Dornbusch, Wilhelm Nölling, and Richard Layard (MIT Press, 1993), 199; Bullock, *Ernest Bevin,* 362.

45. Michael L. Hoffman, "British Workmen Lose Utopian Glow," *New York Times,* February 23, 1947.

46. Bullock, *Ernest Bevin,* 362.

47. Cohen, *Palestine and the Great Powers,* 222–23; Radosh and Radosh, *A Safe Haven,* 207.

11. CYRUS AND STALIN

1. Thomas W. Devine, *Henry Wallace's 1948 Presidential Campaign and the Future of Postwar Liberalism* (University of North Carolina Press, 2015), 42, 48.

2. Joseph P. Lash, *Eleanor: The Years Alone* (W. W. Norton, 1972), 88–89.

3. Ronald Radosh and Allis Radosh, *A Safe Haven: Harry S. Truman and the Founding of Israel* (HarperCollins, 2009), 207–11.

4. William W. Epley, "America's First Cold War Army, 1945–1950," Land Warfare Paper No. 32 (August 1999).

5. Alonzo L. Hamby, *Man of the People: A Life of Harry S. Truman* (Oxford University Press, 1995), 453–54.

6. "Discussion of the Report of the First Committee on the Establishment of a Special Committee on Palestine," United Nations, *General Assembly, Seventy-Seventh Plenary Meeting,* May 14, 1947.

7. Michael J. Cohen, *Palestine and the Great Powers, 1945–1948* (Princeton University Press, 2014), 261.

8. Ibid., 252–54.

9. "Rev. J. S. Grauel, 68, A Supporter of Israel," *New York Times,* September 10, 1986.

10. Benny Morris, *1948: The First Arab-Israeli War* (New Haven: Yale University Press, 2008), 45–46.

11. Ibid., 48; United Nations Special Committee on Palestine, "Report to the General Assembly, Volume 1," 1947.

12. "U.N. Assembly Establishes Ad Hoc Committee on Palestine; Will Start Meetings Thursday," *Jewish Telegraph Agency,* September 23, 1947.

13. Cohen, *Palestine and the Great Powers,* 280–83.

14. Peter Grose, "The Partition of Palestine 35 Years Ago," *New York Times,* November 21, 1982.

15. "United Nations: Just Beginning," *Time,* December 8, 1947.

16. Cohen, *Palestine and the Great Powers,* 298.

17. Alan Bullock, *Ernest Bevin: Foreign Secretary, 1945–1951* (W. W. Norton, 1983), 449–50.

18. Pierre Birnbaum, *Leon Blum: Prime Minister, Socialist, Zionist* (Yale University Press, 2015), 156–58.

19. Lash, *Eleanor,* 116–20.

20. Wilson D. Miscamble, *George F. Kennan and the Making of American Foreign Policy, 1947–1950* (Princeton University Press, 1993), 94.

21. Arnold Krammer, *The Forgotten Friendship: Israel and the Soviet Bloc, 1947–53* (University of Illinois Press, 1974), 74–77.
22. Morris, *1948*, 274.
23. "Editorial Note," *Foreign Relations of the United States*, 1947, Volume V, 916.
24. "Memorandum by the Director of the Policy Planning Staff (Kennan) to the Secretary of State," *Foreign Relations of the United States, 1948, Volume V, Part 2, The Near East, South Asia, and Africa*, 545–54.
25. "Memorandum by the Director of the Policy Planning Staff (Kennan) to the Under Secretary of State (Lovett)," *Foreign Relations of the United States, 1948, Volume V, Part 2, The Near East, South Asia, and Africa*, 573.
26. "The Palestine Partition Plan is manifestly unworkable . . ." *Foreign Relations of the United States, 1948, Volume V, Part 2*, 600 601.
27. "Editorial Note," *Foreign Relations of the United States*, 1948, Volume V, Part 2, 633.
28. "Report by the Central Intelligence Agency," *Foreign Relations of the United States*, 1948, Volume V, Part 2, 666.
29. "Memorandum by Mr. George H. Butler of the Policy Planning Staff to the Under Secretary of State (Lovett)," *Foreign Relations of the United States, 1948*, Volume V, Part 2, 619–25.
30. Morris, *1948*, 112.

12. Cyrus Agonistes

1. Benny Morris, *1948: A History of the First Arab-Israeli War* (Yale University Press, 2008), 75–77.
2. Howard M. Sachar, *A History of the Jews in America* (Vintage, 1993), 604.
3. Michael J. Cohen, *Palestine and the Great Powers, 1945–1948* (Princeton University Press, 2014), 345.
4. Morris, *1948*, 206.
5. John C. Rogers, "Its Decision in Palestine May Decide the Fate of U.N.," *New York Herald Tribune*, February 22, 1948.
6. Cohen, *Palestine and the Great Powers*, 348.
7. David McCullough, *Truman* (Simon & Schuster, 1992), 607.
8. William S. White, "Marshall Said to Explain U.S. Shift on Partition as Step to Aid Peace," *New York Times*, March 25, 1948.
9. Cohen, *Palestine and the Great Powers*, 335.
10. Alonzo L. Hamby, *Man of the People: A Life of Harry S. Truman* (Oxford University Press, 1995), 409.
11. Eleanor Roosevelt to Harry S. Truman, March 22, 1948; McCullough, *Truman*, 612.
12. Eleanor Roosevelt, "March 26, 1948," *My Day*.
13. Harry S. Truman, *Off the Record: The Private Papers of Harry S. Truman* (University of Missouri Press, 1997), 127.
14. Morris, *1948*, 88.
15. Ibid., 201.
16. Arnold Krammer, *The Forgotten Friendship: Israel and the Soviet Bloc, 1947–53* (University of Illinois Press, 1970), 59–61.

17. Krammer, *The Forgotten Friendship*, 83, 88–94.
18. Ernest Tucker, *The Middle East in Modern World History* (Taylor & Francis, 2016), 359.
19. Morris, *1948*, 206.
20. William Claiborne, "Palestinian Guerrillas Put Aside Differences to Train in U.S.S.R.," *Washington Post*, November 17, 1980.
21. Krammer, *The Forgotten Friendship*, 80–81.
22. Morris, *1948*, 206.
23. Tom Segev, *One Palestine, Complete: Jews and Arabs Under the British Mandate* (Abacus, 2000), 452.
24. Cohen, *Palestine and the Great Powers*, 363–64.
25. Ibid., 372–74.
26. "Memorandum of Conversation, by Secretary of State," *Foreign Relations of the United States, 1948*, Volume V, Part 2, *The Near East, South Asia, and Africa*, 972–74.
27. Morris, *1948*, 168–71.
28. Howard Sachar, *A History of Israel: From the Rise of Zionism to Our Time* (Alfred A. Knopf, 2007), 310.
29. Ilan Pappé, "The State and the Tribe: Egypt and Jordan, 1948–88," in *Jordan in the Middle East: The Making of a Pivotal State, 1948–1988* (Routledge, 2013), 162.
30. Thomas Mayer, "Egypt's 1948 Invasion of Palestine," *Middle Eastern Studies* 22, no. 1 (1986): 31.
31. Mahmud A. Faksh, "The Alawai Community of Syria: A New Dominant Political Force," *Middle Eastern Studies* 20, no. 2 (1984): 139.
32. Clark Clifford, *Counsel to the President: A Memoir* (Random House, 1991), 13.
33. "Memorandum of Conversation, by Secretary of State," *Foreign Relations of the United States, 1948*, Volume V, Part 2, *The Near East, South Asia, and Africa, 974*.
34. Clifford, *Counsel to the President*, 11–12; "Memorandum of Conversation, by Secretary of State," *Foreign Relations of the United States, 1948*, Volume V, Part 2, *The Near East, South Asia, and Africa, 974*.
35. Harry S. Truman, *Memoirs by Harry S. Truman*, vol. 2, *Years of Trial and Hope* (Signet, 1965), 145.
36. Ibid., 188–90; "Editorial Note," *Foreign Relations of the United States, 1948*, Volume V, Part 2, *The Near East, South Asia, and Africa, 737*.
37. Michael Oren, "The Diplomatic Struggle for the Negev, 1946–1956," *Studies in Zionism* 10, no. 2 (1989): 200.
38. Robert H. Ferrell, *Harry S. Truman: A Life* (University of Missouri Press, 1994), 311.
39. Ian J. Bickerton, "President Truman's Recognition of Israel," *American Jewish Historical Quarterly* 58, no. 2 (1968): 173–240.
40. Cohen, *Palestine and the Great Powers*, 357.
41. "Editorial Note," *Foreign Relations of the United States, 1948*, Volume V, Part 2, *The Near East, South Asia, and Africa, 993*.
42. *Eleanor and Harry: The Correspondence of Eleanor Roosevelt and Harry S. Truman*, ed. Steve Neal (Scribner, 2002), 141–49.
43. Truman, *Years of Trial and Hope*, 193–94.

13. THE COLD PEACE

1. "Lublin/Majdanek Concentration Camp: Conditions," United States Holocaust Museum.

2. Dan Stone, *The Liberation of the Camps: The End of the Holocaust and Its Aftermath* (Yale University Press, 2015), 37–40.

3. U.S. Census Bureau, *Statistical Abstract of the United States, 89th edition* (U.S. Government Printing Office, 1968), 92.

4. "387,000 Deaths Confirmed in WWII Air Raids in Japan; Toll Unknown in 15 Cities: Survey," *Mainichi Japan*, August 23, 2020.

5. Barbara Salazar Torreon and Sofia Plagakis, "Instances of Use of United States Armed Forces Abroad, 1798–2020," *Congressional Research Service*, July 20, 2020.

6. John Pomfret, *The Beautiful Country and the Middle Kingdom: America and China, 1776 to the Present* (Henry Holt, 2016), 10, 18–19.

7. Staley Lebergott, "Labor Force and Employment, 1800–1960," in *Output, Employment, and Productivity in the United States After 1800*, ed. Dorothy S. Brady (National Bureau of Economic Research, 1966), 119.

8. David Killingray, "The Black Atlantic Missionary Movement and Africa, 1780s–1920s," *Journal of Religion in Africa* 33, no. 1 (2003): 14.

9. Dana L. Robert, "The Influence of American Missionary Women on the World Back Home," *Religion and American Culture: A Journal of Interpretation* 12, no. 1 (2002): 59–89.

10. U.S. Department of Veterans Affairs, "Military Health History Pocket Card—Vietnam"; Graham A. Cosmas, *The Joint Chiefs of Staff and the War in Vietnam, 1960–1968*, Part III (Office of the Chairman of the Joint Chiefs of Staff, 2009), 167.

11. U.S. Government Accountability Office, "Military Presence: U.S. Personnel in the Pacific Theater" (August 1991), 70. Figures in this chapter adjusted to 2019 dollars using Federal Reserve Bank of Minneapolis' Inflation Calculator.

12. Stephen Daggett, "Costs of Major U.S. Wars," *Congressional Research Service*, June 29, 2010; Office of Management and Budget, "Historical Tables: Budget of the U.S. Government" (February 26, 2009), 48.

13. "American War and Military Operations Casualties: Lists and Statistics," *Congressional Research Service*, July 29, 2020.

14. Bernard Gwertzman, "U.S. Papers Tell of '53 Policy to Use A-Bomb in Korea," *New York Times*, June 8, 1984.

15. D. E. Mungello, "Reinterpreting the History of Christianity in China," *The Historical Journal* 55, no. 2 (2012): 533–34.

16. "Report by the Central Intelligence Agency," *Foreign Relations of the United States, 1948*, Volume V, Part 2, *The Near East, South Asia, and Africa*, 1240–48.

17. Douglas Little, "Cold War and Covert Action: The United States and Syria, 1945–1958," *Middle East Journal* 44, no. 1 (1990): 51–75.

18. Jerome Slater, *Mythologies Without End: The US, Israel, and the Arab-Israeli Conflict, 1917–2020* (Oxford University Press, 2020), 94–99.

19. Michael Doran, *Ike's Gamble: America's Rise to Dominance in the Middle East* (Free Press, 2017), 245–49.

20. U.S. Energy Information Administration, "U.S. Net Imports of Crude Oil."

21. Doran, *Ike's Gamble*, 76.
22. State Information Service, "The Egyptian Stock Exchange," https://www.sis .gov.eg.
23. U.S. Agency for International Development, "Foreign Aid Explorer: The Official Record of U.S. Foreign Aid."
24. Author's calculations using statistics obtained from: Comptroller General of the United States, "Summary of United States Assistance to Jordan," August 8, 1973; Israel Minister of Foreign Affairs, "Population of Israel—General Trends and Indicators," December 4, 1998; Jeremy M. Sharp, "U.S. Foreign Assistance to the Middle East: Historical Background, Recent Trends, and the FY2011 Request," Congressional Research Service, June 15, 2010; UNRWA Commissioner-General, "Report of the Commissioner-General of the United Nations Relief and Works Agency for Palestine Refugees in the Near East," July 1, 1969–June 30, 1970.
25. Elie Podeh, "To Unite or Not to Unite—That Is Not the Question: The 1963 Tripartite Unity Talks Reassessed," *Middle Eastern Studies* 39, no. 1 (2003): 157.
26. Guy Ziv, "Shimon Peres and the French-Israeli Alliance, 1954–9," *Journal of Contemporary History* 45, no. 2 (2010): 407.
27. Matti Friedman, *Spies of No Country: Israel's Secret Agents at the Birth of the Mossad* (Algonquin Books, 2019).
28. Dennis Ross, *Doomed to Succeed: The U.S.-Israel Relationship from Truman to Obama* (Farrar, Straus & Giroux, 2016), 64–65.
29. Zaki Shalom, "Kennedy, Ben-Gurion and the Dimona Project, 1962–1963," *Israel Studies* 1, no. 1 (1996): 3–33.
30. "Memorandum of Conversation," *Foreign Relations of the United States, 1961–1963*, Volume XVIII, *Near East, 1962–1963*, 276–83.
31. "Johnson Puzzled over Lack of Jewish Support for His Vietnam Policy," *Jewish Telegraphic Agency*, September 7, 1966.
32. Max Frankel, "Jewish Leaders Deny Johnson Linked Israel and War Support," *New York Times*, September 13, 1966; "Goldberg Sees Jewish Leaders in Effort to Mend Johnson Rift," *New York Times*, September 14, 1966.
33. Michael B. Oren, *Power, Faith, and Fantasy: America in the Middle East, 1776 to the Present* (W. W. Norton, 2007), 525.
34. Ibid., 533.
35. Ibid., 527.

14. Alignment

1. Associated Press, "Mrs. Meir Says Moses Made Israel Oil-Poor," *New York Times*, June 11, 1973.
2. Federal Reserve, "The Postwar Drain on Foreign Gold and Dollar Reserves," *Federal Reserve Bulletin*, April 1948; United Nations Department of Economic Affairs, "World Economic Report," *United Nations Publications*, June 1949, 7, 54–57, 69–70.
3. "Paper Prepared in the Department of the Treasury," *Foreign Relations of the United States, 1969–1976*, Volume III, *Foreign Economic Policy; International Monetary Policy, 1969–1972*, 179–88; Department of Treasury, "Require-

ments for a Secure U.S. Balance-of-payments Position," Washington National Records Center, Department of the Treasury, Office of International Monetary Affairs, September 10, 1971.

4. Interview with Henry Kissinger, October 14, 2021.
5. Carroll Kilpatrick, "Nixon Forces Firing of Cox; Richardson, Ruckelshaus Quit," *Washington Post*, October 21, 1973.
6. Craig R. Whitney, "Willy Brandt Quits Post in Wake of Spy Scandal; Asks Scheel to Take Over," *New York Times*, May 7, 1974.
7. Craig R. Whitney, "Helmut Schmidt Sworn In as West German Chancellor," *New York Times*, May 17, 1974.
8. Nan Robertson, "French Name Poher Interim President," *New York Times*, April 4, 1974.
9. Nan Robertson, "Giscard Is Inaugurated; Departs from Tradition," *New York Times*, May 28, 1974.
10. David Butler and Dennis Kavanagh, *The British General Election of October 1974* (Macmillan, 1975), 275.
11. "Tanaka Quits in Japan," *New York Times*, November 26, 1974.
12. Vassilis Fouskas, "Reflections on the Cyprus Issue and the Turkish Invasions of 1974," *Mediterranean Quarterly* 12, no. 3 (2000) 98–113.
13. "1974: Rebels Seize Control of Portugal," BBC.
14. *Public Papers of the Presidents of the United States: Richard M. Nixon, 1969* (U.S. Government Printing Office, 1999), 279.
15. Daniel Yergin, *The Prize* (Free Press, 1991), 26–34.
16. Monthly figures from U.S. Energy Information Administration, "U.S. Net Imports of Crude Oil."
17. Yergin, *The Prize*, 612–32.
18. Michael Corbett, "Oil Shock of 1973–74," *Federal Reserve History*, November 22, 2013; U.S. Energy Information Administration, "U.S. Crude Oil First Purchase Price."
19. Office of Energy Efficiency & Renewable Energy, "Fact #915: March 7, 2016 Average Historical Annual Gasoline Pump Price, 1929–2015," U.S. Department of Energy; U.S. Energy Information Administration, "Motor Vehicle Mileage, Fuel Consumption, and Fuel Economy, 1949–2010."
20. Greg Myre, "Gas Lines Evoke Memories of Oil Crises in the 1970s," NPR, November 10, 2012.
21. U.S. Census Bureau, "Money Income in 1973 of Families and Persons in the United States," July 1974.
22. David Frum, *How We Got Here: The 70's* (Basic Books, 2000), 318.
23. Connie De Boer, "The Polls: Attitudes Toward the Arab-Israeli Conflict," *The Public Opinion Quarterly* 47, no. 1 (1983): 123.
24. Avner Cohen, "The Last Nuclear Moment," *New York Times*, October 6, 2003.
25. Martin Indyk, *Master of the Game: Henry Kissinger and the Art of Middle East Diplomacy* (Alfred A. Knopf, 2021), 135–39, 169.
26. Ibid., 233.
27. Abraham Rabinovich, *The Yom Kippur War: The Epic Encounter That Transformed the Middle East* (Schocken, 2004), 493.
28. Carleton Jones, "When Agnew Resigned," *Baltimore Sun*, October 6, 1991.

29. Lesley Oelsner, "Judges Rule 5–2," *New York Times*, October 13, 1973.
30. Cohen, "The Last Nuclear Moment."
31. Interview with Henry Kissinger, October 14, 2021.
32. William B. Quandt, "How Far Will Israel Go?," *Washington Post*, November 24, 1991.
33. "Transcript of Telephone Conversation Between Secretary of State Kissinger and the President's Deputy Assistant for National Security Affairs (Scowcroft)," *Foreign Relations of the United States, 1969–1976*, Volume XXV, *Arab-Israeli Crisis and War, 1973*, 441.
34. Lyle J. Goldstein and Yuri M. Zhukov, "A Tale of Two Fleets: A Russian Perspective on the 1973 Naval Standoff in the Mediterranean," *Naval War College Review* 57, no. 2 (2004): 48.
35. Tim Weiner, *One Man Against the World: The Tragedy of Richard Nixon* (Henry Holt, 2015), 289–92.
36. Martin A. Klein, *Historical Dictionary of Slavery and Abolition* (Rowman & Littlefield, 2014), 21.
37. Stephen Daggett, "Costs of Major U.S. Wars," *Congressional Research Service*, June 29, 2010. Figures in this chapter adjusted to 2019 dollars using Federal Reserve Bank of Minneapolis' Inflation Calculator.
38. Michael C. Jensen, "U.S. Arms Exports Boom, Particularly to the Mideast," *New York Times*, April 14, 1975.
39. Doyle McManus, *Free at Last!* (New American Library, 1981), 241.
40. Joseph J. Collins, "The Soviet Invasion of Afghanistan: Methods, Motives, and Ramifications," *Naval War College Review* 33, no. 6 (1980): 53.
41. U.S. Agency for International Development, "Foreign Aid Explorer: The Official Record of U.S. Foreign Aid."
42. Rachel Bronson, *Thicker Than Oil: America's Uneasy Partnership with Saudi Arabia* (Oxford University Press, 2008), 158–60.
43. Bernard Gwertzman, "Reagan Says U.S. Has Not Altered Policy on Israel," *New York Times*, February 17, 1982.
44. "Israel's Qualitative Military Edge and Possible U.S. Arms Sales to the United Arab Emirates," *Congressional Research Service*, October 26, 2020.
45. Wolf Blitzer, "The AIPAC Formula," *Moment*, November 1981, 23.
46. "Algeria and France Settle Bitter Dispute on Oil," *New York Times*, December 16, 1971.
47. Associated Press, "Saudis Said to Buy Rest of Aramco," *New York Times*, September 4, 1980.
48. Fuad Itayim, "Overhaul for Mideast Oil," *New York Times*, October 15, 1972.
49. Ann E. Healy, "Tsarist Anti-Semitism and Russian-American Relations," *Slavic Review* 42, no. 3 (1983): 408–25.
50. George Perkovich, "Soviet Jewry and American Foreign Policy," *World Policy Journal* 5, no. 3 (1988): 438–40.

15. THE GREAT MISCALCULATION

1. Joseph Stalin, "Problems of the Collective-Farm Movement," *Pravda*, March 2, 1930.

2. United Nations Security Council, Resolution 678, November 29, 1990.

3. Michael Schwirtz, Anne Barnard, and C. J. Chivers, "Russia and Georgia Clash Over Separatist Region," *New York Times,* August 8, 2008; Vikas Bajaj and Michael M. Grynbaum, "For Stocks, Worst Single-Day Drop in Two Decades," *New York Times,* September 29, 2008.

4. Office of Policy Development and Research, Department of Housing and Urban Development, "Homeownership—Past, Present, and Future," Summer 1994; U.S. Census Bureau, "Homeownership Rate for the United States," Federal Reserve Bank of St. Louis.

5. Kenneth T. Jackson, *Crabgrass Frontier: The Suburbanization of the United States* (Oxford University Press, 1987), 283.

6. William I. Hitchcock, *The Age of Eisenhower: America and the World in the 1950s* (Simon & Schuster, 2018), 118.

7. "For Our Country," The Book of Common Prayer (Episcopal Church in the United States, 1928), 36.

8. U.S. Census Bureau, "We, the Americans: Blacks," September 1993, 2.

9. Patrick Bayer and Kerwin Kofi Charles, "Divergent Paths: Structural Change, Economic Rank, and the Evolution of Black-White Earnings Differences, 1940–2014" (National Bureau of Economic Research, November 2016), 40.

10. Board of Governors of the Federal Reserve System, "Households; Owners' Equity in Real Estate, Level," Federal Reserve Bank of St. Louis.

11. Edward N. Wolff, "Household Wealth Trends in the United States, 1962 To 2016: Has Middle Class Wealth Recovered?" (National Bureau of Economic Research, November 2017), 51.

12. U.S. Census Bureau, "Quarterly Residential Vacancies and Homeownership, First Quarter 2021," April 27, 2021.

13. H. L. Dam, "The Black-White Economic Divide Is as Wide as It Was in 1968," *Washington Post,* June 4, 2020.

14. Emily Moss, Kriston McIntosh, Wendy Edelberg, and Kristen Broady, "The Black-White Wealth Gap Left Black Households More Vulnerable," *Brookings Institute,* December 8, 2020.

15. James Hansen, *Storms of My Grandchildren: The Truth About the Coming Climate Catastrophe and Our Last Chance to Save Humanity* (Bloomsbury, 2009), 222–36.

16. The Great MacGuffin and the Quest for the Holy Grail

1. Israel Ministry of Foreign Affairs, "Israel-PLO Recognition-Exchange of Letters Between PM Rabin and Chairman Arafat—Sept 9, 1993," September 9, 1993.

2. The timeline of these events is drawn from Dennis Ross, *Doomed to Succeed: The U.S.-Israel Relationship from Truman to Obama* (Farrar, Straus & Giroux, 2016).

3. Ibid., 243.

4. R. Jeffrey Smith, "Pakistan's Nuclear-Bomb Maker Says North Korea Paid Bribes for Know-how," *Washington Post,* July 6, 2011; Larry A. Niksch, "North Korea's Nuclear Weapons Development and Diplomacy," *Congressional Research Service,* January 5, 2010.

5. Dennis Ross, "Don't Play with Maps," *New York Times,* January 9, 2007.

6. Ross, *Doomed to Succeed,* 296–97.

7. Michael Doran, *Ike's Gamble: America's Rise to Dominance in the Middle East* (Free Press, 2017), 90–93.

8. See, for example: Agence France-Presse and *Times of Israel* Staff, "Top Iran Revolutionary Guard Warns Netanyahu Will Have to 'Flee into the Sea,'" *Times of Israel,* October 5, 2018; Amir Vahdat and Jon Gambrell, "Iran Leader Says Israel a 'Cancerous Tumor' to Be Destroyed," Associated Press, May 22, 2020.

9. Michael Fry and Miles Hochstein, "The Forgotten Middle Eastern Crisis of 1957: Gaza and Sharm-el-Sheikh," *The International History Review* 15, no. 1 (1993): 62.

10. Ross, *Doomed to Succeed,* 82–95.

11. United Nations Security Council, Resolution 425, March 19, 1978; United Nations Security Council, Resolution 426, March 19, 1978.

12. Shaan Shaikh and Ian Williams, "Missiles and Rockets of Hezbollah," *Missile Threat,* Center for Strategic and International Studies, June 26, 2018, last modified August 10, 2021.

13. "Scenes from Hell: 1995 Srebrenica Genocide in Photos," *Associated Press,* July 10, 2020.

14. George Perkovich, "Soviet Jewry and American Foreign Policy," *World Policy Journal* 5, no. 3 (1988): 453–55.

15. Noah Lewin-Epstein and Yinon Cohen, "Ethnic Origin and Identity in the Jewish Population of Israel," *Journal of Ethnic and Migration Studies* (June 2018), 9.

16. Shlomo Avineri, *Herzl: Theodore Herzl and the Foundation of the Jewish State* (Weidenfeld & Nicolson, 2014), 179–82.

17. Washington Institute for Near East Policy, "Settlements and Solutions."

18. Martin Indyk, *Master of the Game: Henry Kissinger and the Art of Middle East Diplomacy* (Alfred A. Knopf, 2021), 61–76, 549–50.

19. Efraim Karsh, "The Palestinians, Alone," *New York Times,* August 1, 2010.

20. Clyde Mark, "Palestinians and Middle East Peace: Issues for the United States," *Congressional Research Service,* April 26, 2005.

21. Scott Lasensky, "Paying for Peace: The Oslo Process and the Limits of American Foreign Aid," *Middle East Journal* 58, no. 2 (2004): 220.

22. Anas Iqtait, "Economic Desperation and Dependence Are Driving the Palestinian Authority's Political Decisions," Middle East Institute, December 2, 2020.

17. Right Nation

1. Theodor Herzl, *The Complete Diaries of Theodor Herzl* (Herzl Press and Thomas Yoseloff, 1960), 83–84.

2. Robert North Roberts, Valerie A. Sulfaro, and Scott J. Hammond, *Presidential Campaigns, Slogans, Issues, and Platforms: The Complete Encyclopedia* (Greenwood, 2012), 231–32.

3. Michael Perman, *Road to Redemption: Southern Politics, 1869–1879* (University of North Carolina Press, 1983), 80, 173–74.

4. Ibid., 231–34.
5. Arthur S. Link, "The Progressive Movement in the South, 1870–1914," *The North Carolina Historical Review* 23, no. 2 (1946): 177–88.
6. "Per Capita Personal Income by State, Annual," Federal Reserve Bank of St. Louis.
7. U.S. Census Bureau, "A Half-Century of Learning: Historical Statistics on Educational Attainment in the United States, 1940 to 2000," April 6, 2006.
8. U.S. Census Bureau, "United States Summary," 1940 Census, 83.
9. A. F. Hinrichs, "Wages in Cotton-Goods Manufacturing," U.S. Bureau of Labor Statistics, November 1938, 71.
10. George Brown Tindall and Wendell Holmes Stephenson, *The Emergence of the New South, 1913–1945: A History of the South* (LSU Press, 1967), 77.
11. John Chandler Bancroft Davis, Henry Putzel, Frank D. Wagner, and Henry C. Lind, *United States Reports: Cases Adjudged in the Supreme Court at October Term, 1963* (U.S. Government Printing Office, 1964), 533.
12. Darren Dochuk, *Anointed with Oil: How Christianity and Crude Made Modern America* (Basic Books, 2019), 67–70.
13. Ibid., 426–29.
14. Ibid., 412, 426.
15. Daniel Bell, "The Cultural Contradictions of Capitalism," *The Public Interest,* Fall 1970.
16. Rodney Stark and Roger Finke, "Catholic Religious Vocations: Decline and Revival," *Review of Religious Research* 42, no. 2 (2000): 125.
17. Steven Miller, *Billy Graham and the Rise of the Republican South* (University of Pennsylvania Press, 2011), 28.
18. Joe Carter, "FactChecker: Are All Christian Denominations in Decline?," *The Gospel Coalition*, March 17, 2015.
19. Billy Graham, *Just as I Am: The Autobiography of Billy Graham* (HarperCollins, 2007), 149.
20. "Sickle for the Harvest," *Time,* November 14, 1949, 63; "A New Evangelist Arises," *Life,* November 21, 1949, 97.
21. Edmund Wilson, "The Scrolls from the Dead Sea," *The New Yorker,* May 6, 1955.
22. James Brooke, "Yigael Yadin, Famed Israeli, Dies; Was Archeologist and War Hero," *New York Times,* June 29, 1984.
23. Joel Greenberg, "Benjamin Mazar, 89, Israeli Biblical Archaeologist," *New York Times,* September 11, 1995.
24. Steven Erlanger, "King David's Palace Is Found, Archaeologist Says," *New York Times,* August 5, 2005.
25. Sean Savage, "At 3.1 Million Members, CUFI Continues to Promote Israel Support as Core Christian Value," *Jewish News Syndicate*, July 22, 2016.
26. "387,000 Deaths Confirmed in WWII Air Raids in Japan; Toll Unknown in 15 Cities: Survey," *Mainichi Japan,* August 23, 2020.
27. Diego Lopes da Silva, Nan Tian, and Alexandra Marksteiner, "Trends in World Military Expenditure, 2020," *Stockholm International Peace Research Institute,* April 2021: 2.

18. Apocalypse Now: Israel Policy Under George W. Bush

1. Peter Baker, *Days of Fire: Bush and Cheney in the White House* (Doubleday, 2014), 204.
2. Dennis Ross, *Doomed to Succeed: The U.S.-Israel Relationship from Truman to Obama* (Farrar, Straus & Giroux, 2016), 243.
3. Thomas L. Friedman, "Israel, Ignoring Bush, Presses for Loan Guarantees," *New York Times,* September 7, 1991.
4. Ronald Reagan, *An American Life* (Simon & Schuster, 1990), 419; George W. Bush, *Decision Points* (Crown, 2010), 399–400.
5. Elliott Abrams, *Tested by Zion: The Bush Administration and the Israeli-Palestinian Conflict* (Cambridge University Press, 2013), 6–8.
6. Joel Greenberg, "Sharon Touches a Nerve, and Jerusalem Explodes," *New York Times,* September 29, 2000.
7. Bush, *Decision Points,* 398.
8. David Samuels, "The Aspiring Novelist Who Became Obama's Foreign-Policy Guru," *New York Times,* May 5, 2016.
9. United States Department of Justice, "Amerithrax Investigation Summary," February 19, 2010: 1–3.
10. Gavin W. Jones, "A Demographic Perspective on the Muslim World," *Journal of Population Research* 23, no. 2 (2006): 246.
11. Ann Byle, "LaHaye, Co-Author of Left Behind Series, Leaves a Lasting Impact," *Publishers Weekly,* July 27, 2016.
12. Israel Ministry of Foreign Affairs, "Suicide and Other Bombing Attacks in Israel Since the Declaration of Principles (September 1993)."
13. Bush, *Decision Points,* 229.
14. A. J. C. Edwards, *Nuclear Weapons, the Balance of Terror, the Quest for Peace* (State University of New York Press, 1986), 238.
15. "Bush Official: Libya's Nuclear Program a Surprise," CNN, December 19, 2003; Stephen Farrell, "Israel Admits Bombing Suspected Syrian Nuclear Reactor in 2007, Warns Iran," Reuters, March 20, 2018.
16. Pew Research Center, "Public Attitudes Toward the War in Iraq: 2003–2008," March 19, 2008.
17. Colin Powell, "Remarks to the United Nations Security Council," February 5, 2003.
18. Abrams, *Tested by Zion,* 122–23.
19. I addressed these arguments at length here: Walter Russell Mead, "Jerusalem Syndrome," *Foreign Affairs,* November/December 2007.
20. Bush, *Decision Points,* 404.
21. Ibid., 400–403.
22. Kirk Semple, "U.N. Resolution Condemns Israeli Barrier," *New York Times,* October 22, 2003.
23. Abrams, *Tested by Zion,*163.

19. Israel and the Exceptional American Left

1. Pew Research Center, "Issues and the 2008 Election," August 21, 2008.
2. Anne Barnard, Andrew E. Kramer, and C. J. Chivers, "Russians Push Past Separatist Area to Assault Central Georgia," *New York Times*, August 10, 2008.
3. Nicholas Eberstadt, "Our Miserable 21st Century," *Commentary*, March 2017.
4. Moritz Kuhn, Moritz Schularick, and Ulrike I. Steins, "Income and Wealth Inequality in America, 1949–2016," *Journal of Political Economy* 128, no. 9 (September 2020): 3469–3519.
5. Jeffrey M. Jones, "In U.S., Obama Effect on Racial Matters Falls Short of Hopes," *Gallup*, August 11, 2016.
6. "The Polls: Western Partisanship in the Middle East," *The Public Opinion Quarterly* 33, no. 4 (1969): 630; Maud S. Mandel, *Muslims and Jews in France: History of a Conflict* (Princeton University Press, 2014), 81.
7. J. A. Klinghoffer, "The Transformation of the Holocaust Legacy," *Shofar* 14, no. 2 (1996): 70.
8. Naseer H. Aruri and Natali Hevener, "France and the Middle East, 1967–1968," *Middle East Journal* 23, no. 4 (1969): 487, n13.
9. Martin Gilbert, *Israel: A History*, rev. ed. (Harper Perennial, 2008), 283.
10. Joshua Muravchik, *Making David into Goliath: How the World Turned Against Israel* (Encounter Books, 2015), 14.
11. Michelle Mart, "Eleanor Roosevelt, Liberalism, and Israel," *Shofar* 24, no. 3 (2006): 58.
12. "'Show of Shows' Nets $80,000 for War Fund," *New York Times*, March 14, 1944.
13. "An Appeal by Black Americans for United States Support to Israel," *New York Times*, June 28, 1970.
14. "Black Americans to Support Israel Committee," *New York Times*, November 23, 1975.
15. Henning Sussner, "Still Yearning for the Lost Heimat? Ethnic German Expellees and the Politics of Belonging," *German Politics & Society* 22, no. 2 (71): 2004: 1–5.
16. Vidhi Doshi and Nisar Mehdi, "70 Years Later, Survivors Recall the Horrors of India-Pakistan Partition," *Washington Post*, August 14, 2017.
17. Martin Smith, *Burma: Insurgency and the Politics of Ethnicity*, rev. ed. (Dhaka: The University Press, 1999), 98.
18. Alper Kaliber, "Re-engaging the Self/Other Problematic in Post-Positivist International Relations: The 1964 Expulsion from Istanbul Revisited," *Southeast European and Black Sea Studies* 19, no. 3 (2019): 365.
19. Daniel Geary, "'Becoming International Again': C. Wright Mills and the Emergence of a Global New Left, 1956–1962," *Journal of American History* 95, no. 3 (2008): 730; Giuseppe Morosini, "The European Left and the Third World," *Social Justice* 2 (1980): 71.
20. Barack Obama, *A Promised Land* (Crown, 2020), 627–29.
21. "Exit polls 2012: How the Vote Has Shifted," *Washington Post*, November 8, 2012.

22. Joseph L. Grabill, *Protestant Diplomacy and the Near East: Missionary Influence on American Policy, 1810–1927* (University of Minnesota Press, 1971), 163, 231, 307–8.
23. Lydia Saad, "Americans' Views Toward Israel Remain Firmly Positive," Gallup, February 29, 2016.

20. Cool Hands, Hot World

1. Shadi Hamid, *Islamic Exceptionalism: How the Struggle over Islam Is Reshaping the World* (St. Martin's, 2016), 103.
2. Barack Obama, *A Promised Land* (Crown, 2020), 627.
3. Ibid., 637–41.
4. Office of the Press Secretary, The White House, "Remarks by President Obama to the Turkish Parliament," April 6, 2009; Office of the Press Secretary, The White House, "Remarks by the President on a New Beginning," June 4, 2009.
5. Ben Rhodes, *The World as It Is: A Memoir of the Obama White House* (Random House, 2019), 100–107.
6. David D. Kirkpatrick, "Named Egypt's Winner, Islamist Makes History," *New York Times,* June 24, 2012.
7. David D. Kirkpatrick, "Army Ousts Egypt's President; Morsi Is Taken into Military Custody," *New York Times,* July 3, 2013.
8. David D. Kirkpatrick, "At Swearing-in, Ex-General Vows 'Inclusive' Egypt," *New York Times,* June 8, 2014.
9. Rhodes, *The World as It Is,* 109–20.
10. Tim Gaynor and Taha Zargoun, "Gaddafi Caught Like 'Rat' in a Drain, Humiliated and Shot," *Reuters,* October 21, 2011.
11. United Nations Security Council, Resolution 1973, March 17, 2011.
12. Office of the United Nations High Commissioner for Human Rights, "'Detained and Dehumanised': Report on Human Rights Abuses Against Migrants in Libya," December 13, 2016.
13. Spencer S. Hsu and Ann E. Marimow, "Screams, Explosions and Fire in Benghazi: Bodyguard Details Ambassador's Last Moments," *Washington Post,* October 3, 2017.
14. Rebecca Elliott and Luis Santiago, "A Decade in Which Fracking Rocked the Oil World," *Wall Street Journal,* December 17, 2019.
15. U.S. Energy Information Administration, "U.S. Field Production of Crude Oil."
16. Nancy Gibbs and John F. Dickerson, "Inside the Mind of George W. Bush," *Time,* September 6, 2004.
17. Rick Klein, "Obama's Evolving Take on Meeting with Iran," *ABC News,* July 21, 2008.
18. Office of the Press Secretary, The White House, "Remarks by President Barack Obama in Prague as Delivered," April 5, 2009.
19. Michael Crowley, "Hillary Clinton's Secret Iran Man," *Politico,* April 3, 2015.
20. "George Mitchell Named Special Envoy for the Middle East," *CNN,* January 22, 2009.

21. Ministry of Foreign Affairs, "Address by PM Netanyahu at Bar-Ilan University," June 14, 2009.
22. Ari Rabinovitch, "Israeli Settlement Freeze Ends with Peace Talks in Doubt," *Reuters*, September 26, 2010.
23. Ben Birnbaum and Amir Tibon, "The Explosive, Inside Story of How John Kerry Built an Israel-Palestine Peace Plan—and Watched It Crumble," *The New Republic*, July 20, 2014.
24. United Nations Security Council, Resolution 2334, December 23, 2016.
25. Jodi Rudoren and Isabel Kershner, "Arc of a Failed Deal: How Nine Months of Mideast Talks Ended in Disarray," *New York Times*, April 28, 2014.
26. Uri Friedman, "Martin Indyk Explains the Collapse of the Middle East Peace Process," *The Atlantic*, July 3, 2014.
27. Birnbaum and Tibon, "The Explosive, Inside Story of How John Kerry Built an Israel-Palestine Peace Plan—and Watched It Crumble."
28. Martin Indyk, "The Middle East Isn't Worth It Anymore," *Wall Street Journal*, January 17, 2020.
29. Birnbaum and Tibon, "The Explosive, Inside Story of How John Kerry Built an Israel-Palestine Peace Plan—and Watched It Crumble."
30. Ibid.
31. "Jewish, Arab Fertility Rates in Israel on Par for First Time," *Times of Israel*, November 15, 2016.
32. "H. E. Dr. Ola Awad, Palestinian Central Bureau of Statistics (PCBS) President Presents a Brief on the Status of Palestinian People at the End of 2020," Palestinian Central Bureau of Statistics, December 31, 2020.
33. Elhanan Miller, "Right-Wing Annexation Drive Fueled by False Demographics, Experts Say," *Times of Israel*, January 5, 2015.
34. David B. Green, "Rage, Neglect and Transfer: The Israeli Arab Region Lieberman Wants to 'Give' to the Palestinians," *Haaretz*, December 11, 2017.
35. Palestinian Center for Policy and Survey Research and the Evens Program in Mediation and Conflict Management, "Palestinian-Israeli Pulse: A Joint Poll," October 26, 2020.
36. Jodi Rudoren and Anne Barnard, "Israeli Military Invades Gaza, with Sights Set on Hamas Operations," *New York Times*, July 17, 2014; David D. Kirkpatrick, "Arab Leaders, Viewing Hamas as Worse Than Israel, Stay Silent," *New York Times*, July 30, 2014.
37. Scott Clement and Carol Morello, "New Poll Shows How Sharply Partisan the Debate on Iran Deal Has Become," *Washington Post*, September 1, 2015.
38. "Support for Iran Nuclear Agreement Falls," Pew Research Center, September 8, 2015.
39. Richard Halloran, "Majority in Congress Urge Reagan Not to Sell AWACS to Saudi Arabia," *New York Times*, June 25, 1981.
40. Andrew J. Pierre, "Arms Sales: The New Diplomacy," *Foreign Affairs* (Winter 1981/82).
41. Manu Raju, "How the White House Kept Democrats from Killing the Iran Deal," *CNN*, September 11, 2015.
42. "New Poll: U.S. Jews Support Iran Deal, Despite Misgivings," *Jewish Journal*, July 23, 2015.

43. Robert P. Jones and Daniel Cox, "Chosen for What? Jewish Values in 2012," *Public Religion Research Institute,* April 3, 2012.

44. "AJC 2015 Survey of American Jewish Opinion," *American Jewish Committee,* September 11, 2015.

45. Birnbaum and Tibon, "The Explosive, Inside Story of How John Kerry Built an Israel-Palestine Peace Plan—and Watched It Crumble."

21. AMERICAN CRISIS AND THE FATE OF THE JEWISH PEOPLE

1. Frank Newport and Riley Brands, "Gallup Review: Americans, Immigration and the Election," *Gallup,* October 27, 2016.

2. Jennifer Agiesta, "Most Say Race Relations Worsened Under Obama, Poll Finds," *CNN,* October 5, 2016.

3. Jeffrey M. Jones, "Last Trump Job Approval 34%; Average Is Record-Low 41%," Gallup, January 18, 2021.

4. Stephen Farrell, "Why Is the U.S. Moving Its Embassy to Jerusalem?," *Reuters,* May 7, 2018.

5. Lara Jakes and David M. Halbfinger, "In Shift, U.S. Says Israeli Settlements in West Bank Do Not Violate International Law," *New York Times,* November 18, 2019.

6. Vanessa Romo, "Trump Formally Recognizes Israeli Sovereignty over Golan Heights," *NPR,* March 25, 2019.

7. "First Jerusalem-Born American Gets U.S. Passport That Lists 'Israel' as Birthplace," *Reuters,* October 30, 2020.

8. Quint Forgey, "'The Dawn of a New Middle East': Trump Celebrates Abraham Accords with White House Signing Ceremony," *Politico,* September 15, 2020.

9. Andrew Witherspoon and Courtenay Brown, "Southern States Won the Most Auto Manufacturing Jobs," *Axios,* December 16, 2018.

10. Richard Deitz and James Orr, "A Leaner, More Skilled U.S. Manufacturing Workforce," *Current Issues in Economics and Finance* 12, no. 2 (February/March 2006), 4.

11. Heather Long, "Reality Check: U.S. Manufacturing Jobs at 1940s Levels," *CNN,* April 7, 2017.

12. "Real Wage Trends, 1979 to 2019," *Congressional Research Service*, December 28, 2020.

13. Office of Immigration Statistics, U.S. Department of Homeland Security, "2019 Yearbook of Immigration Statistics" (September 2020), 5.

14. Abby Budiman, "Key Findings About U.S. Immigrants," Pew Research Center, August 20, 2020.

15. H. L. Dam, "The Black-White Economic Divide Is as Wide as It Was in 1968," *Washington Post,* June 4, 2020.

16. Robert Weisbrot and G. Calvin Mackenzie, *The Liberal Hour: Washington and the Politics of Change in the 1960s* (Penguin, 2008), 48.

17. James F. Peltz, "As Defense Cuts Deepen, Southern California's Aerospace Industry Is Down but Not Out," *Los Angeles Times,* September 26, 1993.

18. "Israel Premier and Parliament to Move to Jerusalem; Ben Gurion Reads Declaration," *Jewish Telegraphic Agency,* December 14, 1949.

19. Kimberly Katz, "Administering Jordanian Jerusalem: Constructing National Identity," in *Jerusalem: Idea and Reality,* ed. Tamar Mayer and Suleiman A. Mourad (Taylor & Francis, 2008), 260.

20. Larry Rohter, "Obama's Comments on Israel Stir Criticism in U.S.," *New York Times,* June 7, 2008.

21. Raphael Ahren and *Times of Israel* Staff, "US Confirms No More Presidential Waivers for Jerusalem Embassy Act," *Times of Israel,* May 8, 2019.

22. Mark Landler, "Trump Recognizes Jerusalem as Israel's Capital and Orders U.S. Embassy to Move," *New York Times,* December 6, 2017.

23. Matt Korade, Kevin Bohn, and Daniel Burke, "Controversial US Pastors Take Part in Jerusalem Embassy Opening," *CNN,* May 14, 2018.

24. Bill Chappell, "U.S. Closes Jerusalem Consulate That Gave Palestinians a Link to Washington," NPR, March 4, 2019.

25. Sewell Chan, "Nearly Every Former U.S. Ambassador to Israel Disagrees with Trump's Jerusalem Decision," *New York Times,* December 7, 2017.

26. Ben Sales, "Proud Boys Leader Trying to Rebrand the Group as Explicitly Antisemitic," *Jerusalem Post,* November 12, 2020.

27. "Trump Ally Alex Jones: The Emanuel Brothers Are the Leaders of 'The Jewish Mafia,'" Media Matters, October 25, 2016.

28. Collier Meyerson, "Can You Be a Zionist Feminist? Linda Sarsour Says No," *The Nation,* March 13, 2017.

29. Eric Cortellessa, "In Platform, Movement for Black Lives Accuses Israel of 'Genocide,' Backs BDS," *Times of Israel,* August 3, 2016.

30. Peter Jamison and Valerie Strauss, "D.C. Lawmaker Says Recent Snowfall Caused by 'Rothschilds Controlling the Climate,'" *Washington Post,* March 18, 2018.

31. Jack Dutton, "Marjorie Taylor Greene's 'Jewish Space Lasers' Conspiracy Theory Met with Derision, Jokes," *Newsweek,* January 29, 2021.

Index

Illustration Credits

Edward I: Wikimedia Commons

Increase Mather: Wikimedia Commons

Roger Williams: Wikimedia Commons

Garibaldi: Wikimedia Commons

Pliny Fisk: Wikimedia Commons

John D. Rockefeller: Library of Congress

Anthony Ashley-Cooper, 7th Earl of Shaftesbury: Wikimedia Commons

Philipp, Prince of Eulenburg and Hertefeld: Wikimedia Commons

Kaiser Wilhelm II: Wikimedia Commons

Russian soldiers at remains of Armenian Sheykhalan in 1915: Wikimedia Commons

Czar Alexander III: Wikimedia Commons

Karl Lueger: Wikimedia Commons

Senator Henry Cabot Lodge: Library of Congress

Ellis Island: New York Public Library

Arthur James Balfour: Library of Congress

Benjamin Disraeli: Library of Congress

Henry Morgenthau, Sr.: Library of Congress

Pastor John Hagee: Courtesy of CUFI. @ Hagee Ministries

Alfred Dreyfus: Wikimedia Commons

Theodor Herzl: Wikimedia Commons

Adolph Ochs: Wikimedia Commons

1936 Olympics: Wikimedia Commons

Henry Morgenthau Jr., left, and Rabbi Stephen S. Wise: Library of Congress

Grand Mufti of Jerusalem Mohammed Amin al-Husseini and Hitler: Library of Congress

Clement Attlee, Harry Truman and Josef Stalin: National Archives

Ernest Bevin and Clement Attlee: National Archives

Eleanor Roosevelt: National Archives

David Ben Gurion: Fritz Cohen, State of Israel Government Press Office. License permission information: https://gpophoto.gov.il/haetonot/Eng_ShowPage.aspx?id=30

Harry Truman and Henry Wallace: National Archives

1947 Winter storms: National Library of Wales

Chaim Weizmann: Wikimedia Commons

John Stanley Grauel: United States Holocaust Memorial Museum, courtesy of Murray T. Aronoff

Joseph Stalin: Wikimedia Commons

Jewish Quarter Refugees: Wikimedia Commons

George F. Kennan: Wikimedia Commons

Secretary of State George C. Marshall: US Department of State

Declaration of the Establishment of the State of Israel: Wikimedia Commons

Recognition of the new state of Israel: National Archives

Ehud Avriel: Wikimedia Commons

Paul Robeson : National Archives

Martin Luther King Jr.: Wikimedia Commons

Senator Bernie Sanders: Σ, CC BY-SA 4.0 <https://creativecommons.org/licenses/by-sa/4.0>, via Wikimedia Commons

Dwight Eisenhower and John Foster Dulles: Library of Congress

Lyndon Baines Johnson: National Archives

Nixon, Kissinger and Golda Meir: Library of Congress

Billy Graham: Wikimedia Commons

George W Bush: Wikimedia Commons

Donald Trump and Benjamin Netanyahu: Official White House Photo

A NOTE ABOUT THE AUTHOR

WALTER RUSSELL MEAD is a Distinguished Fellow at Hudson
Institute, Professor of Foreign Affairs and Humanities at Bard
College, and the Global View Columnist at *The Wall Street Journal*. His books include *Special Providence* and *God and Gold*.
A native of South Carolina, he lives in Washington, D.C.

A NOTE ON THE TYPE

This book was set in Minion, a typeface produced by the Adobe Corporation specifically for the Macintosh personal computer and released in 1990. Designed by Robert Slimbach, Minion combines the classic characteristics of old-style faces with the full complement of weights required for modern typesetting.

Composed by North Market Street Graphics,
Lancaster, Pennsylvania

Printed and bound by Berryville Graphics,
Berryville, Virginia

Designed by Cassandra J. Pappas